CHARICLES.

SCENE THE FIRST.

THE FRIENDS OF YOUTH.

NOT far from the ruins of Mycenæ, those primæval witnesses of the grandeur of the earliest Grecian princes,
which, stupendous even in their downfall, have endured for
upwards of three thousand years, is seen a narrow defile,
winding northwards between precipitous walls of rock, and
leading to the hill whereon Cleonæ, probably, whilome stood,
and which, though insignificant in size, is famous from the
eulogy of Homer.[1] This confined way was anciently the
main road from Argos to Corinth, and passable for carriages;[2]

---

[1] The topographical portion of
this book, though of minor importance, was one of considerable difficulty. In the absence of personal acquaintance with the region described, the author has carefully perused
all the most important works on the
subject. Besides the accounts of
Strabo and Pausanias, the following
books have been consulted. Gell's
Itinerary of the Morea; Dodwell's
*Classical and Topographical Tour
through Greece*; Leake's *Travels in
the Morea*; Pouqueville's *Voyage
dans la Grèce*; and the *Expédition
de Morée*. For the position of Cleonæ,
see Strabo, viii. 6, 19 : Κλεωναὶ δ'
εἰσὶ πόλισμα ἐπὶ τῇ ὁδῷ κείμενον
τῇ ἐξ Ἄργους εἰς Κόρινθον ἐπὶ
λόφου περιοικουμένου πανταχόθεν
καὶ τετειχισμένον καλῶς· ὥστ' οἰκείως εἰρῆσθαί μοι δοκεῖ τὸ ἐϋκτιμέ-
νας Κλεωνάς. Leake says that there

is still a hamlet of four or five houses
called Clenas (Κλέναις), although
Curtési, a larger village, is usually
supposed to occupy the site of the
ancient town.

[2] Two roads formerly led from
Cleonæ to Argos. Paus. ii. 15, 1 :
ἐκ Κλεωνῶν δέ εἰσιν ἐς Ἄργος ὁδοὶ
δύο. ἡ μὲν ἀνδράσιν εὐζώνοις, καὶ
ἐστὶν ἐπίτομος. ἡ δὲ ἐπὶ τοῦ καλουμένου Τρητοῦ, στενὴ μὲν καὶ αὐτὴ
περιεχόντων ὀρῶν, ὀχήμασι δέ ἐστι
ὅμως ἐπιτηδειοτέρα. One of them
was named Κοντοπορία. Athen. ii.
p. 43 : διὰ τῆς Κοντοπορίας καλουμένης, κατὰ τὴν ἀκρώρειαν προσβαί-
νουσιν εἶναι κρήνην νᾶμα ἀνιεῖσαν
χιόνος ψυχρότερον. The name is also
mentioned by Polyb. xvi. 16, 4, 5 ;
and its direction from Corinth said
to be ἔγγιστα πρὸς δύσεις χειμερι
νάς. But whether by this is to be un-

but in our time, from its neglected state, it presents difficulties even to a traveller on horseback.[3] The western
side of the defile is skirted by a brook, which, rising to
the north, here forces itself through a dense overgrowth
of bushes. The rugged rocks are indented by numerous
fissures and caverns, one of which is now, as it was in
the time of Pausanias, pointed out as the lair of the Ne-
mean lion.[4] The whole surrounding region presents the
aspect of a mountainous chain severed and intersected in
various directions. Over the western heights the pillars
of the Temple of Jupiter serve to mark the former site of
Nemea; whilst two leagues southward of Mycenæ, the
ancient Argos still survives in its modern transformation.[5]

It was in the last month of the 111th Olympiad, that
a youth, whose years could scarcely have exceeded those
of an Ephebus, was proceeding along this road. He was
mounted on a dark-coloured steed,[6] bearing no brand, it

---

derstood the carriage-road mentioned
by Pausanias, or the foot-path. is still
undetermined. Müller, in his *Dorians*, i. p. 79, declares for the former;
Leake, on the contrary (iii. 328),
thinks it more likely that the shorter
road, which now leads by Aion Oros,
is meant; and there is some weight
in one of his three reasons for this opinion, viz. that Ptolemæos found the
cold spring on the height (κατὰ τὴν
ἀκρώρειαν), an expression which would
scarcely suit the carriage-road. And
Dodwell (p. 208) says of the Κοντοπορία : 'This was probably not the
way which passed through Nemea.'
On the other hand, it is certain that
Pausanias does not call the hill, but
the coach-road itself, Τρητὸς, for he
says, § 4, ἀνελθοῦσι δὲ ἐς τὸν Τρητὸν
καὶ αὖθις τὴν ἐς Ἄργος ἰοῦσιν ἐστι
Μυκηνῶν ἐρείπ.α ἐν ἀριστερᾷ.

[3] Pouquev. iv. 48 : 'Elle est ac-
tuellement dans un tel état de dégra-

dation, qu'on a quelque difficulté a
y voyager à cheval.'

[4] Pausan. *supra*: ἐν τούτοις τοῖς
ὄρεσι τὸ σπήλαιον ἔτι δείκνυται τοῦ
λέοντος. Cf. Dodwell, p. 207; Leake,
p. 329.

[5] *Expédition de Morée*, ii. 147:
'Distance totale, 2 heures 5 minutes.'

[6] In the heroic age carriages were
frequently used for long journeys.
In the historic period people mostly
went on foot, and carriages are an
exception, not the rule ; (see notes
23 and 26 to Sc. VII.). Even em-
bassies travelled thus, as appears
from Æschin. *De Falsa Leg.* p. 272.
Still there are instances of horses
being used, and Demosthenes thus
accompanies Philip's ambassadors as
far as Thebes. *Ib.* 282 : ἐμισθώσατ'
αὐτοῖς ὅτ' ἀπῇεσαν ὁρικὰ ζεύγη καὶ
συμπαρῄει ἐφ' ἵππου. Cf. *in Ctesiph.*

is true, to mark him of celebrated blood, but of a strength
and mettle not unworthy of the noble form that bestrode
him. The rider lacked not breadth of chest and shoulders,
but his frame was rather slim and supple, than thick-
set and muscular. His slightly tanned neck rose proudly
and freely, but in the animation of his blue eye was
blended a languishing expression, betokening him one that
longed to love and to be loved. Beneath the broad brim of
his dark travelling cap crowded an abundance of light-
coloured locks, while a delicate down besprinkled his cheeks
and chin. His whole appearance, his noble carriage and
finely-chiselled profile, bespoke a youth of good descent
and careful nurture.[7]

A single slave, apparently scarce ten years senior to
his master, was his only attendant, and strode along man-
fully in the wake of the steed; though the drops of sweat
that ran down his forehead, shewed that the bundle on his
shoulders containing the coverlet for the night, and other
appliances necessary for a journey, was no light burden for
a hot sunny day in the month of *Skirophorion*.[8]

---

p. 467. In Xenophon's *Sympos.* 9, 7,
some of the guests even arrive at Callias' house on horseback, or perhaps,
as Schneider supposes, order their
steeds to be brought for the journey
home. In writing the foregoing description, Lucian, *Asin.* § 1, and
Appul. *Metam.* i. p. 12, have been
kept in view.

[7] An almost verbal imitation of
Cybele's description of Theagenes.
Heliod. *Æthiop.* vii. 10: εὐρὺς τις
ἦν τὰ στέρνα καὶ τοὺς ὤμους, καὶ τὸν
αὐχένα ὄρθιον καὶ ἐλεύθερον ὑπὲρ
τοὺς ἄλλους αἴρων, καὶ εἰς κορυφὴν
τοὺς ἅπαντας ὑπερέχων, γλαυκιῶν
τὸ βλέμμα καὶ ἐπέραστον ἅμα καὶ
γοργὸν προσβλέπων, ὁ καταβόστρυ-
χός που πάντως ἐκεῖνος, τὴν παρειὰν
ἄρτι ξανθῷ τῷ ἰούλῳ περιστέφων.

[8] Every one of respectable condition was accompanied out of doors
by one or more slaves; (see Excursus
on *The Slaves*;) so also on a journey
slaves attended, to carry the sleeping-
apparatus, στρώματα, and the other
baggage. Aristoph. *Av.* 615:

οὕτω μὲν εἰσίωμεν. ἄγε δὲ, Ξανθία,
καὶ Μανόδωρε, λαμβάνετε τὰ στρώματα.

Cf. *Ran.* 12. Xenoph. *Memor.* iii. 13, 6,
is very explicit: Ἄλλου δὲ λέγοντος,
ὡς παρετάθη μακρὰν ὁδὸν πορευθεὶς,
ἤρετο αὐτὸν, εἰ καὶ φορτίον ἔφερε.
Μὰ Δί', οὐκ ἔγωγ', ἔφη. ἀλλὰ τὸ
ἱμάτιον. Μόνος δ' ἐπορεύου, ἔφη, ἢ
καὶ ἀκόλουθός σοι ἠκολούθει; Ἠκολούθει, ἔφη. Πότερον, ἔφη, κενὸς, ἢ
φέρων τι; Φέρων, νὴ Δί', ἔφη, τά τε
στρώματα καὶ τὰ ἄλλα σκεύη. The
pack or receptacle for these things

The two wayfarers had arrived at a spot where the wall of rock on the east curved inwards semicircularly, leaving space for a green carpet-like lawn, surrounded by a thick bosquet of blooming myrtles and oleanders; between which a holly-bush here and there protruded the points of its glistening leaves, as if to protect the luxuriant foliage. Just at the foot of this leafy curtain, amidst the boulders scattered around, exuberant ferns extended their bright-green fans; and the nakedness of the rocks was sparingly, though picturesquely clothed with branches of red-fruited arbutus, and tufts of the yellow-blossomed sage.[9] The rider drew up, and turning to his slave, said, 'Manes, how high is the sun?' 'The fourth hour is passed for certain,' replied the other. 'Let us stop here then; 'twere hard to find a more inviting spot for our morning meal. The projecting rocks will shield us from the burning rays of the sun; while these moss-grown boulders seem placed purposely for the repose of the wanderer, and the spring which bubbles from the rock up yonder, promises us a refreshing draught.' With these words he sprang from his horse, rubbed the foam and froth from his

was called στρωματόδεσμον : Plato, Theæt. p. 175; Æschin. de Falsa Leg. 273: συνηκολούθουν δ' αὐτῷ ἄνθρωποι δύο στρω;ματόδεσμα φέροντες, ἐν δὲ τῷ ἑτέρῳ τούτων ὡς αὐτὸς ἔφη, τάλαντον ἐνῆν ἀργυρίου. It was afterwards called στρωματεύς, Poll. vii. 79 ; x. 137. Pollux seems not to restrict their use to the journey. The weight borne by the slaves was sometimes considerable. It is true silver money is not meant in the passage of Æschines ; but see Theophr. Char. 30: τῷ ἀκολούθῳ ἐπιθεῖναι μεῖζον φορτίον, ἢ δύναται φέρειν. Even when the master was on horseback, still the slave followed on foot, though part of the baggage may have been carried by the horse. Lucian, Asin. 1 ἵππος δέ με κατῆγε καὶ τὰ σκεύη,

καὶ θεράπων ἠκολούθει εἷς.

[9] These are the plants and shrubs which really grow in this region. See Pouqueville, p. 148: 'le Trété, dans lequel coulent la rivière et les eaux de la source de Rito au milieu d'un fourré épais de myrtes, de lauriers-roses et d'arbustes.' The holly, ilex aquifolium, Linn., Græcè πρῖνος ἀγρία, is also to be found between Corinth and Nemea: 'une campagne couverte de petits buissons et de houx. Expéd. de Morée, iii. 35. The strawberry-tree, arbutus unedo, is indigenous throughout Greece. The yellow sage, salvia pomifera, σφάκος, (now ἀλησφακία) abounds in the vicinity. Dodwell, 228, says: 'This plant is common in the rocky places in Greece.'

neck and back with a handful of leaves, and then turned
him loose to enjoy himself among the tall grass, at which,
in passing, he had already nibbled hastily.[10] Meanwhile
Manes had lost no time in depositing his bundle, and
drew from it bread, Sicilian cheese, and dried figs, with
some fresh ones gathered on the road; not to mention
leeks and onions collected in the same manner, and set
apart by him for his private use.[11] A small skin full of
Mendæan wine—a present from their host at Argos—
and a silver drinking cup,[12] completed the preparations
for the frugal breakfast, the best relish for which was
their morning's exercise.

Manes soon clambered up to the eminence, where the
spring spouted forth abundantly from the rock, and
brought the earthen vessel filled with water, whose cool-
ness proved an admirable freshener to the wine, already
somewhat flat from the warmth of the day.

The youth had concluded his repast, and was reposing

---

[10] Vid. Appul. *Metam.* i. p. 13.

[11] There is no doubt that Grecian
hospitality allowed the wayfarer to
eat of the fruit growing by the roadside. Plato, *Leg.* viii. p. 845: ἐὰν δὲ
ξένος ἐπιδημήσας ὀπώρας ἐπιθυμῇ φαγεῖν, διαπορευόμενος τὰς ὁδοὺς, τῆς μὲν
γενναίας (ὀπώρας, γενναίων σταφυ-
λῶν ἢ σύκων) ἁπτέσθω, ἐὰν βούληται,
μεθ' ἑνὸς ἀκολούθου, χωρὶς τιμῆς,
ξένια δεχόμενος· τῆς δὲ ἀγροίκου
λεγουένης καὶ τῶν τοιούτων ὁ νόμος
εἰργέτω μὴ κοινωνεῖν ἡμῖν τοὺς ξένους. The distinction between ὀπώρα
γενναία, and ἀγροῖκος, is explained
by the context. He evidently means
certain sorts of grapes; for instance,
those not used for must, but for the
table. Afterwards, speaking of apples, pears, pomegranates, &c., he
says: ξένῳ δὲ, καθάπερ ὀπώρας, ἐξέστω
καὶ τῶν τοιούτων μέτοχον εἶναι.

Leeks and onions were very much
esteemed, especially by the lower
orders. See Plutarch, *Symp.* iv. 4, 3 :
τὸ μὲν γὰρ Ὁμηρικὸν ἐκεῖνο, κρόμυον
ποτοῦ ὄψον, ναύταις καὶ κωπηλάταις
μᾶλλον ἢ βασιλεῦσιν ἐπιτήδειον ἦν.
See also Excursus on *The Meals.*

[12] As with the Germans, so among
the Greeks, in every family not quite
indigent were to be found some
little articles of silver-plate, such as
cups, and so forth, serving partly for
sacrifices, partly for the table. See
Cic. *Verr.* iv. 21. Drinking vessels are
frequently mentioned, and they were
also carried on a journey. An instance
occurs in Demosth. *in Timoth.* p. 1193.
The κυμβίον (Id. in *Euerg.* 1156),
which belonged to the freed-man was
doubtless of silver, else the plunderers
would never have so maltreated the
woman in order to obtain it.

comfortably on the mossy slab, when a second traveller
wound round the corner of the crag, and made straight
for the spot, with which he seemed already to be well
acquainted. He was on foot and unaccompanied ; and his
dress, though respectable, did not betoken particularly
flourishing means ; but his powerful figure and resolute
bearing were admirably united with a litheness and activity of limb, which could only have been acquired by a
complete course of training in the *Gymnasium*. The
manly beauty of his features corresponded well with the
symmetry of his person. That lively eye beneath the
lofty brow, which was encircled by a wreath of raven locks,
betrayed an acute understanding, and keen powers of observation ; while the well-turned mouth, besides a slight
expression of shrewdness, bespoke much good humour and
benevolence. His form might be well likened to that of a
Hermes in the flush of incipient manhood. He seemed
neither surprised nor annoyed at finding the resting-place
pre-occupied, for he walked up, and with a friendly salutation greeted the first comer, who returned it with no less
cordiality, and invited the other to a share of the natural
retreat.   For a few moments the stranger examined
thoughtfully the features of the stripling. Some dim and
distant reminiscence of a similar face, seen of yore, seemed
gradually to dawn upon his mind. 'We seem bound to
the same goal,' was his answer, as he presently loosened
the clasp of his *chlamys*, and proceeded to accept the
invitation.   'I have observed the footmarks of your
steed ; you are on your way to Cleonæ.' 'Certainly,'
replied the other, 'by Cleonæ to Corinth.'   'In that case
we can travel in company, that is, if you will tarry till I
have got cooler, and mounted to yonder fountain, which
the benevolent nymph pours forth to refresh the traveller.'
'Right willingly,' replied the fair-haired one ; 'but there
is no need to toil up the ascent. Go, Manes, fill the *hydria* anew, and bring hither the goblet and wine, that I
may pledge my future companion in a cup of welcome.'

The offer was gratefully accepted, and Manes soon returned
with the sparkling beverage. 'May every drop in this
goblet,' said the youth, as he presented it to the stranger,
'become a never-failing fountain of hearty good-will between us. You possess, in a wonderful degree, the gift of
winning a man's confidence: though but a moment since
we were perfect strangers, I already feel marvellously
drawn towards you: I hope we shall be friends.' 'Zeus
Philios grant it be so,' replied the other as he received
the cup and emptied it. His look again rested on the
stripling, whose features he seemed to scan attentively.
'Peradventure, however, we are not quite such strangers
to each other as you think,' continued he ; 'and this is
not perhaps the first time that we have partaken of the
same salt.[13] At all events we are compatriots, for though
your speech has somewhat of a foreign accent, there is no
mistaking the Athenian ; so I shall have to put only half
the question of the Homeric heroes :

Who art thou, and whence among men ? Where dwellest thou, where
dwell thy parents ?

'Doubtless,' rejoined with a smile the person to
whom this query was addressed, 'doubtless, I can lay
claim to the name of an Athenian burgher ; but it is
no wonder if, after six years' absence, I do not speak
the dialect of my native city with such purity as you.
But to answer the other portion of the question ; my
name is Charicles, son of Charinos ; a family of some distinction, even though it cannot trace its descent either
from Hercules or Hermes.[14] But I am the sole surviving

---

[13] Ἁλῶν κοινωνεῖν was a proverbial expression for ὁμοτράπεζον γενέσθαι. Lucian, Asin. 1.

[14] The desire of having a long an-
cestral tree, and of claiming descent
if possible from some god or hero,
need not excite our wonder in the

case of the Greeks, who assigned
to the whole human race a divine
origin of no very remote date ; while
the genealogies of the heroic age afforded abundant materials on which
the heralds of a later time might exercise their ingenuity. When also, so
strict a line of demarcation existed

scion of my race, born to the great joy of my father, after
he had been married six years without having an heir,
that is, if,'—he stopped thoughtfully and earnestly surveyed a ring on the fourth finger of the left hand. 'If
what your mother told you be true,' laughingly rejoined
the other, who, to judge from the expression of his face,
had now become convinced of what before he had only
surmised. 'That is a point on which we cannot do
better than imitate Telemachus, and hope for the best.
But what was the cause of so lengthened an absence from
Athens? Now-a-days Attic burghers migrate not unfrequently to the richer plains of Asia.[15] Mayhap your father
also was one of those whose motto is, "There rest, where
you fare best."[16] Or did he fancy that he would be
better able to finish your education abroad? Are you
not afraid that this may prove a reproach to you in a
city, where the great boast of an exemplary burgher is,
to have avoided all unnecessary journeyings?'[17] 'Oh'
no,' replied Charicles. 'It was no such motive that in-

---

between strangers and citizens, and
certain families enjoyed ancient privileges, pride of ancestry might naturally be expected, though it was often
pitied or derided by sensible men.
See Aristoph. *Nubes*, 48, where the
words, ἔγημα Μεγακλέους τοῦ Μεγακλέους ἀδελφιδῆν, allude no doubt to
Alcibiades, who boasted his descent
on the father's side from Ajax, while
his mother Deinomacha, daughter of
Megacles, belonged to the race of the
Alcmæonidæ. The orator Andocides
traced his descent, we are told, to
Ulysses, and thence to Hermes and
Zeus. Plut. *Alcib.* 21; *Dec. Orat. vit.*
iv. p. 347. An instructive passage on
the worth of such old nobility occurs
in Plato, *Theæt.* 174, and is the more
valuable as the philosopher was himself on both sides of ancient and noble
families.

[15] This had happened earlier. Thus
Helos pleads in his father's favour:
εἰ δ' ἐν Αἴνῳ χωροφιλεῖ, τοῦτο οὐκ
ἀποστερῶν γε τῶν εἰς τὴν πόλιν
ἑαυτὸν οὐδενὸς, οὐδ' ἑτέρας πόλεως
πολίτης γεγενημένος, ὥσπερ ἑτέρους
ὁρῶ τοὺς μὲν εἰς τὴν ἤπειρον ἰόντας
καὶ οἰκοῦντας ἐν τοῖς πολεμίοις τοῖς
ὑμετέροις, καὶ δίκας ἀπὸ ξυμβόλων
ὑμῖν δικαζομένους. Antiph. *de Cæde
Herod.* p. 744. Nobody was prohibited
from so doing (Plato, *Crito*, 51), but
still it could not be acceptable to the
state.

[16] The principle, *ubi bene, ibi
patria*, is not new. It is the leading
idea of the *Aves* of Aristophanes, and
Hermes is made to express the sentiment quite plainly in *Plut.* 1151:
πατρὶς γάρ ἐστι πᾶς', ἵν' ἂν πράττῃ τις εὖ.

[17] See Plato, who says: Ταῖς δὲ

duced my father to change his abode; no one could
have been more anxious than he to give his son a genuine

πλείσταις πόλεσιν, ἅτε οὐδαμῶς εὐ-
νομουμέναις, οὐδὲν διαφέρει φύρεσθαι
δεχομένους τε αὐτοῖς ξένους, καὶ αὐτοὺς εἰς τὰς ἄλλας ἐπικωμάζοντας
πόλεις, ὅταν ἐπιθυμήσῃ τις ἀποδη-
μίας ὅπῃ οὖν καὶ ὁπότε, εἴτε νέος,
εἴτε καὶ πρεσβύτερος ὤν. Leg. xii.
p. 950. He disapproves of the liberty
being conceded to every one of travelling when and where he would :
Πρῶτον μὲν νεωτέρῳ ἐτῶν τετταράκοντα μὴ ἐξέστω ἀποδημεῖν μηδαμῇ
,ιηδαμῶς. ἔτι δὲ ἰδίᾳ μηδενὶ, δημοσίᾳ δ'
ἔστω κήρυξιν ἢ πρεσβείαις, ἢ καί τισι
θεωροῖς. p. 951. No such prohibi-
tive law actually existed anywhere ;
though the words ταῖς πλείσταις πόλεσι may indicate that certain restrictions were occasionally enforced.
Most Athenians had to make frequent
journeys on business, but travelling
into other countries, merely for pleasure, and with no important object,
was another matter ; and it was the
duty of a good burgher not to indulge
in such absence. So in Plato, Crito,
52, Socrates says : Καὶ οὔτ' ἐπὶ θεω-
ρίαν πώποτε ἐκ τῆς πόλεως ἐξῆλθες,
ὅτι μὴ ἅπαξ εἰς 'Ισθμὸν, οὔτε ἄλλοσε
οὐδαμόσε, εἰ μή ποι στρατευσόμενος.
οὔτε ἄλλην ἐποιήσω ἀποδημίαν πώποτε, ὥσπερ οἱ ἄλλοι ἄνθρωποι, οὐδ'
ἐπιθυμία σε ἄλλης πόλεως, οὐδ' ἄλλων νόμων ἔλαβεν εἰδέναι · ἀλλὰ
ἡμεῖς σοι ἱκανοὶ ἦμεν καὶ ἡ ἡμετέρα
πόλις. How far any control was exercised iu the matter is hard to say ;
yet it seems certain that passports
were required for a journey abroad.
Thus in Aves, 1212. Peisthetæros asks
Iris on her entering the new state,

σφραγῖδ' ἔχεις παρὰ τῶν πελαργῶν ; 'IP. τί
    τὸ κακόν ;
Π. οὐκ ἔλαβες ; 'IP. ὑγιαίνεις μέν ; Π. οὐδὲ
    σύμβολον
ἐπέβαλεν ὀρνίθαρχυς οὐδείς σοι παρών ;

on which the Scholiast remarks, οἷον
σύμβολον ἐπὶ τῷ συγχωρηθῆναι παρελθεῖν. Cf. Plaut. Capt. ii. 3, 90,
where Roman customs are by no
means necessarily intended. Another
remarkable passage, Trin. iii. 3, 65,
almost seems to hint at some sort of
police for the surveillance of persons
arriving. The σφραγὶς of Aristophanes is nothing but the passport accredited with the state-seal, or the seal
itself. See Böckh's Publ. Econ. p. 207.
A fact of great interest we gather
from Strabo, who tells us, (ix. 3, 1,)
that the Ozolæ had the evening-star
engraved on their state-seal : ἔχουσί
τε ἐπὶ τῇ δημοσίᾳ σφραγῖδι τὸν ἕσπερον
ἀστέρα ἐγκεχαραγμένον. The σύμβολον is not quite the same, being
any object given a person as his credentials or token of recommendation.
So a line quoted from Euripides by
Eustath. ad Iliad. vi. 169 :

ξένοις τε πέμπειν σύμβολ', οἳ δράσουσί σ' εὖ.

The purpose and nature of these σύμβολα is more clear from Lysias de
Bonis Aristoph. 628, ὅτι ἔλαβε σύμβολον παρα βασιλέως τοῦ μεγάλου
φιάλης μὲν χρυσῆς. And again, p. 629,
πολλῶν γὰρ ἀγαθῶν καὶ ἄλλων χρημάτων εὐπορήσειν διὰ τὸ σύμβολον
ἐν πάσῃ τῇ ἠπείρῳ. The same kind
of accrediting was usual in private
transactions, though here the σύμβολον was merely an impression of the
signet-ring. Plaut. Pseud. i. 1, 53 :

Ea causa miles hic reliquit symbolum,
Expressam in cera ex anulo suam imagi-
    nem,
Ut qui huc afferret ejus similem symbolum,
Cum eo simul me mitteret.

Cf. ib. ii. 2, 52 ; Bacchid. ii. 3, 29 ; and
Plutarch, Artax. 18. Of this description, too, are the σύμβολα mentioned
in Poll. ix. 71, which are similar to the

Attic education.[18] Often have I heard him talk with
indignation of those fathers who appointed, as their sons'
pedagogues, uneducated slaves with their language full
of barbarisms ; or who showed themselves indifferent as
to the selection of a proper school for their children.
Even in the choice of a nurse for me he was vastly particular. The distress which prevailed at the period of my
birth gave him the opportunity of gaining the services of
a respectable female of the middle class, who was reduced
to rather indigent circumstances ; and all my attendants
moreover, both male and female, were subjected to a strict
scrutiny, to ascertain whether they were thoroughly Greek
in speech and habits. Even now, I recall to mind with
pleasure, how the aged Manto, while the other slaves were
all busy at the loom around my mother, would beguile
the winter's evening with pleasant stories. But, it was
not till some time after, that I perceived the difference
between these sensible tales and legends, and the absurd
ghost-stories, of which nurses and waiting-maids are
usually so fond. Then again, my pedagogue !—he was,
to be sure, a cross old fellow, who was rather hard upon
me at times, if I chanced to use my left hand instead
of my right at meals, or sat with one leg across the other,
or if, on my way to school, I peradventure lifted up my
eyes from the dirt in the street just to have a peep at
some swallow, that was being greeted joyfully as the
harbinger of spring.[19] But after all, he did so merely

---

tesseræ hospitales ; and so also those
referred to in an Athenian inscription,
a decree in honour of Strato of Sidon :
ποιησάσθω δὲ καὶ σύμβολα ἡ βουλὴ
πρὸς τὸν βασιλέα τὸν Σιδωνίων, ὅπως
ἂν ὁ δῆμος ὁ ᾿Αθηναίων εἰδῇ, ἐάν τι
πέμπῃ ὁ Σιδωνίων βασιλεὺς δεόμενος
τῆς πόλεως, καὶ ὁ βασι εὐς ὁ Σιδωνίων εἰδῇ ὅταν πέμπῃ τινὰ ὡς αὐτὸν ὁ
δῆμος ὁ ᾿Αθηναίων. *Marmor. Oxon.* ii.
24 ; Böckh, *Corp. Inscr. Gr.* i. p. 126.
As Böckh remarks, these σύμβολα

have nothing to do with the state-
treaties which are also called by the
same name; but are the ambassadors'
credentials, and therefore are also in
some sort *tesseræ hospitales.*

[18] See *Excursus* on Scene I. for all
the details respecting education.

[19] The Greek longed, even more
eagerly than we do, for the return of
the bird of spring. Hence the prover-

because he was full of notions about Old-Attic subordination and decorum.'

'Your father must have been a man of great wealth,' remarked the other, 'or he would scarce have paid more attention to these touches of Attic refinement than to a slave's general usefulness.' 'He was far from rich,' answered Charicles, 'and, besides, he had expended considerable sums on Trierarchies, Choregies, and other patriotic contributions; but in every thing connected with my education he spared no outlay; and I can well remember how wroth he once was with a friend, for advising him to send me to the cheaper school of Elpias at the *Theseion*,[20] instead of to Hermippos, of whose reputation as a teacher, at that time, you have doubtless heard.'

The youth smiled, and said, 'He is not unknown to me; but then, how came it that your father left Athens, and kept you so long away from it?' 'It was no voluntary act on his part,' rejoined the other; 'but an unlucky concatenation of events, of which some worthless sycophants took advantage, to effect his exile. You, surely, recollect the consternation at Athens, after the luckless battle of Chæronea?'

'Recollect it! Never will the terror of that day, on which the unhappy tidings arrived, fade from my memory. Even now I see in fancy the people rushing hurriedly through the streets to the assembly;—free-born dames standing at their doors, almost forgetful of decorum, amid their painful anxiety; and tremblingly questioning the

---

bial exclamation of joy, ὥρα νέα, χελιδών. Thus in Aristoph. *Equit.* 419,

σκέψασθε, παῖδες· οὐχ ὁρᾶθ'; ὥρα νέα, χελιδών,

and the comic lament of Mnesilochus, *Thesmoph.* 1:

'Ω Ζεῦ, χελιδὼν ἆρα πότε φανήσεται.

Our own proverb, too, 'One swallow does not make a summer,' was identically current among the Greeks. Aris-

tot. *Ethic. Nic.* i. 6, μία γὰρ χελιδὼν ἔαρ οὐ ποιεῖ. So also the gled-kite, ἴκτινος, which returned still earlier, was saluted with joy. *Aves.* 712. And *ib.* 500, we have προκυλινδεῖσθαι τοῖς ἰκτίνοις. Cf. Schol. on the passage

[20] The school mentioned Demosth. *de Corona*, 270, where Æschines and his father performed menial offices. Cf. Apollon. and Liban. *Vit. Æschin.*

passers-by as to the safety of their husbands, their fathers,
and their brothers;—hoary veterans, long released by law
from military service, parading the streets in the habiliments of war;—and what a wound was inflicted on
Attic pride, when the slaughter of three thousand of her
burghers reduced the city to the desperate resource of
manumitting the slaves, making the allies free burghers,
and reinstating the infamous in the social privileges which
they had forfeited.'[21]

'Your description is a faithful one,' continued Charicles. 'Though but a boy, scarcely more than fourteen at
that time, and troubling myself little about public matters,
I can speak to the depression that universally prevailed;
and there were few families, methinks, who were more
painfully alive than ours to the horrors in prospect for
them. My father had taken ship only a few hours before
the dreadful tidings came.[22] He had advanced a large
sum to a Lycian merchant, to trade with wine and other
goods to Crete, and return to Athens with a cargo of
Egyptian corn;[23] the proper period for the merchant's
return had elapsed some time, when my father heard that
the ship had run into Epidauros, and the freight been sold.
Alarmed, not only for the safety of his capital, but also for
his own, lest he should be accused of lending money for
illegal traffic,[24] he seized the opportunity, though ill at the

---

[21] Word for word from Lycurg. in
Leocr. p. 165.

[22] Lycurgus says, τὸ γεγονὸς πάθος
τῷ δήμῳ προσηγγέλλετο. It would
seem that the news first reached the
Prytaneion, and was then told to the
people, as appears from comparing
this with the transactions on the taking of Elateia. ἑσπέρα γὰρ ἦν. ἧκε δ'
ἀγγέλλων τις ὡς τοὺς πρυτάνεις, ὡς
Ἐλάτεια κατείληπται. . . τῇ δ' ὑστεραίᾳ ἅμα τῇ ἡμέρᾳ οἱ μὲν πρυτάνεις
τὴν βουλὴν ἐκάλουν εἰς τὸ Βουλευτή-

ριον· ὑμεῖς δ' εἰς τὴν ἐκκλησίαν ἐπο-
ρεύεσθε . . . καὶ μετὰ ταῦτα, ὡς εἰσῆλθεν ἡ βουλή, καὶ ἀπήγγειλαν τὰ
προσηγγελμένα ἑαυτοῖς, καὶ τὸν ἥ-
κοντα παρήγαγον, κ.τ.λ. Demosth.
de Coron. 284.

[23] The manner in which concerns
of this kind were conducted, appears
from the orations of Demosthenes
against Lacritos and Dionysodoros.
See Böckh, *Publ. Econ.* p. 132—139.

[24] There was a law which forbade any Athenian to lend money for

time, of embarking in a vessel bound for that port, being determined to call his fraudulent debtor to a personal account. He succeeded in finding him, and extracted a promise of payment immediately on the cargo being sold : the excitement of the journey had, however, made him worse, and he was so powerfully affected at the account of the misfortunes of Athens, which, soon after, arrived at Epidauros, that he fell violently sick, and could not leave the place. The rascally Lycian profited by his illness, and, with the unsold portion of his cargo, set sail for Athens, where circumstances gave him a prospect of obtaining a better market ; and where my father, only half convalescent, found him on his return. The city had recovered from its panic, there being no immediate calamity in view, as Philip had conducted himself with moderation ; this was, however, only the signal for all sorts of nefarious intriguing against all who might seem in any way to have been connected with these disasters.' 'I can guess the upshot,' exclaimed the stranger. 'Your father was doubtless accused of deserting his country in the moment of danger, contrary to the express decree of the people.' [25]

' Just so. Nobody would have ever dreamt of preferring such a charge, had not the vile Lycian, in order to escape from his liabilities, and avoid the two-fold accusation, bribed two notorious sycophants. At first my father treated their threatened accusation with contempt ;—but when he met here and there a growing coldness among his acquaintance, and learnt that two powerful demagogues, his personal foes, were about to appear against him, he began to consider the danger of staking his life on a moment of passionate excitement ; he bethought him of the untimely fate of Lysicles and others,[26] and of the disgrace

---

the purpose of buying corn destined for foreign ports. See Böckh, *ibid.* p. 85, and Demosth. *in Lacrit.* 941.

[25] Lycurg. *in Leocr.* p. 147.

[26] He was condemned to death on the accusation of Lycurgus. See the fine passage of the oration, preserved in Diod. Sic. xvi. 88.

that might ensue to his family; and with the consciousness
of perfect innocence, he determined to evade the accusation.

'It was indeed a moment of sorrow and consternation when my father, who had secretly made all the necessary preparations for departure, told us one evening that
we must leave Athens, and sojourn in the land of the
stranger. Instead of embarking openly by day, and in the
presence of a crowd of leave-taking friends, we stole in the
dead of night through the small gate, towards the shore,
where the ship was waiting for us, and on board of which
our slaves had already placed the baggage.[27] We first
sailed for Trœzene, but as severe epidemic disorders were
then prevailing there,[28] we departed and went to Sicily, and
abode five years at Syracuse. It was but a few months
ago that news reached my father that his friends had succeeded in establishing his innocence, and procuring permission for his return; but the intelligence arrived too late, as
the next day was the last he had to live. My mother had
died a few months previously, and so I am returned alone,
full of tearful regret, and yet of yearning anticipation;
for, after all, nothing can replace one's fatherland. Fair
too, above all towns beside, is Athens; though my father
was wont to assert that it was full of attraction for the
visitor, but replete with dangers to its own inhabitants.'[29]

'His remark was a just one,' said the other. 'What

---

[27] The flight of Leocrates has
served as the type here, with but few
changes. συσκευασάμενος ἃ εἶχε μετὰ
τῶν οἰκετῶν ἐπὶ τὸν λέμβον κατεκό-
μισε, τῆς νεὼς ἤδη περὶ τὴν ἀκτὴν
ἐξορμώσης· καὶ περὶ δείλην ὀψίαν
αὐτὸς μετὰ τῆς ἑταίρας Εἰρηνίδος
κατὰ μέσην τὴν ἀκτὴν διὰ τῆς Πυλί-
δος ἐξελθὼν πρὸς τὴν ναῦν προσ-
έπλευσε καὶ ᾤχετο φεύγων. Lycurg.
p. 148. Cf. ib. p. 178, where the departure from the harbour is depicted,
ὑπὸ πάντων τῶν φίλων ὁρώμενοι καὶ
ἀποστελλόμενοι. Cf. Antiph. de Venef. p. 613. Lucian, Amores, 6.

[28] Isocr. Ægin. 12, gives a somewhat similar account of the misfortunes of a family, and adds, ὅτι τὸ
χωρίον (Τροιζῆνα) ἐπυνθάνετο νοσῶ-
δες εἶναι. Epidemic, not endemic
disorders must be meant.

[29] According to Ælian, Var. Hist.
xii. 52, Isocrates compared Athens
to a courtesan, whose charms might
excite a temporary pleasure, though
no one would choose to have her for a
wife: καὶ οὖν καὶ τὴν Ἀθηναίων πόλιν
ἐνεπιδημῆσαι μὲν εἶναι ἡδίστην, καὶ
κατά γε τοῦτο πασῶν τῶν κατὰ

the pupil is to the eye, that is Athenæ to Hellas. But its people are volatile and fickle; as easily inspired with any noble thought, as they are hurried away into acts of injustice and atrocity;—now moved even to tears by the tragic end of an Œdipus, or the woes of unhappy Trojan women,—now hastening from thence, to entangle the house of a fellow-citizen in a web of malicious trickery, and plunge it into ruin and despair; a spoiled child, full of vanity and humours; basking in the sunshine of a former age, the spots of which are hidden by the light of noble deeds; pluming itself on the empty name of pure Hellenic blood, and on having been the first to recognize law and justice, while it yet fosters in its bosom a most venomous brood of worthless sycophants, and subjects every law to the caprice of the moment; with the name of freedom for ever in its mouth, yet threatening every careless word that may not please the people's humour with death or banishment. And then again its character presents a most pleasing union of the grave and gay. Blithe and gladsome is the life of the Athenian, who is ever contented, provided he has something to wrangle about or laugh at. He is equally capable of appreciating the grandest creations of the tragic stage, and the most farcical caricatures of comedy; he enjoys alike the society of the most staid philosopher, and of the flightiest *hetæra*. Penurious is he at home, and mean at the table of the money-changer, but most lavish when he wishes to cut a grand figure in a *choregia*, or pass for an admirer of *vertu*.'[30]

τὴν Ἑλλάδα διαφέρειν· ἐνοικῆσαι δὲ ἀσφαλῆ μηκέτι εἶναι.

[30] When Aristotle was asked his opinion of Athens—τίς ἐστιν ἡ τῶν Ἀθηναίων πόλις; he answered, παγκάλη. ἀλλ' ἐν αὐτῇ

ὄγχνη ἐπ' ὄγχνη γηράσκει, σῦκον δ' ἐπὶ σύκῳ.

Ælian, *Var. Hist.* iii. 36. This witty application of Homer's line has the same point as the simile of Isocrates, and in both we read the voice of antiquity, which, though extolling the renown of Athens, complains no less loudly of the want of personal security there; which is to be ascribed partly to the form of the government, partly to the idiosyncrasy of the Athenian people. The words of Philo, ii.

'My father thought of them pretty much as you do,' said Charicles. 'But, as you now know more about me

467 : ὅπερ ἐν ὀφθαλμῷ κόρη, ἢ ἐν ψυχῇ λογισμὸς, τοῖτ' ἐν Ἑλλάδι Ἀθῆναι, and those of Dicæarch. *Stat. Græc.* p. 10 : ὅσον αἱ λοιπαὶ πόλεις πρός τε ἡδονὴν καὶ βίου διόρθωσιν τῶν ἀγρῶν διαφέρουσι, τοσοῦτον τῶν λοιπῶν πόλεων ἡ τῶν Ἀθηναίων παραλλάττει, are a just tribute to the intellectual and mercantile supremacy of Athens. And Athenæus, i. p. 20, comparing various cities, says : Ἀλεξανδρέωι μὲν τὴν χρυσῆν, Ἀντιοχέων δὲ τὴν καλὴν, Νικομηδέων δὲ τὴν περικαλλῆ, προσέτι δὲ

Τὴν λαμπροτάτην πόλεων πασῶν, ὁπόσας ὁ Ζεὺς ἀναφαίνει,

τὰς Ἀθήνας λέγω. Cf. Alciph. *Epist.* ii. 3 : ὅλην ἐν ταῖς Ἀθήναις τὴν Ἑλλάδα, ὅλην τὴν Ἰονίαν. But besides this external splendour. Athens might boast of being a genuine patron of science and art, a very temple of the muses, and a school for all Greece. So Thucyd. ii. 41 ; and Isocr. *Paneg.* p. 63 : τοσοῦτον ἀπολέλοιπεν ἡ πόλις ἡμῶν περὶ τὸ φρονεῖν καὶ λέγειν τοὺς ἄλλους ἀνθρώπους, ὥσθ' οἱ ταύτης μαθηταὶ τῶν ἄλλων διδάσκαλοι γεγόνασι. But the vanity of the inhabitants was so assiduously fostered by the orators and demagogues, that an arrogant contempt of other states sprung up among them. Even Demosthenes betrays this weakness, *de Fœd. Alex.* p. 218 ; and Isocr. *adv. Callim.* 19, says : νῦν δὲ εὐδαιμονέστατοι καὶ σωφρονέστατοι τῶν Ἑλλήνων δοκοῦμεν εἶναι. Every funeral oration teems with their former great deeds in behalf of Greece, and puts prominently forward their claim to the dubious honour of being the only Autochthones in Greece. Of more significance than this inflated common-place, are the earnest words of

Lycurgus, *in Leocr.* p. 170 : (ὁ δῆμος) ὃς πρῶτον ἐπὶ τῷ αὐτόχθων εἶναι καὶ ἐλεύθερος ἐσεμνύνετο · and the chorus in Aristoph. *Vespæ*, 1076, says, Ἀττικοὶ, μόνοι δικαίως εὐγενεῖς αὐτόχθονες. The notion αὐτόχθων εἶναι has been variously interpreted. Originally it meant that the people of Attica were indigenous, neither having been expelled from anywhere, nor having immigrated of their own accord, but τὴν χώραν ἀεὶ οἱ αὐτοὶ οἰκοῦντες. Thucyd. ii. 36. Lesbon. *Protrept.* p. 22, is even more explicit : οἱ μὲν ἄλλοι πάντες Ἕλληνες ἐκ τῆς σφετέρας αὐτῶν μεταστάντες οἰκοῦσιν ἕκαστοι αὐτῶν, ἐξελάσαντες ἑτέρους, καὶ αὐτοὶ ἐξε λαθέντες ὑφ' ἑτέρων, καὶ κατὰ τοῦτι δύο φέρεσθε καυχήματα ἀρετῆς. οὔτι γὰρ ἐξηλάθητε τῆς σφετέρας αὐτῶι ὑπὸ οὐδαμῶν ἀνθρώπων, οὔτε ἐξελά σαντες ἑτέρους αὐτοὶ οἰκεῖτε. They also considered themselves γηγενεῖς, *i.e.* earth-born, in the literal sense of the word. So Demosth. *Funebr.* p. 1390 : οὐ γὰρ μόνον εἰς πατέρ' αὐτοῖς καὶ τῶν ἄνω προγόνων κατ' ἄνδρα ἀνενεγκεῖν ἑκάστῳ τὴν φύσιν ἔστιν, ἀλλ' εἰς ὅλην κοινῇ τὴν ὑπάρχουσαν πατρίδα, ἧς αὐτόχθονες ὁμολογοῦνται εἶναι μόνοι γὰρ πάντων ἀνθρώπων ἐξ ἧσπερ ἔφυσαν, ταύτην ᾤκησαν καὶ τοῖς ἐξ αὐτῶν παρέδωκαν · and Plato, *Menex.* p. 237: αὐτόχθονας καὶ τῷ ὄντι ἐν πατρίδι οἰκοῦντας καὶ ζῶντας, καὶ τρεφομένους οὐχ ὑπὸ μητρυιᾶς, ὡς ἄλλοι, ἀλλ' ὑπὸ μητρὸς, τῆς χώρας ἐν ᾗ ᾤκουν. The idea that in Attica the pure Grecian blood could have ever been adulterated with that of foreigners, is scouted in *Menex.* p. 245 : ἀλλ' αὐτοὶ Ἕλληνες, οὐ μιξο βάρβαροι, οἰκοῦμεν · and again in Isocr. *Paneg.* p. 55 : ταύτην γὰρ οἰκοῦ μεν, οὐχ ἑτέρους ἐκβαλόντες, οὐδ'

than my mere name, tell me yours also : I seem to have
an indistinct notion that we have met in days of yore.'

'Charicles!' exclaimed the youth, as he walked up and
looked straight into the other's face. 'I knew you at our
very first salute ; but you have no recollection of me, I see.

ἐρήμην καταλαβόντες, οὐδ' ἐκ πολλῶν ἐθνῶν μιγάδες συλλεγέντες, ἀλλ'
οὕτω καλῶς καὶ γνησίως γεγόναμεν,
ὥστ' ἐξ ἧσπερ ἔφυμεν, ταύτην ἔχοντες ἄπαντα τὸν χρόνον διατελοῖμεν,
αὐτόχθονες ὄντες. Antisthenes (Diog.
Laert. vi. 1) ridiculed the immense
value attached to this distinction,
and classed them with snails: ἔλεγε
μηδὲν εἶναι κοχλιῶν καὶ ἀττελέβων
εὐγενεστέρους. In proportion as the
Athenians loved to be flattered about
their ancient renown, so they could
not endure to hear reproof or any
unpleasant truths; and thus in a state
that plumed itself on being freest of
the free, freedom of speech was fet-
tered by the caprice of the public.
This intolerance is animadverted on
by Isocrates, de Pace, 5 : ἐγὼ οἶδα
μὲν, ὅτι πρόσαντές ἐστιν ἐναντιοῦ-
σθαι ταῖς ὑμετέραις διανοίαις καὶ ὅτι,
δημοκρατίας οὔσης, οὐκ ἔστι παρρησία, πλὴν ἐνθάδε μὲν τοῖς ἀφρο-
νεστάτοις καὶ μηδὲν ὑμῶν φροντί-
ζουσιν, ἐν δὲ τῷ θεάτρῳ τοῖς κωμῳδο-
διδασκάλοις . . . . πρὸς δὲ τοὺς ἐπι-
πλήττοντας καὶ νουθετοῦντας ὑμᾶς
οὕτω διατίθεσθε δυσκόλως, ὥσπερ
τοὺς κακόν τι τὴν πόλιν ἐργαζομέ-
νους. Again Aristot. de Repub. v. 10:
καὶ γὰρ ἡ δημοκρατία ἡ τελευταία
τυραννίς ἐστιν· and he adds: καὶ γὰρ
ὁ δῆμος εἶναι βούλεται μόναρχος.
διὸ καὶ ὁ κόλαξ παρ' ἀμφοτέροις
ἔντιμος. Cf. Plutarch, Demosth. 26;
and Aristoph. Equit. passim. And
what was this δῆμος? Euthydemos
replies, τοὺς πένητας τῶν πολιτῶν,
(Xenoph. Memor. iv. 2, 37,) which

is a better definition than those of
the philosophers. Aristot. de Rep.
vi. 2. See Hermann's Gr. Staatsalt.
for a capital estimate of the character of the δῆμος. The inordinate
taste for litigation was a special
trait of the Athenian public. See
the apposite remark, Lucian, Icaromen. 16: τοὺς Αἰγυπτίους γεωρ-
γοῦντας ἐπέβλεπον. καὶ ὁ Φοίνιξ δὲ
ἐνεπορεύετο, καὶ ὁ Κίλιξ ἐλῄστευε.
καὶ ὁ Λάκων ἐμαππιγοῦτο, καὶ ὁ
Ἀθηναῖος ἐδικάζετο. So also Xenoph.
de Repub. Athen. 3, 2, and Aves, 40:

Ἀθηναῖοι δ' ἀεὶ
ἐπὶ τῶν δικῶν ᾄδουσι πάντα τὸν βίον.

The character of the people, as
shewn in the Market, the Gymnasium,
and the Theatre, will be discussed
hereafter. The preceding estimate of
the Athenian character will scarcely
appear too severe to an unprejudiced
student of the orators. See Dio Chrysos. Or. xiii. p. 427, and xxxi. p. 574.
The distinction drawn between the
Ἀττικοὶ and Ἀθηναῖοι, (Dicæarch.
Stat. Græc. p. 9,) will not hold at all ;
there are a hundred instances to prove
the mixture of excellent and despicable qualities in the Athenian character. What Pliny relates of Par-
rhasios is much to the point: 'Pinxit
et Demon Atheniensium, argumento
quoque ingenioso. Debebat namque
varium, iracundum, injustum, incon-
stantem, eundem exorabilem, clemen-
tem, misericordem, gloriosum, excel-
sum, humilem, ferocem fugacemque
et omnia pariter ostendere.' Nat.
Hist. xxxv. 10, 36.

C

And yet, there was a time, when we saw each other daily,
and my poverty withheld you not from being my friend
and playmate. What! have you forgotten the poor lad,
who was a drudge in that very school of Hermippos, and
performed menial offices to which he had not been born?
Who used to mix the ink, sweep out the school-room, and
cleanse the benches with a sponge?'[31]

'Ctesiphon!' cried the stripling, as he rushed forward,
and seized his friend by the hand. 'Yes! it is indeed you;
my feelings were more truthful than my memory, and told
me from the first that we must have once been friends.
But how could I have forgotten you? How have become
forgetful of the thousand acts of kindness which you did me
in preference to all others? How you used to give me little
cork carriages carved by your own hand; or caught for
me whirring cockchafers, and fastened a thread deftly to
their legs; and afterwards, how you, being yourself quick
at ciphering, would teach me all the little artifices of the
science; so that even the stern pedagogue took a liking to
you and was pleased to see us in company, notwithstanding
your being my senior by a year or two, and that the cut of
a lad's coat usually made all the difference with him. Forgotten it? Oh! no. But your beard so disguises you,
my friend. And who could ever recognise in that athletic
frame, embrowned by the sun, the pale, weakly boy of my
school-days? Moreover, we have not met for eight years.
How came it, by the bye, that you left Hermippos in such
a hurry?'

'Of that presently,' replied Ctesiphon. 'It is nigh
mid-day: let us try by that time to reach Cleonæ; it is
still eighty stadia from thence to Corinth.'[32]

The friends broke up their bivouac. Charicles took

---

[31] Demosth. *de Coron.* 313, relates
this of Æschines.

[32] Strabo, viii. 6, 19: διέχουσι δ'
αἱ Κλεωναὶ τοῦ μὲν Ἄργους σταδίους
εἴκοσι καὶ ἑκατὸν, Κορίνθου δ' ὀγδοήκοντα. On which Dodwell, *Class.
Tour*, ii. p. 206, observes, that it
'agrees nearly with two hours and
a half that it took us to reach it, from
that place,' though in the *Expédit.
de Morée*, 3 hrs. 4 m. are assigned.

the bridle of his charger, which Manes had again bitted, drew it over his head, and thus led him along, walking side by side with Ctesiphon, who beguiled the way with the recital of his fortunes during the last eight years.

The father of Ctesiphon [33] was an Athenian citizen, well to do in the world; and having only one son surviving from a former marriage, he took for a second wife his brother's daughter. The offspring of this alliance were Ctesiphon, and a younger sister. The father, who was engaged in large mercantile transactions with distant countries, had occasion to go to the Pontus and Chersonesus. Before quitting Athens, he resolved, in case anything should befall him on his journey, to entrust his will to his brother, who was bound to his children by a double tie; and, at the same time, he committed to his custody, partly in cash, partly in bonds and mortgage deeds, a fortune of more than fifteen talents. He never returned. The faithless guardian concealed his death till he had got hold of the papers which the deceased had left under seal. He then broke the sad news, disposed of the widow in marriage, though not with all the dowry that had been intended for her, and undertook the education of Ctesiphon, who was not eight years old, and of his younger sister, as well as the maintenance of their elder step-brother. When the latter had attained his twentieth year, and was declared of age, the uncle summoned them all three, asserted that their father had only left a property of twinty *minæ* in silver and thirty gold *staters*, that he had himself expended a sum far exceeding this on their education and nurture, and it was quite out of his power to take any further charge of them. 'You are a man now,' so he addressed the eldest, 'it is your business to care for your brother and sister.' With this he turned the unfortunate orphans out of their father's own house—which he himself now occupied—badly clothed,

---

[33] The history of Ctesiphon's youth is taken from a classical model. Lysias, *adv. Diogeiton*, p. 894—903.

and worse shod, without a slave to attend on them, without a bed for the night, or a single iota of their father's property. The younger ones were utterly helpless. Their mother had been dead about a year; the elder brother sought employment in foreign service, and nobody stood by them to substantiate the charge against their infamous guardian. A decayed relative, himself in great penury, took charge of the orphans. He used to officiate at the aforementioned school, in the capacity of assistant, and thinking that the boy he had adopted ought to contribute something to their support, he made him perform menial duties, for which his birth had certainly not destined him. Ctesiphon's intelligent manner and obliging behaviour won him many a friend among the boys who came to the school, and on the death of one of them, an only son, the father, a rich burgher, who had conceived a predilection for Ctesiphon, then fourteen, adopted him as his son. ' My benefactor also is now dead,' said Ctesiphon in conclusion, ' and I have just been to Argos to receive a debt, due to me as part of my inheritance, which, though not very considerable, still affords me the means of living in the simple fashion that I love. Luckily I preferred the high road, which is more shady, to the shorter route by the foot-path, and so have been the first to welcome you on your return to your fatherland. But tell me one thing, how come you at Cleonæ, on your way from Sicily?'

' Our ship,' answered Charicles, ' put in at the port of Epidauros. I resolved to go the rest of the journey by land, and took the route by Argos, because the shorter cut over the mountains to Corinth would have been more hurtful to my horse's feet,[34] and also because I wished to visit an old friend of my father's at Argos.'

---

[34] Beckmann, in his *History of Inventions*, has, with tolerable success, attempted to show that horse-shoes were unknown before the fourth century of our era. Ottfr. Müller, on the contrary, believes that a horse-shoeing scene is represented on a certain antique Attic vase. Socks or sandals, however, were tied on the feet of beasts of burden: these were

In the course of this colloquy the friends had arrived in the plain, which was overlooked by the town of Cleonæ, its houses built on a slope, and rising terrace-fashion one above another.[35] There they rested for a brief while, and then continued their journey to Corinth.

---

regular ὑποδήματα, and hence (Lucian, *Asin.* 16) the metamorphosed ass is called ἀνυπόδετος.

[35] Dodwell, *Class. Tour*, ii. p. 206: 'On the side of the hill are six ancient terrace-walls of the third style of masonry, rising one above another, on which the houses and streets were situated.' Comp. Leake, *Travels in the Morea*, iii. p. 325.

SCENE THE SECOND.

CORINTH.

THE sun had sunk low in the west, when the two friends, emerging from a little wood of cypresses and pines, found themselves in sight of the mighty city, mistress of two seas, which, while it lay on the high-road between southern and northern Greece,[1] connected also with its double haven the eastern and the western world.

Not many *stadia* off, the proud Acropolis arose before them, hiding the chief part of the city by its steep northern slope, although detached houses and villas might be descried, reaching down to the plain on the south. To the right of the road, and on the verge of the wood, was an artificial basin, encompassed with stone seats which invited the wanderer to repose. A number of young female slaves, with their dress girt up high, were just then busy filling their earthen *hydria* at the crystal stream that leapt in three jets from amidst festoons of flowers, sculptured—as well as the youths holding them—in marble relief.[2]

Not far from this charming spot the friends separated. Ctesiphon, who intended to put up at the hospitable abode of an acquaintance, turned to the left, making for the Sicyonian gate; while Charicles pursued the road, which, after threading plantations of olive and pomegranate, led to the *Craneion.* Having no friends or acquaintance what-

---

[1] On this happy situation of Corinth, see Strabo, viii. 6, 19: Ὁ δὲ Κόρινθος ἃ νεὶὸς μὲν λέγεται διὰ τὸ ἐμπορεῖον, ἐπὶ τῷ Ἰσθμῷ κείμενος καὶ δυοῖν λιμένων κύριος, . . . καὶ ῥᾳδίας ποιεῖ τὰς ἑκατέρωθεν ἀμοιβὰς τῶν φορτίων. Owing to the perils of the passage round Cape Malea, goods were usually trans-shipped across the Isthmus: ἀγαπητὸν ἦν . . . τοῖς ἐμπό-ροις ἀφεῖσι τὸν ἐπὶ Μαλεὰς πλοῦν εἰς Κόρινθον κατάγεσθαι τὸν φόρτον αὐτόθι. So Dio Chrysos. *Or.* viii. p. 276, says: ὅτι ἡ πόλις ὥσπερ ἐν τριόδῳ τῆς Ἑλλάδος ἔκειτο.

[2] Near Mistra a spring so enclosed may still be seen. *Exped. de Morée,* ii. pl. 42.

soever in the city, he purposed looking for one of those
houses in which the traveller can purchase a good reception
and entertainment. His friend at Argos had mentioned
to him the house of one Sotades, who was reputed to be
a tolerably reasonable man, and very solicitous for his
guests' comfort; and our young hero, not being averse to
pleasure and gaiety, was glad to hear that the female
portion of the household was as free from restraint in its
intercourse with the other sex, as it was personally attractive. Nay, it was even asserted, that they had long
been initiated by brilliant torch-light into the mysteries
of Aphrodite: [3] and report said that their mother was
not the person to reject a well-filled hand, that sued for
the favours of her daughters, though, outwardly, they
avoided the appearance of regular *hetæræ*.[4] It is true that
Ctesiphon had cautioned the inexperienced Charicles, and

---

[3] Comp. the expression, Lucian,
Navig. 11 : Μῶν ἐρωτικόν τί ἐστιν;
οὐδὲ γὰρ τοῦτο ἀμύητοις ἡμῖν ἐξα-
γορεύσεις, ἀλλ' ὑπὸ λαμπρᾷ τῇ δᾳδὶ
καὶ αὐτοῖς τετελεσμένοις.

[4] In a set of pictures illustrative
of Greek customs, it was quite impossible to leave out the *hetæræ*,
who gave such a peculiar colouring
to Grecian levity, and exercised so
potent a sway over the life of the
younger members of the community.
Abundant materials for such a sketch
exist, for the Greeks made no secret
of matters of this kind; the difficulty
has rather been not to sacrifice the
vividness of the picture of the ordinary intercourse with these women,
to the demands of our modern sense
of propriety. But without describing
the enormities that characterise the
symposia where these *hetæræ* were
present, it seemed desirable to enter
a good deal into details. All the
features of the picture, even to the
minutest details, are taken, almost

without exception, from the classics;
especially from the speech against
Neæra, and from that of Lysias on the
murder of *Eratosthenes*; besides Lucian's *Toxaris, Asinus,* and *Dialogi
Meretricii*; as well as from Appuleius,
Heliodorus, and the comedians. The
narrative given by Demosth. *in Neær.*
p. 1366, forms the outline of the story,
and the details are supplied from
Lysias and elsewhere. The passage
in Demosthenes is as follows: Ἐπαί-
νετον γὰρ τὸν Ἄνδριον ἐραστὴν ὄντα
Νεαίρας ταυτησὶ παλαιὸν καὶ πολλὰ
ἀνηλωκότα εἰς αὐτήν, καὶ καταγόμενον
παρὰ τούτοις ὁπότε ἐπιδημήσειεν
Ἀθήναζε διὰ τὴν φιλίαν τῆς Νεαίρας,
ἐπιβουλεύσας ὁ Στέφανος οὑτοσὶ,
μεταπεμψάμενος εἰς ἀγρὸν, ὡς θύων,
λαμβάνει μοιχὸν ἐπὶ τῇ θυγατρὶ τῆς
Νεαίρας ταυτησὶ, καὶ εἰς φόβον καταστήσας πράττεται μνᾶς τριάκον-
τα· καὶ λαβὼν ἐγγυητὰς τούτωι
Ἀριστόμαχόν τε τὸν θεσμοθετή-
σαντα, καὶ Ναυσίφιλον τὸν Ναυσινί
κου τοῦ ἄρξαντος υἱὸν, ἀφίησιν, ὡς
ἀποδώσοντ' αὐτῷ τὸ ἀργύριον.

depicted the perils, that here, more than elsewhere, awaited him who suffered himself to be entangled in their
seductive toils. He had well explained the meaning of
the proverb:—

Non cuivis homini contingit adire Corinthon,[5]

adding instances of merchants who had been forced to
leave both ship and freight in the clutches of the greedy
hetœræ.

But Charicles had firmly assured his monitor that he
would not stay at Corinth more than three days; nor did
he suppose that, in so short a sojourn, he would need even
a tithe of the two thousand *drachmœ* that he had with
him. It was in the best possible spirits therefore that
he directed his steps to the *Craneion,* in the vicinity of
which Sotades lived.

The place that went by this name[6] was by far the
most frequented point of Corinth. Here was an evergreen
cyprus-grove, in which lay the shrine of Bellerophon, and
the temple of Aphrodite Melanis,[7] the goddess in whose
service more than a thousand *hierodulæ* ministered to the
pleasures of the countless stream of strangers.[8] A source

---

[5] Strabo, viii. 6, 20: Οὐ παντὸς
ἀνδρὸς ἐς Κόρινθον ἔσθ' ὁ πλοῦς.

[6] The oldest mention of the Κράνειον or Κράνιον, and perhaps the
only one, previous to the destruction
of Corinth, occurs in Xenoph. *Hist.
Gr.* iv. 4, 4. Diog. Laert. vi. 77. calls
it a *gymnasium:* ἐν τῷ Κρανείῳ τῷ
πρὸ τῆς Κορίνθου γυμνασίῳ, and Suidas
says, Κράνειον· φυτὸν, καὶ τὸ γυμνάσιον. But Pausanias, ii. 2, 4, says
nothing of this, and apparently makes
it merely a pleasure-grove: πρὸ δὲ
τῆς πόλεως κυπαρίσσων ἐστὶν ἄλσος
ὀνομαζόμενον Κράνειον. Perhaps, on
the rebuilding of the city, the place
lost its former destination. That it
was a very agreeable resort, appears
from Plut. *de Exsil* 6.

[7] Pausanias, *supra:* ἐνταῦθα Βελ-
λεροφόντου τέ ἐστι τέμενος, καὶ
Ἀφροδίτης ναὸς Μελανίδος. Concerning Aphrodite Melanis, see Pausan. viii. 6, 2. Whether this was the
temple in which were the thousand
hierodulæ, is nowhere distinctly
stated, but it would seem not improbable. See Excursus on *The Hetæræ.*

[8] The merchants of antiquity, who
were often absent from home for
years, as ἔμποροι or ναύκληροι,
doubtless often yielded to the temp-
tations thrown in their way at the
several places they visited. Cf. Isocr.
Ægin. 2: πλάνης δὲ γενόμενος καὶ
διαιτηθεὶς ἐν πολλαῖς πόλεσιν ἄλλαις τε γυναιξὶ συνεγένετο. ὧν ἔνιαι
καὶ παιδάρι' ἀπέδειξαν, ἃ ἐκεῖνος

of wealth, doubtless, to the temple and city, but to the
easily-inveigled sailor, of more certain destruction than the
whirlpool of the all-engulphing Charybdis. On the monument of Lais hard by stood, like a warning-sign, the
lioness, holding in her claws the captive ram, an easily intelligible symbol of her life.[9] What a strange chance was
it, that, at no very distant period, this identical spot should
be selected for the burial-place of Diogenes of Sinope ; just
as though this example of unnatural abstinence was intended as a contrast to the memorial of wanton licentious-
ness. The vicinity of the hetæræ,[10] and the pleasantness
of the place, drew hither daily a vast number of residents
and strangers, and by a natural consequence, abundance
of hawkers, who exposed their goods for sale. Damsels
with bread and cakes, others with chaplets and *tæniæ*, boys
with baskets full of fruit, plied their trade, offering their
wares to the loungers.[11]

If people congregated here merely for pleasure and
amusement, such was not the case in the street leading
from the harbour of Cenchrea, which presented a most
animated scene of business and traffic. Man and beast were
everlastingly busied in transporting the contents of the
vessels to the town or to the harbour of Lechæon, or from
thence to the eastern harbour. In one place might be
seen numberless beasts of burden carrying Byzantine corn
to the city; waggons meeting each other, some conveying

οὐδὲ πώποτε γνήσια ἐνόμισε, καὶ δὴ
καὶ τὴν ταύτης μητέρα ἐν τούτοις
τοῖς χρόνοις ἔλαβεν. Hence seaports
generally, the Piræus for instance,
abounded with πόρναι and πόρνοι.
Cf. Terent. *Phorm.* iv. 1 ; and Plaut.
Epid. iv. 1, 13.

[9] Pausan. *supra*: Τάφος Λαΐδος,
ᾧ δὴ λέαινα ἐπίθημά ἐστι κριὸν
ἔχουσα ἐν τοῖς προτέροις ποσίν.

[10] Dio Chrysos. *Or.* viii. p. 276,
says of Diogenes of Sinope: μετέβη

εἰς Κόρινθον κἀκεῖ διῆγεν, οὔτε οἰκίαν
μισθωσάμενος, οὔτε παρὰ ξένῳ τινὶ
καταγόμενος, ἀλλ' ἐν τῷ Κρανίῳ
θυραυλῶν. ἑώρα γὰρ ὅτι πλεῖστοι
ἄνθρωποι ἐκεῖ συνίασι διὰ τοὺς λιμέ-
νας καὶ τὰς ἑταίρας.

[11] Alciphr. *Epist.* iii. 60 : 'Ως γὰρ
ἐλούσαντο οἱ πολλοὶ καὶ μεσοῦσα
ἡμέρα ἦν. σταφύλους ἐθεασάμην καὶ
εὐφυεῖς νεανίσκους οὐ περὶ τὰς οἰκίας,
ἀλλὰ περὶ τὸ Κράνειον εἰλουμένους,
καὶ οὗ μάλιστα ταῖς ἀρτοπώλισι καὶ
ὀπωροκαπήλοις ἔθος ἀναστρέφειν.

the wines of the Grecian isles to the west; and others
taking the equally renowned growths of Sicily and Italy
to the cities of Greece. In another, carefully packed
marble statues, the masterpieces of the Attic studios,[12]
were being conveyed by surefooted mules, to be submitted
to the judgment of Sicilian connoisseurs. Here, again,
the scarcely less valuable works in bronze, of Corinth and
Sicyon, were about to be shipped for the towns of Asia
Minor: not to mention the variety of costly products, and
what not, which the innumerable chests and bales contained. The choicest aromatics from the scented plains of
Araby, the costly web of the forests of Ind, its ivory and its
curious woods; gorgeous tapestries, the toilsome produce
of Babylonish ingenuity, the wool of Milesian flocks, the
gauze drapery wrought by maidens of Cos,—all found their
way to this emporium of an hemisphere.

Charicles, in pleased surprise, strode through the
crowd, which presented a phenomenon to which he was
unused. During the six years of his absence, the picture
of Athenian life had been nearly effaced from his recollection. The Sicilian towns which he had seen, were so deserted, that the wild beast made his lair there, and the
suburbs were not unfrequently the scene of the chase.[13]

---

[12] Works of art, such as images
of the gods, were exported in great
quantities, not merely on order, but
also on speculation, as is evident from
the story of Apollonios, who met a
ship's-load of them in the Piraeus.
ἐρομένου δὲ τοῦ ᾿Απολλωνίου, τίς ὁ
φόρτος; Θεῶν, ἔφη, ἀγάλματα ἀπάγω
ἐς ᾿Ιωνίαν, τὰ μὲν χρυσοῦ καὶ λίθου,
τὰ δὲ ἐλέφαντος καὶ χρυσοῦ. ᾿Ιδρυσό-
μενος, ἢ τί; ᾿Αποδωσόμενος, ἔφη, τοῖς
βουλομένοις ἱδρύεσθαι. Philostr. Vit.
Apoll m. Tyan. v. 20. The love of art
in Sicily appears from Cic. in Verr. iv.

[13] Plutarch, Timoleon, 22: ἡ μὲν
ἐν Συρακούσαις ἀγορὰ δι᾿ ἐρημίαν

οὕτω πολλὴν καὶ βαθεῖαν ἐξέφυσεν
ὕλην, ὥστε τοὺς ἵππους ἐν αὐτῇ
κατανέμεσθαι, τῶν ἱππικόμων ἐν τῇ
χλόῃ κατακειμένων. αἱ δ᾿ ἄλλαι πόλεις πλὴν παντελῶς ὀλίγων ἐλάφων
ἐγένοντο μεσταὶ καὶ συῶν ἀγρίων.
ἐν δὲ τοῖς προαστείοις καὶ περὶ τὰ
τείχη πολλάκις οἱ σχολὴν ἄγοντες
ἐκυνηγέτουν. This refers to a period
ten years before the date of this narration. Many other towns were in a
similar state. So Dio Chrysos. Or. vii.
p. 233, speaking of a town in Euboea,
says: βλέπετε γὰρ αὐτοὶ δήπουθεν,
ὅτι τὸ γυμνάσιον ὑμῖν ἄροιραν πε-
ποιήκασιν· ὥστε τὸν ῾Ηρακλέα καὶ
ἄλλους ἀνδριάντας συχνοὺς ὑπὸ τοῦ

Syracuse itself, which Timoleon had found so desolate that horses pastured on the tall grass which overgrew the market-place, had recovered but little of its former animation. But here was a scene to which the busy hum of the Piræus, or the liveliness of the Athenian *agora*, could alone afford a comparison. He asked a boy, who offered him fruit for sale, if he could show him Sotades' domicile. ' Oh, you mean the father of the pretty Melissa and Stephanion ?' replied the urchin. ' He lives no great way off,' added he, and forthwith he offered his services as a guide, and, at Charicles' bidding, tripped gaily along before him.

The house of Sotades was not a common inn [14] that

θέρους ἀποκεκρύφθαι, τοὺς μὲν ἡρώων, τοὺς δὲ θεῶν. καὶ ὅτι καθ' ἡμέραν τὰ τοῦ ῥήτορος τούτου πρόβατα ἔωθεν εἰς τὴν ἀγορὰν ἐμβάλλει καὶ κατανέμεται περὶ τὸ βουλευτήριον.

[14] As has been shewn in *Gallus*, 2nd Ed. p. 353, it is erroneous to suppose that there were no inns among the ancients, or that their use was confined to the lowest class of travellers. Of course there was nothing of the kind in the Homeric age. People on a journey, in those days, found a hospitable reception in the house of a stranger, and thus arose ties of friendship which even extended to their posterity. This beautiful custom even reaches down to the historic era. Herod. vi. 35, Οὗτος ὁ Μιλτιάδης (ὁ Κυψέλου, 'Αθηναῖος) κατήμενος ἐν τοῖσι π. οθύροισι τοῖσι ἑωυτοῦ, ὁρέων τοὺς Δολόγκους παριόντας, ἐσθῆτα ἔχοντας οὐκ ἐγχωρίην καὶ αἰχμὰς, προσεβώσατο· καί σφι προσελθοῦσι ἐπηγγείλατο καταγωγὴν καὶ ξείνια· and a law of Charondas prescribes, ξένον πάντα τὸν ἐν τῇ ἑαυτοῦ πατρίδι σεβόμενον, καὶ κατὰ τοὺς οἰκείους νόμους, εὐφήμως καὶ οἰκείως προσδέχεσθαι καὶ ἀποστέλλειν, μεμνημένους Διὸς Ξενίου,

ὡς παρὰ πᾶσιν ἱδρυμένου κοινοῦ θεοῦ, καὶ ὄντος ἐπισκόπου φιλοξενίας τε καὶ κακοξενίας. Stob. *Tit.* xliv. 40. See Ælian, *Var. Hist.* iv. 1. But when intercourse grew more frequent and towns like Corinth and Athens were overflowing with strangers, it is natural to suppose that the want of inns became felt. At the great Grecian festivals, for instance, the majority of the strangers could have no other house to lodge at but an auberge. Wealthy individuals, even at a later period, were very hospitable to strangers: so Xenoph. *Œcon.* 2, 5: ἔπειτα ξένους προσήκει σοι πολλοὺς δέχεσθαι, καὶ τούτους μεγαλοπρεπῶς. See also Plato, *Protag.* p. 315, where the house of Callias is crammed with guests, but these were some of them friends, some bidden guests, and others persons of distinction. Other persons had to put up at an inn, πανδοκεῖον, καταγώγιον, κατάλυσις. See Plato, *Leg.* xii. p. 952. At festivals, however, places of shelter were provided in the vicinity of the temples at the public expense. Schol. to Pind. *Olym.* xi. 55: τὸ γὰρ ἐν κύκλῳ τοῦ ἱεροῦ καταγωγίοις διείληπτο. Cf. Ælian, *Var. Hist.* iv. 9. It does not appear whether these καταγώγια

took in every stranger seeking shelter and entertainment : or where travellers of all grades might reckon on obtaining protection from the inclemency of the weather, or a place of temporary repose. Particular guests only were free of the house, and they mostly were well-known, and accustomed to visit it several times a-year, and then to make a lengthened stay.[15] Indeed it was no secret to many in Corinth, that the two damsels, whom Sotades called his daughters, were the main support of the family, in like manner as their mother Nicippe—who commonly went by the sobriquet of Ægidion—had formerly been the Amalthea that procured subsistence.[16] Sotades, however, pretended

---

or σκηναί, erected on such occasions, offered anything besides shelter. It was usual for travellers to provide the necessaries of the journey for themselves, and many probably lived entirely in their own tents. See Plutarch, *Alcib.* 12. There was a similar arrangement at the temple of Aphrodite at Cnidos : ἦν δ' ὑπὸ ταῖς ἄγαν παλινσκίοις ὕλαις ἱλαραὶ κλισίαι τοῖς ἐνεστιᾶσθαι θέλουσιν, εἰς ἃ τῶν μὲν ἀστικῶν σπανίως ἐπεφοίτων τινές· ἀθρόος δ' ὁ πολιτικὸς ὄχλος ἐπανηγύριζεν, ὄντως ἀφροδισιάζοντες. Lucian, *Amor.* 12. The most important building of the kind was that erected near the *Heræon*, on the site of Platæa, after its destruction by the Spartans : ᾠκοδόμησαν πρὸς τῷ Ἡραίῳ καταγώγιον διακοσίων ποδῶν, πανταχῇ κύκλῳ οἰκήματα ἔχον κάτωθεν καὶ ἄνωθεν. Thucyd. iii. 68. But these public establishments did not exclude the existence of private inns also, and perhaps the σκηνῖται, in an inscription about a Bœotian festival, refers to this. Böckh, *Corp. Inscr. Gr.* No. 1625. That these inns were used by the wealthy classes, as well as by the poor, would in itself be probable, even were there no instances of this

being the case. Thus the ambassadors from Athens to Philip lodge everywhere in inns, πανδοκείοις. Æsch. *de Falsa Leg.* p. 272 : οὐδ.ὶs αὐτῷ συσσιτεῖν, ὅτ' ἐξῄειμεν ἐπὶ τὴν ὑστέραν πρεσβείαν, ἤθελεν, οὐδὲ ἐν ταῖς ὁδοῖς, ὅπου δυνατὸν ἦν, εἰς ταὐτὸ πανδοκεῖον καταλύειν. Cf. Plutarch, *de San. tuend.* 15; *de Vitios. pud.* 8· *de Esu carn.* 5; Liban. *Or.* xxiv. p. 79. So Dionysos enquires as to the inns on the road to Hades : Aristoph. *Ranœ,* 114. As with the Romans, (*Gallus,* p. 356,) so among the Greeks, the trade of the innkeeper was deemed highly contemptible, first, because entertainment for gain is totally at variance with the duties of the ξενία; and, secondly, because of the villany and extortion of these people. See Plato, *Leg.* xi. p. 918 : πάντα τὰ περὶ τὴν καπηλείαν καὶ ἐμπορίαν καὶ πανδοκίαν γένη διαβέβληταί τε καὶ ἐν αἰσχροῖς γέγονεν ὀνείδεσιν. Cf. Theophr. *Char.* 6.

[15] Epænetos is just a case in point. Demosth. *in Neær.* p. 1366.

[16] Plutarch, *de Aud. Poët.* 8, mentions a similar instance. As Nico was nicknamed Αἴξ, so Nicippe might

before strangers to be ignorant of the course of life which his daughters followed, and the cue of the mother, who played her part to admiration, was to take advantage of his apparent strictness, and so to pursue her plans to greater advantage.[17]

Under the boy's guidance, Charicles soon reached the house, which looked rather insignificant outside, but was situate near the Cenchrean gate, in one of the busiest spots, where there was a strong muster of taverns and various retail shops.

The vicinity of the *Craneion* and the street leading to the harbour, brought numbers of people to the spot; and here the garlick-chewing sailor, as well as the beau reeking of perfume—the one at the price of a couple of oboles, which was perhaps half his day's earnings,[18] the other making light of a handful of silver—were accustomed to indulge themselves, each after his own peculiar fashion.

Charicles rewarded his guide with a few coppers,[19] and

---

very well have received the sobriquet Αἰγίδιον. See Excursus on *The Hetæræ.*

[17] It was so with Nicarete and her seven girls. Demosth. *in Neær.* p. 1351. προσειποῦσα αὐτὰς ὀνόματι θυγατέρας, ἵν' ὡς μεγίστους μισθοὺς πράττοιτο τοὺς βουλομένους πλησιάζειν αὐταῖς, ὡς ἐλευθέραις οὔσαις. Neæra made a similar use of her marriage with Stephanos. *Ib.* p. 1359.

[18] What were the wages per diem for common labour, cannot be accurately stated. Lucian, *Tim.* 6, mentions four oboles, and this certainly refers to his own time. See Böckh's *Publ. Econ. of Athens,* p. 117. So again, *Epist. Saturn.* 21. we read, ὀνειροπολεῖν, εἰ πόθεν ὀβολοὶ τέσσαρες γένοιντο, ὡς ἔχοιμεν ἄρτων γοῦν ἢ ἀλφίτων ἐμπεπλησμένοι καθεύδειν. The daily pay of a rower is

fixed elsewhere (*de Electro,* 3) at two oboles only. εἰ δὲ ἦν τι τοιοῦτον, οἴει ἡμᾶς δυοῖν ὀβολοῖν ἕνεκα ἐρέττειν ἂν ἢ ἕλκειν τὰ πλοῖα πρὸς ἐναντίον τὸ ὕδωρ, οἷς ἐξῆν πλουτεῖν.

[19] For some services, however, much more pay, in comparison, was demanded. See Böckh's observations on Aristoph. *Ran.* 173, in his *Publ. Econ. of Athens,* p. 117. Fees and gratuities were demanded on the most frivolous pretences. So Lucian, *de Merc. Cond.* 14 : εὐθὺς οὖν πρόσεισι παραγγέλλων τις, ἥκειν ἐπὶ τὸ δεῖπνον, οὐκ ἀνομίλητος οἰκέτης, ὃν χρὴ πρότερον ἵλεων ποιήσασθαι, παραβύσαντα ἐς τὴν χεῖρα, ὡς μὴ ἀδέξιος εἶναι δοκῇς, τοὐλάχιστον πέντε δραχμάς· ὁ δὲ ἀκκισάμενος καὶ Ἄπαγε, παρὰ σοῦ δ' ἐγώ; καὶ Ἡράκλεις, μὴ γένοιτο, ἐπειπὼν, τέλος ἐπείσθη. Akin to these douceurs were the

was proceeding to the house-door, when the lad hailed him, and pointed to a strong-built man, in slovenly habiliments, and of audacious mien, who proved to be Sotades himself, just returning home. The youth therefore turned, and briefly informed him that he wished for entertainment for a few days, and had been recommended to his house by a friend at Argos. With the eye of a *trapezites*, going to lend money, the man scanned him from head to foot, dwelling complacently on the stately charger and good-looking heavily-laden slave, and then said half surlily : ' Mine is not a house of call for every chance stranger, and you might have done better at the adjacent inn. I have daughters whose beauty brings suitors enough already before my doors, and it is a delicate matter to receive striplings like you into my somewhat confined domicile; but notwithstanding, as you have been sent to me by my friend at Argos, you shall be welcome ; no attention shall be spared to make you and your horse comfortable.' So saying, he opened the door, called a slave to take the steed, and bid Charicles enter, he and Manes following after.

The man's brusque tone, and whole appearance, had not created a particularly pleasant impression on the youth, and an air of disorder visible in the entrance-hall, was little calculated to raise the inmates in his estimation. In one corner lay fragments of broken wine-stoups, in another relics of withered garlands ; [20] while from the interior sounded a buzz of heterogeneous voices, with now and then the stave of a song. One might have fancied that the noise proceeded from a drinking party ; but this could not be, as the master of the house had but just entered.

---

presents given to one's own servants at certain annual festivals, as Christmas-boxes are with us. So Lucian, *ib.* 19 : ἅπερ ἐν ἑορταῖς ἐτησίοις εἰκὸς ἡμᾶς παρέξειν · and Athen. x. p. 437, says : τῇ δὲ ἑορτῇ τῶν Χοῶν ἔθος ἐστὶν Ἀθήνῃσι πέμπεσθαι δῶρά τε καὶ τοὺς μισθοὺς τοῖς σοφισταῖς.

[20] Plutarch, *de Cohib. Ira*, 15, describes the appearance presented by the house of a dissipated person : διὸ τῶν μὲν ἀσώτων ταῖς οἰκίαις προσιόντες αὐλητρίδος ἀκούομεν ἑωθινῆς καὶ πηλὸν, ὥς τις εἶπεν, οἴνου, καὶ σπαράγματα στεφάνων, καὶ κραιπαλῶντας ὁρῶμεν ἐπὶ θύραις ἀκολούθους

In point of fact, the latter seemed half perplexed, half angry at it, and hurried his guest up a flight of stairs to the upper story, where he assigned him a pleasant apartment, such as Charicles had scarcely expected to find in the house. ‘I hope this will suit you,’ was his host’s remark. ‘But you have travelled some distance,’ he continued, ‘and your weary limbs must need refreshment.[21] Go, Pægnion,’ said he to a lad of some fifteen years old, ‘bring oil, strigils, and linen-cloths, and show the stranger to the nearest bath.[22] Take care also that his evening meal be not deficient in wine and solids.’ Hereupon he took his leave, and the boy soon arriving with the needful apparatus, led Charicles to the bath, on returning from which he found supper ready, though he soon dispensed with Pægnion’s services, as rest and sleep were what he most needed.

But the tranquil god would not sink upon his heavy eye-lids so soon as he desired. Indistinct cries and wild laughter ever and anon penetrated to his chamber from below. It was now night, and yet Charicles heard stormy knockings at the outer door, and swarms of *Comastæ* rushing noisily in. He fancied he could distinctly catch the name of Stephanion. Was not that the very name by which the boy had called one of the daughters? The domestic discipline here, thought he, must be rather more lax than my friend at Argos was aware of.

But on the other hand, the father’s harsh, nay almost repulsive manner, hardly tallied with his supposition: persons of his supposed class behaved in a manner quite the reverse,

---

[21] With the ancients the chief antidote to fatigue was the bath. So Aristoph. *Ranæ*, 1279, where Dionysos says:

ἐγὼ μὲν οὖν ἐς τὸ βαλανεῖον βούλομαι.
ὑπὸ τῶν κόπων γὰρ τὼ νεφρὼ βουβωνιῶ.

And again, Aristot. *Probl.* i. 39, p. 663: διὰ τί τοὺς μὲν θερινοὺς κόπους λουτρῷ ἰᾶσθαι δεῖ, τοὺς δὲ χειμερινοὺς

ἀλείμματι; Also Lucian, *Lexiph.* 2: χαίρω δὲ μετὰ κάματον ἀπολουόμενος· and Athen. i. p. 24: ἴσασι δὲ καὶ λουτρὰ ἄκη πόνων παντοῖα.

[22] Lucian, *Asin.* 2: εἶτα πέμπε αὐτὸν εἰς βαλανεῖον· οὐχὶ γὰρ μετρίαν ἐλήλυθεν ὁδόν· and more at large, Appul. *Metam.* i. p. 72.

and fawned amiably on their future victim. Still the ladies
must be pretty well known, for the urchin had mentioned
them by name. They were comely, too, by all accounts; so,
be the character of the house what it might, Charicles determined to make their acquaintance next day, at all hazards.

The opportunity presented itself more quickly than he
had expected. Next morning, when he was just going out,
Sotades approached, and requested the favour of his company at their family breakfast. ' I am in general very
cautious about introducing my daughters to strange men,
but somehow, your eyes betoken so much modesty, your
brow such earnestness, and so much wisdom hovers on
your lips, that I am certain I shall have nothing to fear
from you.'

The stripling accepted the courtesy with a smile. A
sudden light seemed to break over the character of his
host, whose chief object was evidently to shun inconvenient
notoriety. This made the youth all the more curious, and
probably he had never waited for the breakfast hour with
so much impatience.

At last the oft-consulted *gnomon* [23] proclaimed that the
moment had arrived when the hospitable inmates of the
mansion expected the stranger's presence.

The damsels were indeed beautiful. Stephanion's tall
figure, her raven locks, falling in rich luxuriance down her
rosy neck, the full black orbs beneath the finely-arched
and jetty eyebrows, that ripe *embonpoint* so manifest even
through the thickness of her dress, were qualities that
called to mind the ideal of a Hera : but her attractions
seemed as nothing to Charicles, who was lost in the contemplation of Melissa, her younger sister. A naïve and
merry being was she, just budding into womanhood, not
one to dazzle by any lofty regularity of beauty, but with
a nameless grace in every movement of her softly-swelling

---

[23] Concerning the gnomon and the division of the day into hours, consult
Note 3 to Scene XII.

THE PRIVATE LIFE

OF

THE ANCIENT GREEKS.

CHARICLES

OR

ILLUSTRATIONS

OF THE

PRIVATE LIFE OF THE ANCIENT GREEKS

WITH NOTES AND EXCURSUSES

FROM THE GERMAN OF PROFESSOR BECKER

TRANSLATED BY THE

REV. FREDERICK METCALFE, M.A.

FELLOW OF LINCOLN COLLEGE, OXFORD

NEW EDITION

LONDON

LONGMANS, GREEN, AND CO.

AND NEW YORK: 15 EAST 16th STREET

1895

Πρᾶγμα βραχὺ πολλάκις καὶ ῥῆμα καὶ παιδιά τις ἴμφασιν ἤθους
ἐποίησε μᾶλλον ἢ μάχαι μυοιόνεκροι.—Plutarch.

ADVERTISEMENT

TO

THE THIRD EDITION

———+·——

IN the first edition of the English translation of
Becker's *Charicles*, many of the author's quotations
from Greek and Latin writers were merely referred to,
some left unnoticed, or only the pith of them inserted.
Other curtailments were likewise introduced, partly in
deference to the wishes of the publisher, who desired to
keep down the bulk of the book. In the two subsequent
editions, at the suggestion of several English scholars,
many of these citations have been given at length, and
some of the omitted matter incorporated. It only remains further to add, that the simultaneous call for a
new edition of *Charicles*, and its companion *Gallus*,
and the extensive use of these works in our public
schools and universities, quite justify the idea which
the translator formed of the high value which classical
students would be likely to attach to both works.

OXFORD : *June* 20, 1866.

TRANSLATOR'S PREFACE.

———◆———

THE motto from Plutarch prefixed to *Charicles*, while it intimates the scope and object of the author, is an eloquent though brief argument for the utility of such a work. This description of the every-day pursuits and lighter occupations of the Greeks, this glimpse at their domestic scenes, and introduction, so to speak, to the interior of their dwellings, not only infuse additional zest into the student's survey of their life as a nation; but will also prove no mean auxiliary in estimating the motives and springs of their public actions as chronicled by the historian; pretty much on the same principle that we are prone to contemplate the doings of public men with more curious interest, should we happen also to enjoy their private personal acquaintance. The words of Böttiger respecting Rome admit of application here : ' We gain a correcter and deeper insight into the private life, a look, as it were, behind the *postscenia* of a people, whose public virtues and vices we are too apt to pronounce judgment on with reference solely to the universal history of the world and of nations.' The learned author here quoted, who for fifty years so successfully prosecuted his antiquarian and archæological researches, may be pronounced the originator of this species of antique domestic literature.

In his *Kleine Schriften* he has investigated many points here discussed afresh, though frequently with the same conclusion, by Becker; and his *Sabina,* or *Morning*

Scenes at the Toilette of a rich Roman Lady, probably supplied the first hint for the construction of *Gallus* and *Charicles*. Still, though *Sabina* displays great powers of combination and research, and is in some respects more attractive and readable than either of Becker's productions, yet it falls far short of them in comprehensiveness and finish. Moreover, *Charicles* is the first work devoted to the private manners and customs of Greece. It is dedicated to the veteran Professor Hermann, and is a very meet pendant to its predecessor *Gallus*.

We possess in these works compendious portraitures, tableaux vivants as it were, representing private life at Rome and Athens; and by looking on this picture and then on that, much knowledge may be derived alike instructive and suggestive. In the former we behold the favourite of Augustus, stern in his sense of honour; majestic and dignified even in his pleasures; fond of art, though his devotion for it, true to the imitative nature of his countrymen, is rather of a formal and acquired than inborn and imaginative cast. He is the type of his nation, who loved to adorn their palaces and villas with works of Greek art, as with so many pieces of elegant furniture; thus verifying the proverb, that the wolf's-milk which suckled their progenitors never became a real fountain of the muses. They were the great borrowers of their day, adapting themselves to foreign habits and institutions with marvellous facility, doing violence to nature, and trampling over obstacles physical and moral. How perfectly antipodes to them in all the phases of their character were the children of Dædal Greece!

What a remarkable phenomenon is the Athenian, that creature of impulse, all gushing with nature and vivacity, sudden and quick; with wits as clear as his own 'pure

air,' and temperament not less light than ' the soil.' Un-like the Roman race, they are studious, as by intuition, ' of arts that polish life, inventors rare ;' combining sim-plicity and beauty as no nation ever combined them before or since, and unfolding the most delicate bloom of æsthetic culture almost before their alphabet was complete. 'A people who,' in the words of an ingenious writer, ' con-ceived all that was beautiful in art and profound in philo-sophy ; who became the instructress of all liberal sciences and arts ; the teacher alike of her own times and posterity.' The Greek is essentially the personification of exclusive-ness, indigenous beyond belief, and local in his tastes and habits; the Roman is a citizen of the world. Such then, not to trace their character further, or follow it into its darker details, are the people whose customs and habits the author has proposed to investigate ; and nobody can deny the interest and importance of the theme. His hero is not to our mind so attractive as Gallus. In addition to his historical interest as a poet, the Roman moved in much better and more refined society than our Greek, and there was more individuality and vividness in his portrait. But the author has in his preface given satisfactory reasons for selecting a character of this kind.

It now remains to say a few words on the labours of the translator. The same alterations have been made in the position of the Scenes, Notes, Excursus and Plates, as in *Gallus*. It has also been deemed advisable to depart occasionally from the author's principle of ὀνομάζειν τὰ σῦκα σῦκα ; by an over-tenacious adherence to which his narrative has here and there become offensive to good taste, without much being gained thereby. Accordingly, one entire Excursus has been left out, and the one on the ἑταῖραι much curtailed, though the translator rather regrets

the necessity of making the latter omissions, for it seems to him that this part of the work throws much light on the Excursus relating to the Women; by illustrating the consequences resulting from the Athenian mode of treating married women.[1] Again, all iteration, to which the learned author seems unduly propense, has been avoided as much as possible; many quotations have often been merely referred to, some left unnoticed, when it seemed unnecessary to multiply authorities, or only the pith of them, and that part strictly bearing upon the subject, inserted. In consequence of these alterations, some passages had to be remodelled, and rather adapted in English than literally translated. But at the same time everything of moment has been carefully retained ; and it is hoped that, as it was the translator's intention to make the English version as widely useful as possible, the liberties he has thus taken in greatly reducing the bulk of the work will meet with the approbation of the English scholar ; and that the value of the book, which is in high estimation in Germany, will not have been diminished by this Procrustean operation.

Lastly, the favour extended to his adaptation of *Gallus*, encourages him to hope that this attempt at presenting another most learned and clever work in an English form will be productive of a similar result.

London: *May* 1845.

---

[1] For further information on this subject, see a very able article on Greek female society, *Quarterly Review*, Vol. xxii. p. 163.

SCENE THE ELEVENTH.

SCENE THE TWELFTH.

XX   CONTENTS.

Gyms
Baths
social activities
Games →

Pg.
311, 313
314 +

CONTENTS.

----◆----

CHARICLES.

Attic life, therefore, so varied and comprehensive in its phases, and so abundantly illustrated by contemporary literature, must serve as the norma for the rest of Greece, and the usages of other states can only be considered in a comparative point of view. Doric customs have, moreover, been already investigated by Manso, Müller, and Hoek ; so that the author has generally contented himself with noticing those points in which their conclusions seem to be manifestly erroneous.

If he has occasionally failed in arriving at the truth, he can plead in mitigation that in most cases he has had to commence from the very foundations, no edifice existing on which to rear a superstructure. But where wrong, he will thankfully submit to be set right, and will carefully attend even to criticism which he considers to be erroneous, since it will afford an opportunity for the more extended investigation of disputed points.

in the Greek sense of the word. It does not, moreover appear necessary that an excessive σκυθρωπασμὸς should be essential in conducting every scientific enquiry; on the contrary, it would seem that in the treatment of many phases of antiquity a certain tone of irony is more appropriate.

The rest of the arrangement is similar to that of *Gallus*: but it is hoped that the explanations contained in the Notes and Excursuses will be found more comprehensive and elaborate.

The Classical authorities which bear out the assertions here put forward, have, for the most part, been cited in extenso; for this seemingly cumbrous procedure is the only one which can be really satisfactory to the student. In every case the recognised and most recent editions have been employed, and the greatest care has been taken to secure accuracy in the references and citations.

That Attic customs have been those chiefly portrayed, can be no matter of surprise. Greece being divided into many small states, each of which had its own peculiarities in customs and manner of life, all these nuances ought of course to be noticed in a general picture of Greek life. But there is, unfortunately, a great deficiency of original materials for such a work. Little is known except in reference to Athens and Sparta; and in the latter state, with her bizarre institutions, all individuality is so utterly destroyed, and such an undue and unnatural importance is given to her political strength and the renown of the people as a whole, that she must be considered as an anomaly in the social condition of Greece; and thus the mode of life which was there prevalent can by no means be taken as representative of that generally established

former work prevents, however, the introduction of the necessary detail. In Böttiger's *Kleine Schriften* many of the points in question are discussed, and many of his observations, those for instance on the Grecian Dress, are very valuable. Some of his enquiries are, however, absurdly frivolous ; for instance, his investigations as to the use of pocket-handkerchiefs by the Grecian ladies. Jacobs' works, *Die Erziehung der Hellenen zur Sittlichkeit.* and his *Beiträge zur Gesch. d. weibl. Geschlechts*, are of a more serious tendency, and are written in a remarkably clever and attractive manner. Yet neither of these productions can be considered as anything more than enthusiastic apologies for certain flagrant vices rife among the Hellenes. He who undertakes faithfully to describe the character of a people, ought not, while he gives prominence to its nobler features, to place a screen before the blemishes that deform it. An excellent essay, which estimates, on impartial principles, the religious and moral development of the Greeks, Limburg Brower's *Histoire de la Civilisation morale et religieuse des Grecs*, only reached the author while this treatise was in the press ; he rejoices to find that with respect to the darker vices of the Greek people he has himself arrived at nearly the same results as this learned and unbiased writer.

The author of *Charicles*, discarding the incomplete labours of his predecessors, has uniformly gone to the fountain-head, and has carefully perused, with reference to his present object, the whole range of Greek literature down to the time of Aristotle. Of the succeeding writers down to the fourth century, he has gone through the most important, more especially Theophrastus, Strabo, Plutarch, Lucian, Athenæus, Pausanias, Ælian, Diogenes Laertius, Dio Chrysostom, Libanius, Maximus Tyrius, and Philostratus; also the Erotic writers, Alciphron, Artemidorus, and others, as well as the grammarians, Pollux, Harpocration, Suidas, Hesychius, Photius, Phrynichus, Timæus, Eustathius, and other Scholiasts. The later Roman historians have also been consulted, though in a more cursory manner. There is not one of these writers from whom materials of greater or less value have not been derived. But more regard has been paid to every minute intimation in authors of the better period, than to the most explicit explanations of the grammarians, which are often founded solely on well-known passages of classic writers, or are forced into accordance with the customs of a later age. The Attic orators have proved by far the most valuable sources of information, for by them Greek manners are incidentally depicted with a reality and naturalness which is wanting in the lofty and ideal conceptions of the tragic and lyric poets, or in the caricatures of the comedians, as well as in the phantasies of Utopian philosophers, or the pragmatical reflections of philosophical historians. Though less weight has been attached to the writers of later periods, yet there appears to be no reason to suspect their testimony in general; and though it is seen at a glance that manners greatly degenerated, yet we still recognise all the more important features; and thus Plutarch bears witness that the character of the Athenians, in his day, and their whole mode of life, both in serious as well as in more trivial concerns, were the same as in preceding times.

Another important point to be taken into account was the genuineness of the writings quoted; but here less stress has always been laid on the name of the writer, than on the date, or the recognised antiquity of the production. Everybody knows that the speech against Neæra, that of

Andocides against Alcibiades, certain dialogues of Plato, the second book of Aristotle's Œconomics, the *Apophtheg-mata Laconica* attributed to Plutarch, and many other treatises, are spurious or doubtful; but they have stood from time immemorial among the works of those writers whose names they bear.

The mass of materials being so overwhelming, it is very possible that some omissions may have occurred, but it is hoped that nothing has been neglected which might have been decisive on any of the mooted questions

In addition to these literary stores, much information has been derived from extant works of art; and the rich collection of illustrated archæological works in the university library of Leipsic has proved of the greatest service. These materials, it is true, do not throw so much light on Grecian as on Roman customs, for no buried town has been discovered, with its baths, houses, and household furniture; nevertheless the Greek specimens extant, especially the painted vases, are, so far as they go, of a very high value, inasmuch as they belong to an early period, which is not the case with those of Italy.

In a work descriptive of state antiquities the form here adopted would have been unsuitable, because unsystematic. But the case is different in an attempt to illustrate the checkered and numberless phases of private life, which do not admit of any very strict classification. The Scenes had to be written with inconceivable care and caution, in order to combine the scattered traits, and give unity to the picture, and all imaginative licence on the part of the writer had to be rigidly suppressed. But this was the only way of accomplishing the prescribed task ; except by the composition of *Adversaria in modum*

a

Turnebi, which seems, of all methods, the least happy and the most repulsive. Mere pedantic disquisitions on habits and customs would have been like anatomical plates, wherein we can trace, to their minutest details, all the bones, muscles, nerves, and blood-vessels; though we can form no idea, from these dismembered and deformed parts, of the human body as a whole. The Scenes, then, are intended to give this *tout ensemble*, this portraiture of Greek life; and if the writer has in any measure been successful, he thinks that a desirable object will have been achieved, since nothing of the kind is to be found in the writings of antiquity.

It must not however be supposed that this work partakes, to any great extent, of the character of a romance. The materials previously collected, on being classified, seemed spontaneously to suggest the course of the narrative, and it will be seen, on comparing the text of the Scenes with the Notes and Excursuses, that the former consist almost entirely of excerpted passages of Greek authors.

It did not seem desirable, as was done in *Gallus*, to link the narrative to any historical occurrence, because among the Greeks the private life of every important personage is much harder to separate from the public doings than at Rome, and it would thus have been necessary to encroach frequently on a department of investigation of which the writer desired to be independent. For the same reason a point of time has been selected in which public life had begun to fall into the background, while the egotistic spirit of the age gave a greater prominence to individual interests. The consequence has been, that whereas the Roman scenes wore more of a tragic aspect, these are couched rather in the tone of comedy.

sius; but the results of the investigations of these writers
are widely scattered about in commentaries, so that the
student would only be repaid for the labour of wading
through them by obtaining a number of insulated notices,
without acquiring any systematic information on the
subject. A careful perusal of the Greek authors shows,
moreover, that all that these commentators have gleaned
stands in much the same relation to what they have overlooked, as does the paltry produce of a sand-washing to
the yield of an exhaustless gold-mine.

In later times, several acute investigators have laboured
in the field of Attic law and polity, and these researches
have occasionally thrown light on the relations of private
life. But no comprehensive work, illustrative of the
every-day occurrences of Grecian life has as yet been
undertaken, for neither Nitzsch's Description of the Greeks,
nor Potter's compilation, deserve to be mentioned in the
present state of antiquarian science. Barthelemy's Travels
of the Younger Anacharsis, though a meritorious performance for its time, is anything but satisfactory to
those who have become acquainted with the Greeks from
their own literature.   The figures often resemble antique
statues attired in French court costume and lace ruffles ;
they are like pictures by Le Brun or Coypel, where the
artist's subjective conception has entirely effaced the antique character of the original, and where the clever
treatment of the details is no recompense for the failure
of the attempt as a whole.

In the works which have lately been written on
Grecian customs and institutions, such as Wachsmuth's
Hellenischer Alterthumskunde, and Müller's *History of the
Dorians,* somewhat more has been done to illustrate pri-
vate life. The comprehensiveness of the plan of the

AUTHOR'S PREFACE.

— ✦ —

THE author has been encouraged in offering this work
to the public by the favourable reception which his
work on Roman manners has met with, and which served
to convince him that an illustration of that portion of
antique life was by no means unacceptable. Less has
hitherto been done, in this respect, for Greece than for
Rome. The earlier philologists either ignored this department of Grecian Antiquities, or merely made occasional
allusions to it; while they drew parallels between the features of Grecian and of Roman life, or identified them, in
a most unwarrantable manner. The Italians, for instance,
who seem to have felt themselves especially called, by the
mementos of early grandeur and magnificence around them,
and by the classic atmosphere which they inhaled, to an
investigation of antiquity, have, above all others—perhaps
from a proud contempt of everything not Roman—either
utterly disregarded Greek customs, or handled them after
a very desultory and faulty method. In the collections of
Gronovius and Grævius, and of their successors, Sallengre
and Polen, we are usually presented with an undigested
and confused medley of passages, quoted without any regard either to the context, the period referred to, or the
value of the author, and these are often brought forward in support of the most marvellous hypotheses. Exceptions, it is true, must be made in favour of a few great
names, such as Casaubon, Salmasius, and perhaps Meur-

limbs, that was irresistibly bewitching. So careful and proper was their toilet that Charicles began to waver in his preconceived opinion; yet the easy familiarity with which Melissa seated herself between him and her mother, and their free way of partaking of the wine,[24] and joining in the conversation, little accorded with the reserve of Grecian virgins.

Indeed they seemed gradually to lay aside their dis-guise. Melissa's glances, and all her movements, became anything but correct, and when in the temporary absence of Sotades, Charicles handed her the goblet, she carefully applied her lips to the very place that his had touched.[25] The youth, burning with passion, caught the vessel from her hand, and did the same, upon which the damsel leaned lovingly towards him, and the clasp that fastened the chi-ton over her shoulder became loosened, as if by accident, at the same moment. Unable to restrain himself, he imprinted a hasty kiss on her dazzling shoulder, and the gentle slap with which she punished his presumption, showed that it was not considered an insult. Sotades here returned, and breakfast ended. Melissa's eyes seemed to say, ' I hope we shall meet again,' and Charicles took his leave completely enthralled. He needed no further enticement: breakfast had been the trap; and he was now helplessly ensnared.[26]

---

[24] Xenoph. de Rep. Lac. 1, 3: οἴνου γε μὴν ἢ πάμπαν ἀπεχομένας ἢ ὑδαρεῖ χρωμένας διάγουσιν.

[25] This was a silent declaration of love, or a sign of mutual under-standing. Ovid, Amor. i. 4, 31; Lucian, Dial. Meretr. 12: καὶ πιὼν ἂν ἐκείνη μὲν ὑπέδειξας τὸ ποτήριον, ἀποδιδοὺς δὲ τῷ παιδὶ πρὸς τὸ οὖς ἐκέλευες. εἰ μὴ Πυραλλὶς αἰτήσειε, μὴ ἂν ἄλλῳ ἐγχέαι. Achill. Tat. ii 9: ᾠνοχόει δὲ ὁ Σάτυρος ἡμῖν καί τι ποιεῖ ἐρωτικόν. Διαλλάσσει γὰρ

τὰ ἐκπώματα καὶ τὸ μὲν ἐμὸν τῇ κόρῃ προστίθησι, τὸ δὲ ἐκείνης ἐμοί. καὶ ἐγχέων ἀμφοτέροις καὶ ἐγκερα-σάμενος ὤρεγεν. Ἐγὼ δὲ ἐπιτηρήσας τὸ μέρος τοῦ ἐκπώματος ἔνθα τὸ χεῖλος ἡ κόρη πίνουσα προσέθιγεν ἐναρμοσάμενος ἔπινον ἀποστολι-μαῖον τοῦτο φίλημα ποιῶν καὶ ἅμα κατεφίλουν τὸ ἔκπωμα.

[26] See the striking comparison, Plaut. Asin. i. 3, 63:

　　　... auceps ego,
Esca est meretrix, lectus illex est, amatores aves.

That the damsels were hetæræ, was clear enough ; but the very veil of secrecy they adopted made them the more alluring. Dismissing, for the present, all intentions of departing, he could think of nothing but a second interview with his charmer. Manes was put a poor hand in such matters, or he could have used his services ; as it was, he must apply to some one in the household.

' Pægnion,' said he the same evening to the slave who waited on him, ' wilt thou earn some money ? ' ' Ah ! that I will,' replied he. ' It won't be difficult,' continued Charicles. ' I love the beautiful Melissa ; try to procure me an interview to-night.' ' What sort of a notion is this that you've got about the daughter of a respectable family—? ' ' Pish ! ' interrupted Charicles ; ' I know the extent to which your respectability will reach. Don't assume astonishment ; it suits you ill. But no more of that. Bring me to Melissa, and ten drachmæ are your reward.'

' Ten drachmæ ? ' repeated the slave,—' no, it won't do. Melissa herself won't object, I dare say : she has been half beside herself ever since she saw you. She weeps, and keeps repeating your name ; she can't live without you. We all believe that you have mixed some love-potion in her cup.' ' Well, and why won't it do ? ' asked Charicles ; ' her mother won't mind, surely ? ' ' She is not so strait-laced as all that,' replied the menial ; ' and with the family's narrow means, I take it, some four or five gold pieces will go far towards persuading her to open to you the door of the parthenon. But isn't Sotades at home ? and you see how jealously he guards his daughters.' ' Ah ! there's the rub,' said Charicles with a knowing laugh ; ' but perhaps Nicippe will be able to remove that difficulty. Away, Pægnion ; no more disguise. Tell the mother that a mina of silver is hers if she accomplish my desire to-morrow evening. Off with you, and earn your ten drachmæ.' ' Ten drachmæ ! ' repeated the boy a second time. Why I'm fifteen years old.' ' Well then, fifteen drachmæ,' said the youth ; ' but now be off, and mind

what you're about.' Pægnion departed, assuring Charicles
that the project should not fail by any fault of his ; but
that nevertheless he thought it would be hardly feasible.

It was scarce dawn when Charicles sprang from his
couch. His sleep had not been sound, and towards morning he fancied he had heard a noise, as if the inner and
outer doors were opened.[27] The thought that a favoured
lover was creeping off, disturbed him. Pægnion made his
appearance before long, and his self-satisfied air announced
good news. He informed Charicles that his master proposed going to Sicyon to-day on business, and would be
obliged by the loan of his horse. He would only be absent
two nights, and Charicles of course did not intend leaving
Corinth before then. Charicles fancied he saw through
the meaning of the journey, and felt relieved at getting
rid of so great an impediment to his wishes on such easy
terms. He therefore immediately assented.

Pægnion brought nothing fresh from Melissa, and on
being interrogated about the opening of doors in the night,
alleged as the reason, that the light[28] had become ex-
tinguished, and a female slave had, towards morning, gone
to fetch one from a neighbour's.[29]

Charicles persuaded himself into the belief that this
was true.

Sotades had set off, noon was long passed, and Chari-

---

[27] Lysias, *de Cæde Erat.* p. 20 :
ἀναμιμνησκόμενος, ὅτι ἐν ἐκείνῃ τῇ
νυκτὶ ἐψόφει ἡ μέταυλος θύρα καὶ
ἡ αὔλειος. Consult the Excursus on
The House.

[28] The use of a night-light was
not general, although not uncommon.
Mention of it occurs in Aristoph.
Eccles. 8 ; Lucian, *Catapl.* 27 ; Plut.
Pelop. 11 ; and on the other hand, in
Nub. 18 ; Theoph. *Char.* 18 ; and
Theocr. xxiv. 48, it is not lit till
wanted.

[29] Lysias, *de Cæde Erat.* p. 15 :
ἐρωμένου δέ μου, τί αἱ θύραι νύκτωρ
ψοφοῖεν, ἔφασκε τὸν λύχνον ἀποσβε-
σθῆναι τὸν παρὰ τῷ παιδίῳ, εἶτα
ἐκ τῶν γειτόνων ἀνάψασθαι. ἐσιώπων
ἐγώ, καὶ ταῦτα οὕτως ἔχειν ἡγούμην.
Neighbours did not scruple to beg
a light, even at night. So Xenoph.
Mem. ii. 2, 12 : οὐκοῦν καὶ τῷ γεί-
τονι βούλει σὺ ἀρέσκειν, ἵνα σοι καὶ
πῦρ ἐναίῃ, ὅταν τούτου δέῃ. Other
small services were willingly rendered. See Theophr. *Char.* 10 ;
Aristoph. *Eccles.* 446.

cles still waited for the message that Pægnion was to bring
him. The place of rendezvous was one of the arcades
in the Agora, where he used to meet Ctesiphon. He had
already made his friend a confidant of his hopes, and had
induced him to prolong his stay for another day, though
much against the will of Ctesiphon, who had again warned
him. But the ycuth could see nothing dangerous in the
game, which was one of such very common occurrence. He
paced to and fro in great impatience, when at last the boy
approached. The news he brought was favourable; he
had succeeded in talking the mother over, and Melissa was
impatiently expecting him; and as soon as all were asleep
in the house, he would lead the youth where Dionysos and
Aphrodite, the inseparable deities of joy, would be ready
to receive him.[30] 'Only don't forget,' he added, 'to hand
the mother the mina of silver, when she opens the door,
and bethink you of my services also.'

In the hospitable house where Ctesiphon was staying,
six young men, including himself and his friendly host,
had just met for a *symposion*, and unguents were being
handed round, and wine mingled. The lively discourse of
the party betokened them all to be men of the same sort,
addicted to pleasure, and well acquainted with the merits
of the Corinthian beauties. 'You'll have to keep me a
day longer,' said Ctesiphon to his host. 'The friend who
bore me company hither has lent his horse to his lodging-
house keeper, and Sotades—such is his name—won't be
back for two days.' 'Sotades?' exclaimed one of the
company; 'you don't mean the would-be papa of my Stephanion?' 'And of the charming Melissa?' cried another.
'So the girls are called, I believe,' said Ctesiphon. 'You

---

[30] Eurip. *Bacchæ*, 729:

οἴνου δὲ μηκέτ' ὄντος οὐκ Κύπρις.

So also Aristot. *Prob.* xxx. 1, p. 953:

ὀρθῶς Διόνυσος καὶ 'Αφροδίτη λέγονται μετ' ἀλλήλων εἶναι.

know the man then? he went to-day on a journey to
Sicyon.' 'Impossible!' cried the second; 'I spied him
but a short while ago, stealing along in the dusk of the
evening towards the Isthmian gate; I knew him well,
spite of his pains to muffle himself up. And, strange
enough, just afterwards I met a slave of his, who, now I
think of it, was leading a fine-looking horse.' 'All is not
right,' said the first, starting up. 'Stephanion sent me
a message to-day, pleading sickness as an excuse for her
not being able to receive me this evening. I hope that
the girl who is my property for . . . .' 'Don't disturb
yourself,' said Ctesiphon; 'my friend loves her sister
Melissa.' 'In that case, some danger, doubtless, threatens
him. This Sotades is the most rascally of pimps, and
it would not be the first time that he had allured a
stranger, and then accused him of being the seducer of his
daughters.'[31] 'Well, then,' cried Ctesiphon's host, 'the
best thing for us to do, is to make all speed to Sotades'
house, and see if we can't prevent a knave's trick.' This
proposal met with universal approbation, particularly as
Glaucos wished to assure himself personally about Stephanion's indisposition, while the rest of the party reckoned on
having an amusing scene in an hetæra-house. 'But they
will never let us in,' interposed one of the guests. 'Oh!
be easy on that score,' said Glaucos; 'I have the key of
the garden-door, which leads directly to the women's
apartments. Nicippe herself let me have it for a couple of
gold staters, so long as Stephanion is mine. And even
suppose the bolt inside were shot forward, I can take the
whole door off its hinges.[32] But let us be quick. We
shall, I hope, soon return to our cups.'

---

[31] This is the history of Stephanos
and Epænetos. See note 4; and Demosth. *in Nœr.* 1366 and 1359.

[32] This is the back-door of the
house, usually called θύρα κηπαία.

See Excursus on *The House.* That a
fastened door could thus be opened,
appears from Lucian, *Dial. Meretr.*
xii.: τὴν αὔλιον εὗρον ἀποκεκλεισ
μένην ἐπιμελῶς· μέσαι γὰρ νύκτες
ἦσαν. ουκ ἔκοψα δ᾽ οὖν, ἀλλ᾽ ἐπάρας

Charicles was at the summit of his wishes. At the door of the small room, which Nicippe had fastened outside, Pægnion stood listening; for he was prevented by the tapestry within from peeping through the little hole which he had bored through the door to satisfy his curiosity on such occasions.[33] He now glided gently away towards the house-door. This he cautiously opened, and peered out into the darkness of the night. A group of five or six men, who had come down the street from the town, were standing at a small distance, and he felt rather uneasy at the circumstance. But they presently disappeared into a narrow lane that led along the garden wall to the next street. He kept jingling the fifteen drachmæ in his hand with much satisfaction,[34] and then stole lightly but quickly down the street. At the fourth house he stopped and tapped. He was admitted, and not many seconds after, four men came out of the door, accompanied by three slaves and Pægnion.[35] One of the men—it was Sotades—purchased two links in a neighbouring shop, and having lighted them,[36] advanced with the others towards his house. 'Shut the doors,' said he to Pægnion as soon as they had entered; 'the bird is safe enough now, but unbidden guests might come in.' They stole noiselessly to the chambers of the women.

Charicles reclined on a couch, which smelt sweetly of roses,[37] with the beautiful Melissa in his arms; she was clad in the slightest manner, and she clung closely to him, her arms clasped around his neck. On a sudden the door was dashed open with a tremendous blow, and Sotades

---

ἠρέμα τὴν θύραν (ἤδη δὲ καὶ ἄλλοτε ἐπεποιήκειν αὐτὸ) παραγαγὼν τὸν στροφέα παρῆλθον ἀψοφητί.

[33] Mart. xi. 45, 6:
puncta, lasciva quæ terebrantur acu.

[34] Appul. *Metam.* ii. 154.

[35] Lysias, *de Cæde Erat.* 27.

[36] Lysias, *ib.*: καὶ δᾷδας λαβόντες

ἐκ τοῦ ἐγγυτάτου καπηλείου εἰσερχόμεθα. On the use of torches and lamps, see Notes 1 and 5 to Sc. IX.

[37] Lucian, *Asin.* 7: τῶν δὲ στρωμάτων ῥόδα πολλὰ κατεπέπαστο, τὰ μὲν οὕτω γυμνὰ καθ' αὑτὰ τὰ δὲ λελυμένα, τὰ δὲ στεφάνοις συμπεπλεγμένα. Appul. *Metam.* ii. p. 126.

rushed in with his myrmidons, like one frantic.[38] 'Villain!'
he exclaimed, advancing on the youth, 'is it thus that you
abuse my hospitality? Is it thus you disgrace the house,
and seduce the daughter of an honest man?' The youth had
risen up. 'Seduce your daughter, indeed! why it's notorious
that her charms support your house!' 'You lie,' screamed
Sotades. 'Friends, ye know the blameless reputation of
my roof, and I call you to witness, that I have caught this
good-for-nothing fellow on this couch, with my daughter
in his arms. Seize him, slaves, and bind him.' Charicles,
who was young and powerful. attempted, but in vain, to
break through his assailants. The contest was an unequal
one, and Sotades, by the help of his slaves, soon mastered
and bound him. 'A sword ho!' cried he: 'he shall
atone with his life for the stain he would bring upon my
house.' 'Sotades!' exclaimed the youth, 'take care how
you commit a crime that will not go unrevenged. I did
not wish to stain your house. Your wife has herself received a mina of silver from me for her part in the transaction. But even granted that I have really injured you,
what can you gain by killing me? Take a ransom, and let
me go free.' 'Not I,' said Sotades: 'the law kills you by
my hand. You have deserved death,' he continued after a
slight pause; 'but I will have pity on your youth. Give
me three thousand drachmæ, and you shall be free.'[39] 'I
have not so much by me,' replied Charicles, 'nor any

---

[38] The whole description is from
Lysias, (de Cæde Erat. p. 28) with but
little variation: ὥσαυτες δὲ τὴν θύραν
τοῦ δωματίου οἱ μὲν πρῶτοι εἰσιόντες
ἔτι εἴδομεν αὐτὸν κατακείμενον παρὰ
τῇ γυναικί, οἱ δ᾽ ὕστερον ἐν τῇ κλίνῃ
γυμνὸν ἑστηκότα. ἐγὼ δ᾽, ὦ ἄνδρες,
πατάξας καταβάλλω αὐτὸν, καὶ τὼ
χεῖρε περιαγαγὼν εἰς τοὔπισθεν καὶ
δήσας ἠρώτων, διὰ τί ὑβρίζει, εἰς τὴν
οἰκίαν τὴν ἐμὴν εἰσιών; κἀκεῖνος
ἀδικεῖν μὲν ὡμολόγει, ἠντιβόλει δὲ
καὶ ἱκέτευε μὴ αὐτὸν κτεῖναι, ἀλλ᾽
ἀργύριον πράξασθαι. ἐγὼ δ᾽ εἶπον,
ὅτι οὐκ ἐγώ σε ἀποκτενῶ, ἀλλ᾽ ὁ
τῆς πόλεως νόμος. This occurred in
Athens, but there is no doubt it will
hold for Corinth also. See Excursus
on The Women.

[39] This was the sum extorted by
Stephanos from Epænetos; Demosth.
in Neær. 1367.

friends here to help me to make up the sum.[40]　But there
are two thousand drachmæ in my valise, which shall be
yours.'　'I accept your terms,' said Sotades, 'but only on
condition that you quit Corinth by break of day.　And you,
unworthy daughter,' said he to Melissa, who had hid her
face in the cushion of the couch, 'may think yourself
fortunate, if I do not follow the example of that Athenian,
and consign you alive to the tomb, along with the horse of
your paramour.'[41]

These last words he had pronounced with much pa-
thos:—a peal of shrill laughter answered him from the
entrance of the room.　It was Ctesiphon and his friends,
who had gained the door unobserved.　'Dog[42] of a pimp,'

---

[40] A praiseworthy custom prevailed, not only at Athens, but elsewhere, by which friends considered it
their duty to help, to the best of their
power, a friend suddenly thrown into
pecuniary difficulties.　This kind of
contribution (ἔρανος) has been most
satisfactorily illustrated by Casaubon
on Theophr. *Char.* 15 ; cf. Meier and
Schöman, *Att. Proc.*, on the twofold
kind of ἔρανος.

[41] Æschin. *in Timarch.* p. 175 :
ὥστ᾽ ἀνὴρ εἷς τῶν πολιτῶν εὑρὼν τὴν
ἑαυτοῦ θυγατέρα διεφθαρμένην καὶ
τὴν ἡλικίαν οὐ καλῶς διαφυλάξασαν
μέχρι γάμου, ἐγκατῳκοδόμησεν αὐτὴν
μεθ᾽ ἵππου εἰς ἐρημον οἰκίαν, ὑφ᾽ οὗ
προδήλως ἔμελλεν ἀπολεῖσθαι διὰ
λιμὸν συγκαθειργμένη. καὶ ἔτι νῦν
τῆς οἰκίας ταύτης ἕστηκε τὰ οἰκόπεδα
ἐν τῷ ὑμετέρῳ ἄστει, καὶ ὁ τόπος
οὗτος καλεῖται 'παρ᾽ ἵππον καὶ
κόρην.' Cf. Heracl. Pont. *Polit.* 1.

[42] As was mentioned in *Gallus*,
p. 76, the names of animals, in some
respects despicable, were not usual
among the ancients as terms of abuse.

Sometimes, however, instances do
occur.　Κύων is well known : πίθηκος
occurs, Demosth. *de Coron.* p. 307 ;
and κέρκωψ, Alciphr. *Epist.* i. 28.
As *vervex* in Latin so πρόβατον is
used in Lucian, *Alex. seu Pseudom.*
15 : (ἀνθρώπων) οὐδὲν ἐοικότων σιτο-
φάγοις ἀνδράσιν, ἀλλὰ μόνη τῇ μορφῇ μὴ οὐχὶ πρόβατα εἶναι διαφερόν-
των· and the proverb in Suidas, προ-
βατίου βίον ζῆν.　See also Lucian,
Demon. 41.　So also ὄνος is used,
Plutarch, *Gryll.* 10 : Νῦν μὲν οὖι,
Γρύλλε, μεταβέβλησαι σὺ, καὶ τὸ
πρόβατον λογικὸν ἀποφαίνεις καὶ
τὸν ὄνον ; Lucian, *Jup. Trag.* 31 :
γόητα μὲν εἶναι τοῦτον, ἡμᾶς δὲ
ὄνους κανθηλίους, νὴ Δία, καὶ ἡμιόνους, τοὺς πιστεύοντας αὐτῷ, καὶ
ὄνον αἱ ἀκρίδες τὸν νοῦν ἔχοντας.
Diog. Laert. vii. 170 ; and Lysippus,
quoted in Dicæarch. *Stat. Græc.* 10 :
　　εἰ μὴ τεθέασαι τὰς Ἀθήνας, στέλεχος εἶ·
　　εἰ δὲ τεθέασαι, μὴ τεθήρευσαι δ᾽, ὄνος.
Not only the stupidity, but also the
laziness of the beast is had regard to.
Aves, 1327 :
　　πάνυ γὰρ βραδύς τίς ἐστιν, ὥσπερ ὄνος.
See also Lucian, *Pisc.* 34, and Plut. *de*

cried Ctesiphon's host, springing forward, ' how dare you
bind a free man, and extort money from him?' 'What
right have you to question me? why do you force your way
into my house?' retorted Sotades sharply, though evidently
taken aback. 'The man has dishonoured my house.' Another burst of laughter interrupted him. 'Dishonoured
your house, forsooth! shall I tell you to whom Stephanion
belongs for two months by your written contract? or who,
last night, enjoyed Melissa?' Meanwhile Glaucos and the
rest had entered. 'Tell me, Sotades,' exclaimed one of
them, 'which marriage may these daughters of yours be
by? It strikes me, that scarce ten years have elapsed
since the notorious *hetœra* Ægidion became your wife,
and brought you these girls, who would in vain hunt for
their fathers all Greece over.'[43] Sotades turned pale, the
witnesses whom he had brought with him slipped out,
Ctesiphon rushed towards Charicles and loosed the cords
with which he was bound. 'You shall pay for this,' shouted
Sotades, gnashing his teeth, and striking his hands together in a perfect fury.[44] 'Congratulate yourself,' replied

---

Is. et Osir. 31. The word λίθος is also
applied to simple-minded heavy individuals. So *Nubes*, 1202. When Aris-
tippus was asked what advantage his
son would derive from instruction, he
answered, Καὶ εἰ μηδὲν ἄλλο, ἕν γ'
οὖν τῷ θεάτρῳ οὐ καθεδήσεται λίθος
ἐπὶ λίθῳ. Diog. Laert. ii. 72; Terent.
Heaut. iv. 7, 3: 'Quid stas, lapis?'
And *Hecyr.* ii. 1, 17 : 'quæ me omnino
lapidem, non hominem putas.' Insen-
sibility or apathy is also censured
under this term, Lucian, *Dial. Mer.*
xii.: Ὦ τῆς ἀγριότητος, τὸ δὲ μὴ
ἐπικλασθῆναι δακρυούσης, λίθος, οὐκ
ἄνθρωπός ἐστι. Cf. Dio Chrysos.
Or. xxi. p. 506. The epithet σιδηροῦς
is used like λίθινος. Lysias *in Theomn.*
p. 363: ἀλλ' εἰ μὴ σιδηροῦς ἐστιν,
κ.τ.λ. Other terms of abuse are to

be found in Aristophanes, some of
them very coarse. This perhaps
strikes us more than it would the
Greeks, whose ears were accustomed
to the phrases in question.

[43] This was the case with the reputed daughters of Stephanos. Demosth. *in Neœr.* 1367 : καὶ ὡμολόγει
μὲν (ὁ 'Επαίνετος) χρῆσθαι τῇ ἀνθρώπῳ, οὐ μέντοι μοιχός γε εἶναι·
οὔτε γὰρ Στεφάνου θυγατέρα αὐτὴν
εἶναι, ἀλλὰ Νεαίρας, τὴν δὲ μητέρα
αὐτῆς συνειδέναι πλησιάζουσαν αὐτῷ,
ἀνηλωκέναι τε πολλὰ εἰς αὐτὰς, τρέφειν τε, ὁπότε ἐπιδημήσειε, τὴν οἰκίαν ὅλην.

[44] Lucian, *Somn.* 14 : ἡ δὲ ἀπο-
λιφθεῖσα τὸ μὲν πρῶτον ἠγανάκτει

Ctesiphon's host, ' if we, from a regard to your daughters'
friends, don't bring you before a court of justice. But now
have your baggage conveyed to my house, Charicles, and
abide with me till your departure.' With this all seven
went up to Charicles' room. Sotades and Melissa alone
remained behind. ' You stupid, you!' said the pimp, ' you
forgot the garden-gate.'

καὶ τὼ χεῖρε συνεκρότει, καὶ τοὺς
ἐδόντας ἐνέπριε. Clapping the hands
is also a token of joy. See Jacobs on
Achill. Tat. i. 7.

SCENE THE THIRD.

THE ANCESTRAL ABODE.

THREE days after the events above recorded, the friends landed at the Piræus. Charicles, somewhat ashamed, and out of humour with himself, had willingly listened to Ctesiphon's proposal to go by sea, which was shorter, instead of continuing their journey by land through Megara. A ship, too, chanced to be just weighing anchor, and was ready to convey him thither, slave, horse, and all, for the moderate sum of one drachma; while Ctesiphon, who was unattended and without baggage, had only three oboles to pay.[1]

The youth's heart beat, oh how quickly! as he put foot on his native soil, and greeted the well-known spots, associated with so many happy memories of days gone by. Just the same bustling life as formerly; the same throng and pressure of the multitude, streaming towards the great emporium, where merchants from all parts of the world had exposed samples of their wares,[2] to sell them to travellers from every land. Nowhere could a more tempting assortment be met with, and though elsewhere an article might be sought in vain, yet in this central mart

---

[1] We learn from Plato, *Gorg.* p. 511, how very low passage-money, ναῦλον, was: ἐὰν μὲν ἐξ Αἰγίνης δεῦρο σώσῃ, οἶμαι δύ᾽ ὀβ λοὺς ἐπράξατο· ἐὰν δὲ ἐξ Αἰγύπτου ἢ ἐκ τοῦ Πόντου, ἐὰν πάμπολυ, ταύτης τῆς μεγάλης εὐεργεσίας, σώσασα ἃ νῦν δὴ ἔλεγον, καὶ αὐτὸν καὶ παῖδας, καὶ χρήματα καὶ γυναῖκας, ἀναβιβάσασα εἰς τὸν λιμένα δύο δραχμὰς ἐπράξατο. It rose considerably at a later period, for Lucian mentions four oboles, instead

of two, as the fare from Athens to Ægina. *Navig.* 15: καίτοι πρῶτον καὶ ἐς Αἴγιναν ... οἶσθα ἐν ἡλίκῳ σκαφιδίῳ πάντες ἅμα οἱ φίλοι τεττάρων ἕκαστος ὀβολῶν διεπλεύσαμεν. See Böckh's *Publ. Econ. of Athens*, p. 118.

[2] The building where these samples, δεῖγματα, were exposed, was itself called Δεῖγμα. See Excursus on *The Markets and Commerce.*

of Grecian commerce all imaginable commodities were
assembled, only waiting for a purchaser.[3] On this account
the harbour became a sort of second town, provided with
all that either resident or stranger might require,—taverns,
inns, workshops of all sorts, and houses of ill fame,[4] as well
as the benevolent establishment of the physician.[5] The
prospect, too, of making a ready livelihood, no doubt
attracted thither plenty of swindlers and sycophants, who
even formed organized societies,[6] ever ready to assist in
the dishonest practices of the knavish dealer, or in fleecing
the unsuspecting foreigner. Naturally enough, numbers
of citizens resorted hither daily, to meet some stranger, or
to await the arrival of a friend, or perhaps only for a
lounge on the pier or among the shops, and to amuse
themselves with the animated scene.[7]

But the pleasure which Charicles felt was alloyed by
the painful feeling of finding himself almost a stranger
amongst his fellow-citizens. While Ctesiphon repeatedly

---

[3] Isocr. *Paneg.* p. 60 : 'Εμπόριον
γὰρ ἐν μέσῳ τῆς Ἑλλάδος τὸν Πειραιᾶ κατεσκεύασατο, τοσαύτην ἔχονθ'
ὑπερβολὴν, ὥσθ' ἃ παρὰ τῶν ἄλλων
ἐν παρ' ἑκάστων χαλεπόν ἐστι λαβεῖν,
ταῦθ' ἅπαντα παρ' αὐτῆς ῥᾴδιον εἶναι
πορίσασθαι. Though Corinth was
the chief place of transit, yet the
Piræus was the most important
market for foreign goods.

[4] At least one of those public
establishments mentioned in the Excursus on *The Hetæræ* was in the
Piræus. Aristoph. *Pax,* 165 : ἐν
Πειραιεῖ παρὰ ταῖς πόρναις. So
Suidas : Κεραμεικοί. δύο τόποι Ἀθήνησιν. ἐν δὲ τῷ ἑτέρῳ εἰστήκεισαν αἱ
πόρναι. Cf. Bekker, *Anecd. Gr.* i.
p. 275. A third is mentioned, Steph.
de Urb. : Σκίρος. Ἔστι καὶ ἕτερον
Σκίρον τόπου Ἀττικοῦ ... ἐν δὲ τῷ
τόπῳ τούτῳ αἱ πόρναι ἐκαθίζοντο.

[5] Æschin. *in Timarch.* 65 : ἐκάθητο ἐν Πειραιεῖ ἐπὶ τοῦ Εὐθυδίκου
ἰατρείου.

[6] Demosth. *in Zenoth.* p. 885.
ἔστιν ἐργαστήρια μοχθηρῶν ἀνθρώπων συνεστηκότων ἐν τῷ Πειραιεῖ.
From the context of which passage,
compared with *in Pantæn.* 978, it
appears that there was a regularly
organised band of sharpers, who were
in league with one another. Demosth.
in Bœot. ὄνομ. p. 995, also calls it
ἐργαστήριον συκοφαντῶν.

[7] Demosth. *in Lacr.* 932 : οὗτοι
δὲ περιεπάτουν ἐν τῷ δείγματι τῷ
ἡμετέρῳ, καὶ ἡμεῖς προσιόντες διελε-
γόμεθα, κ.τ.λ. Theophr. *Char.* 23 :
Ὁ δὲ ἀλαζὼν τοιοῦτός τις, οἷος ἐν
τῷ Δείγματι ἑστηκὼς διηγεῖσθαι
ξένοις, ὡς πολλὰ χρήματα αὐτῷ
ἐστιν ἐν τῇ θαλάττῃ.

met with acquaintances, and was more than once tugged by
the cloak from behind,[8] and affectionately greeted, Charicles, who had left the city when a boy, passed through the
crowd unnoticed.   Still he consoled himself with the hope
that old acquaintanceships would speedily be renewed, and
fresh ones made as well.

Ctesiphon did not at first go to his lodgings; having
met his slave at the place of debarcation, he had dispatched him home to await his arrival.   He himself directed his steps to the Lyceion, where he reckoned on
meeting a great number of his friends, preparing themselves by gymnastics and the bath for the approaching hour
of repast.   Charicles accompanied him on his road.   The
house of his father's friend, to whose good offices he was
indebted for his return, and to whom he was now going to
pay his respects, abutted, as he understood, on the Itonian
gate, near the Olympieion, so that the Phalerian road,
which diverged to the right from the Long Walls, was no
bad way for him to the city.

How happy he felt at seeing the stream of the Ilissus,
sacred to the Muses, which, though not deep, came coursing along, so pure and transparent in its hollow bed! 'Oh!
let us put off our sandals,' said he to his friend, 'and
lave our feet in the cool water as we walk along the
stream.[9]   I have often done so as a boy, when my pedagogue let me stroll out beyond the Palæstra.   Not far
from hence is the place where, as the legend goes, Oreithyia
was ravished by Boreas; a sweetly pretty spot in sooth,
and worthy to have been the play-ground of the royal

---

[8] This was the common method of
attracting the attention of one with
whom a person wished to speak.
Plato, *de Repub.* i. p. 327, also speaking of the Piræus: καί μου ὄπισθεν ὁ
παῖς λαβόμενος τοῦ ἱματίου, κ.τ.λ.
So also *ib.* p. 449 : ὁ δὲ Πολέμαρχος …
ἐκτείνας τὴν χεῖρα καὶ λαβόμενος
τοῦ ἱματίου ἄνωθεν αὐτοῦ παρὰ τὸν

ὦμον. Plaut. *Epid.* i. 1, 1 : 'Quis pro-
perantem me prehendit pallio?' And
Appul. *Met.* ii. p. 120 : 'a tergo arri-
pens eum lacinia prehendit.'

[9] Plato, *Phædr.* p. 229. The value
of such pictures is much enhanced by
their extreme rarity.

maid.[10]   Look where that big platanus yonder rears its
leafy head high above its fellows; that was ever my
favourite spot.   That noble tree with wide-spread arms,
and round it the shady bushes of agnus castus, whose
blossoms fill the air with fragrant odours; the lovely
spring of freshest water that runs in front of the platanus;
the cool quivering of the air so peculiar to the place; the
summer-song of the cicadæ chanting in innumerous choirs;
and above all, the tall luxuriant grass, affording so soft a
couch to those who seek repose:—every thing, in short,
unites to render the spot the loveliest retreat that can be
imagined.' [11]

'Strange man,' said Ctesiphon; 'why, you speak as if

---

[10] Plato, *ibid.*

[11] We should hardly credit that
so sentimental a picture of this lovely
spot belonged to the antique; but
these are in fact the very words which
Plato puts into the mouth of Socrates;
ibid. 230 : Νὴ τὴν Ἥραν, καλή γε ἡ
καταγωγη. ἥ τε γὰρ πλάτανος αὕτη
μάλα ἀμφιλαφής τε καὶ ὑψηλή, τοῦ
τε ἄγνου τὸ ὕψος καὶ τὸ σύσκιον
τάγκαλον καὶ ὡς ἀκμὴν ἔχει τῆς
ἄνθης, ὡς ἂν εὐωδέστατον παρέχοι
τὸν τόπον. ἥ γε αὖ πηγὴ χαριεστάτη
ὑπὸ τῆς πλατάνου ῥεῖ μάλα ψυχροῦ
ὕδατος, ὥς γε τῷ ποδὶ τεκμήρασθαι.
νυμφῶν τέ τινων καὶ Ἀχελῴου ἱερὸν
ἀπὸ τῶν κορῶν τε καὶ ἀγαλμάτων
ἔοικεν εἶναι. εἰ δ' αὖ βούλει τὸ εὔ-
πνουν τοῦ τόπου ὡς ἀγαπητόν τε καὶ
σφόδρα ἡδύ. θερινόν τε καὶ λιγυρὸν
ὑπηχεῖ τῷ τεττίγων χορῷ. πάντων
δὲ κομψότατον τὸ τῆς πόας, ὅτι ἐν
ἠρέμα προσάντει ἱκανὴ πέφυκε κα-
τακλινέντι τὴν κεφαλὴν παγκάλως
ἔχειν. No doubt it is true, as Müller
(*Handb. d. Archäol.* p. 445) observes,
that the Greek mind was not much
addicted to the romantic contemplation of nature; and certainly no

author of the better age has even
attempted to portray a landscape;
and this well agrees with the utter
neglect of landscape-painting, which
was never attempted till a very recent
period, and then never rose to medio-
crity.   The Greeks wanted that deep
and warm perception of the charms
of inanimate nature which is so universal in our time; and it is clear
that Plato's enthusiasm for natural
scenery was looked on as strange and
uncommon by the ancients.   Hence
the above passage is frequently alluded to; even by Strabo, ix. 1, 24;
and the matter-of-fact Plutarch seems
to have not liked it at all.   *Amat.* 1 :
ἄφελε τοῦ λόγου τὸ νῦν ἔχον ἐποποιῶν
τε λειμῶνας καὶ σκιὰς, καὶ ἅμα κιττοῦ
τε καὶ λάκκων διαδρομὰς, καὶ ὅσα ἄλλα
τοιούτων τόπων ἐπιλαβόμενοι γλί-
χονται τὸν Πλάτωνος Ἰλισσὸν καὶ
τὸν ἄγνον ἐκεῖνον, καὶ τὴν ἠρέμα
προσάντη πόαν πεφυκυῖαν, προθυ-
μότερον ἢ κάλλιον ἐπιγράφεσθαι.
Among the few other passages betraying a more genial sense of the
delights of nature may be mentioned
Nubes, 1005, quoted *infra,* note 13;
and Sophoc. *Œd. Col.* 16.   See also

I were a stranger to whom you must describe the beauties of the place. Do you suppose that all this is not as well known to me as to you, and that I have never set foot beyond the city-walls?'[12]

'Pardon me,' said the youth. 'My father early accustomed me to derive innocent pleasure from the joys which nature offers: to revel in the spring-tide in the odour of the blossoms, in the silver-dashed leaves of the poplar, in the whispering of the elms and platanus.[13] The recollection of the blissful hours that I whiled away in such-like joys, and beneath yon platanus, made me forget that my description was unneeded by you. And yet,' he added, 'there are many people, who the live-long year do nothing but jostle about in the throng of human beings, and have no sympathy for all these beauties, or rather, have no notion that they exist.'

Engaged in conversation such as this, they reached the neighbourhood of the Itonian gate, where Charicles parted from his friend, in search of Phorion's house, while Ctesiphon pursued his way to the Gymnasium. They had agreed to meet next morning in the market-place, by the tables of the money-changers, whither Charicles was called by his own pecuniary affairs.

The house of Phorion lay in an out of the way place, not far from the city-wall; its outside looked as gloomy and uninviting as the owner himself was by common

---

Humboldt's *Cosmos*, Vol. ii. § 1. It is absurd to suppose, as some have done, that Plato was ridiculing the line, Hom. *Il.* ii. 307:

καλῇ ὑπὸ πλατανίστῳ, ὅθεν ῥέεν ἀγλαὸν ὕδωρ.

[12] The answer of Phædros, in Plato, *ibid.*

[13] Cf. the Parænesis of the Δίκαιος λόγος. Aristoph. *Nub.* 1005:

ἀλλ' εἰς Ἀκαδημίαν κατιὼν ὑπὸ ταῖς μορι-
αις ἀποθρέξεις,
στεφανωσάμενος καλάμῳ λευκῷ μετὰ σώ-
φρονος ἡλικιώτου,
σμίλακος ὄζων καὶ ἀπραγμοσύνης, καὶ λεύ-
κης φυλλοβολούσης,
ἦρος ἐν ὥρᾳ χαίρων, ὁπόταν πλάτανος πτε-
λέᾳ ψιθυρίζῃ.

report described to be. Charicles had already learnt from
his friend that this man was generally supposed to be very
rich, but at the same time inordinately stingy. From the
account that had reached him of his moody disposition and
eccentricities, he did not look forward to an over friendly
reception ; still he remembered that Phorion was formerly
an intimate friend of his father, and that it was he who
had now—if not personally, at all events indirectly, and
by a considerable pecuniary sacrifice [14]—obtained permission for him to return from exile. And above all, a
common friend, in Syracuse, of Phorion and his father,
had given him letters containing the strongest recommendations ; [15] so that there could not possibly be any one in
Athens whom he had such cogent reasons for visiting.

In a shop near the gate stood an aged crone, of whom
Charicles enquired if she could show him the house of
Phorion.[16] 'To be sure I can,' she replied, ' he lives hard
by. D'ye see the windows yonder, overlooking the gate,
and the house-door, beside which the two Hermæ stand ?
That's his house. But if you are going to visit him as a
guest, I would advise you first to look after some supper
for yourself, and fodder for your horse.' [17] ' Why so ?' said

---

[14] That a free use of the purse was
the successful method of procedure
in such cases, appears from Xenoph.
de Republ. Athen. 3, 3 : λέγουσι δέ
τινες, ἥν τις ἀργύριον ἔχων προσίῃ
πρὸς βουλὴν ἢ δῆμον, χρηματιεῖται.
ἐγὼ δὲ τούτοις ὁμολογήσαιμ' ἂν,
ἀπὸ χρημάτων πολλὰ διαπράττεσθαι
Ἀθήνῃσι.

[15] Such letters of introduction
were not uncommon. We have an
instance in the seventh letter of Isocrates, p. 607, which contains such
a recommendation. Αὐτοκράτωρ γάρ
ὁ τὰ γράμματα φέρων οἰκείως ἡμῖν
ἔχει . . . διὰ δὴ ταῦτα πάντα βουλοίμην
ἄν σε καλῶς αὐτῷ χρήσασθαι καὶ

συμφερόντως ἀμφοτέροις ἡμῖν, καὶ
γενέσθαι φανερὸν, ὅτι μέρος τι καὶ
δι' ἐμὲ γίγνεται τῶν δεόντων αὐτῷ.
Cf. Lucian, Asin. 1 : γράμματα δὲ
αὐτῷ ἐκόμιζον οἴκοθεν, ὥστε οἰκῆσαι
παρ' αὐτῷ.

[16] After Appul. Met. i. 65.

[17] Lucius gives the same advice,
Lucian, Asin. 3. It was not thought
necessary that the host should provide
his stranger-guest with board as well
as lodging, though he usually sent
him presents of provisions, ξένια.
Vitruv. vi. 7, 4 : 'Nam cum fuerunt
Græci delicatiores et fortuna opulen-
tiores hospitibus advenientibus in-

Charicles, not loth perhaps to glean some particulars concerning the character of the man. ' Isn't Phorion rich ? ' ' Rich enough, I believe ye,' said the woman ; ' but not so rich as he is stingy ; and besides he'll hardly admit an Athenian to his house, much less a foreigner. But there are reasons for that.' ' And what are they ?' asked Charicles curiously. ' Because,' said she, ' he possesses the Hermes-wand,[18] and is all day seeking for hidden treasures by spells and divination. But it is easy to see from his looks that riches so gotten bring him no good,[19] for, with all his treasures, he leads a wretched life. His children are dead, and he scarcely dares put his head out of doors by day ; and at night, they say, he skulks about the house guarding his buried hoard, with his eye on the party-wall that separates his house from the next, for fear of burglary, and is so timorsome that the slightest noise frightens him out of his wits, and he even takes the pillars of his house for thieves.'[20] ' But,' said Charicles, ' I fancy having heard that Phorion was not once in such ill-odour ? '

---

struebant triclinia, cubicula, cum penu cellas, primoque die ad coenam invitabant, postero mittebant pullos, ova, olera, poma, reliquasque res agrestes.' These presents were also sent by other acquaintances, besides the host. Appul. *Met.* ii. p. 15.

[18] Manifold miracles were ascribed to the Hermes-wand, a magic rod, whose virtues found acceptance with many. τοῦτ' ἔστι τὸ τοῦ Ἑρμοῦ ῥαβδίον· οὗ θέλεις, φησὶν. ἄψαι, καὶ χρυσοῦν ἔσται. Arrian, *Epict. Diss.* iii. 20. Cf. Cic. *Off.* i. 44.

[19] The belief implied in the proverb, 'Ill-gotten goods never prosper,' prevailed also among the ancients. This prohibited wealth included hidden treasure taken up by one not a descendant of the person

who buried it. So Plato, *Leg.* xi. 913 : ἃ μὴ κατέθου μὴ ἀνέλῃ. Heliod. *Æthiop.* v. 5 : τουτῶν συγκειμένων ἀνεδύοντο τοῦ σπηλαίου κειμηλίων μὲν ἄλλων τῶν ἐναποκειμένων οὐδενὸς θιγόντες· τὸν γὰρ ἀπὸ σύλων πλοῦτον βέβηλον ἐδοκίμαζον.

[20] Lucian, in his humorous piece, *Somnium seu Gallus*, 29, makes Micyllos enter the abode of Simon, a rich miser, by night, when he is sleeplessly guarding his treasures. Simon says, δέδια γοῦν, μή τις ὑπορύξας τὸν τοῖχον ὑφέληται ταῦτα. . . ἅπασαν περίειμι διαναστὰς ἐν κύκλῳ τὴν οἰκίαν· . . τίς οὗτος ; ὁρῶ σέ γε, ὦ τοιχωρύχε, μὰ Δία· ἐπεὶ κίων γε ὢν τυγχάνεις, εὖ ἔχει. Cf. Molière's *L'Avare*, Act iv. sc. 7 : 'Qui est-ce ? Arrête. Rends-moi mon argent, coquin.—Ah, c'est moi.'

E

'Stingy he ever was,' rejoined the crone, 'but it is only
for about the last five years that he has been as he now
is. 'Twas then he bought the house of a burgher, who
had to leave the town, and in this, so folks say, he found
a great treasure, hidden under a statue of Hermes that
stood in the court-yard,[21] and since then he has never
ceased grubbing for new treasures.' These words manifestly disturbed Charicles. Five years! just so long ago
had his father's house been sold, and such a statue stood
actually in the court. Could Phorion be the possessor of
the mansion, and really have become master of the wealth
which had perhaps been hidden by some ancestor of the
family? He thanked the woman, and hastened to become
acquainted with Phorion, who now assumed a much greater
importance in his eyes.

The portrait drawn of him by the crone, contained
that usual quantum of exaggeration with which the lower
orders talk of the faults of those who chance to be in
better circumstances than their neighbours. Moreover,
Phorion certainly gave cause sufficient for such reports,
for though rich, he lived in a house, large enough, it is
true, but of excessively shabby exterior; and though he
had hundreds of slaves, who worked for him as handy-
craftsmen, chiefly in the mines, he kept but a single male
domestic, who, together with a cross-grained porter, and
a solitary maid, completed his household.[22] He was never
seen abroad but on business, either going to the tables
of the money-changers, or into the bazaars of the Piræus,
or to the courts of justice. He frequented none of the
customary places of amusement and resort, but stopped at
home with locked doors, within which visitors could rarely
obtain admission.[23] An elderly man, who lived with him,

---

[21] Lucian, *Navig.* 20: ἀνορωρύχθω
θησαυρὸς ὑπὸ τὸν Ἑρμῆν τὸν λίθινον,
ὅς ἐστιν ἡμῖν ἐν τῇ αὐλῇ, μέδιμνοι
χίλιοι ἐπισήμου χρυσοῦ.

[22] Lucian, *Asin.* 1, says of Hipparchos, ὅτι μίαν θεράπαιναν τρέφοι.

[23] Taken entirely from Plutarch's
sketch of Nicias: οὔτε συνεδείπνε

was his only companion, and generally received the persons
who desired speech with Phorion, excuse being made for the
master of the house on the plea of pressing engagements,
which prevented his appearance.[24]   This man, according
to popular belief, served Phorion as soothsayer at his frequent sacrifices, to direct him where to seek for hidden
treasure, or, it might be, only to discover the most advan-
tageous spots for sinking mines.[25]   But, besides this, he
passed for a man of profound learning, to whose care
Phorion committed his well-stocked library, and his collection of choice works of art and of curiosities of all
sorts ; for in such matters he was quite a connoisseur. The
library was for those times considerable enough.   In it
were to be found not only the writings of the most renowned poets from Homer downwards, of whose works
there were several copies,[26]—which, judging from their
colour, and their wormeaten state, were of great antiquity
—but also the compositions of the philosophers, orators,
and historians. Artemidoros, so he was called, had bestowed
much pains in obtaining fine and accurate copies, and, if
possible, the autograph manuscript of the authors themselves ; and he had really succeeded in getting from a frank-
incense-dealer some comedies of Anaxandrides which the
composer, not having obtained the price he demanded, had

τινὶ τῶν πολιτῶν, οὔτε κοινολο-
γίαις, οὔτε συνδιημερεύσεσιν ἐνέ-
βαλλεν ἑαυτὸν, οὐδ' ὅλως ἐσχόλαζε
ταῖς τοιαύταις διατριβαῖς. . . . εἰ δὲ
μηδὲν ἐν κοινῷ πράττειν ἔχοι, δυσ-
πρόσοδος ἦν καὶ δυσέντευκτος, οἰκου-
ρῶν καὶ κατακεκλεισμένος.   Nic. 5.

[24] Plutarch, ibid.: Οἱ δὲ φίλοι
τοῖς ἐπὶ ταῖς θύραις φοιτῶσιν ἐνετύγ-
χανον καὶ παρητοῦντο συγγνώμην
ἔχειν, ὡς καὶ τότε Νικίου πρὸς δημοσίας χρείας τινὰς καὶ ἀσχολίας ὄντος.

[25] See Plutarch, ibid. 4. Augury
was often employed to discover hid-

den hoards. Aves, 598 :

τοὺς θησαυροὺς τ' αὐτοῖς δείξουσ', οὓς οἱ
    πρότεροι κατέθεντο
τῶν ἀργυρίων· οὗτοι γὰρ ἴσασι. λέγουσι δὲ
    τοι τάδε πάντες·
Οὐδεὶς οἶδεν τὸν θησαυρὸν τὸν ἐμὸν, πλὴν εἰ
    τις ἄρ' ὄρνις.

[26] Lucian, adv. Indoct. 7, shows
that people were not content with
one copy of an author only : ἐπεὶ δὲ
ἐν τοῖς ἄλλοις καὶ τὸν Ὅμηρον ἐπρίω
πολλάκις.   See Excursus on Bookselling and Libraries.

destined for waste-paper.[27] Doubtless the good Phorion was occasionally imposed upon, and had some dearly-priced copy palmed off on him as a genuine autograph. Who could say whether those tragedies of Sophocles, this history of Herodotus, were from the authors' own hand; or whether those mysteriously treasured-up strips were the remnants of the condemned writings of Protagoras, saved from the flames;[28] and those eight rolls! were they one of the copies which Demosthenes had made of the history of Thucydides, or were they all still in the possession of the rapid orator?

Equally valuable, in its way, was the collection of curious works of art, and of historic *souvenirs*. Among other things were to be seen the tablets of Æschylus, rescued from the unhallowed hands of Dionysios:[29] the stick with which Antisthenes was supposed to have menaced old Diogenes, with similar curiosities. Beside these lay marvellous specimens of patience and ingenuity: tiny

---

[27] Chamæleon, ap. Athen. ix. p. 374: Πικρὸς δ' ὢν τὸ ἦθος ('Αναξανδρίδης) ἐποίει τι τοιοῦτον περὶ τὰς κωμῳδίας. ὅτε γὰρ μὴ νικῴη, λαμβάνων ἔδωκεν εἰς τὸν λιβανωτὸν κατατεμεῖν καὶ οὐ μετεσκεύαζεν ὥσπερ οἱ πολλοί.

[28] This was the first instance of the confiscation and public burning of a book, on account of its doubting the existence of the gods. Diog. Laert. ix. 52: καὶ τὰ βιβλία αὐτοῦ κατέκαυσαν ἐν τῇ ἀγορᾷ, ὑπὸ κήρυκα ἀναδεξάμενοι παρ' ἑκάστου τῶν κεκτημένων.

[29] Lucian, *adv. Indoct.* 15, relates of Dionysios the younger: Οὗτος τοίνυν πυθόμενος, ὡς ἐγγελᾶται (τραγῳδίαν ποιήσας), τὸ Αἰσχύλου πυξίον, εἰς ὃ ἐκεῖνος ἔγραφε, σὺν πολλῇ σπουδῇ κτησάμενος αὐτὸ ᾤετο ἔνθεος ἔσεσθαι καὶ κάτοχος ἐκ τοῦ πυξίου. So also Neanthos had

obtained by a bribe the putative lyre of Orpheus, preserved in the isle of Lesbos (*ib.* § 13). He also mentions the prices which other relics of the kind had fetched: Καὶ τί σοι τὸν 'Ορφέα ἢ τὸν Νέανθον λέγω, ὅπου καὶ καθ' ἡμᾶς αὐτοὺς ἐγένετό τις καὶ ἔτι ἐστὶν, οἶμαι, ὃς τὸν 'Επικτήτου λύχνον τοῦ Στωικοῦ κεραμεοῦν ὄντα τρισχιλίων δραχμῶν ἐπρίατο; . . Χθὲς δὲ καὶ πρῴην ἄλλος τις τὴν Πρωτέως τοῦ Κυνικοῦ βακτηρίαν, ἣν καταθέμενος ἤλατο εἰς τὸ πῦρ, ταλάντου κἀκεῖνος ἐπρίατο. Doubtless in Lucian's time this *penchant* was more frequent than in Alexander's; but when the Tegeates showed as valuable κειμήλια the skin of the Calydonian boar, and the Thebans the bones of Geryon, it may well be conjectured that at an earlier date private persons indulged in such tastes.

little works in ivory, among which was a chariot and four which a fly might cover with its wings; while an ant, the size of life, and a sesame-corn, on which, in golden letters, two lines of Homer were inscribed, attracted particular attention.[30] Delicate objects of wax-work appeared to be the owner's especial hobby; for in these the collection was richest; the fruits of numerous kinds, in form and colour closely imitating nature, were wonderful efforts of art.[31] On things like these Phorion lavished considerable sums, whereas in other respects his mode of life was simple in the extreme, indeed so much so, that he was accounted miserly by those who were not aware how often he por-

---

[30] These μικρὰ ἔργα of the artists Callicrates and Myrmecides are repeatedly mentioned. See Sillig. *Catal. Artif.* Their precise date is unknown, though they probably flourished toward the end of the Alexandrian era.

[31] For some account of the ancient wax-work, consult Böttiger's *Sabina.* His error of supposing wax-work chaplets to be alluded to in Martial, has been pointed out in *Gallus*, p. 363. That the art of working in wax (κηροπλαστικὴ, Poll. vii. 165), was extensively practised, is beyond dispute. Thus a Cupid modelled in wax is mentioned by Anacreon (x. 1), and the term κηροπλάστης occurs in Plato, *Timæus*, p. 74, and κηροτέχνης in Anacr. v. 9. Cf. Cic. *Verr.* iv. 13, *fingere e cera.* Fruit, and the like, was often imitated (Diog. Laert. vii. 177), for instance pomegranates (Arrian, *Diss. Epict.* iv. 5), or apples (Athen. vii. p. 254; Lamprid. *Heliog*. 25). But that the art was universal, and indispensable on account of the symbolic festival of Adonis, as Böttiger supposes, will be difficult to prove. He and Corsini are wrong in placing that festival between winter and spring, as they conjecture from Plutarch, *Nic.*

13. The departure of the fleet, there mentioned, did not take place till summer, as appears from Thucyd. vi. 30 : θέρους μεσοῦντος ἤδε ἡ ἀναγωγὴ ἐγίγνετο. And this tallies with Plato, *Phædr.* 276 : πότερα σπουδῇ ἂν θέρους εἰς 'Αδώνιδος κήπους ἀρῶν χαίροι. So also Theophr. *Hist. Plant.* vi. 7 : ἐν ὀστράκοις δὲ, ὥσπερ οἱ 'Αδώνιδος κῆποι, σπείρεται τοῦ θέρους. The season of the festival being summer, and not the end of winter, the imaginary necessity for the use of wax-fruits entirely disappears, though waxen images of Adonis may have been used. That these were employed seems probable from Plutarch, *supra*: καὶ προὔκειτο πολλαχόθι τῆς πόλεως εἴδωλα καὶ ταφαὶ περὶ αὐτά. Lastly, the *Xenia* of Martial are groundlessly supposed by Böttiger to have been wax-fruits; if the poet really intended artificial fruits, they were most likely of clay. Cf. Plin. xxxv. 12. 45; and Petron. 68: 'Mirabar, inquam, nisi omnia ista sunt de strunto (*sic*), aut certe de luto: vidi Romæ Saturnalibus ejusmodi cœnarum imaginem. Cf. Mart. xiv. 182:

Ebrius hæc fecit terris, puto, monstra Prometheus,
Saturnalitio lusit et ipse luto.

tioned the daughters of poor burghers, or remitted the
payment of money lent to persons in distress.

Charicles had arrived at the door of the house, and
knocked pretty sharply with the copper ring.[32] It was

---

[32] Although the house-door was
not locked in the day-time, still nobody thought of entering without
previously tapping, or otherwise announcing himself, and waiting for
permission to enter. Plutarch, *Cimon*,
17 : καὶ γὰρ θύραν κόψαντας ἀλλοτρίαν, οὐκ εἰσιέναι πρότερον, ἢ τὸν
κύριων κελεῦσαι. *De Curios.* 3 : Καίτοι μὴ κόψαντά γε θύραν εἰς οἰκίαν
ἀλλοτρίαν οὐ νομίζεται παρελθεῖν.
Xenoph. *Symp.* 1. 11 : Φίλιππος δ' ὁ
γελωτοποιὸς κρούσας τὴν θύραν εἶπε
τῷ ὑπακούσαντι εἰσαγγεῖλαι ὅστις
τε εἴη. The usual method was to tap,
except among the Spartans, who
called out. Plutarch, *Inst. Lac.* 31 :
ἔθος ἦν αὐτοῖς μηδὲ κόπτειν τὰς
αὐλείους θύρας, ἀλλ' ἔξωθεν βοᾶν.
See also Eurip. *Phœn.* 1067 ; *Iphig.
in Taur.* 1267 ; and Plautus, *passim*.
The expression for tapping is κόπτειν,
though the Attic writers, Xenophon
for instance, sometimes use κρούειν,
but hardly κροτεῖν, which the grammarians pronounce unattic. The
word ψοφεῖν was used of the noise
made on opening the door to go out.
Lucian, *Solœc.* 9 : καὶ εἴ τίς γε νῦν
ψοφοίη τὴν θύραν εἰσιών, ἢ ἐξιὼν
κόπτοι, τί φήσομέν σε πεπονθέναι ;
The generally received explanation of
the two last-mentioned words, and
which has been adopted from the old
grammarians, namely, that one was
used of knocking outside, and the
other inside, is very strange, and dis-
agrees with what is known of the construction of the door. So Suidas :
Κόπτω· ἐπὶ τῶν ἔξωθεν τὴν θύραν
κρούοντων τὸ κόπτειν λέγεται· ἐπὶ δὲ
τῶν ἔσωθεν ψοφεῖν. ἱκανῶς δὲ διέστειλε

τοῦτο Μένανδρος ἐπὶ μὲν τῶν ἔξωθεν) ἐ-
γων κόψω τὴν θύραν, ἐπὶ δὲ τῶν ἔσωθεν.
ἀλλ' ἐψόφηκε τὴν θύραν τις ἐξιών.
Cf. Helladius, *Chrest.* p. 25. He
informs us that the doors anciently
opened outwards, and that a person
tapped before going out for fear of
jostling anyone without: ἔξωθεν γὰρ
αὐτὰς ἀνατρέποντες ἔνδοθεν ἐξῄεσαν.
πρότερον δὲ τῇ χειρὶ ψόφον ἐποίουν
κρούοντες ἐπὶ τῷ γνῶναι τοὺς ἐπὶ
τῶν θυρῶν καὶ φυλάξασθαι, μὴ πλη-
γεὶς ἑστὼς λάθῃ τῶν θυρῶν ὠθουμέν-
ων ἄφνω. This explanation, like so
many others, appears merely to have
been invented to explain an obscure
phrase. The word seems never used
to denote an intentional knocking;
thus we either have ἡ θύρα ψοφεῖ, οr
ψοφεῖ τις ἐξιών, or thirdly, ψοφεῖ τις
τὴν θύραν. Now, as is shown in the
Excursus on *The House*, for the door
to open outwards, was an exceptional
case, and this would invalidate the
generality of the explanation of Helladius. Again, the phrase often occurs
where an intentional noise would by
all means have been avoided; thus
when the lover creeps out at night, in
Lysias, *de Cæde Erat.* p. 20, we read :
ὅτι ἐν ἐκείνῃ τῇ νυκτὶ ἐψόφει ἡ μέταυλος θύρα καὶ ἡ αὔλειος. So also Heliod. *Æthiop.* i. 17. So that we must
conclude that the grammarians laid
down this distinction without any immediate knowledge of the matter ; so
even Plutarch, *Popl.* 20 : τὰς δὲ Ἑλ-
ληνικὰς (θύρας) πρότερον οὕτως ἔχειν
ἁπάσας λέγουσιν (ἐκτὸς ἀνοιγομένας),
ἀπὸ τῶν κωμῳδιῶν λαμβάνον-
τες, ὅτι κόπτουσι καὶ ψοφοῦσι τὰς
αὐτῶν θύρας ἔσωθεν οἱ προϊέναι μέλ-

some time before the porter came and pushed back the bolt. And even then, he only opened the door a little, and seeing the youth in travelling costume, said grumpily, 'What d'ye want? He's engaged.' With this he again closed the door. Charicles knocked a second time, but the slave, as he secured the fastenings inside, cried out, 'Don't you hear? he's not at liberty.'[33] 'But, my good man,' importuned the youth, 'just tell your master that it is Charicles, the son of Charinos, with letters for him from Syracuse.' The slave went growling away. At last however he returned, unfastened the door, and said in somewhat more friendly tones, 'Master will see you.'

Phorion had just reclined, together with Artemidoros, to his frugal meal. He did not rise from the small table, on the entrance of Charicles, but offered his hand and saluted him warmly. The youth presented his credentials, which the other opened, having first carefully scrutinised the seal. 'You had no need of these recommendations,' said he, when he had read them. 'I had hoped to have seen your father again within these walls, but I learnt some days ago that his ashes repose in a foreign soil. His son is however not the less welcome on that account. You must content yourself with temporary quarters here, till you have rendered your father's house habitable.' 'My

---

λοντες. The reason why κόπτει is always used of the person entering, and ψοφεῖ of the person going out, is, that the first must knock to be let in, while the latter is only audible from the noise incidental to his opening the door to go out. This noise, ψόφος, is even made by those who enter after having knocked. Thus Plato, Symp. p. 212: καὶ ἐξαίφνης τὴν αὔλειον θύραν κρουομένην πολὺν ψόφον παρασχεῖν· and Lucian, Dial. Mer. xii.: ἔκοψα δ' οὖν, ἀλλ' ἐπάρας ἠρέμα τ ν θύραν . . . παραγαγὼν τὸν στροφέα παρῆλθον ἀψοφητί. Metal rings were fixed on the door to tap

with, as in Homer, the κορῶναι. They were named ῥόπτρα, also κόρακες. See Harpocr. ῥόπτρον: and Posidippos, quoted by Pollux, x. 22 : κόρακ κρούεθ' ἡ θύρα. They were also called ἐπισπαστῆρες, or ἐπίσπαστρα, because they also served to pull the door to from without. Lucian, Amor. 16; Herod. vi. 91. In Plutarch's time they appear to have become unusual. De Curios. 2: ἀλλὰ νῦν μέν εἰσι θυρωροί, πάλαι δὲ ῥόπτρα κρουόμενα πρὸς ταῖς θύραις αἴσθησιν παρεῖχεν.

[33] Plato, Protag. p. 314.

father's house?' said the youth, astonished. 'You suppose it is sold, don't you?' replied Phorion. 'Quite right; and the precipitation of the banker, whom your father in the haste of his flight, charged with the sale, nearly prevented me from preserving for you the home of your fathers, and the shrine of your household gods.[34] I heard, only just in time, that it was advertised for sale. I bought it; it has been uninhabited ever since; and I will restore it to you to-morrow, if you do not think the forty minæ it cost me too high a price.'

Charicles was overwhelmed with surprise and delight. 'Was this the language of such a man as Ctesiphon and the woman had described? A suspicion certainly did flash across his mind, that he had purchased it for the sake of the treasure; but if Phorion's intentions were really dishonest, what could hinder him from continuing in possession of the mansion, which was perhaps of double the value mentioned? He therefore thanked the old man with warmth, and expressed his willingness to repay the forty minæ next day.

'Let my slave now conduct you to your apartment,' said Phorion, 'and thence into the bath, that you may come back and share our homely fare.'

The apartment destined for the guest was in a smaller house abutting on the main building, with an entrance through the party-wall, and consequently, it afforded the convenience of retirement and quiet, without fear of interruption. Charicles, however, only purposed to stay here till his own house could be made ready for his reception. With earliest morn he sprang from his couch, impatient beyond measure to see once more the dear scenes of his happy childhood. Phorion had expressed a wish to accompany him. Charicles during the evening became more and more convinced that though the man's character was full of eccentricities, it in no way justified the unwarrant-

---

[34] See Excursus on *The Grecian House*

able reports in circulation about him. Still he was unable
to rid himself entirely of his suspicions about the treasure.
While conversing about his father's house, he could not
suppress a query concerning the statue of Hermes : Phorion responded with ill-concealed confusion, and a smile
flitted across the solemn lips of Artemidoros. Was it
possible that the fellow was content with his rich booty,
and now intended playing the magnanimous ? He was still
sunk in cogitations like these, when his host's servant
brought him bread and wine for breakfast, and announced
that his master was ready to go out. Just dipping a few
slices of bread into the wine,[35] Charicles hurried away with
Manes to join Phorion, who was already on the threshold,
and behind him a slave, bearing a sealed casket.[36] There
was something mysterious about the man to-day, he spoke
in monosyllables, and kept looking round at the slave, as if
fearing to lose him.

It was still very early, but the streets were already
full of busy passengers ;—men, who wished to catch their
friends at home, before they went out[37]—boys, who were
on their way to school or the gymnasium, attended by
their pedagogues—women and female slaves, who were up
betimes to fetch water from the Enneacrynos[38]—countryfolks bringing their productions to market[39]—chapmen of

---

[35] This was the usual first breakfast, taken directly after rising, called
ἀκράτισμα. See Excursus on *The
Meals.*

[36] The slave in attendance carried
the money his master required. So
Theophr. *Char.* 23, where the brag-
gart, who pretends he wants to buy a
carpet for two talents, scolds his slave
for not having brought the money.

[37] Such visits were made in the
earliest hours of the morning. Xenoph. *Œcon.* 11, 14: Ἐγὼ τοίνυν
ἀνίστασθαι μὲν ἐξ εὐνῆς εἴθισμαι,

ἡνίκα ἔτι ἔνδον καταλαμβάνοιμι, εἴ
τινα δεόμενος ἰδεῖν τυγχάνοιμι. See
also Plato, *Protag.* 311, where Hippocrates calls Socrates before day-break,
in order to pay Protagoras a visit :
μήπω, ὦ 'γαθὲ, ἐκεῖσε ἴωμεν. πρωὶ
γάρ ἐστιν· ἀλλὰ δεῦρο ἐξαναστῶμεν εἰς τὴν αὐλήν, καὶ περιϊόντες
αὐτοῦ διατρίψωμεν, ἕως ἂν φῶς γέ-
νηται· εἶτα ἴωμεν.

[38] Aristoph. *Lys.* 327. See Excursus on *The Women.*

[39] Plutarch. *Arat.* 8. See Excursus
on *The Markets and Commerce.*

all descriptions, preparing for the avocations of the day. In
short, all was life and bustle the moment day broke.

The two now rounded a corner of the Tripod-street,
and in a few moments Charicles stood before the well-
known house, and greeted the tutelar deities who guarded
the entrance. The agyieus, formed in the antique fashion,
like a cone, stood still unscathed; the laurel, spreading its
branches around, was also there, healthy and green as of
yore, and *vis-à-vis* was the head of a Hermes, decked by
some passer-by with a chaplet and ribands, and which
seemed to cast a benign look of welcome on the exile
returned. Phorion, with his three-toothed key,[40] opened
the door, whose creaking hinges told plainly that they
were unaccustomed to revolve. Charicles strode with a
sad kind of joy into the hall of the deserted mansion. The
cell of the porter was empty; rusty lay the chain of the
watchful dog; in the colonnades round the court, and in the
open porticos of the andronitis, swallows had built their
nests, and busy spiders wove their gossamer meshes about
the capitals of the pillars. Green moss had begun to cover
the passage-floors, and the vacant space was overgrown
with rank grass. Here stood the statue of the god, who
was reported to have guarded the hidden treasures; but
the pedestal, which supported it, seemed to the youth
altered. Formerly, he thought, it sank a little deeper
into the ground on one side, but now it appeared to stand
level. He went nearer, to convince himself of the fact; a
change had evidently been made, for the red veins in the
stone which used to face the entrance were now on the
opposite side.

Phorion had marked his astonishment, and apparently
guessed what thoughts were passing in his bosom. With
friendly earnestness he drew nigh and grasped the youth's
hand.[41] 'Have you too, perchance, heard the report, that

---

[40] See *Gallus*, p. 283 : *clavis Laconica*.

[41] Seizing the hand was considered,
even in Homer's time, as a token of
great friendship and familiarity: ἔν τ'

the god kept watch over hoards concealed beneath his
feet?' Charicles replied by an embarrassed silence. ' The
report did not lie,' continued Phorion. ' When I purchased
this mansion, hoping to restore it to your father at some
time or other, I perceived that the base of the statue was
leaning to one side, and its fall was imminent. I caused
it to be removed, and discovered underneath a pot containing two thousand staters of the purest gold. Thus,'
said he, as he took the heavy casket from the slave, ' thus
I restore thee the sum, which some forefather of thy family
buried, in the hope, no doubt, that it would be found by
some one of his descendants.'

Surprise and shame prevented Charicles from replying.
' Full well I know,' proceeded Phorion, ' what's the talk
of the town ; but heaven forefend that I should put finger
on moneys that never belonged to ancestor of mine. Never
will I pray the gods to disclose to me such treasures, nor
will I have aught to do with the soothsayers, who would
advise me to take up what has been entrusted to the lap
of earth ; for could the riches so gained ever compare in
worth with the cheerful consciousness of integrity, and of
nobility of soul ? Could I prize wealth before the peace of
mind resulting from honesty?'[42] ' Excellent man !' exclaimed Charicles, tears of emotion standing in his eyes,
' how like a deity do you appear to me ! You recall
me to my native land, you install me in my paternal abode,
which I had given up for lost, and deliver to me faith-

ἄρα οἱ φῦ χειρί. Cf. Antiph. de Choreut. p. 785. It was a captatio bene-
volentiæ, as prensare was with the
Romans. Xenoph. de Repub. Athen.
i. 18 : καὶ ἀντιβολῆσαι ἀναγκάζεται
ἐν τοῖς δικαστηρίοις καὶ εισιοντος
τοῦ ἐπιλαμβάνεσθαι τῆς χειρός.

[42] A translation of the beautiful
passage in Plato, Leg. xi. 913. So,
' What should it profit a man though
he gain the whole world and lose his

own soul?' The above is not the only
passage in a profane writer, breathing
forth ideas of morality, which are
often thought peculiar to Christianity.
Cf. Plaut. Trin. i. 2, and v. 2, 4.

Si quid amicum erga bene feci, aut consului
    fideliter,
Non videor meruisse laudem : culpa caruisse
    arbitror.
Nam beneficium, homini quod datur pro-
    prium, pro suo sumpserit :
Quod datum utendum est, id repetundi copia
    est, quando velis.

fully the riches that were hidden in the darkness of the earth.' 'May the gods grant you to inhabit the house with more luck than your father!' said the old man. 'Now go and look about you, and give orders for its restoration. Should you want my council or help, come to me; but not a word of what has passed between us.' Thus saying, he squeezed the youth's hand, and withdrew with the slave.

Charicles stood for a long time, as if in a dream, before the image of the god, at whose feet he had deposited the sealed casket : full of admiration of the noble-minded man, and of shame for his own suspicions, and on the other hand full of joy, at having not only recovered his father's mansion, but also increased his property so materially. At last he awoke from his reverie, and commenced a survey of the house. Passing through the middle door, he entered the apartments of the women. Here was his mother's parlour; there the saloon, where by the light of the lamps he had played, amidst the circle of females, at the feet of his nurse, or had listened to her tales. Deep melancholy seized him, at the desolation that reigned around, and at finding himself alone in the spacious chambers. He determined to purchase some slaves, and other necessary appliances, without loss of time. Moreover it was now time to go to the market, to find Ctesiphon, and the banker to whom he was recommended; he therefore gave the casket of gold to Manes, and bid him follow him.

SCENE THE FOURTH.

THE TRAPEZITÆ.

THE market-place was filling fast when Charicles entered it. Traders had set up their wattled stalls all
over it, with their goods exposed on tables and benches.
Here the female bakers had piled up their round-shaped
loaves and cakes, and were pursuing with a torrent of
scolding and abuse the unlucky wight who happened, in
passing by, to upset one of their pyramids.[1] There sim-
mered the kettles of the women, who sold boiled peas and
other vegetables;[2] in the crockery-market, hard by, the
pot-men were descanting on the goodness of their wares.
A little way off, in the myrtle-market, chaplets and fillets
were to be sold, and many a comely flower-weaver received orders for garlands, to be delivered by her in the
evening.[3] All the wants of the day, from barley-groats
up to the choicest fish, from garlick to the incense of the
gods; clear pure oil, and the most exquisite ointments;
fresh-made cheese, and the sweet honey of the bees of Hy-
mettus; cooks ready to be hired; slaves, male and female,

---

[1] Philocleon when drunk offends
in this manner, though he gets out of
the scrape pretty easily. Aristoph.
Vesp. 1389. These ladies, however,
had, on occasion, a perfect Billings-
gate vocabulary at command. *Ranæ*,
857: λοιδορεῖσθαι ὥσπερ ἀρτοπώλιδας.

[2] As at Rome inferior articles of
diet, as *tepidum cicer, tomacula*, &c.
were sold hot to the lower classes
(*Gallus*, p. 465, &c.), so it was also at
Athens. See *Lysist.* 560, where Phylarchos buys λέκιθον, pease-porridge,
παρὰ γραός. See Excursus on *The
Markets and Commerce*. The sau-

sage-dealers also sat in the market,
Equit. 1246.

[3] Chaplets were either sold ready-
made, in the market, or orders were
given for them there, for the *symposia*.
Plutarch, *Arat.* 6: καὶ μετὰ μικρὸν
ἑωρᾶτο τῶν οἰκετῶν αὐτοῦ δι' ἀγορᾶς
ὁ μὲν στεφάνους φέρων, ὁ δὲ λαμπάδας ὠνούμενος, ὁ δὲ τοῖς εἰθισμένοις
παρὰ πότον ψάλλειν καὶ αὐλεῖν γι-
ναίοις διαλεγόμενος. See Aristoph.
Thesmoph. 458; and *Anthol. Pal.* v.:

Ἡ τὰ ῥόδα, ῥοδόεσσαν ἔχεις χάριν· ἀλλὰ τί
   πωλεῖς;
   σαυτὴν ἢ τὰ ῥόδα, ἠὲ συναμφότερα·

to be sold,—each and all were to be found at their customary stands. There were others, who went about crying their wares, while every now and then a public crier crossed the ground, announcing with stentorian voice the arrival of some goods to be sold, or the sale of a house, or perhaps a reward for the apprehension of a robber or a runaway slave.[4] Slaves of both sexes, as well as free-men, kept walking up and down, bargaining, and inspecting the stalls, in search of their daily requirements. Some too lingered, longer than seemed necessary, near a pretty shop-woman; or approached some fruiterer's basket, and commenced a friendly chat, under cover of which, while some person was buying, or having a drachma changed, they would pilfer the fruit.[5]

The fish-market bell was just ringing as a signal that the hour of business had arrived, and forthwith all streamed in that direction, to lose no time in completing this all-important purchase. The way to the money-changers led Charicles directly across this part of the market. And it was truly amusing to behold how the eager buyers tried all their arts of persuasion, to move the hard-hearted dealers, who stuck doggedly to their prices. 'What's the price of these two pike, if I take the pair?' asked a greedy *gourmand* in his hearing. 'Ten oboles,' answered the fishmonger, scarce deigning to look up. 'That's too much,' said the other. 'You'll let me have them for eight, I'm sure?' 'Yes, one of them,' was the reply. 'Nonsense,' said the would-be purchaser; 'come, here are eight oboles.' 'I told you the price, sir; and if you don't like it, you can go elsewhere,'[6] said the

---

[4] On the public criers, see note 4, Sc. xi.

[5] Theophr. *Char.* 11: πληθυού-σης τῆς ἀγορᾶς πρ σελθὼν πρὸς τὰ κάρυα, ἢ τὰ μύρτα, ἢ τὰ ἀκρόδρυα, ἑστηκὼς τραγηματίζεσθαι ἅμα τῷ πωλοῦντι προσλαλῶν. So Lysistratos

gets change for a drachma in the fish-market; Aristoph. *Vesp.* 788:

... δραχμὴν μετ' ἐμοῦ πρώην λαβὼν ἐλθὼν διεκερμά:ιζεν ἐν τοῖς ἰχθύσι.

[6] After Alexis, ap. Athen. vi. p. 224. The passage is quoted in the Excursus on *The Markets and Commerce.*

inexorable dealer, with the most perfect nonchalance. Such scenes as this were of frequent occurrence; and Charicles would have liked to witness more of them, but that Manes was with him, bearing the important casket.

In the arcade occupied by the *trapezitæ*, he encountered Ctesiphon, walking to and fro, and waiting for him. How delighted he would have been to communicate his good fortune to his friend, but the strange old man had straitly charged him not to mention it. Of course, the fact of his having repurchased his paternal abode could not be kept secret; moreover, he felt it incumbent on him to undeceive Ctesiphon, who shared in the common opinion with regard to Phorion. ' It is incomprehensible,' he remarked, in conclusion, ' how a person, who is uprightness and magnanimity itself, could ever have obtained the reputation of being a miser and usurer.'

' So goes the world,' said Ctesiphon. ' The many judge by external appearances, and thus the rogues are accounted patterns of virtue, whilst the motives of the upright man are misconstrued. When you met me, I was just indulging in a somewhat similar contemplation. Look yonder, under the portico, at that vinegar-faced man [7] with a long beard, who goes sneaking along by the wall, unshod, aping the Spartan fashion with his sorry cloak,[8] and seeming not to notice the bustle around him.

---

[7] Βλέπειν νᾶπυ, κάρδαμα, or ὀρίγανον, said of sour-looking persons. *Equites*, 631 :

κάβλεψε νᾶπυ καὶ τὰ μέτωπ' ἀνέσπασε.

It is said also of an earnest and solemn aspect. Eustath. *ad Iliad.* xvi. 200 : ἐκ τούτων δὲ παρενεχθέντες ἄλλοι ἔγραψαν ἐπὶ τοιούτων ἀνδρῶν εὐτελέστερον τὸ βλέπειν αὐτοὺς νᾶπυ, ἢ ὀρίγανον, ἤγουν δριμεῖς εἶναι. *Vesp.* 453 :

. . . ἵν' εἴδηθ' οἷον ἐστ' ἀνδρῶν τρόπος ὀξυθύμων καὶ δικαίων καὶ βλεπόντων κάρδαμα.

[8] When Athens, after the Peloponnesian war, grew more effeminate and luxurious, certain persons affected to imitate the simplicity of Spartan manners and costume, in contradistinction to Athenian habits; this was called λακωνίζειν, and the men Λακωνισταί. But like the imitators of Wallenstein, in Schiller's drama, they confined themselves solely to externals. Plato, *Protag.* p. 342 : καὶ οἱ μὲν ὦτά τε κατάγνυνται μιμούμενοι αὐτοὺς, καὶ ἱμάντας περιειλίττονται, καὶ φιλογυμναστοῦσι, καὶ βραχείας ἀναβολὰς φοροῦσιν, ὡς δὴ τούτοις κρατοῦντας τῶν Ἑλλήνων τοὺς Λακεδαμονίους.

Would not any one take him for a model of manly earnestness, and pristine simplicity? Yet, when he meets his associates by night in their haunt, I assure you that there is no possible abomination in which they do not indulge.[9] Generally, indeed,' he continued, ' any one who wishes to know mankind will find it very instructive to walk up and down here, and make his observations. Look at that man advancing towards us, followed by three slaves. He looks proudly straight before him on the ground, to escape saluting any one; his robe reaches to his very ankles, and more than one ring adorns his fingers; he talks loudly with his slaves of silver goblets, drinking horns, and bowls, so that the passers-by may hear, and puffs himself out, till the city seems almost too small for him.[10] Now, who do you think he is? A fellow of the meanest extraction, who has lately emerged from extreme indigence to great riches, and is now seen nowhere but in the arcade of the trapezitæ. Not contented with his name, he has lengthened it by two syllables, and instead of Simon, calls himself Simonides,[11]

Plutarch, *Phoc.* 10: Ἦν δέ τις Ἀρχιβιάδης, ἐπικαλούμενος Λακωνιστής, πώγωνά τε καθειμένος ὑπερφυῆ μεγέθει καὶ τρίβωνα φορῶν ἀεὶ καὶ σκυθρωπάζων. Cf. Demosth. *in Con.* p. 1267.

[9] Demosth. *ibid.*: ἐπειδὰν δὲ συλλεγῶσι καὶ μετ' ἀλλήλων γένωνται, κακῶν καὶ αἰσχρῶν οὐδὲν ἐλλείπουσι.

[10] The sketches here given derive their sole value from being literally taken from the Greek classic authors. It is interesting to notice such similarity between a Greek ὑπερηφανείᾳ ἐπίφθονος and νεόπλουτος, and an upstart *parvenu* of the present day. The purse-proud inflation of these fellows, who are well characterised by Suidas under the proverb γενναῖοι ἐκ βαλαντίου, is graphically pourtrayed by other writers also. Demosth. *in Mid.* p. 565: καὶ τρεῖς ἀκολούθους ἢ -έτταρας αὐτὸς ἔχων διὰ τῆς ἀγορᾶς

σοβεῖ, κυμβία καὶ ῥυτὰ καὶ φιάλας ὀνομάζων οὕτως, ὥστε τοὺς παριόντας ἀκούειν. And again, *ibid.* p. 579: ἡ πόλις αὐτὸν οὐ χωρεῖ. And Theophr. *Char.* 24: (ὑπερηφάνου) ἐν ταῖς ὁδοῖς πορευόμενος μὴ λαλεῖν τοῖς ἐντυγχάνουσι κάτω κεκυφώς. Cf. *De Falsa Leg.* 442; *Adv. Pantæn.* 981; Aristoph. *Eccl.* 631, and *Nub.* 362. The instance in the text is from Lucian, *Somn. s. Gall.* 14. Cf. idem, *Quom. Hist. conscrib.* 20: ἐοίκασιν οἰκέτῃ νεοπλούτῳ, ἄρτι τοῦ δεσπότου κληρονομήσαντι, ὃς οὐδὲ τὴν ἐσθῆτα οἶδεν ὡς χρὴ περιβάλλεσθαι, οὐδὲ δειπνῆσαι κατὰ νόμον, κ.τ.λ. Most likely Plato had a real instance in view, when he mentions the slave grown rich, who wishes to marry his master's daughter. *De Repub.* vi. p. 495.

[11] Lucian, *Somn. s. Gall.* 14. The description of Simon suddenly ad-

just as if this made him a different man. Not long ago I
saw him in sordid garments, carrying home somebody's
marketing, for a trifling consideration; at present, he
would be vastly indignant, if a badly dressed person
presumed to address him.[12] Just cast your eyes to the
right, on the haggard man in the fish-market, with black
matted hair, who sidles about, not buying anything himself, but watching everybody else; he is a most dangerous
sycophant and glides about the market like a scorpion,
with his venomous sting all ready, spying out whom he
may surprise with misfortune and ruin, and from whom he
can most easily extort money, by threatening him with an
action dangerous in its consequences. You won't see him
speak or associate with any one, but, as the painters en-
compass the shades of the wicked in Hades with the terrific
phantoms of cursing and slander, of envy, discord, and
strife, so also are his attendants. It is the very bane of
our city, that it cherishes and protects this poisonous
brood, and uses them as informers, so that even the honest
man must flatter and court them, in order to be safe from
their machinations.'[13]

---

vanced to wealth: ἔναγχος γοῦν ἐγὼ
μὲν ἰδὼν προσιόντα. Χαῖρε, ἔφην, ὦ
Σίμων. ὁ δὲ ἀγανακτήσας, Εἴπατε,
ἔφη, τῷ πτωχῷ, μὴ κατασμικρύνειν
μου τοὔνομα· οὐ γὰρ Σίμων, ἀλλὰ
Σιμωνίδης ὀνομάζομαι.

[12] The line of demarcation between the different classes of society,
was by no means so distinctly drawn
among the Greeks, as it is in our days.
Mechanics were to be seen in company
with persons of higher station. Lysias, de Inval. 743, and the fragment
of Plutarch, de Anim.: 'Ο δὲ Νικανδᾶς
ἦ/ σκυτοτόμος, ἄλλως δὲ τῶν ἐν
παλαίστραις γεγονότων καὶ πολλοῖς
συνήθης καὶ γνώριμος. Some, however, were foolish enough to be
ashamed of knowing an inferior, and

the poor man perhaps did not like to
come near his betters, when in his
shabby habiliments. Lucian, Somn.
seu Gall. 9: καὶ ἐγὼ μὲν προσειπὼν αὐτὸν, ὥσπερ εἰώθειν, δεσπότην ἀπηλ-
λαττόμην, ὡς μὴ καταισχύναιμι αὐτὸν, ἐν πενιχρῷ τῷ τρίβωνι συμ-
παρομαρτῶν.

[13] The description of the sycophant is from Demosth. in Aristog.
p. 786: πορεύεται διὰ τῆς ἀγορᾶς,
ὥσπερ ὄφις ἢ σκορπίος. ἠρκὼς τὸ
κέντρον, ἄττων δεῦρο κἀκεῖσε, σκο-
πῶν τίνι ξυμφοράν, ἢ βλασφημίαν,
κακόν τι προστριψάμενος καὶ καταστήσας εἰς φόβον ἀργύριον πράξ-
εται· οὐδὲ προσφοιτᾷ πρός τι τούτων τῶν ἐν τῇ πόλει κουρείων ἢ
μυροπωλείων. . . μεθ' ὧν δ' οἱ ζωγρά-

F

'It is no doubt a great reproach to Athens,' said Charicles ; 'but do you know what is more strange to my eye than all the persons you have pointed out? Those striplings there, lounging about among the unguent-girls. Only look how coxcombically and affectedly they strut about, as loose as if their necks were broken ; how they sprawl out their hands for the purpose of gently titillating their heads with the tips of their fingers, or of carefully arranging their hair, the blackness of which was most likely purchased in the market here. To me, nothing is more nauseous than a young man with such a woman's

---

φοι τοὺς ἀσεβεῖς γράφουσιν ἐν "Αιδου, μετὰ τούτων, μετ' ἀρᾶς καὶ βλασφημίας, καὶ φθόνου, καὶ στάσεως, καὶ νείκους περιέρχεται. This fearful nuisance of sycophancy, (on the etymology of the word, see Plut. Sol. 24, and Athen. iii. p. 74,) inseparable as it was from a democracy like that of Athens, demands a few words here. The Athenians coincided with Cicero's opinion respecting Rome (pro Rosc. Amer. 20): 'Accusatores multos esse in civitate utile est, ut metu contineatur audacia.' The state desired to have them, and rewarded their services, at least indirectly. Consequently there were persons who ostensibly obtained a livelihood as hired informers, but whose chief gains were derived from the hush-money they extorted. Demosth. in Neær. 1359 : οὐ γάρ πω ἦν ῥήτωρ, ἀλλ' ἔτι συκοφάντης τῶν παραβοώντων παρὰ τὸ βῆμα καὶ γραφομένων μισθοῦ καὶ φαινόντων καὶ ἐπιγραφομένων ταῖς ἀλλοτρίαις γνώμαις, κ.τ.λ., and ib. p. 1358 : οὐ γὰρ ἦν αὐτῷ ἄλλη πρόσοδος, ὅ τι μὴ συκοφαντήσας τι λάβοι. If their charge was proved to be calumnious they were liable to punishment, but the trade of συκοφαντεῖν μισθοῦ was, at least in later times, hardly forbidden by law. Isocr. de Perm. 497 :

ὑμεῖς δὲ τοσοῦτον ἀπέχετε τοῦ κολάζειν αὐτοὺς, ὥστε τούτοις χρῆσθε καὶ κατηγόροις καὶ νομοθέταις περὶ τῶν ἄλλων. The indulgence granted to this nefarious brood is quite in keeping with Æschin. in Timarch. 45, where, among other rights of which the ἡταιρηκὼς was deprived, is mentioned μηδὲ συκοφαντείτω μισθωθείς. This is not, as some suppose, a mere malicious extension of the law, by Æschines. Naturally enough, the rich and distinguished were most exposed to the chicanery of these people, and many a one was compelled to purchase their forbearance, in order to avoid being the victim of their accusations; for however groundless might be the charge, the issue was always doubtful. Xenoph. Symp. 4, 30 : Ἐγὼ τοίνυν ἐν τῆδε τῇ πόλει ὅτε μὲν πλούσιος ἦν πρῶτον μὲν ἐφοβούμην, μή τίς μου τὴν οἰκίαν διορύξας καὶ τὰ χρήματα λάβοι καὶ αὐτόν τί τε κακὸν ἐργάσαιτο· ἔπειτα δὲ καὶ τοὺς συκοφάντας ἐθεράπευον, εἰδὼς, ὅτι παθεῖν μᾶλλον κακῶς ἱκανὸς εἴην ἢ ποιῆσαι ἐκείνους. See Memor. ii. 9, where Crito, by Socrates' advice, takes a sycophant into his pay to countermine another who was badgering him. Cf. Aristoph. Acharn. 817; Equit. 260.

face, and delicate voice, and all reeking with perfume, and
holding in his hand, ten to one, a bouquet or odoriferous
fruit.[14] What an utter difference there is between life, as
here seen in the forum, and the description my father gave
me of it as taken from his younger years, when such mere
boys, as those yonder, avoided the market-place entirely,
or, if their path obliged them to go that way, hurried
across it with shame and blushes.'[15]

'Those days are long gone by,' said Ctesiphon: 'we
are young men too, and, notwithstanding, we are here in
the market-place.'

'Yes, but not without pressing reasons,' retorted Charicles; 'and you remind me just in time, that I have to
call on Diotimos and Lycon, the trapezitæ. I wish you
would accompany me. My business is of such a nature
that it cannot be transacted without witnesses;[16] you are
more experienced than I, so your counsel may stand me in
good stead. These money-changers are not always the
most honest people imaginable, being apt to lead the inexperienced by the nose,[17] with their promises and subter-
fuges.' Ctesiphon willingly acceded to his friend's request.

---

[14] The main features of this picture of Attic dandyism are from
Lucian, *Rhet. præc.* 11: πάγκαλον
ἄνδρα, διασεσαλευμένον τὸ βάδισμα,
ἐπικεκλασμένον τὸν αὐχένα, γυναικεῖον τὸ βλέμμα, μελιχρὸν τὸ φώ-
νημα, μύρων ἀποπνέοντα, τῷ δακτύλῳ
ἄκρῳ τὴν κεφαλὴν κνώμενον. But
as early as the time of Aristophanes,
such coxcombs figured in the market:

τὰ μειράκια ταυτὶ λέγω, τὰν τῷ μύρῳ
ἃ στωμυλεῖται τοιαδὶ καθήμενα κ.τ.λ.

Equit. 1372; and again, *Vesp.* 687:

ὅταν εἰσελθὸν μειράκιόν σοι κατάπυγον,
    Χαιρέου υἱός,
ὡδὶ διαβὰς, διακινηθεὶς τῷ σώματι καὶ τρυ-
    φερανθείς;

That it was by no means uncommon
to carry flowers or fruits in the hand,

is clear from Athen. xii. p. 553: διὰ
τί μετὰ χεῖρας ἄνθη καὶ μῆλα καὶ
τὰ τοιαῦτα φέρομεν;

[15] See Excursus on *Education*.

[16] Generally, no witnesses were
present at the transactions at the
bankers' tables: τὰ μὲν γὰρ συμβό-
λαια τὰ πρὸς τοὺς ἐπὶ ταῖς τραπέζαις ἄνευ μαρτύρων γίγνεται. Isocr.
Trapez. p. 515. This was not because
such a security was looked upon as
useless, but because it might produce
more harm than good, from letting
others into the secret of the business
transacted.

[17] This homely phrase would not

The trapezitæ, at whose hands Charicles had to receive
the greatest part of his patrimony, were very different
individuals. Diotimos, a man now advanced in years, bore,
universally, a reputation for the highest integrity. Not
only had he been Charinos' banker, but also his friend
and confidant. When the latter, through dread of the
accusation, resolved on leaving Athens, he charged his
trusty and well-approved banker with the sale of his
house, his slaves, and chattels, and at the same time commissioned him to call in all his moneys out at interest.[18]
No inconsiderable amount must still be in his hands, and
Charicles now went to ask for it.

Diotimos was just engaged in paying a sum of money
to a man, apparently a foreigner. Upon the table, from
which he swept up the coin, after having found it right,
lay a slip of paper, being his bond for the amount. 'You
have received from me the sum, in ready cash, and all
correct,' said the banker; 'and you leave nothing for it
but a small piece of paper, that perhaps cost you two chal-
cûs. But remember that the law is on my side, and will defend my right.'[19] The man asseverated his wish to fulfil all
the terms of the contract, and then departed. Diotimos then
reached his ledger, wrote a few words in it, deposited the
paper in a box containing several others, and then turned

---

have been introduced, had it not been
a Greek proverb. 'Ῥινᾶν, in a fragment
of Menander is, perhaps, not from
ῥίς, but from ῥίνη, a file (so in Latin,
deruncinare); though the old grammarians derive it from the first. Cf.
a fragment of Pherecrates, ap. Clem.
Alex. Strom. vii. p. 847. But the
phrase, ῥινὸς ἕλκειν occurs frequently
in Lucian, Deor. Dial. vi. 3; Hermot.
73: καὶ διὰ τοῦτο εἷλκεν ὑμᾶς τῆς
ῥινός: and Philops, 23, ἀπὸ ῥινὸς
ἕλκειν also occurs.

18 Leocrates was in a similar

plight when he fled to Megara. Lycurg. in Leocr. p. 152: καὶ δεηθεὶς τοῦ
κηδεστοῦ πρίασθαι παρ' αὐτοῦ τἀνδ-
ράποδα καὶ τὴν οἰκίαν ἀποδόσθαι
ταλάντου· ἐπὶ τούτοις προσέταξε
τοῖς τε χρήσταις ἀποδοῦναι τὰ ὀφει-
λόμενα καὶ τοὺς ἐράνους διενεγκεῖν,
τὸ δὲ λοιπὸν αὐτῷ ἀποδοῦναι.

19 After Demosth. in Dionysod.
1283: λαβὼν γὰρ ἀργύριον φανερὸν
καὶ ὁμολογούμενον, ἐν γραμματιδίῳ
δυοῖν χαλκοῖν ἐωνημένῳ καὶ βιβλιδίῳ
μικρῷ πάνυ τὴν ὁμολογίαν καταλέ-
λοιπε τοῦ ποιήσειν τὰ δίκαια.

to a second individual, who was waiting in company with
a very common-looking personage. ' I have purchased,'
said the first, ' from this man here a slave for two minæ.
By reference to my account-book I find there must be
seven hundred drachmæ lying with you in my name. Pay
the man his money.'[20] The trapezites again looked in his
book. ' In the main,' said he, ' you are right in your cal-
culations ; except that you forget the agio on three hundred and fifty Æginetan drachmæ which I paid to Paseas
for the ivory you bought.' This the man could not dispute : the two minæ were paid, and the men went away.

Now for the first time, Diotimos regarded the young
men, who had remained somewhat apart. ' Who are
you ? ' he enquired of Charicles, who now stepped forward,
'and what do you want ? ' ' I am Charicles, the son of
Charinos, and am returned from Syracuse. For my credentials, behold here my father's signet-ring, which is well
known to you. I come, as his heir, to require back the
money that still remains in your hands.' ' So Charinos is
dead ? ' exclaimed the banker. ' We have placed his ashes
in Sicilian earth,' said the youth, ' until his most faithful
servant shall have brought them here, to deposit them in
the tomb of his forefathers.'[21] The old man covered his
face and wept.[22] ' According to my father's will,' said
Charicles after a while, when the other had become more
composed, ' you must still have in your possession one talent
and four thousand drachmæ, which, in all probability, I
shall soon require.' ' It is not exactly as you say,' replied

---

[20] A private person did not usually
keep much money by him, but made
all his larger payments at the money-
changer's table; he was said, χρῆσθαι
τῇ τινος τραπέζῃ. Instances of this
abound in the comic writers. A book
was kept of current income and ex-
penditure. Aristoph. Nub. 19 :

ἅπτε, παῖ, λύχνον·
κἄκφερε τὸ γραμματεῖον, ἵν᾿ ἀναγνῶ λαβὼν,
ὁπόσοις ὀφείλω, καὶ λογίσωμαι τοὺς τόκους.

Cf. Plaut. Curc. i. 2, 89 :

Ibo intro atque intus subducam ratiun-
culam,
Quantillum argenti mihi apud trapezitam
siet.

[21] See Excursus on The Burials.

[22] Isocr. Trapez. 521 : ἐγκαλυψ-
άμενος ἔκλαε.

Diotimos; 'but certainly, your father could not possibly
know that. It is only lately that three thousand drachmæ
more were paid to me on his account; and, besides that, the
capital has grown much larger by interest. You will have
more than two talents and a half to receive from me.'

He then explained to the youth how he had, by degrees, sometimes with difficulty, and not till after some
years, contrived to get in all the moneys which were owing
to his father by foreign merchants. From one man, only,
at Andros, he had obtained nothing, since he had not been
to Athens for several years, and Diotimos himself was too
old to undertake a sea-voyage. 'You will do best,' said
he, 'to go thither yourself, unless you wish to leave the
two thousand drachmæ in the lurch. Moreover,' he continued, 'your father, before the disaster which befell him,
had ordered some statues, which he intended for the Acropolis. They are still at the artist's, in the street of the
Sculptors. It is to be hoped you will act in the spirit of
your father, and not withhold from the gods those honours
which he had destined for them.' [23]

Charicles thanked the worthy man for the fidelity
with which he had transacted his father's concerns, and
did not scruple to entrust to him the two thousand
darics contained in the casket, until he had use for
them. From thence he went, accompanied by Ctesiphon,
to a second trapezites. This man was a stranger to him,
and his business with him was of a singular nature.

---

[23] The peculiar imposts on the
burghers of Athens, in the shape of
λειτουργίαι, are well known. See Xenophon, *de Republ. Athen.* i. 13; and
Böckh's *Publ. Econ.* p. 448–466. Then
again, ἀναθήματα were usually made
by victorious Choregi. But other
burghers, of their own accord, dedicated statues of brass or marble, in the
temples and on the Acropolis, perhaps
only that in case of need they might be
able to remind the state of these sacri-

fices in its behalf. Isæus, *de Dicæog.
her.* p. 113: καὶ τούτων μαρτύρια ἐν
τοῖς ἱεροῖς ἀναθήματα ἐκεῖνοι ἐκ τῶν
περιόντων, μνημεῖα τῆς αὐτῶν ἀρετῆς, ἀνέθεσαν· τοῦτο μὲν, ἐν Διονύσου
τρίποδας, οὓς χορηγοῦντες καὶ νικῶν-
τες ἔλαβον· τοῦτο δ' ἐν Πυθίου, ἔτι
δ' ἐν ἀκροπόλει. ἃς ἀπαρχὰς τῶν
ὄντων ἀναθέντες, πολλοῖς, ὡς ἀπὸ
ἰδίας κτήσεως, ἀγάλμασι χαλκοῖς καὶ
λιθίνοις κεκοσμήκασι τὸ ἱερόν. Cf.
ibid. p. 116, and Plato, *Leg.* xii. p. 956

When he was purposing to leave Syracuse, the same friend who had recommended him to Phorion, proposed that he should leave the greater portion of his property in his hands, in return for which he would allow him to draw upon him to the same amount in Athens. 'What? said he, 'will you expose all your substance to the dangers of a long sea-voyage, where storms, and pirates, not to mention the dishonesty of the sailors themselves, threaten you? I have three talents in Athens, at Lycon's the trapezites: leave me that sum here, and he shall pay it you again there.'[24] Charicles had accepted the proposal, and had with him a letter from the Syracusan, ordering the banker to pay the bearer, and also containing the symbolon, which, by virtue of a previous understanding, was to serve as a credential to the person commissioned to receive the money. For greater security, Phorion was also referred to, as a guarantee of the person's identity if Lycon required it.

Seated behind his table, Charicles found a gloomy man of an unhealthy shrivelled appearance. Beside him lay the scales, with which he had just weighed a lot of silver coins that had been paid him.[25] On the other side, his hand rested on a quantity of papers, apparently yellow with age. Before him he had a counting-table, being probably engaged in reckoning the interest due upon one of the bonds.[26] With some repugnance Charicles walked up

---

[24] See Isocr. *Trapez.* p. 526: ἐγὼ γὰρ ... μέλλοντος Στρατοκλέους εἰσπλεῖν εἰς τὸν Πόντον, βουλόμενος ἐκεῖθεν ὡς πλεῖστ᾽ ἐκκομίσασθαι τῶν χρημάτων, ἐδεήθην Στρατοκλέους, τὸ μὲν αὐτοῦ χρυσίον ἐμοὶ καταλιπεῖν, ἐν δὲ τῷ Πόντῳ παρὰ τοῦ πατρὸς τοὐμοῦ κομίσασθαι, νομίζων μεγάλα κερδαίνειν, εἰ κατὰ πλοῦν μὴ κινδυνεύοι τὰ χρήματα. ἄλλως τε καὶ Λακεδαιμονίων ἀρχόντων κατ᾽ ἐκεῖνον τὸν χρόνον τῆς θαλάττης.

[25] From their weighing the coin thus, the *trapezitæ* were contemptuously called ὀβολοστάται, and their business ὀβολοστατική. *Nubes*, 1155. And Aristot. *de Republ.* i. 10 : τῆς δὲ μεταβλητικῆς ψεγομένης δικαίως ... εὐλογώτατα μισεῖται ἡ ὀβολοστατική. Lucian, *Necyom.* 2 : ἁρπάζουσιν, ἐπιορκοῦσι, τοκογλυφοῦσιν, ὀβολοστατοῦσιν.

[26] Alciphr. *Epist.* i. 26 : Εἶτα

to this man, and briefly explained his business. At the
mention of the Syracusan, the trapezites contracted his
brows more than ever. 'I did not know,' said he, 'that
Sosthenes had so large a claim upon me. Has he forgotten that I have had to disburse eight hundred drachmæ
for him, to the Heracleote? Look here at my book.
What stands there? Sosthenes, son of Phormion, of Syracuse, has deposited two talents. Out of these, eight
hundred drachmæ to be paid to Phrynion, the Heracleote,
who will be introduced by Epicrates the Piræan. You
see there remain only four thousand drachmæ.'[27] 'Quite
right,' answered Charicles; 'Sosthenes also mentioned
that to me; but in the month of Elaphebolion, on his return from Pontus, he paid you afresh two talents, and two
thousand drachmæ, so that he wants three talents from
you.' The trapezites was evidently confused, and tried to
conceal it by the vehemence of his speech. 'What are
you to me?' said he abusively. 'How do I know who you
are? Any sycophant might come and demand money
in another person's name.' 'You have not given me time,'
said the youth, 'to present you my credentials. Here is
the letter of Sosthenes. Do you know his seal?' 'It
seems to be his signet,' said the money-changer sullenly.
'And here is the symbolon inside, which will doubtless be
familiar to you.' 'Perhaps a forged one,'[28] muttered the
other, as he ill-humouredly opened the letter, and read it

καταλαμβάνω πρεσβύτην, ὀφθῆναι
ῥικνὸν, συνεσπακότα τὰς ὀφρῦς, χαρ-
τίδια ἀρχαῖά τινα, σαπρὰ δὲ διὰ τὸν
χρόνον, ὑπὸ κόρεων καὶ ⸺ητῶν ἡμί-
βρωτα διὰ χειρὸς κατέχοντα. Cf.
Lucian, Tim. 14.

[27] The single passage, which affords any insight into the method of
book-keeping pursued by the bankers,
is in Demosth. adv. Callipp. 1236:
εἰώθασι δὲ πάντες οἱ τραπεζῖται,
ὅταν τις ἀργύριον τιθεὶς ἰδιώτης ἀπο-

δοῦναι προστάττῃ, πρῶτον τοῦ θέντος
τοὔνομα γράφειν καὶ τὸ κεφάλαιον
τοῦ ἀργυρίου, ἔπειτα παραγράφειν·
τῷ δεῖνι ἀποδοῦναί δεῖ. καὶ ἐὰν μὲν
γιγνώσκωσι τὴν ὄψιν τοῦ ἀνθρώπου,
ᾧ ἂν δέῃ ἀποδοῦναι, τοσοῦτον μόνον
ποιεῖν, γράψαι, ᾧ δεῖ ἀποδοῦναι. ἐὰν
δὲ μὴ γιγνώσκωσι, καὶ τούτου τοὔνομα προσπαραγράφειν, ὃς ἂν μέλλῃ
συστήσειν καὶ δείξειν τὸν ἄνθρωπον,
ὃς ἂν δέῃ κομίσασθαι τὸ ἀργύριον.

[28] See note 17, Scene I. p. 8.

half aloud. But when he came to Phorion's name, he became silent, and stared gloomily before him, as though meditating some way of escape. 'Lycon,' interrupted Ctesiphon at this juncture, ' don't be inventing any new tricks. It is still fresh in people's memories how, not long ago, you bubbled the Byzantine merchant, when he came to require the money deposited with you. The whole city knows how you got out of the way the only slave who was acquainted with the fact, and then, not only denied the claim, but also suborned witnesses to prove that your creditor had borrowed six talents of you.[29] The man, however, obtained his rights by the aid of Phorion, whose name now threatens you a second time; so take warning.'

The trapezites seemed desirous of giving an angry answer, but, suddenly, his eye became fixed on an object in the distance. In fact he saw Phorion himself, coming towards the money-changers' tables. 'Who wants to deny anything?' said he in embarrassment. ' But I have not got the sum at hand, nor, were I to go round to all the tables,[30] could I find anyone to lend me three talents. Come hither again on the morrow, Charicles, and I will take care that you shall have the money.' ' Very well; and I will bring Phorion along with me to dispel all doubts as to my identity.' ' Oh! there will be no need for that,' rejoined the money-changer hastily ; ' the symbolon is right ; you will receive the money.'

During these negotiations, noon had nearly arrived, and the market began to grow thinner and thinner. ' It's time that we breakfasted,' said Ctesiphon as they departed. ' Let us repair to one of the houses where young men are wont to assemble at this hour. You will be sure to meet with some of your early friends.'

---

[29] Pasion is accused of an exactly similar piece of villany. See Isocr. *Trapez.* 7.

[30] The bankers were often, doubtless, under the necessity of obtaining mutual credit. See Plaut. *Curc.* v. 3, 4.

SCENE THE FIFTH.

————◆◇◆————

THE HABITS OF YOUTH.

THE house to which Ctesiphon conducted his friend, as being the nearest of the kind, was inhabited by a freed-man, named Discos, who derived no inconsiderable gains from the young persons who resorted to it.[1] Not a few of them congregated there daily, either to try their luck at the astragali or dice, or to see a fight between the cocks or the quails, of which Discos kept great numbers, or perhaps only to discuss the news of the day, the merits of the horses or dogs which they had purchased, the last citharistria that had been ravished, or the hetæræ lately come out. Not unfrequently, too, several united in a symposion, each clubbing his share in the expense; and no one was a greater adept at humouring the tastes of the young people than Discos, whether from the excellence of his cookery, the goodness of his Chian wine, or the beauty of the flute-girls. These merry-makings did not always pass

————————————————

[1] There is no lack of passages to show that at this period there were places of this sort in Athens, where young gallants (νέοι) resorted to drink, dice, and so forth. Isocr. *Areop.* 18: Τοιγαροῦν οὐκ ἐν τοῖς σκιραφείοις οἱ νεώτεροι διέτριβον, οὐδ' ἐν ταῖς αὐλητρίσιν, οὐδ' ἐν τοῖς τοιούτοις συλλόγοις, ἐν οἷς νῦν διημερεύουσιν. The word σύλλογοι, here used, may mean either the company assembled, or the place where they came together. See Plato, *Leg.* vi. p. 764; Æschin. *in Ctesiph.* p. 517; Lysias, *Olym.* p. 912; Aristot. *Probl.* xxix. 14: ἐν τοῖς κοινοτάτοις συλλόγοις τε καὶ συνόδοις, which may comprehend baths, palæstra, and the market-place; though the word συλλέγεσθαι is generally used in connexion with gaming and drinking. See Dem. *in Con.* 1267; and so Plautus (*Bacch.* i. 1, 147; *Trin.* ii. 2, 33) uses conciliabula as the equivalent of σύλλογοι. A place of the kind is mentioned, Æschin. *in Timarch.* p. 78: ἀλλὰ διημέρευσεν ἐν τῷ κυβείῳ, οὗ ἡ τηλία τίθεται καὶ τοὺς ἀλεκτρυόνας συμβάλλουσι, καὶ κυβεύουσι. The houses where these symposia were held, belonged to freed-men and other people of low condition. Terent. *Eunuch.* iii. 5, 59: apud libertum Discum: and perhaps a meaning of this kind should be attached to Demosth. *in Con.* p. 1258: ἔπινον γὰρ ἐνταῦθα . . παρὰ Παμφίλῳ τῷ κναφεῖ.

off without rioting and violence, and it was but a few
months since, that, in consequence of a dispute about a
favourite boy, whom Discos protected, a mob of drunken
fellows had broken into the house by night, smashed all
the furniture, scattered the astragali and dice-boxes about
the street, and killed the cocks and the quails. As for the
owner, they tied him to a pillar, and so severely chastised
him, that his cries alarmed the neighbours, who came running together from their beds to find the cause of the
disturbance.[2] Nevertheless, Discos, by discreet management of his young guests, sometimes too, as it was reported, by the help of false dice, knew how to indemnify
himself for such losses.

When Charicles and Ctesiphon entered, they encountered plenty of visitors. In one room a party of dice-
players were sitting or standing, just in the very heat of
a dispute as to whether a throw was good or not; in
another chamber, some persons, after indulging in a late
breakfast, had already, thus early, sat down to a carouse,
quite at variance with established usage,[3] and were getting
rid of the time, by playing at odd and even, rather for
fun than gain ; while others practised at spinning a coin
placed upright on its rim, which they suddenly brought to
a stand-still by putting their finger upon it.[4] In the
court-yard were others engaged in animated discourse on

---

[2] We see from the comedians how
liable to such maltreatment those
were who lived by καπηλεία, πορνο-
βοσκία, and so forth. The incident
in the text is borrowed from Æschin.
in Timarch. p. 82: εἰσπηδήσαντες
νύκτωρ εἰς τὴν οἰκίαν, οὗ ᾤκει ὁ Πιττάλακος, πρῶτον μὲν συνέτριβον τὰ
σκευάρια καὶ διεῤῥίπτουν εἰς τὴν ὁδὸν
ἀστραγάλους τέ τινας διασείστους καὶ
φιμοὺς, καὶ κυβευτικὰ ἕτερα ὄργανα·
καὶ τοὺς ὄρτυγας καὶ τοὺς ἀλεκτρυόνας οὓς ἠγάπα ὁ τρισκακοδαίμων
ἄνθρωπος, ἀπέκτειναν, τὸ δὲ τελευ-

ταῖον δήσαντες πρὸς τὸν κίονα αὐτὸν
τὸν Πιττάλακον ἐμαστίγουν τὰς ἐξ
ἀνθρώπων πληγὰς οὕτω πολὺν χρόνον, ὥστε καὶ τοὺς γείτονας αἰσθέ-
σθαι τῆς κραυγῆς.

[3] Demosth. *in Con.* p. 1257: ἔπινον
ἑκάστοτε οὗτοι τὴν ἡμέραν, ἐπειδὴ
τάχιστα ἀριστήσειαν, ὅλην.

[4] This game, often erroneously
called χαλκισμὸς, is explained in the
Excursus on *The Games.*

the qualities of two horses.   The question at issue was,
whether a coppa-stallion, lately purchased for twenty minæ
by one of the disputants, was superior to the samphoras
of the other ;[5] and both of the owners contended with such

---

[5] On the pursuits and amusements
of the young, see the Excursus on
Education.   One of the chief follies
of the young gallants was the inordinate love of fine horses, for which
they paid most ridiculously high
prices. Xenoph. *de Off. Mag. Eq.* 1,
12 : μανικαὶ ἱππώνειαι.   Many were
ruined by it. The breeds marked
with the *koppa* and *san* (see Buttman's
Greek Gram.) were called κοππατίας,
and σαμφόρας.   Aristoph. *Nubes*, 23,
and 122, on the first of which passages
the Scholiast remarks : κοππατίας
ἵππους ἐκάλουν οἷς ἐγκεχάρακτο τὸ
κόππα στοιχεῖον, ὡς σαμφόρας τοὺς
ἐγκεχαραγμένους τὸ σάν.   See also the
Scholiast to Lucian, *adv. Indoct.* 5
(κοππαφόρας).   The brand was on
the buttock. Anacreon, 55 : ἐν ἰσ-
χίοις μὲν ἵπποι πυρὸς χάραγμ'
ἔχουσι.   But there were other
brands, καυστήρια, besides these two.
So Strabo, v. 1, 9, speaking of an
Italian breed, says καυστηριάσαι τε
τὰς ἵππους λύκον καὶ κληθῆναι λυκο-
φόρους τάχει μᾶλλον ἢ κάλλει δια-
φερούσας· τοὺς δ' ἀπ' ἐκείνου διαδε-
ξαμένους τό τε καυστήριον φυλάξει
καὶ τοὔνομα τῷ γένει τῶν ἵππων.
The Scholiast to Aristophanes states
that the appellation βουκέφαλος had
a similar origin; and on vases we see
other marks, one, for instance, something like a wheel, and a serpent on
the Pegasus. Tischbein. *Vas.* i. p. 1.
We are told that the preference was
given to mares, but on the vases
mares are hardly ever represented,
while stallions are not unfrequent.
Gelding does not seem to have been
common, as Strabo (vii. 4, 8) confines

that operation to the Scythians and
Sarmatians : ἴδιον δὲ τοῦ Σκυθικοῦ
καὶ τοῦ Σαρματικοῦ παντὸς ἔθνους τὸ
τοὺς ἵππους ἐκτέμνειν εὐπειθείας
χάριν. The colour was quite as much
a matter of taste and fashion as with
us. So the ψαρὸς ἵππος, *Nub.* 1225.
Horses of different colours appear to
have been preferred for a four-in-
hand. Eurip. *Iphig. Aul.* 218 : τοὺς
μέσσου ζυγίους λευκοστρίκτῳ τριχὶ
βαλίους, τοὺς δ' ἔξω σειραφόρους . . .
πυρρότριχας. The prices were proportionably high. Strepsiades paid
twelve minæ (nearly £50) for the kop-
pa-stallion, *Nub.* 21; and in Lysias, *de
Maled.* p. 307, a horse is pawned for
the same sum. Isæus, *de Diaog. her.*
p. 116, names three *minæ* (about £12)
as a low price. See Böckh's *Publ. Econ.
of Athens*, p. 74. After horses came
dogs, which also fetched high prices.
Plutarch, *Alcib.* 9. See Xenoph. *Mem.*
iii. 11, 7; *de Ven.* 3, for an account of
the different breeds.   Great care was
bestowed on sporting dogs. Plato,
de Repub. v. 459 ; Plut. *Amat.* 21 ;
Xenoph. *de Ven.* 7.   The most celebrated breeds were the Laconian, Mo-
lossian, and Cretan. Μελιταῖα κυνίδια, lap-dogs, were also kept; according to Strabo, they were of Sicilian
origin; vi. 2 : Πρόκειται δὲ τοῦ Παχύ-
νου Μελίτη, ὅθεν τὰ κυνίδια, ἃ καλοῦσι Μελιταῖα· though Pliny, *N. H.*
iii. 26, gives another account : ' Ab his
Corcyra, Melæna cognominata. . inter
quam et Illyricum Melita, unde catu-
los Melitæos appellari Callimachus
auctor est.'   The absurd extreme to
which this hobby was carried appears
from Lucian, *de Merc. Cond.* 34; and

vehemence for the honour of their steeds, that something serious might have been apprehended, had not another contest in the court arrested the attention of all.

Discos had repaired the loss of his cocks and quails, among the latter was one, that had hitherto been victor in every engagement, and by which he had already won more than a mina. This only the more excited the emulation of those who had been beaten, and at this very moment, a fresh bet had been made, and a slave was bringing the stand, whereon was marked the circle, within which the struggle was to be confined.[6] The youth who had made

---

this was the case even at an earlier period. Theophr. *Char.* 21: καὶ κυναρίου δὲ τελευτήσαντος αὐτῷ μνῆμα ποιῆσαι, καὶ στυλίδιον ποιήσας ἐπιγράψαι· Ὁ καλὸς Μελιταῖος. Next in order came cocks and quails, which were kept for fighting. On this subject see the following note. The passion for pigeons, which afterwards went to such lengths at Rome, also prevailed. The Σικελικαὶ περιστεραὶ were most prized. Theophr. *supra.* Other birds may probably have been kept; and Plato, *Theæt.* p. 197, mentions something like an aviary: ὥσπερ εἴ τις ὄρνιθας ἀγρίας, περιστερὰς ἤ τι ἄλλο, θηρεύσας οἴκοι κατασκευασάμενος περιστερεῶνα τρέφοι. Pheasants were a special article of luxury. See Aristoph. *Nub.* 108 :

εἰ δοίης γ' ἐμοὶ
τοὺς Φασιανοὺς οὓς τρέφει Λεωγόρας.

About which the Scholiasts are divided as to whether horses or birds are meant, though the latter is the more probable; cf. Callixenos ap. Athen. ix. p. 387 : εἶτα ἐφέροντο ἐν ἀγγείοις ψιττακοὶ καὶ ταῷ. καὶ μελεαγρίδες, καὶ Φασιανοὶ, καὶ ὄρνιθες Αἰθιοπικοὶ πλήθει πολλοί : and Ptolemæus Euerg. ap. Id. xiv. p. 654 : Τά τε τῶν Φασιανῶν, οὓς τετάρους ὀνομάζουσιν,

οὓς οὐ μόνον ἐκ Μηδίας μετεπέμπετο, ἀλλὰ καὶ νομάδας ὄρνιθας ὑποβαλὼν ἐποίησε πλῆθος, ὥστε καὶ σιτεῖσθαι. τὸ γὰρ βρῶμα πολυτελὲς ἀποφαίνουσιν. Pheasants are first mentioned as a dish in Athenæus, and Alciphr. iii. 7 ; though they had long been thus used at Rome. At a later period, we meet with birds that talk, and even pipe tunes. Philostr. *Vit. Apoll.* i. 7 : ὥσπερ οἱ ὄρνιθες, ἃ μανθάνουσι παρὰ τῶν ἀνθρώπων. τὸ γὰρ χαῖρε, καὶ τὸ εὖ πράττε, καὶ τὸ Ζεὺς ἵλεως οἱ ὄρνιθες εὔχονται, οὐκ εἰδότες ὅ τι λέγουσιν : and vi. 36 : ἐδίδασκε δὲ αὐτοὺς λαλεῖν τε ὅσα οἱ ἄνθρωποι καὶ τερετίζειν ὅσα οἱ αὐλοί. Monkeys also were kept for amusement. Theophr. *Char.* 21 ; Plaut. *Mil.* ii. 2, 7.

[6] Cock- and quail-fighting was common throughout Greece. At Athens it was a political institution, and took place annually by law from the time of the Persian wars. Ælian, *Var. Hist.* ii. 28 : Μετὰ τὴν κατὰ τῶν Περσῶν νίκην Ἀθηναῖοι νόμον ἔθεντο, ἀλεκτρυόνας ἀγωνίζεσθαι δημοσίᾳ ἐν τῷ θεάτρῳ μιᾶς ἡμέρας τοῦ ἔτους. The exhibition of these pugnacious creatures was set up as an instructive example of bravery. See Lucian, *de Gymn.* 37 : ὁρᾶν τὰ ὄρνεα

the match, confident of the courage of his bird, took the
quail with much caution from under his left arm, and set
it carefully in the ring. 'Who'll bet that it goes out of
the ring,' cried he, ' plague it as you will ?' Several accepted the challenge, but as often as the bird was touched
with the finger, or seized by the feathers of the head, it
made a spirited and successful defence against its assailant

διαπυκτεύοντα μέχρι τῆς ἐσχάτης
ἀπαγορεύσεως. According to Paus.
ix. 22, 4. and Suidas, the cocks of
Tanagra and Rhodes were specially
noted as μάχιμοι or ἀθληταὶ, and
to render them more pugnacious they
had heating garlick given them beforehand. Thus we have ἐσκοροδισ-
μένος μάχῃ. Equit. 494; on which see
the explanation by the Scholiast; so
also Xenoph. Sympos. 4, 9 : ἔνιοι τοὺς
ἀλεκτρυόνας σκόροδα στίσαντες συμβάλλουσι. They were also armed with
an artificial spur, πλῆκτρον or κέντρον. Schol. to Aves, 759 : Πλῆκτρα
δέ εἰσιν ἔμβολα χαλκᾶ τὰ ἐμβαλλό-
μενα τοῖς πλήκτροις τῶν ἀλεκτρυό-
νων. Great attention was bestowed
both upon them and upon the quails.
Plato, Leg. viii. p. 789: λαβόντες ὑπὸ
μάλης ἕκαστος τοὺς μὲν ἐλάττονας εἰς
τὰς χεῖρας, μείζους δ' ὑπὸ τὴν ἀγκά-
λην ἐντὸς, πορεύονται περιπατοῦν-
τες σταδίους παμπόλλους ἕνεκα τῆς
εὐεξίας, οὔτι τῆς τῶν αὐτῶν σωμάτων, ἀλλὰ τῆς τούτων τῶν θρεμμά-
των. Contests of this kind are found
represented in the inferior works of
art. See Bracci, Memor. d. Antichi
Incis. i. 10, 3. A victorious cock with
a palm-branch is depicted on a lamp.
Antich. d'Ercol. viii. p. 67. Perhaps
the passion for quail-fights was even
greater. Cf. Aristot. Hist. Anim. ix.
9. See Athen. xi. p. 464, ὀρτυγομανία.
The persons whose business it was
to catch and tame them were called ὀρτυγοθῆραι and ὀρτυγοτρόφοι.

Plato, Euthyd. p. 290; Poll. vii. 136.
But besides contests with each other,
a particular game was played with
them, called ὀρτυγοκοπία. See Poll.
ix. 107 : ἔσθ' ὅτε δὲ ὁ μὲν ἵστη τὸν
ὄρτυγα, ὁ δὲ ἔκοπτε τῷ λιχανῷ, ἢ
τὰ ἐκ τῆς κεφαλῆς πτερὰ ἀπέτιλλε,
καὶ εἰ μὲν ἐγκαρτερήσειεν ὁ ὄρτυξ, ἡ
νίκη μετὰ τοῦ θρέψαντος αὐτὸν ἐγί-
νετο· ἐνδόντος δὲ καὶ ὑποφυγόντος
ὁ κόπτων ἢ ὁ τίλλων ἐνίκα : and
Schol. on Aristoph. Av. 1297, where,
instead of ἐν πυρῷ read ἐν γύρῳ. So
also Suidas. There was a frame or
board (τηλία), and on this a ring
was drawn, or else the board was of a
circular shape with a raised rim, and
within this the fights took place, as
well as the ὀρτυγοκοπία. Æschin. in
Timarch. p. 78 : ἀλλὰ διημέρευσεν ἐν
τῷ κυβείῳ, οὗ ἡ τηλία τίθεται, καὶ
τοὺς ἀλεκτρυόνας συμβάλλουσι, καὶ
κυβεύουσι. Pollux, supra: καὶ τηλίᾳ
μὲν ὁποίᾳ τῇ ἀρτοπώλιδι κύκλον
ἐμπεριγράψαντες ἐνίστασαν τοὺς
ὄρτυγας ἐπὶ ταῖς μάχαις ταῖς πρὸς
ἀλλήλους. ὁ δὲ ἀνατραπεὶς καὶ ἐκ-
πεσὼν τοῦ κύκλου ἡττᾶτο αὐτός τε
καὶ ὁ τοῦ ὄρτυγος δεσπότης. Schol.
on Aristoph. Plut. 1037 : καὶ δὴ καὶ
ἰδίως ἐκαλεῖτο τηλία περίφραγμα
σανίδων ἐν τῇ ἀγορᾷ, ἐν ᾧ ἄλφιτα
ἐπιπράσκοντο. καὶ ὀρτυγοτρόφοι
τοὺς ὄρτυγας συνέβαλλον ἐν τούτῳ.
The stake was sometimes the quail,
sometimes money. Pollux, supra: καὶ
ποτὲ μὲν ἐπ' αὐτοῖς διετίθεντο τοῖς
ὄρτυξι, ποτὲ δὲ καὶ ἐπ' ἀργυρίῳ.

Discos now brought his bird. 'Is it for the quails or for money?' enquired the youth. 'I should not lose my bird in any case,' replied Discos; 'but I never stake him.' 'Very well,' said the first, 'for fifty drachmæ then.' The tiny champions were set opposite, and had scarcely caught sight of each other, ere their feathers ruffled up, and they darted furiously at one another with outspread wings. Neither budged an inch. Often as the battle was renewed, each maintained his ground, or occupied his adversary's; and for some time the victory was doubtful. 'I'll bet another fifty against you, Discos!' exclaimed one of the by-standers, who were all watching the contest with passionate delight; but hardly were the words spoken when Discos' bird, as if infuriated at the doubts about his valour, charged with redoubled impetuosity against his foe, who, stunned by the blow, flew, after a short resistance, far beyond the boundaries of the arena. 'Vanquished! vanquished!' cried a host of voices; while the owner of the beaten bird seized his champion with great expedition, and spoke loudly into his ear, in order, if possible, to efface from its recollection the cry of the victor,[7] which was meanwhile overwhelmed with applause, and borne off by Discos in triumph.

Charicles and Ctesiphon, after finishing their break-fast, had joined the spectators, and the gamesters alone had taken no notice of what was passing. But now the din waxed louder and louder, and from words the company at play had proceeded to blows. The attacks of all seemed directed against an elderly man, apparently of humble con-dition, who, either by good luck, or foul play, had won all the money that had been staked, and was now in danger of seeing it wrested back from him by force. Patiently as a Spartan at the altar of Orthia, did he endure the blows that were levelled at him from all sides; resolved to part with his life rather than his winnings, which he had partly

---

[7] Poll. ix. 109: τοὺς δὲ ἡττηθέν-τας ἔρτυγας ἐμβοήσαντες κατὰ τὸ οὖς αὐτοὺς ἐξιῶντο, ἤθην ἀνεργα-ζόμενοι (ἐνεργαζόμενοι?) τῆς τοῦ νενικηκότος ωνῆς.

concealed in the folds of his chiton, and partly clutched in his hands, which were convulsively pressed together. But all his resistance was in vain; while some forcibly opened his hands, others tore his garment, and plundered him, at the same time thumping and beating him; till at last he fled from the house, amid a peal of laughter, with a black eye, and the clothes half torn from off his back.[8] 'It serves him right,' shouted some of those who had assembled in the court; 'why does he intrude himself into such company?' 'But won't he go and lodge a complaint?' enquired Charicles. 'What, for being drubbed at play?' said one; 'he'll not dream of such a thing.' 'But, have ye heard,' he continued, 'that Ctesippos was condemned yesterday?' 'To be sure,' replied a second; 'or rather his father; in a trifle of some two thousand drachmæ.'

'Which Ctesippos?' asked Charicles; while several to whom the circumstance was new, at the same time stepped forward. 'The son of Ctesias,' replied the first. 'You all know the jovial set of fellows, who from so often getting into rows were yclept the *triballi*. Well, it's that Ctesippos.' 'And why was he convicted?' pursued Charicles. 'A joke, I assure ye, a mere joke,' was the answer, 'which might very well have been excused in young gallants intoxicated at the time.' 'No, no,' said a third, 'it was past a joke. I have been accurately informed of the whole transaction, and was myself a witness to their disgraceful behaviour before the diætetæ. It would be a bad look-out for the public security, if such conduct were to go unpunished.' 'Prythee, tell us then,' said Ctesiphon, 'how it was, who is the accuser, and what the crime.' 'There was a certain man of unexceptionable character,' replied the other, 'Aristophon by name,[9] who some time ago,

---

[8] This tale is from Alciph. *Epist.* ii. 54: καὶ οἱ μὲν πὺξ ἔπαιον, οἱ δὲ διέσχιζον τὸ ἱμάτιον. ἐγὼ δὲ ἀπρὶξ εἰχόμην τῶν κερμάτων, ἀποθανεῖν πρότερον ἢ προέσθαι τι ἐκείνοις τῶν ἐμοὶ πεπορισμένων αἱρούμενος, κ.τ.λ.

[9] This is a fair sample of the goings on of a large section of the younger people. Other instances of

when out on a campaign, laid a complaint before the stra-
tegos against this Ctesippos for rudeness and indecorum,
and caused him to be punished ; ever since which, he has
been pursued with rancorous hatred both by father and
son. A short time back, he went out with a friend in the
dusk of the evening for a stroll in the market-place, and
there met Ctesippos half seas over. The latter, directly
he saw him, croaked out some unintelligible threat or other,
and then went towards Melite, where, as it afterwards
turned out, his father and several friends had assembled
for a debauch. To them he explained what an excellent
occasion now offered itself for taking vengeance on Aristophon ; and forthwith they all sallied out into the market-
place. Meanwhile Aristophon had turned, and met them
almost at the same spot. Two of them seized his companion and held him fast ; while Ctesippos and his father,
and a third man, fell upon Aristophon, tore off his clothes,
threw him into the dirt, beat him, stamped upon him with
their feet, and discharged at him a torrent of the lowest
abuse. While he thus lay, all helpless, Ctesias placed
himself before him, crowing like a cock after a victory, and
flapping his arms against his body in the manner of wings.[10]
They then made off, taking his clothes with them, and
their victim was assisted from the ground by some passers-

---

violence occur, for example, the cases
of Euergos and Meidias in Demosthenes, of Simon and Eratosthenes in
Lysias, of Timarchos in Æschines ;
whence it appears that public security
was at a discount, and that there was
good cause for the frequently-ex-
pressed fears of λωποδυσία and τοι-
χωρυχία. The instance in the text
is from Demosth. *in Con.* p. 1257,
which has been translated word for
word. The assigned penalty of two
thousand drachmæ is quite in rule, for
there is no doubt that damages could
be obtained in a δίκη αἰκίας. See

Meier and Schömann, *Attic. Process.*
p. 549. So too the story related by
Diog Laert. vi. 42, of Meidias, who
struck Diogenes in the face, saying,
'My banker has three thousand drachmæ at your service.' This will, however hardly warrant the inference
that the sum named was the precise
legal penalty for the assault.

[10] Demosth. *supra* : ἥδε γὰρ τοὺς
ἀλεκτρυόνας μιμούμενος τοὺς νενι-
κηκότας. οἱ δὲ κροτεῖν τοῖς ἀγκῶσι·
αὐτὸν ἠξίουν ἀντὶ πτερύγων τὰς
πλευράς.

by, so shockingly maltreated that he has been under the
doctor's hands ever since.'

'By my troth!' exclaimed Charicles, 'if that's a joke,
I don't know what violence is.' 'How so?' retorted the
apologist of Ctesippos; 'you must remember he was drunk
at the time, and allowances must be made for youth. I
know many sons of most distinguished families, who have
got into rows about hetæræ; and as for bad words, how
many there are who call each other by the foulest names,
just in fun.'[11] 'I can't say that I think that even such
proceedings are exactly praiseworthy,' continued the nar-
rator; 'but even if they could plead intoxication in palliation of their offence, nothing could at all justify their
atrocious conduct afterwards. Aristophon naturally brought
an action against them for the assault, and when the cause
was about to come on before the diætetes, he begged me
and others of his friends to be present. The defendants
kept us waiting for a long time before they appeared. It
was not until evening that father and son showed themselves, with some of their fraternity, and then only to bring
into contempt the solemnity of justice and the sacredness
of the place ; for without endeavouring to rebut the accusation, or even looking at the depositions, they sought to
waste the time by miserable tom-fooleries. They led us
singly to the altar, and swore by the dog and the platanus,[12] that the boy was the son of an hetæra, and had

---

[11] This was the defence which
Conon actually made. Demosth. p.
1261. Cf. Lysias, in Sym. p. 160.

[12] This occurs also, Demosth. ibid.,
excepting the oath by the dog and the
platanus: ἐποίησαν μὲν γὰρ ἔξω μέ-
σων νυκτῶν τὴν ὥραν (τῆς διαίτης),
οὐδὲ τὰς μαρτυρίας ἀναγιγνώσκειν
ἐθέλοντες, οὐδὲ ἀντίγραφα διδόναι,
τῶν τε παρόντων ἡμῖν καθ᾽ ἕνα οὐ-
τωσὶ πρὸς τὸν βωμὸν ἄγοντες καὶ
ἐξορκίζοντες καὶ γράφοντες μαρτυ-

ρίας, οὐδὲν πρὸς τὸ πρᾶγμα· ἀλλ᾽ ἐξ
ἑταίρας εἶναι παιδίον αὐτῷ τοῦτο καὶ
πεπονθέναι τὰ καὶ τά. Oaths generally do not seem to have been very
religiously observed; while conversation appears to have been pretty frequently interlarded with such expressions as μὰ τὸν Δία, νὴ τὸν Ἡρακλέα,
νὴ τὴν Ἥραν, and the like. Plato,
Leg. xi. p. 917 : ἔπαινος δὲ ὅρκος τε
περὶ παντὸς τοῦ πωλουμένου ἀπέστω.
Socrates considered it wrong to swear
by a deity, though he used such exple-

undergone this and that; or wrote down evidence concerning things that had not the remotest connexion with
the point at issue.[13] Now if such disgraceful behaviour,
and such contempt of the laws were to remain unpunished,
what safeguard, I should like to know, should we have
against any insult or offence whatever?'

'You are quite in the right,' said an elegant youth,
who had come from the drinking-room to listen to the
story. 'I like to have my joke as well as another, and
don't stick at a slight squabble when there is a woman
in the case, but heaven forfend that I should have aught
to do with such a mad set as your triballi. I knew
Ctesippos of old; he was one of the roughest and most
unruly boys at Hermippos' school, and often had a taste
of the master's rod for his ill-natured pranks.'

The name of Hermippos drew Charicles' eyes to the
speaker. 'By Hercules,' he exclaimed, 'it's Lysiteles!'
and hastened up to him. 'Charicles!' said the person
thus accosted, in astonishment, 'you here? when did you
come?' 'I returned yesterday from Syracuse,' was the
answer. 'So, hail to thee, friend of my youth!' said Lysiteles. 'We'll celebrate your return with a carouse.[14]

---

tives as νὴ τὸν κύνα, τὴν πλάτανον,
τὴν χῆνα. Philostr. *Vit. Apollon.*
vi. 19: ὤμνυ γὰρ ταῦτα οὐχ ὡς θεοὺς,
ἀλλ' ἵνα μὴ θεοὺς ὤμνυ. The oath
κατὰ χηνὸς was very common. So
Aves, 520:

Λάμπων δ' ἔτι καὶ νῦν ὄμνυσιν τὸν χῆν'
ὅταν ἐξαπατᾷ τι.

Indeed τὸν χῆνα seems to have been
a trick of the tongue for τὸν Ζῆνα.
So Zeno swears by the caper, κάππα-
ρις, Diog. Laert. vii. 32; and some
one else, by the cabbage, κράμβη.
Eustath. *ad Od.* xix. 396.

[13] Demosth. *supra*. This was done
merely to fritter away the time.

[14] It was a custom, often alluded
to by Plautus, to give a banquet to a
friend on his safe return home. So
Bacch. iii. 6, 7 : Salvus quom peregre
advenis, cœna dabitur. *Stich.* iii. 2,
17 :

'Cœnabis apud me, quoniam salvus advenis;'

and *Epidicus*, i. 1, 5. Plutarch, *Symp.*
v. 5, 1 : ἐν ταῖς ὑποδοχαῖς, ἃς ἐποιεῖτο
τῶν φίλων ἕκαστος ἑστιῶν ἡμᾶς ἥκον-
τας ἀπὸ τῆς Ἀλεξανδρείας. The same
occurred at departure, προπέμπειν.
Ibid. iv. 3, 2 : θύοντας θεοῖς καὶ προ-
πέμποντας φίλον καὶ ξενίζοντας. Cf.
Plaut. *Bacch.* i. 1, 61 :

Ego sorori meæ cœnam hodie dare volo
viaticam.

To-day you are my guest.' 'I thank thee for the invitation,' replied Charicles; 'but I am already engaged to
dine with the noble friend in whose house I am at present
quartered.' 'Good! so you'll come to-morrow instead,'
said the young man; 'and now give me your hand that
you will be there.'[15] 'Be it so,' assented Charicles; 'but
where?' 'At my house in the Cerameicos; you recollect
it, don't you? We are undisturbed, and you need not
fear that a crabbed old governor will send the jolly spirits
packing.[16] You'll meet with some more of your acquaintances.' He had several questions more to put, but Charicles postponed answering them till next day, as it was
time for him to be moving.

It was now the first hour after noon, and in the streets
of the city the bustle had sensibly moderated. The main
business of the day was transacted; the market-place was
still; and the shops of the artisans alone wore their usual
busy aspect. All the elements of social life with which the
centre of this great city had so recently been thronged,
had suddenly been scattered in all directions, and the busy
crowd had dispersed, only to re-appear in a different form
in the Gymnasia and other such places of resort without
the walls. Hence the paths leading to the Academy, to
the Lyceion, and the Cynosarges, were just then most frequented. The free burgher, not confined to the close
atmosphere of his domicile by any base handicraft, sought
these places of meeting; perhaps in order to whet his
appetite for the approaching meal by some invigorating
exercise, and by a warm or cold bath, or, it might be, only
by a constitutional in the Dromos; or perhaps he amused
himself by being a spectator of the feats of dexterity and
skill exhibited by the wrestlers, and by gazing at the

---

[15] So Eurip. *Helen.* 838:
ἐπὶ τοῖσδε τοίνυν δεξιᾶς ἐμῆς θίγε,
though this was on a more important
occasion.

[16] Plato, *de Republ.* viii. p. 569:
ὥσπερ πατὴρ υἱὸν μετὰ ὀχληρὰν
συμποτῶν ἐξελαύνων.

magnificent figures, there stripped to view; or perhaps he sought intellectual amusement in learned and attractive converse.

Charicles, too, after making a few purchases, directed his steps towards the Gymnasium, to indulge in its amusements, a pleasure of which he had long felt the want; and then after a bath he purposed going to Phorion's. From earliest childhood he had been accustomed by his father to gymnastic exercises. The lessons of the pædotribæ were quite as important in his eyes as his son's visits to school; and when the lad had grown into a youth, he encouraged him to attempt the more arduous exercise of the palæstra. Though he was averse to the one-sided exertions of the athletæ, yet a sensible course of gymnastics—as well as chariot-driving and the chase, together with the intercourse of learned men—ranked with him as the only occupations befitting a free-born youth. 'Our character,' he often observed to his son, 'depends on our avocations, and a man's mind takes its colour from the nature of his pursuits. He who consumes his days in paltry occupations or vulgar toil, can no more feel lofty aspirations and manly courage rising within his bosom, than can pusillanimity and a grovelling habit of thought find a place in the soul of him whose pursuits are noble and honourable.'[17]

---

[17] Taken from the speech περὶ συντάξεως, attributed to Demosthenes: p. 173. So Plato, *Leg.* viii. 846, would banish all artisans from his commonwealth, manual labour being inconsistent with τὸν κοινὸν τῆς πόλεως κόσμον. It is difficult to obtain just views on the social position of this branch of the community. Solon's law is well known: υἱῷ τρέφειν τὸν πατέρα μὴ διδαξάμενον τέχνην ἐπάναγκες μὴ εἶναι. (Plutarch, *Sol.* 22.) But in practice this was ineffective, for we find universally that no free-born youth would demean himself by any occupation of the kind. Thucydides, again (ii. 40), makes it the boast of Athens, that her sons could take a share in public affairs, as well as manage their own trade; thus totally contradicting Plato. This much is certain, that at this period the advantages arising from trade were appreciated at Athens, and that it was favoured accordingly; though it was considered unworthy of a free-man to work at it himself; and in this Plato, Xenophon and Aristotle agree. Plato, *Charm.* 163, is clearest on the sub-

Charicles was therefore well practised in the usual exercises; he was a quick runner, and skilful leaper: he
hurled the discus and javelin with strength and dexterity,
played at ball to admiration, and when at Syracuse was
accounted one of its first wrestlers. Boxing, and the
pancration, his father could never endure, and he used to
praise the Spartan laws which forbade such contests.

Full of happy recollections of bygone days, our young
hero walked along through the gate of Diochares, and
the gardens leading to the Lyceion. He found the Gymnasium very full of company. In the arcades surrounding
the peristyle were groups of men, young and old, engaged
in discourse of various kinds. Here a sophist, seated
amidst his scholars, was discussing by the method of inter-
rogation, the pros and cons of some doctrine of ethics.
The large semicircular bench of marble, on which he sat,
could only accommodate half his auditory, so the others

---

ject: but trade is there not considered
disgraceful in itself, though not befitting everybody; but handicrafts,
βαναυσία καὶ χειροτεχνία (de Republ.
ix. p. 590), are pronounced against on
ethical grounds; for the mind suffers,
he thinks, as well as the body, from
such occupations; ibid. vi. p. 495:
ὥσπερ τὰ σώματα λελώβηνται, οὕτω
καὶ τὰς ψυχὰς συγκεκλασμένοι τε καὶ
ἀποτεθρυμμένοι διὰ τὰς βαναυσίας
τυγχάνουσιν. Xenoph. Œcon. 4, 2,
is not a whit more favourable: τῶν
δὲ σωμάτων θηλυνομένων καὶ αἱ ψυ-
χαὶ πολὺ ἀρρωστότεραι γίγνονται.
And Aristotle (de Republ. viii. 2) in
propounding what a νέος ἐλεύθερος
ought to learn, speaks out still more
plainly; and the words, ἡ δὲ βελτίστη
πόλις οὐ ποιήσει βάναυσον πολίτην,
leave no doubt as to his own opinion;
and though in a few Grecian towns
trade held a somewhat higher place,
yet the above sentiment prevailed in
Greece, and indeed pervaded the

whole of the ancient world. Herodot.
ii 167, after speaking of Egypt, says:
Εἰ μὲν νῦν καὶ τοῦτο παρ' Αἰγυπτίων
μεμαθήκασιν οἱ Ἕλληνες, οὐκ ἔχω
ἀτρεκέως κρῖναι, ὁρέων καὶ Θρήικας
καὶ Σκύθας, καὶ Πέρσας, καὶ Λυδοὺς,
καὶ σχεδὸν πάντας τοὺς βαρβάρους
ἀποτιμοτέρους τῶν ἄλλων ἡγημένους
πολιητέων τοὺς τὰς τέχνας μανθά-
νοντας καὶ τοὺς ἐκγόνους τούτων.
τοὺς δὲ ἀπαλλαγμένους τῶν χειρω-
ναξιέων γενναίους νομιζομένους εἶναι
καὶ μάλιστα τοὺς ἐς τὸν πόλεμον
ἀνειμένους. μεμαθήκασι δ' ὦν τοῦτο
πάντες οἱ Ἕλληνες καὶ μάλιστα Λακεδαιμόνιοι   ἥκιστα δὲ Κορίνθιοι
ὄνονται τοὺς χειροτέχνος. Wealthy
burghers, however, often employed
slaves as artisans, but this was considered perfectly correct, and was
practised by the most distinguished
citizens, as for instance by the father
of Demosthenes. See Böckh's Publ.
Econ. of Athens, pp. 45, 69, 475; and
the Excursus on The Slaves.

stood in front to catch the wisdom that proceeded from his
mouth. Here a rhetorician was making a critical examination of a speech elaborated by one of his pupils. In
several places little knots had formed, and were talking of
the important occurrences in Asia. News had just arrived
from the Macedonian host, announcing the continuance of
the siege of Tyre, and some assayed a display of their
topographical acquirements, by drawing in the sand with
their sticks [18] a plan of the city and its position.[19] In the
great court many were engaged in all kinds of exercises.
while others were already hurrying to warm or cold
baths, or anointing their limbs with pure oil in the Elæo
thesion.

Charicles strode through the Palæstra, to the exercise
grounds in the open air. Here several were running races,
amid the loud acclamations of the beholders, who encouraged
first one, then another.[20] Others stood ready to jump, with
the leaping-weights in their hands. On the course near
the Xystos, a contest of a peculiarly interesting nature
appeared to be going on. A dense ring of spectators
had formed around, and many were leaving, while others
streamed towards the spot. 'That's Ctesiphon, I'm sure,
he is the soul of the Gymnasium,' cried a voice near Cha-

---

[18] Böttiger, *Vaseng.* ii. p. 61, has
spoken of the custom of carrying a
stick out of doors; cf. Casaubon,
on Theophr. 21. Böttiger's assumption that the rest of Greece first
imitated the Laconian usage, after the
Sparian Hegemonia, seems groundless. Lysias, *de Inval.* p. 748: ὅτι μὲν
δυοῖν βακτηρίαιν χρῶμαι τῶν ἄλλων
μιᾷ χρωμένων, proves the habit to
have been general. Cf. Schol. to
Aristoph. *Plut.* 272. Young as well
as old carried a cane, which was indeed
quite a *sine qua non* to a careful
dresser. Athen. xii. p. 543: σκίπωνί τε
ἐστηρίζετο᾽ χρυσᾶς ἕλικας ἐμπεπαι-
σμένῳ. Cf. *ib.* xi. p. 509; and xii. p. 513.

[19] So Plutarch, *Alcib.* 17, talking of
Sicily: ὥστε πολλοὺς ἐν ταῖς παλαίστραις καὶ τοῖς ἡμικυκλίοις καθέζεσθαι, τῆς τε νήσου τὸ σχῆμα καὶ
θέσιν Λιβύης καὶ Καρχηδόνος ὑπο-
γράφοντας.

[20] Isocr. *Evag.* 32: καὶ πᾳ ῶ καὶ
ποιήσω ταὐτὸν, ὅπερ ἐν τοῖς γυμνι-
κοῖς ἀγῶσιν οἱ θεαταί. καὶ γὰρ ἐκεῖνοι
παρακελεύονται τῶν δρομέων οὐ τοῖς
ἀπολελειμμένοις, ἀλλὰ τοῖς περὶ τῆς
νίκης ἁμιλλωμένοις. Dio Chrysost.
Orat. xxviii. p. 531: τοὺς μέν τινας
ἑωρῶμεν ἐν τῷ δρόμῳ τρέχοντας κα
κραυγὴ τῶν παρακελευομένων ἦν.

ricles, who had also joined the throng, but could see
nothing, in consequence of the dense mass of persons before
him.[21] He stood on tiptoe, and could then just perceive the
head of one of the wrestlers. It was really his friend who
had been contending. But the struggle had already come
to an end. Ctesiphon had cleverly discovered his adversary's
weak point, had supplanted, and brought him to the earth.
A boisterous shout of applause succeeded. The ring
opened, and Charicles saluted his friend, who willingly
accepted his challenge to have a throw with him also.
Ctesiphon had unquestionably the advantage in strength,
but Charicles wrestled with so much caution, and made
such excellent use of every chance that offered, that the
match lasted some time, and although his antagonist was
again the conqueror, yet he at least earned the praise of
being himself a most accomplished wrestler. The friends
then went arm in arm to the bath, after which Charicles
made the best of his way to the house of Phorion.

---

[21] Dio Chrysost. ibid.: ὁρῶμεν
οὖν πάνυ πολλοὺς ἑστηκότας πρὸς
τῇ ἐξέδρᾳ τοῦ Ἡρακλέους καὶ ἑτέρους
ἀεὶ προσάγοντας, τοὺς δὲ καὶ ἀπιόν-
τας διὰ τὸ μὴ δύνασθαι ἰδεῖν. τὸ μὲν
οὖν πρῶτον ἐπειρώμεθα ὁρᾶν ὑπερ-
κύπτοντες, καὶ μόλις ἑωρῶμεν τοῦ
γυμναζομένου τὴν κεφαλήν.

SCENE THE SIXTH.

———◦———

THE BANQUET.

FROM the first dawn of day the house of Lysiteles had been in a state of great commotion, for the young gallant was bent on celebrating, with more than usual expense, the return of the playmate of his childhood. Every luxury to be found in the Athenian market had been procured; and not content with leaving his slaves to make the requisite purchases, he had gone to the fish-market in person, to select the finest Copaic eels and the largest sea-pike. A first-rate cook had been hired, chaplets were bespoken, *recherché* unguents bought, and graceful female flute-players and dancing-girls engaged. In the spacious saloon, which Lysiteles had selected for the scene of their nocturnal feast, the couches were all set ready, and on tables of elegant design was a grand display of silver goblets and bowls of various sizes. Youthful slaves, in high-girt semi-transparent chitons, hurried through the halls and saloons, set things in order and cleaned them, spread embroidered tapestry over the mattresses of the couches, smoothed the pillows, which were of a gay striped pattern, scoured vessels, and did not rest, till all the preparations for the reception of the guests had been completed.

The gnomon had long displayed a shadow of more than ten feet in length, when Charicles returned from the Academy, where Manes had met him by appointment, bearing the full-dress garments, and fashionable half-shoes. The day had flown rapidly while he was selecting numerous articles necessary for the commencement of his future establishment. Every thing had turned out according to his wishes; a blissful future opened before him, and he walked along in cheerful mood towards the house where the feast of friendship was preparing for him.

He was not far from his destination, when he perceived

Ctesiphon, who was coming from the Lyceion, and on his way to his own habitation. 'Quick, Manes,' he said to the slave behind him; 'you see Ctesiphon yonder? Run to him and tell him to wait for me.'[1] The slave did as he was commanded; he soon overtook Ctesiphon, fast as he was walking, and seizing him by the garment, bid him wait until Charicles should arrive. 'Where is he?' asked Ctesiphon, turning round. 'Here he comes behind us,' answered the slave, as Charicles joined them, and saluted his friend. 'Bless me,' cried Ctesiphon, 'what a buck you are; pray whither are you bound?' 'To a dinner at Lysiteles',' answered Charicles; 'I promised yesterday to go; are not you invited too?' Ctesiphon answered in the negative. 'Oh! it would be too bad, were I to miss you from the circle of old friends whom I shall meet there. What if I bid you come along with me uninvited?' 'If you bid me,' said Ctesiphon, jocosely, 'of course I can't help myself.' 'Away we go then,' said Charicles; 'let us verify the adage: "To the exquisite banquet the exquisites go self-bidden."' 'But prythee invent some apology, for I shall assert that I was invited by you.' 'We'll concoct something as we go along,' said his friend, 'only let us be moving.'[2]

They found the door of the hospitable mansion open; and a slave, who met them in the hall, ushered them into the saloon, where most of the other guests were already reclining on the couches. Lysiteles advanced to meet them with friendly salutations. 'Ah! Ctesiphon,' he exclaimed, as he saw them enter, 'you are come in the very nick of time to join us at the banquet; or if aught else brings you hither, defer it till another time. I looked all over the city for you yesterday, to invite you, but could not find

---

[1] It will be unnecessary here to cite in full the authorities from which the following account has been compiled, since they will be fully discussed in the Excursus on *The Meals*. The incident above is imitated from Plato, *de Republ.* i. p. 327.

[2] Taken from the excellent description, Plato, *Symp.* p. 174.

you.'[3] 'Charicles has given me an invite in your name
then,' answered Ctesiphon ; 'for he forced me to come along
with him.' 'Capital!' cried their polished host ; 'here's a
place for you next Glaucon ; you, Charicles, will lie by
me.   Take off their sandals, slaves, and wash their feet,
that they may recline.' The slaves unfastened the thongs
of their shoes, and others brought silver basins, into which,
from beautifully-shaped ewers of the same metal, they
poured over the feet of the new comers, who sat meanwhile
upon the couches, not water only, but golden wine, to which
an additional fragrance was imparted by an admixture of
odoriferous balsam.[4] While the two friends were luxuri-
ating in this lavishly sumptuous bath, which though it took
Charicles rather by surprise, yet merely raised a smile in
Ctesiphon, some of the guests went up and saluted the
former.   They were all acquaintances of his boyish days—
Polemarchos and Callicles, Nausicrates and Glaucon—who
now frankly shook hands with their old playmate, and reminded him of a thousand incidents of days long past.
'Enough, enough!' at last cried one of the party, as he
lolled on his couch ; 'that will do, friends, take your places,
and let us fall to.'

'By my troth, Euctemon,' said Lysiteles, 'it is high
time.   Water, ho! for the hands, slaves, and then serve
up what you've got.   Think that you entertain us, and
that we are your guests, and so have a care that you may
merit our praise.' [5]

The order was speedily executed, water and towels
were handed round ; then the slaves, two and two,[6] brought
in the tables, and loaded them with comestibles ; while
others presented bread of the finest quality in tiny baskets
woven of slips of ivory.[7]   At this juncture a loud knock-

---

[3] Plato, *Symp.* p. 175. See Excursus on *The Meals*.

[4] Plutarch, *Phoc.* 20. See Excursus on *The Meals*.

[5] Plato, *Symp.* p. 175. See Excursus on *The Meals*.

[6] See Excursus on *The Meals*.

[7] Athenæus, iv. p. 130: τραγή-

ing was heard at the outer door, and a slave came in to
announce that Stephanos, the jester, was outside, and
begged to inform the company that he was plentifully provided with every thing requisite for enjoying an abundant
repast at a stranger's table.

'How say ye, my friends!' asked the lord of the
mansion; 'it will hardly do, methinks, to shut the door on
him. Let him in.'[8] This however was quite unnecessary,

ματά τ' ἐν πλεκτοῖς ἐλεφαντίνοις
ἐπεδόθη πᾶσι.

[8] When Carystius (Athen. VI. p.
235) asserted that the character of a
parasite, as one of the *dramatis personæ* of comedy, was first invented
(εὑρηθῆναι) by Alexis, he probably
only meant that this poet first distinguished such a character by the name
παράσιτος; for such personages as
κόλακες or γελωτοποιοὶ had long
been of common occurrence, as is
sufficiently shown by a fragment of
Epicharmus quoted by Athenæus directly afterwards:

Συνδειπνέω τῷ λῶντι, καλέσαι δεῖ μόνον,
καὶ τῷ γα μὴ λιῶντι, κωὐδὲν δεῖ καλεῖν.
τηνεὶ δὲ χαρίεις τ' εἰμὶ καὶ ποιέω πολὺν ·
γέλωτα καὶ τὸν ἐστιῶντ' ἐπαινέω.

Philippos, described in Xenoph.
Symp. i. 11, served as the original
here. The name parasite had at first
no evil signification, but was applied
to persons of consideration, who were
appointed to assist the magistrates
and priests in the celebration of sa-
crificial feasts. Athen. vi. p. 234.
According to Clearchos (Athen vi.
p. 235) this usage still subsisted after
Alexander's time. Ἔτι δὲ παράσιτον
νῦν μὲν τὸν ἕτοιμον, τότε δὲ τὸν εἰς
τὸ συμβιοῦν κατειλεγμένον. ἐν γοῦν
τοῖς παλαιοῖς νόμοις αἱ πλεῖσται τῶν
πόλεων ἔτι καὶ τήμερον ταῖς ἐντι-
μοτάταις ἀρχαῖς συγκαταλέγουσι

παρασίτους. The parasites of Comedy
may be divided into three classes, in
all of which obtrusiveness and sensuality is the common trait. Firstly
the γελωτοποιοὶ, who deal in jokes,
often at their own expense, and are
content to be the butts of the company, provided they can get enough
to eat and drink: such were Ergasilus
in the *Captivi*, and Gelasimus in the
Stichus, of Plautus, as well as Xenophon's Philippos. Next come the
κόλακες, or *assentatores*, who are
always flattering their patrons : such
were the Kolax or Struthias of Menander, the Gnatho of Terence, and
the Artotrogus in the *Miles Gloriosus*
of Plautus. The third *nuance* is that
of the θεραπευτικοὶ, who earned a
place at table by all kinds of little
attentions and services, and were
somewhat akin to the *femmes d'intrigue* of the French comedies. See
Plutarch, *de Adul.* 23 : πιστὸς ἔρωτος
ὑπηρέτης καὶ περὶ λύσιν πόρνης ἀκρι-
βὴς, καὶ πότου δαπάνης ἐκκαθᾶραι
λογισμὸν οὐκ ἀμελὴς, οὐδὲ ῥᾴθυμος
ἐν δείπνων παρασκευαῖς, θεραπευτι-
κὸς δὲ παλλακίδων · πρὸς δὲ κηδεστὰς
ἀποθρασύνεσθαι κελευσθεὶς, καὶ συν-
εκβαλεῖν γαμετὴν ἄτεγκτος καὶ
ἀδυσώπητος. Cf. *de Educ.* 17. Phormio in Terence, and Curculio in
Plautus are samples, and, upon the
whole, the parasites in the *Asinaria*
and *Menæchmi*. Such characters, a

as the parasite was already at the door of the saloon, and
said, ' I am, as ye well know, Stephanos the jester, who
never refused when invited by any of you to a meal;
wherefore it would not be fair were ye now to decline my
invitation. I have brought a whole budget of good things.'
' Very well,' said Lysiteles ; ' and besides, there are only
nine of us, so lie you down next to Mantitheos, and be my
guest.'

Fresh dishes, on which the Sicilian *artiste* had displayed
his skill, were served up in profusion. ' Really,' said
Glaucon, 'no Attic meal this, but a Bœotian one!'[9] 'Quite

---

little caricatured perhaps, are copied
from real life, and would undergo any
indignity for the chance of a good
dinner : οὓς οὔτε πῦρ, οὔτε σίδηρος,
οὔτε χαλκὸς εἴργει μὴ φοιτᾶν ἐπὶ
δεῖπνον, as Plutarch says. The description of Chærephon quoted from
Alexis by Athen. iv. p. 164, is from
the life :

> ὅπου γάρ ἐστιν ὁ κέραμος μισθώσιμος
> ὁ τοῖς μαγείροις, εὐθὺς ἐξ ἑωθι. οῦ
> ἕστηκεν ἐλθών· κἂν ἴδῃ μισθούμενον
> εἰς ἑστίασιν, τοῦ μαγείρου πυθόμενος
> τὸν ἑστιῶντα, τῆς θύρας χασμωμένης
> ἂν ἐπιλάβηται, πρῶτος εἰσελήλυθεν.

These fellows had a talent for finding
out where a banquet was going on,
and would waylay people at the baths
or elsewhere, and force their company on them as guests. Eupolis,
ap. Athen. vi. p. 236 ; Lucian, *de
Parasit.* 51. Athenæus, vi. p. 249,
says of the parasites at the table of
Dionysius the younger : ἀποπτύοντος
δὲ τοῦ Διονυσίου πολλάκις παρεῖχον τὰ
πρόσωπα καταπτύεσθαι· καὶ ἀπολεί-
χοντες τὸν σίαλον, ἔτι δὲ τὸν ἔμετον
αὐτοῦ, μέλιτος ἔλεγον εἶναι γλυκύ-
τερον. So Diog. Laert. ii. 67 ;
Plutarch, *de Occulte Viv.* v. p. 611,
relates a still more disgusting story,
which, though it may be exaggerated,
sufficiently shows in what reputation

these fellows stood. They mostly
attached themselves to young people,
with whom they could play their
cards to more advantage ; at a later
period, however, they seem to have
been regarded as a necessary ap-
pendage at the tables of the rich.
So Lucian, *de Parasit.* 58 : ὅτι πλούσιος ἀνήρ, εἰ καὶ τὸ Γύγου χρυσίον
ἔχει, μόνος ἐσθίων πένης ἐστὶ καὶ
προϊὼν ἄνευ παρασίτο. πτωχὸς δοκεῖ
. . . . . καὶ πλούσιος ἄνευ παρασί-
του ταπεινός τις καὶ εὐτελὴς φαί-
νεται. The female parasites, κο-
λακίδες, or κλιμακίδες, Plutarch, *de
Adul.* p. 192, were of quite a different
order. Athen. vi. p. 256 ; Val. Max.
ix. 1.

[9] The Bœotians were renowned
above all other Greeks for πολυ-
φαγία, and the comedians have not
failed to turn this to good account.
So also Plutarch, *de Esu Carn.* 6 :
τοὺς γὰρ Βοιωτοὺς ἡμᾶς οἱ 'Αττικοὶ
καὶ παχεῖς καὶ ἀναισθήτους καὶ ἠλι-
θίους μάλιστα διὰ τὰς ἀδηφαγίας προσ-
ηγόρευον. With this compare the
proverb Βοιωτία ὗς, as also Pind.
Olymp. vi. 152, and the passage of
Eubulos, quoted by Athenæus, x. p.
417 :

right,' interrupted Euctemon, always most in his element
when he saw a well-spread table before him, 'none of
your Attic dinners for me, where your fiddle faddles are
served up on dainty dishes. Just look at those Copaic
eels; there is Bœotian luxury for you ! By Jove, the lake
must have sent its most ancient inhabitants to the Athenian market.'

'Ah!' said Stephanos, who had already made one or
two futile attempts at raising a laugh, 'that must indeed
be a happy lake, which always carries such dishes within it,
and keeps always drinking, and yet never is too full !'—'of
water!' broke in Callicles with a laugh; 'but you are a
prodigy far greater; for put down ever so much wine,
you have never had enough.'

Amidst a variety of gossip, the meal was brought to a
close, though much too early for Stephanos; and Lysiteles,
perceiving that the company would partake of nothing
more, made a sign to the slaves, who with obedient ala-
crity handed water and sweet-smelling smegma wherewith
to wash the hands, while others bore off the viands, and
swept the fragments from the floor.   After this, garlands
of myrtle and roses,[10] party-coloured ribands, and per-

Πονεῖν μὲν ἄμμες καὶ φαγεῖν μάλ' ἀνδρικοὶ
καὶ καρτερῆσαι, τοὶ δ' Ἀθηναῖοι λέγειν
καὶ μικρὰ φαγέμεν, τοὶ δὲ Θηβαῖοι μέγα.

More important still are the words of
Polybius, *Fragm.* xx. 4, 7 : ὁρμήσαν-
τες πρὸς εὐωχίαν καὶ μέθας οὐ μόνον
τοῖς σώμασιν ἐξελύθησαν, ἀλλὰ καὶ
ταῖς ψυχαῖς. Cf. *ib.* xx. 6, 5. So
devoted were they to feasting and
idleness, that, according to Athen.
iv. p. 148, when Alexander destroyed
their city, their whole property was
no more than four hundred and forty
talents.

[10] The chaplets were always distributed after the meal, just before
the πότος began and the libation was

made. Athen. xv. p. 685 : Ἡ δὲ
τῶν στεφάνων καὶ μύρων πρότερον
εἴσοδος εἰς τὰ συμπόσια ἡγεῖτο τῆς δευ-
τέρας τραπέζης. Cf. Plutarch, *Sept.
Sap. Conv.* M. Myrtle was for the
most part the material of these chaplets, and hence the part of the market
where they were sold was called αἱ
μύρριναι. The rose ranked highest
among the flowers that were interwoven in the chaplet (Achill. Tat. ii.
1 : βασιλεὺς τῶν ἀνθέων), hence the
Demos in Aristoph. *Equit.* 966, is to be
ἐστεφανωμένος ῥόδοις. But the vio-
let and the ambiguous ὑάκινθος were
also employed. Theocr. *Id.* x. 28 :
καὶ τὸ ἴον μέλαν ἐντὶ καὶ ἁ γραπτὰ ὑά-
κινθος·

fumed unguents, were distributed all round, and a domestic
came forward with a golden bowl, into which he poured
undiluted wine from a silver can, by way of libation.
Two pretty flute-girls, in all the freshness of blooming
youth, then entered the saloon.   Lysiteles seized the bowl,
poured some wine out of it, and exclaiming, ' To the good
Genius !' took a draught, and then handed the vessel to
Charicles, who lay on his right, that it might pass round
the table.   The maidens accompanied this ceremony with
subdued and solemn tones, until the last of the guests had
returned the cup.   On this, the party waxed merrier, the
minstrels struck up the hymn of praise, and this being
ended, the slaves brought in the dessert, and placed on the
table the crater, tastefully ornamented with dancing bac-
chanals.

   ' And now first of all, my friends,' exclaimed Glaucon,
rising, ' what's to be the rule of drinking this evening ? ' [11]
   ' I vote that we have no rules at all,' replied Ctesiphon,

---

ἀλλ' ἔμπας ἐν τοῖς στεφάνοις τὰ πρῶτα
    λέγονται.

Violet-chaplets were in special favour
among the Athenians (Aristoph.
Acharn. 636), hence the name ἰοστέ-
φανοι. Chaplets were often formed
of a great variety of flowers. Cf.
Anthol. Pal. iv. 1, and v. 74 :

Πέμπω σοι, Ῥοδόκλεια, τόδε στέφος, ἄνθεσι
    καλοῖς
  αὐτὸς ὑφ' ἡμετέραις πλεξάμενος παλάμαις,
  ἔστι κρίνον, ῥοδέη τε κάλυξ, νοτέρη τ' ἀνε-
      μώνη,
  καὶ νάρκισσος ὑγρὸς, καὶ κυαναυγὲς ἴον.

Also *ib.* 147 :

Πλέξω λευκόϊον, πλέξω δ' ἁπαλὴν ἅμα
    μύρτοις
  νάρκισσον, πλέξω καὶ τὰ γελῶντα κρίνα.
πλέξω καὶ κρόκον ἡδὺν, ἐπιπλέξω δ' ὑάκινθον
  πορφυρέην, πλέξω καὶ φιλέραστα ῥόδα,
ὡς ἂν ἐπὶ κροτάφοις μυροβοστρύχου Ἡλιο-
      δώρας
  εὐπλόκαμον χαίτην ἀνθοβολῇ στέφανος.

Besides myrtle, the leaves of the

white-poplar and the ivy were used.
Theocr. ii. 121 :

κρᾶτι δ' ἔχων λεύκαν, Ἡρακλέος ἱερὸν ἔρνος,
πάντοτε πορφυρέῃσι περιζώστρῃσιν ἑλικτάν.

Here   the   πορφυραῖ   περιζῶστραι
must be *tæniæ*, which were fastened
on the chaplet. Cf. Plato, *Symp.*
p. 212, where Alcibiades comes to
Agathon's, wearing such a chaplet :
καὶ ἐπιστῆναι ἐπὶ τὰς θύρας ἐστε-
φανωμένον αὐτὸν κιττοῦ τινι στε-
φάνῳ δασεῖ καὶ ἴων, καὶ ταινίας
ἔχοντα ἐπὶ τῆς κεφαλῆς πάνυ πολλάς. In the neighbourhood of Pan-
dosia, on the west coast of Italy,
whither Persephone was said to have
come to pluck flowers, it was held disreputable to wear purchased flowers
at festivals : see Strabo, vi. 1, 5.

[11] Plato, *Symp.* p. 176. See Excursus on *The Symposia.*

'but leave it free to every one to drink what he likes.'
'Out upon you,' said Polemarch; 'we must have an
Archon, man! that's the main thing at a carouse.' 'Yes,
by Jove!' said Nausicrates, 'an Archon we must have.
I will submit to his laws, even if he should command me
to carry that lovely fluting-girl about in my arms, or to
kiss the pretty cup-bearer, who stands yonder, like a
roguish Eros.'[12] The majority of the guests seconded
him. 'So now then for the astragali,' said Lysiteles,
'that the best throw may determine who is to be king.'
'Not so,' cried Polemarch; 'for we might chance to be
blessed with that sober Ctesiphon, or that sponge Stephanos, for our president. I propose that we choose
Glaucon king; he understands right well how to admi-
nister the functions of the office.' This proposition was
approved of, and Glaucon declared his readiness to accept
office, as conductor of the symposion. 'Now then,' said
he, with serio-comic mien, 'I order you slaves, in the first
place, to mix the wine well. The adage says:

Five drink, or three, but drink not ever four.

We'll take care to avoid the last; but it is old Chian that
our friend is treating us to, which will bear the water well;
so mix two parts water to one of wine. And put some snow
into it, which will make it all the fresher; or if you've
got none, some of Stephanos's frigid jokes will do as well;
after which, pour out into the little cups; we'll begin with
these, and finish up with the larger. But briskly round,
I say, with the wine, and don't forget to have a large
goblet ready for those who have to drink fines.'

'But, Glaucon, allow me,' interrupted Ctesiphon; 'you
talk of nought but drinking; shan't we imprimis have some
games, or singing, or conversation wherewith to amuse us
at our cups?'[13] 'Ay to be sure!' said Glaucon; 'but first

---

[12] Lucian, *Saturn.* 4. See Excursus on *The Symposia.*

[13] The words of Eryximachos.
Plato, *Symp.* p. 214: πῶς οὖν, ὦ
Ἀλκιβιάδη, ποιοῦμεν; οὕτως οὕτε τι

for the wine.' From the hand of the slave he received the *cylix*; 'Zeus Soter!' he exclaimed, and drank; the rest followed his example. 'Now, friends, in the next place, what's to be done?' he continued. 'Anything but learned discourse,' cried Euctemon, and Polemarch agreed with him. 'Philosophy,' said they, 'is like the lady of the house: neither the one nor the other has any business at a symposion.' 'No more has gambling,' added Nausicrates; 'it only breeds contention, and then farewell to jollity.' 'Let us have a song then,' proposed Glaucon. 'Or guess riddles?' said Ctesiphon. 'Riddles for ever!' cried Charicles; 'I love the griphæ above everything else, they give rise to so much fun.' This motion found most seconders. 'Good,' said Glaucon; 'to him who guesses right I give one of the *tæniæ*; and the person who set the riddle must give him a kiss. He who fails to solve it, must drink off this goblet of unmixed wine. But for you, Stephanos.' he added, laughing, 'salt water will be poured out in place of wine, or else, full well I know that you will never guess right. Of course, each one proposes his enigma to his right-hand neighbour. So here's for you first, Ctesiphon. Listen,' he said, after thinking a moment:

> We're sisters twain, one dying bears the other;
> She too expires, and so brings forth her mother.[14]

'That's easily guessed,' answered Ctesiphon without hesitation; 'the sisters are night and day, who by turns die, and bring forth each other.' 'Right,' said Glaucon; 'thus I deck your brow with this fillet, and here's my kiss. It's your turn now!'

Ctesiphon begged for a short space to reflect, and then turned to Lysiteles and said:

λέγομεν ἐπὶ τῇ κύλικι, οὔτε τι ᾄδομεν; ἀλλ' ἀτεχνῶς, ὥσπερ οἱ διψῶντες, πιόμεθα;

'A riddle of the tragedian Theo-

dectes. Athen. x. p. 451:

εἰσὶ κασίγνηται διτταί, ὧν ἡ μία τίκτει τὴν ἑτέραν, αὐτὴ δὲ τεκοῦσ' ὑπὸ τῆσδε τεκνοῦται,

A thing, whose match or in the depths profound
Of ocean, or on earth can ne'er be found;
Cast in no mortal mould, its growth of limb
Dame Nature orders by the strangest whim;
'Tis born, and lo! a giant form appears;
Towards middle age a smaller size it wears;
And now again, its day of life nigh o'er,
How wondrous! 'tis gigantic as before.[15]

'A strange sort of creature that!' said Lysiteles; 'and one I shall hardly hit upon. Great in its childhood, little in its prime, and big again at last. Ah! I have it,' he suddenly exclaimed; 'one need only look at the gnomon; it is the shadow, which is great in the morning, and then contracts, till, towards evening, it again increases.' 'He's guessed it!' cried the whole party, and Lysiteles received a tænia and a kiss.

'Now Charicles,' said he, 'it's your turn to guess:'

Nor mortal fate, nor yet immortal thine,
Amalgam rare of human and divine;
Still ever new thou comest, soon again
To vanish fleeting as the phantom train;
Ever invisible to earthly eye,
Yet known to each one most familiarly.[16]

'Your riddle is somewhat vague and obscure,' said Charicles after a little consideration; 'but if I mistake not, the solution is sleep, isn't it? But you should have made it plainer. Now mind, Euctemon,' he proceeded, 'my riddle is full of contradictions. Beware of the penalty.' 'As for the penalty, I can get over that, but you surely won't deprive me of your kiss!' 'By the bye,' cried

---

[15] Also by Theodectes, *ibid.*:

Τίς φύσις οὔθ' ὅσα γαῖα φέρει τροφός, οὔθ'
    ὅσα πόντος,
οὔτε βροτοῖσιν ἔχει γυίων αὔξησιν ὁμοίαν;
ἀλλ' ἐν μὲν γενέσει πρωτοσπόρῳ ἐστὶ
    μεγίστη,
ἐν δὲ μέσαις ἀκμαῖς μικρά, γήρᾳ δὲ πρὸς
    αὐτῷ
μορφῇ καὶ μεγέθει μείζων πάλιν ἐστὶν ἁπάν-
    των.

[16] From Alexis, ap. Athen. x. p. 449:

Οὐ θνητὸς, οὐδ' ἀθάνατος, ἀλλ' ἔχων τινὰ
σύγκρασιν, ὥστε μήτ' ἐν ἀνθρώπου μέρει,
μήτ' ἐν θεοῦ ζῆν, ἀλλὰ φύεσθαί τ' ἀεὶ
καινῶς, φθίνειν τε τὴν παρουσίαν πάλιν,
ἀόρατος ὄψιν, γνώριμος δ' ἅπασιν ὤν.

Glaucon, 'there is one thing we have forgotten. Suppose
the riddle is not solved, must the next try to guess?'
'Not so,' said Ctesiphon ; 'whoever can guess it first gets
the riband and kiss ; but if he guesses wrong, let him
drink the fine.' This was agreed to, and turning to
Euctemon, Charicles spoke thus :

> Know'st thou the creature, that a tiny brood
> Within her bosom keeps securely mewed?
> Though voiceless all, beyond the ocean wide
> To distant realms their still small voices glide.
> Far, far away, whome'er t' address they seek
> Will understand; yet no one hears them speak.[17]

This proved too much for Euctemon's acumen. Hard
as he tried to unriddle the mystery of the dumb speakers,
it was all of no avail, and he had to drink the fine. ' I
know!' cried Stephanos : ' it is the city ; and her children
are the speakers, who cry out so that their voice may be
heard far across the sea in Asia and Thrace.' A roar of
laughter followed. ' But, Stephanos,' said Charicles, ' did
you ever see an orator that was dumb ? he must then be
impeached thrice for *paranomia*, and condemned.'[18] ' Salt-
water,' screamed several voices ; and, though he tried hard
to get off, Stephanos was forced to drink off the goblet of
brine. ' I will tell you the meaning of the enigma,' Ctesiphon now said : ' it is a letter, and its children that
it conceals within it are the characters, which, mute
and voiceless, speak only to him to whom the letter is
addressed.' ' Bravo!' cried Glaucon ; ' how ever will you
find room on your head for all the *tœniæ* that you're
earning to-day ?' It was now Euctemon's turn. ' You'll
have to drink too,' said he to Nausicrates, who had mean-

---

[17] This riddle, one of the best
extant, is proposed in the *Sappho* of
Antiphanes ; Athen. x. p. 450 :

Ἔστι φύσις θήλεια βρέφη σώζουσ' ὑπὸ κόλ-
ποις
αὐτῆς. ὄντα δ' ἄφωνα βοὴν ἵστησι γεγωνὸν,

καὶ διὰ πόντιον οἶδμα καὶ ἠπείρου διὰ πάσης,
οἶς ἐθέλει θνητῶν· τοῖς δ' οὐ παρεοῦσιν
ἀκούειν
ἔξεστιν· κωφὴν δ' ἀκοῆς αἴσθησιν ἔχουσιν

[18] This too is all from Antiphanes.

time pulled one of the flute-players on to his couch ; ' tell
me what this is : '

> A man it is, and a man 'tis not ;
> 'Tis always carried, yet it legs hath got :
> Ordered to come to every dinner,
> Yet sure to come unbid, the sinner !
> Though fond of cups, ne'er drinks, but then
> It swallows more than any ten.

' Oh ! ' said Nausicrates, ' the subject is not far off.
That's no other than Stephanos.' ' I ? ' said the parasite ;
' that's false. Alack, nobody bids me to a banquet. The
world has grown so serious, that no one laughs at me
now.' [19] ' Quite right ! ' retorted Nausicrates ; ' as a wreath
it is ordered, and as a parasite you come uninvited, and
drink more than ten others.' Thus it went the round of
the guests, till at last it came to Stephanos. ' Now you
will stare,' said he :

> Nine moons roll by ere infants see the light ;
> Ten years the elephant, that beast of might,
> Bears in her vasty womb the embryo freight :
> But longer still, I bear a monster great ;
> Greater, still greater, stronger grows it ever,
> Yet, woe is me ! delivered am I never.[20]

' Egad ! ' exclaimed Glaucon, ' I had rather not have
guessed it either, that I might not have that beard of
thine to hug : but it is so very palpable ; for that it is
hunger which you carry in your paunch, we can all very
well comprehend.'

The fun was kept up in this manner for some time,
until the dancers, whom Lysiteles had ordered entered

---

[19] The complaint of Philip,
Xenoph. *Symp.* 1, 15 : 'Επεὶ γὰρ
γέλως ἐξ ἀνθρώπων ἀπόλωλεν, ἔρρει
τὰ ἐμὰ πράγματα. Πρόσθεν μὲν γὰρ
τούτου ἕνεκα ἐκαλούμην ἐπὶ τὰ
δεῖπνα, ἵνα εὐφραίνοιντο οἱ συνόντες,
δι' ἐμὲ γελῶντες· νῦν δὲ τίνος ἕνεκα
καὶ καλεῖ μέ τις. Cf. Plaut. *Capt.*
iii. 1, 10.

[20] A witticism of Gelasimus, Plaut.
Stich. i. 3, 14 :

Audivi sæpe (verbum) hoc volgo dicier
Solere elephantum gravidam perpetuos
    decem
Esse annos : ejus ex semine hæc certe est
    fames ;
Nam jam complures annos utero hæret meo

the saloon. A man, whose trade it was to exhibit such performances, led in a graceful girl, and a handsome lad, who were followed by a female flute-player.[21] The circle of couches was extended, and the *danseuse* advanced to the side which was left open. The boy took the cithara, and struck the strings to the accompaniment of the flute. The sound of the cithara presently ceased, the maiden took some hoops, and, as she danced to the tune of the flute, whirled them into the air, and caught them one after the other as they fell, with remarkable skill. More and more hoops were handed to her, till at least a dozen were hovering aloft betwixt her hands and the ceiling ; while the grace of her movements, together with the dexterity she evinced, elicited loud applause from the spectators.

‘ Really, Lysiteles,’ said Charicles, ‘ you are entertaining us right royally. Not only do you set before us a noble feast, but also provide pleasures for the eye and ear.’

‘ Pay attention,’ said the friendly host ; ‘ she will soon exhibit greater skill.’ A large hoop, set all round with pointed knives, was now brought in, and placed upon the ground. The damsel commenced dancing afresh, and threw a summersault [22] right into the centre of the hoop,

---

[21] Xenoph. *Symp.* 2, 1 ; from which well-known scene this is taken with slight alterations. The Syracusan appears to have presented himself at the house of Callias without previous arrangements, though as a matter of course he received money for the display of his company : ταῦτα δὲ καὶ ἐπιδεικνὺς, ὡς ἐν θαύματι, ἀργύριον ἐλάμβανεν.

[22] The simple way of dancing, which consists merely in rhythmical movement of the body, gave place at an early period to grotesque feats of agility ; thus even in Homer (*Il.* xviii. 605,) we meet with κυβιστῆρες, who threw regular summersaults, as we

learn from Plato, *Symp.* p. 190 : ὥσπερ οἱ κυβιστῶντες καὶ εἰς ὀρθὸν τὰ σκέλη περιφερόμενοι κυβιστῶσι κύκλῳ. At a later time, to excite additional interest, they jumped over pointed weapons. Plato, *Euthyd.* p. 294 : ἐς μαχαίρας γε κυβιστᾶν καὶ ἐπὶ τροχου δινεῖσθαι. See Xenophon, § 11 : μετὰ δὲ τοῦτο κύκλος εἰσηνέχθη περίμεστος ξιφῶν ὀρθῶν. εἰς οὖν ταῦτα ἡ ὀρχηστρὶς ἐκυβίστα τε καὶ ἐξεκυβίστα ὑπὲρ αὐτῶν. The στρόβιλος (Poll. iv. 101)seems to have been different from δινεῖσθαι ἐπὶ τροχοῦ, which would appear rather to be alluded to by Cic. *in Pison.* 10: ‘cumque ipse nudus in convivio saltaret, in quo ne tum quidem, cum illum suum saltatorium

and then out again, repeating the feat several times, till
the beholders grew quite nervous, and Nausicrates springing up, begged that a stop might be put to the perilous
game, lest the lovely creature should meet with an accident.
The boy next made his *début*, and danced with such art as
to give still greater effect to the matchless symmetry of his
form.   His whole figure was in expressive motion; it was
impossible to tell whether the hands, the neck, or the feet,
had most share in producing the impression which the
gracefulness of his postures worked among the spectators.[23]

---

versaret orbem, fortunæ rotam per-
timescebat.' Male and female κυβιστῆρες are represented in many antique
works of art. Cf. Tischbein, *Engravings from ancient Vases*, i. 60.

[23] Desirable as would be a discussion of the whole art of ancient
dancing, and for which moreover
there is no lack of material, still, as
most of the dances belong to the
theatrical representations and public
festivals, such an investigation would
be beyond the scope of the present
work. A few general remarks must
here suffice. The fundamental notion
of all Greek dancing is the bodily
expression of some inward feeling
(σώματος or νοήματος μίμησις); and
that which poetry effected by words
(λέξις), dancing had to do by movement, κίνησις. Hence the intimate
connection which was conceived to
subsist between the two arts, the
latter being supposed to be a development of the natural action accompanying recitation. Plato, *Leg.* vii.
p. 814 and 816. Lucian well observes
(*de Salt.* 69) that in no other art is
so equal an activity of the mind and
body required ; for the leading idea
must, as it were, penetrate the whole
body, in order that each of its movements may be a speaking expression

of it. Plutarch (*Symp.* ix. 15, 2,)
divides the action of the dance into
φορὰ, σχῆμα and δεῖξις, of which the
first two are related to one another
in the same way as φθόγγοι and
διαστήματα in Music, while of the
δεῖξις he observes, οὐ μιμητικόν ἐστιν,
ἀλλὰ δηλωτικὸν ἀληθῶς τῶν ὑποκειμένων. But the chief characteristic
of Grecian dancing, and that which
elevates it into a fine-art, is, that it
did not consist in mere senseless evo-
lutions, but was the outward representation of an inward idea, which all
the limbs took their due share in expressing. Xenoph. *Symp.* 2, 16:
ὅτι οὐδὲν ἀργὸν τοῦ σώματος ἐν τῇ
ὀρχήσει ἦν, ἀλλ' ἅμα καὶ τράχηλος
καὶ σκέλη καὶ χεῖρες ἐγυμνάζοντο.
Since too the arms and hands were the
most capable of expressive action,
dancers were termed χειρόσοφοι and
χειρονόμοι. Lucian, *Rhet. Præc.* 17;
and *Lexiph.* 14. So Plutarch, *Fragm.
de Anim.* 8: καὶ ὀρχεῖται ὁ ἄνθρωπος,
ἀλλὰ ταῖς χερσί. Cf. Antiph. ap.
Athen. iv. p. 134: οὐχ ὁρᾷς ὀρχού-
μενον ταῖς χερσὶ τὸν βάκηλον; But
the Greeks had also their *pirouettes*
and *battements*, as appears from Lucian, *de Salt.* 71: τὴν μὲν οὖν γε σύντο-
νον κίνησιν τῆς ὀρχηστικῆς καὶ στρο-
φας αὐτῆς. καὶ περιαγωγὰς, καὶ πηδή-
ματα, καὶ ὑπτιασμοὺς τοῖς μὲν ἄλλοις

Immense applause fell to his share also, and many of the company even preferred the boy's performance to that of the girl.

'But now,' said Glaucon, 'let them rest themselves. Lysiteles, order the *cottabos*,[24] that we too may display our skill.' 'Yes, the cottabos, the cottabos!' they all cried, and the word seemed to have exerted quite an electric effect upon the whole party. 'Ha!' cried Ctesiphon to Charicles, 'this is a Sicilian game; you must be a greater adept at it than any of us.' 'I have had some practice therein,' answered he; 'but the game is possibly a still greater favourite at Athens than in its native land.' 'But how shall we play it?' enquired one, 'with the *manes*, or

---

τερπνὰ εἶναι συμβέβηκεν ὁρῶσι.   See Poll. iv. 99 : ῥικνοῦσθαι, ὅπερ ἦν τὸ τὴν ὀσφὺν φορτικῶς περιάγειν.   Also Eustath. *ad Odyss.* ix. 376 : ἀναπηδήσαντες εἰς ὕψος πρὸ τοῦ κατενεχθῆναι ἐπὶ γῆν παραλλαγὰς πολλὰς τοῖς ποσὶν ἐποίουν. Though the art of dancing was so highly prized; though it served to give éclat to the festivals and shows; and though the guests of the symposia dearly loved to see the feats of a skilful *artiste*; still in private life it was little practised, and there seems to have arisen almost a prejudice against it; and though in Homer the sons of Alcinous gain renown by their dexterity in this accomplishment, yet, at a later period, it seems to have been considered incompatible with the dignity of a man. We know from Herodot. vi. 129, the opinion of Cleisthenes hereupon, and how Hippocleides, by suffering himself to be seduced to the dance, lost his bride; indeed it was usually looked upon as an admonitory symptom of incipient intoxication. So Alexis ap. Athen. iv. p. 134 :

ἄπαντες ὀρχοῦντ' εὐθὺς, ἂν οἴνου μόνον ὀσμὴν ἴδωσι.

To dance was also thought a symptom

of the highest state of transport that could be induced by wine. See Xenoph. *Hier.* 6, 2 ; hence the epithet παροίνιοι ὀρχήσεις, Athen. xiv. p. 629 : ἦν δέ τις καὶ Ἰωνικὴ ὄρχησις παροίνιος· and Lucian, p. 288 : τὸ Φρύγιον τῆς ὀρχήσεως εἶδος, τὸ παροίνιον καὶ σιμποτικόν, μετὰ μέθης γιγνόμενον, ἀγροίκων πολλάκις πρὸς αὔλημα γυναικεῖον ὀρχουμένων. Of these private dances there are but scanty notices; one however, called ἄνθεμα, is mentioned by Athen. *Ib.*: ἦν δὲ καὶ παρὰ τοῖς ἰδιώταις ἡ καλουμένη ἄνθεμα.   It was accompanied by these words :

Ποῦ μοι τὰ ῥόδα, ποῦ μοι τὰ ἴα, ποῦ μοι τὰ καλὰ σέλινα ;
Ταδὶ τὰ ῥόδα, ταδὶ τὰ ἴα, ταδὶ τὰ καλὰ σέλινα.

Social dances, in which both sexes might take part, such as Plato desires (*Leg.* vi. p. 771), do not appear to be mentioned anywhere. Consult however Aristoph. *Lysist.* 408 :

Ὦ χρυσοχόε, τὸν ὅρμον, ὃν ἐπεσκεύασας ὀρχουμένης μου τῆς γυναικὸς ἑσπέρας, ἡ βάλανος ἐκπέπτωκεν ἐκ τοῦ τρήματος.

[24] See Excursus on *The Games.*

the bowls?'   'With the manes,' decided Glaucon; 'there's
then more room to display one's skill.'

A tall candelabrum was set in the midst of the circle.
From this was suspended the balance, so adjusted, that
when the scale-pan descended smartly, it must strike the
head of the manes, placed beneath. Glaucon now stepped
forward, his arm bent, with the cylix in his hand, and
jerked the residue of the wine towards the scale. But only
a few drops hit it, and the plate merely oscillated a little
from side to side.   'He loves me not,' said he, retiring in
vexation to his seat.   'You should discharge it more in a
stream,' said Ctesiphon.   He took the cup, and the humid
volley flew like a ball into the scale-plate, which descended,

---

[25] See *Gallus*, p. 498, for the custom of wearing garlands on the breast,
ὑποθυμίδες or ὑποθυμιάδες. They

sometimes occur on monuments. See
Winkelm. *Monum. ined.* 200.

A vase-painting from Tischbein, *Engrav.* II. 45, supposed to represent Dionysos and
Ariadne. The chair (καθέδρα) is of a shape that frequently occurs; on it is a skin
(κώδιον) instead of a cushion: on the seat of Dionysos is a panther-skin; on his head is
a garland, and one also on his breast (ὑποθυμιάς).

and rang repeatedly against the bronze head beneath.
Thus the game went round again and again. At one
time the throw succeeded, at another it did not. Glaucon,
too, had the luck, eventually, to obtain a better augury as
to his loves ; but Ctesiphon surpassed them all.

  ' Yes,' said Glaucon, ' he understands throwing the wine
away, better than drinking it ; but now he must do the
latter also. A larger beaker there ! that will hold at least
ten cyathi, and also a breast-garland.[25] We will drink in
a circle. What's the harm if we do get a little wetted ? [26]
The earth drinks, the plants drink, and as they are re-
freshed by the water of heaven, so is the spirit of man
cheered by wine. It lulls our cares to sleep, as poppy-
juice and mandrake do the senses, and wakes us up to
merriment, as oil nourishes the flame.'[27] A large goblet
was brought, and seized by Glaucon, who turning to the
right, exclaimed : ' Friendship and love to thee, Ctesiphon : '[28]—he then emptied the measure, without drawing
breath. ' By my troth, you force me now to break my
determination,' exclaimed Ctesiphon. ' Oh ! don't be
alarmed,' cried Stephanos : ' I know of a first-rate specific ;
if you get drunk to-day, drink again to-morrow, that will
set you right.'[29] ' Eat bitter almonds,' said Euctemon ;
' that's a sure receipt for being able to stand much
liquor.'[30]

---

[26] A euphemism for being drunk
is βαπτίζεσθα.. So Plato. *Symp.*
p. 176 : καὶ γὰρ καὶ αὐτός εἰμι τῶν
χθὲς βεβαπτισμένων. One slightly
touched or hit was called ἀκροθώραξ
(Latinè. *ictus* or *saucius*). Plutarch,
Symp. iii. 8, 1 : τοῦ δὲ ἀκροθώρακος
ἔτι μὲν ἰσχύειν τὸ φανταστικὸν, ἤδη
δὲ τεταράχθαι τὸ λογιστικόν.

[27] Xenoph. *Symp.* 2, 24 : τῷ γὰρ
ὄντι ὁ οἶνος ἄρδων τὰς ψυχὰς τὰς
μὲν λύπας, ὥσπερ ὁ μανδραγόρας
τοὺς ἀνθρώπους, κοιμίζει, τὰς δὲ φι-
λοφροσύνας, ὥσπεο ἔλαιον φλόγα,
ἐγείρει.

[28] See the Excursus on *The Symposia.*

[29] οἴνῳ τὸν οἶνον ἐξελαύνειν, or
κραιπάλην κραιπάλῃ, was a proverb.
Antiphan. apud Athen. ii. p. 44 ; and
Plutarch, *de San. Tuend.* 11.

[30] Topers resorted to various de-
vices to prevent or allay drunkenness.
Aristotle recommends sweet wine,

Pledging now became the order of the day, and the party grew more uproarious. Several called for drinking horns.[31] Nausicrates held one of the flute-players locked in his embrace, the other knelt near Callicles, and beat the tabor ;[32] the cottabos was forgotten.

Meanwhile the dancers had gone away. At this moment their owner re-appeared, and informed the guests

---

cabbage, and olives. *Probl.* iii. 12, 17. and 35. This property of cabbage, ῥάφανος, or κράμβη, Athenæus endeavours to establish by sundry quotations from the poets (i. p. 34). Bitter almonds are also mentioned as a specific by Plutarch, *Symp.* i. 6, 4. Cf. Athen. ii. p. 52. It has been remarked in *Gallus*, p. 497, that the στέφανοι and ὑποθυμιάδες were also deemed antidotes against the effects of wine. According to Diod. Sic. iv. 4, it was on this account that Dionysos wore the μίτρα round his brow.

[31] The common forms of drinking-vessels which perpetually recur on monuments, are the κύλιξ, the φιάλη, and the καρχήσιον, or, what much resembles it, the κάνθαρος. The κύλιξ occurs most frequently, and when empty is generally held by one of its two handles. The φιάλη, a kind of saucer, without handle or foot, was laid on the palm of the left hand, whilst the right sometimes holds a drinking-horn. These were called κέρατα or ῥυτά, and occur in manifold shapes. The original and oldest shape, is that of the simple bullock's horn (Gerhard, *Auserl. Gr. Vasenb.* 16, 23, 25,) but the pointed end of this was afterwards transformed into the figures of divers beasts. Athenæus, (xi. p. 497,) according to the present text, dates its invention from the time of Ptolemy Philadelphus, though he had previously quoted the word ῥυτὰ from

Demosthenes (*in Mid.* p. 565). The supposition that something has been omitted in the passage of Athenæus, and that the account refers to the δικέρας, is very probable. The proper ῥυτὸν had an opening in the bottom, from which the wine poured into the mouth of the drinker. See the fresco, *Pitt. d'Ercol.* v. pl. 46 ; see also Dorotheos of Sidon ap Athen. *supra*; τὰ ῥυτὰ κέρασιν ὅμοια εἶναι, διατετρημένα δ᾽ εἶναι· ἐξ ὧν κρουννιζόντων λεπτῶς κάτωθεν πίνουσιν· ὠνομάσθαι δὲ ἀπὸ τῆς ῥύσεως. Inasmuch as the ῥυτὸν differed nothing in form from the κέρας, it is not surprising that the name is also applied to similarly shaped vessels having no opening. According to the kind of head in which the lower end of the *rhyton* terminated, so was it named, as for example, γρύψ, κάπρος, ἵππος, Πήγασος, and so on. See Woodcuts in Excursus on *The Meals*, and on *The Symposia* ; also Panofka *Recherches, etc.* pl. v.; Tischbein, *Collection of Engravings from Anc. Vases*, ii. 7. With regard to the material, see Note 22 to Scene viii.

[32] In a vase-painting, (Tischbein, ii. 55,) a παῖς, who is not one of the συμπόται, kneels at the lower end of the κλίνη, and beats the τύμπανον, whilst the αὐλητρίς, standing by the second κλίνη, blows the double flute. So also in Millin, *Peint. d. Vas. Gr.* i. 38. See Woodcuts in the Excursus on *The Symposia.*

that he was about to exhibit a mimic dance. Helena would receive Paris in her thalamos, and be persuaded to elope with him.[33] A gorgeous couch was here introduced, and then Helena entered in bridal array. All her motions and gestures indicated an inward struggle ; she was evidently expecting her lover. Gracefully she sank down on the purple coverlet of the bed, and when the flutes struck up a Phrygian melody, announcing the approach of the seducer, her bosom heaved with stronger emotion : she rose not to

---

[33] See Xenoph. *Symp.* 9, 2, where the Syracusan informs the company that Ἀριάδνη εἴσεισιν εἰς τὸν ἑαυτῆς τε καὶ Διονύσου θάλαμον. μετὰ δὲ τοῦθ' ἥξει Διόνυσος ὑποπεπτωκὼς παρὰ θεοῖς, καὶ εἴσεισι πρὸς αὐτὴν, ἔπειτα παιξοῦνται πρὸς ἀλλήλους. This announcement is like the prologue of the dramas, serving to prepare the spectator for what is to follow : though perfect μιμητικὴ ought not of course to require such an explanation beforehand. See Lucian, *de Salt.* 62. But this pompous prelude was quite to be expected from one like the Syracusan stroller. Such spectacles seem to have been common in Xenophon's day. So in Longus, (*Pastor,* ii. p. 67,) the fable of Pan and Syrinx, which had just before been related, is introduced as a mimic dance. Οἱ δὲ μάλα ταχέως ἀναστάντες ὠρχήσαντο τὸν μῦθον τοῦ Λάμωνος. ὁ Δάφνις Πᾶνα ἐμιμεῖτο, τὴν Σύριγγα Χλόη. ὁ μὲν ἱκέτευε πείθων, ἡ δὲ ἀμελυῦσα ἐμειδία. ὁ μὲν ἐδίωκε καὶ ἐπ' ἄκρων τῶν ὀνύχων ἔτρεχε, τὰς χηλὰς μιμούμενος· ἡ δὲ ἐνέφαινε τ ν κάμνουσαν ἐν τῇ φυγῇ, κ.τ.λ. But other dances, also, not exactly representing a legend, were ἐπιλήνιος ὄρχησις, for instance, were decidedly of a mimic character. *Ibid.* p. 66 : Δρύας δὲ, ἀνασ ὰς καὶ κελεύσας συρίζειν διονυσιακὸν μέλος, ἐπιλήνιον

αὐτοῖς ὄρχησιν ὠρχήσατο, καὶ ἐᾠκει ποτὲ μὲν τρυγῶντι, ποτὲ δὲ φέροντι ἀῤῥίχους, εἶτα πατοῦντι πρὸς βότρυς, εἶτα πληροῦντι τοὺς πίθους, εἶτα πίνοντι τοῦ γλεύκους. The interesting tale in Lucian, *de Salt.* 63, about the Cynic Demetrios, in Nero's time, shows that the mimic art must afterwards have reached a high degree of perfection. This man blamed and ridiculed mimic dances ; but a celebrated performer begged him first to see him dance, before he condemned the art. Upon this he represented, quite alone, (αὐτὸς ἐφ' ἑαυτοῦ), the story of the infidelity of Aphrodite, and so perfect was his delineation of the characters, that the Cynic cried out in astonishment, ἀκούω, ἄνθρωπε, ἃ ποιεῖς, οὐχ ὁρῶ μόνον, ἀλλά μοι δοκεῖς ταῖς χερσὶν αὐταῖς λαλεῖν. As Lucian remarks, (§37,) the mimic art took its subjects from the παλαιὰ ἱστορία only ; and this statement is confirmed by Xenophon's Ariadne, by the Ἀφροδίτης καὶ Ἄρεος μοιχεία, above referred to. and by the Ἑλένης ἁρπαγὴ, which, along with many other instances, is mentioned by Lucian, *Ib.* § 45. The words of Xenophon have been closely followed here, though the *dramatis personæ* have been changed. See Millingen, *Uned. Monum.* ii. 12, and Tischbein, *Homer nach antiken*, vii. 3.

meet him, stifling with difficulty her desire to do so. Paris
came dancing in, his eyes full of an expression of the ten-
derest affection. He sat down on the bed, and with supple
arms clasped the peerless form. And when she, full of
shame, and yet full of love, returned his fond embrace,
a universal tumult arose, and the spectators, unable to
contain themselves, swore it was no acting, but a reality ,
the boy and the girl loved each other, there was no doubt
about it.

'My sandals, slave !' cried Nausicrates. 'Whither
away ?' enquired Lysiteles. 'To see Antiphile, my soul's
idol.' Not a few of the guests rose to go ; though Glaucon, Euctemon, and Stephanos protested that they would
not budge an inch till the bowl was drunk out. 'Kindle
torches there,' cried Lysiteles,[34] 'and light the gentlemen
out.' 'Thanks to thee,' cried Charicles, extending to him
his hand ; 'my chaplet shall deck the Hermes before thy
door.'[35]

---

[34] Respecting the lighting-appa-
ratus, see Notes 1 and 5 to Scene IX.

[35] See the tale about Xenocrates,
Athen. x. p. 437: καὶ λαβὼν τὸν
χρυσοῦν στέφανον καὶ ἀναλύων τῷ

Ἑρμῇ τῷ ἱδρυμένῳ ἐπὶ τῆς αὐλῆς
ἐπέθηκεν, ὥσπερ εἰώθει καὶ τοὺς ἀν-
θινοὺς ἑκάστοτε ἐπιτιθέναι στεφάνους, ἑσπέρας ἀπαλλασσόμενος ἂς
αὐτόν.

SCENE THE SEVENTH.

THE TRITON.

IT was one of the last days of the month of Hecatombæon, and the sun's golden orb, rising above the ocean-mirror, began to illumine with its rays the pediment of the citadel, and the lofty statue of the tutelar goddess, who seemed gazing earnestly over her awakening city, as she looked towards the placid sea, where new-born light was still struggling with the mists of the morning. At this moment a ship, more beautiful than any before seen in the roads of Piræus, weighed anchor in the harbour. Though of an unusual size and stoutness of build, it glided lightly and buoyantly over the watery expanse, impelled vigorously by stalwart oarsmen, whose voices kept time in a rude sailor-chorus.[1] A fresh westerly breeze waved the purple

---

[1] In order that the oars might keep time, a sort of chaunt, κέλευσμα, was universally used, at least in larger ships ; a κελευστής, appointed for the purpose, leading, and the rowers chiming in. So Æschyl. *Pers.* 403 :

εὐθὺς δὲ κώπης ῥοθιάδος ξυνεμβολῇ
ἔπαισαν ἅλμην βρύχιον ἐκ κελεύσματος.

The κελευστής, inasmuch as the quickness or slowness of the time depended upon him, exercised considerable influence on the crew: οἷον καὶ ἐν τριήρει, ἔφη, ὅταν πελαγίζωσι καὶ δέῃ περᾶν ἡμερίους πλοῦς ἐλαύνοντας, οἱ μὲν τῶν κελευστῶν δύνανται τοιαῦτα λέγειν καὶ ποιεῖν, ὥστε ἀκονᾶν τὰς ψυχὰς τῶν ἀνθρώπων ἐπὶ τὸ ἐθελοντὰς πονεῖν, κ.τ.λ. Xenoph. *Œcon.* 21, 3 ; cf. *de Republ. Athen.* 1, 2 ; and Ovid, *Trist.* iv. 1. 7 :

In numerum pulsa brachia versat aqua.

That the κέλευσμα was sung, and was something more than mere beating time, is clear from Lucian, *Catapl.* 19, where Cyniscos, not possessing an obolus to pay Charon for his passage, offers as an equivalent his services at the oar. Charon accepting the proposal, he inquires : Ἦ καὶ ὑποκελεῦσαι δεήσει ; ΧΑΡ. Νὴ Δί᾽, ἤνπερ εἰδῇς κέλευσμά τι τῶν ναυτικῶν. ΚΥΝ. Οἶδα καὶ πολλά, ὦ Χάρων, τῶν ναυτικῶν. ἀλλ᾽ ὁρᾷς, ἀντεπηχοῦσιν οὗτοι δακρύοντες, ὥστε ἡμῖν τὸ ᾆσμα ἐπιταραχθήσεται. On which the Scholiast remarks : Ὡς ἐν τοῖς πλοίοις λέγειν εἰώθασι κελεῦσαι, ᾠδὴν δὲ λέγει ναυτικήν, ἣν ὑποκέλευσμα καλεῖ, διότι ἑνὸς καταρχομένου οἱ ἄλλοι ὑπήκουον τὸ ᾀδόμενον, ὥσπερ καὶ ὅτε τὴν ὀθόνην τῶν πλοίων μετὰ τῆς κεραίας ἐπὶ τὸν ἱστὸν ἀναφέρουσιν. So in the *Ranæ.* 205, the frogs sing the κέλευσμα. On board triremes a flute gave the time, and there was a τριηραύλης on purpose. Demosth. *de*

pennon, and swelled the white sail, which swept over the water like an impending cloud. The briny flood yielded to the deep-ploughing keel, while the spray bedewed the gaily painted sides, ever and anon spirting up to the gilded figure-head—a Triton with distended cheeks, blowing a conch, the tutelary genius of the vessel, and which thence derived its name.[2] The master, a merchant of Hera-

---

Coron. p. 270. So Dionysodoros, the flute-player, prided himself that his performances had never taken place on board a trireme. Diog. Laert. iv. 22. Cf. Max. Tyr. *Diss.* iii. p. 47.

[2] Every ship had its peculiar device to distinguish it, and this was usually called the παράσημον. What this was, its significance, and its position in the ship, are discussed by Scheffer, *de Milit. Nav.* ; and by Enschedé, in his *Diss. de tutelis et insignibus navium* ; though this refers more to Roman than to Grecian vessels. The παράσημον was sometimes the figure of a deity, sometimes of a beast, or other striking object; but where it was placed is doubtful. The passage in Æschylus, *Sept. Cont. Theb.* 193: τί οὖν; ὁ ναύτης ἆρα μὴ εἰς πρωραν φυγὼν πρύμνηθεν εὗρε μηχανὴν σωτηρίας; does not mean, as has been supposed, that the sailor flees to the images of the gods placed at the prow, but only, as the context shows, that he flies from one place to another, as the Theban women had done. No doubt the παράσημον is often mentioned as being at the πρώρα. Herod. iii. 37: ἔστι γὰρ τοῦ Ἡφαίστου τὤγαλμα τοῖσι Φοινικηΐοισι Παταΐκοῖσι ἐμφερέστατον, τοὺς οἱ Φοίνικες ἐν τῆσι πρώρῃσι τῶν τριήρεων περιάγουσι. And the Scholiast adds: θεοὶ οἱ Παταϊκοὶ Φοινικικοὶ ἐν ταῖς πρύμναις ἱδρυμένοι. So again, Herod. iii. 59: καὶ τῶν νεῶν καπρίους ἐχουσέων τὰς

πρώρας ἠκρωτηρίασαν, where the expression, πρῶραι κάπριαι does not refer to the figure-head, but to the peculiar build of the ships. Yet it is placed in the prow by Diod. Sic. iv. 47: Διαπλεῦσαι γὰρ αὐτόν φασιν οἱ μὲν ἐπὶ νεὼς προτομὴν ἐπὶ τῆς πρώρας ἐχούσης κριοῦ· and Schol. to Apoll. *Rhod.* ii. 168: ἐπὶ κριοπρώρου σκάφους ἔπλευσεν. Euripides, however, places it in the stern. *Iphig. in Aul.* 232:

χρυσέαις δ' εἰκόσιν
κατ' ἄκρα Νηρῇδες ἑστασαν θεαί,
πρύμναις σῆμ.' Ἀχιλλεΐου στρατοῦ.

Ibid. 263:

πρύμνας σῆμα ταυρόπουν ὁρᾶν
τὸν πάροικον Ἀλφεόν.

So also *Ib.* 240; and 248: τοῖς δὲ Κάδμος ἦν χρύσεον δράκοιτ' ἔχων ἀμφὶ ναῶν κόρυμβα. where the same place is doubtless meant, though the grammarians restrict the word κόρυμβα to the decorations of the prow, as opposed to ἄφλαστα. See *Etymol. M.* ἄφλαστον. The poets, however, do not seem to have adhered very rigorously to this distinction. Apollonius has, ii. 603: Ἔμπης δ' ὀφλάστοιο παρέθρισαν ἄκρα κόρυμβα. Cf. Eustath. *ad Iliad.* ix. 241.

Two things seem clear from the passages of Euripides: first, that every state had its peculiar σημεῖον or ἐπίσημον, which served to distinguish all ships belonging to it. Thus a Pallas was the σημεῖον of Athens, as appears

clea, strode the deck in high spirits.[3] Having disposed
of his cargo of wheat to advantage, he had freighted the
ship with oil, and sundry productions of Attic industry,
which he intended for the markets of Pontus. But he designed first to steer for Chios, to complete his cargo with
wine, and then to touch at Andros to land some passengers,
and to take in water, for which that rocky island was famed.
He was ruminating over his fortunate adventure, and

---

from the Scholion on the *Acharn.* 521:
Παλλάδια δὲ ἐν ταῖς πρώραις τῶν
τριήρων ἦν ἀγάλματά τινα ξύλινα τῆς
Ἀθηνᾶς καθιδρυμένα, ὧν ἐπεμελοῦντο
μέλλοντες πλεῖν. Thus we have Ἀττικὸν σημεῖον, Polyæn. *Strateg.* iii.
11, 11 ; and Περσικὰ σημεῖα, *Ib.* viii.
53, 1. In the second place this universally used ἐπίσημον was on the after
part of the ship, though the scholiast
just cited asserts the contrary. But
surely the poet is as good an authority
as the scholiast, who most likely was
under a misapprehension ; for, besides this general σημεῖον, which was
a national distinction, there was
doubtless in the fore-part of each ship
a special device, by means of which
the individual ships might be distinguished, and this was properly the
παράσημον. At least this was more
particularly the case with all private
ships, all of which would not perhaps
have the state-symbol also. From this
παράσημον the ship derived its name.
Lucian, *Navig.* 5 : καταντικρὺ δὲ ἀνά-
λογον ἡ πρώρα ὑπερβέβηκεν ἐς τὸ
πρόσω μηκυνομένη, -ὴν ἐπώνυμον τῆς
νεὼς θεὸν ἔχουσα, τὴν Ἶσιν ἑκατέρωθεν. Thus in the bas-relief referred
to in Note 4, a helmeted Minerva appears on the πρώρα as a παράσημον.
With this compare Ovid, *Trist.* i.
10, 1. That every ship had its proper
name, is expressly stated by Palæph.
29 : ὄνομα δὲ ἦν τῷ πλοίῳ Πήγασος,
ὡς καὶ νῦν ἕκαστον τῶν πλοίων ὄνομα
ἔχει. This name was written upon the

ship. Poll. i. 86 : τὸ δὲ ὑπὲρ τὸ προῦχον
ἀκροστόλιον ἢ πτυχὶς ὀνομάζεται,
καὶ ὀφθαλμός, ὅπου καὶ τοὔνομα τῆς
νεὼς ἐπιγραφουσι. Also Eustath. *ad
Iliad.* xiv. 717 : πτυχὴ δέ ἐστιν, ὅπου
οἵ τε ὀφθαλμοὶ ζωγραφοῦνται καὶ τὸ
τῆς νεὼς ὄνομα ἐπιγράφεται. See
also Hippocr. *Epist.* iii. p. 786 ; and
Palæph. 30: ἐγέγραπτο δὲ ἐπὶ τοῦ
πλοίου "ἵπποι ὑπόπτεροι." Such
an inscription may have often served
without any further παράσημον.

Fritzsche infers from Aristoph,
Ran. 48, that the names of living persons were given to ships; but perhaps
the poet only uses the two-fold meaning of ἐπιβατεύειν, to give an unexpected turn to the dialogue. *Ran.*
1433, has also been adduced, though
with very little probability, to show
there were ships which bore the names
of Cleocritos and Cinesias. The thing
is not impossible in itself, even though
no instance could be adduced ; but that
triremes were ever named after private
individuals does not appear probable.

---

[3] The ships of the ναύκληροι were
partly decked, partly not. Antipho, *de
Cæde Herod.* p. 715 : ἐν ᾧ μὲν γὰρ
ἐπλέομεν, ἀστέγαστον ἦν τὸ πλοῖον,
εἰς ὃ δὲ μετέβημεν, ἐστεγασμένον.
τοῦ δὲ ὑετοῦ ἕνεκα ταῦτ' ἦν. Cf.
Alciphr. *Epist.* i. 12. The passengers
resorted mostly to the deck, κατά-
στρωμα, which is opposed to the κοίλη
ναῦς. Herod. iii. 118, 119 ; Lucian
Navig. 5.

calculating how far the profits of the voyage would go
towards covering the expense of his new vessel. The passengers too—what with the fineness of the weather, and
the prospect of a quick passage—were in excellent spirits,
and inhaled with great zest the fresh morning air; some
chiming in with their voices, others beating time with their
feet to the monotonous chaunt of the crew.

Aft, near the cheniscos,[4] where stood the steersman, who
grasped the rudder with practised hands, were two young
men, who complacently surveyed the vessel, and at their
side was a third, who seemed in less cheerful mood, and
appeared to gaze regretfully at the city which was rapidly
receding from his view. 'A noble bark,' exclaimed the one,
'it must be a quarter of a stadium in length,[5] and, as I am
told, it draws a depth of water equal to its breadth. Only
look at that giant mast, that mighty sail, and the beautiful
arrangement of the rigging! And yet it obeys the helm
as readily as a fishing-boat.' 'At any rate,' replied the
person thus addressed, 'we have done better in waiting a

---

[4] The χηνίσκος, properly a πρω-
τομὴ χηνός, or goose-neck, is often
mentioned as a part of the ship, but it
is doubtful whereabouts it was. The
Etymol. M. says: χηνίσκος τὸ τῆς
πρώρας μέοος, οὗ ἀπήρτηνται αἱ
ἄγκυραι, ὃ καὶ τῆς τρόπιδός ἐστιν
ἀρχή. εἰσὶ δ' οἳ μᾶλλον τὸ τῆς πρύ-
μνης ἔφασαν ἄκρον, πρὸς ὃ ἐπιζεύ-
γνυνται αἱ ἐπωτίδες τῆς νεώς. In
several ancient seals it is distinctly
placed in the fore, in others in the
after part of the vessel, sometimes at
both ends; now turned outwards, and
then again bent inwards towards the
ship. It appears most probable, however, that its proper place was the
after-part, πρύμνα. Lucian, Navig.
5: ὡς δὲ ἡ πρύμνα μὲν ἐπανέστηκεν
ἠρέμα καμπύλη, χρυσοῦν χηνίσκον
ἐπικειμένη, and Ver. Hist. ii. 41: ὅτε
γὰρ ἐν τῇ πρύμνῃ χηνίσκος ἄφνω
ἐπτερύξατο καὶ ἀνεβόησε. Cf. Eu-

stath. ad Iliad. vii. 86; ad Odyss. xii.
408; see also Plate vi. 2, in Goro v.
Agyagfalva's Wanderungen durch
Pompeii, which represents an allego-
rical relief from Pompeii, in which the
χηνίσκος is conspicuously represented
in the stern. As appears from the
above-cited passage from Lucian, it
was gilt, as well as the παράσημα, with
which, however, it must not be confounded. See also Lucian, Jup. Trag.
47.

[5] It may be doubted whether, at
the time in question, merchant-ships
were built of such a size, but the one
described by Lucian, (Navig. 5,) was
considerably larger: ἡλίκη ναῦς. εἴκοσι καὶ ἑκατὸν πήχεων ἔλεγεν ὁ
ναυπηγὸς τὸ μῆκος, εὖρος δὲ ὑπὲρ τὸ
τέταρτον μάλιστα τούτου καὶ ἀπὸ
τοῦ καταστρώματος ἐς τὸν πυθμένα,
ᾗ βαθύτατον κατὰ τὸν ἄντλον, ἐννέα
πρὸς τοῖς εἴκοσι.

few days, than if we had trusted our lives to that rickety craft of the Byzantine. The owner, too, is more to my taste; his whole bearing inspires confidence; and at sea, you know, it makes all the difference, whether you are in the hands of an honest man, or of a rogue who in the hour of danger looks only to his own safety, and leaves the rest to shift for themselves.' 'I take him to be honest enough,' said the first; 'but in any exigency, I should not make so sure of his constancy. Why at such a period even the firm ties of friendship will relax; in the desire of self-preservation every other consideration is lost, and the instinctive love of life overwhelms all feeling for another.'[6] 'After all,' interposed the third, who had joined the speakers, 'I am a mere fool for exposing myself so needlessly to the dangers and privations of a voyage. You, Charicles, have a considerable sum to receive at Andros; and you, Ctesiphon, intend to sell an estate of yours at Chios;[7] whilst I have been mad enough to go with you, for no earthly purpose, but just to see the vintage of the noble Chian wine (which I should do far better to drink quietly at home at Athens); and here I am rolling about on this ship till I positively feel quite queer, instead of rocking lovingly and merrily on the knee of my Antiphile. And, what is worse than all, you have dawdled and dawdled, till we shall certainly arrive too late for the vintage.' 'Be easy on that score, Nausicrates,' answered Charicles, with a smile; 'with this wind we can make Andros before night-fall:[8] to-morrow you will be at Chios, and in ten or twelve days, again, perhaps, embrace your Antiphile.'

Meanwhile the Triton glided swiftly along the coast of

---

[6] From Eugène Sue's *Salamander*: cf. Achill. Tat. iii. 3.

[7] See Terent. *Phorm.* iv. 3, 75.

[8] From what Bröndsted says of his passage to Ceos, it must have been easy to go from Athens to Andros in a day. In Homer's time only four days were required from Lesbos to the Peloponnese. *Odyss.* iii. 180:

τέτρατον ἦμαρ ἔην, ὅτ' ἐν Ἄργεϊ νῆας ἐΐσας
Τυδεΐδεω ἕταροι Διομήδεος ἱπποδάμοιο
στῆσαν.

Attica; the sun rose higher in the sky, and the passengers commenced preparations for breakfast. The three friends followed their example, though Nausicrates was a long time in settling the preliminaries. While the other passengers deposited themselves without more ado on the bare deck, he made his two slaves unpack his travelling couch, and spread over it a costly carpet, and arrange the cushions with exquisite nicety. This, however, would not do—the sun was too hot for him, so the couch had to be shifted to a position where the sail afforded a shade.[9] At length he succeeded in selecting the spot where he could proceed to breakfast with the least possible annoyance.

The passengers were so occupied in animated conversation, that the vessel's speed gradually diminished without their perceiving it. The breeze, at first so fresh, flagged by degrees, and the hour of noon brought a dead calm. The sail hung loosely from the mast, and the rowers had to labour harder with the oar. A pale streak in the sky to the south-east, whose breadth kept gradually increasing, made the practised steersman uneasy. 'We shall have a storm,' said he to the owner, who had approached him; 'let us steer for Ceos, and take refuge in its safe harbour.' The Heracleote thought otherwise. 'There will be rain,' said he, 'that's all; and, before it comes, we shall perhaps have got to Andros. Put your helm to larboard, and keep close along Euboea, so that in case of accident we may be within reach of the havens of Carystos or Geraestos. But I have no fear.' The steersman shook his head doubtfully, and the event too soon proved the truth of his prediction. The storm gathered with an incredible rapidity; the heavens, lately so serene, became shrouded in sombre grey;

---

[9] The Attic fopling in Alciphron, *Epist.* i. 12, is the original of this sketch: οὐ γὰρ ἀνεχόμενος τῶν ξύλων τῆς ἁλιάδος ἐπί τε ταπήτων τινῶν ξενικῶν καὶ ἐφεστρίδων κατακλινεὶς (οὐ γὰρ οἶός τε ἔφασκεν εἶναι κεῖσθαι, ὡς οἱ λοιποί, ἐπὶ τῶν καταστρωμά- των, τὴν σανίδα οἶμαι νομίζων λίθου τραχυτέραν) ᾔτει παρ' ἡμῶν, σκιὰν αὐτῷ μηχανήσασθαι, τὴν τοῦ ἱστίου σινδόνα ὑπερπετάσαντας, ὡς οὐδαμῶς οἶός τε ὢν φέρειν τὰς ἡλιακὰς ἀκτῖνας.

single puffs broke the calm, and heralded the coming tempest.

The helmsman altered the ship's course, steering right down on Euboea; but it was too late. With mad fury the hurricane burst forth; the waves upheaved themselves in wrathful strife, and black clouds turned the bright day into a twilight broken only by the fitful gleam of the lightning athwart the sky.[10] In vain did the sailors attempt to take in the canvas. On one side only they succeeded;[11] and this but increased the danger, for the tempest pounced furiously on the other portion of the sheet, and nearly threw the vessel on her beam-ends.

Wilder and wilder blew the gale; the waves rose mountain-high; at one moment the Triton sank into the abyss, the next she was in the clouds. The creaking of the mast, the snapping of the rigging, the shouts of the crew, the lamentations of the women who were on board, all increased the horrors of the scene. The rain poured down in such torrents that nothing could be seen; no one knew which way the vessel was being hurried; and all thought that the next second she would strike upon a rock. At length a gust fiercer than the rest seized the mast, which cracked and broke. 'She's sprung a leak,' cried several voices; 'over with the cargo!' 'Open the oil-jars,' exclaimed a voice above the rest, 'and smooth the sea.'[12] A host of hands forthwith set to work to lighten the ship:

---

[10] The whole description of the shipwreck is taken from Achill. Tat. iii. 1, seqq.

[11] Achill. Tat. *supra*. καὶ ὁ κυβερνήτης περιάγειν ἐκέλευε τὴν κεραίαν. καὶ σπουδῇ περιῆγον οἱ ναῦται πῇ μὲν τὴν ὀθόνην ἐπὶ θάτερα συνάγοντες ἄνω τοῦ κέρως βίᾳ (τὸ γὰρ πνεῦμα σφοδρότερον ἐμπεσὸν ἀνθέλκειν οὐκ ἐπέτρεπεν), πῇ δὲ πρὸς θάτερον μέρος, φυλάττοντες τοῦ πρόσθεν μέτρου, καθ' ὃ συνέβαινεν

εὔριον εἶναι τῇ περιαγωγῇ τὸ πνεῦμα. The whole passage, however, is somewhat obscure, and seems to suppose a disposition of the sails and yards, to which we are unaccustomed. In the relief above referred to, the yards, and apparently the sails also, seem to consist of two portions, united by thongs or ropes.

[12] The belief that the sea might be calmed by pouring oil upon it, is of ancient date. Plutarch, *Quæst.*

earthen vessels and chests were pitched overboard. The
owner yielded to necessity, and consigned his own venture,
along with the passengers' luggage, to the tender mercies
of the deep. But all was of no avail, the ship sank deeper
and deeper ; and there being now no hope of saving her, the
owned signed to the helmsman to have the boat got ready.
He himself was the first to spring into it, followed by the
helmsman and crew, who immediately began to cut the
rope.[13]

A fierce struggle now arose between those in the boat and
the passengers left on board the ship, who struck at them
with oars and poles, trying to prevent the cutting of the
rope, which would destroy their last faint hope of escape ;
whilst the others as obstinately defended themselves, fearful
that the boat would sink if more got into it. Meanwhile,
the powerful hand of Ctesiphon had grasped the rope,
drawing the boat close alongside the Triton. 'Quick!
Charicles,' cried he ; and then leapt after his friend, drag-
ging with him the trembling Nausicrates. Several essayed
to follow, but few only succeeded ; most of them fell short
into the sea. Severed by axes, the rope at length gave
way, and the boat parted from the ship amid the loud
curses of those left behind. Too soon were these destined

Nat. 12, discusses the question: διὰ
τί τῆς θαλάττης ἐλαίῳ καταρραινομέ-
νης γίνεται καταφάνεια καὶ γαλήνη ;

[13] Achill. Tat. iii. 3 : Τέλος δ' ὁ
κυβερνήτης ἀπειπὼν ῥίπτει μὲν τὰ
πηδάλια ἐκ τῶν χειρῶν, ἀφίησι δὲ τὸ
σκάφος τῇ θαλάσσῃ καὶ εὐτρεπίζει
ἤδη τὴν ἐφολκίδα καὶ τοῖς ναύταις
ἐμβαίνειν κελεύσας τῆς ἀποβάθρας
ἦρχεν. Οἱ δὲ εὐθὺς κατὰ πόδας ἐξήλ-
λοντο. Ἔνθα δὴ καὶ τὰ δεινὰ ἦν καὶ
ἦν μάχη χειροποίητος. Οἱ μὲν γὰρ
ἐπιβάντες ἤδη τὸν κάλων ἔκοπτον ὃς
συνέδει τὴν ἐφολκίδα τῷ σκάφει,
τῶν δὲ πλωτήρων ἕκαστος ἔσπευδε
μεταπηδᾶν, ἔνθα καὶ τὸν κιβερνητην

ἑωράκεσαν ἐφέλκοντα τὸν κάλων· ο,
δὲ ἐκ τῆς ἐφολκίδος μεταβαίνειν οὐκ
ἐπέτρεπον κ.τ.λ. Ἔνθα δή τις ἀπὸ
τῆς νεὼς νεανίσκος εὔρωστος λαμβά-
νεται τοῦ κάλω καὶ ἐφέλκεται τὴν
ἐφολκίδα καὶ ἦν ἐγγὺς ἤδη τοῦ σκάφους. ηὐτρεπίζετο δὲ ἕκαστος, ὡς,
εἰ πελάσειε, πηδήσων εἰς αὐτήν. Καὶ
δύο μὲν ἢ τρεῖς ηὐτύχησαν οὐκ ἀναι-
μωτί· πολλοὶ δὲ ἀποπηδᾶν πειρώ-
μενοι ἐξεκυλίσθησαν τῆς νεὼς κατὰ
τῆς θαλάσσης. Ταχὺ γὰρ τὴν ἐφολκίδα ἀπολύσαντες οἱ ναύται πελέκει
κόψαντες τὸν κάλων, τὸν πλοῦν
εἶχον, ἔνθα αὐτοὺς ἦγε τὸ πνεῦμα·
οἱ δὲ ἐπὶ τῆς νεὼς ἐπηρῶντο κατα-
δῦναι τὴν ἐφολκίδα.

to be accomplished; for at the very moment when the Triton sank into her watery grave, and the last cry of agony burst from the perishing souls on board, a giant billow overwhelmed the skiff itself, and buried in the waves all but a few who clutched desperately at pieces of wreck which floated round them.

Pallidly rose the sun on the succeeding morn, throwing a dim and melancholy light over the devastations of the previous day, which were but too plainly indicated by the stranded wreck, and the corpses of the drowned mariners which had been cast on shore. The storm had ceased, although the swell had not yet subsided, and the breakers still foamed furiously on the rocky strand of Euboea.[14] In a tiny bay, sheltered from the more savage violence of the waves by projecting rocks, lay, high on the beach, what seemed to be the lifeless body of a young man. Beside it knelt a slave, who was endeavouring to restore animation to the stiffened limbs, by diligent chafing and rubbing. He now and then would cast a glance at the pale and beautiful countenance, and wipe away the foam and salt water that trickled down on it from the fair-coloured locks.

While he was thus engaged, a third figure appeared on the cliffs above. To judge from his apparel, his net and basket, he was a slave, despatched to secure the finny requisites for his master's breakfast, and at the same time he was apparently spying about, on his own account, for any chance booty that the storm of yesterday might have thrown in his way.[15] On perceiving the group

---

[14] Τὰ Κοῖλα τῆς Εὐβοίας was that part of the coast of Euboea which reached from Chalcis to Geraestus. Strabo, x. 1: ὅτι τῆς Εὐβοίας τὰ Κοῖλα λέγουσι τὰ μεταξὺ Αὐλίδος καὶ τῶν περὶ Γεραιστὸν τόπων. It was a very dangerous spot for shipping. Dio Chrysost. Or. vii. p. 222: καὶ ταῦτ᾽, εἶπεν, ἔστι τὰ Κοῖλα τῆς Εὐβοίας, ὅπου κατενεχθεῖσα ναῦς οὐκ ἂν ἔτι σωθείη. σπανίως δὲ σώζονται καὶ τῶν ἀνθρώπων τινές.

[15] The *Rudens* of Plautus served as

below, he descended, impelled by curiosity, and approaching the slave, who was so intently engaged that he had not yet observed him, demanded what he was about. 'Heaven be praised that you have come!' exclaimed the other springing to his feet. 'Our ship was lost in the storm · we were thrown up here on a piece of the wreck, and my lord has almost perished with wet and fatigue. Help me to try and revive him.' 'Blockhead!' said the fisherman . ' and so you throw away your chance of becoming free? He sleeps sound enough; let him alone; and be off yourself whither you will. To-day you save his life, and to-morrow, perhaps, you will wear chain and collar. Away, I say. You will never have such a chance again.' 'So you would advise,' answered the slave, 'and so would many more; but may Zeus forfend that I should desert my lord, whom I played with when we were boys, and lived with in a foreign land. Besides, 'tis better to live with a good and generous master, than, with the empty name of free man, to drag on a miserable life. But now, no more of that; your master, perhaps, lives close at hand?' 'A short stadium hence,' replied the fisherman; 'his country-house is just behind the cliff.' 'Run, then,' cried the slave; 'run and say that a noble Athenian has been shipwrecked; pray him to send hither wine and dry garments. Make haste, and you shall be richly rewarded for your trouble.' The fisherman shook his head; but setting down his net and basket, he disappeared.

The slave redoubled his exertions, and the wan limbs, he fancied, began to reassume something of the colour of life. He next applied his cheek to the nostrils and mouth, laying his hand at the same time on the heart of his master. 'He breathes,' cries the slave, bounding up in

---

the original in the following picture. The house of Dæmones is in like manner near the sea; so likewise Gripus has gone out to fish on his master's account: iv. 1, 6:

Sed Gripus servus noster quid rerum gerat, Miror, de nocte qui abiit piscatum ad mare.

See statues of fishermen with the basket in *Mus. Pio-Clem.* II. 32, 33.

ecstasy; ' and I feel his heart still beats, feebly though it
be!' Snatching up a handful of wild thyme, he rubbed it
briskly in his hands, and held it before the face. The
youth moved, and for a moment opened his eyes, but closed
them again. 'Charicles!' cried the honest slave, 'awake!'
The other again unclosed his eyelids, and attempted to
raise himself. 'Manes,' said he, with feeble accents, ' is it
you? Where are we?' 'Safe,' answered the slave, 'and
on dry land.' 'And Ctesiphon?' enquired his master.
Manes turned away his face, and was silent. 'Poor Ctesiphon! poor Nausicrates!' sobbed the youth, the tears
flowing from his eyes. 'May be, they are also saved,'
interposed the slave; 'who knows? As I was hauling you
on to the board which brought us hither, I saw them
grasp hold of a fragment of the stern, big enough to bear
them both.' 'You have saved my life, Manes,' said Charicles, taking hold of his attendant's hand; 'the moment
we return to Athens you shall be free.' 'Yet allow me to
remain in your house,' replied the faithful domestic. 'But
now, pray, be mindful of yourself. Let me lead you where
the sun has warmed the air.'

While the youth, assisted by Manes, was endeavouring
to rise, the fisherman returned. He brought with him
wine and bread in a basket, and was followed by two other
slaves with blankets and dry clothes. On hearing of the
disaster, the kind-hearted owner of the neighbouring villa
had ordered the survivors to be conveyed to his abode,
where a bath was being prepared with all speed. The
warm dry clothing and the genial heat of the wine soon
infused new strength and animation into the chilled limbs
of Charicles; but he sat silent and abstracted, recalling to
himself the scene of yesterday, and sick at heart with the
loss of his dearest friend on earth.

Manes, reinvigorated by his share of the dry clothing
and restoratives, had mounted the projecting cliff, and was
gazing seaward over the still agitated waters. His eye
became suddenly riveted on a dark object, that seemed

gradually nearing the shore, urged onward by the current
He called the fisherman, and asked him what it was. 'A
piece of timber,' replied the man; 'belike a bit of your
ship.' 'No such thing,' retorted Manes, who could now
discern more plainly the outline of the object; 'it is a boat.
Surely no fishermen have ventured out in such weather?'
'By Poseidon, they would be mad, an' they had; may be
'tis some fishing-boat that the storm has driven out to sea.'
'No, no!' cried Manes; 'there is somebody aboard of her,
rowing hard in to shore.' The skiff drew nearer, and three
men became plainly distinguishable on board. Two of
them had oars; the third sat between them doing nothing.
At this moment Charicles, attracted by the conversation,
approached the speakers. As he gazed fixedly at the
advancing skiff, a presentiment came over him, which he
scarce dared confess even to himself. And now the boat
essayed to land; but as it approached, it was repeatedly
borne back again by the violence of the surf, till at last a
prodigious wave carried the frail bark, far better than the
expertest steersmen could have hoped, right over the
rocks, on to the shallowest place upon the beach.[16] Out
sprang the man who stood in the bows, and held her fast
with one had, while with his other he assisted a second
person, apparently weak and exhausted, to land; the third
then followed, violently pushing out the boat, which was
immediately stove in upon the rocks. 'That's Ctesiphon,
as I live!' cried Manes. 'I almost think you are right,'
said Charicles. 'So surely as you are Charicles,' replied
the domestic; 'and Nausicrates is with him.' 'Away
then,' cried the master; 'run and guide them hither.'

Manes was right: when the boat upset, Ctesiphon and
Nausicrates had clung to the ship's rudder, which had been
unshipped and was floating by; the steersman had done

---

[16] Plaut. *Rudens*, i. 2, 75:

Ut afflictantur miseræ! Euge, euge, per-
  bene!
Ab saxo avortit fluctus ad litus scapham,
Neque gubernator umquam potuit rectius.

Cf. Dio Chrysost. *supra*: τὸ μὲν δὴ
ἀκάτιον εἰς τραχύν τινα αἰγιαλὸν
ὑπὸ τοῖς κρημνοῖς ἐκβαλόντες διέ-
φθειραν.

the same, and thus had they endured through the horrors of the night, in momentary danger of being swept off and engulphed by every wave. As morning dawned, Ctesiphon espied, floating not far off, an empty fishing-skiff, which had, probably, been loosened from its moorings by the fury of the tempest, and thus carried out to sea. ' A God-send for our rescue !' he cried, as he dashed into the sea, gallantly cleaving the flood with his brawny arms. The steersman followed his example, and they both reached the skiff in safety, and managed to assist Nausicrates, whose strength was utterly exhausted, in getting aboard. At first they tried to reach the coast of Attica, but were forced to abandon the attempt ; so, resigning themselves to the current, they were carried by it to the Eubœan coast, where, to their astonishment and delight, they found the friend whom they supposed had perished ; and they soon received, under a hospitable roof, that attention which their exhausted frames required.

They spent two days at the country-house in recruiting; and then, the weather having cleared, and the clouds, which had enveloped the peaks of Eubœa,[17] being dissipated, the three friends debated as to what was next to be done. ' Carystos is not far hence,' said Ctesiphon ; ' we had best take ship there, and return at once to Athens.' ' Not for worlds !' exclaimed Nausicrates ; ' I'll not tempt the for-bearance of Poseidon a second time. I shall take the shortest route to Athens, and once there, catch me ever again venturing one foot out to sea ! if I do, I give Poseidon leave to treat me as he just now threatened to do.[18] But how can I possibly travel to Athens in such a plight as this ? I have lost all my baggage, besides two

---

[17] Dio Chrysost. *supra*: βουλοί-μην δ' ἂν ἔγωγε καὶ μετὰ πέντε ἡμέ-ρας λῆξαι τὸν ἄνεμον· ἀλλὰ οὐ ῥᾴδιον, εἶπεν, ὅταν οὕτω πιεσθῇ τὰ ἄκρα

τῆς Εὐβοίας ὑπὸ τῶν νεφῶν, ὥς γε νῦν κατειλημμένα ὁρᾷς.

[18] Plaut. *Most.* ii. 2, 1.

slaves, of whom one alone cost me five minæ, the last new moon but one. That would not so much matter, had but my Persian carpet been saved. As it is, I have not a garment fit to appear in, and you yourselves are no better off. Listen, therefore, to my advice; it can't be more than two days' journey to Chalcis, and a friend of mine lives there, who pays me an annual visit at the Dionysia. We will make use of him; he shall provide us with new suits, and then we will start for home.'

This proposal was agreed to; and though Ctesiphon had his laugh at the timidity of the un-Salaminian[19] Nausicrates, he allowed that under existing circumstances it would be insane to think of continuing their journey. Their amiable host provided them with a vehicle drawn by mules, and he himself accompanied them for some distance on horseback.[20]

Nausicrates' scheme was doomed to be frustrated, for he discovered that his friend was from home, having gone for his health to the medicinal spa of Ædepsos, distant about a day's journey; and that a fortnight might elapse before he returned. Charicles and Ctesiphon now proposed crossing over at once to the mainland; but their friend was of a different opinion. ' I have often,' said he, 'heard my friend talk with rapture of the delightful mode of living at these baths; and now that we are so near, it would be unpardonable not to pay them a visit. Listen,—these rings are of great value; I will pawn them,[21] and we can thus procure a scanty wardrobe, and then proceed to visit

---

[19] 'Ασαλαμίνιος. Aristoph. *Ran.* 204.

[20] Æschin. *de Falsa Leg.* p. 282. See Note 6 to Sc. 1.

[21] Money was frequently lent on pledges; for instance even on a horse, while things of less value were often left in pawn for small sums. Aris-

toph. *Plut.* 450:

πο̃ιον γὰρ οὐ θώρακα, ποίαν ἀσπίδα
οὐκ ἐνέχυρον τίθησιν ἡ μιαρωτάτη;

At Athens it was forbidden to pawn arms. See Böckh's *Public Econ. of Athens,* p. 129. Aristoph. *Lysist.* 113:

κἂν εἴ με χρείη τοὔγκυκλον
τουτι καταθεῖσαν ἐκπιεῖν αὐθημερὸν,

appears to allude to pawning clothes.

my friend at the spa.' He expatiated so alluringly on the
pleasures of the spot, that they actually decided on proceeding thither—and in truth, Ædepsos[22] was a place that
well merited even a more distant pilgrimage. Besides its
many natural beauties, which made it a charming place
of residence, the celebrity of the waters had caused the
erection of several handsome dwelling-houses and other
edifices. The neighbourhood abounded in game of all sorts,
and the variety of choice fish caught in the deep limpid
bays of the coast was well worthy of the table of the most
fastidious epicure. Many resorted to the place, not merely
from Eubœa, but from the mainland ; and whilst some
came to reap benefit from the waters, the sole object of
others was the pleasant society and the luxurious mode of
life. The height of the season was towards the end of
spring; but, though autumn was now beginning, there
was no lack of visitors.

The next morning found the three friends already on
their road to Ædepsos. Although no admirer of pedes-
trian excursions, yet on this occasion Nausicrates was very
content to overlook the fatigue of such a manner of travelling, in the feeling of security he derived from being
again on *terra firma*, and in the anticipation of the expected pleasures of the far-famed spot.

---

[22] This may perhaps be an ana-
chronism. No evidence has been adduced to show that at so early a period
any one of the numerous spas of
Greece was able to attract from a
distance those who were in pursuit of
health or of amusement. Afterwards,
however, Ædepsos became quite a
Grecian Baiæ. Plutarch, *Sympos.*iv.4,
gives the following account of it: Τῆς
Εὐβοίας ὁ Αἴδηψος, οὗ τὰ θερμὰ,
χωρίον ἐστὶν αὐτοφυὲς πολλὰ πρὸς
ἡδονὰς ἔχον ἐλευθερίους, καὶ κατεσκευασμένον οἰκήσεσι καὶ διαίταις,
κοινὸν οἰκητήοιον ἀποδέδεικται τῆς

Ἑλλάδος, κ.τ.λ. In later times,
indeed, numerous thermæ are mentioned : Λεβεδίοις δὲ τὰ λουτρὰ ἐν τῇ
γῇ θαῦμα ἀνθρώποις ὁμοῦ καὶ ὠφέλεια
γίνεται. Ἔστι δὲ καὶ Τηΐοις ἐπὶ τῇ
ἄκρᾳ λουτρὰ τῇ Μακρίᾳ, κ.τ.λ.
Pausan. vii. 5, 5. Thus too we read of
one in Elis : λουομένοις δὲ ἐν τῇ πηγῇ
καμάτων τέ ἐστι καὶ ἀλγημάτων
παντοίων ἰάματα. Pausan. vi. 22, 4.
Warm springs were in an especial
manner held sacred, as appears from
Aristotle, *Probl.* xxiv. 19, where he
discusses the question : Διὰ τί τὰ
θερμὰ λουτρὰ ἱερά;

It was nearly noon when they encountered a litter
borne by four slaves.[23] Four stalwart bearers followed
behind, to relieve the others from time to time ; and the
whole appearance of the equipage proclaimed its owner to
be a person of considerable wealth. Probably it was some
invalid who had wooed in vain the healing Nymphs of
Ædepsos ; for the curtains on both sides of the litter were
closed, and the bearers strode cautiously along, for fear of
stumbling, or causing any concussion.

Passing the *cortége*, our travellers kept on their road,
which skirted a brook, overgrown with thickets of under-
wood. They had not gone far, when they heard female
voices close at hand, in the direction of the brook, accom-

---

[23] The use of litters was probably
introduced from Asia into Greece at
an early period, although the Greek
εὐτέλεια would most likely divest this
mode of conveyance of much of the
luxury attached to it in the East.
Their use appears to have been, for
the most part, confined to women.
So Suidas, s. v. φορείων, says, πλέγμα
ποιήσαντες ἐκ λύγων φορεῖον τύπῳ
γυναικείων δέρμασι βοείοις ἐπιπλά-
σαντες ἀκατεργάστροις. For a man
to employ them without special cause,
was considered worthy of reproach.
Dinarchos, *in Demosth.* p. 29, mentions
it as a sign of τρυφή. τρυφῶν ἐν τοῖς
τῆς πόλεως κακοῖς καὶ ἐπὶ φορείου
κατακομιζόμενος τὴν εἰς Πειραιᾶ ὁδὸν
καὶ τὰς τῶν πενήτων ἀπορίας ὀνειδί-
ζων. Hence they were hardly ever
used except in cases of personal infirmity : and thus even in the time of
Pericles the mechanician Artemon,
who used a litter because he was lame,
gained the nickname of Περιφόρητος.
Anacr. ap. Athen. xii. p. 533; Plutarch,
Pericl. 27. For sick persons it was
a simple bed rather than a litter, and
hence it was often also called κλίνη.
Lysias, *de Vuln. Præm.* p. 172; Andoc.

de Myst. p. 30. The regular litters,
like those of the Romans, (see *Gallus,*
p. 341, seq.,) were constructed for a
recumbent posture, and were covered
in, as appears from the passage just
quoted from Suidas. There were also
rideaux at the sides. Plutarch,
Eumen. 14 : 'Ακούσας δ' ὁ Εὐμένης
ἧκε πρὸς αὐτοὺς δρόμῳ τοὺς κομί-
ζοντας ἐπιταχύνας, καὶ τοῦ φορείου
τὰς ἑκατέρωθεν αὐλαίας ἀνακαλύψας
προὔτεινε τὴν δεξιὰν γεγηθώς. Eu-
menes was carried because he was ill.
When the Macedonian rule introduced
luxury more and more into Greece,
the litter, no doubt, became more
splendid. Thus at Corinth Antigonus
sends Nicæa to the theatre ἐν φορείῳ
κεκοσμημένῳ βασιλικῶς. Plutarch,
Arat. 17. The bearers were usually
four in number. Lucian, *Epist.*
Saturn. 28 : ἐς γῆρας ἀφικόμενον
τοῖς αὐτοῦ ποσὶν, ἀλλὰ μὴ φοράδην
ἐπὶ τεττάρων ὀχούμε ον. Id. *Somn.*
seu Gallus, 10 : φοράδην ὑπὸ τεττάρων κεκομισμένον. Hence, perhaps,
are to be explained the four talents,
which Artaxerxes gave to the bearers
of Pelopidas. Plutarch, *Pelop.* 30,
Cf. Lucian, *Cyn.* 9.

panied by much merriment and laughter. Approaching
the spot, they beheld through a break in the bushes a most
fascinating spectacle. By the margin of the brook sat a
blooming fair one, dabbling with her feet in the brawling
stream, and behind her a female slave held a parasol [24] to

---

[24] A parasol, σκιάδειον, was an
indispensable article to a Grecian, or
at least to an Athenian lady; it was
usually carried by a female slave; but
on festivals this service was performed
by the daughters of the Metœci. So
in Aristoph. *Thesmoph.* 821, the
chorus of women taunt the men who
had thrown away their σκιάδειον, the
shield. These parasols occur frequently on vases. The accompanying
figure is taken from Millin, *Peintures
de Vases Antiques*, ii. pl. 70. See
also, Paciaudi *de umbellæ gestatione.*

shade her delicate form from the scorching rays; whilst
another of more tender age knelt on the ground, and joked
confidentially with her mistress. A little way off a male
slave was packing up the breakfast things, which had been
spread among the tall grass;[25] and on the road close by
was a carriage drawn by mules,[26] the driver of which was

This parasol much resembled ours,
being constructed of moveable ribs,
so that it could be put up or down as
required.

τὰ δ' ὦτα γάρ σου, νὴ Δί', ἐξεπετάννυτο,
ὥσπερ σκιάδειον, καὶ πάλιν ξυνήγετο.

Aristoph. *Equit.* 1347, on which the
Scholiast observes: ἐκτείνεται δὲ καὶ
συστέλλεται πρὸς τὸν κατεπείγοντα
καιρόν. Cf. Ovid, *Art. Am.* ii. 209:

Ipse tene distenta suis umbracula virgis.

They were occasionally carried by
men, but this was considered a mark
of effeminacy. Aristoph. *Aves*, 1507,
does not prove this, but a fragment of
Anacreon, quoted by Athen. xii. p.
534, does: καὶ σκιαδίσκην ἐλεφαντίνην φορέει γυναιξὶν αὔτως. In later
times, instead of a parasol, women
wore on the head a θολία, which was
something like a modern straw-hat.
Poll. vii. 174: θολία δ' ἐκαλεῖτο
πλέγμα τι θολοειδές, ᾧ ἀντὶ σκιαδίου
ἐχρῶντο αἱ γυναῖκες. See Scholiast
on Theocr. xv. 39; and Harpocr. s.v.
Θόλος.

[25] This description is from Eurip.
Iphig. Aul. 410:

ἀλλ' ὡς μακρὰν ἔτεινον, εὔρυτον παρὰ
κρήνην ἀναψύχουσι θηλύπουν βάσιν,
αὐταί τε πώλοί τ', ἐς δὲ λει, ᾿νων χλόην.
καθεῖμεν αὐτὰς, ὡς βορᾶς γευσαίατο.

[26] Very little can be said of the
carriages of the Greeks, and even
their general shape is a subject in-
volved in doubt. Of names even we
have but a scanty list, the general

terms ζεῦγος and ὄχημα being mostly
employed. The use of carriages was
very limited, and he who used one in
the city and environs was always set
down as effeminate or proud. So Demosth. *adv. Phænipp.* p. 1046: ἀπο-
δόμενος τὸν πολεμιστήριον ἵππον καταβέβηκεν ἀπὸ τῶν ἵππων καὶ ωτ'
ἐκείνου ὄχημα αὑτῷ τηλικοῦτος ὢν
ἐώνηται, ἵνα μὴ πεζῇ πορεύηται.
τοσαύτης τρυφῆς μεστὸς οὗτός ἐστι.
This explains the anecdote in Diog.
Laert. iv. 3: Speusippos, while going
to the Academy in a carriage, met Diogenes, and saluted him with a Χαῖρε,
to which the Cynic replied: 'Αλλὰ μὴ
σύ γε, ὅστις ὑπομένεις ζῆν τοιοῦτος
ὤν. Cf. Aristoph. *Thesm.* 811. It
was considered arrogant even in women. Demosth. *in Mid.* p. 565. Hence
Lycurgus, the orator, caused a law to
be enacted, that the women should
not drive to Eleusis, that the poorer
classes might not feel the distinction.
Plutarch, *Dec. Or. Vit.* iv. p. 378.
His own wife, however, transgressed
the law, and he had to silence the
sycophants with a talent. Timoleon
drove into the assembly, and continued in his carriage during the de-
bate; but he did so because he was
blind. Plutarch, *Timol.* 38. It is
a mark of distinction in Andoc. *de
Myst.* p. 23: τὸν δὲ τῶν κακῶν τούτων αἴτιον Διοκλείδην, ὡς σωτῆρα
ὄντα τῆς πόλεως ἐπὶ ζεύγους ἦγον
εἰς τὸ πρυτανεῖον στεφανώσαντες.

As regards the different kinds of
carriages, the meagre account of Poll.

conversing with a second slave, whose dress bespoke him
to be a eunuch.

The trio stood enchanted, their eyes fixed on the sporting maidens, who, casting aside the irksome trammels of
stiffness and formality, were giving loose to the exuberance
of their spirits. The younger female attendant, who appeared to be regarded rather as a companion than a slave,
now brought a handful of flowers, which she had just
culled, and as she showered them into the lap of her mistress, whispered something in her ear, which might not be
heard even by the bushes around. In pretended wrath,
the lady seized her gold-embroidered shoe, to strike her
offending domestic; but in the attempt it slipped from
her hand, and flew into the brook.

The maidens all set up a scream, when Charicles, with
rash resolve, dashed down, and rescued the floating shoe.
The women screamed louder than ever, and essayed to
flee; but in the twinkling of an eye Charicles gallantly
handed the slipper to the damsel, who rose blushing and
confounded, and looked around, but in vain, for her veil

---

x. 51, must suffice. Strangely enough,
he speaks as if carriages were only
used early in the morning: ἀλλ' εἰ
μὲν αἰωρήσει τῇ δι' ὀχημάτων χρῷτό
τις περὶ τὴν ἔω, θέρους ὄντος. πρινὴ
τὸν ἥλιον περιφλέγειν, τὰ εἴδη τῶν
ὀχημάτων ἰστέον, εἴτε ἅρματα, εἴτε
ὄχους, εἴτε ἁμάξας, εἴτε λαμπήνας
αὐτὰ προσήκει καλεῖν. ἔστι δὲ τοὔνομα ἡ λαμπήνη ἐν τῇ Σοφοκλέους
Ναυσικάᾳ καὶ ἐν τοῖς Μενάνδρου
ἁλιεῦσιν. To these names may be
added ἅρμα, ἀπήνη, and ὄχημα; but
these are either general terms, or
are used to denote carriages not in
ordinary use, and this may also be
said of the Lacedæmonian κάναθρον.
Müller, Dorians, ii. p. 292. We learn
also that carriages were adapted partly for sitting, and partly for lying
down in; they were partially covered;

and were sometimes on two, sometimes on four wheels. Poll. x. 52 : τὰ
δὲ ἐνθρόνια, τὰ δὲ εἰς τὸ κατακλῖναι
ἐνεύναια, τὰ δὲ κατάστεγα, καὶ στε-
γαστά, καὶ καμάραι· οὕτω γὰρ ὠνό-
μασεν Ἡρόδοτος· καὶ Ξενοφῶν δὲ ἐν
τῇ Παιδείᾳ τὸ ἐστεγασμένον μέρος
τῆς ἁμάξης ὑποσημαίνων ἔφη, καὶ
κατέκλιναν καὶ κατεκάλυψαν τὴν
σκηνήν· καὶ τὰ μὲν τετράκυκλα, τὰ
δὲ δίκυκλα. Mules were frequently
used: on them was placed an easy
saddle with a back to it, ἀστράβη,
(clitella,) but this word came afterwards to be used for the beast itself.
Demosth. in Mid. p. 558: ἐπ' ἀστράβης ὀχούμενος ἐξ Ἀργούρας τῆς Εὐβοίας. With this compare Lysias, de
Inval. p. 747: εἰ γὰρ ἐκεκτή μην
οὐσίαν, ἐπ' ἀστράβης ἂν ὠχούμην,
and Machon, ap. Athen. xiii. p. 582.

and mantle, which had been left behind at the spot where
they had breakfasted. Charicles too felt no little emotion;
he fancied that he had never in his existence beheld a form
more lovely, or more fascinating features. The sparkling
brilliancy of her eyes was mingled with a look of soft
rapture; a profusion of light hair descended on her neck
in luxuriant ringlets, while the finely-pencilled arch of the
eyebrows was of a jetty black: in the delicate whiteness
of her cheeks rose a soft tinge of natural vermilion; the
mouth was like a rose-bud, just on the point of unfolding
its leafy chalice;[27] and her whole person possessed an
irresistible charm of youthful loveliness. For a few moments only was the happy Charicles permitted to revel in
the contemplation of such surpassing beauties; the cries of
the female slaves had summoned the male attendants, and
the females fled faster than ever, on seeing Nausicrates
and Ctesiphon also approach. Many a longing lingering
look did Charicles cast after the disappearing carriage,
which he regretted he could not follow.

His pleasant reverie was disagreeably broken by Manes,
who informed him that he had learnt, in conversing with
the driver of the vehicle, that it was the family of a rich
Athenian, who was aged and infirm, and was being conveyed home from Ædepsos in the litter. The fair en-
chantress was this person's wife, but Manes was unable
to tell his name. 'What, married?' cried Charicles, in
agitation. 'And to a sick old fellow?' continued Nausicrates. 'By Hera, though, she was beautiful; tender and
lovely as Aphrodite, with the life and bloom of an Artemis.
Ay! ay! the statues of both goddesses must have stood in
her mother's *thalamos*.'[28]

---

[27] The description of Leucippe in
Achill. Tat. i. 4: ὄμμα γοργὸν ἐν
ἡδονῇ· κόμη ξανθή, τὸ ξανθὸν οὖλον·
ὀφρὺς μέλαινα, τὸ μέλαν ἄκρατον·
λευκὴ παρειά, τὸ λευκὸν εἰς μέσον
ἐφοινίσσετο καὶ ἐμιμεῖτο πορφύραν,
οἷον εἰς τὸν ἐλέφαντα Λυδία βάπτει
γυνή· τὸ στόμα ῥόδων ἄνθος ἦν, ὅταν

ἄρχηται τὸ ῥόδον ἀνοίγειν τῶν φύλ-
λων τὰ χείλη. The ὄμμα γοργὸν ἐν
ἡδονῇ, in this passage, corresponds
to the expression, τῶν ὀφθαλμῶν τὸ
ὑγρὸν ἅμα τῷ φαιδρῷ, in Lucian,
Imag. 6.

[28] Such effects were commonly

The friends continued their journey; but Charicles had
turned silent and thoughtful, and the banter of his com-
panions was manifestly unpleasing to him. The attractions,
also, of the baths were quite lost upon him, and in spite of
their Chalcian host's kind endeavours to make their stay
as agreeable as possible, Charicles would only stop a day
or two, and incessantly urged his friends to return, since
pressing business called him to Athens. At length Nausicrates yielded to his solicitations, though much against his
inclination, since he was successfully endeavouring to console himself for his recent calamities with the pleasures the
place afforded. 'Pressing business, no doubt!' he would
say snappishly to Charicles; 'that fair apparition is the
real magnet [29] of attraction to Athens. But what's the
good? she is married, you know.' The colour that suffused
the cheek of Charicles showed that Nausicrates was right
in his conjecture; still, as the other persisted that he must
be in Athens by a certain day, Nausicrates was at last
obliged to yield the point.

---

attributed to the frequent survey of
beautiful statues, and even Empedocles noticed the supposed fact.
Plutarch, *de Plac. Philos.* v. 12: Ἐμπεδοκλῆς τῇ κατὰ τὴν σύλληψιν φαντασίᾳ
τῆς γυναικὸς μορφοῦσθαι τὰ βρέφη.
πολλάκις γὰρ εἰκόνων καὶ ἀνδριάν-
των ἠράσθησαν γυναῖκες, καὶ ὅμοια
τούτοις ἀπέτεκον. On this hinges
the whole plot in Heliodor. *Æthiop.*
iv. 8, where the queen of the Æthio-
pians declares that she has brought
forth a white child, because she had
the image of Hesione before her. See
Galen. *Hist. Phil.* xix. p. 329. The
same author states elsewhere: ἐμοὶ δὲ
καὶ λόγος τις ἀρχαῖος ἐμήνυσεν, ὅτι
τῶν ἀμόρφων τις δυνατὸς εὔμορφον
θέλων γεννῆσαι παῖδα, ἐποίησε γράψαι ἐν πλατεῖ ξύλῳ εὐειδὲς ἄλλο
παιδίον καὶ ἔλεγε τῇ γυναικὶ συμ-
πλεκόμενος ἐκείνῳ τῷ τύπῳ τῆς γρα-

φῆς ἐμβλέπειν. ἡ δὲ ἀτενὲς βλέπουσα
καὶ ὡς ἔστιν εἰπεῖν ὅλον τὸν νοῦν
ἔχουσα, οὐχὶ τῷ γεννήσαντι, ἀλλὰ
τῷ γεγραμμένῳ ὁμοίως ἀπέτεκε τὸ
παιδίον. *De Therica*, xiv. p. 254.
The reader may attach what credit
he chooses to Oppian, *Cyneg.* i. 361,
where it is stated that the Lacedæmonians placed before their pregnant
ladies pictures representing

Νιρέα καὶ Νάρκισσον, εὔμμελίην δ' Ὑάκινθον.

[29] The comparison of a fascinating
woman with a magnet, λίθος Ἡρακλεία, or Μαγνῆτις, occurs in classic
writers. Lucian, *Imag.* 1: εἰ δὲ κἀ-
κείνη προσβλέψειέ σε, τίς ἔσται
μηχανὴ ἀποστῆναι αὐτῆς; ἀπάξει
γάρ σε ἀναδησαμένη, ἔνθα ἂν ἐθέλῃ,
ὅπερ καὶ ἡ λίθος ἡ Ἡρακλεία δρᾷ
τὸν σίδηρον. Cf. Achill. Tat. i. 17.

K

SCENE THE EIGHTH.

—◦◦—

THE INVALID.

IT was now two months since Charicles had returned to Athens; but that peace of mind and cheerfulness which accompanied him on board the Triton, had not been the partners of his return. His property had, by Phorion's assistance, been securely and advantageously invested: slaves had been purchased, and his abode fitted up with every convenience. The walls and ceilings of the chambers and saloons were decorated in a light and cheerful style, so that in the opinion of every body it was an excellent and commodious abode. The possessor alone was dissatisfied, and felt lonely in the empty cheerless rooms. But even in the convivial circle he was not happy. The turmoil of the market-place was irksome, and the spirit-stirring life of the Gymnasium disturbed his reveries; his highest pleasure was a stroll to the great platanus-tree, where, in the grateful privacy of the spot, he could bury himself in undisturbed meditation.

' You are in love,' his friends would often say jokingly, when the petals of an autumnal flower in his garland happened to drop off.[1] ' To be sure I am,' had formerly been his laughing retort; but now he did not relish the sally; and the mounting colour proclaimed that now at all events the proverb held good. Some well-meant advice of Phorion's had had the most serious effect upon him. One day, he had shown this friend of his father's over his

---

[1] When leaves fell from a chaplet, it was looked upon as a sign of the wearer's being in love. See Callimachus, 45:

'Ελκος ἔχων ὁ ξεῖνος ἐλάνθανεν· ὡς ἀνιηρὸν
πνεῦμα διὰ στηθέων, εἶδες, ἀνηγάγετο;
τὸ τρίτον ἡ γῆ ἔπινε, τὰ δὲ ῥόδα φιλλοβο-
λοῦντα

τὠνδρὸς ἀπὸ στεφάνων πάντ' ἐγένοντο
χαμαί.

and the discussion in Athen. xv. p. 669: διὰ τί δὲ λέγονται, τῶν ἐστε-
φανωμένων ἐὰν λύωνται οἱ στέφανοι,
ὅτι ἐρῶσι.

newly-furnished dwelling. Among other things the women's apartments had not been omitted; and, in fact, matters almost looked as if a bride were daily expected at the house. 'You've done quite right, my friend,' was Phorion's remark; 'but this is not enough. Seek out now a discreet housewife, to preserve thee from the follies of youth, and to bring a blessing on thy house withal. Choose for thyself a damsel of equal rank, not dowerless, for then she will not assume her due position in the household;[2] nor yet a great heiress, or thine own independence will be bartered for her portion. You are nearly a stranger in this city, so let me woo for you. Pasias, my brother's son, has a daughter, a comely child, both modest and thrifty; if you desire it, I will solicit her hand for you.' Charicles made no answer to this proposal; for although he felt that Phorion was right, and that a happy marriage would be the best means of driving from his heart the image of the fair unknown, yet he could not endure the idea of uniting himself for life with a girl of whom he knew nothing. He had communicated Phorion's plan to his friend Ctesiphon, who, on hearing it, betrayed an extraordinary emotion. He answered so evasively that Charicles could not comprehend the meaning of his behaviour. On the other hand, he placed entire confidence in the rectitude of Phorion's intentions, and, by entertaining the offer, he would have an opportunity of displaying his gratitude to his benefactor.

Occupied with such thoughts as these, he was one evening crossing the market-place, toward sunset on his way to the *Cerameicos*, when he felt himself pulled by the cloak. He turned round, and before him stood an aged female slave, making gestures, expressive partly of alarm partly of delight. 'Charicles!' she cried; 'oh dearest Charicles, is it really you?' He now recognised the crone. It was Manto, the nurse of his childhood, who was sick

---

[2] Menandr. *Sent. Sing.* 371 :
νύμφη δ' ἄπροικος οὐκ ἔχει παῤῥησίαν.

Comp. Excursus on *The Women.*

when Charinos fled from Athens, and so had remained
behind with the greater number of the slaves. She narrated how a wealthy man, Polycles by name, had purchased
the whole of the slaves left by his father, and herself
among the number. ' You know him surely,' she continued; ' he was an intimate friend of your father.' ' I
remember to have heard the name frequently,' replied
Charicles. ' Ah! and many is the time he has mentioned
you,' proceeded Manto ; ' but he has been laid up for
many months past with a grievous malady, against which
all his treasures avail him nothing ; while we, poor bodies,
are all sound and well '— as she said this, she spat three
times before her[3]—' but he'll be right glad, I warrant,

---

[3] The superstitious usage, πτύειν
εἰς κόλπον, had two significations,
both of which may perhaps be traced
to a common origin. Firstly, it was
supposed possible thus to appease
the vengeance of Nemesis consequent
on self-glorification, or for having
cherished and expressed over-san-
guine expectations. Secondly, it was
done on seeing any one afflicted with a
bad complaint, such as insanity or epi-
lepsy, or on witnessing the misfortune
of another ; and it was supposed that
by this means a like evil could be
averted from oneself. This idea is
nowhere more distinctly expressed
than in Plin. Nat. Hist. xxviii. 4, 7 :
' Despuimus comitiales morbos, hoc
est, contagia regerimus. Simili modo
et fascinationes repercutimus dextræ-
que clauditatis occursum. Veniam
quoque a deis spei alicujus audacioris
petimus in sinum spuentes.' Also
Theocr. vi. 39, where Polyphemus
says :

ὡς μὴ βασκανθῶ δὲ, τρὶς εἰς ἐμὸν ἔπτυσα
κόλπον.

and the Scholiast correctly remarks :
ποιοῦσι γὰρ καὶ μέχρι τοῦ νυν μάλιστα τοῦτο αἱ γυναῖκες τὸ νεμε-
σητὸν ἐκτρεπόμεναι. Καλλίμαχος·
Δαίμων, τοὶ κόλποισιν ἐπιπτύουσι
γυναῖκες. Cf. the obscure and corrupt
passage quoted by Plut. Symp. v.
7, 4. Another instance occurs in
Lucian, Navig. 15, where Lycinus
checks Adimantus, who is puffed up
with visions of wealth and fortune,
with the words, ὑπερμαζᾷς γε, ὦ
'Αδείμοντε, καὶ ἐς τὸν κόλπον οὐ
πτύεις. The second case, where the
spectator of another man's misfortune
desires to avert the same calamity
from himself, is passed over by Pliny
with the words, Despuimus comitiales
morbos, and he omits in sinum. See
also Plaut. Capt. iii. 4, 18 :

Et illic isti, qui sputatur, morbus interdum
    venit.

But whatever the Roman custom may
have been, the Greeks certainly used
πτύειν εἰς κόλπον in such cases, as is
plain from Theoph. Char. 16, where a
token of the δεισιδαίμων is said to be :
Μαινόμενόν τε ἰδὼν ἢ ἐπίληπτον
φρίξας εἰς κόλπον πτύσαι. Cf.
Tibull. i. 2, 97. We may add also that
both significations of the custom become identical when we consider that
ridicule and commiseration equally

to hear you are come back.' Hereupon followed a stream
of questions, interrupted now by sobs, now by fits of
laughter ; and Charicles would never have satisfied all her
queries, had not she suddenly bethought herself that she
had better take home the vegetables which her mistress
had sent her out to purchase.

Polycles was, as Manto had stated, a very wealthy
man. His country estates, his houses in the city and
Piræus, and his numerous slaves, yielded him, with no
trouble, a secure income ; which, however, was as nothing
compared to that which he derived from the ready money
lying at the money-changers', or lent out elsewhere, at a
high rate of interest. Those who were more intimate with
the state of his affairs, were convinced that his property
amounted in all to more than fifty talents. He had
remained single till his fifty-fifth year, and then, in compliance with his late brother's dying request, he had married his only surviving daughter, Cleobule, a blooming girl
of sixteen. But in the midst of the festivity of the marriage-feast, he was attacked with apoplexy, which had been
succeeded by tedious and painful illness. No means of
relief had been neglected. The veteran family physician, a
man of no mean skill, had called in the advice of other
medical men, but the resources of their art were exhausted
without success :—neither their exertions, nor the tender-
ness of Cleobule, who nursed the patient like a dutiful
daughter, availed to reunite the ruptured threads of his
existence. Polycles was not satisfied with applying for
aid to the successors of Æsculapius, but tried the efficacy
of certain charms ; while interpreters of dreams [4] were

imply an elevation of oneself over
another.

[4] The interpretation of dreams
was one of the oldest and most natural
provinces of μαντική ; and from the

time of Homer, who makes dreams
the ministers of the gods to incite men
to action, down to the latest period of
declining heathenism, we find ὀνειρό-
πολοι, ὀνειροκρίται, or ὀνειρομαντεις
in requisition, and the prophetic

consulted, expiations placed in the cross-ways,[5] and aged
women reputed to have the power of curing diseases by
mysterious arts and magic songs, had been summoned to
attend. Whole days and nights had also been passed by the
sufferer in the temple of Æsculapius,[6] but to no purpose.

---

visions of the night propitiated by
anxious ceremonies. These are described in numerous passages: thus in
Æschyl. *Pers.* 200, which, though
Atossa is the speaker, of course
alludes to Grecian usages:

καὶ ταῦτα μὲν δὴ νυκτὸς εἰσιδεῖν λέγω.
ἐπεὶ δ' ἀνέστην καὶ χεροῖν καλλιρρόου
ἔψαυσα πηγῆς, ξὺν θυηπόλῳ χερὶ
βωμῷ προσέστην, ἀποτρόποισι δαίμοσι
θέλουσα θῦσαι πέλανον, ὧν τέλη τάδε.

This sprinkling with water usually
pertained to such an ἀποτροπιασμός.
So, again, Aristoph. *Ran.* 1338:

ἀλλά μοι, ἀμφίπολοι, λύχνον ἅψατε,
κάλπισί, τ' ἐκ ποταμῶν δρόσον ἄρατε, θέρ-
μετε δ' ὕδωρ,
ὡς ἂν θεῖον ὄνειρον ἀποκλύσω.

These passages are confirmed by
Xenoph. *Symp.* 4, 33: καὶ ἐάν τι ὄναρ
ἀγαθὸν ἴδῃς τοῖς ἀποτροπαίοις θύεις ;
So, again, Theoph. *Char.* 16: καὶ
ὅταν ἐνύπνιον ἴδῃ πορεύεσθαι πρὸς
τοὺς ὀνειροκρίτας, πρὸς τοὺς μάντεις,
πρὸς τοὺς ὀρνιθοσκόπους ἐρωτήσων,
τίνι θεῷ ἢ θεᾷ προσεύχεσθαι δεῖ. On
which Casaubon has remarked that it
was considered in some measure an
ἀποτρόπαιων to tell a dream to the
face of day. Eurip. *Iphig. Taur.* 42:

ἃ καινὰ δ' ἥκει νὺξ φέρουσα φάσματα,
λέξω πρὸς αἰθέρ', εἴ τι δὴ τόδ' εἰς ἄκος.

Cf. Sophocl. *Electr.* 416. The dream-
interpreters made a regular trade of
their pretended art, and exacted fees
for their services. Aristoph. *Vesp.* 52:

εἶτ' οὐκ ἐγώ, δοὺς δύ' ὀβολούς, μισθώσομαι
οὕτως ὑποκρινόμενον σαφῶς ὀνείρατα.

In Alciphr. *Epist.* iii. 59, two drachmæ are the fee. Dreams dreamt
towards morning, 'post mediam noc-

tem, quum somnia vera,' (Hor. *Sat.*
I. 10, 33,) were regarded as the most
significant, and to these, therefore, the
dream-interpreters confined themselves. Philostr. *Vit. Apollon. Tyan.*
ii. 37: οἱ γὰρ ἐξηγηταὶ τῶν ὕψεων,
οὓς ὀνειροπόλους οἱ ποιηταὶ καλοῦσιν
οὐδ' ἂν ὑποκρίναιντο ὄψιν οὐδενὶ
οὐδεμίαν, μὴ πρότερον ἐρόμενοι τὸν
καιρὸν ἐν ᾧ εἶδεν. ἂν μὲν γὰρ ἕῳς ᾖ
καὶ τοῦ περὶ τὸν ὄρθρον ὕπνου, ξυμ-
βάλλονται αὐτὴν, ὡς ὑγιῶς μαντευο-
μένης τῆς ψυχῆς, κ.τ.λ.

[5] The belief that sickness and
other evils could be got rid of by
means of καθάρματα placed at the
cross-ways, is well known. The
throwing them into flowing water is
chiefly mentioned by Roman authors;
nor does the passage in Theocr. xxiv.
92, seem properly referable to this
custom. The Roman usage is often
alluded to. See Virg. *Ecl.* viii. 101;
Tibull. iv. 4, 7; Ovid, *Metam.* xv. 327.

[6] This too appears to have been
much in vogue; so much so, that
apartments were provided in the
temples of this god, in which sick
persons might reside. Pausan. ii. 27,
2: τοῦ ναοῦ δέ ἐστι πέραν, ἔνθα οἱ
ἱκέται. τοῦ θεοῦ καθεύδουσιν. Again,
x. 32, 8: Σταδίοις δὲ ἀπωτέρω Τιθο-
ρέας ἑβδομήκοντα ναός ἐστιν Ἀσκληπιοῦ ... ἐντὸς μὲν δὴ τοῦ περιβόλου
τοῖς τε ἱκέταις καὶ, ὅσοι τοῦ θεοῦ
δοῦλοι, τούτοις μὲν ἐνταῦθά εἰσι καὶ
οἰκήσεις. See Aristoph. *Plut.* 410,
653; cf. Plaut. *Curc.* i. 1, 61; ii. 1.

At last, hearing of a happy cure effected, in a similar case, by the baths of Ædepsos, he repaired thither for the benefit of the waters; but the Nymphs had refused their succour; and, some days ago, the doctor had declared that the patient would never need any herb more, save the parsley.[7]

Next day Charicles was on the point of going out. The previous evening, he had come to the resolution of marrying, and he had determined that Phorion should play the suitor for him. At this moment a slave rapped at the door, on an errand from Polycles. Weak as the patient was, he had expressed great pleasure on hearing that the son of his old friend was in Athens, and now sent to say he wished to see him once more before his end, which he felt was drawing nigh. Charicles could not refuse a request expressive of so much kindliness, and therefore promised to attend. 'It were better to come along with me at once,' said the slave. 'My master is very low now, and his friends have just met at his bed-side.' 'Well, lead on,' said Charicles, not unwilling to put off for a time his intended visit to Phorion; 'lead on, I follow you.'

When they approached the residence of Polycles, they found a slave standing before the open door in order to

---

Probably some temples were accounted more efficacious than others. Thus Bdelycleon took his father to Ægina. Aristoph. *Vesp.* 122 :

διέπλευσεν εἰς Αἴγιναν· εἶτα συλλαβὼν νύκτωρ κατέκλινεν αὐτὸν εἰς Ἀσκληπιοῦ.

So also many persons sought for aid at the oracle of Amphiaraos, near Oropos, and threw a gold or silver coin into the holy spring. Lastly, between Tralles and Nysa, not far from Acharaca, there was a village with a shrine sacred to Pluto and Persephoné, and a Χαρώνιον ἄντρον, whither sick people were brought. Strabo, xiv. 1, 44 : λέγουσι γὰρ δὴ

καὶ τοὺς νοσώδεις καὶ προσέχοντας ταῖς τῶν θεαν τούτων θεραπείαις φοιτᾶν ἐκεῖσε καὶ διαιτᾶσθαι ἐν τῇ κώμῃ πλησίον τοῦ ἄντρου παρὰ τοῖς ἐμπείροις τῶν ἱερέων, οἳ ἐγκοιμῶνται τε ὑπὲρ αὐτῶν καὶ διατάττουσιν ἐκ τῶν ὀνείρων τὰς θεραπείας.

[7] Σέλινον, *apium*, was especially used for decking tombs. Hence the adage mentioned by Plutarch, *Timol.* 26: ὅτι τὰ μνήματα τῶν νεκρῶν εἰώθαμεν ἐπιεικῶς στεφανοῦν σελίνοις· καὶ παροιμία τις ἐκ τούτου γέγονε, τὸν ἐπισφαλῶς νοσοῦντα, Δεῖσθαι τούτου τοῦ σελίνου.

prevent any one from rapping too loudly, and so disturbing his lord. Charicles entered, and everything that he saw corroborated Manto's testimony concerning the wealth of the possessor. Even the sick chamber, into which he was admitted after a slight delay, was furnished with peculiar magnificence. Before the door hung a costly piece of tapestry, wrought in rich and varied colours, the product of Babylonish industry. The sick man's bed [8] was over-

---

[8] The account given of the Roman bed in *Gallus* (pp. 285–291) will, in its chief points, be also applicable to the Grecian couch; but the particulars which Pollux gives are more copious, and will, if properly investigated, make the matter very plain. In Homer we have simply a bedstead and coverlet, and there is no mention of a mattress of any kind. In later times also, the beds of the poorer classes were probably of this description. Instead of a mattress, stout coverlets, especially κώδια, sheepskins, were often spread underneath. Plutarch, *Dec. Or. Vit.* iv. p. 379, relates of the orator Lycurgus: Ἐμελέτα δὲ νυκτὸς καὶ ἡμέρας, οὐκ εὖ πρὸς τὰ αὐτο⁻χεδια πεφυκὼς, κλινιδίου δὲ αὐτῷ ὑποκειμένου, ἐφ' ᾧ μόνον ἦν κώδιον καὶ προσκεφάλαιον, ὅπως ἐγείροιτο ῥᾳδίως καὶ μελετῴη.

But the εὐνὴ, the complete bed of a wealthy Greek, consisted of the following parts: κλίνη, ἐπίτονοι, τυλεῖον or κνέφαλον, προσκεφάλαιον, and ἐπιβλήματα or περιβλήματα. The κλίνη, or bedstead, was of very simple construction. Its four sides, ἐνήλατα, Attic κραστήρια (Phryn. p. 178) were not so much boards, as posts or bars jointed into one another, and supported by the feet. Only at the end where the head lay was there a back, ἀνάκλιντρον or ἐπίκλιντρον. Poll. x. 34: μέρη δὲ κλίνης καὶ ἐνή-

λατα καὶ ἐπίκλιντρον· ... Σοφοκλῆς δ' ἐν Ἰχνευταῖς Σατύροις ἔφη, ἐνήλατα ξύλα τρίγομφα διατορεῦσαί σε δεῖται. Cf. Id. vi. 9. Occasionally there was a board at the foot as well as at the head of the bed, but this was unusual. A bedstead of this kind, κλίνη ἀμφικνέφαλος, is mentioned by Pollux, x. 35, as having belonged to Alcibiades. This reading, however, seems to be corrupt; for besides the unintelligibility of the phrase, the word κνέφαλον is totally different from προσκεφάλαιον: there seems to be no doubt that ἀμφικέφαλος is the correct reading.

The κλίνη was usually of wood; hence ἐνήλατα ξύλα. Valuable woods were often employed, as maple, σφένδαμνος, Poll. x. 35, or box-wood, *ibid.* § 34. but most likely these were only used as veneer, at least χαμεύνη παράκολλος (*ibid.* § 36) leads to this supposition. Passow's explanation, 'a low couch, to one end only of which was attached an ἀνακλιντήριον, on which the head rested: being called ἀμφίκολλος, if it had one at both ends,' is not only at variance with the etymology, but also contradicts Pollux, § 34, who evidently speaks of the material only. That veneering was practised among the ancients, has been mentioned in *Gallus*, p. 295. There is no doubt, too, that frames of bronze were likewise in request. When, however,

hung with a purple Milesian coverlet, from under which
peeped the ivory feet. Soft party-coloured pillows sup-

Pollux adds, (x. 35) σὺ δ᾽ ἂν καὶ ἐλεφαντίνην εἴποις καὶ χελώνης, we
must refer the tortoise-shell altogether to a later period; while with
regard to the ivory, Timæus, ap.
Ælian, *Var. Hist.* xii. 29, mentions
as a proof of the excessive luxury
prevailing at Acragas: ὅτι ἀργυροῖς
ληκύθοις καὶ στλεγγίσιν ἐχρῶντο καὶ
ἐλεφαντίνας κλίνας εἶχον ὅλας. Cf.
Dio Chrysos. *Or.* xiii. 434. The feet
of the κλίνη, however, were frequently
of more valuable material; ivory, for
instance, or the precious metals. So
in Poll. x. 34, ἀργυρόπους; and Clearchos, ap. Athen. vi. p. 255: κατέκειτο
δι᾽ ὑπερβάλλουσαν τρυφὴν ἐπὶ ἀργυρό-
ποδος κλίνης. So also Plato Com. ap.
Id. ii. p. 48:

Κᾆτ᾽ ἐν κλίναις ἐλεφαντόποσιν καὶ στρώμασι πορφυροβάπτοις
κᾶν φοινικίσι Σαρδιανικαῖσιν κοσμησάμενοι
κατάκεινται.

The κλῖναι captured from the Persians at Platæa were ἐπίχρυσοι καὶ
ἐπάργυροι. Herodot. ix. 80, 82.

Girths were stretched across the
κλίνη to support the mattress. Poll.
§ 36: καὶ μὴν τό γε τῇ κλίνῃ ἢ τῷ
σκίμποδι ἐντεταμένον, ὡς φέρειν τὰ
τυλεῖα, σπαρτία, σπάρτα, τόνος,
κειρία· τάχα δὲ καὶ σχοῖνος καὶ σχοι-
νία, καὶ κάλοι. The general name for
them was τόνος. Aristoph. *Lysist.*
923. Thus used, they were called
κειρία: mere cords were used for the
commoner kinds of beds. Aristoph.
Aves, 814:

Σπάρτην γὰρ ἂν θείμην ἐγὼ τῇ 'μῇ πόλει;
οὐδ᾽ ἂν χαμεύνῃ, παῖνν γε κειρίαν ἔχων.

These girths supported a mattress,
called κνέφαλον or τυλεῖον, also τύλη.
See Lobeck on Phryn. p. 173. This
was covered with linen or woollen

ticking, or even with leather. Poll.
x. 40, and again, §39, from Sophocles,
λινορράφῃ τυλεῖα. The stuffing, τὸ
ἐμβαλλόμενον πλήρωμα, ὃ γνάφαλον
καλοῦσι (Poll. 41), was usually flocks
of wool, and thus κνέφαλον (κνάφα-
λον) derives its name from κναφεύς.
Some vegetable material was also
employed, Poll. 41: ἡ μέντοι καλουμένη λυχνὶς ἀνθήλη ἐκαλεῖτο, though
what is meant by λυχνὶς, is another
matter: neither Hesychius nor the
Etymol. M. give a satisfactory explanation.

On the ἐπίκλιντρον lay, as is
abundantly manifest from the antiques, a round cushion, προσκεφάλαιον, which served the purpose of a
pillow; but occasionally there are also
a couple of four-cornered ones behind.
The expression ποτίκρανον (Poll. vi.
9) is identical in meaning. Cf. Theocr.
xv. 3. The προσκεφάλαια ὑπαυχένια,
Poll. x. 38, were those employed at
night, whereas those used at the δεῖπνον are called ὑπαγκώνια στρώματα,
because it was the custom to lean upon
the elbow. See Poll. vi. 10. In the vase-
paintings the covers of these cushions
are almost invariably represented as
striped, and usually of brilliant colours.
They were perhaps stuffed with feathers, though this is uncertain; for the
πτίλωτὰ mentioned by Poll. x. 38
appear to mean something different.

Over the κνέφαλον were spread
coverlets, which bear manifold desig-
nations, Poll. vi. 10: περιστρώματα,
ἐπιβλήματα, ἐφεστρίδες, χλαῖναι,
ἐπιβόλαια, δάπιδες, κ.τ.λ., besides
the τάπητες and ἀμφιτάπητες, Id. vi.
9. The latter were shaggy on both
sides, the former only on one: ἀμφιτάπητες οἱ ἐξ ἑκατέρου δασεῖς. τά-

ported his back and head; and the hard pavement of
the floor was covered, after the Asiatic fashion, with a soft

πητες δὲ οἱ ἐκ θατέρου. The other
names either require no explanation,
or do not admit of any certain one.
This article afforded occasion for the
display of great extravagance: and
though the various kinds mentioned
by Pollux (x. 42) belong rather to the
symposium, still it is certain that
magnificent coloured coverlets were
used also for the beds. There was,
moreover, little or no difference between the couches used for meals,
and those employed for sleeping purposes, except that the former were
distinguished by the greater elegance
of their coverlets and cushions. So a
fragment of Phylarchos ap. Athen. iv.
p. 142, which refers to Sparta in her
degenerate time: στρωμναί τε (παρε-
σκευάζοντο) τοῖς μεγέθεσιν οὕτως
ἐξησκημέναι πολυτελῶς καὶ τῇ ποι-
κιλίᾳ διαφόρως, ὥστε τῶν ξένων
ἐνίους τῶν παραληφθέντων ὀκνεῖν
τὸν ἀγκῶνα ἐπὶ τὰ προσκεφάλαια
ἐρείδειν. We may well conceive that
the bed would be correspondingly
magnificent also. According to Plutarch, *Dec. Or. Vit.* iv. p. 366, Isocrates had a προσκεφάλαιον κρόκῳ
διάβροχον. The Asiatics, however,
regarded the Greek bed as a very
common affair in comparison with
their own. Athen. ii. p. 48: πρῶται
δὲ Πέρσαι, ὥς φησιν Ἡρακλείδης, καὶ
τοὺς λεγομένους στρώτας ἐφεῦρον,
ἵνα κόσμον ἔχῃ ἡ στρῶσις καὶ εὐά-
φειαν. And presently, Ἀρταξέρξης
σκηνήν τε ἔδωκεν αὐτῷ διαφέρουσαν
τὸ κάλλος καὶ τὸ μέγεθος καὶ κλίνην
ἀργυρόποδα, ἔπεμψε δὲ καὶ στρώματα
πολυτελῆ καὶ τὸν ὑποστρώσοντα,
φάσκων οὐκ ἐπίστασθαι τοὺς Ἕλληνας ὑποστρωννύειν. Cf. Plutarch,
Pelop. 30. The most celebrated
στρώματα came from Miletus, at least

in early times, Aristoph. *Ran.* 542,
and also from Corinth, as appears
from Antiphanes ap. Athen. i. p. 27:
ἐκ Κορίνθου στρώματα. Carthage also
is mentioned in a line from Hermippos, *ibid.* p. 28:

Καρχηδὼν δάπιδας καὶ ποικίλα προσκεφα-
         λαια.

Lastly, there is a remarkable passage
in Poll. vi. 10, where coverlets of feathers are mentioned: ὅτι δὲ καὶ πτί-
λοις τὰ κνέφαλα ἐφήπλουν, Εὔβουλος
ἐν Ἀγχίσει διδάσκει. καὶ πτερωτὰ καὶ
πτιλωτὰ προσκεφάλαια ὀνομάζουσι.
This passage confirms what was said
in *Gallus*, p. 288, about the *plumarii*
They wrapped themselves up in these
coverlets at night, though a special
night-dress, ἐνεύναιον, was put on.
Poll. x. 123. In winter furs were used.
Plato, *Prot.* p. 315: Ὁ μὲν οὖν Πρό
δικος ἔτι κατέκειτο ἐγκεκαλυμμένος ἐν
κωδίοις τισὶ καὶ στρώμασι, καὶ μάλο
πολλοῖς ὡς ἐφαίνετο. The κώδιοι
is a sheep-skin, προβάτου δορὰ, as we
are informed by Pollux. vii. 16. But
the σισύρα is particularly mentioned
as a night-coverlet, thus in Aristoph.
Nub. 10:

ἐν πέντε σισύραις ἐγκεκορδυλημένος.

Cf. *Eccles.* 347; *Aves*, 122; *Lysist.*
933. This also was used in winter
(*Eccl.* 421), and is perhaps nothing
but a κώδιον. Poll. vii. 70. says: ἡ
δὲ σισύρα περίβλημα ἂν εἴη ἐκ διφθέρας.
The use of this kind of coverlet was
perhaps confined to the less wealthy,
who would have to content themselves
with much less sumptuous appliances.
We must allow for the comic exaggeration in the description of a poor man's
bed given in Aristoph. *Plut.* 540:

πρὸς δέ γε τούτοις ἀνθ' ἱματίου μὲν ἔχειν
   ῥάκος, ἀντὶ δὲ κλίνης

carpet, and the couch resting upon this, was thus rendered
still more easy and elastic.[9] Close by stood a round
table, whose three bronze goat's feet sustained its maple
top.[10] In one corner of the apartment a magnificent

στιβάδα σχοίνων κόρεων μεστὴν, ἢ τοὺς
εὔδοντας ἐγείρει.
καὶ φορμὸν ἔχειν ἀντὶ τάπητος σαπρόν·
ἀντὶ δὲ προσκεφαλαίου
λίθον εὐμεγέθη πρὸς τῇ κεφαλῇ.

Cf. *Lysist.* 916, where are mentioned
all the parts belonging to an ordinary
bed, as κλινίδιον, τόνος, ψίαθος,
προσκεφάλαιον, and σισύρα. The
frame of the common bed is called
σκίμπους, ἀσκάντης, and κράββατος.
Socrates slept on a σκίμπους. Plato,
Protag. p. 310. The three words are
precisely identical in meaning, though
κράββατος is rejected by Attic writers.
See *Nubes*, 633, and 709; Poll. x. 35;
vi. 9; Eustath. *ad Il.* xvi. 608; and
ad Odyss. xxiii. 184: Λέχος δὲ δῆλον
ὅτι τὴν κλίνην λέγει, ἣν οἱ ὕστερον
καὶ ἀσκάντην καὶ σκίμποδα ἔλεγον, ὡς
δηλοῖ ὁ γράψας οὕτως· ἀσκάντης
Ἀττικῶς, συνηθέστερον δὲ ὁ σκίμπους,
ὁ δὲ κράββατος, φησὶ, παρ' οὐδενί.
Cf. Suid. and Hesych. Gerhard, *Pit-
ture Tarquin.* p. 29. The χαμεύνη
or χαμεύνιον was nothing more than
a shake-down. Theocr. xiii. 34:

ἐκβάντες δ' ἐπὶ θῖνα κατὰ ζυγὰ δαῖτα
πένοντο
δειελινοὶ, πολλοὶ δὲ μίαν στορέσαντο χα-
μεύνην·
λειμὼν γάρ σφιν ἔκειτο μέγας, στιβάδεσσιν
ὄνειαρ.

On this the Scholiast remarks: στιβάδα δὲ καλοῦσι τὴν ἐξ ὕλης χορτώ-
δη κατάστρωσιν. Cf. Plutarch, *Lycurg.* 16: ἐκάθευδον . . . ἐπὶ στιβάδων,
ἃς αὐτοὶ συνεφόρουν τοῦ παρὰ τὸν
Εὐρώταν πεφυκότος καλάμου. The
word φυλλάδες, Poll. vi. 9, probably
means the same thing. Afterwards
χαμεύνιον signified a bed low, and

near the ground, and was hence opposed to the taller κλίνη, and was that
used by the poorest class, being of
reeds, bast-mat, or rushes. Liban.
Orat. xxxvii. ἐν χαμευνίοις δεῖ σε
καθεύδειν, ἢν κελεύω, καὶ πάλιν ἐπὶ
κλίνης, ἢν ἐπιτρέπω. And Poll. x. 43:
καὶ μὴν τοῖς μὲν οἰκέταις ἐν κοιτῶνι ἢ
προκοιτῶνι, ἢ πρὸ προκοιτῶνος ἀναγ-
καῖα σκεύη, χαμεύνια καὶ ψίαθοι, καὶ
φορμοὶ καὶ σάμαξ. ἔστι δὲ ὁ σάμαξ
ῥὶψ καλάμου τοῦ καλουμένου σάκτου.
μάλιστα δὲ ἐπὶ στρατιᾶς τούτῳ ἐχρῶντο. The ψίαθος was a mat of this
kind; see Poll. x. 175, 178, and vi. 11:
and φορμὸς is perhaps the same thing.
Theocr. xxi. 13: νέρθεν τὰς κεφαλᾶς
φορμὸς βραχύς.

[9] Xenoph. *Cyrop.* viii. 8, 16: ἐκείνοις (Μήδοις) γὰρ πρῶτον μὲν τὰς
εὐνὰς οὐ μόνον ἀρκεῖ μαλακῶς ὑπο-
στρώννυσθαι, ἀλλ' ἤδη καὶ τῶν κλινῶν
τοὺς πόδας ἐπὶ ταπίδων τιθέασιν,
ὅπως μὴ ἀντερείδῃ τὸ δάπεδον, ἀλλ'
ὑπείκωσιν αἱ τάπιδες: and again,
Memor. ii. 1, 30: οὐ μόνον τὰς στρω-
μνὰς μαλακὰς, ἀλλὰ καὶ τὰς κλίνας
καὶ τὰ ὑπόβαθρα ταῖς κλίναις παρα-
σκευάζεις. What the arrangement of
the ὑπόβαθρα διαγώνια was, is, however, doubtful.

[10] Maple, σφένδαμνος, seems to
have been much prized. Athen. ii.
p. 49: Τράπεζαι ἐλεφαντόποδες τῶν
ἐπιθημάτων ἐκ τῆς καλουμένης σφεν-
δάμνου πεποιημένων. Κρατῖνος
Γαυριῶσαι δ' ἀναμένουσιν ὧδ' ἐπηγλαϊσμέ-
ναι
μείρακες φαιδραὶ τράπεζαι τρισκελεῖς σφεν-
δάμνιναι.

tripod, apparently of Corinthian or Sicyonian workmanship.
held a copper coal-pan,[11] for the autumn air was chilly.

Around the bed were placed chairs of ebony, inlaid
skilfully with golden tendrils,[12] and each provided with a
coloured cushion. Upon one of these sat the doctor, a
demure elderly man, of simple yet dignified exterior. His
short beard, as well as his dark locks, now sprinkled with
the snows of life's winter, were arranged with peculiar care,
and, together with the dazzling whiteness of his robe,
showed him to be one who studied a modest neatness of
person, and avoided in his appearance whatever might
create an unpleasing impression.[13] He had deposited a
plain *étui*, containing his instruments and medicines, on the
table near him, while with his right hand he felt the sick
man's pulse.

At his side stood three friends of the family,[14] their
gaze fixed inquiringly on the physician's countenance;
while at the foot of the bed an aged slave, with clasped
hands,[15] was gazing intently on his dying master. Long

Three-footed tables were called τρίποδες, but they also bore the name of
τράπεζαι. Thus we have τράπεζα
τετράπους, τρίπους, and μονόπους,
Poll. x. 80, and 69. The disk, ἐπίθημα, of the τρίπους, was usually
round, and was sometimes a horizontal section of the whole trunk, like the
Roman *orbes*. Poll. § 81 : τὸ δ᾽ ἐπίθημα τοῦ τρίποδος κύκλον καὶ ὅλμον
προσήκει καλεῖν. Poll. *supra*: ἐν δὲ
τοῖς Δημιοπράτοις καὶ τράπεζά τις
μονόκυκλος πέπραται. See *Gallus*,
p. 294.

[11] These coal-pans, ἀνθράκια, ἐσ-
χάρια, also λάρκοι and φορμοὶ (Poll.
x. 100, and vii. 110), served partly as
stoves, as in Italy. See *Gallus*, p. 278;
Stuart, *Antiq. of Athens*, I. pl. 19.

[12] Covers or cushions were placed
on the very simple, yet beautifully

shaped settles, and were also called
προσκεφάλια, or ποτίκρανα, though
they were used for sitting on. Plato,
de Repub. i. p. 328 : καθῆστο δὲ
ἐστεφανωμένος ἐπί τινος προσκεφαλαίου τε καὶ δίφρου. Cf. Theocr.
xv. 2. See Excursus on *The Theatres*.

[13] After Galen *in Hippocr. Epid*,
xvii. 2. See Excursus on *The Doctors*.

[14] There were numerous visitors
on the sick, so as even to be burden-
some. See Note 16. This is taken
from Demosth. *Aphob.* 2, p. 840,
where three relations surround the
sick-bed. In the reliefs, the death of
Meleager, for instance, several persons are always present.

[15] Clasping the hands—with us a

and silently did the leech hold the sick man's wrist, and
at last let it go, though without uttering a word that
might encourage hope.

The slave who had conducted Charicles now approached,
and first whispered his arrival to the doctor, with whose
assent [16] he further announced it to his master. The sick
man pushed back the felt cap,[17] which he had drawn down
over his forehead, and extended his right hand to Charicles. 'Joy to you,[18] son of my friend,' he murmured

---

sign of devotion or of excessive grief—
is not properly an antique attitude,
still instances occur in which something of the kind is met with as an
expression of the latter passion. For
instance, in a fresco at Pompeii, representing Medea about to kill her
children, the pedagogue stands in the
background, with his hands in this
posture. There is also a relief, representing a servant in a like attitude
beside a sick-bed. But to clasp the
hands round the knees, while in a sitting position, is mentioned as a token
of the deepest grief. Böttiger has adduced as an instance, Appul. *Metam.*
iii. p. 173: 'Complicitis denique pedi-
bus ac palmulis inter alternas digito-
rum vicissitudines super genua con-
nexis, sic grabatum coxim insidens
ubertim flebam.' Cf. Dio Chrys. *Or.*
xvi. p. 458: μέλαιναν ἐσθῆτα καὶ συμ-
πλοκὰς χειρῶν, καὶ ταπεινὰς καθέδρας. So too Basil. *Hom.* ii. p. 63: οἱ
γεωργοὶ δὲ ταῖς ἀρούραις ἐπικαθή-
μενοι καὶ τὰς χεῖρας κατὰ τῶν γονά-
των συμπλέξαντες· τοῦτο δὲ τῶν
πενθούντων σχῆμα. These are the
καθίσεις ἄμορφοι of Plutarch, *Consol.
ad Uxor.* iii. p. 456. In other cases,
clasping the hands was supposed to
act as a spell. Thus, 'adsidere gra-
vidis, vel, cum remedium alicui adhi-
beatur, digitis pectinatim inter se
implexis veneficium est.' Plin. *Nat.*

Hist. xviii. 6, 17. So Juno sits at the
threshold of Alcmena, ' digitis i nter
se pectine junctis,' Ovid, *Metam.* ix.
299. Wringing the hands, also, can
hardly be adduced as a customary
symptom of grief at any early period ;
we have, however, τὼ χεῖρε συντρί-
ψας in Heliod. *Æthiop.* vii. p. 307.

[16] Galen *in Hippocr. Epid.* xvii. 2,
directs that the doctor shall decide as
to the admission of visitors: ταῦτα
δὲ πολυπραγμονήσας ὁ ἰατρὸς αὐτὸς
ἐργάσεται καὶ διατάξει.

[17] The word πιλίδιον, which is
used to denote such a head-dress for
the sick, can hardly be translated
otherwise. See Plato, *de Repub.* iii.
p. 406 : ἐὰν δέ τις αὐτῷ (τῷ κάμνοντι)
μακρὰν δίαιταν προστάττῃ, πιλίδιά
τε περὶ τὴν κεφαλὴν περιτιθεὶς καὶ
τὰ τούτοις ἑπόμενα, κ.τ.λ. Cf. Plut
adv. Colot. 33. See Excursus on *The
Dress.*

[18] Nothing is harder to translate
than the conventional formulæ of salutation. The ordinary Greek greeting,
χαῖρε, literally 'rejoice,' or 'joy with
you,' answers, doubtless, to our 'Good
day,' but this would sound ridiculous
if transferred to a classic idiom; while,
on the other hand, the literal English
equivalent of χαῖρε sounds no less

feebly; 'and thanks for fulfilling my wish. I was present
at the festival of naming you, and thus you stand now at
my dying bed.' 'Health to you also,' answered Charicles,
'and joy, although now you are in pain and anguish.

---

strange to us. The phrase χαῖρε or
χαίρειν (κελεύω), was the oldest, and,
at the same time, most universal form
of salutation among the Greeks, and
was used both for meeting and taking
leave, and corresponds therefore both
to *salve* and *vale*. Though anything
but appropriate on some occasions, as
in cases of suffering or misfortune,
still, as being the usual phrase, it was
employed all the same, though sometimes with a qualifying ὅμως, as in
Æschyl. *Pers.* 845:

ὑμεῖς δὲ πρέσβεις, χαίρετ᾽, ἐν κακοῖς ὅμως.

In place of this ancient form, others
afterwards came into use. Thus
from Lucian, *de Saltat.* 76, we learn
that καλῶς ἔχε was said to the
sick. He tells us that a very lanky
dancer appearing on the stage at
Antioch, ἐπεβόησαν, Καλῶς ἔχε, ὡς
νοσοῦντι. In Lucian's time a new
distinction appears to have arisen
between the various salutations that
were in use, and this occasioned the
treatise ὑπὲρ τοῦ ἐν τῇ προσαγορεύ-
σει πταίσματος. He informs us that
though ὑγιαίνειν might be said at
other times of the day, yet in the
morning χαῖρε alone was used. ἀφι-
κόμενος παρὰ σὲ, ὡς προσείποιμι τὸ
ἑωθινὸν, δέον τὴν συνήθη ταύτην
φωνὴν ἀφεῖναι καὶ χαίρειν κελεύειν,
ἐγὼ δ᾽ ὁ χρυσοῦς ἐπιλαθόμενος ὑγιαίνειν σε ἠξίουν, εὔφημον μὲν καὶ τοῦτο,
οὐκ ἐν καιρῷ δὲ, ὡς οὐ κατὰ τὴν ἕω.
Pro lapsu inter salut. 1. We further
learn that at an earlier period, at least
in the time of Alexis and Philemon,
no such distinction existed, and that
ὑγιαίνειν, and εὖ πράττειν, were customary. The first is the Pythagorean

salutation; the second, according to
Lucian, § 4, was first introduced by
Plato; according to Diog. Laert. x. 14,
by Epicurus as a superscription of his
letters. We have all three in a fragment of Philemon, quoted by Lucian
§ 6:

Αἰτῶ δ᾽ ὑγίειαν πρῶτον, εἶτ᾽ εὐπραξίαν,
τρίτον δὲ χαίρειν, εἶτ᾽ ὀφείλειν μηδενί.

In the time of Aristophanes, the ancient χαῖρε (ἀρχαιοτάτη φιλικὴ προσ-
φώνησις, Eustath. *ad Il.* ix. 197)
seems to have been regarded as old-
fashioned, and to some extent it became the mode to say ἀσπάζομαι.
Aristoph. *Plut.* 322:

Χαίρειν μὲν ὑμᾶς ἐστιν, ὦ ἄνδρες δημόται,
ἀρχαῖον ἤδη προσαγορεύειν καὶ σαπρόν·
ἀσπάζομαι δέ.

See *Nub.* 1145, where Socrates says
Στρεψιάδην ἀσπάζομαι. It appears
from Herodotus, ii. 89, that it was
customary to greet with words;
though afterwards it became the
fashion to kiss the hand, breast, or
knee of a superior. Lucian, *Nigrin.* 21:
οἱ δὲ σεμνότεροι καὶ προσκυνεῖσθαι
περιμένοντες, οὐ πόρρωθεν, οὐδ᾽ ὡς
Πέρσαις νόμος, ἀλλὰ δεῖ προσελ-
θόντα καὶ ὑποκύψαντα, καὶ πόρρωθεν τὴν ψυχὴν ταπεινώσαντα καὶ
τὸ πάθος αὐτῆς ἐμφανίσαντα τῇ τοῦ
σώματος ὁμοιότητι, τὸ στῆθος ἢ τὴν
δεξιὰν καταφιλεῖν. Also *Alexand.*
55: προὔτεινέ μοι κῦσαι τὴν δεξιὰν,
ὥσπερ εἰώθει τοῖς πολλοῖς. This
usage is evidently borrowed from ob-
servances in the worship of the gods;
see Lucian, *de Sacrif.* 12: ὁ δὲ πένης
ἱλάσατο τὸν θεὸν φιλήσας μόνον τὴν
αὑτοῦ δεξιάν.

May the gods transform into lightsome day the dark night
that now encompasses you.'[19] 'Nay,' said Polycles ; 'I
am not to be deceived. I am not one of those who, when
they meet with suffering or misfortune, send for a sophist
to console them.[20] Rather tell me something of the fate

---

[19] The words of Atossa when she
hears the news of the life of her son
(*Persæ*, 306),

καὶ λευκὸν ἦμαρ νυκτὸς ἐκ μελαγχίμου,

seem to contain a far more natural
solution of the adage, λευκὴ ἡμέρα,
than the far-fetched derivations that
have been given. Plutarch, *Pericl.*
27, says it originated from an incident
in the Samian war, in which Pericles
divided the Athenian troops into eight
companies, and every day one of these
was always allowed to rest. They
drew lots for it, and that company
which drew the one white bean rested.
He adds, διὸ καί φασι, τοὺς ἐν εὐπα-
θείαις τισὶ γενομένους λευκὴν ἡμέραν
ἐκείνην ἀπὸ τοῦ λευκοῦ κυάμου προσαγορεύειν. The more usual derivation is from the Scythian or Thracian
custom of marking those days on
which they had been prosperous with
a white, the others with a black
pebble. Suidas says : λευκὴ ἡμέρα.
Φύλαρχος γάρ φησι, τοὺς Σκύθας
μέλλοντας καθεύδειν ἄγειν τὴν φαρέτραν καί, εἰ μὲν ἀλύπως τύχοιεν
τὴν ἡμέραν ἐκείνην διαγαγόντες, καθ-
ιέναι εἰς τὴν φαρέτραν ψῆφον λευ-
κήν· εἰ δὲ ὀχληρῶς, μέλαιναν. After
death these were counted. See Plin.
Nat. Hist. vii. 40, 41.

[20] The philosophers of antiquity
seem in some sort to have undertaken
the care of souls, at all events they
frequently administered consolation
at times of suffering and sorrow.
Dio Chrysostom is very explicit. *Or.*
xxvi. p. 529 : πεπόνθασι γὰρ δὴ οἱ

πολλοὶ πρὸς τοὺς ἐκ φιλοσοφίας
λόγους, ὥσπερ, οἶμαι, πρὸς τὰ τῶι
ἰατρῶν φάρμακα. οὔτε γάρ τις ἐκείνοις εὐθὺς πρόσεισιν, οὐδὲ ὠνεῖται,
πρὶν ἢ περιπεσεῖν φαιερῷ νοσή-
ματι καὶ ἀλγῆσαί τι τοῦ σώματος·
οὔτε τῶν τοιούτων λόγων ἀκούειν
ἐθέλουσιν ὡς τὸ πολύ, ὅτῳ ἂν μὴ
λυπηρόν τι ξυνενεχθῇ καὶ τῶν δο-
κούντων χαλεπῶν. . . Κἂν ἀπολέσας
τύχῃ τινὰς τῶν οἰκείων, ἢ γυναῖκα, ἢ
παῖδα, ἢ ἀδελφὸν, ἀξιοῦσιν ἀι̣ικ-
νεῖσθαι τὸν φιλόσοφον καὶ παρη-
γορεῖν. See Plutarch, *de Superstit.*
7. It is related of Antiphon : ἐν
Κορίνθῳ τε κατεσκευασμένος οἴκημά
τι παρὰ τὴν ἀγορὰν προέγραψεν,
ὅτι δύναται τοὺς λυπουμένους διὰ
λόγων θεραπεύειν. καὶ πυνθανόμενος
τὰς αἰτίας παρεμυθεῖτο τοὺς κάμνοντας. Plut. *Dec. Or. Vit.* iv. p. 344.
See Phot. *Bibl.* Cod. 259. Similar
instances occur elsewhere ; so Aristoph. *Plut.* 177 :

Φ. λέψιος δ' οὐχ ἕνεκά σου μύθους λέγει ;

and we know from Dio Chrysost. *Or.*
xi. p. 323, how fond the Greeks were
of listening to amusing tales, whether
true or not. Many persons turned to
their own profit the superstition of
others. See Isocrates, *Ægin.* 2, p. 551.
Cf. Plato, *de Repub.* ii. p. 364 :
ἀγύρται δὲ καὶ μάντεις ἐπὶ πλουσίων
θύρας ἰόντες πείθουσι, κ. τ. λ. And
Dio Chrysost. *Or.* xxx. p. 553. Demosthenes taunts Æschines with
having pursued an occupation of the
kind ; *de Coron.* p. 313 ; and it is
related of Epicurus : σὺν τῇ μητρὶ
περιϊόντα αὐτὸν ἐς τὰ οἰκίδια καθαρ-

of thy family.' The youth, accordingly, delivered a brief recital of the fortunes of his house since the flight from Athens.

The sick man evinced so much emotion in the course of the narration, that at last the doctor motioned Charicles to break off. ' Is the draught ready that I ordered to be prepared ? ' he enquired of a slave who just then entered. ' Manto will bring it immediately,' was the reply. 'Manto?' exclaimed Polycles ; ' why not Cleobule ? ' ' She heard that gentlemen were with you,' replied the slave. ' They are only near friends of the family,' said the sick man ; ' she need not mind them. I prefer taking the draught from her.' The slave departed to inform the lady of his master's wishes, and the doctor again felt the patient's pulse, whilst the bystanders stood aside.

One of the three, who had been addressed as Sophilos, had seized Charicles by the hand, and retired with him to a corner of the room. His age was between fifty and sixty, and his exterior bespoke affluence, as well as polish and good breeding. Time had furrowed his brow, and rendered grey his locks ; but his firm carriage and active step betokened one still vigorous, and he conversed with all the vivacity of youth. A gentle earnestness and good-humoured benevolence beamed in his countenance, and his whole appearance was calculated to awaken confidence, and attract the beholder.[21]

μ.ὺς ἀναγινώσκειν. These καθαρμοὶ were connected with the recitation of mysterious spells. Of the same kind were the magic sentences serving as amulets, ἀλεξιφάρμακα, like the Ἐφέσια γράμματα. So a fragment of Menander :

Ἐφέσια τοῖς γαμοῦσιν οὗτος περιπατεῖ λέγων ἀλεξιφάρμακα.

The interpretation of dreams has already been discussed. See Note 4, Sc. VIII. A kindred art to this is mentioned by Alciphron, Epist. iii. 59. The πινάκια there mentioned seem to be analogous to the Roman sortes, and the operation may be compared to our cutting of cards. No doubt a great number of persons made a living as οἰωνισταὶ, ἀγυρταὶ, τερατοσκόποι and γόητες, though their trade stood in very ill odour.

[21] Periplectomenes in the Miles of Plautus, iii. 1, has served as the original of Sophilos.

As Charicles recounted the misfortunes of his family, Sophilos had listened with sympathy, and, when he now further questioned Charicles about many passages in his life, his glance dwelt on the youth with peculiar satisfaction. Whilst they were engaged in low-toned conversation, the hanging was pushed aside, and Cleobule entered, followed by a female slave. Nearly overcome with timidity, she did not dare to raise her eyes, but kept them fixed on the glass phial [22] in her right hand, and she hastened to

---

[22] Though the invention of glass falls in the days of early Phœnician legend, still from this we cannot infer how soon articles of this material came into common use in Greece. It seems to have been long ranked with precious stones, and was always called λίθος (*Nubes*, 766); whilst later, crystal is called ὕαλος ὀρωρυγμένη (Achill. Tat. ii. 3). In Herodot. ii. 69, where we read, ἀρτήματά τε λίθινα χυτὰ καὶ χρύσεα ἐς τὰ ὦτα ἐνθέντες, the name ὕαλος does not seem to be even known, so that it must then have been still a rarity. For these λίθινα χυτὰ are of glass, as is manifest from a comparison of the above passage with Plato, *Tim.* p. 61 : τό τε περὶ τὴν ὕαλον γένος ἅπαν ὅσα τε λίθων χυτὰ εἴδη. The first mention of the name, and at the same time of glass utensils, occurs *Acharn.* 73 :

ξενιζόμενοι δὲ πρὸς βίαν ἐπίνομεν
ἐξ ὑαλίνων ἐκπωμάτων καὶ χρυσίδων
ἄκρατον οἶνον ἡδύν.

But here, as in Herodotus, it is evident that such vessels are costly rarities, for the ὑάλινα ἐκπώματα are mentioned along with vessels of gold, and the passage is descriptive of magnificence and luxury. By degrees glass became more common, and not only drinking vessels, but also large bowls were made of this material. Pausan. ii. 27, 3 : γέγραπται δὲ ἐνταῦθα καὶ

Μέθη, Παυσίου καὶ τοῦτο ἔργον, ἐξ ὑαλίνης φιάλης πίνουσα· ἴδοις δ' ἂν ἐν τῇ γραφῇ φιάλην τε ὑάλου καὶ δι' αὐτῆς γυναικὸς πρόσωπον. In Athenæus, iv. p. 129, in the description of the wedding-feast of Caranos the Macedonian, mention occurs of a glass bowl which measured two cubits in diameter : ὑαλοῦς πίναξ δίπηχύς που τὴν διάμετρον. But the period when the use of glass became most common, was when its manufacture, and particularly the art of polishing it, arrived at such wonderful perfection in Alexandria. Athen. xi. p. 1012 : κατασκευάζουσι δὲ οἱ ἐν 'Αλεξανδρείᾳ τὴν ὕαλον μεταρρυθμίζοντες πολλάκις πολλαῖς ἰδέαις ποτηρίων παντὸς τοῦ πανταχόθεν κατακομιζομένου κεράμου τὴν ἰδέαν μιμούμενοι. Consult *Gallus*, pp. 303 and 373. See also the description of a crystal vase in Achill. Tat. ii. 3 : ὑάλου μὲν τὸ πᾶν ἔργον ὀρωρυγμένης· κύκλῳ δὲ αὐτὸν ἄμπελοι περιέστεφον ἀπὸ τοῦ κρατῆρος πεφυτευμέναι. Οἱ δὲ βότρυς πάντῃ περικρεμάμενοι· ὄμφαξ μὲν αὐτῶν ἕκαστος, ὅσον ἦν κενὸς ὁ κρατήρ· ἐὰν δὲ ἐγχέῃς οἶνον, κατὰ μικρὸν ὁ βότρυς ὑποπερκάζεται καὶ σταφυλὴν τὴν ὄμφακα ποιεῖ. Cf. Strabo, xvi. 2, 25.

The commonest drinking vessels were of burnt clay, κεράμεια. Those manufactured in Attica were very celebrated, and were exported in con-

present to her sick husband and uncle the potion which it contained; the physician having first mingled in it something from his drug-box. She next smoothed the pillow, bending affectionately over her husband, as if to enquire whether he felt any relief.

The eyes of all present were fastened on this picture of dutiful affection, but the gaze of Charicles especially seemed riveted to the spot. When Cleobule entered, he was conversing with Sophilos, with his back to the door, and she on her part was so entirely occupied with tending the sick man, that her face had not once been turned towards the group behind her. Yet there was something in that graceful figure that awoke scarcely stifled emotions in his breast. It was the very image of the apparition by the brook. There was the same delicate structure and youthful swell of the limbs, though they were now enveloped in a dress of more ample folds; the same profusion of blond tresses, though now gathered in a gold-coloured caul; and that very same gracefulness of movement, though modified of course by the altered circumstances.

The physician next prescribed a bath for his patient. This was easily effected, as Polycles had apartments constructed for the purpose in his own house, which were fitted up with every requisite appliance. They bore a miniature resemblance to the larger public baths; although Polycles, being stricken in years, had seldom any use for the cold bath, confining himself to one of a warmer character. There

---

siderable quantities. See Herod. v. 88; Aristoph. *Acharn.* 900; Athen. i. p. 28; xi. pp. 480, 484. There was also throughout Greece an important internal traffic in these pottery wares, and certain kinds were even imported into Athens. Eubulos, quoted in Athen. i. p. 28, praises Κνίδια κεράμια, Σικελικὰ βατάνια, Μεγαρικὰ πιθάκνια. See Plut. *de vit. Ær. al.* 2; and Athen.

xi. p. 464. Besides these, there were utensils of brass, silver, and gold, often embossed. Demosth. *in Euerg.* p. 1155: ὑδρία χαλκῆ πολλοῦ ἀξία. Again *in Timoth.* p. 1193, we have φιάλαι λυκιουργεῖς δύο, worth 237 drachmas. For further information see Dodwell, *Class. Tour,* ii. p. 200, and Welcker, in the *Rhein. Mus.* for 1839.

was also a regular sudatory, and in it the laver[23] used in taking the hotter baths. Orders were given for raising

---

[23] The Roman baths have been very fully discussed in *Gallus*, pp. 366-397, and as what has there been said is, for the most part, applicable to the baths of Greece, it will not be necessary to repeat it here; and besides the absence of accurate information respecting the Grecian baths of the better age, leaves us to infer many of the details from the analogy of the baths of Rome. Here, therefore, the method of bathing will be alone investigated. The daily bath was by no means so indispensable with the Greeks as it was with the Romans; nay, in some instances the former nation looked on it as a mark of degeneracy and increasing effeminacy, when the baths were much frequented. But so far as the bath was necessary to cleanliness, its neglect was considered a matter of reproach. So *Lysistr.* 280 : ῥυπῶν, ἀπαράτιλτος, ἐξ ἐτῶν ἄλοντος. And *Nubes*, 835:

ὧν ὑπὸ τῆς φειδωλίας
ἀπεκείρατ' οὐδεὶς πώποτ', οὐδ' ἠλείψατο
οὐδ' ἐς βαλανεῖον ἦλθε λουσόμενος.

It was said in ridicule of the Dardans that they only washed thrice in their lives, τρὶς ἐν τῷ βίῳ λούονται μόνον, ὅταν γεννῶνται, καὶ ἐπὶ γάμοις, καὶ τελευτῶντες. Nicol. Damasc. quoted by Stobæus, *Tit.* v. 51. Yet the frequent use of the bath in the βαλανείοις was deemed a τρυφὴ in the better period, and persons of simple habits abstained from it. So Plato, *Symp.* p. 174, relates of Socrates, ἔφη γὰρ οἱ Σωκράτη ἐντυχεῖν λελουμένον τε καὶ τὰς βλαύτας ὑποδεδεμένον, ἃ ἐκεῖνος ὀλιγάκις ἐποίει: and in Plutarch, *Phoc.* 4, we read, Φωκίωνα γὰρ οὔτε γελάσαντά τις, οὔτε κλαύσαντα ῥᾳδίως Ἀθηναί-

ων εἶδεν, οὐδ' ἐν βαλανείῳ δημοσιεύοντι λουσάμενον. Demosth. *adv. Polycl.* p. 1217, speaks of it as a mark of the bad discipline of a ship's crew: διεφθαρμένον μὲν πλήρωμα καὶ εἰωθὸς, ἀργύριον πολὺ προλαμβάνειν, καὶ ἀτελείας ἄγειν τῶν νομιζομένων ἐν τῇ νηῒ λειτουργιῶν, καὶ λούσθαι ἐν βαλανείῳ. Hence the youth in Sparta was καὶ λουτρῶν καὶ ἀλειμμάτων ἄπειρος. Plutarch, *Lyc.* 16. But it was only the βαλανεῖα, that is, the warm baths, θερμὰ λουτρὰ, which were censured, and in early times they were not even allowed within cities. Athen. i. p. 18: προσφάτως δὲ καὶ τὰ βαλανεῖα παρῆκται, τὴν ἀρχὴν οὐδὲ ἔνδον τῆς πόλεως ἐώντων εἶναι αὐτά. So the Δίκαιος λόγος, *Nubes*, 991, advises the youth βαλανείων ἀπέχεσθαι, and maintains this opinion against the question which the Ἄδικος λόγος puts, 1045,

καίτοι τίνα γνώμην ἔχων ψέγεις τὰ θερμὰ λουτρά;
Δ. ὅτιὴ κάκιστόν ἐστι καὶ δειλὸν ποιεῖ τὸν ἄνδρα.

Plato, *Leg.* vi. p. 761, wishes to confine the use of warm baths to old people, γεροντικὰ λουτρὰ θερμὰ παρέχοντας. See Plutarch, *de San. Tuend.* i. p. 515: and *Symp.* viii. 9.

The βαλανεῖα were either public, δημόσια, (Xen. *de Repub.* 2, 10,) or private establishments, ἴδια, ἰδιωτικὰ, though the latter terms may also be supposed to denote baths in private houses, which also naturally existed. In some vase-paintings the bathing tubs bear the inscriptions ΔΗΜΟΣΙΑ and ΙΔΙΑ. See Tischbein, *Coll. of Engr.* i. pl. 58, from which the accompanying cut is taken. A public bath is to be understood in Diog. Laert. vii.? 2.

this apartment to a moderate temperature, previous to the patient being carried thither. Cleobule hastened to

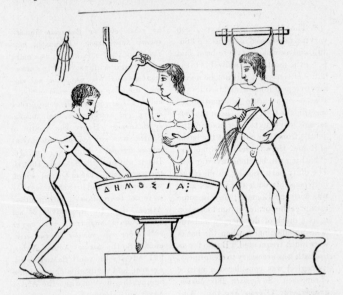

where Zeno is mentioned as τῶν εἰς τὴν ἐπισκευὴν τοῦ λουτρῶνος συμβαλλομένων εἷς. A private bath is mentioned by Isæus, *de Dicæog. her.* p. 101, and in Id. *de Philoctem. her.* p. 140, we hear of such an one being sold for three thousand drachmas. A βαλανεῖον ἰδιωτικὸν is referred to by Plutarch, *Demetr.* 24, and also by Alciphron, *Epist.* i. 23. In these baths, and in the public ones as well, the βαλανεὺς received a trifle, ἐπίλουτρον. So *Nubes*, 835, where Socrates and his scholars abstain from bathing for the sake of economy. See *Ranæ*, 710; Lucian, *Lexiph.* 2: σὺ δὲ, ὦ παῖ, στλεγγίδα μοι καὶ βύρσαν, καὶ φωσώνια, καὶ ῥύμματα ναυστολεῖν ἐς τὸ βαλανεῖον καὶ τοὐπίλουτρον κομίζειν. ἔχεις δὲ χαμάζε παρὰ τὴν ἐγγυοθήκην δύ᾽ ὀβολώ. Schol. τὸ ἐπίλουτρον δὲ τὸ ἐν τῇ συνηθείᾳ

βαλανικὸν, and that this is to be understood of the public baths, appears from Athen. viii. p. 351: ἐν Φασήλιδι δὲ πρὸς τὸν παῖδα διαμφισβητοῦντος τοῦ βαλανέως περὶ τοῦ ἀργυρίου· ἦν γὰρ νόμος πλείονος λούειν τοὺς ξένους· ᾿Ω μιαρὲ, ἔφη, παῖ, παρὰ χαλκοῦν με μικροῦ Φασηλίτην ἐποίησας.

Of the arrangement of the baths we know extremely little, for Lucian's *Hippias* refers to a bath arranged in the taste of a later age. It is rather remarkable that in the vase-paintings we never meet with any basin or tub, wherein the bathers might stand or sit. There is always a round or oval basin, resting on one foot, beside which the bathers stand quite naked to wash themselves. These basins are doubtless the λουτῆρες and λουτήρια. See Moschion apud Athen. v. p. 207. The ὑπόστατον, Poll. x.

superintend in person the needful preparations, and as she
turned round to go towards the door, her eye fell upon

46, is the leg or foot whereon the
vessel rested. Nevertheless we cannot doubt but that there were also
tubs in the baths, which one might
get into. They were called πύελοι
(in Homer ἀσάμινθοι). See Schol. on
Aristoph. *Equit.* 1060: ' τὰς πυέλους
καταλήψεσθ' ἐν βαλανείῳ.' τὰς ἐμ-
βάσεις. πύελος γὰρ ὄρυγμα, ἐμβατὴ ἔνθα ἀπολούονται, and Pollux, vii. 166,
quotes a fragment of Aristophanes :

ἀλλ' ἀρτίως κατέλιπον αὐτὴν σμωμένην
ἐν τῇ πυέλῳ.

Some of them were calculated to contain several persons, as we see from a
passage of Eupolis ap. Poll. vii. 168 :
λέγει γοῦν ἐν Διαιτῶντι, εἰς βαλανεῖον εἰσελθὼν μὴ ζηλοτυπήσῃς τὸν
συμβαίνοντά σοι εἰς τὴν μάκτραν.
So that, in the main points, the λουτήρ answers to the Roman *labrum*,
and the πύελος to the *alveus*.

In the βαλανεῖον there was also
frequently a vapour-bath or sudatory,
πυρία, πυριατήριον. Herodot. iv. 75,
mentions it as usual; also Eupolis
apud Poll. ix. 43 ; Aristot. *Probl.* ii.
11 ; 29; and 32. There seems to
have been nothing in the Grecian
sweating-baths similar to the Roman
concamerata sudatio, with its *Laco-
nicum* ; but the bathers sat, on the
contrary, in separate tub-like compartments. This is what is meant by
the πυρίας χαλκᾶς in the fragment of
Moschion, referred to above. See also
Athen. xii. p. 519 : παρὰ Συβαρίταις
δ' εὑρήθησαν καὶ πύελοι, ἐν αἷς κατα-
κείμενοι ἐπυριῶντο. These πύελοι
used in the vapour-baths were also
called πυρίαι. Phrynich. *Epit.* p. 325.
A bathing establishment also was not
complete without an anointing room,
ἀλειπτήριον, which is probably the

same as the *elæothesium* of Vitruvius.
See Poll. vii. 166. It is doubtful
whether an ἀποδυτήριον, in which to
deposit the clothes, was an essential
portion of the baths ; it was probably
of later date. Though Lucian talks
of such a place, where ἱματιοφυλα-
κοῦντες (Lat. *capsarii*) are stationed,
yet in Aristotle's time such people
were unknown, and the bathers
looked after their own clothes : for
in discussing the punishment to be
awarded, ἐὰν μέν τις ἐκ βαλανείου
κλέψῃ, he says, ἐν δὲ τῷ βαλανείῳ. . .
ῥᾴδιον τῷ βουλομένῳ κακουργεῖν.
οὐδὲν γὰρ ἰσχυρὸν ἔχουσι πρὸς τὴν
φυλακὴν οἱ τιθέντες, ἀλλ' ἢ τὸ αὑτῶν ὄμμα. *Probl.* xxix. 14. See
Theoph. *Char.* 8 ; Diog. Laert. vi.
52 ; Athen. iii. p. 97.

The question whether there were
common baths for women, can only
be answered from the monuments.
There are many very wanton vase-
paintings representing women washing together at a λουτήρ. Tischbein,
Coll. of Engr. iii. 35 ; iv. 26 ; 27 ; 28.
Millin, ii. 9, &c. A vessel in the
Museum at Berlin is especially interesting ; a woman's bath of very
remarkable construction is depicted
on it. Water descends upon the
bathers in a shower, from certain
heads of animals fixed to the capitals
of the pillars of the bath-room. If
these representations do not refer to
baths in private houses, it would appear that there were common baths
for women, and perhaps even public
ones. The almost illegible inscription on the λουτήρ, in Tischbein, iv.
28, looks very much like ΔΗΜΟΣΙΑ,
though this is far from certain. At
Athens, it is true that nothing of the

Charicles, who was standing near it.   Suddenly she started
as though she had seen the Gorgo's head, or some spectre

kind would be admissible; but in other
towns, those of Magna Græcia for
instance, where the women were under less restraint, it might well have
been the case.

In the vase-paintings the women
are in a state of nudity, except in a
single instance where one has a slight
shift, χιτώνιον. See the woodcut.
Poll. x. 181, says: τὸ μέντοι δέρμα, ᾧ
ὑποζώννυνται αἱ γυναῖκες λουόμεναι,
ἢ οἱ λοῦντες αὐτὰς, φᾶν λουτρίδα ἔξεστι καλεῖν Θεοπόμπου εἰπόντος ἐν
Παισί,

τηνδὶ περιζωσάμενος φᾶν λουτρίδα
κατάδεσμον ἥβης περιπέτασον.

Φερεκράτης δὲ ἐν Ἵππῳ καταλέγων
τὰ ἐργαλεῖα τῆς παιδοτριβικῆς

ἤδη μὲν φᾶν λούμενοι περιζώννυνται.

But neither of the passages he quotes

refer to women ; and such a περίζωμα
or ὑπόζωμα is never represented. Cf.
Jacobs, Animadv. ad Anthol. iv. p.
224.   The other necessaries, such as
oil, towel and strigils, were brought
from home by slaves. See Gallus,
p. 393. For the form of the strigil or
scraper στλεγγὶς or ξύστρα (Phryn.
p. 229; 460), the handle of which was
hollow, see Aristoph. Thesm. 556 :

ἐπεὶ τόδ' οὐκ εἴρηχ', ὁρᾷς, ὡς στλεγγίδας
   λαβοῦσαι
ἔπειτα σιφωνίζομεν τὸν οἶνον.

It was usually of iron, among the
Spartans of cane (Plut. Inst. Lac.
32), at Acragas, according to Ælian,
Var. Hist. xii. 29, of silver, as well
as the λήκυθοι. Sometimes it was of
peculiar shape, as we see from vases
and gems. Millin, Peint. d. Vas.

risen out of Hades; and the glass phial would have dropped from her hand, had not the doctor caught it. With a

---

ii. 45; 63. Concerning the oil, see Theophr. *Char.* 11. The ῥύμμα, however, was mostly provided by the βαλανεὺς, thus in Aristoph. *Lysist.* 377, the woman says,

εἰ ῥύμμα τυγχάνεις ἔχων, λουτρόν γέ σοι
παρέξω.

Ran. 710: ὁ πονηρότατος βαλανεὺς, ὁπόσοι κρατοῦσι κυκησιτέφρου, ψευδονίτρου κονίας καὶ Κιμωλίας γῆς. Schol. ταῦτα τοιαῦτα καθάρματά ἐστιν, οἷς οἱ λουόμενοι χρῶνται τῶν βαλανέων πωλούντων. For the various sorts, lye, κονία, (Plato, *de Repub.* iv. p. 430,) alkaline salts, nitre, νίτρον, fuller's earth, γῆ Κιμωλία, &c., see Beckmann's *History of Inventions*. What resemblance the σμήματα or σμήγματα bore to our soap cannot be determined. See *Gallus*, p. 378.

It was invariably the rule to be soused with cold water immediately after either a warm or a sweatingbath. Plutarch, *de primo frig.* 10: ἱκανῶς δὲ καὶ ὁ τῶν μετὰ λουτρὸν ἢ πυρίαν περιχεαμένων ψυχρὸν ἀνιὼν ἀτμὸς ἐνδείκνυται κ.τ.λ. Cf. Fragm. *in Hesiod.* περιχεόμενοι κατὰ κρατός τε καὶ ὤμων, and Paus. ii. 34, 2, complains that at the hot springs of Methana, λουσαμένῳ δὲ ἐνταῦθα οὔτε ὕδωρ ἐστὶν ἐγγὺς ψυχρὸν, οὔτε ἐσπεσόντα ἐς τὴν θάλασσαν ἀκινδύνως νήχεσθαι. Cf. Plato, *de Repub.* i. p. 344: ὥσπερ βαλανεὺς ἡμῶν καταντλήσας κατὰ τῶν ὤτων ἀθρόον καὶ πολὺν λόγον. So Lucian, *Demosth. encom.* 16. This dashing with cold water was performed by the βαλανεὺς and his assistants, παραχύται. Plutarch, *de Invid.* 6: and *Apophth. Lac.* 49. The vessel used for the operation was called ἀρύταινα, and perhaps also ἀρύβαλλος, as Poll. vii. 166, supposes

from the passage in *Equit.* 1090, though the Scholiast explains it differently. See Athen. xi. p. 1039; and Theophr. *Char.* 9: δεινὸς δὲ καὶ πρὸς τὰ χαλκεῖα τὰ ἐν τῷ βαλανείῳ προσελθὼν καὶ βάψας ἀρύταιναν βοῶντος τοῦ βαλανέως αὐτὸς αὑτοῦ καταχέασθαι. In a vase-painting, Tischbein, i. 58, is represented a boy in the character of a παραχύτης with the ἀρύταινα, and in Moses, *Collect. of Ant. Vas.* p. 14, there is a woman over whom the water is being poured. It may be added, that the παραχύται also brought the hot water. See Athen. xii. p. 518.

The hour of bathing was, in the better period, that preceding the chief meal, δεῖπνον, of this no proof need be adduced. In later and more degenerate days, noon is sometimes mentioned. Lucian, *Lexiph.* 4: καὶ γὰρ ὁ γνώμων σκιάζει μέσην τὴν πόλον· καὶ δέος μὴ ἐν λουτρίῳ ἀπολουσάμεθα κ.τ.λ., and Alciph. *Epist.* iii. 60: ὡς γὰρ ἐλούσαντο οἱ πολλοὶ καὶ μεσοῦσα ἡμέρα ἦν. But, even at an earlier period, voluptuaries bathed several times a day. See Menander, quoted by Athen. iv. p. 166:

καίτοι νέος ποτ' ἐγενόμην κἀγὼ, γύναι·
ἀλλ' οὐκ ἐλούμην πεντάκις τῆς ἡμέρας
τότ', ἀλλὰ νῦν.

See also the fragment of Simonides in Meineke, p. 127:

λοῦται δὲ πάσης ἡμέρας ἀπο ῥύπον
δὶς, ἄλλοτε τρὶς, καὶ μύροις ἀλείφεται.

Still, even then the bath was regarded for the most part as a preliminary to a meal. See Artemidor. *Oneirocr.* i. 64: νῦν δὲ οἱ μὲν οὐ πρότερον ἐσθίουσιν, εἰ μὴ λούοιντο· οἱ δὲ καὶ ἐμφαγόντες· εἶτα δὴ λούονται μέλλοντες δειπνήσειν. καὶ ἔστι νῦν τὸ βαλα-

deep blush, and downcast eyes, she rushed hurriedly past
the young man, who was himself so surprised and confused,
that he did not hear the question which Sophilos just
then put to him.   It was now necessary to leave the
sick chamber, and he was not sorry to do so.   Approaching the bed, he expressed a hope that its tenant would
amend, and then hastened from the chamber in a tumult
of contending emotions.

νεῖον οὐδὲν ἄλλο ἢ ὁδὸς ἐπὶ τροφήν.
At that time, games, such as the cottabos, were played at the baths. See
Diog. Laert. vi. 46.   In winter, the
baths, particularly the firing-place,
served for the poor to stay and warm
themselves, if the βαλανεύς allowed
it.   Aristoph. *Plut.* 951:

ΔΙΚ. καὶ μὴν ἐπειδὴ τὴν πανοπλίαν τὴν
      ἐμὴν
ἔχων βαδίζεις, ἐς τὸ βαλανεῖον τρέχε·
ἔπειτ' ἐκεῖ κορυφαῖος ἑστηκὼς θέρου.
κἀγὼ γὰρ εἶχον τὴν στάσιν ταύτην ποτέ.
ΧΡ. ἀλλ' ὁ βαλανεὺς ἕλξει **θύραζ**' αὐτόν.

Cf. also, *ib.* 535, which latter passage
is admirably illustrated by Alciphr.
Epist. i. 23 : ἐβουλευσάμην οὖν 'Οδύσ-
σειον βούλευμα, δραμεῖν εἰς τοὺς θό-
λους ἢ τὰς καμίνους τῶν βαλανείων·
ἀλλ' οὐδὲ ἐκεῖσε συνεχώρουν οἱ τῶν
ὁμοτέχνων περὶ ταῦτα κυλινδούμενοι
. . . ὡς οὖν ᾐσθόμην, οὐκ εἶναί μοι εἰς
ταῦτα εἰσιτητέον δραμὼν ἐπὶ τὸ
Θρασύλλου βαλανεῖον ἰδιωτικῆς οἰκίας εὗρον τοῦτο κενὸν καὶ καταβα-
λὼν ὀβολοὺς δύο καὶ τὸν βαλανέα
τούτοις ἵλεων καταστήσας ἐθερόμην.

SCENE THE NINTH.

THE WILL.

IT was one of those blustering nights, so common at the commencement of Mæmacterion. The wind blew from Salamis, driving before it the scud of black rain-clouds over the Piræus; and when they opened for a moment, the crescent of the waning moon would peer forth, throwing a transient glimmer on the distant temples of the Acropolis. In the streets of the sea-port, generally so full of bustle, reigned deep repose, only broken by the dull roaring of the sea, or the groaning of the masts, as some more violent gust swept through the rigging of the vessels yet remaining in the harbour. Occasionally too some half-intoxicated sailor would stagger lanternless[1] from the wine-shops

---

[1] As the streets were not lighted, (see *Gallus*, p. 80, Note 19,) it was enjoined by custom, or perhaps even by authority, that all who went out after dusk should be preceded by a slave with a light. Torches, δᾳδες, φανοί, δεταί, λαμπάδες, λαμπτῆρες, mostly purchased at the time from a κάπηλος, were used for this purpose. See Lysias, *de Cæde Erat.* p. 27; Nicostr. ap. Athen. xv. p. 700; Plutarch, *Arat.* 6; Aristoph. *Eccles.* 692, 978; *Vesp.* 1331. They consisted of a bundle of pine-splints, (hence δεταί, and in Athen. xv. p. 700: ἔκ τινων ξύλων τετμημένων δέσμη,) or of other dried woods, probably made more inflammable by means of pitch. Thus the tendrils of the vine were used. *Lysistr.* 308 :

τῆς ἀμπέλου δ᾽ ἐς τὴν χύτραν τὸν φαιὸν ἐγκαθέντες,
ἄψαιτες εἶτ᾽ ἐς τὴν θύραν, κριηδὸν ἐμπέσοιμεν.

On which the Scholiast remarks : ἐκ

δὲ τῶν ἀμπελίνων τὰς λαμπάδας κατεσκεύαζον εἰς ἔξαψιν, ὡς καὶ ἐν Λημνίαις φησί. In the early times, however, no mention occurs of the pitch-torches of oakum, *funalia*, or the wax-torches, so much used by the Romans. See Note 5, *infra*. They used also lanterns of horn, called φανοί, but by the Attics λυχνοῦχοι. Among many other passages we may refer to Phryn. *Ecl.* p. 59 : Φανός· ἐπὶ τῆς λαμπάδος, ἀλλὰ μὴ ἐπὶ τοῦ κερατίνου λέγε. τοῦτο δὲ λυχνοῦχον. Phot. *Lex.* p. 238 : Λυχνοῦχον· τὸν κεράτινον φανὸν, ἀπὸ τοῦ λύχνον ἐν αὐτῷ περιέχεσθαι, φανὸς δὲ ἡ ἐκ ξύλων λαμπάς· Athen. xv. p. 699: ὅτι δὲ λυχνοῦχοι οἱ νῦν καλούμενοι φανοὶ ὠ᾽ ομάζοντο Ἀριστοφάνης ἐν Αἰολοσίκωνι παρίστησι·

Καὶ διαστίλβον θ᾽ ὁρῶμεν
ὥσπερ ἐν καινῷ λυχνούχῳ
πάντα τῆς ἐξωμίδος.

Translucent horn seems to have been

towards the harbour; or some footpad would sneak along the sides of the houses, ready to pounce on the cloak of a belated passenger, and hiding cautiously behind a Hermes or an altar whenever the bell of the night-patrol was heard.[2]

In a small room of a house situated some distance from the harbour, a young man of unprepossessing exterior lay stretched upon a low couch, which was too short for his figure. His hollow eyes and sunken cheeks, the carelessness of his demeanour, his hasty way of draining the cup in his right hand, and the coarse jokes that from time to time escaped him, sufficiently marked him as one of those vulgar

---

the usual material for these lanterns. See a fragment quoted by Athenæus, supra:

κερατίνου τε φωσφόρου λύχνου σέλας.

See Gallus, p. 314. In this lantern the lamp was placed. See Vesp. 246. In the absence of such a lantern, a pot or basket supplied its place. So Acharn. 453: σπυρίδιον διακεκαυμένον λύχνῳ. How general the use of such lights was, is shown by the manner in which the Chorus in the Clouds, 612, extols the moon, for saving people this expense:

πρῶτα μὲν τοῦ μηνὸς εἰς δᾷδ' οὐκ ἔλαττον ἢ
    δραχμὴν,
ὥστε καὶ λέγειν ἅπαντας ἐξιόντας ἑσπέρας·
μὴ πρίω, παῖ, δᾷδ', ἐπειδὴ φῶς Σεληναίης
    καλόν.

See also the fragment of Epicharmus quoted in the following note, where the parasite very characteristically steals about without a light.

[2] The altars and Hermæ before the houses, the public monuments and the arcades, were well adapted for nocturnal hiding-places. See Andoc. de Myst. p. 19. Nocturnal depredators, who stole people's clothes, λωποδύται, would avail themselves of them. The often-expressed fear of such characters proves how numerous they

were at Athens. Antipho. de Cæde Volunt. p. 631: ἔστι δὲ οὐκ ἀπεικὸς, ὡς οὗτοί φασιν, ἀλλὰ εἰκὸς, ἀωρὶ τῶν νυκτῶν πλανώμενον ἐπὶ τοῖς ἱματίοις διαφθαρῆναι. The nightly patrols, περίπολοι, seem to have apprehended suspicious characters whom they found in the street, at least so says the parasite in a fragment of Epicharmus, ap. Athen. vi. p. 236:

λύχνον δ' οὐχ ὁ παῖς μοι συμφέρει·
ἕρπω δ' ὀλισθάζων τε καὶ κατάσκοτος
ἔραμος. αἴ κα δ' ἐντύχω τοῖς περιπόλοις,
τούτοις ἀγαθὸν ἐπιλέγω τοῖς θεοῖς, ὅτι
οὐ λῶντι παίων, ἀλλὰ μαστιγῶντί με.

These περίπολοι, as can be abundantly shown, carried a bell to ascertain whether the watch were awake and at their posts, and the latter were probably required to answer at the sound of the same. Aves, 842, 1159; Schol. on the former passage: οἱ περίπολοι τὰς φυλακὰς περισκοποῦντες, ἐρχόμενοι ἐπὶ τοὺς φύλακας κώδωνας εἶχον καὶ διὰ τούτων ἐψόφουν, πειράζοντες τὸν καθεύδοντα, καὶ ἵνα οἱ φυλάττοντες ἀντιφθέγγωνται. Cf. Hesych. s. v. κωδωνίσαι and κωδωνοφορῶν. See also Plutarch, Arat. 7, concerning the surprisal of Sicyon: Ἀναβάντων δὲ τῶν πρώτων ὁ τὴν ἑωθινὴν φυλακὴν παραδιδοὺς ἐφώδευε κώδωνι καὶ φῶτα πολλὰ καὶ θόριβο· ἦν τῶν ἐπιπορευομένων.

roués, who were accustomed to waste the day at the dice-board, and devote the night to riot and debauchery. On the table near him, beside the nearly empty punch-bowl, stood a lamp with a double wick, whose light abundantly illumined the narrow chamber. There were also the remnants of the frugal supper that he had just concluded, and a second goblet, which a slave, who sat upon another couch opposite the young man, replenished pretty frequently. Between them was a draught-board which the slave was eyeing attentively, whilst the other surveyed it with tolerable indifference. The game was by no means even. The menial evidently had the advantage; and he now made a move which reduced his adversary to great straits.

'A stupid game, this!' exclaimed the youth, as he tossed the pieces all in a heap; 'a game where it's all thinking, and nothing won after all. Dicing for me,' he added with a yawn. 'But what has got Sosilas? It must be past midnight; and such weather as this, I should not over-enjoy the walk from the town to the haven.' 'He's gone to Polycles,' replied the slave. ''Twas said he would not live till morning, and Sosilas seems vastly concerned about him.' 'I know,' answered the youth; 'but then why did he send for me, just at this time of all others? The morning would have done quite as well; and I must needs leave a jolly party, forsooth; and here I am, hang it, and have to stand my own wine; for not a drop has the old hunks provided.' 'All I know,' replied the slave, 'is, that he bade me fetch you, wherever you were, as he must have speech with you this very night without fail.' 'Then why doesn't he come?' retorted the other, peevishly. 'Did he go unattended?' 'Syrus went with him; he'll come to no harm. And even suppose he didn't return,' continued the slave with a smile; 'why, you're his next relation and heir, aren't you? Two houses in the city, besides this here—a carpenter's shop,[3] and may be some

---

[3] See Excursus on *The Slaves*.

five or six talents in ready cash :—in sooth, no such bad
heritage!' The youth lolled back complacently on the
couch. 'Yes, Molon,' said he, ' when he's once out of the
way, then '——At this moment came a violent rap at the
outer door. 'There he is !' cried the slave, as he hastily
caught up the draught-board and one of the goblets,
smoothed down the cushion and coverlet of the couch he
had been sitting on, and stationed himself at the stripling's
elbow, as if he had been waiting on him.

Steps were now audible in the court-yard, and a gruff
voice was heard giving orders to a slave in harsh accents.
The door opened, and in walked a man with a large beard,
and dark and forbidding features. He was wrapped, after
the Spartan fashion, in a short mantle of coarse thick texture, and wore Laconian shoes. In his hand was a stout
cudgel, with its handle bent in the form of a cross.[4] The
sight of the drinking cups and the unwonted illumination of
the chamber made him forget the greeting. He approached
the slave in a rage. ' Ah! you knave !' cried he, raising
his stick ; ' what d'ye mean by these two burners, and such
large wicks ?[5] Does not the winter consume oil enough

---

[4] In ancient reliefs and paintings,
representing scenes from comedy, are
to be seen old men with sticks whose
handles curl inwards in a serpentine
fashion. See *Mus. Borb.* i. 20; iv. 24.

[5] So Strepsiades says, Aristoph.
Nub. 57 :

οἴμοι, τί γάρ μοι τὸν πότην ἧπτες λύχνον;
δεῦρ' ἐλθ', ἵνα κλάῃς. Θ. διὰ τί δῆτα
κλαύσομαι ;
Σ. ὅτι τῶν παχειῶν ἐνετιθεῖς θρυαλλίδων.

Similarly the chorus, *Vesp.* 251, forbids the wick to be drawn out too
much :

τί δὴ παθὼν τῷ δακτύλῳ τὴν θρυαλλίδ' ὠθεῖς;
καὶ ταῦτα τοὐλαίου σπανίζοντος, ὦ 'ρόητε.
οὐ γὰρ δάκνει σ', ὅταν δέῃ τίμιον πρίασθαι.

The oil-lamp, λύχνος, was the only
sort of light the Greeks had for household use. Perhaps in more ancient

times chips of wood, or pieces of pine,
burning in a chafing-dish, answered
the purpose; but when manners grew
more refined, this method of lighting
was entirely superseded by the lamp,
and torches were used only out of
doors. Athen. xv. p. 700, says : οἱ
παλαιὸν δ' εὕρημα λύχνος· φλογὶ δ'
οἱ παλαιοὶ τῆς τε δᾳδὸς καὶ τῶν
ἄλλων ξύλων ἐχρῶντο: but this refers
to the very earliest period only ; and
when he wrote, the lamp had been
known for perhaps nearly a thousand years. Wax and tallow lights
are scarcely ever mentioned, and then
only in the very latest times, and by
the Roman name. κανδῆλαι. Athen.
p. 701 : Ἐμοὶ δὲ, παῖ δωρόδειπνε,
ἀσσαρίου κανδήλας ποίω. Moreover
they are here used as a substitute for

without this? And you, Lysistratos '— he here turned to
the youth—' seem to make yourself quite at home in my
house?' 'Oh! to be sure, uncle,' answered the other,
drily ; ' wine on credit from the tavern, since yours is safe
under lock and key. Do you suppose I'm going to wait

---

torches. Suidas, very improperly, derives the word from the Greek:—ἀπὸ
τοῦ καίειν δῆλα.

The lamps were usually of burnt
earth (τροχήλατοι, Eccles. 1—5,) or
of metal. Their form is well known:
they had sometimes one, sometimes
two or more orifices for the wick,
which from their likeness to the nostrils were called μυκτῆρες and μύξαι;
hence λύχνοι δίμυξοι, τρίμυξοι, &c.
Poll. ii. 72. The wick, Atticè θρυαλ-
λὶς, otherwise ἐλλύχνιον and φλόμος,
(Poll. vi. 103; x. 115,) was, partly at
least, made of the woolly leaves of a
plant, which was thence called φλόμος λυχνῖτις. Dioscor. iv. 106; Plin.
xxv. 10, 74; Hesych. Φλόμος· πόα
τις, ἧ καὶ ἀντὶ ἐλλυχνίου χρῶνται·
ἡ αὐτὴ δὲ καὶ θρυαλλίς. Also Phot. p.
95: Θρυαλλίς· ἐσχάρα· λύχνος· ἀκτίς·
καὶ βοτάνη πρὸς λύχνον ἁρμόζο.σα.
As the lamps were generally small
and low, and without feet, they were
set upon a stand, λυχνίον or λυχνιον,
also λυχνία or λυχνεῖον, (Athen. xv.
p. 700,) the candelabrum of the Romans. What has been said on this
subject in Gallus, p. 313, need not be
here repeated. See especially Athen.
IV. p. 147: (ὑψίλυχνοι αὐγαί); xv.
p. 700; Poll. x. 118. The word ὀβελισκολύχνιον however requires explanation. Poll. 117, says: τὸ δὲ ὀβελισκολύχνιον, στρατιωτικὸν μέν τοι τὸ
χρῆμα· εἴρηται δὲ ὑπὸ Θεοπόμπου
τοῦ κωμικοῦ ἐν Εἰρήνῃ,

ἡμᾶς δ' ἀπαλλαχθέντας ἐν ἀγαθαῖς τύχαις
ὀβελισκολυχνίου καὶ ξιφομαχαίρας πικρᾶς.

And Athen. xv. p. 700, refers to the

same expression of Theopompus,
which however they both seem to have
misunderstood. But Aristot. de Repub. iv. 15, p. 1299, explains the military connexion in which Theopompus
employs the word. Aristotle is speaking of the necessity of assigning, in
small states, several functions to the
same individual, there not being
persons enough singly to undertake
them, and then be succeeded by others.
Small states, however, often require
as many offices as large ones, though
these may not be individually of so
much importance. He then says: διόπερ οὐδὲν κωλύει πολλὰς ἐπιμελείας
ἅμα προστάττειν· οὐ γὰρ ἐμποδιοῦσιν
ἀλλήλαις, καὶ πρὸς τὴν ὀλιγανθρω-
πίαν ἀναγκαῖον τὰ ἀρχεῖα οἷον ὀβε-
λισκολύχνια ποιεῖν. Now as he is
talking of the heaping several offices
on one person, we might fancy the
allusion to be to a candelabrum,
which, obelisk-like, is set with lamps
from bottom to top; but, inasmuch
as Theopompus combines it with
ξιφομάχαιρα, a thing which admitted
of a twofold use, it seems certain that
the comparison refers to something
else than the multitude of the offices;
and we then arrive at another solution,
namely, that a person who is employed
first for this and then for that official
duty, is like the ὀβελισκολύχνιον,
which served both for a spear and a
candlestick, and which would thus
be a very compendious implement
for a soldier,—στρατιωτικὸν χρῆμα,
as Pollux calls it.

here half the night for you, without a drop to drink?'
'I didn't expect to be kept so long,' said the old man,
somewhat softened, as he hastily scanned the apartment.
'You may go,' he said to the slave; 'we don't want you
any more; leave us, and go to bed.' The slave departed:
Sosilas bolted the door, and returned to his nephew.

'He is dead,' whispered he, drawing a long breath;
'Polycles is dead, and a property of sixty talents and more
is left without natural heirs.' The nephew started. 'Well!
and what good is that to us, if we do not come in for
a share?' 'That's just the question,' answered the uncle.
'Lysistratos,' he resumed after a short silence, 'you may
be a rich man, if you will.' 'Will? ay! by Dionysos will I,
and no mistake,' laughed the nephew. 'Only do what
I tell you,' said Sosilas, 'and you have your desire. We
are connected—very distantly, I grant—with Polycles,
for my long-deceased wife and Cleobule's mother were
first cousins. Yet this connexion gives us no title to the
property. But, now, what if a will were produced naming
me heir!' 'You mean a forged one,' said Lysistratos,
musingly; 'but how will it be accredited without you have
his signet ring? And do you suppose Polycles, during his
long illness, has not himself arranged about bequeathing his
property?' The old man quietly opened an adjoining room,
and fetched out of it a box, which he unfastened, and
drew forth a document with a seal. 'Look ye there, read
that,' said he, as he placed it before the youth. 'What's
the superscription?' 'By Dionysos!' cried the youth,
springing to his feet, '"The last will of Polycles." How
came you by this?' 'Very simply,' replied the uncle.
'When Polycles was starting to Ædepsos, and Sophilos,
who had got him in his meshes, was luckily gone upon a
journey, he summoned me, as a relative of his wife's, and
entrusted me with his will, in the presence of the three
witnesses therein named.' 'Capital!' shouted Lysistratos:
'so you can substitute another of your own composing.
But, still, even then, you will want his signet: do you

think you could imitate it ?'[6] 'That would be a dangerous experiment,' replied the uncle ; 'and, besides, you can perceive by the superscription. in what peculiar shaky characters it is written ; so that it would be almost impossible to forge an imitation, nor indeed do we want one.'

Saying this he produced a knife, removed the shell which served as a capsule to the seal,[7] and said, 'See ! that's Polycles' seal, and there is just such another beneath the writing ;[8] and now look at this,' cried he, as he placed side by side with it another seal, hanging by a slip of string. 'By Poseidon ! exactly the same,' exclaimed Lysistratos, in amazement ; 'but I can't conceive what all this is about.' 'You'll understand presently,' replied the uncle. He took the knife, and without hesitation severed the string to which the seal was appended, opened the document, and spread it before his nephew. 'Look,' he said with a malicious grin ; 'supposing "Sosilas" stood *here* instead of "Sophilos," and *there*, "Sophilos" instead of "Sosilas." I should not so much mind then.' The youth read in astonishment 'I' faith !' he exclaimed, 'that were

---

[6] Forgery of seals must have occurred early, for Solon enacted a law against it: δακτυλιογλύφῳ μὴ ἐξεῖναι σφραγῖδα φυλάττειν τοῦ πραθέντος δακτυλίου. Diog. Laert. i. 57. Afterwards it occurred frequently, as may be concluded from Aristoph. *Thesmoph.* 424:

προτοῦ μὲν οὖν ἦν ἀλλ' ὑτοῖξαι τὴν θύραν,
ποιησαμέναισι δακτιλιον τριωβόλου.

Thucydides, i. 132, also relates that Argilios, the ambassador from Pausanias to Artabazos, opened the letter entrusted to him : καὶ παραποιησάμενος σφραγῖδα, ἵνα, ἢν ψευσθῇ τῆς δόξης, ἢ καὶ ἐκεῖνος μεταγράψαι τι αἰτήσῃ, μὴ ἐπιγνῷ, λύει τὰς ἐπιστολάς.

[7] The custom of keeping a seal in a capsule, κόγχη, lest it should be in-

jured, is only mentioned in a single passage, Aristoph. *Vesp.* 585, but the allusion is clear and decisive :

κἂν ἀποθνῄσκων ὁ πατήρ τῳ δῷ καταλείπων
παῖδ' ἐπίκληρον,
κλάειν ἡμεῖς μακρὰ τὴν κεφαλὴν εἰπόντες τῇ
διαθήκῃ
καὶ τῇ κόγχῃ τῇ πάνυ σεμνῶς τοῖς σημείοισιν ἐπούσῃ,
ἔδομεν ταύτην, ὅστις ἂν ἡμᾶς ἀντιβολήσας
ἀναπείσῃ.

And the Scholiast says : ὡς κόγχας ἐπιτιθέντων ταῖς σφραγῖσιν ἀσφαλείας ἕνεκα.

[8] Important documents, although they were to be sealed up, were also, it seems, attested by a seal beneath the writing. Plato, *Leg.* ix. p. 856 ; cf. Demosth. *in Pantæn.* p. 978 ; and *in Aphob.* p. 837.

indeed a master-stroke ; and there are only two letters to
alter ; for, as good luck has it, the fathers' names are the
same. But the seal ?' he added, ' the seal ? how could you
venture to break open the deed ?'

The old man made a second dive into the mysterious
box, and drew out something resembling a signet. 'I learnt
how to make this substance from a cunning fellow who
went about soothsaying. If pressed when soft, upon a seal,
it receives all the characters with perfect accuracy and in
a short time becomes as hard as stone.'[9] The will had been
opened before, and the seal appended to it was merely an
impression of this. 'Can you distinguish between it and
the genuine one ?' ' No, that I can't,' answered the nephew.
' So then, it will be an easy matter to re-seal the deed,
when we have altered the letters in these two places.'
' But how am _I_ to become rich by this ?' now interposed
the youth, suspiciously ; ' _my_ name is not mentioned in the
testament.' ' Listen a moment,' replied the uncle ; ' the
inheritance, as you may have read, is coupled with one
condition—that the heir must marry the widow Cleobule,
and if he object to this, must be content with five talents
as his portion ; but he will have the right of giving the
widow in marriage, along with the rest of the property, to
whomsoever he may judge proper.[10] Now I am too old
to marry again ; and, besides, I was warned against it in a
dream. I dreamt that I wished to take a wife, and went

---

[9] Lucian, _Alexander seu Pseudo-
mantis_, 21, mentions many artifices to
which that impostor had recourse for
opening letters containing inquiries
addressed to him, and then sealing
them again without detection. But
the seal is there of wax, which is
here designedly supposed not to be
the case. He, however, mentions two
methods of taking impressions in a
soft substance which afterwards became hard. The second of these,

which is that intended in the text, he
describes thus : τι-άνου γὰρ ἐς κόλ-
λαν ἐμβαλὼν, ᾗ κολλῶσι τὰ βιβλία,
καὶ κηρὸν ἐκ τούτου ποιήσας, ἔτι
ὑγρὸν ὄντα ἐπετίθει τῇ σφραγῖδι
καὶ ἀφελὼν (αὐτίκα δὲ ξηρὸν γίγνεται καὶ κέρατος, μᾶλλον δὲ σιδήρου
παγιώτερον) τούτῳ δὲ ἐχρῆτο πρὸς
τὸν τύπον. See Note 14.

[10] See Note 20.

to the bride's house to be betrothed to her, but when I
essayed to go away again, the door was fastened, and
could not be opened. Two interpreters of dreams, whom
I consulted, foretold that I should die on the day of my
betrothment;[11] and that is warning enough: but you
shall marry Cleobule, if you will privately cede half the
property to me.' The nephew reflected for a moment.
'It's an unequal partition,' he said at last; 'your share is
unencumbered, while my moiety will be saddled with the
widow.' 'Fool!' retorted Sosilas; 'Cleobule is such a
beauty, that many a man would be glad to take her without any dowry at all; besides which it all depends on me,
you know, whether you get a farthing.' After some hig-
gling, it was finally settled that the uncle should not
receive the five talents over and above his half of the property, but that these should be included in the partition.

'Now hand me the will,' said the old man; 'with this
little sponge I erase the two letters, and the more easily
because the paper is so good.[12] Look! they are now

---

[11] Artemidor. *Oneirocr.* i. 78:
οἶδα δέ τινα, ὃς ἔδοξεν εἰσελθεῖν εἰς
πορνεῖον καὶ μὴ δύνασθαι ἐξελθεῖν.
καὶ ἀπέθανεν οὐ μετὰ πολλὰς ἡμέρας.

[12] The observations in *Gallus*, p.
325, on the paper of the ancients,
are perhaps open to question; owing
chiefly to the uncertainty as to the
meaning of the passage in Pliny, *Nat.
Hist.* xiii. 12, 23, which is the main
source of our knowledge about this
manufacture. Sprengel, *Allgem. En-
cyclop.* explains the words, 'Præpa-
rantur ex eo chartæ, diviso acu in
prætenues, sed quam latissimas phi-
luras;' 'The *inner pith* was split by
a pointed instrument into very thin,
but broad *slices*.' This can hardly be
the meaning, for the inner pith of
the papyrus appears to be much too
porous for the fabrication of paper.

Again, if Pliny had meant that the
stalk was cut into plates or slices, he
would have used the word *laminæ* or
tabellæ, certainly not *philuræ*. Nor
were longitudinal sections made of the
stalk, for each strip would have then
contained all degrees of quality;
whereas Pliny says, 'principatus me-
dio, atque inde scissuræ ordine,' that
is, the strips were such, that the inner-
most one was the best, and they gradually became inferior as they got nearer
the outer part, *propiores cortici*. This
agrees also with what Pliny adds as
to the process of manufacture: 'Pre-
mitur deinde prelis, et siccantur sole
plagulæ atque inter se junguntur,
proximarum semper bonitatis diminu-
tione ad deterrimas. Nunquam plures
scapo, quam vicenæ.' The old explanation of Winkelmann, ii. p. 57 seems
to be the best, that the many bast-

scarce distinguishable. This ink,' continued he, as he produced a little box,[13] and the writing-reed, ' is of just the

---

like skins or layers placed one under another were peeled off, (these are the philuræ,)and thus the strips produced.

The paper of the Nile was known and used in Greece long before the time of Herodotus, for he says, v. 58: καὶ τὰς βύβλους διφθέρας καλέουσι ἀπὸ τοῦ παλαιοῦ οἱ Ἴωνες, ὅτι κοτὲ ἐν σπάνι βύβλων ἐχρέωντο διφθέρῃσι αἰγέῃσί τε καὶ ὀϊέῃσι. The universal name for the paper, as a writing material, is βίβλος; the single leaf is called χάρτης; and when written upon, or designed for such a purpose, it is denominated γραμματεῖον and γραμματίδιον; though these words are sometimes used to mean merely the tablets, πίνακες, δέλτοι, smeared over with softened wax, μάλθη or μάλθα, (Poll. x. 58,) which were also early used. The word μάλθη is explained by Harpocration, Photius, Hesychius and Suidas to be μεμαλαγμένης κηρὸς, and we may readily suppose that the wax was mixed with something to make it less brittle; Suidas also mentions σκληρόκηροι δέλτοι, which would better preserve the writing on them: μόλις μὲν γράφονται, διατηροῦσι δὲ τὰ γραφέντα. These wax tablets were only used for letters, and matters of no permanent moment. A passage in Demosthenes, in Steph. ii. p. 1132, is worthy of attention: Ἔτι τοίνυν κἂν ἀπὸ τοῦ γραμματείου γνοίη τις, ἐν ᾧ ἡ μαρτυρία γέγραπται, ὅτι τὰ ψευδῆ μεμαρτύρηκε. λελευκωμένον τε γάρ ἐστι καὶ οἴκοθεν κατεσκευασμένον. καίτοι τοὺς μὲν τὰ πεπραγμένα μαρτυροῦντας προσήκει οἴκοθεν τὰς μαρτυρίας κατεσκευασμένας μαρτυρεῖν· τοὺς δὲ τὰς προκλήσεις μαρτυροῦντας, τοὺς ἀπὸ ταὐτομάτου προστάν-

τας, ἐν μάλθῃ γεγραμμένην τὴν μαρτυρίαν, ἵνα, εἴ τι προσγράψαι ἢ ἀπαγεῖψαι βουληθῇ, ῥᾴδιον ᾖ. Nothing could be easier than to alter anything written on a wax tablet, and ink-marks could also readily be effaced. The Nile paper, particularly when good, did not, to any great extent, imbibe the writing fluid, which, as we learn from Pliny, resembled our Indian-ink, and could easily be washed off with a wetted finger or a sponge. See Chamæleon ap. Athen. ix. p. 407: ἧκεν εἰς τὸ Μητρῷον, ὅπου τῶν δικῶν ἦσαν αἱ γραφαὶ, καὶ βρέξας τὸν δάκτυλον ἐκ τοῦ στόματος διήλειψε τὴν δίκην τοῦ Ἡγήμονος. Hence the paper might be cleaned, and then used a second time, as παλίμψηστον. See Gallus, p. 328. With regard to the price, all that can be stated is that a piece of paper for a bond cost two chalcus, i.e. a quarter of an obole. Demosth. in Dionysod. p. 1283: λαβὼν γὰρ ἀργύριον φανερὸν καὶ ὁμολογούμενον ἐν γραμματιδίῳ δυοῖν χαλκοῖν ἐωνημένῳ καὶ βιβλιδίῳ μικρῷ πάνυ τὴν ὁμολογίαν κατελοιπε τοῦ ποιήσειν τὰ δίκαια. See Note 19 to Scene IV.

[13] Pollux, iv. 18, and x. 59, mentions among the requirements of a school-boy, the ink-stand, πυξίον, which he also calls μελανοδόχον. The ink, τὸ μέλαν, was not a chemical preparation, but merely a pigment which was prepared for use by rubbing; Demosth. de Corona, p. 313: τὸ μέλαν τρίβειν. Instead of quills, they employed reeds, κάλαμοι γραφεῖς. Poll. x. 61. See Gallus, p. 327. Plutarch, Demosth. 29, relates of that orator, that he used to bite his

same blackness as the writing. There we have it, all right.
Who will assert that it was not always as it now stands?'
'Excellent!' said the nephew; 'now for the seal.' The old
man carefully folded up the deed again, moistened some
clay,[14] tied the string, and impressed the forged stamp upon
the clay. 'There!' said he, 'isn't it the same seal?' 'Well,
that beats everything,' cried Lysistratos, as he compared
the two seals; 'no one will ever dream that it is a forgery.'
A rustling outside the door startled the old man. He
snatched up the will and the other contents of the box,
which he bore off, and fastened the door of the room
adjacent, sealing it for greater security. Then taking the
lamp, he explored the court, to discover, if possible, the
cause of the disturbance. 'It was nothing,' he said, when
he came back; 'most likely the storm which made the
door shake. It will soon be morning; Lysistratos, come
into my bed-chamber, and let us have a short nap.'

The two worthies had not been long gone, when Molon
glided softly into the room, and groped about, in the dark,

---

writing-reed while meditating: καὶ
λαβὼν βιβλίον, ὡς γράφειν μέλλων,
προσήνεγκε τῷ στόματι τὸν κάλαμον, καὶ δακὼν, ὥσπερ ἐν τῷ διανο-
εῖσθαι καὶ γράφειν εἰώθει, χρόνον
τινὰ κατέσχεν, εἶτα συγκαλυψάμε-
νος ἀπέκλινε τὴν κεφαλήν. See also
Plutarch, *Dec. Or. Vit.* iv. p. 376.
A pointed instrument, γραφεῖον, was
used for writing on waxed tablets.
Poll. iv. 18; x. 59. Cf. Plut. *Eumen.* 1.

[14] In early times a kind of earth,
called *cretula* by the Romans, seems
to have been exclusively used for seals,
and it continued to be so employed
after wax had come into vogue. See
Beckmann's *Hist. of Inventions.* The
Greeks named this material ῥύπος.
Aristoph. *Lysist.* 1199:

καὶ μηδὲν οὕτως
οὖ σεσημάνθαι, τὸ μὴ οὐχὶ τοὺς ῥύπους
ἀνασπάσαι.

The double meaning of the word ῥύπος gave occasion to the witty answer of Lais, recorded by Athen. xiii.
p. 585: πρὸς Λαΐδα τὴν Κορινθίαν
ἐραστὴς ἀποσφράγισμα πέμψας ἐκέλευε παραγίνεσθαι. ἡ δ', οὐ δύναμαι,
εἶπε, πηλός ἐστι. See Poll. x. 59.
The document to be sealed was tied
round by a thread, λίνον; or perhaps
it was pierced on the open side, and
the thread drawn through. See Paul.
Sent. xxv. 6. The material for the seal
was then put on the ends of this thread,
part under the knot, part upon it, and
then stamped. See Lucian, *Alex-
and.* 21: βελώνην πυρώσας τὸ ὑπὸ
τὴν σφραγῖδα μέρος τοῦ κηροῦ δια-
τήκων ἐξῄρει καὶ μετὰ τὴν ἀνάγνω-
σιν τῇ βελώνῃ αὖθις ἐπιχλιάνας τὸν
κηρὸν, τόν τε κάτω ὑπὸ τῷ λίνῳ καὶ
τὸν αὐτὴν τὴν σφραγῖδα ἔχοντα,
ῥᾳδίως συνεκόλλα.

for one of the sofas. A gleam of moonlight shone through
the open door; and he hastily seized something that lay
in the folds of the drapery; and then, as quickly and
softly vanished, his gestures denoting the prize to be one
on which he set a high value.

When morning dawned on the house of the deceased,
it found the inmates already busy with preparations for the
burial. An earthen vessel, filled with water, stood before
the door, to signify to the passenger that it was a house
of mourning.[15] Within, the women were occupied in
anointing and laying out the corpse. Cleobule, inexperienced, and woe-begone like an orphan child, had begged
the aid of Sophilos; who, even without solicitation, would
have undertaken to conduct the funeral. She had always
looked on Polycles in the light of an affectionate uncle,
who had indulged her every wish; and now she wept for
him as for a parent; while she applied herself to her
mournful duties, assisted by her mother, whom she had
sent for on the previous evening, as her child-like tremors,
which had been early nourished by nurses' fairy-tales and
ghost-stories, rendered solitude in the house of death in-
supportable.[16]

It was still early, and Sophilos was just debating with

---

[15] See Excursus on *The Burials*;
also Eurip. *Alcestis*, 98 :

πυλῶν πάροιθε δ' οὐχ ὁρῶ
πηγαῖον ὡς νομίζεται
χέρνιβ' ἐπὶ φθιτῶν πύλαις.

Cf. Hesych. s. v. ὄστρακον : ὁπότε τις
ἀποθάνοι γάστραν πρὸ τῶν θυρῶν
ἐτίθεσαν, ἐξ ἄλλης οἰκίας λαμβά-
οντες καὶ πληροῦντες ὕδατος.

[16] The fear of apparitions and of
being alone in the dark is occasionally
mentioned. See the story of Democritus, quoted in the Excursus on *The
Burials*; and Plaut. *Mostell.* ii. 2, 76.
These fears were fostered by a multitude of terrifying stories, of which
several survive. A ghost-story that
may be compared to that of the Marble
Guest occurs in Dio Chrysost. *Or.*
xxxi. p. 618 : τελευτήσαντος δὲ πρᾶγμα πάντων ἀνοητότατον καὶ ἀσεβέ-
στατον ἐποίει. τὸν γὰρ ἀνδριάντα
αὐτοῦ, τὸν ἑστῶτα ἐν μέσῃ τῇ πόλει,
νύκτωρ ἐμαστίγου. τοιγαροῦν εἴτε
ἀπὸ τύχης, εἴτε δαιμονίου τινὸς νε-
μεσήσαντος αὐτῷ, κινηθείς ποτε ἐκ
τῆς βάσεως ἠκολούθησεν ἅμα τῇ
μάστιγι καὶ κτείνει τὸν ἄνδρα. A
somewhat similar story may be found
in Lucian's *Philopseudos*.

the women as to the order of the interment, when Sosilas also made his appearance, with sorrow in his aspect, but exultation in his heart. He had hastened, he said, to bring the will which the deceased had deposited in his hands; as, perhaps, it might contain some dispositions respecting his interment.[17] He then named the witnesses who had been by when he received the will, and whose presence would now be necessary at the opening. Cleobule was somewhat disconcerted to find the document that was to decide her future fate placed in the custody of one to whom, whom early childhood, she had entertained feelings of aversion. Polycles had never been explicit on this head, merely assuring her, in general terms, that she had been cared for. And such she now hoped was the case; but yet she had rather that anybody else had produced the will. Sophilos, on the other hand, did not seem at all put out by the circumstance. He praised Sosilas for

---

[17] That the will was opened immediately on the testator's death is evident from the fact that it often contained dispositions regarding the burial. See Notes 25 and 26. Cf. Lucian, *Nigrin.* 30, whence it also appears that the opening did not take place judicially, as at Rome, but in private before witnesses. It is true that a more public procedure is mentioned in Lucian, *Tim.* 21: καὶ ὁ μὲν νεκρὸς ἐν σκοτεινῷ που τῆς οἰκίας πρόκειται, ὑπὲρ τὰ γόνατα παλαιᾷ τῇ ὀθόνῃ σκεπόμενος περιμάχητος ταῖς γαλαῖς. ἐμὲ δὲ (πλοῦτον) οἱ ἐπελπίσαντες ἐν τῇ ἀγορᾷ περιμένουσι κεχηνότες . . . Ἐπειδὰν δὲ τὸ σημεῖον ἀφαιρεθῇ καὶ τὸ λίνον ἐντμηθῇ, καὶ ἡ δέλτος ἀνοιχθῇ, καὶ ἀνακηρυχθῇ μου ὁ καινὸς δεσπότης κ.τ.λ. We must not, however, infer from this that the practice was prevalent at any early period, for Lucian frequently introduces much that is quite irrele-

vant to earlier Attic customs. On the contrary, we must suppose that the will was opened in private, and not proved before a court till afterwards; and this view is borne out by Demosth. *in Aphob.* ii. p. 837: ἀλλ' ἐχρῆν, ἐπειδὴ τάχιστ' ἐτελεύτησεν ὁ πατὴρ, εἰσκαλέσαντας μάρτυρας πολλοὺς παρασημήνασθαι κελεῦσα. τὰς διαθήκας, ἵν', εἴ τι ἐγένετο ἀμφισβητήσιμον, ἦν εἰς τὰ γράμματα ταῦτ' ἐπανελθεῖν. The μάρτυρας πολλοὺς would not have been required, if the proceedings had been of a judicial character. Nor can we conclude from Demosth. *in Steph.* i. p. 1104, that wills were opened in the presence of diætetes, for in the case there mentioned the matter was already a subject of litigation, and a copy only of the will could be produced. See Meier and Schömann, *Att. Proc.* p. 259.

his punctuality, and desired that the witnesses might be cited to attend; but this, the other said, was not necessary, as he had already sent them notices to that effect.

Before long, the three made their appearance. ' You were present,' said Sosilas to them, ' when Polycles committed his last will to my charge?' They replied in the affirmative. ' You will be ready then to testify that this is the deed which he entrusted to me?' ' The superscription and the seal,' answered one of them, ' are what prove its authenticity. All that we can witness to is, that a testament was deposited with you—not, that this is the identical one in question;[18] still there is no ground for the contrary assumption, since the seal is untouched, and may be recognised as that of Polycles.' ' Do you, therefore, satisfy yourself, Cleobule, that I have faithfully discharged your husband's behest. Do you acknowledge this seal?' With trembling hand Cleobule took the deed. ' An eagle clutching a snake,' said she; ' it is the device of his signet.' She next handed the testament to Sophilos, who also pronounced it all right. ' Open it then,' said Sosilas to one of the witnesses, ' that its contents may be known. My sight is bad; do one of you read for me.'

---

[18] The presence of witnesses at the depositing of a will was considered necessary for several reasons. Firstly, in order that the existence of the testament might not be kept secret; secondly, that the fact of its deposition might be defended against any cavils; next, as an additional security against forgery; and lastly, to prove that the testator was free from any mental infirmity which might incapacitate him, by Solon's law, from any testamentary disposition of his property. See Note 19, *infra*. The witnesses, however, knew nothing of the contents of the will, and therefore could not attest the

authenticity of the same at its opening. Isæus, *de Nicostr. her.* p. 75 : καὶ τῶν διατιθεμένων οἱ πολλοὶ οὐδὲ λέγουσι τοῖς παραγινομένοις ὅ,τι διατίθενται, ἀλλ' αὐτοῦ μόνου τοῦ καταλιπεῖν δια- θήκας μάρτυρας παρίστανται. Cf. Id. *de Apollodori her.* p. 160. Wills, however, were frequently forged, and palmed off as genuine. Aristot. *Probl.* xxix. 3 : διὰ τί ἐνίοις δικαστη- ρίοις τοῖς γένεσι μᾶλλον ἢ ταῖς δια- θήκαις ψηφιοῦνται; ἢ ὅτι γένους μὲν οὐκ ἔστι καταψεύσασθαι, ἀλλὰ τὸ ὂν ἀποφαίνειν. διαθῆκαι δὲ πολλαὶ ψευ- δεῖς ἤδη ἐξελέγχθησαν οὖσαι. Cf. Demosth. *in Macart.* p. 1051; and Lucian, *adv. indoct.* 19.

The string was cut, the document unfolded, and the witness read as follows:

" The testament of Polycles the Pæanian. May all be well; but should I not recover from this sickness, thus do I devise my estate.[19] I give my wife[20] Cleobule, with all my fortune, as set down in the accompanying schedule,[21] —save and except all that is herein otherwise disposed,— to my friend Sosilas, the son of Philo, to which end I

---

[19] The form in which a will was drawn up is well known to us. We have extracts or epitomes of wills in Demosth. *in Steph.* i. p. 1110; *in Aphob.* i. p. 826. Of much greater value, however, are the wills of Plato, Aristotle, Theophrastus, Lycon, and Epicurus, which have been preserved verbatim by Diogenes Laertius. They mostly commence by a kind of title; thus Demosth. *in Steph.* p. 1110: Τάδε διέθετο Πασίων 'Αχαρνεύς: or as in Diog. Laert. iii. 41 : Τάδε κατέλιπε Πλάτων καὶ διέθετο. The formula Ἔσται μὲν εὖ is a common commencement. Diog. Laert. v. 11. : Ἔσται μὲν εὖ· ἐὰν δέ τι συμβαίνῃ, τάδε διέθετο 'Αριστοτέλης. So *ib.* § 51: Ἔσται μὲν εὖ· ἐὰν δέ τι συμβῇ, τάδε διατίθεμαι: and Lycon's will, *ib.* § 69, commences: Τάδε διατίθεμαι περὶ τῶν κατ' ἐμαυτὸν, ἐὰν μὴ δυνηθῶ τὴν ἀρρωστίαν ταύτην ὑπενεγκεῖν. Certain persons were by a law of Solon incapacitated from making a will. Demosth. *in Steph.* ii. p. 1133: τὰ ἑαυτοῦ διαθέσθαι εἶναι, ὅπως ἂν ἐθέλῃ, ἂν μὴ παῖδες ὦσι γνήσιοι ἄρρενες, ἂν μὴ μανιῶν ἢ γήρως, ἢ φαρμάκων, ἢ νόσου ἕνεκεν, ἢ γυναικὶ πειθόμενος, ἢ ὑπὸ τῶν τοῦ παρανόμων, ἢ ὑπ' ἀνάγκης, ἢ ὑπὸ δεσμοῦ καταληφθείς. This can only refer to cases in which the mind was enfeebled, for bodily infirmity was no impedi-

ment. Thus in Isæus, *de Apollod. her.* p. 160: εἴ τις τελευτήσειν μέλλων διέθετο. Cf. Diog. Laert. iv. 44. The document was superscribed with the name of the testator. Demosth. *in Steph.* i. p. 1106: γραμματεῖον ἔχειν, ἐφ' ᾧ γεγράφθαι, Διαθήκη Πασίωνος. At the end, curses were often imprecated against those who should act contrary to its dispositions. Demosth. *Phorm.* p. 960 : ἀλλ' ἐναντία τῇ διαθήκῃ καὶ ταῖς ἀπ' ἐκείνης ἀραῖς γραφείσαις ὑπὸ τοῦ πατρὸς ἐλαύνεις, διώκεις, συκοφαντεῖς.

[20] The Attic laws of inheritance are obscure and difficult. Polycles and Cleobule are here supposed without heirs male, while the latter, as niece of the testator, would be heir at law. There occur instances of a third person being designated as spouse as well as κύριος of the testator's widow. The cases of Demosthenes' father, Demosth. *in Aphob.* may be cited, and perhaps also that of Pasion. Id. *in Steph.* p. 1110. Cf. Diog. Laert. x. 19.

[21] Usually the various goods and chattels are enumerated in the will; here, however, Plato's will has been the model: σκεύη τὰ γεγραμμένα, ὧν ἔχει τὰ ἀντίγραφα Δημήτριος. Diog. Laert. iii. 43.

adopt him as my son.[22]   But should he refuse to marry
her, then I bequeath to him the five talents lying with
Pasion, the money-changer; but I then constitute him
guardian of Cleobule, and he shall give her, with the rest
of the property, to some husband of his own choosing; who
shall take possession of my house.   I give and bequeath
my house on the Olympieion to Theron, the son of Callias;
and the lodging-house in the Piræus to Sophilos, son of
Philo.   To the son of Callipides I bequeath my largest
silver bowl, and to his wife a pair of gold earrings, and
two coverlets and two cushions of the best in my possession; that I may not seem to have forgotten them.[23]   To
my physician, Zenothemis, I leave a legacy of one thousand
drachmæ, though his skill and attention have deserved still
more.[24]   Let my sepulchre be erected in a fitting spot of
the garden outside the Melitic gate.[25]   Let Theron, together with Sophilos and my relatives, see to it that my
obsequies and monument be neither unworthy of me, nor
yet on too sumptuous a scale.[26]   I expressly prohibit
Cleobule and the women, as well as the female slaves, from
cutting off their hair, or otherwise disfiguring themselves.[27]
To Demetrius, who has long been free, I remit his ransom,
and make him a present of five minæ, a himation and a
chiton, in consideration of his faithful services.[28]   Of the

---

[22] See Isæus, de Aristarch. her.
p. 258; and Petit. Leg. Att. 579.

[23] Lycon's will, ap. Diog. Laert. v.
72: Δίδωμι δὲ τῷ Καλλίνου παιδίῳ
θηρικλείων ζεῦγος καὶ τῇ γυναικὶ
αὐτοῦ ῥοΐσκων ζεῦγος, ψιλοτάπιδα,
ἀμφίταπον, περίστρωμα, προσκεφάλαια δύο τὰ βέλιστα τῶν καταλει-
πομένων.

[24] Ibid.: Τιμησάτω δὲ καὶ τοὺς
ἰατροὺς Πισίθεμιν καὶ Μειδίαν, ἀξίους ὄντας καὶ διὰ τὴν ἐπιμέλειαν τὴν
περὶ ἐμὲ καὶ τὴν τέχνην καὶ μείζονος
ἔτι τιμῆς.

[25] Theophrastus' will, ibid. v. 53:
θάψαι δὲ καὶ ἡμᾶς, ὅπου ἂν δοκῇ μάλιστα ἁρμόττον εἶιαι τοῦ κήπου, μηδὲν περίεργον περὶ τὴν ταφὴν, μήτε
περὶ τὸ μνημεῖον ποιοῦντας.

[26] Lycon's will, ibid. v. 70: περὶ δὲ
τῆς ἐκφορᾶς καὶ καύσεως ἐπιμεληθή-
τωσαν Βούλων καὶ Καλλῖνος μετὰ
τῶν συνήθων, ὅπως μήτ᾽ ἀνελεύθερος
γένηται μήτε περίεργος.

[27] See Excursus on The Burials.

[28] Diog. Laert. v. 72: Δημητρίῳ
μὲν ἐλευθέρῳ πάλαι ὄντι ἀφίημι τὰ

slaves, I hereby manumit[29] Parmeno, and Chares,[30] with his child; but Carion and Donax must work for four years in the garden, and shall then be made free, if they shall have conducted themselves well during that period.[31] Manto shall be free immediately on Cleobule's marriage,[32] and shall also receive three minæ. Of the children of my slaves none are to be sold, but are to be kept in the house till they are grown up, and then set free.[33] Syrus, however, shall be sold.[34] Sophilos, Theron, and Callipides will discharge the duties of executors.[35] This testament is placed in the keeping of Sosilas. Witnesses: Lysimachos, son

---

λύτρα καὶ δίδωμι πέντε μνᾶς, καὶ ἱμάτιον καὶ χιτῶνα· ἵνα πολλὰ πεπονηκὼς μετ' ἐμοῦ, βίον εὐσχήμονα ἔχῃ.

[29] The manumission of slaves, and of their children, occurs very frequently in wills. So in Aristotle's will, Diog. Laert. v. 15. Also a female slave is sometimes assigned to a freedman. Thus in Lycon's will: δίδωμι δὲ καὶ Σύρῳ ἐλευθέρῳ ὄντι τέτταρας μνᾶς, καὶ τὴν Μηνοδώραν δίδωμι.

[30] The assertion of Limburg Brower, *Hist. de la Civilisation des Grecs,* i. p. 254, that slaves might not have the same names as freemen, is utterly unfounded. In the above-mentioned wills a host of the most distinguished names are mentioned as being those of slaves; for instance, Dionysios, Philo, Cimon, Callias, Demetrios, Crito, Chares, Euphranor, Agathon, Nicias, &c. Had not this been the case, the law (Gell. ix. 2), that no slave might bear the names Harmodius or Aristogeiton, would have been superfluous.

[31] Diog. Laert. v. 55: Μάτην δὲ

καὶ Καλλίαν παραμείναντας ἔτη τέτταρα ἐν τῷ κήπῳ καὶ συνεργασαμένους καὶ ἀναμαρτήτους γενομένους ἀφίημι ἐλευθέρους. So also Id. v. 73: καὶ Ἀγάθωνα δύο ἔτη παραμείναντα ἀφεῖσθαι ἐλεύθερον.

[32] Aristotle's will. Diog. Laert. v. 15: Τάχωνα δὲ ἐλεύθερον εἶναι, ὅταν ἡ παῖς ἐκδοθῇ.

[33] This humane disposition is also made by Aristotle. *Ib.*: μὴ πωλεῖν δὲ τῶν παιδίων μηδένα τῶν ἐμὲ θεραπευόντων, ἀλλὰ χρῆσθαι αὐτοῖς· ὅταν δ' ἐν ἡλικίᾳ γένωνται, ἐλεύθερα ἀφεῖναι κατ' ἀξίαν.

[34] Theophrastus' will. Diog. Laert. v. 55: Εὔβιον δ' ἀποδόσθαι.

[35] In Theophrastus' will we have: Ἐπιμεληταὶ δὲ ἔστωσαν τῶν ἐν τῇ διαθήκῃ γεγραμμένων "Ιππαρχος, Νηλεὺς, Στράτων, κ.τ.λ. Diog. Laert. v. 56. These ἐπιμεληταί, or executors, are not quite identical with the ἐπίτροποι in Aristotle's or Plato's wills, for the latter took also the office of guardians. See Meier and Schömann, *Att. Proc.* p. 445.

of Strato; Hegesias, of Hegio· and Hipparchos, of Cal-
lippos."

A deathlike stillness reigned among the audience when
the reader had concluded. At the first words Cleobule
had turned pale, and sunk back on a settle half-fainting,
while her mother, who was crying, supported her. Sophilos
placed his hand on his lips, and was lost in thought: the
witnesses mutely surveyed the scene. Sosilas alone seemed
perfectly composed. 'Take courage,' said he, approaching
Cleobule; 'fear not that I will lay claim to the happiness
that Polycles intended for me. I myself too am astonished,
and could easily be dazzled by the tempting prize: but I
am too old to dream of wedding a young bride. Willingly
do I resign the rich inheritance, and shall select for you a
husband more suitable in age.'

Cleobule turned away with a shudder. Sosilas grasped
the will, saying, 'Nothing more is now wanting but the
attestation of the witnesses, that such was the tenor of
the will, when opened.'[36] The witnesses accordingly set
their seals to the writing. 'It is not the only testament
that Polycles has left,' remarked one of them. 'How?
What?' exclaimed Sosilas, turning pale; 'nothing is said
here about the existence of another will.' 'I don't rightly
understand it,' replied the witness; but two days after
you received this, Polycles called me and four others in as
witnesses, on his depositing another document—doubtless
a duplicate of this—in the hands of Menecles, to whose
house he had caused himself to be conveyed.'

The effects of this disclosure on those present were,
as might have been expected, extremely various. Sosilas
stood like one utterly undone; a faint ray of hope glim-
mered in the bosom of Cleobule; Sophilos eyed narrowly
the countenance of the forger, who quailed before his
glance; and the witnesses looked doubtingly at one an-

---

[36] The passage from Demosthenes quoted in Note 17 shows that the witnesses, after opening the will, set their seals to it.

other.   Sosilas at length broke the silence.   'This will,'
said he with some vehemence, ' is genuine ; and even supposing that there is another authentic one in existence, its
contents will of course be the same.'   ' Why! it is indeed
hardly to be supposed,' rejoined Sophilos, ' that Polycles
would have changed his mind in two days : but we must
invite Menecles to produce the copy in his custody, without loss of time.'   A slave here entered, and whispered a
message in his ear.   ' The very thing!' he cried.   ' Menecles is not less punctual than you.   Two of his witnesses
have already arrived, in obedience to his summons; and
he will therefore shortly be here in person.'   The men
now entered.   Sosilas walked up and down the room, and
gradually recovered his composure.   Even should his plans
be unpleasantly disturbed by the contents of the second
will, still a wide field would be open for litigation, in which
he had an even chance of coming off victor.   Menecles
soon arrived with the other two witnesses, and delivered
the will.   The superscription and seal were found to be
correct, and its contents tallied with those of the first,
word for word, with the exception of the two names, which
were interchanged.   At the end was a postscript, to the
effect that an exactly similar testament was deposited
with Sosilas the Piræan.[37]

---

[37] This custom of depositing several copies of a will in the hands of
different persons seems to have been
very common.   In Demosth. *in Steph.*
ii. p. 1137, where we read : διαθηκῶν
οὐδεὶς πώποτε ἀντίγρα·α ἐποιήσατο ·
ἀλλὰ συγγραφῶν μὲν, ἵνα εἰδῶσι καὶ
μὴ παραβαίνωσι, διαθηκῶν δὲ οὔ. τούτου γὰρ ἕνεκα καταλείπουσιν οἱ διατι-
θέμενοι, ἵνα μηδεὶς εἰδῇ, ἃ διατίθενται,
all that is meant is that no open
copies were given, whence the con
tents of a man's will might be divulged
in his lifetime.   This agrees with
Isæus, *de Apollod. Her* p. 160. But

several copies might be left for additional security.   Arcesilaos took this
precaution.   In a letter to Thauma-
sias, in which he commits a copy to
his keeping, we read, κεῖνται δὲ 'Αθή-
νησιν αὗται παρά τισι τῶν γνωρίμων,
καὶ ἐν 'Ερετρίᾳ παρ' 'Αμφικρίτῳ.
Diog. Laert. iv. 44.   So Theophrastus had deposited three copies.   See
his will in Diog. Laert. v. 57 : αἱ διαθῆκαι κεῖνται ἀντίγραφα τῷ Θεοφρά-
στου δακτυλίῳ σεσημασμέναι, μία
μὲν, κ.τ.λ.   The witnesses might. or
might not, be the same ; thus in
Theophrastus' second will we have

The reading of this caused a violent scene, and plenty of abuse and recrimination followed on both sides. Sosilas pronounced it a forgery, and went off declaring that he would make good his claims before a court of law.

The morning of the funeral had arrived; and, before daybreak, a crowd of mourners, and of others actuated merely by motives of curiosity, had collected in and around the house, either to attach themselves to the procession, or merely to be spectators of the pageant. Even the day before, whilst the corpse lay in state, the door was crowded by persons who in the course of their lives had never before crossed its threshold. Several too had evinced much celerity in putting on mourning, being very anxious to establish their claims to a distant relationship with the defunct, when they learnt the property was in dispute, and there seemed a prospect of good fishing in the troubled waters.[38]

Charicles, however, did not present himself within; although perhaps the house possessed greater attractions for him than for any of the others. The impression his late unexpected appearance made on Cleobule had not escaped him, and he held it improper to disturb her duties to the departed by a second visit. Still he could not omit accompanying the funeral procession to the place of interment; and in fact Sophilos, who somehow felt a great liking for the youth, had himself invited him to be present. The old gentleman had paid him several visits, and, in a significant manner, had described how much Cleobule was imperilled by the will, which he was convinced was a forgery. Charicles was perhaps more disquieted at this than even Sophilos himself. Whichever way the matter might be decided, it would of course make no difference

----

μάρτυρες οἱ αὐτοί, but for the third will others are selected. Cf. Lysias, in Diogit. p. 864; Isæus, de Phil-et.

Her. p. 123.

[38] See Aristoph. Equites, 864.

to him personally; for, in case a fraud were detected, the lady would become the wife of Sophilos; and, as regarded himself, he had made up his mind, that, even under the most favourable circumstances, it would never befit one of his years and condition to marry a widow of such large property:[39] he was, nevertheless, pained to think that such a fascinating creature might fall into the power of one who, to judge from all accounts, must be utterly unworthy of her. He had caught only a hasty glimpse of Sosilas at Polycles' house, and therefore was the more inclined to attend the funeral, where he would be sure to obtain a good view of him;—impelled by these reasons, he had repaired to the house of woe at an early hour, but forbore to enter, waiting outside in order to attach himself to Sophilos, as soon as he should come out.

The first ray of the morning sun had not as yet beamed forth, when the procession began to move. In front, the plaintive tones of the flutes resounded in Carian mode; next followed the friends of the deceased, and any others of the male sex who wished to join the train. Behind these came freedmen,[40] bearing the bed, on which lay the corpse, as if asleep, wearing a white robe and garland. The magnificent purple pall was half hidden by numberless chaplets and tæniæ:[41] beside it walked slaves bearing vessels of ointment, and other needful accessories. Behind the bier followed the women, and among them Cleobule, led by her mother. Never, perhaps, had she appeared

---

[39] So Plutarch, *Amat.* 2, says, with regard to a somewhat similar case: Παραδόξου δὲ τοῦ πράγματος αὐτοῦ φανέντος, ἥ τε μήτηρ ὑφεωρᾶτο τὸ βάρος τοῦ οἴκου καὶ τὸν ὄγκον, ὡς οὐ κατὰ τὸν ἐραστήν. See Excursus on *The Women.*

[40] This supposition is the most natural one in the absence of relations. See Excursus on *The Burials.*

[41] The passage of Alciphron, *Epist* i. 36, quoted in the Excursus on *The Burials,* need not lead us to suppose that the bier of young persons only was thus crowned. Plutarch, *Philop.* 21, speaking of Philopœmen's burial, says: Αὐτὴν δὲ τὴν ὑδρίαν ὑπὸ πλήθους ταινιῶν καὶ στεφάνων μόλις ὁρωμένην ἐκόμιζεν ὁ τοῦ στρατηγοῦ τῶν Ἀχαιῶν παῖς, Πολύβιος.

more beautiful; never was it more manifest that the fresh
vermilion which tinged her delicate cheeks was no deceit-
ful work of the cosmetic pencil.[42]

---

[42] There can be no doubt that
painting was almost universal among
the Grecian women. The reason of
this may have been that the οἰκουρεῖν, σκιατραφεῖσθαι, and the ἀεὶ καθῆσθαι of the girls and women robbed
them of their natural freshness and
colour, which they thus endeavoured
to imitate. Thus Ischomachos coun-
selled his young wife to take exercise, that she might do without the
rouge which she was accustomed
constantly to use. Xenoph. Œcon.
10, 10: συνεβούλευον αὐτῇ, μὴ δου-
λικῶς ἀεὶ καθῆσθαι. Cf. Stob. Tit.
lxxiv. 61: Εἰ γὰρ μηδέν τι ὀκνῆσαι
αὐτὴν καὶ περὶ γυμνασίας ἔχειν ἀνα-
πείσαις, ἐνταῦθα εὕροις ἂν καὶ, οὗ
πάλαι ἐπεθυμοῦμεν, τὸν κόσμον τῷ
σώματι. Τοῦ μὲν γὰρ ὑγιαίνειν οὐδὲν ἔμοιγε δοκεῖ ἄλλο τι περίθημα
καὶ περιδέραιον κρεῖττον. Πόρρω δ'
ἂν εἴη καὶ τοῦ δεηθῆναι γυνὴ ὑγιαί-
νουσα καὶ ψιμυθίου, καὶ ὑπ' ὀφθαλμῷ
ὑπογραφῆς, καὶ ἄλλου χρώματος ζω-
γραφοῦντος καὶ ἀφανίζοντος τὰς
ὄψεις. While the women were engaged in their ordinary domestic avocations, paint may have been partially
disused, but it was resumed when they
were going out, or wished to be specially attractive. So in Lysias, de Cæde
Eratosth. p. 15, the woman retouches
her complexion when she goes to meet
her paramour, and the next morning
her husband observes, ἔδοξέ δέ μοι
τὸ πρόσωπον ἐψιμυθιῶσθαι. See Lysistrata, 149; cf. Eccl. 878; Plut.
1064; and Plutarch, Alcib. 39. The
pigments employed were ψιμύθιον, i.e.
cerussa, or white lead, ἄγχουσα or
ἔγχουσα, παιδέρως, συκάμινον, and
φῦκος, which last chiefly supplied the

red tint; all the red colours were derived from the vegetable kingdom. Φῦκος is not mentioned in earlier times;
ἄγχουσα occurs most frequently. Xenoph. Œcon. 10, 2: Ἐγὼ τοίνυν, ἔφη,
ἰδών ποτε αὐτὴν, ὦ Σ., ἐντετριμμέ-
νην, πολλῷ μὲν ψιμυθίῳ, ὅπως λευ-
κοτέρα ἔτι δοκοίη εἶναι, ἢ ἦν, πολλῇ
δὲ ἐγχούσῃ, ὅπως ἐρυθροτέρα φαί-
νοιτο τῆς ἀληθείας κ.τ.λ. Cf. Lysistr. 48; Eccl. 929: and a fragment
of Alexis in Athen. xiii. p. 568:

συμβέβηκ' εἶναι μέλαιναν· κατέπλασε
ψιμυθίῳ.
λευκόχρως λίαν τίς ἐστι· παιδέρωτ' ἐντρί-
βεται.

See Etymol. M. ἐψιμμυθιῶσθαι. The
folly and repulsiveness of the practice
are well pictured by Ischomachos,
Xen. Œcon. 10, 8: Αἰ δ' ἀπάται αὗται τοὺς μὲν ἔξω πως δύναιντ' ἂν
ἀνεξελέγκτως ἐξαπατᾶν, συνόντας δὲ
ἀεὶ ἀνάγκη ἁλίσκεσθαι, ἂν ἐπιχει-
ρῶσιν ἐξαπατᾶν ἀλλήλους. Ἡ γὰρ
ἐξ εὐνῆς ἁλίσκονται ἐξανιστάμενοι
πρὶν παρασκευάσασθαι, ἢ ὑπὸ ἱδρῶ-
τος ἐλέγχονται, ἢ ὑπὸ δακρύων βα-
σανίζονται, ἢ ὑπὸ λουτροῦ ἀληθινῶς
κατωπτεύθησαν. So also an amusing
fragment of Eubulos, ap. Athen.
xiii. p. 557:

Μὰ Δι', οὐχὶ περιπεπλασμέναι ψιμυθίοις,
οὐδ' ὥσπερ ὑμεῖς συκαμίνῳ τὰς γνάθους
κεχριμέναι. κἂν ἐξίητε τοῦ θέρους,
ἀπὸ τῶν μὲν ὀφθαλμῶν ὑδρορρόαι δύο
ῥέουσι μέλανος, ἐκ δὲ τῶν γνάθων ἱδρὼς
ἐπὶ τὸν τράχηλον ἄλοκα μιλτώδη ποιεῖ,
ἐπὶ τῷ προσώπῳ δ' αἱ τρίχες φορούμεναι
εἴξασι πολιαῖς, ἀνάπλεῳ ψιμυθίου.

The eyebrows were painted with a
dark colour, called μέλαν or ἄσβολος.
Alexis, ap. Athen. xiii. p. 568:

τὰς ὀφρῦς πυρρὰς ἔχει τις· ζωγραφοῦσιν
ἀσβόλῳ.

The procession soon approached the garden, in the centre of which the funeral pyre had been erected. The bier having been lifted upon it, unguent vessels and other articles were thrown in, and a blazing pine-link was then applied to the pile, which being constructed of the most inflammable materials, took light at once, and the consuming flame shot high aloft, amid the loud lamentations and sobs of those present. Sincere tears of deepest sorrow were shed by Cleobule. With tottering step she approached the blazing pile, to throw into it a vessel of ointment, as a last libation of love ; when, in her distraction, a sudden draught of air drove the flame towards her without her being conscious of the danger. 'For heaven's sake!' screamed several voices, and Charicles, reckless of everything, darted ahead of all the rest, and with his hands smothered the flame, which had already caught the border of her robe; he then led the trembling Cleobule to her mother, who was hastening towards her.[43]

A part only of the escort tarried till the ashes were collected, and all the rites duly discharged. Of this number was Charicles. But when the bones had been consigned to the ground, and the women had bidden farewell to the new-made grave, he also, with Sophilos, wended his way back towards the city. The possible consequences of the unhappy will formed the topic of conversation. Charicles

---

It was also called στίμμις. Poll. v. 101 : καὶ τὰ ὑπογράμματα καὶ ἡ στίμμις παρ' Ἴωνι ἐν 'Ομφάλη

καὶ τὴν μέλαιναν στίμμιν ὀμματογράφον.

Instances occur of men painting, so Demetrios Phalereus, mentioned by Duris, ap. Athen xii. p. 542. Ischomachos too asks his wife if she would prefer him painted. Xenoph. Œcon. 10, 5. The passage however is evidently corrupt, since ἀνδρείκελον was never used for painting the eyes. We should probably read μίλτῳ ἢ ἀνδρεικέλῳ. In Tischbein's Engravings, ii. 58, is

a vase-painting of a female in a sitting posture occupied in rouging with a brush. This is copied in Böttiger's Sabina, Pl. ix. The operation was also performed with the finger.

[43] After Terent. Andr. i. 1, 102:

In ignem imposita est: fletur. Interea hæc soror,
Quam dixi, ad flammam accessit imprudentius,
Satis cum periclo: ibi tum exanimatus Pamphilus
Bene dissimulatum amorem et celatum indicat.
Adcurrit, mediam mulierem complectitur, etc.

could not conceal how very different an impression Sosilas
had made upon him from what he had expected. To-day
the man had looked so unassuming and devout, and withal
so venerable, that he had well nigh dropped his suspicions.
' Who ever would believe,' said he, ' that beneath this exterior lurked such knavery?' ' You will meet with plenty
more such,' answered Sophilos, ' who go about with the
aspect of lambs, but within are the most poisonous scor
pions ;[44] it is just these that are most dangerous of all.'

At the city-gate they separated. A strange slave
had followed them at a distance all the way. He now
stood still for a moment, apparently undetermined which
of the two he should pursue. ' Youth is more liberal,'
said he half aloud, after reflecting a moment, ' especially
when in love.' With this he struck into the path Charicles had taken, and which led through a narrow lonely
lane, between two garden-walls; here he redoubled his
pace, and soon overtook Charicles. ' Who art thou?' asked
the youth, retreating back a step. ' A slave, as you see,'
was the reply, ' and one who may be of service to you.
You seem interested in Cleobule's fate, eh?' ' What
business is that of yours?' retorted Charicles; but his
blush was more than a sufficient answer for the slave. ' It
is not indifferent to you,' he proceeded, ' whether Sophilos
or Sosilas be the heir.' ' Very possibly; but wherefore
these enquiries? what is this to you, sirrah?' ' More than
you think,' rejoined the slave. ' What shall be my reward if I hand you the proof that one of the two wills is
a forgery?' ' You! a miserable slave!' exclaimed the
youth, astonished. ' The slave is often acquainted with
his master's most secret dealings,' answered the other.
' Come now, what's to be my reward?' ' Freedom, which
is your rightful due for the discovery of such a crime.'[45]

---

[44] Hermipp. *Fragm. Com.* p. 381.
Mein.

[45] It is not here intended to assert

that when a mere private right was
violated, freedom was publicly given
as a μήνυτρα to the slave who in-

'Good,' replied the slave, 'but the freedman must have
the means wherewith to live.'[46] 'That also shall you have;
five minæ are yours, if you speak the truth.' 'Thy name
is Charicles,' said the slave; 'no one hears your promise,
but I'll trust you. My master is Sosilas, and they call me
Molon.' He opened a small bag, and pulled something
out of it with a mysterious air. 'See, here is the signet,'
said he, 'with which the forged will was sealed.' He took
some wax, wetted it, and impressed the seal thereon.
'That is the device of Polycles, an eagle clawing a snake;
you will be the eagle.' He related how he had witnessed
the forgery through a crack in the door; how a rustling
he had made was near betraying him; and how Sosilas, in
his haste to bundle up the things, had unwittingly let the
false stamp drop on the coverlet. 'Now then,' said he,
'haven't I kept my word?' 'By the gods! and so will I,'
cried Charicles, almost beside himself with wonder and joy.
'Not five—no—ten minæ shalt thou have. And now tc
Sophilos with all speed.' 'No!' said the slave, 'I trust to
you. Do you go by yourself, and have me called when
you have need of me.'

---

formed, but the manumission might
be otherwise effected. See Excursus
on *The Slaves.*

[46] After Plaut. *Epid.* v. 2, 60:

PE. Optumnm atque æquissimum oras:
　　soccos, tunicam, pallium
Tibi dabo. EP. Quid deinde porro? PE. Li-
　　bertatem. EP. At postea?
Novo liberto opus est, quod pappet. PE.
　　Dabitur: præbebo cibum.

SCENE THE TENTH.

THE DIONYSIA.

AMONG the festivals which Athens celebrated annually, or at greater intervals,—either in honour of the gods, for the renown and credit of the state, or for the amusement of its burghers—there were doubtless several that laid claim to a greater share of political importance, or a deeper religious significancy, than the rest, as, for example, the Panathenæa and the Eleusinia. But the last-mentioned object — pleasure—was attained most eminently by that feast at which the giver of joy and jollity, Dionysos himself, was worshipped. Almost might it be said, that the original intention of the festival,—to thank the god for the noblest gift brought by the returning seasons, —had been lost sight of in the tumult of passion and unbridled mirth. On these days all sobriety or serious occupation was banished, and the people, one and all, embraced with open arms the myrmidons of the god, Methe and Comos, resigning themselves all too willingly to their sway. To have their fill of enjoyment, with public spectacle and carouse, and to revel self-oblivious in a transport of delight—such was the all-absorbing desire of young and old, the common goal to which all pressed forward ; nay, even the most sober-minded, bidding adieu to the stringency of habit, followed the maxim :

> Ne'er blush with drink to spice the feast's gay hour,
> And reeling own the mighty wine-god's power.

The feast of the city-*Dionysia*,[1] which was celebrated

---

[1] At the Dionysia the most unbridled merriment and drunkenness were the order of the day, and were held quite blameless. Nor was this the case at Athens only : see Plato, *Leg.* i. p. 637. He says elsewhere, in extenuation : πίνειν δὲ εἰς μέθην οὔτε ἀλλοθί που πρέπει, πλὴν ἐν ταῖς τοῦ τὸν οἶνον δόντος θεοῦ ἑορταῖς. *Leg.* vi. p. 775. Indeed, it was considered as an act of gratitude due to the giver of the grape, and under

at the beginning of spring, with the greatest splendour
and festivities, was most popular of all. Not only did it
attract the inhabitants of Attica;[2] but a vast number of
strangers, eager for spectacles and diversion, streamed
into Athens on these anniversaries to share in the fun and
frolic.

The first anniversary of this festival, since Charicles
had returned to Athens, had now arrived. The milder
days of spring had set in early;[3] the winterly rest and
stillness of the port had yielded to new life and animation;
craft were beginning to run in from the neighbouring ports
and islands; and the merchants were fitting out their ships
on any venture that promised a lucrative return.[4] Innumerable guests had poured to the scene of the festival
from all the regions of Greece;[5] every house was kept

Ptolemy Dionysios it was thought a
crime to remain sober; so at least
says Lucian, de Calumn. 16 : παρὰ
Πτολεμαίῳ τῷ Διονύσῳ ἐπικληθέντι
ἐγένετό τις, ὃς διέβαλε τὸν Πλατω-
νικὸν Δημήτριον, ὅτι ὕδωρ τε πίνει
καὶ μόνος τῶν ἄλλων γυναικεῖα οὐκ
ἐνεδύσατο ἐν τοῖς Διονυσίοις. καὶ εἴ
γε μὴ κληθεὶς ἕωθεν ἔπινέ τε πάντων ὁρώντων καὶ λαβὼν Ταραντινί-
διον ἐκυμβάλισέ τε καὶ προσωρχή-
σατο, ἀπολώλει ἄν.

[2] Country folks naturally resorted
to the city-Dionysia, though more
rarely in early times. Isocrates, Areop.
p. 203, says that the ancient inhabitants of Attica were so comfortably off
in their farms, (ὥστε) πολλοὺς τῶν
πολιτῶν μηδ' εἰς τὰς ἑορτὰς εἰς ἄστυ
καταβαίνειν, ἀλλ' αἱρεῖσθαι μένειν
ἐπὶ τοῖς ἰδίοις ἀγαθοῖς μᾶλλον ἢ τῶν
κοινῶν ἀπολαύειν.

[3] By spring is here meant the
milder season of the year generally.
In Attica this may be supposed usually to have set in some time in March;

though occasionally cold weather
might return. Plutarch, Demetr. 12 :
Τῇ δ' ἡμέρᾳ ᾗ τὰ Διονύσια ἐγίνετο,
τὴν πομπὴν κατέλυσαν ἰσχυρῶν πά-
γων γενομένων παρ' ὥραν καὶ πάχνης
βαθείας πεσούσης ἧς οὐ μόνον ἀμπέ-
λους καὶ συκᾶς ἁπάσας ἀπέκαυσε τὸ
ψῦχος, ἀλλὰ καὶ τοῦ σίτου τὸν πλεῖστον κατέφθειρεν ἐν χλόῃ,

[4] Navigation was suspended during the winter. Hesiod, Opp. 619.
The time of the city-Dionysia was the
period when the sea was again considered navigable. Theophr. Char. 3:
τὴν θάλατταν ἐκ Διονυσίων πλώϊμον
εἶναι.

[5] The Dionysia and other festivals
were visited by a very great concourse
of strangers. Xenoph. 1, 11 : ἐπὶ δὲ
τούτων ἕκαστα οἱ μὲν ἰδιῶται ἔρχονται καὶ εἰς πόλεις, ἃς ἂν βούλωνται,
θεαμάτων ἕνεκα καὶ εἰς τὰς κοινὰς
πανηγύρεις. Æschin. in Ctesiph. p.
428 : Κτησιφῶν δὲ (ἀνακηρύττειν κελεύει) ἐν τῷ θεάτρῳ...οὐδὲ ἐκκλησια-
ζόντων 'Αθηναίων, ἀλλὰ τραγῳδοῖν

open for the reception of distant friends; every tavern
was too small to accommodate its crowd of visitors. Many
had even erected booths in the streets and public places,
intending to turn the festival to profit; for, besides the
sight-seers and pleasure-hunters, a mass of the lower classes
had come, in the hopes of picking up something among
such a confluence of idlers. Retail-dealers [6] of all descriptions had arrived; pimps, with their bevies of Corinthian
beauties; jugglers, and strolling mountebanks, laden with
the apparatus of their art, and the decorations of their
booths; [7] all were ready to devote their utmost exertions
to the amusement of the public, and the replenishment of
their own purses.

Charicles was one of the few who could not be allured
into the universal tone of enjoyment. Since the death of
Polycles more than four months had passed, and these had
been to him a period of disquiet and of painful irresolution.
Cleobule's affairs had taken a most happy turn. In addition to the slave's statement, and the production of the
forged signet, another decisive proof had been obtained.
With his usual circumspection and prudence, Polycles had,
during his stay at Ædepsos, deposited a third copy of the
will in the hands of a respectable man there. [8] Of course

ἀγωνιζομένων καινῶν, οὐδ' ἐναντίον
τοῦ δήμου, ἀλλ' ἐναντίον τῶν Ἑλλή-
ρων: and again, ib. p. 434: οἱ δὲ ἀνη-
γορεύοντο ἐνώπιον ἀπάντων τῶν Ἑλλήνων. So Demosth. in Mid. p. 584,
speaking of the insult offered him by
Meidias in the theatre, says, ἡμαρτη-
κότα ἀσελγῶς ἐν πανηγύρει, μάρτυρας τῆς ὕβρεως τῆς αὑτοῦ πεποιημένον οὐ μόνον ὑμᾶς, ἀλλὰ καὶ τοὺς
ἐπιδημοῦντας ἅπαντας τῶν Ἑλλήνων.

[6] See Excursus on *The Markets
and Commerce.*

[7] The θαυματοποιοί, or wandering
jugglers, are mentioned by Plu-

tarch, *de Facie in Orbe Lunæ,* 8:
θαυματοποιοῦ τινος ἀποσκευήν καὶ
πυλαίαν κατανωτισάμενοι καὶ παρέλ-
κοντες. They naturally frequented
public festivals. Dio Chrysostom, *Or.*
viii. p. 278, speaking of the Isthmian
games, says, πολλῶν δὲ θαυματοποιῶν
θαύματα ἐπιδεικνύντων, πολλῶν δὲ
τερατοσκόπων τέρατα κρινόντων. The
Syracusan in Xenophon's *Symposium*
had unquestionably come to Athens
on account of the Panathenæa.

[8] Such caution was necessary.
Diog. Laert. iv. 43: τρεῖς τε διαθή-
κας ποιησάμενος ἔθετο τὴν μὲν ἐν
Ἐρετρίᾳ παρὰ Ἀμφίκριτον, τὴν δὲ

this also testified against Sosilas, and the forgery he had committed was now so manifest, that he might congratulate himself on the magnanimity of Sophilos in not proceeding against him. Charicles had therefore no further cause for alarm about the fate of Cleobule ; but he became the more anxious and uncertain respecting his own destiny, particularly as Sophilos delayed his marriage, and had let fall some expressions which seemed to indicate that he had no intention of ever celebrating it ; nay, he even hinted that he designed his young friend, whom he treated almost like a son, for the bridegroom of the wealthy widow. This it was that rendered our hero so uneasy.

The heart of Charicles leaned, it is true, towards Cleobule, and it pained him to fancy the possibility of her being the bride of another ; but Phorion's warning, not to become dependent on a rich wife, resounded loudly in his ears ; and he was the more alive to the truth of his sage monitor's advice, from his own innate love of freedom and independence. His humble patrimony almost vanished in comparison with the dowry which Cleobule would bring her future husband, and her property, not his, would be the basis of the establishment. ' No !' he had mentally ejaculated, ' " Look out for a wife befitting you," says the proverb,[9] as Ctesiphon, not without reason, lately reminded me : never will I sacrifice to inclination the position that a free man ought to enjoy.' And thus he fancied that by dint of calm reason he had vanquished the passion that filled his bosom : when, on the day preceding the festival, Sophilos came to him, as he often did, with looks of the sincerest friendship. ' I have a weighty business to discuss with you, Charicles,' said he, after the first salutations, ' and I wish, in the celebration of the festival, to be one care lighter. The will of Polycles makes it

---

Ἀθήνησι παρά τινας τῶν φίλων, τὴν δὲ τρίτην ἀπέστειλεν εἰς οἶκον, κ.τ.λ.

[9] τὴν κατὰ σαυτὸν ἕλα. Plutarch, de Educ. Puer. 19. See Excursus on The Women.

imperative on me to give away Cleobule in marriage, and
I have already delayed doing so almost too long. Two
fathers have been suing for her on behalf of their sons,
but neither of them is to my taste, and ——' 'What, are
you not going to wed her yourself then?' hastily interposed Charicles. 'What would you think of me?' replied
Sophilos. 'I'm the wrong side of fifty; brisk and hearty
to be sure; my eye is still undimmed, my limbs robust
and active; and though this hair be grey, yet the intellect is unenfeebled by age;[10] but, notwithstanding, do you
suppose that, at my time of life, I am going to undertake
the cares of a husband and a father, and embitter my
days with a thousand anxieties?[11] I have had my share
of them, and am resolved to pass the remainder of my life
in peace.' 'But can you resist the temptation of so rich
a dower?' enquired Charicles. 'What do I want with
riches?' said Sophilos gravely. 'Have not I more already
than I want, and does not my property nearly equal that
which was left by Polycles? But for whom should I pile
up riches? My sons fell in the wars against Philip—one
son I still might have, if—but why advert now to that
painful subject? Enough! for Cleobule's sake I will never
put forward any claim to the property; the second time
she shall not be wedded to an old man. The choice of
her husband rests with me; but it were better that she
should have one of her own choosing, and, if I err not,
you are the man.' 'I?' cried Charicles in confusion, while
the blood mounted to his cheeks; 'Cleobule choose me?'
The thought of being so near happiness, that he had only
to stretch out his hand to obtain it, had such a powerful
effect on Charicles, that he had to call to mind all the
objections with which calm reflection had combated his
wishes, in order not to prove a deserter of his principles.

---

[10] The words of Periplectomenes,
and the remark of Palæstrio. Plaut.
Mil. iii. 1, 35.

[11] The reason given by Periplectomenes for not wishing to marry.
Ibid. v. 125.

' I thank you,' he replied at length in a collected tone,
' for the twofold happiness you design for me ; but this
marriage would be unsuited to my circumstances.'   ' Unsuited ? ' repeated Sophilos in amazement.   ' A young and
blooming bride, and good and well-mannered withal, with
such a property too, and not suit ?   Or is it because she
is a widow that you hesitate ?   Fool that you must be !
call her a bride rather, a bride of sixteen, whose bridegroom never escorted her to the thalamos, for he was
a dying man from the very hour of the marriage-feast.
Search Athens through, and you will not find a damsel
who could with more confidence enter the grotto of Pan
at Ephesos, where, as they say, the god takes terrible
vengeance on the conscious delinquent.'[12]   ' Not for that,'

---

[12] Achill. Tat. viii. 6, relates that
pure virgins only might enter this
grotto, which Pan had dedicated to
Artemis, and wherein he had hung
up his pipe. Hence, any damsel sus-
pected of incontinence was made to
enter it, and the doors were closed ;
if she was innocent, the clear tones of
the flute were heard, the doors flew
open of themselves, and the maiden
came out scatheless. Were the contrary the case, the flute remained
mute, sounds of wailing reached the
ears, the doors remained closed, and
the female was seen no more. This
story may not have been the pure invention of the writer, but may have
been founded on some local legend,
most likely of considerable antiquity.
Ælian, *Hist. Anim.* xi. 6, mentions
a similar test of virginity in the
dragon's cave at Lanuvium, and this
is elsewhere corroborated ; as also is
what Achilles Tatius relates of the
Στυγὸς ὕδωρ, by which an oath was
tested. Hence the tale about Pan's
grotto need not be considered pure
fiction. Ordeals were as well known

in antiquity as in the middle ages.
The earliest instance of the kind occurs, Sophocl. *Antig.* 264, where the
guards over the corpse of Polyneices
assert their innocence :

ἦμεν δ' ἕτοιμοι καὶ μύδρους αἴρειν χεροῖν
καὶ πῦρ διέρπειν, καὶ θεοὺς ὁρκωμοτεῖν
τὸ μήτε δρᾶσαι, μήτε τῳ ξυνειδέναι
τὸ πρᾶγμα βουλεύσαντι, μήτ' εἰργασμένῳ.

This of course does not refer to tor-
ture, or anything of the kind, but is a
voluntary offer of the speakers to attest their innocence by lifting hot iron,
passing through the fire, and similar
acts. Brunk, incorrectly, it would
appear, compares the θαυμαστὴ ἱερο-
ποιΐα at Soracte. See Strabo, v. 2, 9.
Pliny, *Nat. Hist.* vii. 2, however, clearly shows that this was a piece of mum-
mery got up by the priests to deceive
the credulous people. A similar imposture took place, according to Strabo, xii. 2, 7, at Castabala in Cilicia,
ὅπου φασὶ τὰς ἱερείας γυμνοῖς τοῖς
ποσὶ δι' ἀνθρακίας βαδίζειν ἀπαθεῖς.
A case much more in point occurs in
Pausan. vii. 25, 8, where it is related
that the purity of the priestesses in a

answered Charicles; 'Cleobule is the most loveable creature I have ever seen, but her property does not assort
with mine. I will not live in the house of a wife whom
I have to thank for my good fortune; I will be free and
independent, and owe my position to myself, not to another.' 'You might be right,' rejoined Sophilos, 'with
any other than an innocent, merry creature like Cleobule,
who would never dream of giving herself airs on the
strength of her superior wealth; trust me, all the power
she would ever exercise over you would be that of love.
Come, don't be a fool, and mar Cleobule's happiness and
your own, by pride and obstinacy; for that you love each
other, I know full well. I had wished to affiance you this
very day; but since you raise scruples, we'll talk thereon
when the festival is over.'

The Dionysia had begun, and pleasure was the sole
pursuit of all through the live-long day. Strangers and
citizens paraded the streets in holiday attire, with garlands
on their brows; altars and Hermæ were wreathed with
chaplets; and in every thoroughfare stood huge bowls
filled with the gift of the god, inviting all that liked, to

---

temple in Achaia was put to the proof by making them drink ox-blood, which was thought to be deadly poison: πί-νουσαι δὲ αἷμα ταύρου δοκιμάζονται. ἣ δ' ἂν αὐτῶν τύχῃ μὴ ἀληθεύουσα, αὐτίκα ἐκ τούτου τὴν δίκην ἔχει. Cf. Aristoph. *Equites*, 80; Plutarch, *Themist.* 31, and Scholiast thereon. Another peculiar ordeal was the altar, ἐσχάρα (Heliod. *Æthiop.* x. 8), by which the crimes of παρθενεύειν and perjury were assayed. When a guilty person ascended the altar, flames issued from it spontaneously. Similar to this was the water-ordeal of an oath, to which class belongs the Στυγὸς ὕδωρ already referred to. Achill.

Tat. viii. 12: Ἡ δὲ κρίσις· ἐγγράψας τὸν ὅρκον γραμματείῳ μηρίνθῳ δεδε-μένον περιεθήκατο τῇ δέρῃ. Κἂν μὲν ἀψευδῆ τὸν ὅρκον, μένει κατὰ χώραι ἡ πηγή· ἂν δὲ ψεύδηται τὸ ὕδωρ ὀργί-ζεται καὶ ἀναβαίνει μέχρι τῆς δέρης, καὶ τὸ γραμματεῖον ἐκάλυψε. So the ὕδωρ ὅρκιον and the φρέαρ ἐλέγχου, mentioned by Philostr. *Vit. Apollon.* i. 6, and iii. 14. A sort of wager of battle is also mentioned, Heliod. *Æthiop.* vii. 4. Something of the kind is alluded to by Chæreas, ap. Charit. viii. 4: Σὺ μὲν ἔμελλες τὴν δίκην κρίνειν, ἐγὼ δὲ ἤδη νενίκηκα παρὰ τῷ δικαιοτάτῳ δικαστῇ. πόλεμος γὰρ ἄριστος κρι-της τοῦ κρείττονός τε καὶ χείρονος.

drink to their very heart's content.[13]　Everywhere peals of loud laughter and boisterous mirth assailed the ear; nought was to be seen but troops of merry-makers, and reckless swarms of comastæ, impudently caricaturing the pomp and ceremony of the festal procession.

But the most curious sight of all was the mob that beset the theatre. Since early dawn the seats had been crammed with spectators, who attentively followed the solemn contest of the tragedians, previous to being diverted, a little later, by the more lively fare of the comedians.[14]　From time to time stormy rounds of cheering and applause burst from the serried mass; while at intervals might also be heard a shrill whistling, directed at an obnoxious passage in the play, or the bad performance of some actor, or, perchance, meant for some one among the audience.

Outside the theatre also, sight-seers of more humble pretensions found abundant materials for amusement. Here a puppet-man had set up his little theatre,[15] and, with

---

[13] A Delphian oracle, quoted by Demosth. in Mid. p. 531, enjoined the Athenians,

μεμνῆσθαι Βάκχοιο καὶ εὐευχόρους κατ' ἀγυιὰς
ἱστάναι ὡραίων Βρομίῳ χάριν ἄμμιγα πάντας,
καὶ κνισσᾶν βωμοῖσι, κάρη στεφάνοις πυκάσαντες.

Cf. in Macart. p. 1072 : κατ' ἀγυιὰς κρατῆρας ἱστάμεν. This was also the case at the Dionysia at Pellene in Achaia, and elsewhere. Pausan. vii. 27, 2 : τούτῳ καὶ Λαμπτηρίαν ἑορτὴν ἄγουσι καὶ δᾷδάς τε ἐς τὸ ἱερὸν κομίζουσιν ἐν νυκτὶ καὶ οἴνου κρατῆρας ἱστᾶσιν ἀνὰ τὴν πόλιν πᾶσαν.

[14] Kannegiesser, Die alte kom. Bühne in Athen, has supposed that because the scene of several comedies of Aristophanes is laid early in the

morning, therefore the representation of them commenced at daybreak. But, on the other hand, it is clear from Aves, 785, that the tragedy was acted early, and the comedy in the afternoon :

αὐτίχ' ὑμῶν τῶν θεατῶν εἴ τις ἦν ὑπόπτερος,
εἶτα πεινῶν τοῖς χοροῖσι τῶν τραγῳδῶν ἤχθετο,
ἐκπτόμενος ἂν οὗτος ἠρίστησεν ἐλθὼν οἴκαδε·
κᾆτ' ἂν ἐμπλησθεὶς ἐφ' ἡμᾶς αὖθις αὖ κατέπτετο.

[15] Puppets moved by strings, νευρόσπαστα, are mentioned by Herodotus, ii. 48, as having been introduced from Egypt : ἀντὶ δὲ φαλλῶν ἄλλα σφί ἐστι ἐξευρημένα ὅσον τε πηχυαῖα ἀγάλματα νευρόσπαστα, τὰ περιφορέουσι κατὰ κώμας γυναῖκες, νεῦον τὸ αἰδοῖον, κ.τ.λ. See Lucian, de Syr. dea, 16 ; Aristot. de Mundo,

practised hand, guided the hidden strings that set in motion
the pigmy figures, which performed the most grotesque
antics, to the intense delight of the children and nurses
standing round.[16] Elsewhere a Thessalian exhibited the
dexterity of two damsels, who, with the most infinite cool
ness and agility, made surprising leaps amidst sharp sword-
blades stuck upright in the ground, threw somersaults,[17]
or, sitting down upon a potter's wheel in rapid motion,
read and wrote with ease;[18] whilst the man himself from
time to time opened his mouth wide, and let fly a stream
of sparks among the horrified spectators,[19] or, with apparent difficulty, gulped down swords and daggers.[20] Not
far off a juggler had pitched his tent, taking the prudent
precaution of placing projecting barriers,[21] to keep over

6: ὁμοίως δὲ καὶ οἱ νευροσπάσται
μίαν μήρινθον ἐπισπασάμενοι ποιοῦσι
καὶ αὐχένα κινεῖσθαι καὶ χεῖρα τοῦ
ζῴου, καὶ ὦμον, καὶ ὀφθαλμόν. Cf.
Heindorf, ad Hor. Sat. ii. 7, 82. Persons strolled about, exhibiting them
for a livelihood. Xenoph. Symp. 4,
55: οὗτοι γὰρ τὰ ἐμὰ νευρόσπαστα
θεώμενοι τρέφουσί με.

[16] Plaut. Cist. v. 2, 45:
              Nutrix.....
.... me spectatum tulerat per Dionysia.

[17] On this κυβιστᾶν εἰς μαχαίρας,
see Note 22 to Scene VI. Cf. Athen.
iv. p. 129; and Mus. Borb. iv. 58,
where we actually see represented
this κυβιστᾶν εἰς κύκλον περίμεστον
ξιφῶν ὀρθῶν.

[18] Xenoph. Symp. 7, 2: εἰσεφέ-
ρετο τῇ ὀρχηστρίδι τροχὸς τῶν κε-
ραμεικῶν, ἐφ' οὗ ἔμελλε θαυμασιουρ-
γήσειν: and a little further: καὶ μὴν
τό γε ἐπὶ τοῦ τροχοῦ ἅμα περιδινου-
μένου γράφειν τε καὶ ἀναγιγνώσκειν,
θαῦμα μὲν ἴσως τί ἐστιν.

[19] This trick was well known to
the Greeks. Hippolochos, apud

Athen. iv. p. 129: (εἰσῆλθόν) τινες
καὶ θαυματουργοὶ γυναῖκες, εἰς ξίφη
κυβιστῶσαι καὶ πῦρ ἐκ τοῦ στόματος
ἐκριπίζουσαι γυμναί.

[20] Plutarch, Lyc. 19, where an
Athenian, ridiculing the short Spartan swords, says, ῥᾳδίως αὐτὰς οἱ
θαυματοποιοὶ καταπίνουσιν ἐν τοῖς
θεάτροις. The apparatus used for
performing this feat was nearly the
same as that now employed for the
same purpose. See Achill. Tat. iii. 20,
where Satyros finds in a chest χλαμύδα
καὶ ξίφος τὴν μὲν κώπην ὅσον παλαι-
στῶν τεσσάρων, τὸν δὲ σίδηρον ἐπὶ τῇ
κώπῃ βραχύτατον, δακτύλων ὅσον οὐ
πλείω τριῶν. Ὡς δὲ ἀνελόμενος τὸ ξίφος ὁ Μενέλαος ἔλαθε μετασπρέψας
κατὰ τὸ τοῦ σιδήρου μέρος τὸ μικρὸν
ἐκεῖνο ξίφος, ὥσπερ ἀπὸ χηραμοῦ τῆς
κώπης κατατρέχει τοσοῦτον, ὅσον
εἶχεν ἡ κώπη τὸ μέγεθος· ὡς δὲ
ἀνέστρεψεν εἰς τὸ ἔμπαλιν, αὖθις ὁ
σίδηρος εἴσω κατεδύετο. Τούτῳ δ'
ἄρα, ὡς εἰκὸς, ὁ κακοδαίμων ἐκεῖνος
ἐν τοῖς θεάτροις ἐχρῆτο πρὸς τὰς
κιβδήλους σφαγάς.

[21] Casaubon, on Athen. . p. 19,

curious observers from his apparatus-table. Simple rustics
and fishermen beheld with wonderment how at first the
pebbles lay, one under each of the mysterious cups, then
all are under one, after which they all vanished, finally
reappearing out of the conjuror's mouth.[22] But when,
after causing them to disappear a second time, he finally
drew them all three out of the nose and ears of the
nearest spectator, several of them scratched their heads,
as not knowing what to make of it; and one plain countryman, shaking his head, said to his neighbour, 'I say,
if this chap come near my farm, then good-bye to goods
and gear.'[23] But the heartiest laughter was heard round
the booth of a man who was exhibiting a number of trained
monkeys, dressed in motley suits, with masks before their
faces, and which performed elaborate dances like so many
well-behaved human beings.[24] The trainer's switch kept

---

and on Theophr. *Char.* 6, has discussed the ancient jugglers. Cf.
Beckmann's *History of Inventions*,
from which mainly Böttiger has
compiled his meagre account. He is
quite wrong too in supposing the
performers had nothing erected to
conceal their secret apparatus, for
the contrary is expressly asserted by
Plato, *de Republ.* vii. p. 514 : ὥσπερ
τοῖς θαυματοποιοῖς πρὸ τῶν ἀνθρώπων
πρόκειται τὰ παραφράγματα, ὑπὲρ ὧν
τὰ θαύματα δεικνύσιν.

[22] One of the commonest tricks
was that of passing objects from
under one cup to another (παροψίδες
μικραί). The performers were hence
called ψηφοκλέπται, ψηφοπαῖκται,
ψηφολόγοι. Athen. i. p. 19; Poll. vii.
201. Suidas quotes the words of an
unknown writer : ὥσπερ οἱ ψηφολόγοι τοὺς ὀφθαλμοὺς τῷ τάχει τῆς
μεταθέσεως τῶν ψήφων ἀπατῶντες
συναρπάζουσι. See Artemidor, *Oneirocr.* iii. 56; and Alciphron, *Epist.* iii.

20, is still more explicit in his description : Εἶς γάρ τις, εἰς μέσους παρελθὼν καὶ στήσας τρίποδα, τρεῖς μικρας
παρετίθει παροψίδας. εἶτα ὑπὸ ταύταις ἔσκεπε μικρά τινα καὶ λευκὰ
καὶ στρογγύλα λιθίδια, οἷα ἡμεῖς ἐπὶ
ταῖς ὄχθαις τῶν χειμάρρων ἀνευρί-
σκομεν. ταῦτα ποτὲ μὲν κατὰ μίαν
ἔσκεπε παροψίδα, ποτὲ δὲ, οὐκ οἶδ'
ὅπως, ὑπὸ τῇ μιᾷ ἐδείκνυ, ποτὲ δὲ
παντελῶς ἀπὸ τῶν παροψίδων ἠφά-
νιζε καὶ ἐπὶ τοῦ στόματος ἐφαίνεν.
εἶτα καταβροχθίσας τοὺς πλησίον
ἑστῶτας ἄγων εἰς μέσον, τὴν μὲν ἐκ
ῥινός τινος. τὴν δὲ ἐξ ὠτίου, τὴν δὲ
ἐκ κεφαλῆς ἀνῃρεῖτο.

[23] Alciphr. *ib.* : Μὴ γένοιτο κατ'
ἀγρὸν τοιοῦτο θηρίον· οὐ γὰρ ἁλώ-
σεται ὑπ' οὐδενὸς καὶ πάντα ὑφαι-
ρούμενος τὰ ἔνδον φροῦδά μοι τὰ κατ'
ἀγρὸν ἀπεργάσεται.

[24] Lucian, *Piscat.* 36, mentions an
ape-comedy like this, though his description refers to a somewhat later

them a long while in order, and his man was just collect-
ing the small copper-coins from the bystanders,[25] when
a wag amused himself with throwing some nuts among the
dancers, who, in a twinkling, forgetful alike of all propriety
and the parts they played, made a descent on the prey,
and began scratching and biting each other for the possession of it, to the great amusement of the spectators.[26]
The confusion which ensued was a fine opportunity for the
thieves and cut-purses, who were following their calling in
great force, and levying contributions on the crowd, or at
the tables of the pedlars, where all sorts of wares, clothes,
and ornaments, both false and genuine, were displayed for
sale.[27] Not a few of the purchasers, when they came to
pay, discovered themselves to be minus girdle and purse;
but it was Dionysia-time, and so nobody was disconcerted
by such occurrences.

Whilst all besides resigned themselves to mirth and
joviality, Cleobule sat weeping in her chamber. Her
thoughts were bent on the future; and, occupied with the

---

date. Cf. de Merc. Cond. 5. Dogs,
horses, and other animals were trained for the same purpose. Plutarch,
Gryll. 9: κόρακας διαλέγεσθαι καὶ
κύνας ἄλλεσθαι διὰ τροχῶν περιφε-
ρομένων· ἵπποι δὲ καὶ βόες ἐν θεάτροις κατακλίσεις καὶ χορείας καὶ
στάσεις παραβόλους, καὶ κινήσεις οὐδὲ
ἀνθρώποις πάνυ ῥᾳδίας ἀκριβοῦσιν.

[25] As with us a person goes round
with a plate to the spectators, so the
Greek θαυματοποιοί went round to
collect the θεωρικόν. Theophrastus,
Char. 6, among the tokens of ἀπόνοια,
mentions: ἐν θαύμασι τοὺς χαλκοὺς
ἐκλέγειν, καθ' ἕκαστον παριών, καὶ
μάχεσθαι τοῖς τὸ σύμβολον φέρουσι
καὶ προῖκα θεωρεῖν ἀξιοῦσι. Hence it
appears that they gave to some persons free-admission tickets, which
entitled them to see without paying.

See also Lucian, Asin. 37; Xenoph.
Symp. 2, 1.

[26] Lucian, ibid.: καὶ μέχρι πολλοῦ εὐδοκιμεῖν τὴν θέαν, ἄχρι δή τις
θεατὴς ἀστεῖος, κάρυα ὑπὸ κόλπον
ἔχων, ἀφῆκεν ἐς τὸ μέσον· οἱ δὲ πίθηκοι ἰδόντες καὶ ἐκλαθόμενοι τῆς
ὀρχήσεως τοῦθ', ὅπερ ἦσαν, πίθηκοι
ἐγένοντο ἀντὶ πυρριχιστῶν καὶ ξυνέ-
τριβον τὰ προσωπεῖα καὶ τὴν ἐσθῆτα
κατερρήγνυον, καὶ ἐμάχοντο περὶ
τῆς ὀπώρας πρὸς ἀλλήλους.

[27] Aristoph. Pax, 760:

      ὡς εἰώθασι μάλιστα
περὶ τὰς σκηνὰς πλεῖστοι κλέπται κυπτάζειν
      καὶ κακοποιεῖν.

See Excursus on The Markets and
Commerce. Xenoph. Œcon. 10, 3,
mentions false trinkets, ὅρμους ὑποξύλους.

wishes secretly cherished in her heart, she had not quitted
the house, declining all share in those pleasures which her
sex was permitted by custom to enjoy. For a short time
she had surveyed the festival from a window, but the merry
multitude possessed no attractions for her; there was one
only whom she had desired to see, and she had seen him,
but alas! only to feel to her sorrow that his thoughts were
not occupied with her, for he had directed no kindly gaze
toward the house. Charicles had passed moodily by, his
eyes cast straight before him. 'He loves me not,' she
said to herself, as, with tears in her eyes, she left the
window; 'I am forgotten, and all the oracles have played
me false.' Thus she sat sorrowing in her chamber, her
beautiful head leaning on the white arm which rested on
the side of the chair. Chloris, her favourite and confidential slave, knelt before her, and beside her stood the
aged Manto, trying, with anxious solicitude, to divine the
reason of her tears. 'Art thou unwell, my mistress?' she
enquired; 'hast thou peradventure been blighted by the
evil-eye?[28]   If so, let us send for the old Thessalian crone,
who can counteract each spell.' But Chloris understood
better than Manto what was passing through her mistress'
heart. She had noticed that the youth had found favour
with her lady in the adventure of the brook, and that
since Polycles' death the inclination cherished in secret had
become a consuming passion. Why else would Cleobule
have so often stealthily cracked the leaves of the tele-
philon?[29] or why did she so repeatedly shoot the slippery

---

[28] It is curious to remark how the
belief in the evil-eye has descended to
the present time, and the ὀφθαλμὸς
βάσκανος of the Greeks corresponds
to the *mal-occhio* and *mauvais-œil* of
our day. Δυσμενὴς καὶ βάσκανος ὁ τῶν
γειτόνων ὀφθαλμός, says Alciphron,
Ep. i. 15; and Heliod. *Æthiop.* iii 7,
comments on and defends the popular
superstition. Plutarch devotes a spe-

cial chapter to the subject. *Sympos.*
v. 7: περὶ τῶν βασκαίνειν λεγομένων καὶ βάσκανον ἔχειν ὀφθαλμόν.
There, as in Heliodorus, the notion is
partly derided, partly defended. Not
only the person, but his property could
be affected by βασκανία Virg. *Ecl.*
103. See Note 3 to Scene viii

[29] Just as the leaves of the ox-eye

apple-pips out of her taper fingers against the ceiling?[30] or
so carefully treasure up those trumpery sandals? and to
what must Chloris ascribe the numberless cups and
vases, which her mistress had fractured in her fits of
abstraction?[31]   'Pooh, pooh!' said she to Manto, volun-
teering an answer for Cleobule; 'our mistress wears the
ring with the Ephesian legend on it;[32] and that's a sure

---

daisy, *Chrysanthemum leucanthemum*,
are consulted in Germany as love's
oracle — a game immortalised by
Göthe's Gretchen—so the Greeks
had recourse to more than one μαν-
τεία of this sort in affairs of the
heart. The usual way was to place the
leaf on the ring made by bending the
fore-finger to the thumb, and then to
burst it with a slap of the other hand.
The broad petal of the poppy-flower,
hence called πλαταγώνιον, was used,
as well as that of the anemone; but
the τηλέφιλον is much more frequently mentioned, though it is uncertain whether this word denotes a
particular plant, or was only another
name for the πλαταγώνιον. See Pollux, ix. 27, who apparently does not
distinguish between them: Τὸ δὲ
πλαταγώνιον οἱ ἐρῶντες ἢ ἐρῶσαι
ἔπαιζον· καλεῖται μὲν γὰρ οὕτω καὶ
τὸ κρόταλον καὶ τὸ σεῖστρον, ᾧ
καταβαυκαλῶσιν αἱ τίτθαι ψυχα-
γωγοῦσαι τὰ δυσυπνοῦντα τῶν παιδίων. Ἀλλὰ καὶ τὰ τοῦ τηλεφίλου
καλουμένου φύλλα ἐπὶ τοὺς πρώτους
δύο τῆς λαιᾶς δακτύλους εἰς κύκλον
συμβληθέντας ἐπιθέντες τῷ κοίλῳ
τῆς ἑτέρας χειρὸς ἐπικρούσαντες, εἰ
κτύπον ποιήσειεν εὔκροτον ὑποσχι-
σθὲν τῇ πληγῇ τὸ φύλλον, μεμνῆσθαι τοὺς ἐρωμένους αὐτῶν ὑπελάμβανον. So also Phot. *Lex.* p. 432;
Suidas and Hesych. The Scholiasts
on Theocr. iii. 28, incline however to
the former supposition. But a different sort of augury is there described,

derived not from the sound produced
by the slap, but from the discoloration
of the skin, produced by some corrosive
principle in the leaf or fruit. In the
case of a favourable argury this was
red. On the whole it seems that the
word τηλέφιλον was used to designate
the leaf (or fruit) of every plant used
as an oracle of 'distant love.' See
Anthol. Pal. v. 296 :

Ἐξότε τηλεφίλου πλαταγήματος ἠχέτα βόμ-
        βος
    γαστέρα μαντῷου μάξατο κισσυβίου,
    ἴγνων, ὡς φιλέεις με.

Pollux, ix. 128, mentions another
method, by means of inflated lily-
leaves: Καὶ μὲν καὶ τὸ κρίνον διπλοῦν
ὃν καὶ διάκενον ἔνδοθεν ἐμφυσήσαντες,
ὡς ὑποπλῆσαι πνεύματος πρὸς τὰ
μέτωπα ῥηγνύντες ἐσημαίνοντο τὰ
παραπλήσια τῷ κτύπῳ.

[30] Poll. ix. 128 : Ἔτι τοίνυν τὸ
σπέρμα τῶν μήλων, ὅπερ ἔγκειται
τοῖς μήλοις ἔνδοθεν, ἄκροις τοῖς πρώτοις τῆς δεξιᾶς δύο δακτύλοις συμ-
πιέζοντες ἔτι διάβροχον καὶ ὀλισθη-
ρὸν ὂν, εἰ πρὸς ὕψος πηδήσειεν, ἐσημαίνοντο τούτῳ τὴν εὔνοιαν τὴν παρὰ
τῶν παιδικῶν.

[31] Aristoph. *Thesmoph.* 401 :

    ἐάν γέ τις πλέκῃ
γυνὴ στέφανον, ἐρᾶν δοκεῖ· κἂν ἐκβάλῃ
σκεῦός τι, κατὰ τὴν οἰκίαν πλανωμένη,
ἀνὴρ ἐρωτᾷ, τῷ κατέαγεν ἡ χύτρα;
οὐκ ἔσθ' ὅπως οὐ τῷ Κορινθίῳ ξένῳ.

[32] It was very usual to wear amu-

safeguard against the evil-eye. It is merely a transient
qualm; go and prepare the potion our doctor prescribed
in such a case.'

Away went Manto. Chloris affectionately embraced
her mistress' knees, and giving a roguish peep upwards,
said in dolorous tone, 'Alas! that odious bath.' 'What
mean you?' asked Cleobule, raising herself. 'I mean the
journey to Ædepsos,' answered the abigail; 'that's to
blame for all. We must go to Argyra, and bathe in the
water of the Selemnos,[33] the wondrous efficacy of which
the byssos-seller from Patræ extolled so much the other
day.' 'You silly thing!' scolded the mistress with a deep
blush, ' there you go chattering again !' 'Am I not right ?'
said the slave in coaxing tones; ' but, may be, help is
nearer at hand. How runs the proverb ?   " He who gave

---

lets, προβασκάνια, as a protection
against spells or misfortune. The
Phalli and other obscene emblems
hung about children, or even affixed
to houses, as a safeguard against
fascination, are well known. Plutarch,
Sympos. v. 7, 3 : Διὸ καὶ τὸ τῶν
λεγομένων προβασκανίων γένος οἴονται πρὸς τὸν φθόνον ὠφελεῖν, ἑλκο-
μένης διὰ τὴν ἀτοπίαν τῆς ὄψεως,
ὥστε ἧττον ἐπερείδειν τοῖς πάσχου-
σιν. Rings, also, probably with some
secret token, were deemed a security
against every danger. Aristoph. *Plut.*
883 :

οὐδὲν προτιμῶ σου. φορῶ γὰρ πριάμενος
τὸν δακτύλιον τονδὶ παρ' Εὐδάμου δραχμῆς.

So also a fragment of Antiphanes,
apud Athen. iii. p. 123 :

οὐ γὰρ κακὸν ἔχω μηδ' ἔχοιμ'. ἐὰν δ' ἄρα
στρέφῃ με περὶ τὴν γαστέρ' ἢ τὸν ὀμφαλὸν
παρὰ Φερτάτου δακτύλιός ἐστί μοι δραχμῆς.

So again Charicleia possesses a magic
ring; Heliod. *Æthiop.* iv. 8.   In Lucian, *Philops.* 17, Eucrates, who had
been sadly plagued by ghosts, says he
is free now, μάλιστα ἐξ οὗ μοι τὸν

δακτύλιον ὁ "Αραψ ἔδωκε σιδήρου τοῦ
ἐκ τῶν σταυρῶν πεποιημένον. Ar
amulet bearing certain Ephesian
characters, is mentioned by Anaxilas,
ap. Athen. xii. p. 548 : ἐν σκυταρίοις
ῥαπτοῖσι φορῶν Ἐφεσήϊα γράμματα
καλά. On the subject of these Ephe
sian characters, Photius, who gives in
stances of their efficacy, observes (p
40): ὀνόματα ἄττα καὶ φωναὶ ἀντι
πάθειάν τινα φυσικὴν ἔχουσαι. Hesychius gives the six original words;
cf. Eustath. *ad Odyss.* xix. 247 : ὅτ.
ἀσαφῶς καὶ αἰνιγματωδῶς δοκεῖ ἐπὶ
ποδᾶν καὶ ζώνης καὶ στεφάνης ἐπι
γεγράφθαι τῆς Ἀρτέμιδος τὰ τοιαῦτε
γράμματα.

[33] The little river Selemnos, in
Achaia, was said, in reference to the
myth of its metamorphosis, to be a
cure for the love-sick. Pausan. vii
23, 2 : τὸ ὕδωρ τοῦ Σελέμνου σύμ-
φορον καὶ ἀνδράσιν εἶναι καὶ γυναιξὶν
ἐς ἔρωτος ἴαμα λουομένοις ἐν τῷ πο-
ταμῷ λήθην ἔρωτος γίνεσθαι.

the wound will also heal it." [34] Isn't it so?' Cleobule
turned away her face and wept. 'I knew it long ago,'
continued the domestic; 'but why cry so, my lady?
Hasn't Sophilos left the choice to yourself? and as to
Charicles, his wishes on the matter must be known to
every one who attended at the funeral.' 'He has forgotten me,' said Cleobule mournfully; 'he hates me.' 'Non
sense!' retorted Chloris; 'but if so, we must send for the
woman of Thessaly. I'm told that she has often, by melt-
ing waxen images, and pronouncing charms the while, or
by the magic virtue of the iynx, and other secret arts, led
the hearts of faithless swains back again to their loves.' [35]
'In the name of all the gods, no!' cried Cleobule; 'I have
heard that such love-charms may imperil the life of their
object.' 'Well then,' continued Chloris, 'let us resort to
more simple methods. A half-faded garland from the head
of the damsel, or a bitten apple, has often done wonders.' [36]
'I'm to propose to him myself, then?' said the lady, rising;

---

[34] Ὁ τρώσας αὐτὸς ἰάσεται, originally the answer of the oracle to
Telephos, but afterwards employed
in this sense. Charit. vi. 3: φάρμακον
γὰρ ἕτερον ἔρωτος οὐδέν ἐστι πλὴν
αὐτὸς ὁ ἐρώμενος. τοῦτο δὲ ἄρα τὸ
ᾀδόμενον λόγιον ἦν, ὅτι ὁ τρώσας
αὐτὸς ἰάσεται.

[35] That fertile subject, the magic
arts of the ancients, can be merely
touched on here. The Φαρμακεύτρια
of Theocritus is the most instructive
treatise on this head which Greek
literature supplies. Consult also
Tiedemann, *Kurze Uebersicht d.
Gesch. d. Artes magicæ.* For a case
of poisoning by a φίλτρον, see
Antipho, *de Venef.* pp. 608, 614.

[36] A chaplet that had been worn,
or a bitten apple, served as a declaration of love, or as a substitute for a

billet doux, in the same way as drinking out of the same goblet. Note 25
to Scene II. See Lucian, *Tox.* 13:
καὶ γραμματεῖά τε εἰσεφοίτα παρὰ
τῆς γυναικὸς αὐτῷ καὶ στέφανοι
ἡμιμάραντοι καὶ μῆλά τινα ἀποδε-
δηγμένα καὶ ἄλλα, ὁπόσα αἱ μαστρο-
ποὶ ἐπὶ τοῖς νέοις μηχανῶνται, κατὰ
μικρὸν αὐτοῖς ἐπιτεχιώμεναι τοὺς
ἔρωτας, κ.τ.λ. Also Id. *Dial. Meretr.*
xii.; and Alciphr. *Epist.* iii. 62; and
i. 36; also Theocr. xi. 10, says of
Polyphemus:

Ἤρατο δ' οὔτι ῥόδοις, οὐ μάλοις, οὐδὲ κικίν-
νοις.

Merely throwing an apple at a person
was a declaration of love. *Anth.
Pal.* v. 79:

Τῷ μήλῳ βάλλω σε· σὺ δ', εἰ μὲν ἑκοῦσα
φιλεῖς με
δεξαμένη τῆς σῆς παρθενίης μετάδος.

'no, Chloris, you are not in earnest, surely?' 'Let us have recourse to Sophilos then,' interposed the indefatigable slave; 'besides, old Manto, you know, was once Charicles' nurse. Yes, I have it; she must be our main agent. Just leave it to me, and ere three days have passed I'll bring the truant back.'

SCENE THE ELEVENTH.

————•>•————

THE RING.

DEEP repose was still spread over Athens, and her citizens were dreaming off, at their leisure, the fumes of the festival just ended; when Manto emerged from her mistress's abode, on the secret errand with which Chloris had commissioned her. The streets were still noiseless, although it was past daybreak. A few slaves only had begun their day's avocations, or were busied in attending to the first morning requirements of their lords. Here and there tipsy comastæ, their faded bravery of coronals and tæniæ reeking with ointment, and all dangling from their heads, came reeling homewards from their prolonged debauch, a female flute-player staggering in the van.

Manto hobbled away, without stopping, to the house where Charicles dwelt. Who more desirous than she to promote his marriage with Cleobule! Faithfully attached to the interests of her mistress, she was no less so to Charicles, who had been committed to her fostering care from his earliest infancy. But she was also bound to him by a certain cherished mystery, of which she was now the sole living repository. Nor must it be forgotten that the moment of Cleobule's marriage was that also of her own manumission, and she hoped to pass the remnant of her days in the house of Charicles, released from toils and troubles. Yet there was still something else that spurred on her footsteps. An unlooked-for event threatened suddenly to defeat all her wishes and hopes, and bring about a discovery, the consequences of which could not be foreseen. She too had mingled in the crowd of spectators yesterday; and while intent upon the feats of a rope-dancer, a slave, whose guise was more that of a farm-bailiff than a town servant, had edged through the press, and twitching her cloak, had bidden her, in a tone, partly of entreaty, partly of command, to follow him. Much alarmed, she had done so ; and when they had escaped from the crowd, he sharply eyed her, and asked who was her master. 'My master is dead,' was her answer. The man demanded more hurriedly, whether he had left a son. 'No,' she replied, somewhat perplexed ; 'he had not been married a year when he died.' The slave looked at her for a moment with attention. 'You are certainly the woman,' he then exclaimed, 'who one-and-twenty years ago took up a boy exposed on the altar of Pity, early in the morning. I watched you ; you bore off the vessel [1] with the infant to Nicarete the midwife : she has unfortunately been dead this long while ; but I conjure you by the gods, tell me to whom you gave the boy : it was my master's son, and he has no other.' Manto, confused, tried to get off ; but her trembling plainly showed that the slave was not mistaken. He begged, he conjured, he threatened her, and Manto had very nearly lost her self-possession and confessed the truth ; but the thought that Charicles —for he, in truth, was the boy—might find his parents again in a manner he least desired, restored her presence of mind. To be sure, he could not be of lowly origin ; this was proved by the fine linen cloth that lay by the child, the golden ring with a blue stone ingeniously carved, and also by the collar, and the various gold and silver baubles.[2] But nevertheless, Charicles, who was happy in the recollection of the loved and familiar faces of his supposed parents, and who was, at present, in the independent enjoyment of an ample fortune, might have to make an unpleasant change ; and Cleobule—there was no know-

---

[1] Children were exposed in large earthen vessels, ἐν χύτραις. Mœr. Att. p. 102 : ἐγχυτρισμὸς, ἡ τοῦ βρέφους ἔκθεσις, ἐπεὶ ἐν χύτραις ἐξετίθεντο. See Schol. on *Ranæ*, 1288 : τὸ δὲ ἐν ὀστράκῳ, ἐπεὶ ἐν χύ-ραις ἐξετίθεσαν τὰ παιδία, διὸ καὶ χυτρί-ζειν ἔλεγον. Cf. Schol. on *Vesp.* 228 ; and Hesych. s. v. The sale of children is also alluded to, *Anthol. Pal.* v. 178.

[2] See Excursus on *Education*. See also Heliod. *Æthiop.* iv. 8.

ing what might intervene to thwart her wishes. At all events, she thought it would be better that the revelation should be deferred till after the wedding, and she therefore promised to meet the slave the next new moon, at sunset, near the Acharnian gate, making all sorts of excuses for not saying more at the present moment. 'But how am I to trust you,' answered the slave, 'if I don't know who you are?' 'I swear to thee by the Dioscuri,' was her assurance. 'Women's oaths are fleeting as the water, on which they are written,'[3] he interposed; 'tell me to whom you belong.' 'What good will that be to you?' answered she. 'To one so distrustful as you, that will be but a poor satisfaction; for how would you know after all whether I were speaking the truth?' Without his observing it, she had gradually drawn him back near the spectacle, and profited by the lucky moment to disappear in the tumult.

This it was that urged her to the house of Charicles at so early an hour. She wished at all events to attain one object, before she could be traced out, and the truth come to light prematurely, contrary to her desire. She expected to find the house still in repose, and had intended to wait before it till the inmates were astir; but to her astonishment the door was open, and, on entering the peristyle of the court, she was met by Charicles, who was just giving orders to a slave. 'Quick, quick!' said he; 'take this paper, and fasten it to some pillar in the market-place, so that every one can read it, and bid the crier make known with a loud voice through the streets and in the full market, that whoever has found a gold ring with a

---

[3] Εἰς ὕδωρ γράφειν, or εἰς τέφραν, was a proverbial expression for fruitless undertakings, particularly invalid oaths. So Hellad. *Chrest.* apud Phot. *Bibl.* p. 530: ὁ στίχος ὁ καὶ παροιμιαζόμενος,

ὅρκους ἐγὼ γυναικὸς εἰς ὕδωρ γράφω

ἐστὶ μὲν Σοφοκλέους, τοῦτον δὲ παρῳδήσας ὁ Φιλωνίδης ἔφη,

ὅρκους δὲ μοιχῶν εἰς τέφραν ἐγὼ γράφω. And in Lucian, *Catapl.* 21, Micyllos says: Παίζεις, ὦ Χάρων, ἢ καθ' ὕδατος, φασὶν, ἤδη γράφεις, παρὰ Μικύλλου ἤδη τινὰ ὀβολὸν προσδοκῶν.

blue stone, bearing the device of a running satyr holding
a hare, and will bring it to Charicles, the son of Charinos,
shall receive the reward of two minæ.[4] Give my address,
and add that the ring may easily be recognised, on account
of a flaw in the stone right across the satyr's body.'

Manto had only caught the concluding words. 'You
have lost a ring?' asked she, approaching Charicles, when
the slave had disappeared. 'Yes,' said he, 'a trinket, that
my dying mother gave me, with significant but enigmatical
words.' 'By all the gods!' cried the slave, 'surely not
the ring with the blue stone?' 'The very same,' he replied ;
'but how do you know anything about it?' 'I have seen
it on your finger,' said she, trying to hide her confusion.
'Yet I have seldom worn it in Athens,' answered Charicles.
'Yesterday, at the bath, I took it off, and in some incomprehensible manner it has disappeared ; though I, not
habitually wearing it, did not discover my loss till I went
to bed. I had rather have lost the half of my estate than

---

[4] Things lost, stolen, or found,
runaway slaves, and commodities for
sale, were advertised either by the
public crier, a placard on the walls,
or a board set up in some frequented
spot. See Lucian, *Demon.* 17: 'Επεὶ
δέ ποτε καὶ χρυσοῦν δακτύλιον ὁδῷ
βαδίζων εὗρε, γραμμάτιον ἐν ἀγορᾷ
προτιθεὶς ἠξίου τὸν ἀπολέσαντα,
ὅστις εἴη τοῦ δακτυλίου δεσπότης,
ἥκειν καὶ εἰπόντα ὁλκὴν αὐτοῦ καὶ
λίθον καὶ τύπον ἀπολαμβάνειν. Lucian also travesties the form of proclaiming a fugitive slave. *Fugit.* 26:
εἴ τις ἀνδράποδον Παφλαγονικὸν,
τῶν ἀπὸ Σινώπης βαρβάρων, ὄνομα
τοιοῦτον, οἷον ἀπὸ κτημάτων, ὕπω-
χρον, ἐν χρῷ κουρίαν, ἐν γενείῳ βαθεῖ, πήραν ἐξημμένον καὶ τριβώνιον
ἀμπεχόμενον, ὀργίλον, ἄμουσον, τρα-
χύφωνον, λοίδορον, μηνύειν ἐπὶ ῥητῷ
αὐτονόμῳ. In most cases a fixed reward, μήνυτρα, or σῶστρα, was promised in the advertisement. So in

Xenoph. *Memor.* ii. 10, 1. Cf. Dio
Chrysost. *Orat.* vii. p. 264. The state
also offered large rewards for the discovery of the perpetrators of great
crimes. Thus on the occasion of the
mutilation of the Hermæ, ἦσαν γὰρ
κατὰ τὸ Κλεωνύμου ψήφισμα χίλιαι
δραχμαὶ, κατὰ δὲ τὸ Πεισάνδρου μύ-
ριαι. Andoc. *de Myst.* p. 14. Cf. Plutarch, *Alcib.* 20 ; Böckh's *Public Econ.
of Athens*, p. 248. For the corresponding Roman custom, consult *Gallus*, Note 8 to Scene IV. p. 44. The
usage of proclaiming commodities for
sale some days beforehand is mentioned in the Excursus on *The Markets and Commerce*. In some states
this was compulsory in judicial sales.
See Theophrast, ap. Stob. *Tit.* xliv.
22: Οἱ μὲν οὖν ὑπὸ κήρυκος κελεύουσι
πωλεῖν καὶ προκηρύττειν ἐκ πλειό-
νων ἡμερῶν. Cf. Demosth. *in Ar s-
tocr.* p. 687: οἱ τὰ μικρὰ καὶ κομιδῇ
φαῦλα ἀποκηρυττοντες.

this ring; for, as my mother said, it possesses a secret, the explanation of which is lost for ever along with it. But what's the matter? You tremble; and besides, what brings you here at this early hour?' 'Let us go where we are by ourselves,'[5] replied the crone; 'for I must speak with you.' 'Not now, my good Manto; I must go back to the bath, whither I have already dispatched Manes. Rest awhile here, and await my return.'

The city had gradually awakened to its wonted every-day activity. The market-place was beginning to fill; and though many were missing, who had not yet got over the unpleasant consequences of yesterday's carouse, the soberer section of the community adhered to the usual custom, and met at the regular hour in this focus of city life. Ctesiphon, having found the Gymnasium very thin to-day, was here in hopes of meeting some friends. A number of people were standing before a pillar in the arcade of the Trapezitæ, reading a notice. 'Go and see what it is,' said he to his attendant. The slave ran off, and soon returned quite out of breath. 'Master,' he exclaimed, 'what a lucky fellow our Satyros is! Charicles has lost a ring, and promises two minæ to the person that restores it to him. Satyros is the finder; I saw him yesterday with just such an one, which he had picked up in the street.' 'Or stolen,' replied Ctesiphon; 'for that's just like the fellow. Was not he with me and Charicles at the bath yesterday? To be sure! and Charicles wore two rings.[6] The knave has purloined it. Follow me.'

---

[5] Græcè αὐτοί ἐσμεν. Plato, *Leg.* viii. p. 836. So Plaut. *Cas.* ii. 2, 25: *Nos sumus.*

[6] The free Greek, if not of the very poorest class, wore a ring, not only as an ornament, but as a signet, to attest his signature, or for making secure his property. See Excursus on *The* *Grecian House*; and Notes 6, 7, and 8 to Scene IX. The antiquity of this usage cannot be certainly determined. No trace of it, however, is to be found in Homer. And Pliny, *Nat. Hist.* xxxiii. 1, 4, rightly concludes from Hom. *Od.* viii. 443, that the use of the signet-ring was at that time unknown. Odysseus merely ties the χηλὸς, con-

After a vain hunt, Charicles had returned home, and
was pacing, out of humour, up and down the peristyle of

taining the presents, with a knot
taught him by Circe. The legends of a
later time will not of course prove anything about the customs of the heroic
age. Hence the σφραγίς of Theseus,
ἣν αὐτὸς φέρων ἔτυχεν, mentioned by
Pausan. i. 17, 3, or the sealed letters
of Agamemnon and Phædra, alluded
to by Euripides, *Iphig. in Aul.* 154;
Hippol. 859, cannot here be adduced
in evidence. It is highly probable that
the use of the ring, and the custom of
sealing, came from the East, where it
was common; *e.g.* at Babylon, as is
affirmed by Herodotus, i. 195, and
abundantly attested by the hundreds
of rings and signet cylinders now in
the British Museum and elsewhere.
See Layard, *Discoveries at Nineveh
and Babylon*, pp. 156, 608. One of
the oldest accounts is that of the ring
of Polycrates, though it is uncertain
whether this stone was cut, and
served as a signet, σφραγίς. But
in Solon's time this use of the ring
was common, as is clear from the law
he enacted, (see Note 6 to Scene IX.)
though, from the existence of genuine
signet rings, we cannot infer that they
necessarily contained cut stones. In
later times rings served also as ornaments, and hence several were often
worn, and in the degenerate period
the hands were literally covered with
them. Hippias wore two. Plato,
Hipp. Min. p. 368. But people soon
went beyond this. So Aristoph. *Eccles.* 632, we read σφραγῖδας ἔχοντες,
and again, *Nub.* 332, we have σφρα-
γιδονυχαργοκομῆται, though the Scholiast's explanation is absurd. Demosthenes too adorned his hands with
rings in so conspicuous a manner that,
at a time of public disasters, it was
stigmatised as unbecoming vanity.

Dinarch. *in Demosth.* p. 29: καὶ κατ-
αισχύνων τὴν τῆς πόλεως δόξαν
χρυσὸν ἐκ τῶν δακτύλων ἀναψάμενος
περιεπορεύετο, τριφῶν ἐν τοῖς τῆς
πολεως κακοῖς. And Diog. Laert. v.
1, says of Aristotle, ἐσθῆτί τε (ἦν)
ἐπισήμῳ χρώμενος καὶ δακτυλίοις,
καὶ κουρᾷ. Of the cost of these
articles we have frequent mention.
Thus Ælian, *Var. Hist.* xii. 30, says
of the Tarentines, Ὁμολογεῖ δὲ καὶ
Εὔπολις ἐν τῷ Μαρικᾷ, ὅστις αὐτῶν
εὐτελέστατος, σφραγῖδας εἶχε δέκα
μνῶν. Hence the luxury of the later
ages need not excite our surprise. So
Lucian, *Icaromen.* 18: εἴ τινα ἴδοιμι
ἐπὶ χρυσῷ μέγα φρονοῦντα, ὅτι δακτυλίους τε εἶχεν ὀκτὼ, κ.τ.λ. Id.
Somn. seu Gall. 12: ἐγὼ δὲ τ ν ἐσθῆτα τὴν ἐκείνου ἔχων καὶ δακτυλίους
βαρεῖς ὅσων ἑκκαίδεκα ἐξημμένους
τῶν δακτύλων, κ.τ.λ. The value of
the ring depended in the first instance
on the stone, and more still on the
skill of the engraver. The onyx, Σαρ-
δῶος, σαρδόνυξ, was well adapted for
the display of art, and was therefore
very highly esteemed. See Lucian, *de
Syria dea,* 32; and *Dial. Meretr.* ix.:
εἶχε δὲ καὶ αὐτὸς Παρμένων δακτύλιον ἐν τῷ μικρῷ δακτύλῳ μέγιστον,
πολύγωνον, καὶ ψῆφος ἐνεβέβλητο
τῶν τριχρώμων, ἐρυθρά τε ἦν ἐπι-
πολῆς. The golden sling-formed ring
σφενδόνη, (Plato, *de Repub.* ii. p. 359;
Eurip. *Hippol.* 857,) in which the
stone, ψῆφος, σφραγὶς, was set, was
also highly finished and facetted.
Some rings had no stone, but were
merely of metal, ἄψηφοι. Artemidor.
Oneiroc. ii. 5: Ἀγαθοὶ δὲ καὶ οἱ χρυ-
σοῖ (δακτύλιοι) οἵ γε ψήφους ἔχοντες·
ἐπεὶ οἵ γε ἄψηφοι ἀκερδεῖς τὰς ἐγχει-
ρήσεις σημαίνουσι διὸ τὸ ἄψηφον.
ψῆφον γὰρ καλοῦμεν, ὥσπερ λίθον

the court, when Ctesiphon appeared with a face of joy.
'Cheer up,' cried he, 'your ring is found, and won't cost
you two minæ. The knave that stole it is already fast in
the pillory.' He then recounted briefly how it had been
recovered, and expressed surprise that a cracked ring like
this could be worth so large a reward. Charicles was
about to explain the reason of his setting so high a value

τὸν ἐν δακτυλίῳ, οὕτω καὶ τὸν τῶν χρημάτων ἀριθμόν. As with us, they were sometimes solid, sometimes only plated, but passed off as solid. Artem. *Ib.*: 'Αεὶ δὲ ἀμείνονες οἱ ὁλόσφυροι· οἱ γὰρ κενοὶ καὶ θεῖον ἔνδον ἔχοντες δόλους καὶ ἐνέδρας σημαίνουσι διὰ τὸ ἐμπεριέχειν τὸ ἐγκεκρυμμένον, ἢ μείζονας τὰς προσδοκίας τῶν ὠφελειῶν διὰ τὸ μείζονα τὸν ὄγκον τοῦ βάρους ἔχειν. That women also wore rings cannot be doubted, though the allusions to the fact are very scanty. It would seem that these were not the same as those of the men, but were of amber, and so forth. Artemidor. *Ib.* A snake-shaped ring was discovered in a tomb along with sundry female ornaments. See Stackelberg, *Gräber d. Hell.* pl. 73. The ring was worn on the fourth finger, παράμεσος. The heading of the lost 8th chapter of Plutarch, *Sympos.* iv., runs, Διὰ τί τῶν δακτύλων μάλιστα τῷ παραμέσῳ σφραγῖδας φοροῦσιν; they were therefore so worn usually, μάλιστα, but not invariably. Men did not wear any other gold ornament, at least it was much reprobated if they did. See a fragment of Anacreon, ap. Athen. xii. p. 534:

νῦν δ' ἐπιβαίνει σατινέων, χρύσεα φορέων
    καθέρματα
πάϊς Κύκης, καὶ σκιαδίσκην ἐλεφαντίνην
    φορέει
γυναιξὶν αὔτως.

Whether this word καθέρματα means earrings or ὅρμοι is dubious. It was considered a dishonour, and a token of foreign manners, for men to have their ears bored. Xenoph. *Anab.* iii. 1, 31 : ἀλλὰ τούτῳ γε οὐδὲ τῆς Βοιωτίας προσήκει οὐδὲν, οὔτε τῆς 'Ελλάδος παντάπασιν· ἐπεὶ ἐγὼ αὐτὸν εἶδον, ὥσπερ Λυδὸν, ἀμφότερα τὰ ὦτα τετρυπημένον. Cf. Diog. Laert. ii. 50 ; Aristot. *Probl.* xxxii. 7. Women and girls, however, not only used earrings, ἐνώτια, ἐλλόβια, ἑλικτῆρες, which are seen perpetually on vases, but they also wore numerous articles of jewellery about the neck, (περιδέραια ὅρμοι,) the arms, (ψέλια, ὄφεις,) and on the leg above the ankle, (πέδαι χρυσαῖ, περισκελίδες, περισφύρια). Poll. v. 99. Cf. Aristoph. *Acharn.* 258 ; *Lysistr.* 408 ; *Aves,* 669 ; Lysias, *in Eratosth.* p. 395. How valuable these ornaments sometimes were, appears from Plato, *Alcib.* i. p. 123, where we learn that Deinomache, the mother of Alcibiades, wore a κόσμος, ἴσως ἄξιος μνῶν πεντήκοντα. Cf. Demosth. *in Aphob.* i. p. 817. Concerning a later period, see Lucian, *Amor.* 41 : λίθους 'Ερυθραίους κατὰ τῶν λοβῶν, πολυτά λαντον ἠρτημένας βρῖθος, ἢ τοὺς περὶ καρποῖς καὶ βραχίοσι δράκοντας, ὡς ὤφελον ὄντως ἀντὶ χρυσίου δράκοντες εἶναι. καὶ στεφάνη μὲν ἐν κύκλῳ τὴν κεφαλὴν περιθεῖ, λίθοις 'Ινδικαῖς διάστερος· πολυτελεῖς δὲ τῶν αὐχένων ὅρμοι καθεῖνται καὶ ἄχρι τῶν ποδῶν ἐσχάτων καταβέβηκεν ὁ ἄθλιος χρυσὸς, ἅπαν, εἴ τι τοῦ σφυροῦ γυμνοῦται, περισφίγγων.

on it, when a violent knocking was heard at the house-
door, and Sophilos hurried through the entrance-hall with
hasty steps.   Everything about him evinced an anxious
state of suspense, so much so that he even forgot the salutation.   ' I have just come from the market-place,' said he,
turning to Charicles, ' where the crier was proclaiming that
you had lost a ring.   Tell me, who gave you that ring?'
' It's found,' answered the other; ' for which I have to
thank my friend Ctesiphon here.   Look, here it is.'   Sophilos snatched the ring.   ' The very same !' he exclaimed
vehemently.   ' Tell me, how came you by it?'   ' An odd
sort of question !' replied Charicles.   ' My mother gave it
me on her death-bed.   " Keep it safe," said she, " peradventure it is the best part of thine inheritance.   It can
lead you to fortune, if it should be found by him who
understands its speech."'   ' By Olympian Zeus !' shouted
Sophilos, ' that man has found it, and I am he.   With
this very ring I had my third child exposed, because, fool
that I was, two male heirs seemed quite enough to me at
that time.[7]   One-and-twenty years have rolled by since
then ; that is thine age, and thou art my son !'

The vehemence with which he spoke, and the rejoicing
consequent on the discovery, had brought to the spot every
creature in the house, and among others, Manto, who had
vainly waited to have an interview with Charicles.   She
now seized his knees, and said, ' It was I that raised thee
up from the altar of Pity, and brought thee to thy childless
mother, who had long made preparations for passing the
cheat upon her husband ; and it was no sin to do so, for
Charinos was now content, and you found in them two fond
parents and careful guardians of your infancy.'   ' Manto !'
exclaimed Sophilos, astonished ; ' you are the woman that
artfully dodged my faithful Carion yesterday ?   But stay!
The ring was not the only thing exposed with the child ;
where are the rest ?   Manto was for a moment perplexed,

---

[7] See Longus, *Pastor.* iv. p. 126.

and answered nothing. At last she said, 'There was a collar too, with trinkets, hung round the babe's neck, I confess. I have kept it back, but still have it all safe.' 'So every thing tallies exactly,' exclaimed Sophilos; 'but why refuse my slave an explanation yesterday?' 'How should I know that it was your slave?' said she. 'I feared some unwelcome father might turn up and oppose the match that I'm longing for.' 'In sooth, that was cunning,' replied Sophilos; 'and it is well that you remind me. Charicles, you are my son, and my first paternal command is, that you marry Cleobule. How? still refuse?' 'Father,' said the overjoyed young man, 'I desire no greater happiness.' 'And you will resign Pasias' daughter to me now, won't you?' interposed Ctesiphon. 'To you?' asked Charicles, amazed. 'Ha! I see now the cause of your strange manner: and would you really have made that sacrifice too for me?' 'Willingly,' returned his friend, 'if it would have made you happier.' 'Excellent young man,' said Sophilos; 'I will myself woo her for you, if you like. But now to Cleobule. We must first send word to her, but not by you, Manto, for you'll blurt everything out all at once. Go,' said he to his slave, 'and merely say that I am coming to her with an agreeable attendant. Not a syllable more; do you hear? And you, Charicles, attire yourself as becomes a bridegroom.'

'One word more,' said Charicles to Ctesiphon, as they parted; 'forgive Satyros the punishment; for if he had not filched the ring, I should not now be the lucky man I am.'[8] 'The knave does not deserve it,' replied Ctesiphon; 'but for your sake be it so.'

Little did Cleobule dream of the happy turn of events, which was, on a sudden, about to realise all her fondest

---

[8] In the comedy, slaves who have grievously transgressed are pardoned if the confusion they have caused is satisfactorily cleared up. See the *Andria* and *Heautontimorumenos* of Terence; and the *Epidicus* and *Mostellaria* of Plautus.

wishes. Giving way to her meditations, she had gone with
Chloris into the garden adjoining the house, and whilst the
maid gathered into her lap a heap of odorous violets,[9]
Cleobule stood in tranquil reverie before a tree, and with

---

[9] Little is known of the state of
the art of gardening among the
Greeks, except that it must have been
at a very low ebb, at least as regards
the ornamental part. Böttiger groundlessly blames antiquarians and writers on the subject for making a jump
from the gardens of Alcinoos and the
Paradises of the Persian Satraps to
the box-hedges of Pliny, without regarding the art of gardening among
the Greeks. What can be said on the
subject when the ancients have left
us almost entirely in the dark? The
whole series of writers, down to the
very latest Roman period, contain
hardly a mention of gardens or gardening. Böttiger's treatise on the
subject does not contain one word
about real Greek gardening; he stops
where he ought to begin to instruct.
The reason for the neglect of this
pleasing art by the Greeks is pretty
apparent. Their flora was insignificant, and apart from the improve-
ments of art it was not showy enough
to stimulate the industry of the Greek,
and who, moreover, evidently had but
little sympathy for beauty of landscape. See Note 11 to Scene III. The
groves of the gods were the only
things of the kind, and these were
composed in a great measure of fruit-
trees. See Xenoph. *Anab.* v. 3, 12;
Sophocl. *Œdip. Colon.* 16, sqq. Pausanias, however, (i. 21, 9,) speaking
of a grove of Apollo at Athens, says:
ἔνθα Ἀπόλλωνος κάλλιστον ἄλσος
δένδρων καὶ ἡμέρων καὶ ὅσα τῶν
ἀκάρπων ἡσμὴν παρέχεταί τινα ἢ θέας
ἡδονήν. Plato even speaks, though
rather problematically, of works on
horticulture, *Min.* p. 316: Τίνων οὖν

ἐστι τὰ περὶ κήπων ἐργασίας συγγράμματα καὶ νόμιμα; If such existed,
we may be sure that they treated
rather of the operations of agriculture
or the kitchen-garden, than of flori-
culture. The flowers most cultivated
were those adapted for chaplets, as
violets, roses, parsley, and so on; and
in these perhaps there was a regular
trade. Thus in Demosth. *in Nicostr.*
p. 1251, a rose-plantation, ῥοδωνιὰν
βλαστάνουσαν, is kept by a man whom
we should hardly suspect of doing
so for pleasure only. Excepting the
κήπους εὐώδεις, Aristoph. *Aves,* 1066.
there appears to be no other mention
made of Greek flower-gardens during
the better period. At a later time,
under the Ptolemies, and especially
at Alexandria, great progress appears
to have been made; and the gardeners
there studied particularly to have
roses and other flowers all the year
round, an object which the climate
rendered easy of attainment. Cal-
lixen. ap. Athen. v. p. 196: ἡ γὰρ
Αἴγυπτος τὴν τοῦ περιέχοντος ἀέρος
εὐκρασίαν καὶ διὰ τοὺς κηπεύοντας τὰ
σπανίως καὶ καθ' ὥραν ἐνεστηκυῖαν ἐν
ἑτέροις φυόμενα τόποις ἄφθονα γεννᾷ
καὶ διὰ παντὸς, καὶ οὔτε ῥόδον, οὔτε
λευκόϊον, οὔτε ἄλλο ῥᾳδίως ἄνθος
ἐκλιπεῖν οὐδὲν οὐδέποτ' εἴωθεν. But
whether the art advanced in Greece
itself cannot be determined; for the
parks described by Longus, *Past.* iv.
p. 108, and by Achill. Tat. i. 15, are
only Asiatic παράδεισοι. See Plutarch.
Alcib. 24; Xenoph. *Œcon.* 4, 21. The
Grecian gardens were much simpler
affairs, at least so they are represented
by Longus, *Past.* ii. p. 36: Κῆπός
ἐστί μοι τῶν ἐμῶν χειρῶν,...ὅσα ὥραι

the clasp of her chiton scratched letters in the young
bark.[10]   Suddenly she stopped : ' What was it you said
yesterday, Chloris,' enquired she, ' that when our ears tingle
somebody is thinking about us ?'[11]   ' Most certainly !'
cried the maiden, starting up.   ' But what are you about ?
Well I never,—if you aren't cutting your thoughts on
the tree.   " Handsome," stands here [12]—shall I go on ? " is
Charicles ;" and below, " Handsome is Cleobule."   Hold !'
cried the sportive damsel, ' there is something toward.   A

φέρουσι, πάντα ἔχων ἐν αὑτῷ καθ'
ὥραν ἑκάστην. ᾟρος ῥόδα, κρίνα
καὶ ὑάκινθος, καὶ ἴα ἀμφότερα· θέρους μήκωνες καὶ ἀχράδες, καὶ μῆλα
πάντα· νῦν ἄμπελοι καὶ συκαῖ, καὶ
ῥοιαὶ, καὶ μύρτα χλωρά. And Plutarch, de cap. ex inim. util. 10, says :
ὥσπερ οἱ χαρίεντες γεωργοὶ τὰ ῥόδα
καὶ τὰ ἴα βελτίω ποιεῖν νιμίζουσι,
σκόροδα καὶ κρόμμυα παραφυτεύοντες :
which shows that the flowers were
more grown for cutting than to
ornament the garden ; for the leeks
and onions growing among roses and
violets are scarcely compatible with
æsthetical gardening. On this subject see Gallus, p. 362.

[10] The sentimental lovers' amusement of cutting each other's names in
the bark of trees is mentioned at a
period a little later than that here in
question. See a fragment of Callimachus, preserved in the Schol. to
Aristoph. Acharn. 144 :

'Αλλ' ἐνὶ δὴ φλοιοῖσι κεκομμένα τόσσα φο-
　　ρεῖτε
γράμματα, Κυδίππην ὅσσ' ἐρέουσι καλήν.

Theocr. xviii. 47 :

Γράμματα δ' ἐν φλοιῷ γεγράψεται, ὡς
　　παριών τις
ἀγγνοίῃ, Δωριστί· Σέβου μ', Ἑλένας φυτόν
εἰμι.

So Lucian, Amor. 16, says of the youth
who fell in love with the Venus of
Praxiteles : πᾶς μαλακοῦ δένδρου

φλοιὸς 'Αφροδίτην καλὴν ἐκήρυσσεν.
Cf. Anthol. Pal. ix. 341 ; Aristæn.
Epist. i. 10, Eustath. ad Il. vi. 169.

[11] Lucian, Dial. Mer. ix.: ἦ που,
ὦ Παρμένων, ἐβόμβει τὰ ὦτα ὑμῖν ;
ἀεὶ γὰρ ἐμέμνητο ἡ κεκτημένη μετὰ
δακρύων.

[12] It was very common to express
the emotions of the heart by a καλὸς
or καλή, written with the surname
upon a wall or pillar. Schol. on Aristoph. Vespæ, 98 : ἐπέγραφον δὲ οἱ
'Αθηναῖοι τὰ τῶν καλῶν ὀνόματα
οὕτως· ὁ δεῖνα καλός. ἔγραφον δὲ
κοὶ ἐν τοίχοις καὶ ἐν θύραις καὶ ὅποι
τύχῃ. See Suidas, s. v. ὁ δεῖνα καλός.
Cf. also Plut. Eryll. 7 ; Böttiger, Va·
sengemälde, iii. p. 64 ; Amalthea, iii.
p. 344. These προγράμματα were
very numerous, and the walls and
pillars of the market and Cerameicos
served the purpose, to same extent
of a daily journal. And as in these,
false announcements and accounts of
marriages are inserted, so at Athens
similar malicious reports were also
promulgated. Lucian, Dial. Mer.
iv.: ἔπεμψα οὖν 'Ακίδα κατασκεψο-
μένην· ἡ δ' ἄλλο μὲν οὐδὲν εὗρε,
τοῦτο δὲ μόνον ἐπιγεγραμμένον ἐσι-
όντων ἐπὶ τὰ δεξιὰ πρὸς τῷ Διπύλῳ,
Μέλιττα φιλεῖ 'Ερμότιμον, καὶ
μικρὸν αὖθ.s ὑποκάτω, 'Ο ναύκληρος
'Ερμότιμος φιλεῖ Μέλιτταν.

lucky omen! See how my right eye twitches.'[13] She
turned to the sun, and sneezed: 'Zeus our preserver!'[14]
said she, 'or Aphrodite! But where can that Manto be?'
she added impatiently. 'I haven't seen her the whole
morning,' said Cleobule; 'where is she?' 'She has gone
with the clothes to the wash,'[15] was the ready subterfuge
of the maid.

At this moment a slave hastened in with the message
from Sophilos. Cleobule crimsoned. 'And who is the
attendant?' queried Chloris hastily. 'The servant who
came with the message assured me that he knew no more,'
was the slave's answer. 'Suppose it were a stranger,'
suggested Cleobule: 'Chloris, to-day you again gave me
the chiton without sleeves and lappet. I can't possibly

---

[13] The involuntary twitching of
the eyelids was held a favourable
presage. Theocr. iii. 37:
ἅλλεται ὀφθαλμός μευ ὁ δεξιός· ἆρά γ᾽ ἰδησῶ
αὐτάν;
Cf. Plaut. *Pseud.* i. 1, 105.

[14] From Hom. *Odyss.* xvii. 545, and
numerous other passages, it is plain
that an augury was taken from involuntary sneezing. Absurdly enough,
it has even been supposed that the
δαιμόνιον of Socrates consisted in this.
Plutarch, *de Gen. Socr.* 11: Μεγαρι-
κοῦ τινος ἤκουσα, Τερψίωνος δὲ ἐ-
κείνος, ὅτι τὸ Σωκράτους δαιμόνιον
πταρμὸς ἦν ὅ τε παρ᾽ αὐτοῦ καὶ ὁ
παρ᾽ ἄλλων. The superstition was
widely spread, and undoubtingly believed in. Thus Aristoph. *Aves*, 719:
πταρμὸν ὄρνιθα καλεῖτε. Aristot.
Prob. xxxiii. 7: Διὰ τί τὸν μὲν
πταρμὸν θεὸν ἡγούμεθα εἶναι; So
also, *prob.* 9, and *prob.* 11. Cf. *Anthol.*
Pal. xi. 375; also Suid. and Hesych. s. v. ξυμβόλους. The importance attached to the omen is clearly
seen from Xenoph. *Anab.* iii. 2, 9,
where Xenophon asserts in the coun-

cil: σὺν τοῖς θεοῖς πολλαὶ ἡμῖν καὶ
καλαὶ ἐλπίδες εἰσὶ σωτηρίας. Τοῦτο
δὲ λέγοντος αὐτοῦ πτάρνυταί τις.
ἀκούσαντες δὲ οἱ στρατιῶται, πάντες μιᾷ ὁρμῇ προσεκύνησαν τὸν θεόν.
καὶ Ξενοφῶν εἶπε· Δοκεῖ μοι, ὦ ἄ.,
ἐπεὶ περὶ σωτηρίας ἡμῶν λεγόντων
οἰωνὸς τοῦ Διὸς τοῦ Σωτῆρος ἐφάνη,
εὔξασθαι τῷ θεῷ κ.τ.λ. The usual
form of address in such cases was,
Ζεῦ σῶσον.

[15] Concerning the washing or
scouring of clothes, see *Gallus*, p. 449.
Among the Greeks as well as among
the Romans it was done entirely away
from home, and by people who made
it their exclusive occupation. See
Theophr. *Char.* 10; Machon, ap.
Athen. xiii. p. 582. Πλύνειν was
said of linen clothes, κναφεύειν or
γναφεύειν of woollen ones. Eustath.
ad Od. xxiv. 148: τὸ δὲ πλύνειν, ὃ
νῦν ἐπὶ λινέου φάρους ἐρρέθη, γναφεύειν
ἢ κναφεύειν ἐπὶ τῶν ἐριωδῶν λέγεται.
See Mœr. Attic. p. 242; cf. Aristoph.
Lysistr. 470: Plutarch, *de San. Tuend.* 20.

receive them as I am. Come, dress me directly.' Chloris followed her mistress to her chamber, and opened the capacious chest containing her richest clothes, from which arose the sweet odour of the Median apples placed between the dresses.[16] 'What shall it be?' she enquired. 'A yellow byssos-chiton, or this one embroidered with flowers?' 'By no means,' said Cleobule; 'something simpler than those. Give me the new white diploïs, with the purple stripe down the sides, and the open sleeves. So: now, fasten the sleeves, and give me the girdle. Mind that the border of the lappet is level with the colpos.' The attendant had now finished dressing her mistress 'We've no time for braiding your hair,' said she, 'and that coloured kerchief wrapped round it suits you exquisitely.' Cleobule took the mirror, and surveyed herself. 'Well, it will do,' was her decision; 'but put me on some other sandals. No, not those purple ones embroidered in gold; bring the white pair with the red strings.'

Scarcely had Chloris finished her labours, when Sophilos and a young gentleman were announced. 'Oh! if it were Charicles!' whispered the abigail into the ear of her blushing mistress. And he it was; and a scene followed, such as neither the chisel of the sculptor, nor the limner's pencil, no, nor the style of the poet, would be able to delineate.[17] 'Well I thought,' said Sophilos smiling, to Cleobule, 'that you liked him better than me; but don't let us tarry. The betrothing shall take place to-day, and in three days we'll celebrate the wedding.' [18]

---

[16] Citrons or oranges, Περσικὰ ἢ Μηδικὰ μῆλα, were placed among the clothes, partly on account of the agreeable smell, partly for a protection against the moths. Theophr. *Hist. Pl.* iv. 3: κἂν εἰς ἱμάτια τεθῇ τὸ μῆλον, ἄκοπα διατηρεῖ.

[17] Charit. iii. 8: καὶ ὤφθη θέαμα κάλλιστον, οἷον οὔτε ζωγράφος ἔγραψεν, οὔτε πλάστης ἔπλασεν, οὔτε

ποιητὴς ἱστόρησε μέχρι νῦν. Cf. Plaut. *Asin.* i. 3, 22.

[18] In the comedies the marriage often follows immediately after the betrothal. Plaut. *Trin.* v. 2, 64:

Numquid causæ est, quin uxorem cras domum ducam?

and in the *Aulularia* and *Curculio* the marriage takes place on the same day.

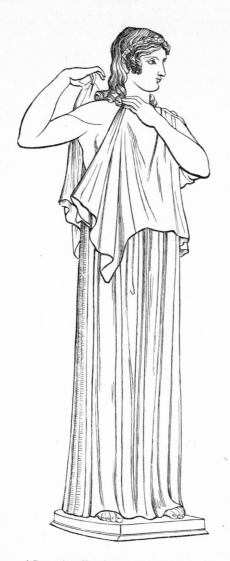

A Bronze from Herculaneum, *Mus. Borb.* ii. 4.

The girl is in the act of fastening the Chiton over the right shoulder, and we see how the lappet, δυπλοΐδιον, is caused by this means. On the side where the seam is, joining the πτέρυγες, are two purple stripes.

SCENE THE TWELFTH.

———◆———

THE WEDDING-DAY.

AND now for one glance at the occurrences of that day whereon Charicles was united to Cleobule. The proposal of Sophilos to hasten the marriage was not at all likely to embarrass a Grecian bride; on the contrary, a courtship lasting several months was a thing quite out of the usual way. All the requisite preparations had been long since made. In like manner as the royal damsel Nausicaa, at the warning of Athena, provided the bridal clothes for herself and her attendants before a husband had been chosen for her;[1] so every Grecian house had always a superfluity of such bravery; and how much more therefore one in which plenty and abundance reigned? As it was, however, what with the ceremony of the affiancing as appointed by law, and the customary sacrifices, both parties found enough to occupy them during the few intervening days. Charicles, in compliance with his father's invitation, had for the present taken up his quarters at his house, in which the women's apartments had been hastily cleaned up, and furnished with everything necessary for the proper reception and convenience of the bride. The wreaths of fresh spring-flowers, ornamenting the door in rich festoons, proclaimed to the passer-by the festal day: while inside the mansion, cooks and slaves were busily making ready for the marriage-feast, which was to be celebrated by a numerous assemblage of the relations and frends of either party. Even Phorion himself, departing from his usual custom, had agreed to be present; and Pasias too, who had already promised Ctesiphon his daughter in marriage, was among those invited.

---

[1] *Odyss.* vi. 27 :

σοὶ δὲ γάμος σχεδόν ἐστιν, ἵνα χρὴ καλὰ μὲν αὐτὴν
ἕννυσθαι, τὰ δὲ τοῖσι παρασχεῖν, οἵ κέ σ' ἄγωνται.

P

In the chamber of Charicles, Manes had arranged the
festal garments designed for the occasion.   These consisted
of a soft chiton of fine Milesian wool, with a himation of
dazzling whiteness, which had been purposely chosen without the usual purple border.   Beside it stood the elegant
half-shoes, their crimson thongs fastened with clasps of
gold.   Chaplets of myrtle-twigs, with violets interwoven,
lay also ready ; and Sophilos had added two silver *alabas-
tra* filled with costly unguents, in case Charicles might like
to make use of them on so special an occasion.   The
bridegroom himself was still at the bath, with Ctesiphon,
previous to going with his friend to fetch away the bride :
for who else could he have preferred for bridegroom's
man ? [2]

The household of Cleobule was not a whit less busy.
The sun had sunk half-way from the meridian, yet the
bridal array was still unfinished.   Cleobule sat upon a
settle in her apartment, which was filled with perfume,
and held the silver disc of the mirror in her hand ; while
Chloris sedulously arranged her hair, and the mother
inserted the pearl-drops in the ears of her daughter.   'Do
make haste,' she cried impatiently to the maid ; 'how in-
tolerably slow you are to-day, and it will be evening anon.

---

[2] The παράνυμφος, or πάροχος,
was certainly a youthful friend of the
νυμφίος.   The passages cited in the
Excursus on *The Women*, though
they do not distinctly say so, still imply it ; moreover, Hesychius explains
ἑταῖρος and παράνυμφος as synonymous.

[3] The various methods of measuring
the day employed by the ancients have
been very fully discussed in *Gallus*,
pp. 315–321 ; but the Greek method
was not precisely the same as that
employed at Rome ; at least the former
nation retained a very ancient method

which never perhaps obtained footing
among the Romans. According to Herod. ii. 109, (on the meaning of the
words πόλος and γνώμων see Bähr's
note,) the Greeks themselves did not
invent the gnomon, having derived it
from Babylon : πόλον μὲν γὰρ καὶ
γνώμονα, καὶ τὰ δυώδεκα μέρεα τῆς
ἡμέρης παρὰ Βαβυλωνίων ἔμαθον οἱ
Ἕλληνες.   But, according to other
accounts, Anaximander was the inventor.   See Suidas, s. v. γνώμων.
Also Diog. Laert. ii. 1 : εὗρε δὲ καὶ
γνώμονα πρῶτος καὶ ἔστησεν ἐπὶ
τῶν σκιοθήρων ἐν Λακεδαίμονι.   The
γνώμων, or στοιχεῖον, as it was also

'Go, Menodora,' she said to another slave, ' go and measure the shadow on the sun-dial [3] in the garden.' ' We

called, was, unquestionably, the most ancient means of measuring the day. It consisted of a perpendicular staff or pillar, the length of whose shadow was measured in feet. An untenable hypothesis was started by Salmasius, that the observer measured his own shadow with his feet, and this has been recently revived by Ideler. The whole is a mistake, arising from a misconception of Hesychius, s. v. ἑπτά-τους σκιά; and of Phot. *Lex.* p. 539. The gnomon is seldom mentioned except in reference to the hour of supper or of the bath : for the first, a shadow ten or twelve feet long is assigned, Aristoph. *Eccles.* 652:

σοὶ δὲ μελήσει
ὅταν ᾖ δεκάπουν τὸ στοιχεῖον λιπαρὸν χωρεῖν
ἐπὶ δεῖπνον·

on which the Scholiast remarks : ἡ τοῦ ἡλίου σκιὰ ὅταν ᾖ δέκα πηχῶν. θέ-λει οὖν εἰπεῖν, ὅτε γίνεται ὀψέ. Menander ap. Athen. vi. p. 243; Poll. vi. 44. See also Suidas, and Hesych: Δωδεκάποδος· οὕτως ἔλεγον ἐλλειπ-τικῶς, στοιχείου ἢ σκιᾶς. οὕτω γὰρ συνετίθεντο ἐπὶ δεῖπνον ἥξειν τοῦ στοιχείου ὄντος δωδεκάποδος, ὡς νῦν πρὸς ὥρας φασί. It seems probable therefore that the gnomon was usually so constructed as to throw a shadow of about twelve feet shortly before sunset, for this was the time at which the δεῖπνον usually took place. A fragment of Eubulos ap. Athen i. p. 8, throws some light on this question :

ὃν φασι παρακληθέντ' ἐπὶ δεῖπνον πρὸς φίλου τινὸς,
εἰπόντος αὐτῷ τοῦ φίλου, ὁπηνίκ' ἂν
εἴκοσι ποδῶν μετροῦντι τὸ στοιχεῖον ᾖ,
ἥκειν, ἕωθεν αὐτὸν εὐθὺς ἡλίου
μετρεῖν ἀνέχοντος· μακροτέρας δ' οὔσης ετι
πλεῖν ἢ δυοῖν ποδοῖν παρεῖναι τῆς σκιᾶς·

ἔπειτα φαίναι μικρον ὀψιαίτερον
δι' ἀσχολίαν ἥκειν παρόνθ' ἅμ' ἡμέρᾳ.

Here the gnomon evidently throws a shadow of twice the length, *i.e.* of twenty-four feet, and the supper hour corresponds to a twenty-foot, instead of a ten-foot shadow, as before. An accurate division of the day into twelve equal hours would of course be unattainable by a method of measurement such as that just described ; no regard being paid to the varying declination of the sun throughout the year. The differences owing to this source would, however, be of less magnitude in the latitude of Greece than in that of England, and were probably disregarded, dinner being served, ὅταν ᾖ δεκάπουν τὸ στοιχεῖον. For the hour of bathing, a six-foot shadow is spoken of, at least in the later period. Lucian, *Cro-nos.* 17 : Λούεσθαι μὲν, ὁπόταν τὸ στοιχεῖον ἑξάπουν ᾖ. Cf. *Somn. seu Gallus,* 9. We must remark, that the word γνώμων was afterwards applied to every ὡρολόγιον, and even to the κλεψύδρα. See Athen. ii. p. 42. The πόλος, or proper sun-dial, also called σκιαθήρας or ἡλιοτρόπιον, is not often alluded to ; though, setting aside the allusion of Herodotus, it appears from Poll. iv. 46, that in the time of Aristophanes it was used, and not the mere gnomon only, as Ideler *Lehrb. d. Chronol.* i. p. 98, would persuade us. Pollux says, τὸ δὲ καλού-μενον ὡρολόγιον ἤπου πόλον ἄν τις εἴποι, φήσαντος Ἀριστοφάνους ἐν Γηρυτάδῃ 'πόλος τοῦτ' ἔστιν· ἑκα-σταποστὴν ἥλιος τέτραπται ;' The πόλος was like a basin, λεκανὶς, in the centre of which stood the vertical staff (γνώμων), and on it the δώδεκα μέρη of the day were marked with lines. Poll. vi. 110; and Alciphr. *Epist.* iii.

have the clepsydra [4] here,' interposed Chloris; ' see how
much water there is left in it; it will run off once more
before sunset.' ' I am sure she's wrong,' said Cleobule;

---

‡ : Ὁ γνώμων οὔπω σκιάζει τὴν ἕκτην . . . εἰ γὰρ καὶ ὅλην καταβαλοῦ-
μεν τὴν κίονα τὴν τὸ πικρὸν τοῦτο
ὡρολόγιον ἀνέχουσαν, ἢ τὸν γνώμονα τρέψομεν ἐκεῖσε νεύειν, οὗ τα-
χίον δυνήσεται τὰς ὥρας ἀποσημαί-
νειν, ἔσται τὸ βούλευμα Παλαμή-
δειον. Suid.: γνώμων· τὸ ἐν τοῖς ἡλιο-
τροπίοις πηγνύμενον, ὅπερ ἐφεῦρεν
Ἀναξίμανδρος καὶ ἔστησεν ἐπὶ τῶν
σκιοθήρων. Cf. Lucian, Lexiph. 4.

[4] The κλεψύδρα as ltitle deserves
the appellation of clock as the gnomon does. The use of the clepsydra
in courts of law is mentioned by Aristophanes, (Acharn. 692; Vesp. 93,
857,) as such a matter of course, that
we conclude that in his time it was no
novelty. We have the fullest information as to its form and structure
from Aristot. Probl. xvi. 8, though
there is still some doubt as to its size
and time of running out. It was a
hollow ball, perhaps flattened a little
at the top, whence from its likeness to
a poppy-head the ball was called κώ-
δεια, or κωδία. For the introduction
of the water, there was at the top an
opening which was extended into a
short neck, αὐλός, which might be
closed by a stopper, (πῶμα, πωμά-
ζειν,) to stop the water from flowing
out, ἐπιλαβεῖν τὸ ὕδωρ. On the
netherside, opposite to this neck, were
several small orifices, τρυπήματα,
forming a kind of colander or filter,
through which the water slowly trickled out. Aristotle is describing various
hydrostatic and pneumatic experi-
ments which may be tried with the
clepsydra, and his description is such
as to leave no doubt as to its construc-

tion. It is plain, however, that he had
not a transparent ball in view; and
we have no authority for supposing
that at that period glass vessels could
be constructed of the size which the
clepsydræ ordinarily were. Indeed,
a fragment of Bato, ap. Athen. iv.
p. 163, precludes the notion of the
clepsydra being transparent :

ἔπειθ' ἔωθεν περιάγεις τὴν λήκυθον
καταμανθάνων τοὔλαιον, ὥστε περιφέρειν
ὡρολόγιον δόξει τις, οὐχὶ λήκυθον.

Smaller ones of glass there may have
been, and, at a later period, were
common. Experience however taught
that this instrument could not be
relied on, the rapidity with which the
water flowed out being influenced by
the temperature. Athen. ii. p. 42 :
συστέλλει δὲ αὐτὸ (τὸ ὕδωρ) καὶ πυκνοῖ
μᾶλλον τὸ ψῦχος. διὸ καὶ ἐν τοῖς
γνώμοσι ῥέον οὐκ ἀναδίδωσι τὰς ὥρας
ἐν τῷ χειμῶνι, ἀλλὰ περιττεύει, βρα-
δυτέρας οὔσης τῆς ἐκροῆς διὰ τὸ πά-
χος. According to Æneas Tact. 22,
this inequality could be remedied by
partially stopping with wax. The
Greeks were acquainted with the
division of the twelve natural hours of
the day, but no hint is ever given of
reckoning by hours; so that in Scene i.
p. 4, instead of the fourth hour, it
would be better perhaps to say, the
time of full market.

Whether the clepsydra was often
used in private life, as well as in
courts of justice, is doubtful; it would
seem probable that it was. A clepsydra belonging to Plato, which served
for the whole night, is described by
Aristocles, ap. Athen. iv. p. 174: λέγεται δὲ Πλάτωνα μικράν τινα ἔν-
νοιαν δοῦναι τοῦ κατασκευάσματος

'it must be later.' Menodora, however, returned with
the assurance that the shadow was only eight feet long,
and it therefore wanted some time yet to evening.

At last Chloris had drawn the bandeau through Cleobule's luxuriant locks, and had fastened the bridal veil [5] on
her head with a golden tiring-pin ; and Menodora twined
the white thongs of the embroidered sandals round the feet
of her mistress.   Her mother then opened an ivory casket,
and took out of it a broad necklace of gold, richly set with
precious stones, and the serpent-shaped armlets, which completed her attire.   Cleobule took the mirror once again, and
surveyed herself in it : the clothes-chests were then locked,
and she awaited with maidenly timidity the arrival of the
escort that was to conduct her away, though her sensations
were far from those of her former wedding-day.

The water-clock had emptied itself a second time, the
sun had completed his course, and the rooms of the house
grew duskier apace, when the carriage destined to carry
home the bride, drawn by stately mules and surrounded
by a numerous band of attendants, drove up to the door,
which was profusely hung with garlands.

The bridegroom and his man, accompanied by the
happy father of the former, now entered and received the
bride from the hands of her mother, in order to escort her
to the carriage, in which Charicles and Ctesiphon took
their seats, one on each side of the veiled fair.   The
mother kindled the marriage-torch, the attendants follow-

νυκτερινὸν ποιήσαντα ὡρολόγιον ἐοι-
κὸς τῷ ὑδραυλικῷ, οἷον κλεψύδραν
μεγάλην λίαν.   See also Athen. xiii.
p. 567, where another instance of
its domestic use occurs.

[5] Numerous as are the extant accounts of marriage solemnities, still
they do not suffice for the construction of a connected and detailed
description of the ceremony.   It is
not known whether, when a widow
was re-married, the same formalities
were observed as at the first marriage ; for instance, the festive escort to her abode, the veiling, the
procession with torches, the *Ana-
calypteria*, and so on.   Some of
these ceremonies were probably
omitted ; but the excuse for their
introduction in this place must be,
that the first marriage might be
considered to have hardly taken
place at all.

ing her example, and thus the procession moved off amid the music of the flutes and the merry song of Hymenæos to the house of Sophilos, where the pair were received on entering, according to an ancient custom, with a symbolical rain of sweetmeats and small coins. They then proceeded at once to the hall, which was brilliantly lighted up for the festival; the couches of the males being arranged on one side of it, and on the other the seats of the females.

After the bride-cakes had been partaken of, as midnight began to approach, Cleobule's mother accompanied the pair to the quiet thalamos: again the loud burden of Hymenæos re-echoed before its closed doors, and never perhaps had the god hovered more delightedly over a bridal-chamber

APPENDIX.

EXCURSUS TO SCENE I.

EDUCATION.

IN attempting to combine a multitude of scattered allusions into a connected account of education among the Greeks, it will be desirable to investigate not only their system of intellectual culture and training in the higher sense of the word, but also to consider the corporeal nurture, the first occupations of the children, their general habits and behaviour, their toys, the ballads and fairy tales of the nurses and attendants, with all the minutiæ of the nursery. Such petty domestic traits are quite as deserving of attention as the instruction conveyed in the public gymnasia, and the schools of the Grammarians.

In this sense the παιδεία commences with the hour of birth; it is the training and bringing up till the moment when the youth became an independent burgher, and under the immediate control of the law. Plato, *Leg.* ii. p. 659. Cf. Heliod. *Æthiop.* i. 13.

Throughout Greece, except in Sparta (Plutarch, *Lycurg.* 16), the new-born babe was wrapped in σπάργανα, immediately after the first bath. So Plato, *Leg.* vii. p. 789: μέχρι δυοῖν ἐτοῖν τὸ γενόμενον σπαργανᾶν. Whether these σπάργανα were mere swaddling-clothes is not quite clear. See Aristot. *de Republ.* vii. 17: πρὸς δὲ τὸ μὴ διαστρέφεσθαι τὰ μέλη (τῶν παιδίων) δι' ἀπαλότητα χρῶνται καὶ νῦν ἔνια τῶν ἐθνῶν ὀργάνοις τισὶ μηχανικοῖς, ἃ τὸ σῶμα ποιεῖ τῶν τοιούτων ἀστραβές. On the fifth day, according to Suidas, the first festival in honour of the family-event was held, the ἀμφιδρόμια, or δρομιάμφιον ἦμαρ, as it is called by Hesychius, who places it on the seventh day: ἔστι δὲ ἡμερῶν ἑπτὰ ἀπὸ τῆς γεννήσεως, ἐν ᾗ τὸ βρέφος βαστάζοντες περὶ τὴν ἑστίαν γυμνοὶ τρέχουσι. The midwife, or some of the women present at the birth, carried the babe round the hearth of the house; hence the name. Plato, *Theæt.* p. 160: μετὰ δὲ τὸν τόκον τὰ ἀμφιδρόμια αὐτοῦ ὡς ἀληθῶς ἐν κύκλῳ περιθρεκτέον τῷ λόγῳ. The house-door was ornamented with garlands, and a feast was given, at which cabbage, ῥάφανος, was a standing

dish, as appears from a fragment of Ephippus preserved by
Athenæus, ix. p. 370:

> ἔπειτα πῶς
> οὐ στέφανος οὐδείς ἐστι πρόσθε τῶν θυρῶν,
> οὐ κνῖσα κρούει ῥινὸς ὑπεροχὰς ὄκρας,
> Ἀμφιδρομίων ὄντων; ἐν οἷς νομίζεται
> ὀπτᾶν τε τυροῦ Χερῥονησίτου τόμους,
> ἕψειν τ' ἐλαίῳ ῥάφανον ἠγλαϊσμένην.

The account of Suidas is as follows: Ἀμφιδρύμια· ἣν πέμπτην
ἄγουσιν ἐπὶ τοῖς βρέφεσιν. ἐν ᾗ ἀποκαθαίρονται τὰς χεῖρας αἱ
συναψάμεναι τῆς μαιώσεως. τὸ βρέφος περιφέρουσι τὴν ἑστίαν
τρέχοντες καὶ δῶρα πέμπουσιν οἱ προσήκοντες ὡς ἐπὶ τὸ πλεῖστον
πολύποδας καὶ σηπίας. It would almost appear from Plato that
 the father did not declare, until this ceremony, whether he would
rear the child; for on him it depended whether the infant should
be brought up or exposed; a barbarity which was actually authorised by law. See Petit. *Leg. Att.* p. 144. Thebes, however,
was an honourable exception to this rule. Ælian, *Var. Hist.* ii. 7:
(νόμος) ὅτι οὐκ ἔξεστιν ἀνδρὶ Θηβαίῳ ἐκθεῖναι παιδίον, οὐδ' εἰς
ἐρημίαν αὐτὸ ῥῖψαι, θάνατον αὐτοῦ καταψηφισάμενος. The offspring of paupers, εἰς ἔσχατα πενήτων, were brought up at the
public expense; which was a more humane regulation than the
proposition of Aristotle, who repudiates ἀπόθεσις, but recommends
ἄμβλωσις as a check to overpopulation! *De Republ.* vii. 16,
p. 1335: πρὶν αἴσθησιν ἐγγενέσθαι καὶ ζωὴν ἐμποιεῖσθαι δεῖ τὴν
ἄμβλωσιν. Still, exposure was not so frequent in regular marriage as has been usually supposed; at least this unhappy fate
fell mostly upon female children, who could even be condemned
outright to death at the father's pleasure. So says Chremes,
Terent. *Heaut.* iv. 1, 21:

> si meum
> Imperium exsequi voluisses, interemptam oportuit.

Children were generally exposed, to escape the trouble of rearing them, or to avoid too great a subdivision of the inheritance.
Longus, *Pastor.* iv. p. 126: Ἄλλοι πατέρες ἐξέθηκαν τοῦτο τὸ
παιδίον, ἴσως παιδίων πρεσβυτέρων ἅλις ἔχοντες. Cf. Terent.
Adelph. v. 3, 23. Illegitimate children were most frequently
exposed: and many a childless wife would profit by this opportunity to obtain an infant, and pass it off as her own. Dio

Chrysost. *Orat.* xv. p. 447 : ἐπίσταμαι γὰρ, ὅτι αἱ μὲν ἐλεύθεραι γυναῖκες ὑποβάλλονται πολλάκις δι᾽ ἀπαιδίαν, ὅταν μὴ δύνωνται αὐταὶ κυῆσαι. This is well illustrated by the words of Demosth. *in Mid.* p. 563 : ἡ μὲν γὰρ ἀπέδοτο εὐθὺς γενόμενον, ἡ δ᾽ ἐξὸν αὐτῇ βελτίω πρίασθαι τῆς ἴσης τιμῆς, τοῦτον ἠγόρασε. Cf. Æschin. *in Timarch.* p. 160 : Κηφισόδωρον τὸν τοῦ Μόλωνος καλούμενον : such children were called σκότιοι. Eustath. *ad Il.* vii. 24. So Eurip. *Troad.* 256 : λέκτρων σκότια νυμφευτήρια. Thus Œdipus is called πλαστὸς by Sophocles, *Œd. Tyr.* 780.

The grand festival was the δεκάτη, celebrated on the tentl day, when the relations and friends were invited to a sacrifice and banquet (δεκάτην θύειν, and ἑστιᾶν) ; and this ceremony was held as a legal proof that the child was recognised as γνήσιος by its father. Isæus, *de Pyrrhi Hered.* p. 60 : ἔτι δὲ καὶ ἐν τῇ δεκάτῃ ταύτης κληθέντες συνεστιᾶσθαι (φάσκοντες). See Demosth. *adv. Bœot. ὀνομ.* p. 1001 ; also Aristoph. *Aves*, 493 ; Plato, *Leg.* vi. p. 784. On this occasion presents were made to the child by the father and mother, the relatives, and even by the slaves, and then also the infant received its name. Aristoph. *Aves*, 922. But according to Aristotle, *Hist. An.* viii. 11, this took place also on the seventh day : τὰ πλεῖστα δ᾽ ἀναιρεῖται πρὸ τῆς ἑβδόμης, διὸ καὶ τὰ ὀνόματα τότε τίθενται : and sometimes perhaps even at the Amphidromia, if we are to believe Hesychius, and the Scholiast on the *Theœtetus* of Plato ; Suidas, however, expressly fixes it on the tenth day : τῇ δεκάτῃ δὲ τοὔνομα τίθενται. The father mostly chose the name, though it could not have been unusual for the mother to do so, as we see from Eurip. *Phœniss.* 57, where Jocasta says :

> τὴν μὲν Ἰσμήνην πατὴρ
> ὠνόμασε. τὴν δὲ πρόσθεν Ἀντιγόνην ἐγώ.

Sometimes the parents fell out on this point ; see the complaint of Strepsiades, the Aristophanic George Dandin ; *Nub.* 60 :

> Μετὰ ταῦθ᾽, ὅπως νῷν ἐγένεθ᾽ υἱὸς οὑτοσὶ,
> ἐμοί τε δὴ καὶ τῇ γυναικὶ, τῇ ᾽γαθῇ,
> περὶ τοὐνόματος δὴ ταῦτ᾽ ἐλοιδορούμεθα.

Strepsiades wished to name the boy Φειδωνίδης, after his grand-father, as was most usual. Cf. Eustath. *ad Il.* v. 546 : Ἰστέον δὲ καὶ ὅτι παλαίτατον ἔθος ἦν, τοὺς ἐγγόνους καλεῖσθαι τοῖς τῶν πάππων ὀνόμασιν. This was particularly the case with the eldest

son, as appears from Demosth. *adv. Bœot. ὀνόμ.* p. 1002 : ἀξιοῖ
δ' αὐτὸς, ὡς δὴ πρεσβύτερος ὤν, τοὔνομ' ἔχειν τὸ τοῦ πρὸς πατρὸς
πάππου. See also Plutarch, *Cimon.* 4. But the son was often
called after his father; as were Demosthenes and Demades; or
the name was slightly changed; thus we have Ναυσίφιλος
Ναυσινίκου, and Καλλίστρατος Καλλικράτους. So also brothers'
names sometimes varied but slightly, as Diodotos and Diogeiton ;
Lysias, *in Diogit.* Lastly, we meet with regular patronymics, as
Φωκίων Φώκου.

We will now digress for a moment to the surnames. The
Greeks had no family or clan names, as is well known ; a single
appellation serving for an individual. But as many persons
might bear this name, to avoid confusion, the father's name was
appended, and this was called πατρόθεν ὀνομάζεσθαι. Xenoph.
Œcon. 7, 3. Cf. Pausan. vii. 7, 4 : ἐπεὶ καλοῦνταί γε οὐ πατρόθεν οἱ Ῥωμαῖοι κατὰ ταὐτὰ "Ελλησιν, ἀλλὰ καὶ τρία, ὁπότε ᾖ
ὀλίγιστα, καὶ ἔτι πλείονα ὀνόματα ἑκάστῳ τίθενται. Attic wit
had also abundant recourse to nicknames, derived either from
some personal peculiarity, or owing to accidental circumstances.
Thus Demosthenes was called Βάταλος, even from childhood.
Æschin. *in Timarch.* p. 139 ; cf. Demosth. *de Cor.* p. 288. So
the poet and orator Dionysios was called Χαλκοῦς. Eustath. *ad
Il.* xxi. 393 : ὃς χαλκοῦς ἐκλήθη διὰ τὸ συμβουλεῦσαι Ἀθηναίοις
χαλκῷ νομίσματι χρήσασθαι. Aristophanes mentions a number
of names of birds used as nicknames; *Aves,* 1291 :

> Πέρδιξ μὲν εἶς κάπηλος ὠνομάζετο
> χωλός.   Μενίππῳ δ' ἦν Χελιδὼν τοὔνομα·
> 'Οπουντίῳ δ' ὀφθαλμὸν οὐκ ἔχων Κόραξ·
> Κόρυδος Φιλοκλέει·   Χηναλώπηξ Θεαγένει·
> 'Ἶβις Λυκούργῳ·   Χαιρεφῶντι Νυκτερίς, κ.τ.λ.

So the frosty tragic poet Theognis was yclept Χίων : *Acharn.*
138 ; *Thesmoph.* 170 ; and how universal the habit was among
the Athenians appears from a fragment of Anaxandrides, ap.
Athen. vi. p. 242 :

> 'Υμεῖς γὰρ ἀλλήλους ἀεὶ χλευάζετ', οἶδ' ἀκριβῶς.
> ἂν μὲν γὰρ ᾖ τις εὐπρεπὴς, 'Ιερὸν γάμον καλεῖτε,
> ἐὰν δὲ μικρὸν παντελῶς ἀνθρώπιον, Σταλαγμόν, κ.τ.λ.

See also the Excursus on *The Hetœrœ.* But to return to the
nursery, and the first treatment of children.

As regards the τροφὴ, Plutarch says, *de Educ. Puer.* 5, that mothers should suckle their own children : δεῖ δὲ αὐτὰς τὰς μη-τέρας τὰ τέκνα τρέφειν καὶ τούτοις ὑπέχειν τοὺς μαστούς. This rule, however, was seldom observed by the wealthy classes, and wet-nurses were in general requisition. But the τίτθη or τιτθὴ (Eustath. *ad Iliad*, vii. 329—τιθήνη means the attendant merely,; was frequently not a slave, but one of the poor ἀσταὶ, who gave her services for hire. Demosth. *adv. Eubulid.* p. 1309 : καὶ γὰρ ὖν ἀστὰς γυναῖκας πολλὰς εὑρήσετε τιτθευούσας. Spartan nurses, who were in great repute for their skill in managing children, were sometimes bought, as for Alcibiades. Plutarch, *Lyc.* 16 : ἦν δὲ περὶ τὰς τροφοὺς ἐπιμέλεια τις μετὰ τέχνης, ὥστ' ἄνευ σπαργάνων ἐκτρεφούσας τὰ βρέφη . . . διὸ καὶ τῶν ἔξωθεν ἔνιοι τοῖς τέκνοις Λακωνικὰς ἐωνοῦντο τιτθάς. καὶ τήν γε τὸν 'Αθη-ναῖον 'Αλκιβιάδην τιτθεύσασαν 'Αμύκλαν ἱστοροῦσι γεγονέναι Λά-καιναν. Plutarch (*e Educ.* 5,) requires for the purpose, τοῖς ἤθεσιν 'Ελληνίδας. Besides being suckled, the children were also fed with honey. See Böckh, ad Pind. *Olymp.* vi. When they could take more substantial nourishment, the τίτθη first chewed the food, and then gave it to the infant, μασωμένη ἐσίτιζεν. Theophr. *Char.* 20 : τὸ παιδίον τῆς τίτθης ἀφελόμενος μασώμενος σιτίζειν αὐτός. See Aristoph. *Equites*, 717. This was also called ψωμίζειν. *Lysistr.* 19. An absurd story of some one who re-tained this habit during his whole life for convenience sake is related by Athenæus, xii. p. 530 : Σάγαριν τὸν Μαριανδυνὸν ὑπὸ τρυφῆς σιτεῖσθαι μὲν μέχρι γήρως ἐκ τοῦ τῆς τίτθης στόματος, ἵνα μὴ μασώμενος ποιήσειεν.

Cradles are first mentioned by Plutarch, *Fragm. in Hesiod.* 45 : Ο δὲ Πλούταρχός φησιν, ὅτι μὴ δεῖ τὰ νεογνὰ ἀκίνητα ἐᾶν καὶ ἀποτίθεσθαι ἐν ἀκινήτοις . . . οἷά τισιν εὐκίνητα κλινίδια μεμηχάνη-ται πρὸς τὴν τῶν παιδίων εὐνήν. Plato knew nothing of them, or he would certainly have mentioned them, *Leg.* vii. p. 789. The σκάφη is often mentioned, it is true; cf. Aristot. *Poet.* 16 ; but though used for a similar purpose, we can in no passage sup-pose a regular cradle to be meant. See Theocr. *Id.* xxiv. 10. Doubtless mothers and nurses went about dandling the baby in their arms, and singing the while. See Plato, *Leg.* vii. p. 790 : ἡνίκα γὰρ ἄν που βουληθῶσι κατακοιμίζειν τὰ δυσυπνοῦντα τῶν παιδίων αἱ μητέρες, οὐχ ἡσυχίαν αὐτοῖς προσφέρουσιν, ἀλλὰ τοὐ-

ναντίον κίνησιν, ἐν ταῖς ἀγκάλαις ἀεὶ σείουσαι· καὶ οὐ σιγὴν, ἀλλά
τινα μελῳδίαν. See Aristot. *Probl.* xix. 38. These lullabies were
called βαυκαλήματα, or καταβαυκαλήσεις. Athen. xiv. p. 618 :
αἱ δὲ τῶν τιτθευουσῶν ᾠδαὶ καταβαυκαλήσεις ὀνομάζονται. See
also Theocr. *Id.* xxiv. 6, where Alcmene is hushing her twins to
sleep :

> Ἀπτομένα δὲ γυνὰ κεφαλᾶς μυθήσατο παίδων·
> εὕδετ᾽ ἐμὰ βρέφεα γλυκερὸν καὶ ἐγέρσιμον ὕπνον·
> εὕδετ᾽ ἐμὰ ψυχὰ, δὔ ἀδελφεῷ, εὔσοα τέκνα·
> ὄλβιοι εὐνάζοισθε, καὶ ὄλβιοι ἀῶ ἵκοισθε.

Cf. Aristoph. *Nubes*, 1383; *Lysistr.* 1410; Lysias, *de cæde
Eratosth.* pp. 10–15.

Children were not encouraged to walk very early. The distinction drawn by Eustathius, *ad Il.* ix. 518 : παιδίον τὸ τρεφό-
μενον ὑπὸ τηθῆς, παιδάριον τὸ περιπατοῦν καὶ ἤδη λέξεως ἀντι-
λαμβανόμενον, is doubtful, though Pollux, ii. 9, says that παιδάριον was the after-appellation of the two. According to Plato,
Leg. vii. p. 794, the boys remained under the hands of the mother
and the nurses till their sixth year, and up to that time were
educated along with the girls.

The baubles, *crepundia*, given to children, have been discussed in *Gallus*, p. 183. Sometimes these were suspended from
the neck, and are so represented in antiques, hence they were
called δέραια or περιδέραια. Eurip. *Ion*, 1430; Aristot. *Poet.* 16.
Children who were to be exposed were provided with them, by
way of γνωρίσματα. Dio Chrys. *Or.* iv. p. 150 : καθάπερ τὰ
δέραια τοῖς ἐκτιθεμένοις παιδίοις, ἵνα μὴ ἀγνοῆται. Also Alciphr.
Epist. iii. 63 : τοῦτο (τὸ παιδίον) μετὰ τῶν σπαργάνων, δέραιά
τινα καὶ γνωρίσματα περιθεῖσαι, ἔδωκαν. Other things were also
given to them. See Longus, *Past.* i. pp. 6, 8; Heliod. *Æthiop.*
ii. 31; Aristænet. *Epist.* i. 1. Such playthings were mostly of
metal, hence the Roman name, *crepundia.* The Greeks had also
regular child's-rattles, πλαταγαὶ, of which Archytas is named as
the inventor, Aristot. *de Republ.* viii. 6 ; and a go-cart, ἁμαξίς, is
mentioned, Aristoph. *Nubes*, 861 :

> κἀγώ τοί ποτε
> ὃν πρῶτον ὀβολὸν ἔλαβον Ἡλιαστικὸν,
> ὅτ᾽ ἐπριάμην σοι Διασίοις ἁμαξίδα.

Cf. Poll. x. 168. Pausanias, v. 20, 1, mentions among the curiosities in the temple of Juno at Olympia, a small bed ornamented

with ivory, said to have been a plaything, παίγνιον, of Hippo-
damia's. Children would sometimes try their hands at construct-
ing similar nick-nacks; Aristoph. *Nubes*, 878 :

> εὐθύς γέ τοι παιδάριον ὢν τυννουτονὶ
> ἔπλαττεν ἔνδον οἰκίας, ναῦς δ᾽ ἔγλυφεν,
> ἁμαξίδας τε σκυτίνας εἰργάζετο,
> κἀκ τῶν σιδίων βατράχους ἐποίει.

See also Lucian's account of himself, *Somn.* 2 : ἀποξέων ἂν τὸν
κηρὸν ἢ βόας, ἢ ἵππους, ἢ καὶ νὴ Δί᾽ ἀνθρώπους ἀνέπλαττον.
Cf. Suidas, s. v. φορμίς. Dolls, κόραι, were usual playthings, and
the κοροπλάθοι, or κοροπλάσται, had always a supply on sale in
the market; they were however different from those in use now,
being made of clay and painted. Cf. Plato, *Theæt.* p. 146 : πηλὸς ὁ τῶν κοροπλάθων. Demosth. *Phil.* i. p. 47 : ὥσπερ γὰρ οἱ
πλάττοντες τοὺς πηλίνους. εἰς τὴν ἀγορὰν χειροτονεῖτε τοὺς ταξι-
άρχους καὶ τοὺς φυλάρχους, οὐκ ἐπὶ τὸν πολεμόν. Lucian. *Prom.
in Verb.* 2 : καὶ τὸ μὲν ὅλον ἐν πηλῷ ἡ πλαστικὴ κατὰ ταὐτὰ
τοῖς κοροπλάθοις. *Lexiphan.* 22 : ὡς νῦν γε ἐλελήθεις σαυτὸν τοῖς
ὑπὸ τῶν κοροπλάθων εἰς τὴν ἀγορὰν πλαττομένοις ἐοικὼς, κε-
χρωσμένος μὲν τῇ μίλτῳ καὶ τῷ κυανῷ, τὸ δ᾽ ἔνδοθεν πήλινός τε
καὶ εὔθρυπτος ὤν. Böttiger, in his *Sabina*, confounds κοροπλάσται with κηροπλάσται; having followed Ruhnken without independent investigation. Wax, it is true, is mentioned, but only
by late writers; Timæus and Suidas say, κηρῷ ἢ γύψῳ, and Harpocration has : κοροπλάθους λέγουσι τοὺς ἐκ πηλοῦ τινος, ἢ κηροῦ,
ἢ τοιαύτης ὕλης πλάττοντας κόρας ἢ κούρους; but these are the
only writers who say a word about wax in the manufacture of
these dolls; all speaking only of πηλός. The very passage in
Pollux (x. 189) descriptive of this art, has been wrongly interpreted by Böttiger; the πλασθέντα κήρινα there mentioned are
merely the cores for the moulds, over which the πηλὸς was laid,
and this wax was afterwards melted out, in order to preserve the
hollow form, λίγδος, or ἡμίλιγδος. From the above passages we
learn that these clay-figures were not merely children's dolls (also
called νύμφαι), but images of all sorts; and indeed the words of
Demosthenes will be devoid of sense unless we understand figures
of warriors, generals, and the like. Mythological subjects were
also common, such as Marsyas bound to the tree; Achill. Tat.
iii. 15 : οἷον ποιοῦσιν οἱ κοροπλάθοι τὸν Μαρσύαν ἐκ τοῦ φυτοῦ

δεδεμένον. There were other amusements, as the hoop, τροχός, the top, ρόμβος, στρόβιλος, not to mention the cockchafer fastened by a thread. Aristoph. *Nubes*, 763:

> λινόδετον ὥσπερ μηλολόνθην τοῦ ποδός.

Cf. Schol. on *Vesp.* 1341: χρυσομηλολόνθιον δὲ ζωΰφιόν τί ἐστι κατὰ κάνθαρον, ξανθὸν, ὃ καὶ κατέχοντες οἱ παῖδες δεσμεύουσιν ἐκ τοῦ ποδὸς καὶ ἀφιᾶσι πρὸς τὸν ἀέρα. Among a number of other games mentioned by Pollux. ix. 122, is the χαλκῆ μυῖα, a sort of blind-man's-buff: Ἡ δὲ χαλκῆ μυῖα, ταινίᾳ τὼ ὀφθαλμὼ περισφίγξαντες ἑνὸς παιδός, ὁ μὲν περιστρέφεται κηρύττων· χαλκῆν μυῖαν θηράσω· οἱ δὲ ἀποκρινάμενοι, θηράσεις ἀλλ᾽ οὐ λήψει, σκύτεσι βυβλίνοις παίουσιν αὐτόν, ἕως τινὸς αὐτῶν λήψεται. Amid the rough manners of Sparta it is interesting to find Agesilaos riding about among his children astride of a cane: μικροῖς τοῖς παιδίοις οὖσι κάλαμον περιβεβηκὼς, ὥσπερ ἵππον, οἴκοι συνέπαιζεν. Plutarch, *Ages.* 25; cf. Ælian, *Var. Hist.* xii. 15.

Generally, however, great caution was exercised in the keeping up one's dignity before children, as is evident from Theocr. *Id.* xv. 11, where Praxinoe having called her husband a φθονερὸν κακὸν, Gorgo bids her not to abuse him, τῶ μικκῶ παρεόντος, and then follows that lady's characteristic fib to her child, οὐ λέγω ἀπφῦν. Plato, *Leg.* v. p. 729, above all, recommends νουθετεῖν, as well as good example, in the correction of children, though castigation was far from uncommon in practice, and was usually administered with the slippers or sandals. Lucian, *Philops.* 28: ἐπεὶ σανδάλῳ γε χρυσῷ ἐς τὰς πυγὰς, ὥσπερ τὰ παιδία, παίεσθαι ἄξιοι ἂν εἶεν οἱ ἀπιστοῦντες. This served in the Grecian schools instead of the ferule used at Rome. Cf. Plutarch, *de sera Num. Vind.* 16. Divers bugbears were also used to frighten children into good behaviour: such were the Ἀκκὼ and Ἀλφιτώ, a sort of bogies. They are alluded to by Chrysippos, apud Plutarch, *de Stoic. Repugn.* 15: ὡς οὐδὲν διαφέροντα τῆς Ἀκκοῦς καὶ τῆς Ἀλφιτοῦς, δι᾽ ὧν τὰ παιδάρια τοῦ κακοσχολεῖν αἱ γυναῖκες ἀπείργουσιν. So also Strabo, i. 2, 6: τοῖς τε γὰρ παισὶ προσφέρομεν τοὺς ἡδεῖς μύθους εἰς προτροπήν· εἰς ἀποτροπὴν δὲ τοὺς φοβερούς. ἥ τε γὰρ Λάμια μῦθός ἐστι, καὶ ἡ Γοργώ, καὶ ὁ Ἐφιάλτης, καὶ ἡ Μορμολύκη. We read also of Ἔμπουσα, a name which is interchanged with Λαμία, or, as a general expression, comprehends the latter. What sort of a notion was attached

to these beings we learn from the story in Philostratus, *Vit.*
Apoll. Tyan. iv. 25 : ἡ χρηστὴ νύμφη μία τῶν Ἐμπουσῶν ἐστιν,
ἃς Λαμίας τε καὶ Μορμολυκίας οἱ πολλοὶ ἡγοῦνται. ἐρῶσι δ᾽ αὖ-
ται οὐκ ἀφροδισίων μὲν, σαρκῶν δὲ, καὶ μάλιστα ἀνθρωπείων ἐρῶσι,
καὶ πάλλουσι τοῖς ἀφροδισίοις, οὓς ἂν ἐθέλωσι δαίσασθαι. See
also what Libanius, in the life of Æschines, says about that person's mother. The general term for all these creatures was μορ-
μολυκεῖα, also βρίκελοι. Eustath. *ad Od.* i. 101. An instance of
the way children were thus terrified occurs in Theocritus, xv. 40,
where Praxinoe says to the child, who runs after her crying,
when she wants to go out :

> οὐκ ἄξω τύ, τέκνου· Μορμὼ, δάκνει ἵππος.
> δάκρυε, ὅσσα θέλεις· χωλὸν δ᾽ οὐ δεῖ σε γενεσθαι.

Naturally enough, superstitious terrors were much increased by
such nonsense.

The nurses and attendants had a store of tales (μῦθοι) for
the amusement of the children, and γραῶν or τιτθῶν μῦθοι have
grown into a proverb. Plato, *Gorg.* p. 527 ; *Hipp. Maj.* p. 286 ;
Lucian, *Philops.* 9. As these legends narrated, for the most
part, the actions of the gods and demigods of the popular superstition,—the ancient mythology embracing the entire domain
of the marvellous—the telling of them might have the greatest
influence on the moral education of the children : and hence
Plato (*Leg.* x. p. 887,) enlarges much on the care to be used in
their selection, and repudiates even Hesiod and Homer, *de Republ.*
ii. p. 377 : οὗτοι γάρ που μύθους τοῖς ἀνθρώποις ψευδεῖς συντιθέν-
τες ἔλεγόν τε καὶ λέγουσι. Plutarch, *de Educ. Puer.* 5, thinks
the nurses should be restrained, μὴ τοὺς τυχόντας μύθους τοῖς
παιδίοις λέγειν, ἵνα μὴ τὰς τούτων ψυχὰς ἐξ ἀρχῆς ἀνοίας καὶ
διαφθορᾶς ἀναπίμπλασθαι συμβαίνῃ : and Aristotle wishes to place
these matters under the supervision of the Pædonomoi ; *de Republ.*
vii. 17 : καὶ περὶ λόγων τε καὶ μύθων ποίους τινὰς ἀκούειν δεῖ τοὺς
τηλικούτους ἐπιμελὲς ἔστω τοῖς ἄρχουσιν, οὓς καλοῦσι παιδονό-
μους. With regard to the character of these fables, see Aristoph.
Vesp. 1182 : ὡς οὕτω ποτ᾽ ἦν μῦς καὶ γαλῆ. See also Philostr.
Vit. Apoll. Tyan. v. 14 ; whence we conclude that the fables of
Æsop were among those most in vogue. Frequently such legends
were handed down in the shape of ballads ; see Aristoph. *Lysistr.*
781, where the chorus sings two such songs, after saying,

μῦθον

βούλομαι λέξαι τιν' ὑμῖν, ὅν ποτ' ἤκουσ'
αὐτὸς ἔτι παῖς ὤν.

Adults as well as children took pleasure in them, so that there
were persons who recited such legends for a livelihood: Philep-
sios perhaps was such an one, see Aristoph. *Plutus*, 177, on which
the Scholiast says: οὗτος πένης ὢν λέγων ἱστορίας ἐτρέφετο.

In process of time the children were entrusted to the care of
a pedagogue. Plato, *Leg.* vii. p. 808. At what age this took
place is uncertain, though Plato (*Ib.* p. 794,) seems to have
had in his eye the end of the sixth year, at which period the
boys were first separated from the girls. Plato, however, only
gives his own ideas on the subject, so that we must be careful
not to reason from his words as to the actual practice, though
in this instance he appears to be supported by other authorities.
This παιδαγωγὸς was a slave. Intelligent and honest persons, and
of polished manners, were obtained if possible, though this could
not always be accomplished. Thus the pedagogues of Menexe-
nos and Lysis are described (Plato, *Lysis*, p. 223,) as ὑποβαρ-
βαρίζοντες. Plutarch, *de Educ. Puer.* 7, speaks very severely
of the want of conscientiousness of parents in his day: τῶν γὰρ
δούλων τῶν σπουδαίων τοὺς μὲν γεωργοὺς ἀποδεικνύουσι, τοὺς δὲ
ναυκλήρους, τοὺς δὲ ἐμπόρους, τοὺς δὲ οἰκονόμους, τοὺς δὲ δανει-
στάς· ὅ,τι δ' ἂν εὕρωσιν ἀνδράποδον οἰνόληπτον καὶ λίχνον, πᾶσαν πραγματείαν ἄχρηστον, τούτῳ φέροντες ὑποβάλλουσι τοὺς
υἱούς. Cf. *Lyc.* 16. *Alcib.* 1. These pedagogues accompanied the
boys to school and the gymnasium, and indeed everywhere. See
Plato, *Lysis*, p. 208. There was a law of Solon's, περὶ παιδαγωγῶν ἐπιμελείας : Æschin. *in Timarch.* p. 35. They carried the
boys' books and other school-requirements, or the cithara, although
special slaves frequently attended for this purpose. Liban. *Or.*
xxiv. p. 81 : οὐ παιδαγωγὸς, οὐχ οἱ τὰ βιβλία τοῖς νέοις ἐπ' ὤμων
φέροντες. Lucian, *Amor.* 44; Poll. x. 59. Whether they remained all the while at the school, as they did at the gymnasium, or returned to fetch their charges, does not appear; for
even though the school-room was called παιδαγωγεῖον (Demosth.
de Coron. p. 313; Poll. iv. 19, 41,) this has nothing whatever to
do with the pedagogue. Older persons, excepting near relations
of the master, were forbidden to enter the school during school-

hours under pain of death. Æschin. in Timarch. p. 38 : καὶ μὴ
ἐξέστω τοῖς ὑπὲρ τὴν τῶν παίδων ἡλικίαν οἷσιν εἰσιέναι τῶν παίδων ἔνδον ὄντων, ἐὰν μὴ υἱὸς διδασκάλου, ἢ ἀδελφὸς, ἢ θυγατρὸς
ἀνήρ. ἐὰν δέ τις παρὰ ταῦτ᾽ εἰσίῃ, θανάτῳ ζημιούσθω. At a
later period this law does not seem to have been strictly observed; for in Theophr. Char. 7, one of the traits of a λάλος is
to enter the palœstræ and schools, and interrupt master and pupils
by talking. Young persons remained under the surveillance of
pedagogues till they reached the age of ephebi. Terent. Andr. i.
1, 24 ; Plut. de Aud. i. p. 141. In Plaut. Bacch. i. 2 ; iii. 1, 3,
is a specimen of a pedagogue of the old stamp, whom the lad will
no longer obey.

After this age the instruction took place entirely away from
home, namely, at the schools and gymnasia. Plato, Prot. p. 320,
does not in the slightest allude to private instruction at home,
as Cramer supposes. It is nowhere definitely stated at what
year the boy commenced going to school. Plato, Leg. vii. p. 794,
τοὺς μὲν ἄρρενας ἐφ᾽ ἵππων διδακάλους καὶ τόξων καὶ σφεν-
δονήσεως, seems to restrict lads to the bodily exercises of the
gymnasium merely, until their tenth year, which time he fixes
for their commencement ἐν γράμμασι: but this could scarcely
have been actually the case; and boys were doubtless sent early
to school, as now-a-days, to keep them out of mischief at home.
Indeed, Lucian says as much, Hermotim. 82 : ἐπεὶ καὶ αἱ τίτθαι
τοιάδε λέγουσι περὶ τῶν παιδίων, ὡς ἀπιτέον αὐτοῖς ἐς διδασκάλου. καὶ γὰρ ἂν μηδέπω μαθεῖν ἀγαθόν τι δύνωνται, ἀλλ᾽ οὖν
φαῦλον οὐδὲν ποιήσουσιν ἐκεῖ μένοντες. Aristotle, de Republ. vii.
17, in the main agrees with Plato in thinking the age μέχρι πέντε
ἐτῶν as unfit either πρὸς μάθησιν, or πρὸς ἀναγκαίους πόνους.
During the next two years he thinks, δεῖ θεωροὺς ἤδη γίγνεσθαι
τῶν μαθήσεων, ἃς δεήσει μανθάνειν αὐτούς. He also thinks gymnastics ought to precede mental instruction, καὶ περὶ τὸ σῶμα
πρότερον ἢ τὴν διάνοιαν, though he does not explain when the
beginning ἐν γράμμασι should take place. Ib. viii. 3.

The state had but little concern with the schools. So Socrates
says : τῆς δὲ σῆς γενέσεως, ὦ Ἀλκιβιάδη, καὶ τροφῆς, καὶ παιδείας, ἢ ἄλλου ὁτουοῦν Ἀθηναίων, ὡς ἔπος εἰπεῖν, οὐδενὶ μέλει.
Plato, Alcib. i. p. 122. There were laws, it is true, respecting
instruction, ἢ οὐ καλῶς προσέταττον ἡμῶν οἱ ἐπὶ τούτοις τεταγ-

μένοι νόμοι, παραγγέλλοντες τῷ πατρὶ τῷ σῷ, σὲ ἐν μουσικῇ καὶ
γυμναστικῇ παιδεύειν, (Plato, *Crito*, p. 50,) but the expression
παραγγέλλειν, used here, does not enable us to ascertain how far
they were carried out; the laws of Solon, mentioned by Æschines,
were all intended to prevent moral abuses; and if there did exist
an express law at Athens which prescribed τοὺς παῖδας διδάσκεσθαι πρῶτον νεῖν τε καὶ γράμματα, (Petit. *Leg. Att.* pp. 12, 239,)
at least no control was exercised.

The state never thought of erecting public institutions, to be
maintained at the general expense. In Demosthenes, *in Bœot.
ὄνομ.* p. 1001, we read, it is true : ἀλλὰ καὶ πρῖν ἡμέτερος φάσκειν
συγγενὴς εἶναι εἰς Ἱπποθοωντίδα ἐφοίτα φύλην εἰς παῖδας χορεύσων.
But even if we adopt the inference drawn from this passage by
Böckh, *Public Econ. of Athens*, p. 121, that the tribes had partly
to provide for the instruction of their youth in music and bodily
exercises, by the appointment of teachers for this purpose, still
such an association would always bear the character of a private
undertaking. The whole passage may, however, with more
probability be understood of Choregia : see Antiph. *de Choreut.*
The words of Aristophanes, *Nubes*, 964, taken in connexion with
the obscurely-phrased law in Æschines, *in Timarch.* p. 35, περὶ τῆς
συμφοιτήσεως τῶν παίδων, are much more applicable to an institution of the kind surmised by Böckh, unless, indeed, they refer
to the χοροὶ ἐγκύκλιοι mentioned just after. What Plato says,
Leg. vii. p. 804, about appointing teachers to be paid at the
public cost, ἐν δὲ τούτοις πᾶσι (διδασκαλείοις καὶ γυμνασίοις)
διδασκάλους ἑκάστων πεπεισμένους μισθοῖς, is purely his own idea,
which was not realised till afterwards. The law of Charondas,
mentioned by Diod. Sic. xii. 13, can be hardly genuine : τὴν γὰρ
γραμματικὴν παρὰ τὰς ἄλλας μαθήσεις προέκρινεν ὁ νομοθέτης . . .
ὅθεν ὡς μεγάλων τινῶν ἀγαθῶν ἀποστερουμένους τοὺς ἀγραμμάτους
διωρθώσατο τῇ νομοθεσίᾳ ταύτῃ καὶ δημοσίας ἐπιμελείας τε καὶ
δαπάνης ἠξίωσε. Such establishments were not founded till a late
period.

The sort of an education the children received depended mainly
on the parent's own conscientiousness; some got none at all, the
sausage-seller for instance ; Aristoph. *Equites*, 1234. This, however, was not usual; and so necessary a thing did daily school-
going seem, that when the women and children of Athens fled to

Trœzen at the time of the Persian invasion, the inhabitants, besides supporting them, paid persons to teach the children. Plutarch, *Themist.* 10 : Καὶ τρέφειν ἐψηφίσαντο δημοσίᾳ, δύο ὀβολοὺς ἑκάστῳ διδόντες, καὶ τῆς ὀπώρας λαμβάνειν τοὺς παῖδας ἐξεῖναι πανταχόθεν, ἔτι δ᾽ ὑπὲρ αὐτῶν διδασκάλοις τελεῖν μισθούς. See also Ælian, *Var. Hist.* vii. 15, where we read that the Mitylenæans, when masters of the sea, punished those allies who revolted, by not allowing their children to be taught, deeming this the severest penalty they could inflict: γράμματα μὴ μανθάνειν τοὺς παῖδας αὐτῶν μηδὲ μουσικὴν διδάσκεσθαι, πασῶν κολάσεων ἡγησάμενοι βαρυτάτην εἶναι ταύτην, ἐν ἀμαθίᾳ καὶ ἀμουσίᾳ καταβιῶναι. The selection of a teacher rested entirely with the parents, and, as might be expected, the choice often fell on incompetent persons. Plutarch, *de Educ. Puer.* 7.

The tutors were, in some degree, under the surveillance of the state, and certain ἀρχαί, probably the παιδονόμοι mentioned by Aristotle, *de Repub.* iv. 15, were appointed by Solon to inspect them, as we are informed by Æschines, *in Timarch.* p. 35 ; and Plato, *Leg.* vi. p. 765, requires: ἄρχων ὁ τῆς παιδείας ἐπιμελητὴς πάσης. But the functions of these persons were confined to the administration of certain laws respecting morality, while the state exercised but little supervision over the qualifications of the tutors or their method of teaching : perhaps the only requirement was that they should be above a certain age, and thus also the χορηγοὶ παίδων were required to be more than forty. Persons therefore taught the elements, not so much from choice and qualifications, as from having no other means of livelihood ; hence the amusing reference in Lucian, *Necyom.* 17, to those who might be supposed to be reduced to this condition in Hades: πολλῷ δ᾽ ἂν οἶμαι μᾶλλον ἐγέλας, εἰ ἐθεάσω τοὺς παρ᾽ ἡμῖν βασιλέας καὶ σατράπας πτωχεύοντας παρ᾽ αὐτοῖς, καὶ ἤτοι ταριχοπωλοῦντας ὑπ᾽ ἀπορίας, ἢ τὰ πρῶτα διδάσκοντας γράμματα. Others were in the service of teachers of repute, as, for instance, was the father of Æschines, as appears from Demosth. *de Coron.* p. 313, a passage which affords many curious details as to the arrangements of an Athenian school-room : δι᾽ ἣν (τύχην) παῖς μὲν ὢν μετὰ πολλῆς ἐνδείας ἐτράφης, ἅμα τῷ πατρὶ πρὸς τῷ διδασκαλείῳ προσεδρεύων, τὸ μέλαν τρίβων, καὶ τὰ βάθρα σπογγίζων, καὶ τὸ παιδαγωγεῖον κορῶν, οἰκέτου τάξιν, οὐκ ἐλευθέρου παιδὸς ἔχων. Cf. *Ib.* p. 270.

A somewhat similar tale is told of Epicurus and his father; Diog
Laert. x. 4 : καὶ σὺν τῷ πατρὶ γράμματα διδάσκειν λυπροῦ τινος
μισθαρίου. It appears that the calling of teachers of the rudi-
ments, τῶν τὰ πρῶτα γράμματα διδασκόντων, stood in no great
repute, and this will elucidate Plutarch, *Alcib.* 7. The children
of wealthy parents of course went to better teachers. Demosthenes relates with honest pride how he went εἰς τὰ προσήκοντα
διδασκαλεῖα. *De Coron.* p. 312.

In default of direct evidence as to the fees ordinarily received
by schoolmasters, we must not be misled by the sums extorted by
the Rhetoricians and Sophists. The schoolmaster's income would
depend on the number of his scholars. See Æschin. *in Timarch.*
p. 34 : οἷς ἐστιν ὁ μὲν βίος ἀπὸ τοῦ σωφρονεῖν, ἡ δ' ἀπορία ἐκ τῶν
ἐναντίων. The customary times of payment are also unknown,
but they would appear to have been monthly, from Theophr.
Char. 30: καὶ τὸν Ἀνθεστηριῶνα τὸν ὅλον μὴ πέμπειν αὐτοὺς
(τοὺς παῖδας) εἰς τὰ μαθήματα διὰ τὸ θέας εἶναι πολλὰς, ἵνα μὴ τὸν
μισθὸν ἐκτίνῃ. A deduction would seem to have been made, pro-
portionate to the time of absence, *Ib.*: καὶ τῶν υἱῶν δὲ μὴ πορευομέ-
νων εἰς τὸ διδασκαλεῖον διὰ τὴν ἀρρωστίαν ἀφαιρεῖν τοῦ μισθοῦ
κατὰ λόγον. Cf. Liban. *Orat.* xxxii. p. 269. At all events, there
appears to have been much irregularity in this matter. So
Demosth. *in Aphob.* i. p. 828, complains that the school account
of Aphobos had run on unpaid during the whole time of his
minority : ὥστε καὶ τοὺς διδασκάλους τοὺς μισθοὺς ἀπεστέρηκε.

At Athens the number of pupils would seem to have been restricted by law. See Æschin. *in Timarch.* p. 34 : πρῶτον μὲν ἣν
ὥραν προσήκει ἰέναι τὸν παῖδα τὸν ἐλεύθερον εἰς τὸ διδασκαλεῖον·
ἔπειτα μετὰ πόσων παίδων εἰσιέναι. We read of a school at Asty-
palæa numbering about sixty boys : ἐνταῦθα ὅσον ἑξήκοντα
ἀριθμὸν παῖδες. Pausan. vi. 9, 3. Sometimes the number ran
very low. In the school of Stratonicos (who, however, taught
the *cithara*, and not grammar) were figures of the nine Muses, one
Apollo, and two pupils, and when asked how many pupils he
had, his reply was, Σὺν τοῖς θεοῖς δώδεκα. Athen. viii. p. 348.
See also Diog. Laert. vi. 69. Many schools were elegantly furnished. The βάθροι were benches for the pupils, probably rising
one above another; whether there were also a θρόνος, like that
from which the Sophists addressed their audience, is uncertain.

Justin, xxi. 5, relates of Dionysius; 'novissime ludimagistrum professus pueros in trivio docebat ;' and this has given rise to the opinion that teaching in the roads and crossways was of common occurrence; but the notion will certainly not hold good of Athens, notwithstanding that Dio Chrysost. *Orat.* xx. p. 264, says, οἱ γὰρ τῶν γραμμάτων διδάσκαλοι μετὰ τῶν παίδων ἐν ταῖς ὁδοῖς κάθηνται. The proverb, ἐκ τριόδου, e trivio, said of anything very common and ordinary, had a different origin, such a spot being συχνῶς πεπατημένον. See Lucian, *de morte Peregrin.* 3.

Instruction began with the early morning, children as well as adults rising at this time. So Plato, *Leg.* vii. p. 808 : ἡμέρας δὲ ὄρθρου τε ἐπανιόντων παῖδας μὲν πρὸς διδασκάλους που τρέπεσθαι χρεών. A law of Solon's enacts that the schools should open μὴ πρότερον ἡλίου ἀνιόντος, and close again, πρὸ ἡλίου δύνοντος. Æschin. *in Timarch.* p. 37. We learn from Thucyd. vii. 29, that this was the case elsewhere; for he tells us that the Thracians surprised Mycalessos ἅμα τῇ ἡμέρᾳ, and butchered the children assembled in a school, ὅπερ μέγιστον ἦν αὐτόθι. It appears also from the law above cited that the schools were opened again in the afternoon, μετὰ τὸ ἄριστον· and so also Lucian, *de Parasito*, 61, says : καί σοι λοιπὸν, ὥσπερ οἱ παῖδες, ἀφίξομαι καὶ ἑῷος, καὶ μετ' ἄριστον, μαθησόμενος τὴν τέχνην. See Excursus on *The Gymnasia.*

Instruction was in three branches : γράμματα, μουσικὴ, γυμναστική. Plato, *Theag.* p. 122 : οὐκ ἐδιδάξετό σε ὁ πατὴρ καὶ ἐπαίδευσεν, ἅπερ ἐνθάδε οἱ ἄλλοι παιδεύονται οἱ τῶν καλῶν κἀγαθῶν υἱεῖς; οἷον γράμματά τε καὶ κιθαρίζειν καὶ παλαίειν καὶ τὴν ἄλλην ἀγωνίαν. Plutarch, *de Audit.* 17 : ἐν γράμμασι καὶ περὶ λύραν καὶ παλαίστραν. Cf. Plato, *Clitoph.* p. 407. But the chief passage is in Aristotle, *de Republ.* viii. 3, who adds a fourth branch, drawing or painting : ἔστι δὲ τέτταρα σχεδὸν, ἃ παιδεύειν εἰώθασι, γράμματα καὶ γυμναστικὴν, καὶ μουσικὴν, καὶ τέταρτον ἔνιοι γραφικήν . . . . δοκεῖ δὲ καὶ γραφικὴ χρήσιμος εἶναι πρὸς τὸ κρίνειν τὰ τῶν τεχνιτῶν ἔργα κάλλιον. We will first consider the γράμματα, as being the most indispensable part of instruction ; for, as is evident from the context, we must take in a higher sense the words of Isocrates, *Panathen.* 83, who says, speaking of the Spartans, οὐδὲ γράμματα μανθάνουσιν. Cf. Plutarch, *Lyc.* 16. In its simplest signification, γράμματα comprehended reading,

writing, and arithmetic. See, however, Plato, *Leg.* vii. p. 809.
In learning to read, the method of dividing into syllables, συλλα-
βίζειν, was used. Dionys. Halic. *de admir. vi dic. in Demosth.*
52 : ταύτην γὰρ (τὴν γραμματικὴν) ὅταν ἐκμάθωμεν, πρῶτον μὲν
τὰ ὀνόματα τῶν στοιχείων τῆς φωνῆς ἀναλαμβάνομεν, ἃ καλεῖται
γράμματα. ἔπειτα τύπους τ᾽ αὐτῶν καὶ δυνάμεις. ὅταν δὲ ταῦτα
μάθωμεν, τότε τὰς συλλαβὰς αὐτῶν καὶ τὰ περὶ ταῦτα πάθη. After
mastering this, the pupils were next instructed on the component
portions of a sentence : κρατήσαντες δὲ τούτων τὰ τοῦ λόγου μόρια·
ὀνόματα λέγω, καὶ ῥήματα, καὶ συνδέσμους ; and then they commenced reading, properly so called : ὅταν δὲ τὴν τούτων ἁπάντων
ἐπιστήμην περιλάβωμεν, τότ᾽ ἀρχόμεθα γράφειν τε καὶ ἀναγινώσκειν, κατὰ συλλαβὴν μὲν καὶ βραδέως τὸ πρῶτον. See Athenæus,
x. p. 453, where we have a metrical alphabet :

> Ἔστ᾽ ἄλφα, βῆτα, γάμμα, δέλτα, θεοῦ πάρ᾽ εἶ,
> ζῆτ᾽, ἦτα, θῆτ᾽, ἰῶτα, κάππα, λάμβδα, μῦ,
> νῦ, ξῦ, τὸ οὖ, πῖ, ῥῶ, τὸ σὰν,, ταῦ ὒ παρὸν,
> φῖ, χῖ τε τῷ ψῖ εἰς τὸ ὦ.

And he then proceeds : ὁ χορὸς δὲ γυναικῶν ἐκ τῶν σύνδυο πεποιημένος αὐτῷ ἐστιν ἔμμετρος ἅμα καὶ μεμελοπεποιημένος τόνδε τὸν
τρόπον· βῆτα ἄλφα βα, βῆτα εἶ βε, βῆτα ἦ βη, βῆτα ἰῶτα βί,
βῆτα οὖ βο, βῆτα ὒ βυ, βῆτα ὦ βῶ. καὶ πάλιν ἐν ἀντιστρόφῳ τοῦ
μέλους καὶ τοῦ μέτρου, γάμμα ἄλφα, γάμμα εἶ, γάμμα ἰῶτα, γάμμα
εὖ, γάμμα ὒ, γάμμα ὦ. καὶ ἐπὶ τῶν λοιπῶν συλλαβῶν ὁμοίως ἑκάστων. There are some interesting passages relating to writing
and ciphering. Copies were given by the teachers ; Plato, *Prot.*
p. 326 : ὑπογράψαντες γραμμὰς τῇ γραφίδι. Plato, however, requires but a small degree of facility in reading as well as writing.
Leg. vii. p. 810 : γράμματα μὲν τοίνυν χρὴ τὸ μέχρι τοῦ γράψαι
τε καὶ ἀναγνῶναι δυνατὸν εἶναι διαπονεῖν· πρὸς τάχος δὲ ἢ κάλλος
ἀπηκριβῶσθαί τισιν, οἷς μὴ φύσις ἐπέσπευσεν ἐν τοῖς τεταγμένοις
ἔτεσι χαίρειν ἐᾶν. Plato, *ibid.* p. 1819, thinks arithmetic should
be learnt as an amusement, and that the abstract ideas of numbers should be presented in as concrete a form as possible, by the
use of apples and the like. Otherwise the fingers were ordinarily
used, not only at school, but in every-day life, or when more
accuracy was needed, counters, ψῆθοι. Aristoph. *Vesp.* 656 :

> καὶ πρῶτον μὲν λόγισαι φαύλως μὴ ψήφοις, ἀλλ᾽ ἀπὸ χειρός.

Cf. Theophr. *Char.* 14 ; 23 ; 24. These ψῆφοι varied in value

according to their place on the counting-board. Polyb. v. 26 :
ἐκεῖναί τε γὰρ κατὰ τὴν τοῦ ψηφίζοντος βούλησιν ἄρτι χαλκοῦν καὶ
παραυτίκα τάλαντον ἴσχουσιν. See also a *bon-mot* ascribed to
Solon by Diog. Laert. i. 59 : ἔλεγε δὲ τοὺς παρὰ τοῖς τυράννοις
δυναμένους παραπλησίους εἶναι ταῖς ψήφοις ἐπὶ τῶν λογισμῶν.
καὶ γὰρ ἐκείνων ἑκάστην ποτὲ μὲν πλείω σημαίνειν, ποτὲ δὲ ἥττω.
See also Plutarch, *Apoph. reg.* p. 691 : καθάπερ οἱ τῶν ἀριθμητι-
κῶν δάκτυλοι νῦν μὲν μυριάδας, νῦν δὲ μονάδα τιθέναι δύνανται,
κ. τ. λ. The fingers were also used to express numbers by
placing them in different positions. Alciph. *Epist.* 26 : οἱ περὶ
τὰς ψύφους καὶ τῶν δακτύλων τὰς κάμψεις εἰλινδούμενοι.

When the children could read, and understand what they read,
the works of the poets were put in requisition, to exercise their
minds, and awaken their hearts to great and noble deeds. Plato,
Leg. vii. p. 810, approves of this, and also recommends commit-
ting whole poems, or select passages, to memory ; and this method
of instruction appears to have been universal ; see Strabo, i. 2, 3 :
λέγουσι πρώτην τὴν ποιητικὴν . . . καὶ τοὺς παῖδας αἱ τῶν Ἑλλήνων
πόλεις πρώτιστα διὰ τῆς ποιητικῆς παιδεύουσι. See too the discourse of Protagoras, Plato, *Prot.* p. 326 : οἱ δὲ διδάσκαλοι τούτων
τε ἐπιμελοῦνται, καὶ ἐπειδὰν αὖ γράμματα μάθωσι καὶ μέλλωσι
ξυνήσειν τὰ γεγραμμένα, ὥσπερ τότε τὴν φωνὴν, παρατιθέασιν
αὐτοῖς ἐπὶ τῶν βάθρων ἀναγιγνώσκειν ποιητῶν ἀγαθῶν ποιήματα,
καὶ ἐκμανθάνειν ἀναγκάζουσιν. Above all, the poems of Homer
were thought to contain, by precept and example, every thing
calculated to awaken national spirit, and to instruct a man how
to be καλὸς κἀγαθός. See Isocr. *Paneg.* 95. So in Xenoph.
Symp. 3, 5, Niceratos says of himself: Ὁ πατὴρ ἐπιμελούμενος
ὅπως ἀνὴρ ἀγαθὸς γενοίμην, ἠνάγκασέ με πάντα τὰ Ὁμήρου ἔπη
μαθεῖν· καὶ νῦν δυναίμην ἂν Ἰλιάδα ὅλην καὶ Ὀδύσσειαν ἀπὸ στόματος εἰπεῖν. For the continuance of the custom in later times,
see Dio Chrysost. *Orat.* xi. p. 308 : κἀκεῖνον μὲν (Ὁμηρον) ὑπολαβ-
εῖν θεῖον ἄνδρα καὶ σοφὸν, καὶ τοὺς παῖδας εὐθὺς ἐξ ἀρχῆς τὰ ἔπη
διδάσκειν.

The study of music began somewhat later; according to
Plato, with the thirteenth year. *Leg.* vii. p. 809. Aristotle, *de
Republ.* viii. 3, speaks admirably of the study of music, as considered from the point of view of his own time; he says it should
not merely be pursued ἡδονῆς χάριν, which he confesses mostly

to be the case, but πρὸς τὴν ἐν τῇ σχολῇ διαγωγὴν, or in order
καλῶς σχολάζειν. It was not a necessary portion of the παιδεια,
οὐχ ὡς ἀναγκαῖον (οὐδὲν γὰρ ἔχει τοιοῦτον) οὐδ' ὡς χρήσιμον,
ὥσπερ τὰ γράμματα, but was accounted a noble and worthy
occupation (ἐλευθέριον καὶ καλὴν) for the hours of recreation and
leisure. The λύρα or κιθάρα, for the distinction is sometimes
neglected, were the chief, or rather the only, instruments which
were thought suited for an ἐλεύθερος. At one period, at Athens,
the flute also was a great favourite, but it soon fell into disuse,
not only because it distorted the face, but especially because it
did not allow the accompaniment of the voice. Aristot. de
Republ. viii. 6. To this victory of the lyra over the flute, the
myth of Marsyas unquestionably alludes. These observations,
however, apply chiefly to Athens, for elsewhere, as at Thebes,
the flute maintained its ground. Maxim. Tyr. Diss. xxiii. 2 :
Θηβαῖοι αὐλητικὴν ἐπιτηδεύουσι, καὶ ἔστιν ἡ δι' αὐλῶν μοῦσα
ἐπιχώριος τοῖς Βοιωτοῖς. Cf. Plutarch, Pelop. 19.

There is no mention of regular vacations at fixed intervals,
though naturally the numerous public festivals, as for example
those in the month Anthesterion, would cause holidays at the
schools. Theophr. Char. 30. There was a law of Solon's which
is mentioned by Æschines, in Timarch. p. 35, περὶ Μουσείων ἐι
τοῖς διδασκαλείοις, καὶ περὶ Ἑρμαίων ἐν ταῖς παλαίστραις, which
Wolf and Reiske have wrongly interpreted of the sacella Musa-
rum, whereas Pollux, i. 37, in the section on the festivals, says,
Μουσῶν Μουσεῖα, Ἑρμοῦ Ἑρμαῖα (ἑορταί): so that most probably such festivals are meant as were obligatory by law. Cf.
Plato, Lysis, p. 206. At all events the Greeks knew nothing
of a four-months' summer-vacation, which K. F. Hermann has,
on very doubtful grounds, assumed for the Roman, or rather the
Italian youth generally. In particular cases, as when the teacher
was unwell, a notice, πρόγραμμα, was posted up on the door.
Lucian, Hermotim. 11 : πινάκιον γάρ τι ἐκρέματο ὑπὲρ τοῦ πυ-
λῶνος, μεγάλοις γράμμασι, λέγον, τήμερον οὐ συμφιλοσοφεῖν.

Attendance at school was continued till the pupils reached
riper years in the Greek sense, which would generally be at the
age of sixteen. Lucian says that he ceased going to school ἤδη
τὴν ἡλικίαν πρόσηβος ὤν : but of course the time might vary as
it does among ourselves; the poorer classes putting their children

early to some trade, whilst the wealthier kept theirs at school
longer; and this is expressly asserted by Plato, *Protag.* p. 326.
This more advanced instruction was imparted by teachers of a
higher order, the Rhetoricians and Sophists, whose charges only
the rich could defray. Thus Aristippos demanded one thousand
drachmæ (Plutarch, *de Educ. Puer.* 7 ; Diog. Laert. ii. 72), and
according to Plutarch, *Dec. Orat. vit.* 4, Isocrates required a like
sum ; and when Demosthenes offered him two hundred, ἐφ' ᾧ τε
τὸ πέμπτον μέρος ἐκμάθῃ, he answered, οὐ τεμαχίζομεν, ὦ Δη-
μόσθενες, τὴν πραγματείαν· ὥσπερ δὲ τοὺς καλοὺς ἰχθῦς ὅλους
πωλοῦμεν, οὕτω κἀγώ σοι, εἰ βούλοιο μαθητεύειν, ὁλόκληρον ἀπο-
δώσομαι τὴν τέχνην. The same author tells us: οὐκ αἰσχύνονται
τέτταρας ἢ πέντε μνᾶς ὑπὲρ τούτων αἰτοῦντες. See also Böckh's
Public Econ. of Athens, pp. 121, 122. The Sophists seem to
have insisted most rigidly on their fees, without abating one jot
to their poorer pupils. See a lively, though of course highly-
coloured scene in Lucian, *Hermotim.* 9 : ἐκεῖνον αὐτὸν, ἐπεὶ τὸν
μισθὸν, οἶμαι, μὴ ἀπεδίδου κατὰ καιρὸν, ἀπήγαγε παρὰ τὸν ἄρχοντα ἔναγχος, περιθείς γε αὐτῷ θοιμάτιον περὶ τὸν τράχηλον, καὶ
ἐβόα, καὶ ὠργίζετο, καὶ εἰ μὴ τῶν σανήθων τινὲς ἐν μέσῳ γειόμενοι
ἀφείλοντο τὸν νεανίσκον ἐκ τῶν χειρῶν αὐτοῦ, εὖ ἴσθι, προσφὺς ἂν
ἀπέτραγεν αὐτοῦ τὴν ῥῖνα ὁ γέρων, οὕτω ἠγανάκτει. But this did
not prevent the lovers of knowledge from purchasing their instruction even at the greatest sacrifices. Thus Cleanthes (Diog.
Laert. vii. 168), and Menedemos and Asclepiades (Athen. iv.
p. 168), worked by night in gardens and mills, in order to be
able to attend by day the classes of the philosophers.

This account of the method of instruction applies chiefly to
Athens itself, but of course there were schools in the small towns
and villages. Thus Protagoras was said in early life, διδάσκειν
ἐν κώμῃ τινὶ γράμματα. Athen. viii. p. 354. Little is known
of the schools of other cities, but the παιδεία, except at Sparta,
was in the main the same. Theophr. *Char.* proem., πάντων τῶν
Ἑλλήνων ὁμοίως παιδευομένων. With the Spartans mental culture was a secondary consideration, and Aristotle, *de Republ.*
viii. 4, justly upbraids them for bringing up their offspring like
animals, θηριώδεις ἀπεργάζονται, though this perhaps applies
rather to a later period. Ælian, *Var. Hist.* xii. 50, says, certainly without ground : Λακεδαιμόνιοι μουσικῆς ἀπείρως εἶχον,

κ. τ. λ. With regard to Thebes, we have a sad report from Aristophanes the Bœotian, apud Plutarch. *de Herod. Malig.* 31. Herodotus wished to open a school there, τοῖς νέοις διαλέγεσθαι καὶ συσχολάζειν, but the magistrates forbade him : ὑπὸ τῶν ἀρχόντων ἐκωλύθη δι᾽ ἀγροικίαν αὐτῶν καὶ μισολογίαν. Dio Chrysost. *Orat.* x. p. 306, makes Diogenes express himself in still severer terms : ἐγὼ δὲ ἤκουσα λέγοντος, ὅτι ἡ Σφίγξ ἡ ἀμαθία ἐστί. ταύτην οὖν καὶ πρότερον διαφθεῖραι τοὺς Βοιωτούς, καὶ νῦν, οὐδὲν αὐτοὺς ἐῶσαν εἰδέναι, ἅτε ἀνθρώπων ἀμαθεστάτους. Whatever measure of truth these accounts may contain, it is at least certain that less was done at Thebes for education than at Athens, for otherwise the more sensible Theban parents would not have sent their sons to school at Athens, as they did. See Æschin. *Epist.* 12, p. 699.

All that has been said hitherto refers to the instruction of the boys merely. We nowhere hear anything of educational institutions for girls ; and, indeed, they would have been incompatible with the universal training of the female sex. Plato, it is granted, desires to have gymnasia for the boys and girls, separate of course. *Leg.* vi. p. 764 : γυμνάσια καὶ διδασκαλεῖα ἀρρένων καὶ κορῶν : and so again ὀρχηστὰς for the boys, and ὀρχηστρίδας for the girls ; *Ib.* viii. p. 813 ; but this is nothing more than a proposition, and was never actually carried out. In Terent. *Phorm.* i. 2, 36, a girl goes, it is true. *in ludum* ; but she is a Citharistria, the property of a *leno,* and she goes thither to learn to play on the cithara. For the free daughter of a burgher to have frequented a school out of her father's house would have been repugnant to every notion of feminine decorum ; so that the meagre instruction they received was at the hands of the mother or the nurses.

Outward propriety, εὐκοσμία, was especially attended to. Plato, *Protag.* p. 326 : μετὰ δὲ ταῦτα εἰς διδασκάλων πέμποντες πολὺ μᾶλλον ἐντέλλονται ἐπιμελεῖσθαι εὐκοσμίας τῶν παίδων, ἢ γραμμάτων τε καὶ κιθαρίσεως. Various minute points of etiquette, such as taking the victuals with the right hand, and so forth, were rigidly enforced by the pedagogue on his pupil. See Plutarch, *Virt. doceri posse,* 2 : καὶ αὐτοὶ διδάσκουσιν οἱ παιδαγωγοὶ κεκυφότας ἐν ταῖς ὁδοῖς περιπατεῖν, ἑνὶ δακτύλῳ τὸ τάριχος ἅψασθαι, δυσὶ δ᾽ ἰχθὺν, σῖτον, κρέας, οὕτω κνᾶσθαι, τὸ ἱμάτιον οὕτως ἀναλαβεῖν. Also Id. *de Educ. Puer.* 7 : τῇ μὲν δεξιᾷ συνεθίζειν τὰ παιδία δέχεσθαι τὰς τροφὰς, κἂν προτείνειε τὴν ἀριστερὰν, ἐπιτιμᾶν. Cf. Id. *de Fort.* 5 : τοὺς παῖδας διδάσκομεν τῇ δεξιᾷ λαμβάνειν τοῦ ὄψου, τῇ δὲ ἀριστερᾷ κρατεῖν τὸν ἄρτον. This custom of always using the right hand for everything is ridiculed by Plato, *Leg.* vii. p. 794, and to this Aristotle alludes, *De Republ.* ii. 12. When walking in the streets, boys were required to look straight before them on the ground, with head downcast, κεκυφότες, as Plutarch says. See Diog. Laert. v. 82. Modesty and respect towards their elders was one of the first duties inculcated on youth. Plato, *Leg.* ix. p. 879 : πᾶς ἡμῖν αἰδείσθω τὸν ἑαυτοῦ πρεσβύτερον ἔργῳ τε καὶ ἔπει. He also assumes, as a matter of course, that νεώτεροι should be silent in the presence of their seniors. *De Republ.* iv. p. 426 : σιγᾶς νεωτέρων παρὰ πρεσβυτέροις, ὡς πρέπει. See a pretty fragment of Menander, in Plutarch, *de San. Tuend.* 18. There is no finer instance of this juvenile αἰδὼς than that of Autolycos in Xenophon's *Symposion*, 3, 12. He takes no part in the conversation, and the blushing modesty with which he replies to a question is very beautifully depicted. That Autolycos is present at a banquet, away from his father's house, is quite an exception to the general custom, the reason being that his ἐραστὴς has given the banquet in honour of his victory, νικητήρια ἑστιᾷ. He also leaves earlier than the rest, Αὐτόλυκος δὲ, ἤδη γὰρ ὥρα ἦν αὐτῷ, ἐξανίστατο εἰς περίπατον. When the father entertained guests at home, the son sometimes appeared and *sat* at table—the adults *reclined*, Αὐτόλυκος μὲν οὖν παρὰ τὸν πατέρα ἐκαθέζετο, οἱ δ' ἄλλοι, ὥσπερ εἰκὸς, κατεκλίθησαν, but even this did not usually take place (Theophr. *Char.* 5); and the children were often sent away to the women's apartments for want of room. Lucian, *Somn. seu Gall.* 11 : τὸν υἱὸν γὰρ ἐγὼ κελεύσω ἐν τῇ γυναικωνίτιδι μετὰ τῆς μητρὸς ἑστιαθῆναι, ὡς σὺ χώραν ἔχῃς.

In more ancient times it was accounted highly improper for youths, even long after they had emerged from childhood, to take part in public business. This was strictly observed at Sparta. Plutarch, *Lyc.* 25 : Οἱ μέν γε νεώτεροι τριάκοντα ἐτῶν τὸ παράπαν οὐ κατέβαινον εἰς ἀγοράν. At Athens this was not so rigorously the case, yet the feeling of αἰδὼς acted as a

powerful restraint. See Lysias, *in Theomnest.* p. 346; Æschin.
in Timarch. p. 178. But matters had somewhat changed in the
time of Æschines. Isocrates, *Areop.* 18, p. 202, praises the good
old ways: οὕτω δ' ἔφευγον τὴν ἀγορὰν, ὥστε εἰ καί ποτε διελθεῖν
ἀναγκασθεῖεν, με‑ὰ πολλῆς αἰδοῦς καὶ σωφροσύνης ἐφαίνοντο τοῦτο
ποιοῦντες. So Isæus, *de Hered. Cleonym.* p. 2 : καὶ τότε μὲν
οὕτως ὑπ' αὐτοῦ (τοῦ πατρὸς) σωφρόνως ἐπαιδευόμεθα, ὥστ' οὐδὲ
ἀκροασόμενοι οὐδέποτε ἤλθομεν ἐπὶ δικαστήριον. Xenophon
Mem. iv. 2, 1, mentions Euthydemos, διὰ νεότητα οὔπω εἰς τὴν
ἀγορὰν εἰσιόντα. The change may in fact be considered to date
from the Peloponnesian war, and hence the complaint of Andocides, *in Alcib.* p. 123 : τοιγάρτοι τῶν νέων αἱ διατριβαὶ οὐκ ἐν
τοῖς γυμνασίοις, ἀλλ' ἐν τοῖς δικαστηρίοις εἰσίν. Aristophanes is
very bitter on the alterations in education generally, contrasting the old habits with the new, in the dialogue between
the Δίκαιος and Ἄδικος λόγος. *Nubes,* 960–994. Lastly, we
may refer to the beautiful portrait of the modest daily life of a
well-ordered youth, as drawn by Lucian, *Amor.* 44 : ὄρθριος
ἀναστὰς ἐκ τῆς ἀζύγου κοίτης τὸν ἐπὶ τῶν ὀμμάτων ἔτι λοιπὸν
ὕπνου ἀπονιψάμενος ὕδατι λιτῷ, καὶ χιτωνίσκον καὶ χλανίδα ταῖς
ἐπωμίαις περόναις συρράψας ἀπὸ τῆς πατρῴας ἑστίας ἐξέρχεται
κάτω κεκυφὼς, καὶ μηδένα τῶν ἀπαντώντων ἐξ ἐναντίου προσβλε-
πων. ἀκόλουθοι δὲ καὶ παιδαγωγοὶ, χορὸς αὐτῷ κόσμιος, ἕπονται
τα σεμνὰ τῆς ἀρετῆς ἐν χερσὶν ὄργανα κρατοῦντες, οὐ πριστοῦ
κτενὸς ἐντομὰς κόμην καταψήχειν δυναμένας, οὐδ' ἔσοπτρα τῶν
ἀντιμόρφων χαρακτήρων ἀγράφους εἰκόιας, ἀλλ' ἢ πολύπτυχοι
δέλτοι κατόπιν ἀκολουθοῦσιν, ἢ παλαιῶν ἔργων ἀρετὰς φυλάτ-
τουσαι βίβλοι. κἂν εἰς Μουσικοῦ δέοι φοιτᾶν, εὐμελὴς λύρα.
But this picture could hardly have been applicable to many
young persons even in earlier times; while such an example of
premature debauchery as Alcibiades presented, (Lysias, *in Alcib.*
p. 536,) must have doubtless exercised a most baneful influence
on the Attic youth. At Athens, there was no lack of *gamins,*
ready for any piece of mischief that might turn up. See Demosth. *adv. Nicostr.* p. 1251.

With his sixteenth year, the Athenian youth entered on a transition period, which lasted two years, and during which he had to
pay particular attention to the exercises of the gymnasium. This
is the time during which Lucian calls himself πρόσηβος, though

the general expression for this interval was ἐπὶ διετὲς ἡβῆσαι. When these two years had elapsed, the youth was admitted among the ephebi, and, with the exception of having to serve the state until his twentieth year as περίπολος, he now entered at once on a freer course of action, and, at least if he belonged to the upper classes, he could follow his own inclination in the selection of an occupation. Many fathers of substantial means endeavoured to bring up their sons to business, as is clear from the comic poets; but those youths who could afford it mostly devoted themselves to the pursuit of pleasure;—to the chase, charioteering, and the company of hetæræ,—or they became disciples of the philosophers; and no passage is clearer on this head than Terent. *Andr.* i. 1, 28:

> Quod plerique omnes faciunt adolescentuli,
> Ut animum ad aliquod studium adjungant, aut equos
> Alere, aut canes ad venandum, aut ad philosophos, etc.

See Plaut. *Merc.* Prol. 40, 61; and Xenoph. *Memor.* i. 6, 14: ὥσπερ ἄλλος τις ἢ ἵππῳ ἀγαθῷ, ἢ κυνὶ, ἢ ὄρνιθι ἥδεται. Nor must we omit the passionate fondness for cock and quail-fighting, and on rearing these birds immense pains were frequently bestowed. The state had no objection to all these amusements; nay, the Areopagus urged the rich to pursue them, quite as much as it did the poor to labour, Isocr. *Areopag.* 17, p. 201: τοὺς δὲ βίον ἱκανὸν κεκτημένους περί τε ἱππικὴν καὶ τὰ γυμνάσια, καὶ κυνηγέσια καὶ τὴν φιλοσοφίαν ἠνάγκασαν διατρίβειν. It was regarded with favour, not only as a harmless way of diverting the unruly passions of youth, but because, if they obtained prizes at the Olympian or other games, they opened a source of honour and renown to the state. Isocr. *de Big.* 14, p. 509: τὰς πόλεις ὀνομαστὰς γιγνομένας τῶν νικώντων. Lysias, *de Bon. Aristoph.* p. 661: αὐτίκα ὅτε ἵππευεν, οὐ μόνον ἵππους ἐκτήσατο λαμπροὺς, ἀλλὰ καὶ ἀθλητὰς ἐνίκησεν Ἰσθμοῖ καὶ Νεμέᾳ. ὥστε τὴν πόλιν κηρυχθῆναι καὶ αὐτὸν στεφανωθῆναι.

In Sparta, where every individual pursuit was entirely discouraged, and where all were brought up after *one* rule, and for the state, there was but little scope for indulging these private tastes. There, also, the youth became a man of eighteen; but the name now imposed upon him, εἴρην, which means ἄρχων generally, sufficiently denotes his position among the public. Plutarch, *Lyc.* 17: Εἴρενας δὲ καλοῦσι τοὺς ἔτος ἤδη δεύτερον ἐκ παίδων γεγονότας· μελλείρενας δὲ τῶν παίδων τοὺς πρεσβυτάτους. Οὗτος

οὖν ὁ εἴρην εἴκοσιν ἔτη γεγονὼς ἄρχει τε τῶν ὑποτεταγμένων ἐν
ταῖς μάχαις, καὶ κατ᾽ οἶκον ὑπηρέταις χρῆται πρὸς τὸ δεῖπνον.
See Müller's *Dorians*, ii. p. 309, Note.

The chief works on Grecian pædagogy, besides Göss, *die
Erziehungswissenschaft nach den Grundsätzen der Griechen und
Römer*, are Friedr. Cramer, *Gesch. der Erziehung und des Un-
terrichts im Alterth.*, and the *Erziehungslehre* of Schwarz. A
small work by Adolph Cramer, *de Educatione Puerorum apud
Athenienses*, is better than either; but the most ingenious, though
it occasionally sacrifices reality to an ideal, is *die Erziehung der
Hellenen zur Sittlichkeit*, by Fr. Jacobs.

EXCURSUS TO SCENE II

THE HETÆRÆ.

IN a general survey of Greek customs, it will be impossible to omit giving an account of a class of the community which the moderns have denounced as most abandoned, and have branded with the utmost contumely; this will be apparent to any one who has merely gained from the Roman comic poets a faint notion of the prominent position which the hetæræ occupied in Grecian life After the excellent treatise on this subject by Jacobs, it might be supposed that further elucidation was needless; but that writer, vivid and truthful though his sketch may be, instead of investigating the matter in all its bearings, has preferred to dwell on the brighter side of his subject. The present writer, on the contrary, has determined not to shrink from a further scrutiny; his intention in this work being to paint the individual traits of character, and not to omit even the minutest features requisite to complete the picture.

In one point he certainly differs from Jacobs, namely, as to the expression of public opinion on the intercourse of married men with hetæræ. Doubtless it was the young unmarried men who chiefly indulged in this vice; but it is also true that men frequently resorted to their old practices after marriage, and this without losing grade in the popular opinion, unless they threw aside all propriety and respect for their wives, as was the case with Alcibiades. Andoc. *in Alcib.* p. 117. In no instance are such proceedings reprehended, but, on the contrary, the language held everywhere plainly shows that it was considered nothing uncommon. See Demosth. *in Neær.* p. 1351. Plato himself, who, in his ideal State, wished to see realised much that was impracticable, nevertheless despaired of the possibility of restricting his citizens to the lawful intercourse of marriage. *Leg.* viii. p. 841. The manner in which these vices were regarded by the women is seen from Aristoph. *Eccles.* 720 :

ΠΡ. ἔπειτα τὰς πόρνας καταπαῦσαι βούλομαι
  ἀπαξαπάσας. ΒΛ. ἵνα τί ; ΠΡ. δῆλον τουτογί·
  ἵνα τῶν νέων ἔχωμεν αὐταὶ τὰς ἀκμάς.
  καὶ τάς γε δούλας οὐχὶ δεῖ κοσμουμένας
  τὴν τῶν ἐλευθέρων ὑφαρπάζειν Κύπριν.

But although the wife could, and often did, reproach her offending
husband, yet probably she could not institute a κακώσεως δίκη
against him.   The instances adduced by Petit, *Leg. Att.* p. 543,
have no reference to hetæræ, and the only passage which is
clearly in point is Alciph. *Epist.* i. 6, where the wife says to
her husband : ἢ οὖν πέπαυσο τῆς ἀγερωχίας. . . . ἢ ἴσθι με παρὰ
τὸν πατέρα οἰχησομένην, ὃς οὐδ᾽ ἐμὲ περιόψεται, καὶ σὲ γράψε-
ται παρὰ τοῖς δικασταῖς κακώσεως.   But here, in addition to the
other causes of complaint, the husband had entirely neglected
his family ; and it would be rash to build an hypothesis on a
single testimony, especially on one of such a date as that just
referred to.   We have moreover the testimony of Plautus, that
the exact contrary was the case; *Merc.* iv. 6, 3 :

> Nam si vir scortum duxit clam uxorem suam,
> Id si rescivit uxor, impune est viro.
> Uxor viro si clam domo egressa est foras,
> Viro fit causa: exigitur matrimonio.
> Utinam lex esset eadem, quæ uxori est, viro.

The public opinion with reference to the intercourse of men with
hetæræ is well illustrated by the decision of the diætetes in the
case of Neæra, to whom both Phrynion and Stephanos laid claim ;
Demosth. *in Neær.* p. 1360 : συνεῖναι δ᾽ ἑκατέρῳ ἡμέραν παρ᾽ ἡμέραν, *Ib.* p. 1361 : κατὰ τάδε διήλλαξαν Φρυνίωνα καὶ Στέφανον,
χρῆσθαι ἑκάτερον Νεαίρᾳ τὰς ἴσας ἡμέρας τοῦ μηνὸς παρ᾽ ἑαυτοῖς
ἔχοντας.

The prevalence of the fear of having a large family, which is
shown by the frequency of the exposure of infants, as well as an
addiction to sensual enjoyments, were both prominent features in
the Greek character, though apt to be discordant in their results ;
and it must not be denied, that in the period of their greatest
refinement, sensuality, if not the mother, was, at all events, the
nurse, of the Greek perception of the beautiful.   A curious proof
of this is afforded by the artifice by which Hyperides procured a
verdict in Phryne's favour, by suddenly rending her garment, and
displaying her beautiful bust before the judges.   See Plutarch,
Dec. Orat. Vit. 9 ; Athen. xiii. p. 590 ; Alciph. *Epist.* 30, 31, 32.

It was thus by an Attic euphemism that those females who did not belong to the very lowest class were termed ἑταῖραι rather than πόρναι. Plutarch, *Solon*, 15 ; Athen. xiii. p. 571 : καλοῦσι δὲ καὶ τὰς μισθαρνούσας ἑταίρας καὶ τὸ ἐπὶ συνουσίαις μισθαρνεῖν ἑταιρεῖν, οὐκ ἔτι πρὸς τὸ ἔτυμον ἀναφέροντες, ἀλλὰ πρὸς τὸ εὐσχημονέστερον.

Jacobs is right in his remark that these women, with the exception of the Milesian Aspasia, were never respected ; though the more decent portion of them were not exactly despised. It will be convenient to class them in certain grades and divisions. The lowest were the common prostitutes kept in the public πορνεῖα, state-institutions, which were first established by Solon. Athen. xiii. p. 569 : καὶ Φιλήμων δ' ἐν Ἀδελφοῖς προσιστορῶν ὅτι πρῶτος Σόλων διὰ τὴν τῶν νέων ἀκμὴν ἔστησεν ἐπὶ οἰκημάτων γύναια πριάμενος. The passage of Philemon here referred to is as follows :

> καί μοι λέγειν τοῦτ' ἐστὶν ἁρμοστὸν, Σόλων,
> μεστὴν ὁρῶντα τὴν πόλιν νεωτέρων.
> τούτους τ' ἔχοντας τὴν ἀναγκαίαν φύσιν
> ἁμαρτάνοντάς τ' εἰς ὃ μὴ προσῆκον ἦν,
> στῆσαι πριάμενόν τοι γυναῖκας κατὰ τόπους
> κοινὰς, ἅπασι καὶ κατεσκευασμένας.

Cf. Dio Chrysost. *Orat.* vii. p. 271. The state also countenanced the proceedings of all such females by levying a tax upon them, which was annually farmed out. The evidence on this point is satisfactory and conclusive ; Æschin. *in Timarch.* p. 134 : θαυμάζει γὰρ εἰ μὴ πάντες μέμνησθ', ὅτι καθ' ἕκαστον ἐνιαυτὸν ἡ βουλὴ πωλεῖ τὸ πορνικὸν τέλος · καὶ τοὺς πριαμένους τὸ τέλος τοῦτο οὐκ εἰκάζειν, ἀλλ' ἀκριβῶς εἰδέναι τοὺς ταύτῃ χρωμένους τῇ ἐργασίᾳ. See Böckh's *Public Econ. of Athens*, p. 333 In these public πορνεῖα the πόρναι were accustomed to stand lightly clad, γυμναί. So Xenarchos ap. Athen. xiii. p. 568 :

> ἃς ἔξεσθ' ὁρᾶν
> εἰληθερούσας στέρν' ἀπημφιεσμένας,
> γυμνὰς, ἐφεξῆς τ' ἐπὶ κέρως τεταγμ'νας·

or, according to Eubulos, ἐν λεπτοπήνοις ὕφεσιν ἑστώσας. The admittance fee was but an obole. See Philemon, ap. Athen. *Ib.* : ἡ θύρα 'στ' ἀνεῳγμένη. εἰς ὀβολός· εἰσπήδησον. A step removed from these were the houses of the πορνοβοσκοὶ, *lenones* and *lenæ*, who gained a livelihood by keeping a number of girls, and into

whose hands children, exposed by their parents, often fell. See
Demosth. *in Neær.* p. 1351, where we read that Nicarete, a freed-
woman, having obtained seven children of this sort in their
earliest infancy, now supported herself by means of them. Cf.
Plaut. *Cistell.*; and Isæus *de Philoctem. Hered.* p. 134. These
wretches, who were more contemned than the hetæræ themselves,
would let out the girls for long periods together, and even to
several persons at the same time, and this does not seem to
have excited jealousy. Demosth. *in Neær.* p. 1353: μετὰ ταῦτα
τοίνυν ἐν τῇ Κορίνθῳ αὐτῆς ἐπιφανῶς ἐργαζομένης καὶ οὔσης
λαμπρᾶς, ἄλλοι τε ἐρασταὶ γίγνονται, καὶ Ξενοκλείδης ὁ ποιητὴς καὶ Ἵππαρχος ὁ ὑποκριτής. καὶ εἶχον αὐτὴν μεμισθωμένοι.
But the πόρναι were sometimes purchased outright from the
πορνοβοσκὸς, either by one or more persons, as was the case
with Neæra herself. Demosth. *in Neær.* p. 1354: μετὰ ταῦτα
τοίνυν αὐτῆς γίγνονται ἐρασταὶ δύο, ... κατατιθέασιν αὐτῆς
(Νεαίρας) τιμὴν τριάκοντα μνᾶς τοῦ σώματος τῇ Νικαρέτῃ καὶ
ὠνοῦνται αὐτὴν παρ᾽ αὐτῆς νόμῳ πόλεως καθάπαξ αὐτῶν δούλην
εἶναι. Another case, where there were also two joint purchasers,
is mentioned by Lysias, *de Vuln. Præm.* pp. 166, 172. Instances
of such sales are very common in the comic writers.

These houses, as well as those before mentioned, are called
πορνεῖα, παιδισκεῖα, (Athen. x. p. 437,) or οἰκήματα, whence the
expressions ἐν οἰκήματι καθῆσθαι, ἐξ οἰκήματος γύναια, &c., and they
are also called ἐργαστήρια (Demosth. *in Neær.* p. 1367; Æschin.
in Timarch. p. 137); which has reference to the expressions
ἐργάζεσθαι τῷ σώματι, or ἀφ᾽ ὥρας ἐργάζεσθαι, Plutarch, *Timol.*
14. But we must distinguish between those houses which anybody was free to enter, and those inhabited by females who had
been let for specified periods, as just described, sometimes under
written contracts; κατὰ συγγραφὰς μισθωθῆναι καὶ γραμματεῖον.
Æschin. *in Timarch.* p. 160; and Plaut. *Asin.* iv. 1. This will
explain the words of Ballio in Plaut. *Pseud.* i. 2, 91. Cf. Antiph.
de Venef. p. 611. Among these females, as appears abundantly
from the comic writers, there were many born to better things,
and with minds far above the vile trade which they were compelled by circumstances to follow: this may be considered as
some palliation of the intercourse with them.

Many hetæræ lived by themselves, and independently. First

among these comes the numerous class of freed-women, comprehending the flute-players, αὐληρτρίδες, and the cither-players, κιθαρίστριαι, who were hired to assist at the domestic sacrifices, (Plaut. *Epid.* iii. 4, 64 ; Millin, *Peint. de Vas. Gr.* i. 8,) and, like the ὀρχηστρίδες, or dancing-girls, served to give zest to the pleasures of the symposia.   But these girls generally followed the profession of hetæræ also; and that this was often the purpose of their presence at such drinking-scenes, is manifest from numerous antiques.   The younger men often assembled at the houses of these persons.   See Isocr. *Areop.* 18, p. 202 : Τοιγαροῦν οὐκ ἐν τοῖς σκιραφείοις οἱ νεώτεροι διέτριβον, οὐδ' ἐν ταῖς αὐλητρίσιν, οὐδ' ἐν τοῖς τοιούτοις συλλόγοις, ἐν οἷς νῦν διημερεύουσιν. Others frequented taverns, as appears from the expression, προσεταιρίζεσθαι ἐς πανδοχεῖον, used by Lucian, *Philopatr.* 9.

Many of those in this class were probably distinguished for wit and vivacity ; but those remarkable personages, who by their intellect and powers of fascination perhaps, rather than by their beauty, exerted such an extensive sway over their age, and who, by the position in which they stood to the greatest men of the day, have secured an historic celebrity, were sprung from a different order.   For Aspasia and the Corinthian Lais, as well as Phryne and Pythionice, were aliens, ξέναι, and Lamia was the daughter of a free Athenian citizen.   Many penniless and unbefriended maidens who went to Athens, Corinth, and the largei cities without any intention of becoming hetæræ, were afterwards, by degrees, borne away into the vortex.   So the Andrian, Chrysis ; Terent, *Andr.* i. 1, 42.   Others, on the contrary, probably repaired to the great cities with the express object of making their *début* in this character.   Among such may be reckoned the Thais and the two Bacchides of Terence, as well as the Bacchides and Phronesium of Plautus, with several mentioned by Athenæus and by other writers.   The lives and characters of nine of the most renowned have been capitally sketched by Jacobs.

Corinth seems to have surpassed all other cities in the number of its hetæræ, to whom the wealth and splendour of the place, as well as the crowd of wealthy merchants, who were not very scrupulous in their habits of life, held out the prospect of a rich harvest.   Nor was it in numbers only that this city was pre-eminent ; but in magnificence, elegance, and luxurious

refinement, if not in genuine cultivation of mind also, its hetæræ
eclipsed even those of Athens; so that Κορινθία κόρη became an
adage expressive of the acme of voluptuousness. So Plato, *Republ.* iii. p. 404, after condemning Συρακουσία τράπεζα, Ἀττικὰ
πέμματα, &c., proceeds: ψέγεις ἄρα καὶ Κορινθίαν κόρην φίλην
εἶναι ἀνδράσι μέλλουσιν εὖ σώματος ἕξειν. Cf. Aristoph. *Plut.* 149.
Strabo, viii. 6, 20, relates that the temple of Aphrodite numbered
above a thousand hetæræ as hierodulæ, whom he describes as
the ruin of foreigners: τό τε τῆς Ἀφροδίτης ἱερὸν οὕτω πλούσιον
ὑπῆρξεν, ὥστε πλείους ἢ χιλίας ἱεροδούλους ἐκέκτητο ἑταίρας, ἃς
ἀνετίθεσαν τῇ θεῷ καὶ ἄνδρες καὶ γυναῖκες. Καὶ διὰ ταύτας οὖν
ἐπολυοχλεῖτο ἡ πόλις καὶ ἐπλουτίζετο· οἱ γὰρ ναύκληροι ῥᾳδίως
ἐξανηλίσκοντο καὶ διὰ τοῦτο ἡ παροιμία φησὶν,

Οὐ παντὸς ἀνδρὸς ἐς Κόρινθόν ἐσθ' ὁ πλοῦς.

As Κορινθία κόρη was a synonym for an hetæra, so κορινθιάζεσθαι
stood for ἑταιρεῖν. Eustath. *ad Il.* ii. 570. Equally significant is
the term ἀνδροκόρινθος applied to the infamous town Heraclea.
Athen. viii. p. 351. So Dio Chrysos. *Orat.* xxxvii. p. 119, says to
the Corinthians: πόλιν οἰκεῖτε τῶν οὐσῶν τε καὶ γεγενημένων ἐπα-
φροδιτοτάτην. Cf. Plutarch, *Prov. Alex.* p. 1270. At Sparta,
on the contrary, particularly in the days of Lycurgic austerity,
hetæræ found no great encouragement, the sturdy manners of the
people comporting best with a *Venus armata.* Plutarch, *de Fort.
Rom.* 4 : ὥσπερ οἱ Σπαρτιᾶται τὴν Ἀφροδίτην λέγουσι διαβαί-
νουσαν τὸν Εὐρώταν τὰ μὲν ἔσοπτρα καὶ τοὺς χλιδῶνας καὶ τὸν
κεστὸν ἀποθέσθαι, δόρυ δὲ καὶ ἀσπίδα λαβεῖν κοσμουμένην τῷ
Λυκούργῳ.

The external life of these females and the intercourse with
them presents a less offensive aspect, when, as sometimes happened, they attracted, not so much by the subtle arts of studied
coquetry, as by their merry sprightliness, and by the well-timed
interchange of unreserved freedom with apparent prudery. But
on closer examination, we may compare them to baskets of
noxious weeds and garbage, covered over with roses. Their disso-
lute habits, their extravagance and debauchery, could not but lead,
in spite of outward show and glitter, to disorder, filth, and penury.
Exceptions of course occurred. On the visit of Socrates, the
house of Theodota, as well as all its inmates, appear, according

to Xenophon's description, to have been perfectly decent and proper. *Memor.* iii. 11, 4 : Ἐκ δὲ τούτου ὁ Σωκράτης ὁρῶν αὐτήν τε πολυτελῶς κεκοσμημένην, καὶ μητέρα παροῦσαν αὐτῇ ἐν ἐσθῆτι καὶ θεραπείᾳ οὐ τῇ τυχούσῃ, καὶ θεραπαίνας πολλὰς καὶ εὐειδεῖς, καὶ οὐδὲ ταύτας ἠμελημένως ἐχούσας, καὶ τοῖς ἄλλοις τὴν οἰκίαν ἀφθόνως κατεσκευασμένην, εἶπε, κ.τ.λ. But the very surprise of Socrates proves that he expected to find the usual absence of decency and comfort. So Terence, *Eun.* v. 4, 12, mentions, ' Harum inluviem, sordes, inopiam.' If we add to this, that they could have seldom felt any genuine affection, and that beneath the mask of devotion lurked trickery and avarice, with constant scheming to plunder their besotted admirers—there is left only a wretched, disconsolate picture of existence, darkened by the gloomy perspective of a time when their charms should have faded away. And this was, generally, the character of professional hetæræ, of whom Thais, as drawn by Menander (Meineke, p. 75), may be taken as a representative :

> θρασεῖαν, ὡραίαν δὲ καὶ πιθανὴν ἅμα,
> ἀδικοῦσαν, ἀποκλείουσαν, αἰτοῦσαν πυκνὰ,
> μηθενὸς ἐρῶσαν, προσποιουμένην δ' ἀεί.

The first rule of life was, ' assimulare amare oportet' (Plaut. *Cist.* i. 1, 98), and this principle is well carried out in the *Truculentus*, i. 2 ; and ii. 1. Cf. Isocrat. *de Pace*, 33, p. 242. So again, Dicæarchos says, speaking of Athens, φυλακτέον δ' ὡς ἔνι μάλιστα τὰς ἑταίρας, μὴ λάθῃ τις ἡδέως ἀπολόμενος. *Stat. Gr.* p. 10. What credit their admirers attached to the sincerity of their professions may be gathered from the quaint words of Aristippos, as reported by Plutarch, *Amat.* 4 : ὡς ἐμαρτύρησεν Ἀρίστιππος τῷ κατηγοροῦντι Λαΐδος πρὸς αὐτὸν, ὡς οὐ φιλούσης, ἀποκρινάμενος, Ὅτι καὶ τὸν οἶνον οἴεται καὶ τὸν ἰχθὺν μὴ φιλεῖν αὐτὸν, ἀλλ' ἡδέως ἑκατέρῳ χρῆται. Cf. Athen. xiii. p. 588.

Alexis, apud Athen. xiii. p. 568. recounts the expedients of the hetæræ for heightening their charms, or replacing those which they had lost. See Note 42 to Scene IX. Many, however, increased their attractiveness by wit and humour, as well as by intellectual acquirements. Though not perhaps possessed of very profound scientific attainments, yet at all events they displayed a degree of learning much above that of the ordinary run of Greek women,

and on this some prided themselves not a little. Athen. xiii. p.583;
καὶ ἄλλαι δὲ ἑταῖραι μέγα ἐφρόνουν ἐφ᾽ αὑταῖς, παιδείας ἀντεχό-
μεναι καὶ τοῖς μαθήμασι χρόνον ἀπομερίζουσαι.   Thus the Arcadian Lastheneia was a pupil of Plato (Athen. xii. p. 546), and
Leontion a hearer of Epicurus (ib. xiii. p. 588).   Still the witticisms of a Lamia, a Mania, or a Gnathæna, of which Athenæus
has preserved so many specimens, are coarse, though pointed,
and would argue that they often descended into real grossness
and immodesty in their conversation.

The price paid by Hipparchos and Xenocleides for Neæra
was thirty minæ, or three thousand drachmæ.   Gnathæna, on
the other hand, demanded one thousand drachmæ as the price
of her daughter's society for a single night; but these μεγαλό-
μισθοι ἑταῖραι had to stoop to lower prices when their beauty
was on the wane.   See the fragment of Epicrates respecting
Lais, which has been preserved by Athenæus, xiii. p. 570:

> ἰδεῖν μὲν αὐτὴν ῥᾷόν ἐστι καὶ πτύσαι.
> ἐξέρχεται δὲ πανταχόσ᾽ ἤδη πιομένη,
> δέχεται δὲ καὶ στατῆρα καὶ τριώβολον,
> προσίεται δὲ καὶ γέροντα καὶ νέον.

Phryne, on one occasion, demands a mina (Athen. xiii. p. 583),
and in other instances the price descends to five (Lucian, Dial.
Mer. xi.), two (Athen. xiii. p. 596), and even the single drachma
which is paid by the Scythian in Aristoph. Thesmoph. 1195.
In cases of longer intimacy presents of clothes, trinkets, and
slaves, were made; and if the lady did not live with her erastes,
as was usually the case, he bore the expense of the symposia they
had together, and often the entire charges of her housekeeping.

In the circle of their suitors, these beauties were fêted, loved,
and idolized; but their position with regard to the community
at large was unenviable enough; for though they were far from
being so despicable in the eyes of their contemporaries as the
same class of persons is at the present day, still they were
always looked on as legitimate objects for wanton mischief and
jokes of all descriptions; as we see from the contemptuous appellations applied to them, πανδοσίαι, λεωφόροι, δημιουργοὶ γυναῖκες, χαλκιδῖται, σποδησιλαῦραι, and so on.   But more biting nicknames were often given them; thus two Athenian hetæræ, and
they τῶν οὐκ ἀσήμων, in addition to their own names of Melissa

and Nicion, bear the sobriquets of Θεατροτορύνη and Κυνάμυια. Athen. iv p. 157. So Nico was yclept Αἴξ, Callisto Ῠς, (Athen. xiii. p. 582), Lais Ἀξίνη (Ælian, *Var. Hist.* xii. 5), and Phanostrata Φθειροπύλη, for the amusing reason, ἐπειδήπερ ἐπὶ τῆς θύρας ἑστῶσα ἐφθειρίζετο. Athen. xiii. p. 586. They were beyond the pale of the ordinary law in all cases of μοιχεία, βία, and προαγωγεία; cf. Demosth. *Mid.* p. 525; Lysias *in Theomn.* p. 361; and Plutarch, *Sol.* 23. See Excursus on *The Markets and Commerce,* where these passages are all discussed at length.

It has been asserted that they were compelled to wear a peculiar dress, and were specially distinguished by garments of divers colours. See Petit, *Leg. Att.* p. 576. Suidas, it is true, says, νόμος Ἀθήνῃσι τὰς ἑταίρας ἄνθινα φορεῖν : but the word νόμος here decidedly means nothing more than custom, or habit; and there certainly never was any law of Solon's to this effect, nor does a single author of the better period hint at any such distinctive attire. The very passages quoted by Petit from Artemidorus and Clemens Alexandrinus contain no proof. The words of the latter (*Pædag.* iii. 2), οὕτω τὴν μοιχαλίδα δεικνύουσι τὰ ἀνθίσματα, mean nothing more than his previous assertion, οὐ γὰρ γυναικὸς, ἀλλ' ἑταίρας τὸ φιλόκοσμον : and the laws of Zaleucos (Diod. Sic. xii. 21), as well as the Syracusan ordinance (Phylarch. apud Athen. xii. p. 521), contained sumptuary restrictions for free women merely, and were not designed for the regulation of the dress of the hetæræ. And Clemens Alex. *Pædag.* ii. 10, plainly alludes to something of the same kind when he says : Ἄγαμαι τῶν Λακεδαιμονίων τὴν πόλιν τὴν παλαιάν, ἣ μόναις ταῖς ἑταίραις ἀνθίνας ἐσθῆτας καὶ χρυσοῦν κόσμον ἐπέτρεψε φορεῖν, ἀφαιρουμένη τῶν δοκίμων γυναικῶν τὴν φιλοκοσμίαν, τῷ μόναις ἐφεῖναι καλλοπίζεσθαι ταῖς ἑταιρούσαις. The courtesan, desirous of looking as attractive as possible, would naturally adopt a gayer and more pretentious dress than the sober habiliments of the Grecian dame, just as she bestowed more pains on the dressing of her hair, though this was certainly not done after any particular fashion prescribed by law. Lucian, *Bis Accus.* 31 : κοσμουμένην καὶ τὰς τρίχας εὐθετίζουσαν εἰς τὸ ἑταιρικόν. So also Id. *Ver. Hist.* ii. 46 : γυναῖκες πάνυ ἑταιρικῶς κεκοσμημέναι. If the hetæræ had been really forced by law to wear a party-coloured dress, the wonder would be why this was never adduced to decide the point, when the question was raised as to whether a woman was an hetæra or not; and in that case it would have been impossible that such an error or dispute could have arisen as that between Stephanos and Epænetos. Demosth. *in Neær.* Hence it is evident that the mistake has been made of supposing this sort of dress to have been compulsory by law, while, in fact, it was only voluntarily adopted by the hetæræ. Respecting the party-coloured garments, see Excursus on *The Dress*

EXCURSUS I. TO SCENE III.

THE GRECIAN HOUSE.

IN the total absence of any remains of a Grecian house, in the scarcity of trustworthy descriptions, and the great confusion of the terms used for its various parts, to re-construct it in a satisfactory manner is no easy task. That the house had its Thyroreion, Peristyle, Gynæconitis and Andronitis, its Thalamos and Amphithalamos, we know, but their relative positions are not so clear. Many writers have blindly followed Vitruvius' hasty account of a Grecian house of his own day, though the construction he describes was certainly not, even then, in universal use, and they utterly disregard the contradictions he meets with from other and more trustworthy authorities; while others throw him overboard, and insist, in direct opposition to his statements, that the front of the house was the ἀνδρωνῖτις, the back the γυναικωνῖτις.

The translators of Vitruvius,—Perrault, Galiani, Ortiz y Sanz, Newton, and Rode,—do little or nothing towards solving the difficulties which present themselves. There are also recent English translations by Wilkins and Gwilt. Of the editors, Stratico and Marini are commonplace and incompetent, but Schneider's is a truly valuable critical edition. But neither in this, nor in his other work, *Epimetrum ad Xenoph. Mem.* iii. 8, 9, does he give any plan, or attempt to explain the construction of the whole house, *dispositio singularum partium*, as Vitruvius expresses it, p. 485. The other works on this subject are Scamozzi, *Architettura*, uncritical in the extreme; Stieglitz, *Archäol. d. Baukunst*, in which Vitruvius is blindly followed; Hirts, *Gesch. d. Bauk.*, a poor affair; Barthélemy, *Anachars.* vol. ii.; and lastly, Böttiger, *Prol.* i. *de Medea Eurip.*, which contains some good remarks interspersed with a few errors. Such being the state of the subject, we can hardly hope to present a complete and satisfactory restoration of the Grecian house; it will not be difficult, however, to rectify many of the absurdities and errors which have been again and again repeated by successive writers.

The Grecian house at the time of our story was entirely different from the palaces of the Homeric chiefs, in which the female
apartments were invariably in the upper story, ὑπερῷον, a construction which was the exception, and not the rule, in after-
times. Hence Voss' plan of the house of Odysseus requires no
comment here. Of the changes which took place in the period
between Homer and the Peloponnesian war, we know next to
nothing; but there is no reason to suppose that the houses at
this latter period differed materially from those in the time of
Solon and the Pisistratidæ. So that the hundred years from the
beginning of the war to the time of Alexander will be the
period now under investigation. After this latter date great
changes probably took place.

Of course the writers who flourished during this epoch are
our best authorities; yet the information which we derive from
them is so detached and disconnected, that it will be better to
attempt, in the first place, to re-construct the house from the
description of Vitruvius (vi. 7), which these scattered notices
will serve to elucidate or correct. The passage in Vitruvius is
as follows: ' Atriis Græci quia non utuntur, neque ædificant, sed
ab janua introeuntibus itinera faciunt latitudinibus non spatiosis,
et ex una parte equilia, ex altera ostiariis cellas, statimque januæ
interiores finiuntur. Hic autem locus inter duas januas græce
θυρωρεῖον appellatur. Deinde est introitus in peristylion : id peristylion in tribus partibus habet porticus ; in ea parte, quæ
spectat ad meridiem, duas antas inter se spatio amplo distantes,
in quibus trabes invehuntur, et quantum inter antas distat ex eo
tertia demta spatium datur introrsus. Hic locus apud nonnullos
προστάς, apud alios παραστὰς nominatur. In his locis introrsus
constituuntur œci magni, in quibus matres familiarum cum lani-
ficis habent sessionem. In prostadii autem dextra ac sinistra
cubicula sunt collocata, quorum unus thalamus, alterum amphi-
thalamus dicitur. Circum autem in porticibus triclinia quotidi-
ana, cubicula etiam et cellæ familiaricæ constituuntur. Hæc
pars Gynæconitis appellatur. Conjunguntur autem his domus
ampliores habentes latiora peristylia, etc.' Also in the description of the Andronitis, which comes next, we read : ' Habent
autem eæ domus vestibula egregia et januas proprias cum digni-
tate, etc.'

According to this account, the house-door opened into an
entrance-hall, on either side of which were the porter's lodge
and the stables. Except with respect to the stables, this agrees
with Poll. i. 77 : εἰσιόντων δὲ πρόθυρα, καὶ προπύλαια καὶ τὸν
μὲν πυλῶνα καὶ θυρῶνα καλοῦσι. This πυλὼν or θυρὼν is the
θυρωρεῖον of Vitruvius. According to him, the entrance-hall was
again provided with a door towards the interior, 'locus inter
duas januas.' There must have been, from the nature of the case,
an opening from it into the peristyle, but whether this was
usually closed by an inner door, as Vitruvius asserts, is doubtful.
The house-door itself was called αὔλειος, or αὐλία θύρα. See a
fragment of Menander (Meineke, p. 87):

> τοὺς τῆς γαμετῆς ὅρους ὑπερβαίνεις, γύναι,
> τὴν αὐλίαν· πέρας γὰρ αὔλιος θύρα
> ἐλευθέρᾳ γυναικὶ νενόμιστ' οἰκίας.

Cf. Pind. Nem. i. 19 ; Eustath. ad Iliad. xxii. 69 : πρώτας θύρας
λέγει τὰς αὐλείους. Now a second door, before the αὐλή, is nowhere
mentioned; but directly the αὔλειος is opened, you always entered
at once into the peristyle. Nay, from Plutarch, de Genio Soer.
17, it is clear that the house-door was visible from the peristyle.
Caphisias, standing in a corner of the peristyle, τινὰ γωνίαν τοῦ
περιστύλου, exclaims : Καὶ τίς οὗτος, ὁ πρὸς ταῖς αὐλείοις θύραις
ἐφεστὼς πάλαι καὶ προσβλέπων ἡμῖν ; So that at all events such
an inner door must not be considered indispensable. Vitruvius
makes the passage lead immediately to the peristyle ; Pollux,
however, says : εἶτα πρόδομοι, καὶ προαύλιον, καὶ αὐλὴ τὸ ἔνδον
ἦν αἴθουσαν Ὅμηρος καλεῖ. From this it would appear that the
peristyle was not separated from the entrance-lodge, θυρωρεῖον,
by a mere wall, but that there were rooms on that side of the
peristyle with doors opening into it. Suidas, Hesychius, and
Photius, moreover, say : πρόδομος· ἡ τοῦ οἴκου παστὰς, or προστάς. This, compared with what Vitruvius says on the προστὰς
in the peristyle, may throw some light upon the subject.

In Pollux αὐλὴ means the same as περιστύλιον, and it corresponds to the cavum ædium of the Roman house, comprehending
the open court in the middle, ὕπαιθρον, and the surrounding
arcades : and from it access was gained to the other parts of the
house. See Plato, Symp. p. 212 ; Plutarch, de Gen. Socr. 32 :
Ὡς δὲ ἀπαγγείλας καὶ κελευσθεὶς ἀνοῖξαι τὸν μοχλὸν ἀφεῖλε καὶ
μικρὸν ἐνέδωκε τὴν θύραν, ἐμπεσόντες ἀθρόοι καὶ ἀνατρέψαντες τὸν

ἄνθρωπον ἵεντο δρόμῳ διὰ τῆς αὐλῆς ἐπὶ τὸν θάλαμον. That it
served as a promenade appears from Plato, *Protag.* p. 311 :
ἀλλὰ δεῦρο ἐξαναστῶμεν εἰς τὴν αὐλὴν, καὶ περιϊόντες αὐτοῦ διατρίψωμεν ἕως ἂν φῶς γένηται. Meals were also taken there, as
we see from Demosth. in *Euerg.* p. 1115 : ἔτυχεν ἡ γυνή μου μετὰ
τῶν παίδων ἀριστῶσα ἐν τῇ αὐλῇ. Here, too, the altar for domestic sacrifice was usually placed. Plato, *de Republ.* i. p. 328 :
τεθυκὼς γὰρ ἐτύγχανεν ἐν τῇ αὐλῇ. Böckh assumes from Cic.
Verr. iv. 2, that there were special *sacraria* in Greek private
houses; but the instance adduced in that passage being from
Sicily, and at a comparatively late period, affords by no means
such a conclusive proof as to early Greek customs as is derived
from Lycurg. *in Leocr.* p. 155 : οὐ γὰρ ἐξήρκεσε τὸ σῶμα τὸ
ἑαυτοῦ καὶ τὰ χρήματα μόνον ὑπεκθέσθαι, ἀλλὰ καὶ τὰ ἱερὰ τὰ
πατρῷα, ἃ τοῖς ὑμετέροις καὶ πατρῴοις ἔθεσιν οἱ πρόγονοι παρέ-
δοσαν αὐτῷ ἱδρυσάμενοι, ταῦτα μετεπέμψατο εἰς Μέγαρα καὶ
ἐξήγαγεν ἐκ τῆς χώρας. As D'Orville, ad Charit. iii. 2, has
observed, portable altars were employed for the purpose of
sacrifice.

According to Vitruvius, this peristyle, which formed a square
or oblong, had arcades on three sides only, namely, on that adjoining the entrance, and on those running parallel to each other
on the right and left. On the side opposite the entrance, and in
a line with the columns at the sides, were two pillars. *antæ*, between which lay a space, open toward the αὐλὴ, but enclosed on
the other three sides, thus forming a kind of vestibule, whose
depth was one third less than its breadth, i. e. the interval between the two pillars. Right and left of this προστὰς, παραστὰς,
or παστὰς, as it was called, were the θάλαμος and ἀμφιθάλαμος ;
and behind these (*introrsus*), the large saloons for the wool-
working: while around the αὐλὴ were the eating and sitting rooms
and cells for the slaves.

This description of Vitruvius would be perfectly intelligible,
were it not that he has all along been talking of the gynæconitis,
which he thus assumes to lie next the street ; and he presently
begins to talk of the andronitis in the words, ' Conjunguntur
autem his domus ampliores.' This, however, is entirely at variance
with all the information as to the women's apartments which we
derive from the Greeks themselves. But before proceeding to
discuss these Greek accounts, we must advert to two erroneous

suppositions that have been often made. First, all the houses
have been universally assumed to have been free and isolated,
and in no way connected with other buildings. Those in the
suburbs and ἐν ἀγροῖς, nay, many in the town, may have been
so, but the majority of houses must have been built close together, and even with party-walls. So Thucydides, ii. 3, speaking
of Platæa, says: καὶ ξυνελέγοντο διορύσσοντες τοὺς κοινοὺς τοίχους παρ' ἀλλήλους, ὅπως μὴ δια τῶν ὁδῶν φανεροὶ ὦσιν ἰόντες.
Also Isæus, *de Philoctem. Hered.* p. 143: τὰ δὲ χρήματα ἔνδοθεν
ἐξεφορήσαντο μετὰ τῆς ἀνθρώπου εἰς τὴν ὁμότοιχον οἰκίαν, ἣν ᾤκει
μεμισθωμένος εἰς τούτων. Plaut. *Mil. Glor.* ii. 1, 62; Demosth.
in Androt. p. 609: τέγος ὡς τοὺς γείτονας ὑπερβαίνειν. None of
the restorations yet proposed will apply to houses such as these.

Secondly, it is frequently assumed that Vitruvius' description
applies not to the ancient houses, but merely to those of later
date; and that in earlier times the houses consisted of two stories,
the andronitis being on the ground-floor, and the upper floor,
ὑπερῷον, being appropriated to the gynæconitis. Now as regards
the period from Homer to the time of the Persian invasion there
is absolute lack of all evidence on the one side or the other, and
the scanty notices extant which refer to the time of the Peloponnesian war, sufficiently prove that at that epoch the apartments
of the women were *not generally* above stairs. The often-quoted
passage in Lysias, *de Cæde Eratosth.* p. 12, runs: οἰκίδιόν ἐστί
μοι διπλοῦν, ἴσα ἔχον τὰ ἄνω τοῖς κάτω, κατὰ τὴν γυναικωνῖτιν
καὶ κατὰ τὴν ἀνδρωνῖτιν. ἐπειδὴ δὲ τὸ παιδίον ἐγένετο ἡμῖν, ἡ μήτηρ
αὐτὸ ἐθήλαζεν. ἵνα δὲ μὴ, ὁπότε λούεσθαι δέοι, κινδυνεύοι κατὰ τῆς
κλίμακος καταβαίνουσα, ἐγὼ μὲν ἄνω διῃτώμην, αἱ δὲ γυναῖκες κάτω.
To this we may add Aristoph. *Eccles.* 961: καταδραμοῦσα τὴν
θύραν ἄνοιξον. These passages no doubt refer to an upper story;
but this does not necessarily show that such was of usual occurrence. What Plutarch relates, *ad Princ. Iner.* 4; *Arat.* 26; and
Pelop. 35, has reference to the two tyrants, Aristippos and Alexander of Pheræ, who take special precautions for their personal
safety; and from this therefore we cannot infer the general practice. Achilles Tatius, ii. 26, says: καὶ ὁ Κλεινίας, ἐν ὑπερῴῳ γὰρ
τὸν θάλαμον εἶχε. But this cannot be quoted as an authority, on
account of the late time at which the author wrote. Now the
house mentioned by Lysias, *suprà*, was a small one, and therefore

its confined plan might have made it necessary for the gynæconitis to be constructed on the upper floor, which would then be
a very suitable position. Moreover, Euphiletos need not have
explained to the judges, οἰκίδιόν ἐστί μοι διπλοῦν, if houses were
commonly so constructed. In another passage Lysias mentions a
gynæconitis which is certainly not in a ὑπερῷον; adv. Simon.
p. 139: ἐλθὼν ἐπὶ τὴν οἰκίαν τὴν ἐμὴν νύκτωρ μεθύων, ἐκκόψας
τὰς θύρας εἰσῆλθεν εἰς τὴν γυναικωνῖτιν. Again, in the house of
Ischomachos, the andronitis and gynæconitis adjoin each other;
Xenoph. Œcon. 9, 5. So in Demosth. in Euerg. p. 1155, Mne-
sibulos and Euergos, passing through the back-door, arrive at the
gynæconitis, and find the women in the αὐλή. Cf. Antipho, de
Venef. p. 611. Nay, even the tragic poets seem sometimes to
have had in view not the houses of the heroic age, but those of
their own; see Œdip. Tyr. 1241–1262, where the λέχη νυμφικὰ,
and therefore also the chambers of Jocasta, can only be supposed
to be on the ground-floor.

All these citations go to prove that, in the historic period, the
women's apartments were not in the ὑπερῷον, except under peculiar circumstances; but the passages referring to the doors which
connected the gynæconitis with the rest of the house, afford still
more conclusive evidence. Xenoph. Œcon. 9, 5: Ἔδειξα δὲ καὶ
τὴν γυναικωνῖτιν αὐτῇ θύραν βαλανείῳ (sic) ὡρισμένην ἀπὸ τῆς
ἀνδρωνίτιδος, ἵνα μήτε ἐκφέρηται ἔνδοθεν ὅ,τι μὴ δεῖ, μήτε τεκνοποιῶνται οἱ οἰκέται ἄνευ τῆς ἡμετέρας γνώμης. The words θύραν
βαλανείῳ ὡρισμένην ἀ. τ. ἀ. are devoid of meaning, as all the
editors agree: the most probable emendation appears to be that
suggested by Professor Hermann, who would read θύρᾳ βαλανωτῷ,
and this conjecture is confirmed by the phrase ὀχεὺς βαλανωτός,
which occurs in a fragment of Parmenides, ap. Sext. Empir.
p. 393. Two reasons are assigned by Xenophon for the andronitis
and gynæconitis being separated by a door that could be kept
locked; first, ἵνα μὴ ἐκφέρηται ἔνδοθεν ὅ,τι μὴ δεῖ, for the valuables and household stores were kept in the women's apartments,
those of the men being devoted more to convivial purposes:
secondly, μήτε τεκνοποιῶνται οἱ οἰκέται ἄνευ τῆς ἡμετέρας γνώμης,
for the slaves also were separated according to their sex, the males
being confined to the andronitis, the females to the gynæconitis.
We learn then from this passage, that the gynæconitis lay beyond

the andronitis, and was separated from it by a single door, elsewhere called μέταυλος, μέσαυλος, or μεσαύλιος. The introduction
of this door is the crucial test of all correct restorations of the
Grecian house ; and it must carefully be remembered, that one
and the same door are denoted by μέταυλος and μέσαυλος, but
that the latter, in its strict meaning, could not be used in every
house instead of the more general word μέταυλος : for Schneider
is quite wrong (Epim. p. 279), in stating that μέταυλος was only
the commoner Attic form of μέσαυλος. Without forgetting the
connexion between μέσος and μετὰ, there appears to be a distinct
reason why μέταυλος is preferred by earlier writers. The best-
known passage in which μέταυλος occurs is in Lysias, de Cæde
Eratosth. p. 20 : ἀναμιμνησκόμενος, ὅτι ἐν ἐκείνῃ τῇ νυκτὶ ἐψόφει
ἡ μέταυλος θύρα καὶ ἡ αὔλειος. All however that we learn from
this is, that in order to arrive at the gynæconitis it was necessary to pass through an interior door : but the point here to be
noticed is, that though this door does not, in this case, connect the
andronitis and gynæconitis (for the latter is in the ὑπερῷον), yet
it is still called μέταυλος. Whereas Mœr. Att. p. 264, says :
μέταυλος, ἡ μέση τῆς ἀνδρωνίτιδος καὶ γυναικονίτιδος θύρα, Ἀττικῶς. μέσαυλος, Ἑλληνικῶς. See Schol. ad Apoll. Rhod. iii. 335 :
ἡ μέσαυλος ἡ φέρουσα εἴς τε τὴν ἀνδρωνῖτιν καὶ γυναικωνῖτιν. Cf.
Plutarch. Symp. vii. 1 : ἡ δὲ μέταυλος αὕτη (ἡ ἐπιγλωττὶς) κλίσιν
ἐπ᾽ ἀμφότερα λαμβάνουσα φθεγγομένων μὲν ἐπιπίπτει τῷ στομάχῳ
σιτουμένων δὲ καὶ πινόντων τῇ ἀρτηρίᾳ. But the greatest weight
is to be attached to a quotation from Ælius Dionysius in Eustath.
ad Iliad. xi. 547 : οἱ δὲ παλαιοὶ σημειοῦνται, ὡς Ἀττικοὶ μὲν τὴν
μέσην θύραν μέσαυλόν φασι, μάλιστα μὲν οὖν τὴν μέσην δυοῖν αὐλαῖν,
ὥς φησιν Αἴλιος Διονύσιος, ἣν καὶ μέταυλον αὐτὸς λέγει πρὸς ὁμοιό-
τητα τοῦ μεθόριον καὶ μεταίχμιον. This explanation, taken in
connexion with the passage in Lysias, enables us to determine the
real meaning of μέταυλος, and its relation to μέσαυλος. In early
times, when a private citizen passed most of his time amid the
grandeur of the public edifices, his own abode was simple enough,
and certainly did not possess two peristyles. Through the αὔλειος
θύρα was the entrance into the αὐλή, which was in the front of the
house, and which was in fact the peristyle, and was surrounded
by the apartments appertaining to the andronitis. Beyond the
peristyle, and separated from it by a door, was the gynæconitis.

s

This door was called μέταυλος, not because it connected the two
departments of the house, but because it lay opposite to the
αὔλειος, across or behind the αὐλή. But when houses were built
on a more extensive plan, with a separate peristyle for both andronitis and gynæconitis, the door that joined them both still continued to be μέταυλος in reference to the αὔλειος; but in so far as
it formed the passage from one αὐλή into the other, it was also at
the same time μέσαυλος, and hence the words of Ælius Dionysius
just quoted from Eustathius: μάλιστα τὴν μέσην δυοῖν αὐλαῖν.
Houses in which there was but a single αὐλή appear to be alluded
to by Plutarch, de Curios. 3 : ἀλλὰ νῦν μέν εἰσι θυρωροὶ, πάλαι δὲ
ῥόπτρα κρουόμενα πρὸς ταῖς θύραις αἴσθησιν παρεῖχεν, ἵνα μὴ τὴν
οἰκοδέσποιναν ἐν μέσῳ καταλάβῃ ὁ ἀλλότριος, ἢ τὴν παρθένον, ἢ
κολαζόμενον οἰκέτην ἢ κεκραγυίας τὰς θεραπαινίδας.

From all this it is clear that in the best period the women as
well as the men lived on the ground-floor, and the latter always
in the front of the house. But we must not suppose that the
lady of the house was excluded entirely from the men's apartments; on the contrary, it was only on the arrival of strangers
that she retired to the gynæconitis; though the virgins remained
there in all cases. Philo, de Special. leg. ii. p. 327 : παρθένοις
μὲν εἴσω κλισιάδων τὴν μεσαύλιον ὅρον πεποιημέναις, τελείαις δὲ
ἤδη γυναιξὶ τὴν αὔλιον. See also Plutarch, Arat. 26.

This construction of a Grecian house, as gathered from the
most trustworthy Greek authors, seems to be in direct contradiction to the description of Vitruvius. The commentators attempt
to reconcile the discrepancy by the most opposite hypotheses.
Perrault, Marini, and Weiske, utterly regardless of Grecian habits,
place the gynæconitis next the entrance, thus making it serve as
a passage to the andronitis. With far greater probability Galiani,
Ortiz, and Rode, suppose that the andronitis and gynæconitis,
instead of being one behind the other, were side by side, and that
the words of Vitruvius, ' Habent autem eæ domus vestibula egre-
dia et januas proprias,' show that each had a separate entrance to
the street. The principal difficulty of this hypothesis is that no
other author gives any hint of such an arrangement. Still in towns
of lax morality, such as Alexandria, it may have been found inconvenient to have to pass through the andronitis to get into the
gynæconitis, and so each may have had its own separate entrance.

Still, even in the time of Vitruvius, such a disposition cannot be supposed the ordinary one; and, moreover, the description of this author appears to belong more to the mansions of the opulent than to the residences of ordinary citizens.

It still remains to inquire why Vitruvius treats first of the gynæconitis as if it were the principal part of the house, when the andronitis would seem naturally to claim an earlier notice, as well from its greater size and more pretentious appearance, as from being the part that was probably first entered. The reason may perhaps have been because the former still retained the original form of the house, while the latter had the appearance of a modern adjunct. Indeed the women's apartments were in reality the most important part of the edifice, containing, as they did, the θάλαμος, and the household stores and other valuables. With regard to the gynæconitis, we may rest assured that the description in Vitruvius will also very well suit the period here in question, except that in his account the μέσαυλος is not opposite to the αὔλειος, but on the side against which the andronitis was built. The remainder of the Roman architect's description contains nothing of moment, and will therefore only supply an occasional hint as we proceed.

In building a house a great point was to have as much sun as possible in winter, and in summer very little. Hence the main front mostly faced the south, or at least the porticoes on this side were built higher. Xenoph. Œcon. 9, 4: καὶ σύμπασαν δὲ τὴν οἰκίαν ἐπέδειξα αὐτῇ, ὅτι πρὸς μεσημβρίαν ἀναπέπταται, ὥστε εὔδηλον εἶναι, ὅτι χειμῶνος μὲν εὐήλιός ἐστι, τοῦ δὲ θέρους εὔσκιος. Memor. iii. 8, 9: οἰκοδομεῖν δεῖ ὑψηλότερα μὲν τὰ πρὸς μεσημβρίαν, ἵνα ὁ χειμερινὸς ἥλιος μὴ ἀποκλείηται. χθαμαλώτερα δὲ τὰ πρὸς ἄρκτον, ἵνα οἱ ψυχροὶ μὴ ἐμπίπτωσιν ἄνεμοι. Cf. Aristot. Œcon. i. 6; so also Vitruvius: 'una (porticus) quæ ad meridiem spectat excelsioribus columnis constituitur.' A peristyle of this sort was called *Rhodiacum*.

The Athenian residences at the time of the Peloponnesian war were certainly neither large nor stately structures. According to Thucydides, ii. 14, the Athenians preferred living on their estates in the country to residing in the city, and hence the country-houses were even superior to those in the town. Isocr. *Areop.* 20, p. 203: ὥστε καλλίους εἶναι καὶ πολυτελεστέρας τὰς οἰκήσεις καὶ

s 2

τὰς ἐπισκευὰς τὰς ἐπὶ τῶν ἀγρῶν, ἢ τὰς ἐντὸς τείχους. Cf
Thucyd. ii. 65 : οἱ δὲ δυνατοὶ (ἐλυποῦντο) καλὰ κτήματα κατὰ
τὴν χώραν οἰκοδομίαις τε καὶ πολυτελέσι κατασκευαῖς ἀπολωλε-
κότες. That the houses in the town were not remarkably commodious or handsome appears from Dicæarch. *Stat. Græc.* p. 8 :
αἱ μὲν πολλαὶ τῶν οἰκιῶν εὐτελεῖς, ὀλίγαι δὲ χρήσιμαι. It was
not till the Macedonian era, when public spirit had gradually decayed, and private persons, not satisfied with participating in the
grandeur of the state, became desirous of emulating it at home,
that the private buildings became more spacious and magnificent,
while public structures were proportionably neglected. Demosth.
Olynth. iii. p. 36 : ἔνιοι δὲ τὰς ἰδίας οἰκίας τῶν δημοσίων οἰκοδο-
μημάτων σεμνοτέρας εἰσὶ κατεσκευασμένοι. ὅσῳ δὲ τὰς τῆς πόλεως
ἐλάττω γέγονε, τοσούτῳ τὰ τούτων ηὔξηται. Id. *in Aristocr.* p.
689 : νῦν δ᾽ ἰδίᾳ μὲν, ἑκάστῳ τῶν τὰ κοινὰ πραττόντων τοσαύτη
περιουσία ἐστὶν, ὥστε τινὲς μὲν αὐτῶν πολλῶν δημοσίων οἰκοδομη-
μάτων σεμνοτέρας τὰς ἰδίας κατεσκευάκασιν οἰκίας.

The Grecian house had not, as the Roman had, a vestibulum,
or vacant space before the house-door. This is clear from the
fact of a tax being imposed by Hippias on such doors as opened
outwards, on account of their encroaching on the space that was
public property. Aristot. *Œcon.* ii. p. 1347 : Ἱππίας ὁ Ἀθηναῖος
τὰ ὑπερέχοντα τῶν ὑπερῴων εἰς τὰς δημοσίας ὁδοὺς καὶ τοὺς ἀνα-
βαθμοὺς καὶ τὰ προφράγματα, καὶ τὰς θύρας τὰς ἀνοιγομένας ἔξω
ἐπώλησεν. The πρόθυρα mentioned by Herodotus, vi. 35, Μιλτιάδης κατήμενος ἐν τοῖσι προθύροισι τοῖσι ἑωυτοῦ, is merely the
ground generally in front of the door. But many houses must
have had an enclosure about them, as appears from the passage
just cited from Aristotle. Similar to these must have been the
δρύφακτοι, whose further extension was forbidden by Themistocles
and Aristides. See Heracl. Pont. *Polit.* i : καὶ τῶν ὁδῶν ἐπεμελοῦντο ὅπως μήτινες ἀνοικοδομῶσιν αὐτὰς, ἢ δρυφάκτους ὑπερτεί-
νωσιν. Before each house stood, usually, its own peculiar altar
of Apollo Agyieus, or an obelisk rudely representing the god
himself, a relic of the ancient τετράγωνος ἐργασία, hence termed
Ἀγυιεύς. It is called κίων εἰς ὀξὺ λήγων ὡς ὀβέλισκος, sometimes
κωνοειδὴς κίων, or βωμὸς στρογγύλος, also Ἀπόλλων τετράγωνος.
Cf. Schol. ad *Vesp.* 875 ; *Thesmoph.* 489 ; Hellad. ap. Phot. *bibl.*
279 ; Harpocration and Suidas, s. v. Ἀγυιᾶς ; Plaut. *Merc.* iv. 1,

10. Sometimes a laurel was planted beside it. Cf. Thucyd. vi.
27 ; Aristoph. *Plut.* 1153. Perhaps some steps led to the house-
door, over which, *boni ominis causa*, or as a sort of βασκάνιον, an
inscription was often placed. Plutarch, Fragm. *Vit. Crat.* v.
p. 874 : ἐπὶ τούτου φασὶ τοὺς "Ελληνας ἐπιγράφειν τοῖς ἑαυτῶν
οἴκοις ἐπὶ τῶν προπυλαίων 'Εἴσοδος Κράτητι Ἀγαθῷ Δαίμονι.
Cf. Diog. Laert. vi. 50 : Νεογάμου ἐπιγράψαντος ἐπὶ τὴν οἰκίαν
' Ὁ τοῦ Διὸς παῖς 'Ηρακλῆς Καλλίνικος ἐνθάδε κατοικεῖ, μηδὲν
εἰσίτω κακόν,' ἐπέγραψε ' Μετὰ πόλεμον ἡ συμμαχία.'

In all houses of consequence there was a porter, θυρωρός : and
though Plutarch, *de Curios.* 3, denies that this was the case in
ancient times, still at the period of the Peloponnesian war the
custom had become very general. The duty of the θυρωρὸς was
not only to let people in, and announce them to his master, but
also to see that nothing was secretly or irregularly carried out
of the mansion. Aristot. *Œcon.* i. 6, p. 1345 : δοκεῖ δὲ καὶ ἐν
ταῖς μεγάλαις οἰκονομίαις χρήσιμος εἶναι θυρωρὸς, ὃς ἂν ᾖ ἄχρη-
στος τῶν ἄλλων ἔργων, πρὸς τὴν σωτηρίαν τῶν εἰσφερομένων καὶ
ἐκφερομένων. The behaviour of this personage is capitally portrayed by Plato, when describing the reception Socrates met with
at the door of Callias ; *Prot.* p. 314 : Δοκεῖ οὖν μοι, ὁ θυρωρὸς,
εὐνοῦχός τις, κατήκουεν ἡμῶν. κινδυνεύει δὲ διὰ τὸ πλῆθος τῶν
σοφιστῶν ἄχθεσθαι τοῖς φοιτῶσιν εἰς τὴν οἰκίαν. ἐπειδὴ γοῦν
ἐκρούσαμεν τὴν θύραν, ἀνοίξας καὶ ἰδὼν ἡμᾶς, "Εα, ἔφη, σοφισταί
τινες. οὐ σχολὴ αὐτῷ. καὶ ἅμα ἀμφοῖν ταῖν χεροῖν τὴν θύραν
πάνυ προθύμως ὡς οἷόν τ' ἦν ἐπήραξε.. καὶ ἡμεῖς πάλιν ἐκρούομεν·
καὶ ὃς ἐγκεκλεισμένης τῆς θύρας ἀποκρινόμενος εἶπεν, Ὦ ἄνθρωποι,
ἔφη, οὐκ ἀκηκόατε, ὅτι οὐ σχολὴ αὐτῷ ; Ἀλλ', ὦ 'γαθὲ, ἔφην ἐγὼ,
οὔτε παρὰ Καλλίαν ἥκομεν, οὔτε σοφισταί ἐσμεν, ἀλλὰ θάρρει,.
Πρωταγόραν γάρ τοι δεόμενοι ἰδεῖν ἤλθομεν, εἰσάγγειλον οὖν. μόγις οὖν ποτε ἡμῖν ὁ ἄνθρωπος ἀνέῳξε τὴν θύραν. A dog also
was often placed at the door, who kept watch when the porter
was away. Apollod. ap. Athen. i. p. 3 ; cf. Theocr. xv. 43 :

τὰν κύν' ἔσω κάλεσον, τὰν αὐλείαν ἀπόκλαξον.

See also Aristoph. *Thesm.* 416 ; *Equit.* 1025 ; *Lysistr.* 1215 :
εὐλαβεῖσθαι τὴν κύνα, a warning which was often written up like
the *cave canem*! of the Romans.

In the accompanying plan, which is intended to represent a

Ground-plan of a large Greek Dwelling-house, with double Peristyle for Andronitis and Gynæconitis.

α. αὔλειος θύρα.

θυρ. θυρωρεῖον or θυρών.

A. αὐλή of the Andronitis.

O. The various saloons and chambers of the Andronitis.

μ. μέταυλος, here a regular μέσαυλος, forming the only communication between the Andronitis and Gynæconitis.

Γ. Court of the Gynæconitis.

γ. The various divisions of the Gynæconitis with the ordinary eating and store-rooms, kitchen, &c.

π. παραστὰς, παστὰς, or προστάς.

θ. θάλαμος and ἀμφιθάλαμος.

I. ἱστῶνες, or rooms for the looms, and woollen manufactures.

κ. κηπαία θύρα, whose precise position is, however, immaterial.

Of course the arrangement of the various chambers, with their doors, windows, and stairs, &c., is arbitrary.

The *Mesaulos* of Vitruvius is most likely the long uninterrupted passage between the Andronitis and Gynæconitis. Inasmuch as it is divided by the door Vitruvius might speak of two passages (*mesaulæ*).

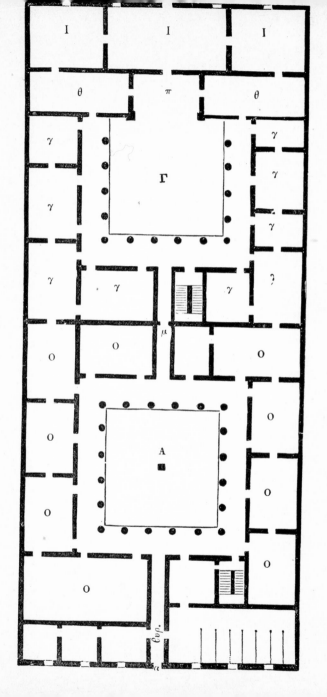

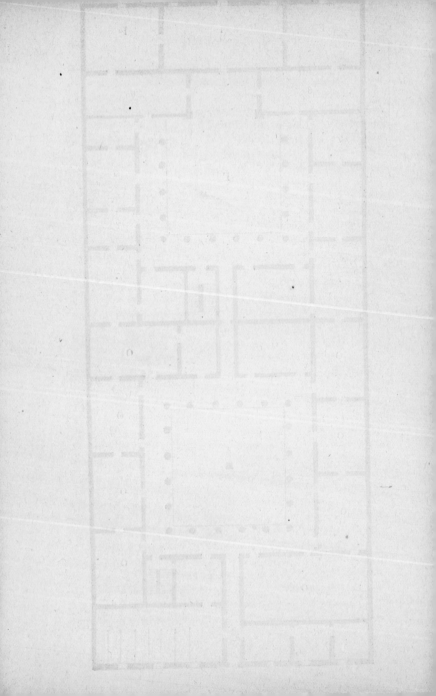

large dwelling-house with a double peristyle, such as might have
been in vogue at the date of our story, everything not essential
has been omitted; while at the same time the particular arrangement of the various rooms and chambers must of course be entirely
hypothetical. Passing through the entrance-hall, or thyroreion,
you first enter the front αὐλή, or peristyle of the andronitis, on
all four sides of which are arcades, στοαί. See Poll. i. 78. That
nearest the entrance, and perhaps also that opposite to it, was
called πρόστοον. Plato, *Prot.* p. 314 : Ἐπειδὴ δὲ εἰσήλθομεν
κατελάβομεν Πρωταγόραν ἐν τῷ προστύῳ περιπατοῦντα. *Ib.* p.
315 : Τὸν δὲ μέτ' εἰσενόησα, ἔφη Ὅμηρος, Ἱππίαν τὸν Ἠλεῖον
καθήμενον ἐν τῷ καταντικρὺ προστόῳ ἐν θρόνῳ. Around the
peristyle were situated the larger saloons, οἶκοι, designed for the
symposia of the men (τρίκλινοι, ἑπτάκλινοι, τριακοντάκλινοι, Plutarch, *Symp.* v. 5, 2), and hence they were also called ἀνδρῶνες.
In Plutarch, *Sept. Sap. Conv.* 2, we also meet with a ἑστιατόριον,
though this appears to have been a building specially designed for
such convivial meetings. In the best period, ἀνδρών is the usual
expression See Xenoph. *Symp.* i. 4, 13 ; Aristoph. *Eccles.* 676 :

> τὸ δὲ δεῖπνον ποῦ παραθήσεις ;
> τὰ δικαστήρια καὶ τὰς στοιὰς ἀνδρῶνας πάντα ποιήσω.

Besides these there was a room with seats for the reception of visitors, ἐξέδρα, and there were also smaller chambers, δωμάτια (Lysias,
de Cœd. Erat. p. 28 ; Aristoph. *Eccles.* 8), called also κοιτῶνες
(Poll. i. 79), and frequently οἰκήματα (Plato, *Prot.* p. 316 ; Achill.
Tat. ii. 19). Here also there may have been store-rooms, as was
the case at Callias's father's. Plato, *Protag.* p. 315. Cf. Aristoph.
Eccl. 14 :

> στοάς τε καρποῦ βακχίου τε νάματος
> πλήρεις.

In the centre of the arcade which faced the entrance, called by
Plato τὸ καταντικρὺ πρόστοον, may be placed with the greatest
probability the μέταυλος θύρα ; which may here be taken in its
proper meaning of μέσαυλος, as already explained. Besides this
there was a third principal door, usually called κηπαία θύρα
(Poll. i. 76), because there was a plot of garden adjoining most
houses. See Demosth. *in Euerg.* p. 1155 : καταβαλόντες τὴν
θύραν τὴν εἰς τὸν κῆπον φέρουσαν. Cf. Plaut. *Most.* v. 1, 4; so
also Lysias, *in Eratosth.* p. 393 : ἔμπειρος γὰρ ὢν ἐτύγχανον τῆς

οἰκίας, καὶ ᾔδειν, ὅτι ἀμφίθυρος εἴη. Lysias also mentions a third, or rather a fourth door, τριῶν δὲ θυρῶν οὐσῶν, ἃς ἔδει με διελθεῖν, ἅπασαι ἀνεῳγμέναι ἔτυχον. The context plainly shows that the αὔλειος cannot have been one of the three doors here mentioned; the one in question may possibly have been one leading out of the garden into the street.

In the time of Vitruvius, and probably also at an earlier period, the gynæconitis was so built that the peristyle had porticoes on three sides only. On the fourth side was the προστὰς, formed by the two antæ (see Plan): behind this were the rooms for female industry, which terminated the mansion; but on the right and left of the προστὰς, and opening into it, were the θάλαμος and ἀμφιθάλαμος, and on the three remaining sides of the peristyle the daily eating-rooms, and all the offices required for household purposes. This tallies very well with the account of Pollux: ὁ δὲ γυναικωνίτης, θάλαμος, ἱστών. ταλασιουργὸς οἶκος, σιτοποϊκὸς, ἵνα μὴ μυλῶνα, ὡς οὐκ εὔφηνμον, ὀνομάζωμεν. εἶτα ὑπτανεῖον, τὸ μαγειρεῖον, ἐρεῖς, ὡς ἀποθῆκαι, ταμεῖα, θησαυροὶ, φυλακτήρια.

The θάλαμος is the matrimonial bed-chamber. Schneider erroneously supposes that at Athens θάλαμος was used to denote a store-room, as it does in Homer. This conclusion is based on Xenoph. Œcon. 9, 3: ὁ μὲν γὰρ θάλαμος ἐν ὀχυρῷ ὢν τὰ πλείστου ἄξια καὶ στρώματα καὶ σκεύη παρεκάλει. It was quite natural however to keep the plate and other valuables in a chest in the bed-chamber. It would almost seem from Lysias, *de Cade Eratosth.* p. 13, that the θάλαμος was in the men's apartments; but the reason of this is because Euphiletos has exchanged lodgings with his wife, while the θάλαμος remained unchanged. The θάλαμος was at a later period usually called παστάς; and though there is some doubt about the signification of this word and of παραστὰς, it would seem that the similar appellation of the antechamber (προστὰς) caused the bed-chamber to be called so also. The use of the *amphithalamos* is not clear, unless it be the sitting-room of the wife and the rest of the family.

When there was an upper story, ὑπερῷον, διῆρες, it certainly did not usually cover the whole space occupied by the ground-floor: in it the slaves mostly lodged. Thus in Demosth. *in Everg.* p. 1156, the female slaves are shut up ἐν τῷ πύργῳ.

This ὑπερῷον may have been sometimes approached by a flight of stairs leading from the street (see *Gallus*, p. 4), and these perhaps are the ἀναβαθμοὶ taxed by Hippias. Aristot. *Œcon.* ii. p. 1347. If the upper story was used for strangers, a separate access of this kind must have been very commodious. Frequently these upper stories may have projected over the area of the ground-floor, like balconies or oriels; these also, τὰ ὑπερέχοντα τῶν ὑπερῴων, were taxed by Hippias. See Poll. i. 81 : εἶτα ὑπερῷα οἰκήματα. τὰ δ' αὐτὰ καὶ διήρη. αἱ δὲ προβολαὶ τῶν ὑπερῴων οἰκημάτων, αἱ ὑπὲρ τοὺς κάτω τοίχους προὔχουσαι, γεισιποδίσματα· καὶ τὰ φέροντα αὐτὰς ξύλα γεισίποδας. The ὑπερῷον was sometimes assigned or let to strangers, as appears from Antipho, *de Venef.* p. 611 : Ὑπερῷόν τι ἦν τῆς ἡμετέρας οἰκίας ὃ εἶχε Φιλόνεως, ὅποτ' ἐν ἄστει διατρίβοι. Vitruvius, however, speaks of special apartments for guests, adjoining the main building, which was doubtless occasionally the case in large houses : ' Præterea dextra ac sinistra domunculæ constituuntur habentes proprias januas, triclinia et cubicula commoda, uti hospites advenientes non in peristylia, sed in ea hospitalia recipiantur.' Cf. Eurip. *Alcest.* 564 : ἐξώπιοι ξενῶνες. But this cannot have been the rule, for no such *hospitalia* are to be found in the house of Callias, in which the guests all lodge under their host's roof. Plato, *Protag.* p. 315. Vitruvius also speaks of *hospitalia* separated from the main building by passages, μέσαυλοι, but the text is evidently corrupt, and has been satisfactorily emended by Schneider. Most likely the μέσαυλος to which Vitruvius alludes is only the passage leading from the andronitis to the gynæconitis, in which was the μέσαυλος θύρα; and the dubious expression *itinera* must be taken to mean only a single passage, as Schneider has remarked.

The roofs were usually flat, so as to afford a place for walking on. Lysias, *adv. Simon.* p. 142 ; Plaut. *Mil.* ii. 2, 3. But there were also pitched roofs, and though gables are restricted to temples (*Aves*, 1108), still this is only to be understood of pediments fronting the street, as appears from Galen. So Pollux, i. 81, speaking exclusively of private houses, says : ἀμείβοντες δὲ εἰσί, ξύλα ἐξ ἑκατέρων τῶν τοίχων ἀλλήλοις ἀντερειδόμενα, πρὸς τὸ τοὺς μέσους ὑψηλοὺς ὀροφους ἀνέχειν δύνασθαι.

The exterior of dwelling-houses, as seen from the street, could

not have been very imposing. Not faced with marble, as among
the Romans, the usual material was common stone, brick, or
wood. Xenoph. *Mem.* iii. 1, 7 : λίθοι καὶ κέραμος κάτω καὶ ἐπι-
πολῆς, ἐν μέσῳ δὲ αἵ τε πλίνθοι καὶ τὰ ξύλα. Over this there
was a coating of plaster, κονίαμα, in the preparation of which
the Greeks were certainly adepts. Demosth. *de Ord. Rep.* p.
175; Plutarch, *Comp. Arist. et Cat.* 4. In Plutarch, *Phoc.* 18,
we read: ἡ δ' οἰκία τοῦ Φωκίωνος ἔτι νῦν ἐν Μελίτῃ δείκνυται,
χαλκαῖς λεπίσι κεκοσμημένη, τὰ δ' ἄλλα λιτὴ καὶ ἀφελής.

The remaining arrangements, and the decoration of the interior, were also characterised by great simplicity, although even
in Xenophon's and Plato's time more care was expended on
these particulars. The floor was decidedly mere plaster; flags
were not used till late, and the first mention of mosaic occurs
under the kings of Pergamus. Nevertheless, in elegant houses
this plaster-floor was sometimes executed tastefully in divers
colours. Cf. Plin. *Nat. Hist.* xxxvi. 25, 60 : ' Pavimenta ori-
ginem apud Græcos habent elaborata arte, picturæ ratione, donec
lithostrota expulere eam.'

The walls, until the fourth century B.C., seem to have been
whitewashed only. The house of Alcibiades is the first instance
of their being painted. Andocid. *in Alcib.* p. 119; Plutarch, *Alcib.*
16. It is immaterial whether the paint was laid on lime or panels,
though the first is the more probable. This innovation, however,
met with opposition. Thus Xenophon, who was very utilitarian
in his principles, decides: γραφαὶ δὲ καὶ ποικιλίαι πλείονας εὐφρο-
σύνας ἀποστεροῦσιν ἢ παρέχουσι. *Memor.* iii. 8, 10; see also
Œcon. 9, 2. Plato, on the other hand, considers ζωγραφία and
ποικ λία as signs of a τρυφῶσα πόλις ; though this, he says, would
be a more agreeable residence than a ὑῶν πόλις. *De Republ.* iii.
p. 372. Hence we gather that painting the interior walls was
not uncommon at that period. We also read of ποικιλίαι or ποικίλματα, which are stucco-ornaments on the cornices and ceilings ;
thus we have ἐν ὀροφῇ ποικίλματα. Plato, *de Republ.* vii. p
529. At a later time, wall-painting, or at all events coloured
ornament, was quite as common as at Pompeii. So Lucian, *Amor.*
34 : ἀντὶ δὲ εὐτελῶν δωματίων ὑψηλὰ τέρεμνα καὶ λίθων πολυτέ-
λειαν ἐμηχανήσαντο, καὶ γυμνὴν τοίχων ἀμορφίαν εὐανθέσι βαφαῖς
χρωμάτων κατέγραψαν.

There were certainly more doors in a Grecian house than has been generally supposed. All the store-rooms, the thalamos, and the various sitting-rooms, had them of course, and perhaps they were only wanting in the saloons and the apartments which all might enter ; these were provided with hangings, παραπετάσματα. Poll. x. 32 : Πρὸ μὲν οὖν κοιτῶνος ἐπὶ ταῖς θύραις παραπετασμάτων σοι δεῖ, εἴτε ἁπλοῦν εἴη τὸ παραπέτασμα λευκὸν ἐξ ὀθόνης, εἴτε καὶ τρίχαπτόν τι βαπτὸν, εἴτε πολύχρουν. The αὐλαία ἔχουσα Πέρσας ἐνυφασμένους, mentioned by Theophrastus, § 5, meant perhaps the same thing. Cf. Poll. iv. 122.

It has been already stated that the house-door sometimes opened outwards; but it was far more usual for it to open inwards, as is apparent from the term ἐνδοῦναι, used of opening, and ἐπισπάσασθαι, or ἐφελκύσασθαι, of shutting. Plutarch, Pelop. 11 : ἅμα τῷ πρῶτον ἐνδοῦναι καὶ χαλάσαι τὰς θύρας ἐπιπεσόντες ἀθρόοι. Id. de Gen. Socr. 32 : τὸν μοχλὸν ἀφεῖλε καὶ μικρὸν ἐνέδωκε τὴν θύραν. He says elsewhere, however, οἱ μὲν ἔξω τὰς θύρας ἐπιστασάμενοι κατεῖχον, (Dio. 57,) and hence the rings or handles on the doors were called ἐπισπαστῆρες. Cf. Note 32, p. 54. That the door usually opened inwards in the time of the Peisistratidæ is clear from the tax already mentioned, though the passages quoted do not, it is true, refer to Athens. Neither is it probable that any change was made afterwards, for, from the time of Themistocles, everything tending to narrow the street was prohibited. It has usually been supposed, however, that the door opened outwards, though there are only two passages that can support this notion : first, the explanation given by Helladius of the words κόπτειν and ψοφεῖν, discussed in Note 32, p. 54 ; and secondly, Vitruv. iv. 6, 6, ‘ et aperturas habent in exteriores partes,’ but he is here speaking of temple doors only, ‘ de ostiorum sacrarum ædium rationibus.’

There are no passages which satisfactorily decide whether the outer-door was locked in the day-time, or merely shut, though the latter would seem more probable. It is certainly an exceptive case when Socrates finds Agathon's door open ; Plato, Symp. p. 174 : ἀι εῳγμένην καταλαμβάνειν τὴν θύραν. This may have been to save the guests the trouble of knocking. The eunuch in Callias' house seems not to have locked the door till he saw Socrates ; Plato, Protag. p. 314 ; and Praxinoe does so because she is going

out; Theocr. xv. 43. In another instance, Demosth. *in Euerg.*
p. 1150, the door stands open, ἔτυχε γὰρ ἡ θύρα ἀνεῳγμένη, which
is strange enough. On the other hand, we may conclude from Plutarch, *Pelop.* 11, that it was not customary to lock up the door
before night : καὶ κεκλεισμένην τὴν οἰκίαν εὗρον ἤδη καθεύδοντος.

The methods of fastening the doors have been discussed in
Gallus, pp. 281–284. The few remaining notices which exist are
hardly explicit enough to reward any further investigation. Yet
we may remark the curious fact that doors had sometimes two
locks. one in and the other outside. Achill. Tat. ii. 19 : Κατα-
κοιμίζουσα δὲ ἀεὶ τὴν Λευκίππην ἡ μήτηρ ἔκλειεν ἔνδοθεν τὴν ἐπὶ
τοῦ στενωποῦ θύραν. ἔξωθεν δέ τις ἕτερος ἐπέκλειε καὶ τὰς κλεῖς
ἔβαλλε διὰ τῆς ὀπῆς. ἡ δὲ λαβοῦσα ἐφύλαττε καὶ περὶ τὴν ἕω,
καλέσασα τὸν εἰς τοῦτο ἐπιτεταγμένον, διέβαλλε πάλιν τὰς κλεῖς,
ὅπως ἀνοίξειε. It is moreover manifest from Lysias, *de Cæde
Erat.* p. 14, that a door that had been locked outside could only
be unlocked again outside. Store-chambers were often sealed, for
the sake of greater security. Plato, *Leg.* xii. p. 954; cf. Aristoph.
Thesmoph. 414–428; *Lysistr.* 1199. When sealed the doors do
not appear to have been locked as well. Diog. Laert. iv. 59.

The assertion that the Grecian houses possessed no windows,
or at least none which looked toward the street, is quite untenable, though we must not expect to find the rows of broad and
staring apertures which characterise our own street architecture.
The Greeks lighted their rooms partly from above, and partly by
means of the doors which opened into the porticoes: yet windows,
θυρίδες, were certainly not uncommon, and they even looked into
the street. See Aristoph. *Thesmoph.* 797, where the women say :

> κἂν ἐκ θυρίδος παρακύπτωμεν, ζητεῖ τὸ κακὸν τεθεᾶσθαι.
> κἂν αἰσχυνθεῖσ᾽ ἀναχωρήσῃ, πολὺ μᾶλλον πᾶς ἐπιθυμεῖ
> αὖθις παρακύψαν ἰδεῖν τὸ κακόν.

Cf. Plutarch, *de Curios.* 13 : ἡμεῖς δὲ τοῖς φορείοις τῶν γυναικῶν ὑποβάλλοντες τὰ ὄμματα, καὶ τῶν θυρίδων ἐκκρεμαννύντες
οὐδὲν ἁμαρτάνειν δοκοῦμεν. So also in Aristoph. *Eccles.* 961, a
window is probably alluded to; and further, Plutarch, *Dio,* 56,
says: οἱ μὲν ἔξω τὴν οἰκίαν περιέστησαν, οἱ δὲ πρὸς ταῖς θύραις
τοῦ οἴκου καὶ ταῖς θυρίσιν ἦσιν : and then adds, Λύκων Συρακού-
σιος ὀρέγει τινὶ Ζακυνθίων διὰ τῆς θυρίδος ἐγχειρίδιον. But the
most decisive evidence on this point is the account given by Vitru-

vius, v. 6, 9, of the house brought on the stage in comedy : ' comicæ autem (scenæ) ædificiorum privatorum et menianorum habent speciem, prospectusque fenestris dispositos imitatione communium ædificiorum rationibus.' Cf. Appul. *Met.* i. p. 67.

The method of warming was by fire-places, though it is supposed that there were no proper chimneys, the smoke escaping through a hole in the ceiling. The καπνοδόκη, Herodot. viii. 137, through which the sun shone, was certainly not a regular chimney ; though it is difficult to understand what became of the smoke, especially when there was an ὑπερῷον ; and the joke in the *Vespæ*, 143, loses its point if we suppose a mere hole in the roof to exist. Consult *Gallus*, p. 279, on this subject. No mention is made of heating the rooms by means of pipes ; though small portable braziers, ἐσχάραι, ἐσχαρίδες, were often used. Plutarch, *Apophth. Reg.* i. p. 717 : Ἐν δὲ χειμῶνι καὶ ψύχει τῶν φίλων τινὸς ἐστιῶντος αὐτὸν, ἐσχάραν δὲ μικρὰν καὶ πῦρ ὀλίγον εἰσενεγκόντος, ἭΙ ξύλα, ἢ λιβανωτὸν εἰσενεγκεῖν ἐκέλευεν. Cf. Aristoph. *Vespæ*, 811. In most cases these were mere coal-tubs, ἀνθράκια. Poll. vi. 89 : ἀγγεῖα οἷς τοὺς ἐμπύρους ἄνθρακας κομίζουσιν ἐσχαρίδας . . . καλοῦσιν. Cf. Id. x. 101.

Böckh in his *Public Economy of Athens*, p. 141, has given such a complete and satisfactory account of the price of the houses, and the rent of the συνοικίαι, which however hardly correspond to the Roman *insulæ*, that nothing need here be added on the subject.

EXCURSUS II. TO SCENE III.

BOOKSELLING AND LIBRARIES.

AS the account of Roman libraries and books in *Gallus*, pp. 322–337, is in a great measure applicable to those of the Greeks, a few supplementary observations only would have been made in this place, had not doubts been raised as to the fact of bookselling being practised as a trade, and even as to the existence of private libraries, before the time of Aristotle. Böckh, in his *Public Econ. of Athens*, p. 47, has denied the existence of any such trade before the time of Plato, and his opinion has been that ordinarily adopted. But as the generally diffused taste of the Greeks for literary productions, and their speculative propensities, which would not readily neglect any opportunity of commercial advantage, raise a strong presumption against the above assumption, it will be worth while to investigate the facts.

The main argument against any trade in books being usual in Plato's time, is an adage quoted by Suidas after Zenobius: λόγοισιν Ἑρμόδωρος ἐμπορεύεται, with the explanation, that Hermodoros being a hearer of Plato, conveyed his discourses to Sicily and sold them : ὁ Ἑρμόδωρος ἀκροατὴς γενόμενος Πλάτωνος τοὺς ὑπ' αὐτοῦ συντεθειμένους λόγους κομίζων εἰς Σικελίαν ἐπώλει. The first mention of this adage occurs in Cicero, *ad Attic.* xiii. 21. On this authority Böckh takes on himself to explain the book-market at Athens, expressly mentioned by Pollux, as being merely the place where blank books without any writing in them were sold. Poll. ix. 47 : ἐν δὲ τῶν κοινῶν βιβλιοθῆκαι, ἢ ὡς Εὔπολίς φησιν, οὗ τὰ βιβλία ὤνια, καὶ αὐτὸ ἐφ' αὑτοῦ· οὕτω γὰρ τὸν τόπον, οὗ τὰ βιβλία, οἱ Ἀττικοὶ ὠνόμαζον. He also interprets in a similar manner the passage where Xenophon, (*Anab.* vii. 5, 14,) speaking of a vessel wrecked at Salmydessos, says : ἐνταῦθα εὑρίσκοντο πολλαὶ μὲν κλῖναι, πολλὰ δὲ κιβώτια, πολλαὶ δὲ βίβλοι καὶ τἄλλα πολλὰ, ὅσα ἐν ξυλίνοις τεύχεσι ναύκληροι ἄγουσιν. These passages as they stand would seem to prove that a trade was carried on in books in the ordinary sense of the word ; but still more unluckily for Böckh's hypothesis, all the best MSS. have πολλαὶ δὲ βίβλογεγραμμέναι: and the question seems to be set at rest by comparing another passage in Pollux, (vii. 210,) where he says, that it was quite as unusual to use βιβλίον of unwritten books, as χάρτης of manuscripts ; so that in the previous passage he cannot mean that the place at Athens called τὰ βιβλία, i. e. οὖ τὰ βιβλία ὄντα, was the market for the mere writing-material, βίβλος. Moreover, we see that this market is mentioned as early as the time of Eupolis ; add to which, βιβλιοπώλης occurs in Aristomenes, also a writer of the old comedy : in conjunction with which word, as if to obviate the possible error of supposing the βιβλιοπώλης a vendor of unwritten books, Pollux quotes the word βιβλιογράφος from Cratinos and Antiphanes, the βιβλιογράφος being the same person with the βιβλιοπώλης, and identical with the Roman *librarius*, i.e. one who multiplied copies of books for sale. See Lucian, *adv. Indoct.* 24 : Τὸ δὲ ὅλον ἀγνοεῖν μοι δοκεῖς, ὅτι τὰς ἀγαθὰς ἐλπίδας οὐ παρὰ τῶν βιβλιοκαπήλων δεῖ ζητεῖν, ἀλλὰ παρ' αὑτοῦ καὶ τοῦ καθ' ἡμέραν βίου λαμβάνειν. σὺ δ' οἴει συνήγορον κοινὸν καὶ μάρτυρα ἔσεσθαί σοι τὸν Ἀττικὸν καὶ Καλλῖνον τοὺς βιβλιογράφους. So also the ψηφισματογράφος, in Aristophanes, *Aves*, 1037, says :

> ψηφισματοπώλης εἰμὶ, καὶ νόμους νεους
> ἥκω παρ' ἡμᾶς δεῦρο πωλήσων.

Neither is there any reason why we should deem fictitious the story respecting Zeno the stoic, related by Diogenes Laertius, vii. 2 : ἀνελθὼν δὲ εἰς τὰς Ἀθήνας ἤδη τριακοντούτης ἐκάθισε παρά τινα βιβλιοπώλην. ἀναγινώσκοντος δὲ ἐκείνου τὸ δεύτερον τῶν Ξενοφῶντος ἀπομνημονευμάτων, ἡσθεὶς ἐπύθετο, ποῦ διατρίβοιεν οἱ τοιοῦτοι ἄνδρες. This strongly confirms the existence of an Athenian book-trade, at least in the time of Alexander.

But we must also recollect that the νέοι at all events, if not the παῖδες, must, without exception, have had copies of Homer, and other poets, which could not always have been transcribed at home. Cf. Aristoph. *Ranæ*, 1114 :

> βιβλίον τ' ἔχων ἕκαστος μανθάνει τὰ δεξιά.

And the example of Euthydemos alone proves that private individuals took great pains to collect the writings of the poets and sophists. Xenoph. *Memor.* iv. 2, 1 : Καταμαθὼν γὰρ Εὐθύδημον τὸν Καλὸν γράμματα πολλὰ συνειλεγμένον· ποιητῶν τε καὶ σοφιστῶν

T

τῶν εὐδοκιμωτάτων, κ.τ.λ. § 8. Εἰπέ μοι, ἔφη, ᾧ Εὐθύδημε, τῷ ὄντι, ὥσπερ ἐγὼ ἀκούω, πολλὰ γράμματα συνῆχας τῶν λεγομένων σοφῶν γεγονέναι; Νὴ τὸν Δί’, ἔφη, ὦ Σώκρατες· καὶ ἔτι γε συνάγω, ἕως ἂν κτήσωμαι ὡς ἂν δύνωμαι πλεῖστα. Νὴ τὴν Ἥραν, ἔφη ὁ Σωκράτης, ἄγαμαί γέ σου, διότι οὐκ ἀργυρίου καὶ χρυσίου προείλου θησαυροὺς κεκτῆσθαι μᾶλλον ἢ σοφίας. Now Euthydemos would never have made the copies himself, this being not at all in character with the life of an Attic νέος, nor were they the work of slaves, like the Roman librarii, for no such class of educated slaves existed in the Grecian house, in which they were entirely devoted to material objects. Besides, the reply of Socrates in the passage just quoted evidently refers to the expense of making the collection. Autographs, it is true, might sometimes be procured from the author or from some other possessor ; for an example of which see Gellius, iii. 17 ; but these were exceptive cases, and in general books must have been obtained through the medium of those who made the transcription and sale of manuscripts their trade. As for the proverb above mentioned, λόγοισι Ἑρμόδωρος ἐμπορεύεται, there was most likely a *double-entendre*, now lost to us, in the word λόγοι: if it meant no more than an imputation against Hermodoros for trading in books, a procedure which grew very common afterwards, it is not very intelligible how the sentence could have become proverbial.

Another passage which has been urged against the existence of libraries in earlier times, occurs in Strabo, xiii. 1, where we read of Aristotle: πρῶτος ὧν ἴσμεν συναγαγὼν βιβλία καὶ διδάξας τοὺς ἐν Αἰγύπτῳ βασιλέας βιβλιοθήκης σύνταξιν. As to the πρῶτος συναγαγὼν, this is sufficiently contradicted by Xenophon's account of the collection of Euthydemos, and also by what is related by Athenæus, i. p. 3, of the large libraries possessed by Euclides, the Athenian Archon, and by Euripides. So that the account of Strabo can only be supposed to mean that Aristotle's library was the first made on a comprehensive plan, and with a scientific arrangement. Even this supposition perhaps goes too far, for a well-arranged library is mentioned in a fragment of the *Linus* of Alexis, apud Athen. iv. p. 164, which is surely something more than a satire on the education of Alexander by Aristotle.

The first libraries for public purposes that we hear of, are those founded by Peisistratos at Athens, and by Polycrates at Samos. See Gell. vi. 17 ; Isidor. *Orig.* vi. 3, 3. But a sort of mythical obscurity pervades these accounts, and our suspicions are increased by the bold conjectures of Gellius and Isidore as to the subsequent destinies of these libraries. Moreover, no mention is made of any other such attempts during the succeeding centuries, until the magnificent Alexandrian institution was founded ; most probably by Ptolemy Soter, though his successor, Ptolemy Philadelphos, may have performed a still more meritorious service by his systematic arrangement of its contents. See Ritschl, *die Alex. Biblioth.* ; Letronne, in the *Journ. des Savants*, Juin 1838. A fortunate emulation excited the kings of Pergamus to imitate the Ptolemies in the boon they conferred on science, and when the literary treasures of Alexandria had been destroyed by fire, the world was fortunate in still possessing the scarcely less valuable library of Pergamus. Plutarch, *Anton.* 58.

As respects Greece itself, the idea of founding public libraries for the advancement of science and letters awoke too late. Public spirit had long yielded to paltry private interests, and had not, on the other hand, been replaced by the liberality of high-minded princes. It was from a Roman emperor, Hadrian, that Athens first obtained a rich and magnificent library. Paus. i. 18, 9. Of the public libraries of antiquity, the best account is that by Petit-Radel, *Recherches sur les Bibliothèques Anciennes et Modernes*.

At a later period, doubtless, private collections greatly increased in number and importance, and after a while individuals made collections of books for parade, and the sake of appearing learned, rather than from any real interest in science. From Lucian's treatise, *adversus Indoctum*, we learn many amusing particulars respecting this Bibliomania, and also about the manifold tricks of the booksellers of the time. See § 1 : ἢ πόθεν γάρ σοι διαγνῶναι δυνατὸν, τίνα μὲν παλαιὰ καὶ πολλοῦ ἄξια, τίνα δὲ φαῦλα καὶ ἄλλως σαπρὰ, εἰ μὴ τῷ διαβεβρῶσθαι καὶ κατακεκόφθαι αὐτὰ τεκμαίροιο, καὶ συμβούλους τοὺς σέας ἐπὶ τὴν ἐξέτασιν παραλαμβάνεις ; Dio Chrysostom speaks still more plainly on the subject of their rogueries ; *Orat.* xxi. p. 505 : Πάντως γάρ τινι τῶν βιβλιοπωλῶν προσέσχηκας ; Διὰ τί δὴ τοῦτό με ἐρωτᾷς ; Ὅτι εἰδότες τὰ ἀρχαῖα τῶν βιβλίων σπουδαζόμενα, ὡς

ἵμεινον γεγραμμένα καὶ ἐν κρείττοσι βιβλίοις· οἱ δὲ τὰ φαυλό-
τατα τῶν νῦν καθέντες εἰς σῖτον, ὅπως τό γε χρῶμα ὅμοια γε-
νηται τοῖς παλαιοῖς, καὶ προσδιαφθείροντες, ἀποδίδονται ὡς παλαιά.
How extensive the trade was, and what a rich selection was to
be found in the booksellers' shops, may be inferred from Lucian,
Ib. § 4: τίς δὲ τοῖς ἐμπόροις καὶ τοῖς βιβλιοκαπήλοις ἤρισεν ἂν
περὶ παιδείας τοσαῦτα βιβλία ἔχουσι καὶ πωλοῦσιν (εἰ τὸ κεκτῆσθαι τὰ βιβλία καὶ πεπαιδευμένον ἀπέφαινε τὸν ἔχοντα); The
highest prices were naturally attached to autographs, and so the
bibliomaniac, whom Lucian ridicules, fancied he had the autograph speeches of Demosthenes, as well as that orator's copy, in
his own handwriting, of the history of Thucydides. *Ibid.* On
the subject of the material used for writing on, see Note 12 to
Scene IX. Many remaining particulars are discussed in the Excursus in *Gallus* on this subject. See also the article *Bibliotheca*.
in the *Real-Encyklop. d. Klass. Alterth.*

EXCURSUS TO SCENE IV.

THE MARKETS AND COMMERCE.

A N investigation as to the precise site occupied by the Athenian market-place, or a discussion of its topographical details, lies beyond the scope of the present work. We purpose
merely to glance at the life and bustle of the Agora; and though
the vividness of such a picture would be much heightened by an
accurate knowledge of the locality, yet this would involve an
entire restoration of the market-place, its buildings, porticoes,
and monuments, and a knowledge of the position of the various
Exchanges, such as no one at present would venture to profess.
On the other hand, we shall not speak of the commerce of
Athens, in so far as it bears on history, political economy, or
private right. Our theme concerns only the outward appear·
ance of the merchants and dealers; our object is to see how, in
speculation and industry, in intrigue and deception, in their purchases and sales, the mercantile spirit of the Greeks, and their
every-day customs, were exhibited. Hence the wine-seller, who
hastens with his samples from house to house; the soldier,
who has peas measured to him in his helmet; the surly fishmonger, who scarce deigns to reply to the customer who grumbles
at his price; the trapezite, assaying the weight of the drachma;
the knavish huckster, with his false weights and measures, are
here, and in this point of view, more interesting than the organi-
zation of the higher branches of commercial polity, the lawsuits
arising from mercantile transactions, or a comparison between
the exports and imports. It is in this light that the following
combination of characteristic traits should be regarded; while
the endless difficulties which interfere with their regular classification must excuse the want of a strict methodical arrangement. Certain cognate matters also, such as the customary
διατριβαὶ, and life in the Ergasteria, naturally come under con-·
sideration at the same time.

In the first place, a word on the topography of the market-
place The ἀρχαία ἀγορὰ, which alone need here be understood,
was by no means a place of regular form, but rather a long

rambling quarter of the town, and this, whether we suppose it
to have reached from the Pnyx, across the Areiopagus, to the
inner Cerameicus, or whether we assign it any other position.
It was adorned with temples and porticoes, altars and statues,
and was shaded by the platanus-trees which Cimon planted.
Plutarch, *Cim.* 13 : ἐκαλλώπισε τὸ ἄστυ, τὴν μὲν ἀγορὰν πλατά-
νοις καταφυτεύσας, κ.τ.λ. When the market-place is spoken of
as a place of ordinary assembly and resort, this must be understood to apply only to a portion of it, the other parts being
appropriated to special purposes, and denominated accordingly.
Cf. Aristot. *de Republ.* vii. 12, p. 1331.

The visit to the market formed part of the usual arrangements of the day. While the Grecian matron was restricted to
the precincts of the house, and the unmarried damsel to the
parthenon, the husband spent the greater part of the day from
home; and all, even those unfettered by the claims of business,
resorted to this place of general assembly, where they found at
once the market, the gymnasia, and baths and tabernæ of all
kinds. Xenophon, *Mem.* i. 1, 10, says of Socrates : Ἀλλὰ μὴν
ἐκεῖνός γε ἀεὶ μὲν ἦν ἐν τῷ φανερῷ, πρωΐ τε γὰρ εἰς τοὺς περιπάτους καὶ τὰ γυμνάσια ᾔει, καὶ πληθούσης ἀγορᾶς ἐκεῖ φανερὸς
ἦν, καὶ τὸ λοιπὸν ἀεὶ τῆς ἡμέρας ἦν ὅπου πλείστοις μέλλοι συνε-
σεσθαι. Cf Plato, *Apol.* p. 17.

The time for resorting to the market was the forenoon,
which is therefore designated by the names πλήθουσα ἀγορὰ,
περὶ πλήθουσαν ἀγορὰν, πληθώρη ἀγορᾶς. The exact hour cannot, however, be fixed with certainty. Suidas, s. v. πλήθουσα
ἀγορὰ, says, ὥρα τρίτη : and again : Περὶ πλήθουσαν ἀγοράν·
περὶ ὥραν τετάρτην, ἢ πέμπτην καὶ ἕκτην. τότε γὰρ μάλιστα
πλήθει ἡ ἀγορά. We may take the third hour as the commencement; but that full market lasted till mid-day is improbable, and at all events is irreconcileable with two passages of
Herodotus, in which the time of πλήθουσα ἀγορὰ is expressly
opposed to μεσημβρία. Herodot. iv. 181; and iii. 104 : θερμότατος
δέ ἐστι ὁ ἥλιος τούτοισι τοῖσι ἀνθρώποισι τὸ ἑωθινὸν, οὐ κατάπερ
τοῖσι ἄλλοισι μεσαμβρίης. ἀλλ᾽ ὑπερτείλας, μέχρις οὗ ἀγορῆς δια-
λύσιος. τοῦτον δὲ τὸν χρόνον καίει πολλῷ μᾶλλον ἢ τῇ μεσαμβρίῃ
τὴν Ἑλλάδα. The end of the market was called ἀγορᾶς διάλυσις,
as we see from the above passage. So also in Xenoph. *Œcon.*

12, 1 : οὐκ ἂν ἀπέλθοιμι, πρὶν παντάπασιν ἡ ἀγορὰ λυθῇ   In the
lapse of centuries, this time probably became changed, and hence
the account of Herodotus may be reconciled with Liban. *Epist.*
1084 : καὶ ταῦτα ἐν τετάρτῳ μέρει τετέλεσταί σοι τῆς ἡμέρας
ἀπὸ πληθούσης ἀγορᾶς εἰς μεσημβρίαν σταθεράν.

But at other hours also the porticoes and shady parts of
the market were frequented by promenaders.   Demosth. *in Con.*
p. 1258 : περιπατοῦντος, ὥσπερ εἰώθειν, ἑσπέρας ἐν ἀγορᾷ μου μετὰ
Φανοστράτου.   Plutarch, *Dec. Or. Vit.* iv. p. 406, says of Hyperides : Ἐποιεῖτό τε τὸν περίπατον ἐν τῇ ἰχθυοπωλίτιδι ὁσημέραι.
Seats were fixed in the porticoes as well as in the gymnasia.   See
Lucian, *Jup. Trag.* 16 : Ἐπεὶ δὲ ταῦτα ἐννοῶν γίγνομαι κατὰ τὴν
Ποικίλην, ὁρῶ πλῆθος ἀνθρώπων πάμπολυ συνεστηκός· ἐνίους μὲν
ἔνδον ἐν αὐτῇ τῇ στοᾷ, πολλοὺς δὲ καὶ ἐν τῷ ὑπαίθρῳ· καί τινας
βοῶντας καὶ διατεινομένους ἐπὶ τῶν θάκων καθημένους.

The shops of the hair-dressers, unguent-sellers, and others,
were also favourite resorts, and the entire avoidance of these
places of *réunion* was censured.   Demosth. *in Aristog.* p. 786 :
οὐ φιλανθρωπίας οὐχ ὁμιλίας οὐδεμιᾶς οὐδενὶ κοινωνεῖ . . οὐδὲ προσφοιτᾷ πρός τι τούτων τῶν ἐν τῇ πόλει κουρείων ἢ μυροπωλίων, ἢ
τῶν ἄλλων ἐργαστηρίων οὐδὲ πρὸς ἕν.   See also Lysias *de Inval.*
p. 754 : ἕκαστος γὰρ ὑμῶν εἴθισται προσφοιτᾶν, ὁ μὲν πρὸς μυρο-
πώλιον, οἱ δὲ πρὸς κουρεῖον, ὁ δὲ πρὸς σκυτοτομεῖον, ὁ δ᾿ ὅπῃ ἂν
τύχῃ.   καὶ πλεῖστοι μὲν ὡς τοὺς ἐγγυτάτω τῆς ἀγορᾶς κατεσκευ-
ασμένους, ἐλάχιστοι δὲ ὡς τοὺς οὐ πλεῖστον ἀπέχοντας αὐτῆς.   Cf.
Isocr. *adv. Callim.* 4. p. 536 ; Aristoph. *Plutus,* 338 ; *Aves,* 1441.
Besides the κουρεῖα, μυροπώλια and ἰατρεῖα, the workshops of
even the common artisans formed fashionable lounges ; of this
kind are the σκυτοτομεῖα, mentioned by Lysias, *supra.*   See
Xenoph. *Memor.* iv. 2, 1: Καταμαθὼν γὰρ Εὐθύδημον.. καθίζοντα
εἰς ἡνιοποιεῖόν τι τῶν ἐγγὺς τῆς ἀγορᾶς, εἰς τοῦτο καὶ αὐτὸς ᾔει
τῶν μεθ᾿ αὐτοῦ τινας ἔχων.   These places sometimes assumed a
political importance from becoming the rendezvous of particular
phylæ, or of the inhabitants of certain quarters.   Lysias, *in
Pancl.* p. 730 : ἐπειδὴ δὲ ἀπεκρίνατο ὅτι Δεκελειόθεν, προσκαλε-
σάμενος αὐτὸν πρὸς τοὺς τῇ Ἱπποθοωντίδι δικάζοντας, ἐλθὼν ἐπὶ
τὸ κουρεῖον τὸ παρὰ τοὺς Ἑρμᾶς, ἵνα οἱ Δεκελεῖς προσφοιτῶσιν.
Cf. *Ib.* p. 732.

We will now proceed to speak of the various classes of mer-

chants and dealers, and of the social position which they held.
Aristotle, *de Republ.* i. 11, p. 1258, divides the whole μεταβλη-
τικὴ into ἐμπορία, τοκισμὸς, and μισθαρνία, and of ἐμπορία he
gives also three subdivisions : τῆς δὲ μεταβλητικῆς μέγιστον μὲν
ἐμπορία. καὶ ταύτης μέρη τρία, ναυκληρία, φορτηγία, παράστασις.
But so comprehensive a signification of the word was unusual,
and Aristotle himself does not adhere to it; *Ib.* iv. 4. The classification, moreover, is at fault in not distinguishing the αὐτο-
πώλης, as well as the ἔμπορος, from the κάπηλος : see Plato, *Polit.*
p. 260. The countryman who carried his produce to the city,
the artisan who sold his work, and the woman who offered for
sale her tæniæ and chaplets, all belonged to the class of αὐτο-
πώλαι. The ἔμπορος was the merchant who imported foreign
goods, and sold them by wholesale. Plato, *Protag.* p. 313. But
the κάπηλοι were the retail dealers, ἐλάττονος πριάμενοι πλείονος
ἀποδῶνται. Xenoph. *Memor.* iii. 7, 6. Cf. Plato, *Polit. supra.*
The most important passage relating to the business of these
κάπηλοι, and the sale of goods in general, occurs in Plato, *de
Republ.* ii. p. 371, q. v. It would seem that the country people
mostly brought their wares to town early, ἤδη θθεγγομένων ἀλεκ-
τρυόνων, and sold them to the κάπηλοι. Plutarch, *Arat.* 8. As
sellers again of bought goods, the κάπηλοι were called also
παλιγκάπηλοι. Aristoph. *Plutus,* 1156 ; Demosth. *in Dionysod.*
p. 1285 ; Poll. vii. 12. Dealers, not only in victuals, but in all
sorts of wares, were called κάπηλοι : so Aristoph. *Pax,* 1210, has
ὅπλων κάπηλος ; Plutarch, *Pericl.* 24, προβατοκάπηλος ; and Eustath. *ad Odyss.* i. 262, ἀνδραποδοκάπηλος. In Lysias *de Cæde
Erat.* p. 27, torches, δᾷδες, are purchased in a καπηλεῖον. But
by the term κάπηλοι, retailers of wine are most frequently meant.
Plato, *Gorg.* p. 518 : ὅτι Θεαρίων ὁ ἀρτοκόπος, καὶ Μίθαικος ὁ
τὴν ὀψοποιίαν συγγεγραφὼς τὴν Σικελικὴν, καὶ Σάραμβος ὁ κάπηλος, ὅτι οὗτοι θαυμάσιοι γεγόνασι σωμάτων θεραπευταί, ὁ μὲν
ἄρτους θαυμαστοὺς παρασκευάζων, ὁ δὲ ὄψον, ὁ δὲ οἶνον. Adul-
teration and short measure were matters of course. Lucian,
Hermot. 59 : ὅτι καὶ φιλόσοφοι ἀποδίδονται τὰ μαθήματα, ὥσπερ
οἱ κάπηλοι, κερασάμενοί γε οἱ πολλοὶ, καὶ δολόσαντες, καὶ κακο-
μετροῦντες. Plutarch, *Timol.* 14 : καθήμενον ἐν μυροπωλ.ω, πί-
νοντα κεκραμένον ἀπὸ τῶν καπηλείων. Cf. Id. *Lysand.* 13, where
Theopompos wittily compares with it the taste of freedom which
the Spartans vouchsafed to Greece.

These retailers not only sold their wares in the market, but had καπηλεῖα all through the town; but it was not thought respectable, especially in the olden times, to take any refreshment in them, as is seen from the anecdote in Plutarch, *Dec. Or. Vit.* iv. p. 400, where Diogenes catching Demosthenes ἐν καπηλείῳ αἰσχυνόμενον καὶ ὑποχωροῦντα, calls out to him: "Ὅσῳ μᾶλλον ὑποχωρεῖς, τοσούτῳ μᾶλλον ἐν τῷ καπηλείῳ ἔσῃ. And Isocrates, *Areopag.* 18, p. 202, speaking of former times, says: ἐν καπηλείῳ δὲ φαγεῖν ἢ πιεῖν οὐδεὶς οὐδ᾽ ἂν οἰκέτης ἐπιεικὴς ἐτόλμησεν. See also Athen. xiii. p. 566: Ὑπερίδης δ᾽ ἐν τῷ κατὰ Πατροκλέους, εἰ γνήσιος ὁ λόγος, τοὺς Ἀρεοπαγίτας φησὶν ἀριστήσαντά τινα ἐν καπηλείῳ κωλῦσαι ἀνιέναι εἰς Ἄρειον πάγον. It is clear, however, that this practice became common in later days. See Eubulos ap. Athen. xi. p. 473. According to Phylarchos, ap. Athen. x. p. 442, and Theopompos, ap. Id. xii. p. 526, the Byzantines were in very bad odour, being said to have even let their own houses, and taken up their abode in taverns, καπηλείοις. A painting at Pompeii, which represents several persons sitting round a table, drinking, refers probably to a καπηλεῖον. Gell, *Pompeiana*, second series, ii. pl. 80.

The whole trade of the κάπηλοι, as well as that of the regular innkeepers, was greatly despised; in fact, trade of any kind was at no time much respected. Plutarch, it is true, relates that Solon was engaged in commerce, and he adds, that this was even said to have been the real object of his travels; while a venture in the oil-trade occupied Plato on his Egyptian journey. Plutarch, *Sol.* 2. An Athenian would readily advance money to others for carrying on mercantile concerns, but it was considered disreputable to take part in them personally; and even ναυκληρία and ἐμπορία were held as a reproach. See Andoc. *de Myst.* p. 68. Aristotle, *de Republ.* i. 10, p. 1258, says: τῆς μεταβλητικῆς ψεγομένης δικαίως: and Plato, *Leg.* xi. p. 918, uses still stronger language: πάντα τὰ περὶ τὴν καπηλείαν καὶ ἐμπορίαν καὶ πανδοκίαν γένη διαβέβληταί τε καὶ ἐν αἰσχροῖς γέγονεν ὀνείδεσιν.

In a still greater degree this was the case with καπηλεία, not only at Athens, but also at Thebes, where nobody who had sold in the market within the last ten years was allowed to take part in the government. Aristot. *de Republ.* iii. 5, p. 1278: ἐν

Θήβαις δὲ νόμος ἦν τὸν δέκα ἐτῶν μὴ ἀπεσχημένον τῆς ἀγορᾶς μὴ μετέχειν ἀρχῆς. Cf. Plato, *Leg.* xi. p. 919. Whether not only the καπηλεία, but every sort of selling in the market, was thought degrading at Athens, is a disputed point. From a very important passage in Demosthenes, we gather that women publicly selling in the market were, in the eye of the law, classed with the women of the town. *In Neær.* p. 1367 : τόν τε νόμον ἐπὶ τούτοις παρεχόμενος, ὃς οὐκ ἐᾷ ἐπὶ ταύταις μοιχὸν λαβεῖν, ὁπόσαι ἂν ἐπ' ἐργαστηρίου κάθωνται, ἢ ἐν τῇ ἀγορᾷ πωλῶσί τί ἀποπεφασμένως, ἐργαστήριον φάσκων καὶ τοῦτο εἶναι [τὴν Στεφάνου οἰκίαν]. But, strangely enough, Lysias, *in Theomn.* p. 361, apparently quotes the same law, but reading ὅσαι δὲ πεφασμένως πωλοῦνται, with the commentary : τὸ μὲν πεφασμένως ἐστὶ φανερῶς· πωλεῖσθαι δὲ βαδίζειν. Also Plutarch, *Sol.* 23, gives the same explanation : ὅσαι πεφασμένως πωλοῦνται, λέγων δὴ τὰς ἑταίρας. Αὗται γὰρ ἐμφανῶς φοιτῶσι πρὸς τοὺς διδόντας. Harpocration and Suidas say : Πωλῶσι. Δημοσθένης ἐν τῷ κατὰ Νεαίρας· Ἡ ἐν τῇ ἀγορᾷ πωλῶσί τι ἀποπεφασμένως. Δίδυμός φησιν ἀντὶ τοῦ πορνεύουσι φανερῶς. πωλεῖν γὰρ τὸ παρέχειν ἑαυτὴν τοῖς βουλομένοις. ἐγὼ δέ φημι ὅτι κυρίως ἔταξε νῦν ὁ ῥήτωρ τὸ πωλεῖν. φησὶ γὰρ τὸν νόμον οὐκ ἐᾷν ἐπὶ ταύτης μοιχὸν λαβεῖν ὁπόσαι ἂν ἐπ' ἐργασ. ἠοίου κάθωνται, ἢ ἐν τῇ ἀγορᾷ πωλῶσί τι ἀποπεφασμένως. Between the two orators, it is hard to decide as to the real import of the law. We cannot escape from the difficulty by supposing that Lysias and Demosthenes do not both allude to the same law, as peculiarities of phrase establish its identity in both cases ; nor can we suppose that either of them misquoted it, or misunderstood its purport. We know, however, from Lysias, *in Nicom.* p. 837, that Nicomachos, being charged with the transcription of the old laws of Solon, indulged in alterations, not of form only, but of matter : ἐπειδὴ δὲ τῶν νόμων ἀναγραφεὺς ἐγένετο (Νικόμαχος), τίς οὐκ οἶδεν, ὅσα τὴν πόλιν ἐλυμήνατο ; προσταχθὲν γὰρ αὐτῷ τεσσάρων μηνῶν ἀναγράψαι τοὺς νόμους τοὺς Σόλωνος, ἀντὶ μὲν Σόλωνος αὐτὸν νομοθέτην κατέστησε, ἀντὶ δὲ τεττάρων μηνῶν ἑξέτη τὴν ἀρχὴν ἐποιήσατο. καθ' ἑκάστην δὲ ἡμέραν ἀργύριον λαμβάνων τοὺς μὲν ἐνέγραφε, τοὺς δ' ἐξήλειφεν. εἰς τοῦτο δὲ κατέστημεν, ὥστε ἐκ τῆς τούτου χειρὸς τεταμιεύμεθα τοὺς νόμους. This νόμος μοιχείας may, therefore, among others, have received a very different shape. Now in the speech against

Theomnestos, Lysias does not quote from the νόμοι ἀναγεγραμ-
μένοι, for he says, p. 356, καί μοι ἀνάγνωθι τούτους τοὺς νόμους
τοῦ Σόλωνος τοὺς παλαιούς. The true solution of the difficulty
may therefore be that the words in the speech against Neæra
are from the new edition of the laws.

The internal evidence, too, tends the same way, for it is in-
trinsically improbable that the selling wares in the market was
made such a *nota dedecoris* by law; and besides, Demosthenes, *in
Eubul.* p. 1308, adduces another law, which forbade making this
traffic an imputation against a person's character: παρὰ τοὺς νόμους, οἳ κελεύουσιν ἔνοχον εἶναι τῇ κακηγορίᾳ τὸν τὴν ἐργασίαν τὴν
ἐν τῇ ἀγορᾷ, ἢ τῶν πολιτῶν, ἢ τῶν πολιτίδων ὀνειδίζοντα τινι.
Originally, as is clear from the context of this passage in Demosthenes, burghers only were allowed ἐν τῇ ἀγορᾷ ἐργάζεσθαι,
without being subject to imposts, the ξένοι having to pay a
tax. Still, such employment was universally despised, and was
only carried on by burghers of the lowest class; cf. Diog. Laert.
ix. 66. Hence ἀγοραῖος denotes a low fellow, and πόνηρος and ἐξ
ἀγορᾶς are phrases of similar significance. Aristoph. *Equites*, 181 :

ὁτιὴ πόνηρος κἀξ ἀγορᾶς εἶ, καὶ θρασύς.

But if such employment was considered unseemly for a man, how
highly unbecoming would it have been for a woman, according
to the Greek notions of feminine decorum, to appear with articles for sale in the market where men were the only purchasers!
Artemidorus, *Oneirocr.* i. 78, after speaking of the hetæræ ἐν
πορνείοις, proceeds : Ἀγαθαὶ δὲ καὶ αἱ ἐπὶ ἐργαστηρίων καθεζόμεναι καὶ πιπράσκουσαί τι καὶ δεχόμεναι ἐμπολὰς, καὶ ὁραθεῖσαι
καὶ μιγεῖσαι. Hence we see that the shop-women, αἱ ἐπὶ ἐργαστηρίων καθεζόμεναι, were placed in the same category with the
hetæræ. It will be therefore impossible to suppose that the
female sellers in the market were not regarded much in the same
light. From Demosth. *in Eubul.* p. 1309, and Æschin. *in Timarch.* p. 118, we gather that female slaves sold in the market
the work they had done for their owners; but this does not
enhance the respectability of such an occupation. The two laws
may therefore have subsisted together.

The sale of goods was variously affected. The wholesale dealer,
ἔμπορος, seems usually to have sold by sample, δεῖγμα. For this
purpose, there was in the Piræus, and probably in other harbours

also, a place used for these sales, which was also itself called
Δεῖγμα. Harpocr. Δεῖγμα· κυρίως μὲν τὸ δεικνύμενον ἀφ' ἑκάστου
τῶν πωλουμένων. ἤδη δὲ καὶ τόπος τις ἐν τῇ Ἀθήνησιν ἐμπορίῳ,
εἰς ὃν τὰ δείγματα ἐκομίζετο, οὕτως ἐκαλεῖτο. See Böckh's *Public
Econ. of Athens*, p. 58. The samples were also carried about from
house to house. Aristobulos, ap. Plutarch, *Demosth.* 23 : Ὅτι
τοὺς ἐμπόρους ὁρῶμεν, ὅταν ἐν τρυβλίῳ δεῖγμα περιφέρωσι. Cf.
Plato, *Leg.* vii. p. 788. So a wine-merchant, οἰνοπώλης, goes
round with a flask under his arm, and sells the wine by this
sample. Diphilos, ap. Athen. xi. p. 499 :

> ὦ τοιχωρύχον
>
> ἐκεῖνο καὶ τῶν δυναμένων, λαγύνιον
> ἔχον βαδίζειν εἰς τὰ γεύμαθ' ὑπὸ μάλης
> καὶ τοῦτο πωλεῖν, μέχρι ἂν, ὥσπερ ἐν ἐράνῳ,
> εἷς λοιπὸς ᾖ κάπηλος ἠδικημένος
> ὑπ' οἰνοπώλου.

The legal restrictions of trade were few.   There were no
trade-guilds, in our sense of the word, nor, properly speaking,
any monopolies, i. e. assignments to individuals of special branches
of trade, though such were occasionally reserved by the State for
itself. See Böckh's *Public Econ. of Athens*, p. 52. A private
citizen could only obtain a μονοπωλία or μονοπώλιον, (Poll. vii.
11,) by buying up some article entirely, as Aristotle relates of
Thales the Milesian, and of a certain Syracusan ; *De Republ.* i. 11.
Nevertheless, Phylarchos, apud Athen. xii. p. 521, seems to allude
to a privilege of this kind : εἰ δέ τις τῶν ὀψοποιῶν ἢ μαγείρων
ἴδιον εὕροι βρῶμα καὶ περιττὸν, τὴν ἐξουσίαν μὴ εἶναι χρήσασθαι
τούτῳ ἕτερον πρὸ ἐνιαυτοῦ.

The retailers of certain articles seem, very commonly, to have
gone about crying them. See Aristoph. *Acharn.* 33 :

> στυγῶν μὲν ἄστυ, τὸν δ' ἐμὸν δῆμον ποθῶν,
> ὃς οὐδεπώποτ' εἶπεν ' ἄνθρακας πρίω,'
> οὐκ ' ὄξος,' οὐκ ' ἔλαιον,' οὐδ' ᾔδη ' π.ρίω.'

So also Plutarch, *Apophth. Lac.* 62: Ἕτερος ἐλθὼν εἰς Ἀθήνας
καὶ ὁρῶν τοὺς Ἀθηναίους τὸ τάριχος ἀποκηρύττοντας καὶ τὸ ὄψον,
κ.τ.λ. See also Note 4 to Scene XI.

The chief part of the traffic was of course confined to the
market-place, and the tabernæ around it. The market-place was
not paved,—indeed street-paving generally was quite an exception to the rule before, and even after, the Roman era. The

οὗτοι λᾶες in the ἀγορὰ of the Phæacians (*Odyss.* vi. 267) are
nothing more than the stone-benches, on which the assembly sat.
Cf. *Ib.* viii. 6: ἐλθόντες δὲ κάθιζον ἐπὶ ξεστοῖσι λίθοισιν. Strabo,
xiv. 1, 37, mentions, as an unusual circumstance, that at Smyrna
there were paved streets, ὁδοὶ λιθόστρωτοι. But the subterraneous
sewers, the want of which he remarks in that city, were in existence at Athens. See Aristoph. *Pax*, 99, and Scholiast. But
the streets, especially in bad weather, could not have been over
clean. See Thucyd. ii. 4.

The various divisions of the market, assigned to the sale of
different goods, seem to have been called κύκλοι. It has been
often supposed that this term referred only to that section devoted to the sale of kitchen-stuff, meat, and so forth; but the
authorities will hardly bear this out. The chief passage on this
subject is Poll. x. 18: Ἵνα δ' ἐπιπράσκετο τὰ σκεύη τῆς ἀγορᾶς,
τὸ μέρος τοῦτο κύκλοι ὠνομάζοντο, ὡς Ἀλεξις ὑποδηλοῦν ἔοικεν ἐν
Καλασίριδι, ποῖ δέ με ἄγεις διὰ τῶν κύκλων. σαφέστερον δὲ ἐν τῷ
Μαινομένῳ Δίφιλος·

> καὶ προσέτι τοίνυν ἐσχάραν, καινὸν κάδον,
> στρώματα, συνὸν, ἀσκόπηραν, θύλακον,
> ὥς που στρατιώτην ἄν τις, ἀλλὰ καὶ κύκλον
> ἐκ τῆς ἀγορᾶς ὀρθὸν βαδίζειν ὑπολάβοι·
> τοσοῦτός ἐσθ' ὁ ῥῶπος, ὃν σὺ περιφέρεις.

Id. vii. 11: καὶ κύκλοι δὲ ἐν τῇ νέᾳ κωμῳδίᾳ καλοῦνται ἐν οἷς ἐπιπράσκοντο τὰ ἀνδράποδα, ἴσως καὶ τα λοιπὰ ὤνια. Also Schol.
ad Aristoph. *Equit.* 137: ὁ δὲ κύκλος Ἀθήνησίν ἐστι καθάπερ
μάκελλος ἐκ τῆς κατασκευῆς τὴν προσηγορίαν λαβὼν, ἔνθα δὴ
πιπράσκεται χωρὶς κρεῶν τὰ ἄλλα ὤνια, ἐξαιρέτως δὲ οἱ ἰχθύες.
In these passages we see that σκεύη, ἀνδράποδα, κρέα, ἰχθῦς, and
in short τὰ ἄλλα ὤνια, are mentioned; and that the whole locality,
in various parts of which these were sold, was called κύκλος or
κύκλοι.

The sellers had also booths, σκηνὰς, apparently of wicker-work.
Harpocr.: Σκηνίτης· ἐν σκηναῖς ἐπιπράσκετο πολλὰ τῶν ὠνίων.
Demosth. *de Coron.* p. 284: τοὺς δ' ἐκ τῶν σκηνῶν τῶν κατὰ τὴν
ἀγορὰν ἐξεῖργον καὶ τὰ γέρρα ἐνεπίμπρασαν. This latter passage
shows that business was not confined to the time of πλήθουσα
ἀγορὰ, for it was evening when the news arrived, which was the
signal for this outrage. The γέρρα here mentioned may doubtless be taken for σκεπάσματα σκηνῶν. Another passage of the

same author presents more difficulties, and implies a different arrangement. *In Neær.* p. 1375 : τοὺς δὲ πρυτάνεις κελεύει τι-θέναι τοὺς καδίσκους ὁ νόμος και τὴν ψῆφον διδόναι προσιόντι τῷ δήμῳ, πρὶν τοὺς ξένους εἰσιέναι καὶ τὰ γέρρα ἀναιρεῖν. Harpocration, in his comment on the last passage, supposes that the wattles, or whatever the γέρρα may have been, were used to block up the approaches to the Pnyx, till the voting was over; while on the contrary, the Scholiast on Aristoph. *Acharn.* 22, says that the passages to the ecclesia were alone left open : ἀνεπετάννυσαν γὰρ τὰ γέρρα καὶ ἀπέκλειον τὰς ὁδοὺς τὰς μὴ φερούσας εἰς τὴν ἐκκλησίαν, καὶ τὰ ὤνια ἀνῄρουν ἐν ταῖς ἀγοραῖς, ὅπως μὴ περὶ ταῦτα διατρίβοιεν. That the γέρρα were barriers of some kind is clear from the Scholion on Lucian, *de Gymn.* 32 : Γέρρον τετράγωνον σκέπασμα ἐκ στερεᾶς βύρσης, ᾧ ἀντὶ ἀσπίδος ἐχρῶντο Σκύθαι . . . Δημοσθένης δὲ ἐπὶ τῶν σκηνῶν καὶ τῶν περιφραγμάτων. See also Eustath. *ad Odyss.* xxii. 184 : Παυσανίας δὲ γράφει οὕτω· γέρρα· σκηνώματα καὶ Περσικὰ ὅπλα . . . καὶ περιφράγματα. Αἴλιος δὲ Διονύσιος, ὅτι γέρρον καὶ οἱ περιπεφραγμένοι τόποι καὶ ἀσπίδες, κ.τ.λ. Festus also, p. 70, explains the Latin word *gerræ*, by *crates vimineæ*. But it is not necessary to suppose that the booth-wattles were used on this occasion, for there may perhaps have been proper γέρρα at hand for the purpose. From the words of the *Etym. M.* τὰ τῶν σκηνῶν περιφράγματα, it would almost seem that the κύκλοι were severally provided with such fences.

Each of the places of sale was called by a name derived from the article sold there, and at Athens the name of the article was itself used to denote the place where it was sold. Harpocr. s. v. δεῖγμα, says : ἔστι δὲ τὸ ἔθος Ἀττικὸν τὸ σημαίνειν ἀπὸ τῶν ἐν τῷ τόπῳ τοὺς τόπους αὐτούς. Poll. ix. 47 : εἰς τοὖψον, καὶ εἰς τὸι οἶνον, καὶ εἰς τὰς χύτρας. Id. x. 19 : ὥσπερ οἱ Ἀττικοὶ ἀπὸ τῶι πιπρασκομένων καὶ τὰ χωρία ὠνόμαζον, λέγοντες εἰς τοὖψον, καὶ εἰς τὰ μύρα, καὶ εἰς τὸν χλωρὸν τυρόν, καὶ εἰς τὰ ἀνδράποδα. There is scarcely an article which does not appear to have had its special place of sale, either in the market-place or elsewhere. Thus Eupolis, ap. Poll. ix. 47 : περιῆλθον εἰς τὰ σκόροδα καὶ τὰ κρόμμυνα, καὶ τὸν λιβανωτὸν, καὶ εὐθὺ τῶν ἀρωμάτων καὶ περὶ τὰ γέλγη.

Some of these appellations require explanation; for instance, γυναικεία ἀγορὰ, a term of doubtful import in Theophr. *Char.* 2:

Ἀμέλει δὲ καὶ τὰ ἐκ γυναικείας ἀγορᾶς διακονῆσαι δυνατὸς ἀπνευστί. The notion that in these κύκλοι, the chief purchasers were women, is erroneous, having been hastily adopted from Pollux, x. 18. At Athens it was a thing unheard of for any free-woman, except those of the lowest class, to make purchases in the market, or at the shop of a κάπηλος. The hetæræ, it is true, did not scruple to perform such offices for themselves. See Machon, ap. Athen. xiii. p. 580 :

> Ἐπεὶ προέβη τοῖς ἔτεσιν ἡ Γνάθαινα, καὶ
> ἤδη τελέως ἦν ὁμολογουμένως σορὸς,
> εἰς τὴν ἀγορὰν λέγουσιν αὐτὴν ἐξίναι
> καὶ τοὔψον ἐφορᾶν καὶ πολυπραγμονεῖν πόσου
> πωλεῖθ᾽ ἕκαστον.

Female slaves also went occasionally on such errands. See Lysias, de Cæde Erat. p. 18 : ἐὰν οὖν λάβῃς τὴν θεράπαιναν τὴν εἰς τὴν ἀγορὰν βαδίζουσαν καὶ διακονοῦσαν ὑμῖν. These however are exceptive cases. If a man did not go marketing himself, he had a slave, ἀγοραστὴς, for the purpose. Athen. iv. p. 171 : ἐκάλουν δὲ καὶ ἀγοραστὴν τὸν τὰ ὄψα ὠνούμενον. Cf. Poll. iii. 126. And it is to be observed that male slaves alone are mentioned in this capacity; so Terent. Andr. ii. 2, 31 :

> etiam puerum inde abiens conveni Chremis
> Ole a et pisciculos minutos ferre obolo in cœnam seni.

But the master generally attended to these matters himself; Æschin. in Timarch. 87 : τίς γὰρ ὑμῶν, ὃς οὐπώποτε εἰς τοὔψον ἀφῖκται καὶ τὰς δαπάνας τὰς τούτων οὐ τεθεώρηκεν ; The comic writers abound in instances in point, and it is only in a special case that the practice is ridiculed by Aristophanes, Lysistr. 557 :

> καὶ μὴν τό γε πρᾶγμα γέλοιον,
> ὅταν ἀσπίδ᾽ ἔχων καὶ Γοργόνα τις, κᾆτ᾽ ὠνῆται κορακίνους.

The name γυναικεία ἀγορὰ cannot, therefore, have been derived from the purchasers. We may suppose, with greater probability, that certain wares were sold principally by females, and that one section of the market was possessed exclusively by these ἀρτοπώλιδες, λεκιθοπώλιδες, ἰσχαδοπώλιδες, στεφανοπώλιδες, and others; or perhaps the name was applied to the locality where articles for women's use were chiefly sold. But the passage in Theophrastus which has given rise to this discussion is itself so

obscure that nothing certain can be inferred from it, and even
Pollux seems to be in doubt as to the true meaning of the word.

The part most frequented, and for the *gourmand* the most
important, was the fish-market, ἰχθῦς, ἰχθυοπωλῖτις, ὄψον. See
Excursus on *The Meals.* The sale was not allowed to begin
before a certain hour, when the signal for commencing was given
by a bell, at the sound of which everybody hurried to the spot.
Plutarch, *Symp.* iv. 4, 2 : ἀλλὰ τοὺς περὶ τὴν ἰχθυοπωλίαν ἀνα-
διδόντας ἑκάστοτε, καὶ τοῦ κώδωνος ὀξέως ἀκούοντας. But the
best elucidation of this occurs in Strabo, xiv. 2, 21, where there
is a capital anecdote of a Citharœdus, whose audience all desert
him when the fish-bell rings, except one who was deaf. 'Sir,
I thank you much for the honour you have done me in not going
like the others at the sound of the bell,' said the Citharœdus
to the deaf man. 'What!' asked he; 'did you say the bell
had rung?' And on the musician answering that it had, εὖ
σοι εἴη, said the other; καὶ ἀναστὰς ἀπῆλθε καὶ αὐτός. Neither
of these passages refers, it is true, to Athens, but no doubt the
custom prevailed there, as well as in other towns.

The surliness and knavery of the fishmongers are pourtrayed
in a very amusing manner by the comic writers. See a passage
of Amphis, ap. Athen. vi. p. 224 (τοὺς ἰχθυοπώλας):

> οὓς ἂν ἐπερωτήσῃ τις, ἢ λαβών τι τῶν
> παρακειμένων ἔκυψεν ὥσπερ Τήλεφος
> πρῶτον σιωπῇ—καὶ δικαίως τοῦτό γε·
> ἅπαντες ἀνδροφόνοι γάρ εἰσιν ἑνὶ λόγῳ—
> ὡσεὶ δὲ προσέχων οὐδὲν οὐδ' ἀκηκοὼς
> ἔκρουσε πόλυπόν τιν'· ὁ δ' ἐπρήσθη, κοὺ λαλῶν
> ὅλα ῥήματ', ἀλλὰ συλλαβὴν ἀφελὼν, τάρων
> βολῶν γένοιτ' ἄν· ἡ δὲ κέστρα κτὼ βολῶν.

A fragment of Alexis, *Ib.* is equally characteristic :

> τοὺς δ' ἰχθυοπώλας τοὺς κάκιστ' ἀπολουμένους
> ἐπὰν ἴδω κάτω βλέποντας, τὰς δ' ὀφρῦς
> ἔχοντας ἐπάνω τῆς κορυφῆς, ἀποπνίγομαι.
> ἐὰν δ' ἐρωτήσῃς, πόσου τοὺς κεστρέας
> πωλεῖς δὔ ὄντας ; δέκ' ὀβολῶν, φησίν.—βαρύ.
> ὀκτὼ λάβοις ἄν; - εἴπερ ὠνεῖ τὸν ἕτερον.—
> ὦ τᾶν λαβὲ καὶ μὴ παῖζε.—τοσουδὶ παράτρεχε.

If the comic writers may be trusted, several laws existed to
restrain their roguery; for instance, they were not allowed to
water their fish. Xenarchos, apud Athen. vi. p. 225 :

ἐπεὶ γὰρ αὐτοῖς οὐκ ἔτ᾽ ἔστ᾽ ἐξουσία
ῥαίνειν, ἀπείρηται δὲ ~οῦτο τῷ νόμῳ.

To evade this restriction a fight is got up near the fish-stall ;
a person falls down, pretending to be stunned by a blow; water
is thrown over him under the pretext of recovering him, and the
fish get watered at the same time. Another law is mentioned
in a fragment of Alexis, ap. Athen. vi. p. 266, which orders the
fishmongers to adhere without abatement to the price first named ;
but this appears merely to have been intended to ridicule Plato's
law on the subject (*Leg.* xi. p. 917), for the poet proceeds to announce, as the most recent improvement in legislation, that the
dealers were not to be allowed to sit down, so that they might
be induced by the fatigue to pass off their goods more quickly.
For the coming season a new ordonnance is announced to forbid
any sale being effected unless the dealer were suspended over his
stall, like the gods upon the stage : ἀπὸ μηχανῆς πωλοῦντες
ὥσπερ οἱ θεοί. Haggling about the price of an article was quite
as common as in modern times. Cf. Theophr. *Char.* 17 : πριάμενος ἀνδράποδον ἄξιον καὶ πολλὰ δεηθεὶς τοῦ πωλοῦντος.

Respecting other parts of the market, as, for instance, the
shambles, there are fewer notices. We may mention, however,
the humorous passage in Aristophanes, *Aves*, 1076, where the
birds set a price on the head of Philocrates, who was probably a
noted poulterer :

ὅτι συνείρων τοὺς σπίνους πωλεῖ καθ᾽ ἑπτὰ τοῦ ᾽βολοῦ.
εἶτα φυσῶν τὰς κίχλας δείκνυσι καὶ λυμαίνεται,
τοῖς τε κοψίχοισιν εἰς τὰς ῥῖνας ἐγχεῖ τὰ πτερά.

There are also some reliefs which represent the sale of game and
poultry. See Zoëga, *Bassiril.* 27, 28.

Bread was seldom made at home, but was usually bought of
women, ἀρτοπώλιδες, who either carried it about, or sold it at
stalls in the market, and elsewhere. Aristoph. *Vesp.* 1389 ; *Ran.*
857. See note 1 to Scene IV.

The chaplet-weavers too had their peculiar locality, which
seems to have been called the myrtle-market. See Aristoph.
Thesmoph. 448 : στεφανηπλοκοῦσα ἐν ταῖς μυρρίναις. This was
in the ἀγορὰ, as appears from v. 457 :

ἀλλ᾽ εἰς ἀγορὰν ὕπειμι· δεῖ γὰρ ἀνδράσι
πλέξαι στεφάνους συνθηματιαίους εἴκοσιν.

Probably the ταινιοπώλιδες, who sold ribands and ready-made

U

head-dresses, were also in the vicinity. Demosth. *in Eubul.* p. 1308.

The place for the sale of wine is mentioned by Isæus, *de Philoct. Her.* p. 134: καθίστησιν Εὐκτήμων ἐπιμελεῖσθαι τῆς ἐν Κεραμεικῷ συνοικίας, τῆς παρὰ τὴν πυλίδα, οὗ ὁ οἶνος ὤνιος. This does not allude to the retail trade, carried on by the κάπηλος, but to the sale of the wine which had been brought to the city in wains. A sale of this kind is represented in two Pompeian pictures, *Mus. Borbon.* iv., where the *amphoræ* are being filled from a large skin. These paintings are the best commentary on the fragment of Alexis, ap. Athen. x. p. 431:

ἐν τοῖς συμποσίοις οὐ πίνετε
ἄκρατον.—οὐ γὰρ ῥᾴδιον. πωλοῦσι γὰρ
ἐν ταῖς ἁμάξαις εὐθέως κεκραμένον, κ.τ.λ.

We must distinguish between the crockery-mart, χύτραι, and the place where the cooks stood with their apparatus waiting to be hired. Poll. ix. 48: Εἴη δ᾽ ἂν καὶ μαγειρεῖα τῶν πόλεως μερῶν, οὐχ ᾗπερ τὰ λοιπὰ τῶν ὑπὸ ταῖς τέχναις ἐργαστηρίων, ἀλλὰ τόπος, ὅθεν μισθοῦνται ὡς τοὺς μαγείρους. There seems also to have been a separate place where cooking-utensils were to be hired: ὅπου ὁ κέραμος μισθώσιμος ὁ τοῖς μαγείροις. Alexis ap. Athen. iv. p. 164.

Not only these necessaries of life, but also articles of luxury, seem mostly to have been sold in the same spot, and not in places scattered about the town. See Theophr. *Char.* 23: Καὶ προσελθὼν δ᾽ εἰς τοὺς ἵππους ὅπου τοὺς ἀγαθοὺς πωλοῦσι, προσποιήσασθαι ὠνητιᾶν. καὶ ἐπὶ τὰς κλίνας ἐλθὼν ἱματισμὸν ζητῆσαι εἰς δύο τάλαντα. This shows that where the κλῖναι, properly the frames only of the couches, were sold, there, very naturally, the coverlets were also to be had.

Lastly, it is in the market-place that the tables of the money-changers, αἱ τράπεζαι, are to be sought. See Plato, *Apol.* p. 17, where the correct reading is, ἐν ἀγορᾷ ἐπὶ τραπεζῶν. Cf. *Hipp. Min.* p. 368. Most likely the higher classes lounged about in the vicinity of these tables. See Theophr. *Char.* 21, where one of the signs of μικροφιλοτιμία is said to be, τῆς ἀγορᾶς πρὸς τὰς τραπέζας προσφοιτᾶν. Of course, certain necessaries,—provisions, for instance,—were to be obtained in other parts of the city. Thucyd. viii. 95: οἱ δὲ ἔτυχον οὐκ ἐκ τῆς ἀγορᾶς ἄριστον

ἱπ:σιτιζόμενοι—οὐδὲν γὰρ ἐπωλεῖτο ἀπὸ προνοίας τῶν Ἐρετριέων
—ἀλλὰ ἐκ τῶν ἐπ᾽ ἔσχατα τοῦ ἄστεος οἰκιῶν. Several articles,
such as salt-fish, were sold outside the gates.   Aristoph. *Equites*,
1246 :

> ΚΛ. καί μοι τοσοῦτον εἰπέ· πότερον ἐν ἀγορᾷ
> ἠλλαντοπώλεις ἐτεὸν, ἢ 'πὶ ταῖς πύλαις ;
> ΑΛΛ. ἐπὶ ταῖς πύλαισιν, οὗ τὸ τάριχος ὤνιον.

The superintendence of the market was intrusted to officers,
called ἀγορανόμοι.   Cf. Böckh, *Public Econ. of Athens*, p. 48,
Meier u. Schömann, *Att. Proc.* p. 90.   Sophilos, as we are told
by Athenæus, vi. p. 228, mentions certain ὀψονόμοι, whose duty
it was to observe whether people lived above their income; this
perhaps is a mere idea of the comedian's; though, according to
Diphilos, ap. Id. p. 227, this was one of the duties of the ἀγορανόμοι at Corinth.   But though these functionaries, ἀγορανόμοι,
σιτοφύλακες, προμετρηταὶ, &c., were able to check petty frauds,
yet there were plenty of ways for plundering the public by wholesale.   The fraudulent accounts of the funds and markets in our
own day had their parallel in antiquity.   See Lysias, κ. τ. σιτο-
πωλ. p. 721 : οὕτω δ᾽ ἄσμενοι τὰς συμφορὰς τὰς ὑμετέρας ὁρῶσιν,
ὥστε τὰς μὲν πρότεροι τῶν ἄλλων πυνθάνονται, τὰς δ᾽ αὐτοὶ λο-
γοποιοῦσιν· ἢ τὰς ναῦς διεφθάρθαι τὰς ἐν τῷ Πόντῳ, ἢ ὑπὸ Λακεδαιμονίων ἐκπλεούσας συνειλῆφθαι, ἢ τὰ ἐμπόρια κεκλεῖσθαι, ἢ
τὰς σπονδὰς μέλλειν ἀποῤῥηθήσεσθαι.

The current coins, their relative value, and their modern equi-
valents, have been adequately discussed by Böckh in his *Public
Econ. of Athens*, pp. 5–30.   Silver seems to have constituted the
ordinary currency.   Very small coins only, such as the χαλκοῦς, or
the δίχαλκον, were of copper.   Gold, at this period, seems to have
been rather an article of merchandise than a medium of exchange ;
hence the word χρυσωνεῖν is used to denote the exchange of gold
for silver.   Isocr. *Trapez.* 21, p. 528.   The difference of the
standard in the different stages gave rise to frequent extortion, and
the agio, καταλλαγὴ, κόλλυβος, on the larger coins was carefully
reckoned.   So Diphilos, ap. Athen. iv. p. 225, says, speaking of
a fishmonger :

> ἔπειτ᾽ ἐὰν τἀργύριον αὐτῷ καταβάλῃς,
> ἐπράξατ᾽ Αἰγιναῖον· ἂν δ᾽ αὐτὸν δέῃ
> κέρματ᾽ ἀποδοῦναι προσαπέδωκεν Ἀττικά.
> κατ᾽ ἀμφότερα δὲ τὴν καταλλαγὴν ἔχει.

Bad money, ἀργύριον κίβδηλον (opposed to δόκιμον), was not of rare occurrence, though to coin it appears to have been punishable by death throughout Greece.   Demosth. *in Timocr.* p. 765 : νόμος ἐστὶν ἁπάσαις, ὡς ἔπος εἰπεῖν, ταῖς πόλεσιν, ἐάν τις τὸ νόμισμα διαφθείρῃ θάνατον τὴν ζημίαν εἶναι.   Cf. Id. *in Leptin.* p. 508.   The oldest example is that of the gilt lead coins of Polycrates of Samos, if indeed we may credit the account given by Herodotus.   The usual expedient in forging (παραχαράττειν, Dio Chrysost. *Or.* xxxi. p. 577) was, before minting, to place a thin film of the precious metal on the piece of iron or copper. See Eckhel. *Doctr. Num.* i. p. 113.

Though there were no regular fairs in Greece, still there was something analogous to the annual marts of Germany.   The occasions of these were the public festivals, πανηγύρεις, whither such numbers of people resorted.   Strabo, x. 5, talking of Delos, says, ἥ τε πανήγυρις ἐμπορικόν τι πρᾶγμα.   At such periods crowds of dealers set up their stalls, so that the festival had much the appearance of a fair.   Dio Chrys. *Or.* xxvii. p. 528 : ἀφικνοῦνται δὲ καὶ πρὸς τὰς πανηγύρεις οἱ μὲν, . . . πολλοὶ δὲ ὤνια κομίζοντες παντοδαπὰ, ἀγοραῖος ὄχλος.   The most detailed account of such a Panegyris occurs in Pausanias, x. 32, 9 ; it relates to that which took place twice a-year at Tithorea in Phocis : τῇ δὲ ἐπιούσῃ σκηνὰς οἱ καπηλεύοντες ποιοῦνται, καλάμου τε καὶ ἄλλης ὕλης αὐτοσχεδίου · τῇ τελευταίᾳ δὲ τῶν τριῶν πανηγυρίζουσι πιπράσκοντες καὶ ἀνδράποδα, καὶ κτήνη τὰ πάντα, ἔτι δὲ ἐσθῆτας καὶ ἄργυρον καὶ χρυσόν.   Cf. Dio Chrysost. *Orat.* viii. p. 278. Hence the Romans translated the word πανήγυρις by *mercatus*, even when referring to the Olympian games.   See Moser, ad Cic. *Tusc.* v. 3 ; Böckh, *Corp. Insc. Gr.* No. 1625.   What Aristotle narrates of the occurrences at a spot on Hæmus, is still more like a fair.   *De Mir. Ausc.* 104 : εἶναι δέ τινα καὶ τόπον ἐν τοῖς ἀνὰ μέσον διαστήμασιν, εἰς ὃν ἀγορᾶς κοινῆς γινομένης πωλεῖσθαι παρὰ μὲν τῶν ἐκ τοῦ Πόντου ἐμπόρων ἀναβαινόντων τὰ Λέσβια καὶ Χῖα καὶ Θάσια, παρὰ δὲ τῶν ἐκ τοῦ Ἀδρίου τοὺς Κερκυραϊκοὺς ἀμφορεῖς.

EXCURSUS TO SCENE V.

THE GYMNASIA.

OF all the peculiar Hellenistic institutions the Gymnasia are perhaps the most important, for none exercised so powerful an influence on the entire development and various phases of Greek life — none at once awakened the noblest feelings, and fostered the most impure passions — none formed to the same extent the incitement to glorious deeds, and the seduction to idle pastimes — none so much enhanced the vigour of the corporeal powers, and at the same time gave them so false a direction — none made men so alive to the beauty and nobility of the human form and opened so broad a field for the grandest creations of art —and lastly, none betrayed youthful innocence into such degrading abuses—as was the case with the exercises of the Gymnasia. At a period when physical strength had usurped many of the prerogatives of intellectual power, it is true that even the rudest nations also cultivated bodily exercises; but in no country was their original intention so entirely lost sight of as in Greece; nowhere did Gymnastics assume so generally the character of agonistics; nowhere were they so much looked on as a diversion; nowhere did the Gymnasia become such universal places of amusement, and such arenas for emulous exertions.

We cannot wonder that the stern Romans, who valued such exercises merely for their military and diætetic advantages, judged unfavourably of Grecian gymnastics. See Plutarch, *Quæst. Rom.* 40: τὸ γὰρ ξηραλοιφεῖν ὑφεωρῶντο Ῥωμαῖοι σφόδρα καὶ τοῖς Ἕλλησιν οἴονται μηδὲν οὕτως αἴτιον δουλείας γεγονέναι καὶ μαλακίας, ὡς τὰ γυμνάσια καὶ τὰς παλαίστρας, πολὺν ἄλυν καὶ σχολὴν ἐντεκούσας ταῖς πόλεσι καὶ κακοσχολίαν, καὶ τὸ παιδεραστεῖν καὶ τὸ διαφθείρειν τὰ σώματα τῶν νέων ὕπνοις καὶ περιπάτοις καὶ κινήσεσιν εὐρύθμοις καὶ διαίταις ἀκριβέσιν, ὑφ' ὧν ἔλαθον ἐκρυέντες τῶν ὅπλων καὶ ἀγαπήσαντες ἀνθ' ὁπλιτῶν καὶ ἱππέων ἀγαθῶν εὐτράπελοι καὶ παλαιστρῖται καὶ καλοὶ λέγεσθαι. This passage requires a little elucidation. In the first place, the explanation given by Wyttenbach of the word ξηραλοιφεῖν is not

satisfactory. The body was anointed either after the bath, or as
a preparation for gymnastic exercises, but this was not universal,
being chiefly practised by the Palæstæ and Pancratiastæ. It is
true that Solon's law, which forbad the practice of gymnastic
exercises to slaves, is once and again quoted by Plutarch as if
ξηραλοιφεῖν only were forbidden, but this is inexact. Æschines,
in Timarch. p. 147, gives the law more correctly : Δοῦλον, φησὶν
ὁ νόμος, μὴ γυμνάζεσθαι, μηδὲ ξηραλοιφεῖν ἐν ταῖς παλαίστραις.
The difference between the Gymnasium and the Palæstra is
manifest from this law, as well as from Lucian, *Paras.* 51 ; but
neither from this passage, nor from such as Plato, *Lys.* p. 204, and
Charm. p. 153, can we deduce the inference that the former was
a public institution, and the latter not. The distinction seems
to have been that the Gymnasium was a place including grounds
for running, archery, javelin-practice, and the like, along with
baths, and numerous resorts for those who only sought amusement ; while the Palæstra. on the other hand, was the regular
wrestling-school, where, originally, wrestling, πάλη, and the pancration, were principally taught and practised. That the Palæstra
was not necessarily a private institution is clear from Xenophon,
de Rep. Athen. ii. 9 : ὁ δὲ δῆμος αὐτὸς αὑτῷ οἰκοδομεῖται ἰδίᾳ παλαίστρας πολλὰς, κ. τ. λ. The distinction which Krause has
attempted to establish, that the παλαίστρα was chiefly for the
use of boys, is quite untenable. Æschines, *in Timarch.* pp. 35,
38, uses the words interchangeably ; and Antipho, *de Cæd. Invol.*
p. 661, speaking of boys only, has, μελετῶν μετὰ τῶν ἡλίκων
ἀκοντίζειν ἐπὶ τῷ γυμνασίῳ. Cf. Lucian, *Navig.* 4, where the
young men betake themselves to the Palæstra. When Solon
forbade slaves both γυμνάζεσθαι, and also ξηραλοιφεῖν ἐν ταῖς
παλαίστραις, all the kinds of gymnastic exercises are included.
Cf. Harpocration, and the *Etymol. M.* s. v. ξηραλοιφεῖν.

The chief points of the above-mentioned charge made by
the Romans against the gymnasia, were, setting aside the evil
of παιδεραστία, that they induced inactivity and idleness ; that
what should have been the main objects, the strengthening and
exercising the body, were lost sight of ; that instead of the use
of weapons, mere unprofitable arts were taught ; and that the
body was too highly fed on unnatural diet to become fitted for
other exertions. Many voices even in Greece itself re-echoed

this imputation, in which, it must be confessed, there is a good deal of truth, especially as respects the athletes, the whole business of whose lives was the exercises of the Palæstra. At Sparta, for instance, πυγμὴ and παγκράτιον were entirely prohibited. See Plutarch, *Apophth. Reg.* i. p. 753 ; and Müller's *Dorians*, ii. p. 313. There, also, athletics were not generally the object of gymnastics. Aristot. *de Republ.* viii. 4.

Many agreed, on this subject, with Lycurgus. So Philopœmen, on being urged to undergo the exercises of the Palæstra, asked whether it would not partly unfit him for the use of his weapons ; and afterwards, when on service, πᾶσαν ἄθλησιν ἐξέβαλεν, ὡς τὰ χρησιμώτατα τῶν σωμάτων εἰς τοὺς ἀναγκαίους ἀγῶνας ἄχρηστα ποιοῦσαν. Plutarch, *Philop.* 3. The useless discipline of the ἀθλητικὴ is described with much point, though with a little rhetorical exaggeration, in a fragment from the *Autolycos* of Euripides, apud Athen. x. p. 413 :

> Κακῶν γὰρ ὄντων μυρίων καθ᾽ Ἑλλάʾα,
> οὐδὲν κάκιόν ἐστιν ἀθλητῶν γένους . . .
> Τίς γὰρ παλαίσας εὖ, τίς δ᾽ ὠκύπους ἀνὴρ,
> ἢ δίσκον ἄρας, ἢ γνάθον παίσας καλῶς
> πόλει πατρώᾳ στέφανον ἤρκεσεν λαβών ;
> πότερα μαχοῦνται πολεμίοισιν ἐν χεροῖν
> δίσκους ἔχοντες, ἢ δι᾽ ἀσπίδων χερὶ
> θείνοντες ἐκβαλοῦσι πολεμίους πάτρας ;

The disadvantages of such one-sided training are further hinted at by Socrates ; Xenoph. *Symp.* 2, 17 : ὥσπερ οἱ δολιχοδρόμοι τὰ σκέλη μὲν παχύνονται, τοὺς δὲ ὤμους λεπτύνονται μηδ᾽ ὥσπερ οἱ πύκται τοὺς μὲν ὤμους παχύνονται, τὰ δὲ σκέλη λεπτύνονται. The πολυσαρκία of the athletes was often ridiculed, and from their dulness of intellect they were called παχεῖς. The *double-entendre* in the word is explained by Eustath. *ad Il.* xxiii. 261. See Plutarch, *de San. Tuend.* 18 : τοῖς ἐν γυμνασίῳ κίοσιν ὁμοίως λιπαροὺς πεποιήκασι καὶ λιθίνους. Hence Hermes says to the athlete, who, παχὺς καὶ πολύσαρκος, wishes to go in Charon's boat, and calls himself γυμνός : οὐ γυμνὸν, ὦ βέλτιστε, τοσαύτας σάρκας περιβεβλημένον. Lucian, *Mort. Dial.* x. 5.

Of course there was a great difference between the exercises of the gymnasia generally, and those of the professional athlete. The contests of the gymnasia also imparted a spirit of activity and emulation to the whole social machinery of the Greeks.

This is well expressed by Lucian, *de Gymn.* 15. But very important disadvantages existed; among which were the encouragement it gave to παιδεραστία, and also the formation of the habit of idle lounging, or, as Plutarch says, πολὺν ἄλυν καὶ σχολὴν ἐντεκεῖν καὶ κακοσχολίαν. Quarrels and enmities were frequently engendered in the palæstra, the evil effects of which were felt in after life. *Palam.* 65: ἔνθα (ἐν παλαίστρᾳ) φιλεῖ ἔριδας πλείστας καὶ λοιδορίας γίνεσθαι.

But that which chiefly offended the Romans, and indeed all non-Grecian nations, was the perfect nakedness both at the customary exercises and at the matches; and this even at the Olympic games, from the time of Orsippos of Megara, or Acanthos the Lacedæmonian. Böckh, *Corp. Inscr. Gr.* No. 1003. The Romans looked on this as a *flagitium*, nor was it less unbecoming in the eyes of the Asiatics. Herod. i. 10: παρὰ γὰρ τοῖσι Λυδοῖσι, σχεδὸν δὲ καὶ παρὰ τοῖσι ἄλλοισι βαρβάροισι καὶ ἄνδρα ὀφθῆναι γυμνὸν ἐς αἰσχύνην μεγάλην φέρει. Plato, *de Republ.* v. p. 452, οὐ πολὺς χρόνος, ἐξ οὗ τοῖς Ἕλλησιν ἐδόκει αἰσχρὰ εἶναι καὶ γελοῖα, ἅπερ νῦν τοῖς πολλοῖς τῶν βαρβάρων, γυμνοὺς ἄνδρας ὁρᾶσθαι. The words which Herodotus (i. 8) puts into the mouth of Gyges, ἅμα κιθῶνι ἐκδυομένῳ συνεκδύεται καὶ τὴν αἰδῶ γυνή, are doubtless a Grecian sentiment, and are well applicable to the male sex also. Cf. Diog. Laert. viii. 43.

It is certain that in nearly all of the Greek states neither matrons nor maidens were allowed to be spectators of gymnastic games. Pausanias, v. 6, 5, relates that the mother of Peisidoros, who accompanied him to the Olympic games, dressed as a gymnastes, discovered herself in the moment when her son was victorious, and only escaped punishment because many of her family had been Olympian victors. On the other hand, the same author says, vi. 20, 6: παρθένους δὲ οὐκ εἴργουσι θεᾶσθαι. That married women, to whom alone the first passage refers, should have been prohibited from appearing on pain of death, while the presence of maidens was allowed, seems so strange, that many critics have supposed the passages hopelessly contradictory. Now it is true that an Attic virgin would never have dreamt of appearing in public, or being present at the games; but this would be quite in keeping with the habits of the Dorians, and the Spartans especially; for these nations allowed virgins much greater freedom

than married women. In Cyrene women were also permitted
to be present. See Böckh, ad Pind. *Pyth.* ix.

Of course it was still more rarely that females appeared as
competitors themselves in running or driving matches, although
they might send carriages to run. See Paus. iii. 17, 6 ; and v.
8, 3. Müller, in his *Dorians*, ii. p. 273, note, seems to fancy
that maidens at least were allowed to compete in person. Now
with regard to Cynisca, the sister of Agesilaos, who was the
most celebrated of these female charioteers, and was the first
who obtained the prize, it is plain that she did not herself drive
the horses, for an *ἀνὴρ ἡνίοχος* is also mentioned ; Paus. vi. 1, 3 :
Πεποίηται δὲ ἐν Ὀλυμπίᾳ παρὰ τὸν ἀνδριάντα τοῦ Τρωΐλου λίθοι
κρηπὶς καὶ ἅρμα τε ἵππων καὶ ἀνὴρ ἡνίοχος, καὶ αὐτῆς Κυνίσκας
εἰκών. If the representation on an ancient vase in Tischb. ii.
28, p. 59, where a female is seen driving a chariot, really refers
to Cynisca, a license taken by the artist must be supposed.

Throughout the Ionic states, and in most of the others except
Sparta, the female sex was excluded from all participation in
gymnastic exercises. Plato, however, is for the Spartan custom,
but his words show that he felt that its introduction would have
run counter to the universally entertained notions of propriety.
See *de Republ.* v. p. 452 ; and *Leg.* vii. p. 804.

But at Sparta it is well known that the maidens, as well as
the youths, practised the exercises of the gymnasium ; and the
mere mention of this fact might here suffice, had not a repugnance
to admitting that nudity was usual in both cases, led to many
passages being interpreted in a sense which their writers could
never have intended, and which the language used cannot possibly
admit. At Sparta, married women alone were excluded from
gymnastic exercises, the maidens being allowed much greater freedom in this respect, as well as in dress, and in their intercourse
with the other sex. This limitation seems to displease Plato, *Leg.*
vii. p. 806 : and it is, moreover, quite an oversight in Lucian, *Deor.*
Dial. xx. 14, when he talks of the already married Helen as γυμνὰς τὰ πολλὰ καὶ παλαιστική : and Aristophanes, *Lysistr.* 82,
has made a similar mistake   The real point at issue is, whether
by the γύμνωσις τῶν παρθένων of Plutarch, is meant actual nudity,
or only very light clothing. Now Plutarch, *Lyc.* 14, says : οὐδὲν
ἧττον εἴθισε τῶν κόρων τὰς κόρας γυμνάς τε πομπεύειν καὶ ἱεροῖς

τισιν ὀρχεῖσθαι καὶ ᾄδειν τῶν νέων παρόντων καὶ θεωμένων· and
since the complete nudity of the κόροι is indisputable, the presumption would be that the same was the case with the maidens.
Too much stress must not, however, be laid on the word γυμνας
in the above passage, since it is undoubtedly used of those who
were clad in the chiton only. See Aristoph. *Lysistr.* 150:

> εἰ γὰρ καθοίμεθ' ἔνδον ἐντετριμμέναι,
> κἂν τοῖς χιτωνίοισι τοῖς ἀμοργίνοις
> γυμναὶ παρίοιμεν, κ.τ.λ.

So Demosth. *in Mid.* p. 583: θοἰμάτιον προέσθαι καὶ μικροῦ γυμνὸν ἐν χιτωνίσκῳ γενέσθαι. The word denotes a still smaller
amount of clothing in Athen. iv. p. 129; and Id. xiii. p. 568:
γυμναὶ ἐν λεπτοπήνοις ὑφεσιν. This signification of γυμνὸς is
confirmed by the accounts we possess of the dress of the Doric
virgins, which was merely a short chiton, without sleeves, and
often not reaching to the knees. See Clem. Alex. *Pæd.* ii. 10:
οὐδὲ γὰρ ὑπὲρ γόνυ, καθάπερ τὰς Λακαίνας φασὶ παρθένους, ἐστο-
λίσθαι καλόν. Also Eurip. *Androm.* 588:

> αἳ ξὺν νέοισιν, ἐξερημοῦσαι δόμους
> γυμνοῖσι μηροῖς καὶ πέπλοις ἀνειμένοις,
> δρόμους παλαίστρας τ', οὐκ ἀνασχετοὺς ἐμοὶ
> κοινὰς ἔχουσι.

The words πέπλοις ἀνειμένοις are explained by Plutarch, *Comp.
Lyc. c. Num.* 3: Τῷ γὰρ ὄντι τοῦ παρθενικοῦ χιτῶνος αἱ πτέρυγες οὐκ ἦσαν συνερραμμέναι κάτωθεν, ἀλλ' ἀνεπτύσσοντο καὶ
συνανεγύμνουν ὅλον ἐν τῷ βαδίζειν τὸν μηρόν. καὶ σαφέστατα
τὸ γινόμενον εἴρηκε Σοφοκλῆς ἐν τούτοις (*Fragm. Helen.* 4) καὶ
τὰν νέοργον, ἇς ἔτ' ἄστολος χιτὼν θυραῖον ἀμφὶ μηρὸν πτύσσε-
ται, Ἑρμιόναν. Cf. Poll. vii. 55: ἐκαλεῖτο δὲ καὶ ὁ μῶν παρθένων οὕτω χιτωνίσκος, οὒ παραλύσαντες ἄχρι τινὸς τὰς πτέρυγας,
ἐκ τῆς κάτω πέζης παρέφαινον τοὺς μηρούς. μάλιστα αἱ Σπαρ-
τιάτιδες, ἃς διὰ τοῦτο φαινομηρίδας ὠνόμαζον. See the Phigalian
reliefs in the British Museum, and other sculptures at Florence
and elsewhere. See also Müller's *Dorians,* ii. p. 274–6, and the
Excursus on *The Dress.* Pausanias and Ælius Dionysius, apud
Eustath. *ad Il.* xiv. 175, explain the word δωριάζειν as follows:
Αἴλιος γοῦν Διονύσιος δωριάζειν φησὶ τὸ παραφαίνειν καὶ παρα-
γυμνοῦν πολύ τι τοῦ σώματος. αἱ γὰρ κατὰ Πελοπόννησον, φησί,
κόραι διημέρευον ἄζωστοι καὶ ἀχίτωνες, ἱμάτιον μόνον ἐπὶ θατέρᾳ
ἐπιπεπορπημέναι. Καὶ ὅρα ἐνταῦθα διαφορὰν χιτῶνος καὶ ἱμα-

τίου. Παυσανίας δὲ καὶ αὐτὸς δωριάζειν φησὶ τὸ παραγυμνοῦσθαι. Δωρικὸν γὰρ, φησὶ, τὸ παραφαίνειν τὸ σῶμα διὰ τὸ μηδὲ ζώνας ἔχειν, τὸ πολὺ δὲ χιτῶνας φορεῖν. ἐν δὲ Σπάρτῃ καὶ τὰς κόρας γυμνὰς φαίνεσθαι. Nor is there any contradiction in Ælius Dionysius calling the Peloponnesian females ἀχίτωνες, while Pausanias says that they generally wore the χιτὼν only. For this garment, being without arms, and merely fastened over the shoulders by agraffes, while below, on one side at least, it was quite open, might, when compared with the Ionian dress, be considered as scarcely a chiton at all. All this, it must be remembered, refers not to the palæstra, but to the dress of girls in every-day life. The only passage referring to the chiton as worn in the palæstræ is the Schol. ad Eurip. *Hecub.* 914: αἱ Λακεδαιμόνιαι γυναῖκες ἐν τοῖς ἀγῶσι μονοχίτωνες ἦσαν, πόρπας ἐφ' ἑκατέρου τῶν ὤμων ἔχουσαι, ὅθεν καὶ δωριάζειν τὸ γυμνοῦσθαι Ἀνακρέων φησί. Other passages, however, seem to speak of actual nudity at these contests, or at least show that the chiton was not worn. See Athen. xiii. p. 566: ἐπαινοῦντες τῶν Σπαρτιατῶν τὸ ἔθος τὸ γυμνοῦν τὰς παρθένους τοῖς ξένοις. Plutarch, *Lyc.* 15: λέγω δὲ τὰς πομπὰς τῶν παρθένων, καὶ τὰς ἀποδύσεις, καὶ τοὺς ἀγῶνας ἐν ὄψει τῶν νέων, ἀγομένων οὐ γεωμετρικαῖς, ὡς φησὶν ὁ Πλάτων, ἀλλ' ἐρωτικαῖς ἀνάγκαις. Whatever the γύμνωσις τῶν παρθένων may mean, the ἀπόδυσις must refer to divestiture of something, and we know that only one garment, the chiton, was ordinarily worn. Cf. Plato, *Leg.* vi. p. 771; and *Ib.* xi. p. 925. Moreover, Theocritus, xviii. 22, seems to allude to a *nuda palæstra*, when he makes the Spartan damsels say:

> Ἄμμες γὰρ πᾶσαι συνομάλικες, ᾗς δρόμος ωὑτός,
> χρισαμέναις ἀνδριστὶ παρ' Εὐρώταο λοετροῖς.

Neither did they restrict themselves to running, and the gentler exercises, but had trials of strength also. Xenoph. *de Rep. Lac.* 1, 4: πρῶτον μὲν σωμασκεῖν ἔταξεν οὐδὲν ἧττον τὸ θῆλυ τοῦ ἄρρενος φύλου. ἔπειτα δὲ δρόμου καὶ ἰσχύος, ὥσπερ καὶ τοῖς ἀνδράσιν, οὕτω καὶ ταῖς θηλείαις ἀγῶνας πρὸς ἀλλήλας ἐποίησε. See also Prop. iii. 12:

> Multa tuæ, Sparte, miramur jura palæstræ,
> Sed mage virginei tot bona gymnasii,
> Quod non infames exercet corpore ludos
> Inter luctantes nuda puella viros

So also Ovid, *Her.* 16, 149 :

> More tuæ gentis nitida dum nuda palæstra
> Ludis et es nudis femina mista viris.

Whatever weight may be attached to these passages, at all events the Latin word *nudus* has not the twofold signification of its Greek equivalent. Nor is there any doubt as to what was the ordinary belief in the times of those writers from whom the details are derived.

That youths were present at these female *agones*, as well as at the dances, is indubitable, though we may question whether they exercised together, as the κοιναὶ παλαίστραι of Euripides would insinuate. This, however, is said to have been usual at Chios; Athen. xiii. p. 566 : ἐν Χίῳ δὲ τῇ νήσῳ καὶ βαδίζειν ἥδιστόν ἐστιν ἐπὶ τὰ γυμνάσια καὶ τοὺς δρόμους καὶ ὁρᾶν προσπαλαίοντας τοὺς νέους ταῖς κόραις.

There are but few other notices of female gymnastics. Pausanias, v. 16, 2, speaking of the Heræa at Elis, says : ὁ δὲ ἀγών ἐστιν ἅμιλλα δρόμου παρθένοις, οὗτοι που πάσαις ἡλικίας τῆς αὐτῆς· . . . θέουσι δὲ οὕτω· καθεῖταί σφισιν ἡ κόμη, χιτὼν ὀλίγον ὑπὲρ γόνατος καθήκει, τὸν ὦμον ἄχρι τοῦ στήθους φαίνουσι τὸν δεξιόν. Also Athenæus, i. p. 24, briefly notices the ball-play of the Corcyrean dames.

The only connected account of the plan of a gymnasium is that given by Vitruvius, and this is both superficial and obscure. According to Ignarra, *de Palæstra Neapolitana*, he had in his eye the gymnasium at Naples, which was of a very different construction from those at Ephesus, Hierapolis, and Alexandria in Troas, the remains of which have been discovered. See Canina, *Archit. Greca*, iii. Newton and Schneider are the only writers who have done any thing to clear up the critical difficulties of the text of Vitruvius, or have attempted to reconcile the discrepancies in his account. All the plans given by the various commentators differ from one another. The accompanying plate is a gymnasium after Newton's plan, which on the whole appears to present the fewest difficulties.

According to Vitruvius the gymnasium consisted of a large prristyle, two stadia, or 1200 feet in circumference, having single rows of pillars on three sides, and on that facing the south, a double row. In the middle of this double portico, and opening upon it, was the Ephebeion, the most spacious of the exercising rooms, which

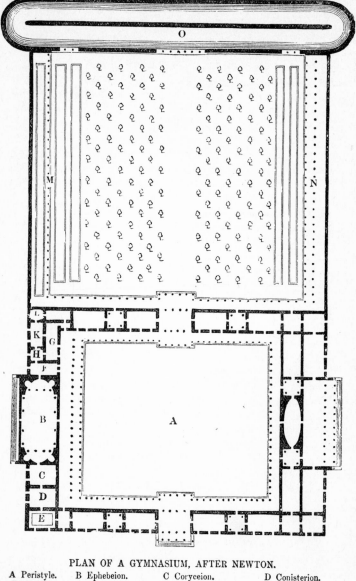

PLAN OF A GYMNASIUM, AFTER NEWTON.

A Peristyle.	**B** Ephebeion.	**C** Coryceion.	**D** Conisterion.
E Cold Bath.	**F** Elæothesion.	**G** Frigidarium.	**H** Hot Bath.
K Sudatio.	**L** Laconicum.	**MN** Porticus stadiatæ.	**M** Simplex.
N Duplex.	**O** Stadium.		

was furnished with seats along the walls, and was designed, it is supposed, for the use of the ephebi. To the right of the Ephebeion was the Coryceion ; next came the Conisterion, and lastly, in the corner of the portico, was the cold bath. On the left side of the Ephebeion lay, first, the Elæothesion for the use of the warm-bathers; next, according to Vitruvius, the frigidarium, though the purpose for which it was designed is doubtful. It has been shown in *Gallus*, p. 385, that frigidarium is the same as frigida lavatio, and the latter is placed by Vitruvius on the opposite side. With Marini, therefore, we would read tepidarium,—an alteration which renders intelligible the words, 'proxime autem introrsus e regione frigidarii collocetur concamerata sudatio.' For if the frigidarium had been the chamber next to the sudatio, Vitruvius could never have said, ' e regione frigidarii.' But it is the frigida lavatio which is here meant, and this being at the opposite end of the portico, the expression ' e regione ' is certainly applicable to it with respect to the sudatio.

In the three remaining arcades of the peristyle were the *exedræ*, saloons, furnished with seats, for the accommodation of the philosophers and rhetoricians, and of all indeed who sought intellectual recreation : ' Constituantur autem in tribus porticibus exedræ spatiosæ, habentes sedes, in quibus philosophi, rhetores, reliquique qui studiis delectantur, sedentes disputare possint.' These exedræ appear to have been usually uncovered ; for Vitruvius says that the *minium* was unsuited for the walls, as they were exposed to the sun, which that colour could not stand. 'vitiatur, et amissa virtute coloris denigratur.' Vitruv. ii. 9, 2. But, of course, there were also roofed rooms, and such are perhaps alluded to by Lucian, *de Gymn.* 16 : ἀλλ', εἰ δοκεῖ, ἐς τὸ σύσκιον ἐκεῖσε ἀπελθόντες καθίσωμεν ἐπὶ τῶν θάκων. The exedræ were sometimes semicircular, as we gather from Plutarch, *Alcib.* 17, ὥστε πολλοὺς ἐν ταῖς παλαίστραις καὶ τοῖς ἡμικυκλίοις καθέζεσθαι. Possibly, however, the last words may not refer to the gymnasium at all. The seats were stone benches, and ran along the walls ; Lucian, *ib.* : καὶ καθέδρα μάλα ἡδεῖα καὶ εὔκαιρος ἐπὶ ψυχροῦ τοῦ λίθου. Cf. Plato, *Charm.* p. 155 ; *Euthyd.* p. 274. There were also probably isolated stone seats, both in the gymnasia, and in other parts of the city. See Lucian, *Demon.* 67. Several such are still extant. Stuart, *Antiq. of Athens,* iii. pp. 19, 29.

The above-mentioned compartments constituted the most important portion of the gymnasium. It is strange that no one has hazarded a conjecture as to the use of the large open space of the peristyle, which according to Vitruvius must have measured, exclusive of the arcades, sixty thousand square feet. Doubtless it served chiefly for gymnastic exercises; and that this was the case in the Lyceion is expressly stated by Lucian, *de Gymn.* 2 : Ἕτεροι δὲ ἐν τῷ αἰθρίῳ τῆς αὐλῆς ,ὸ αὐτὸ τοῦτο δοῶσιν. Cf. Dio Chrysost. *Or.* xxviii. p. 531. The words of Plato, *Lys.* p. 206, οἱ μὲν οὖν πολλοὶ ἐν τῇ αὐλῇ ἔπαιζον ἔξω, have been strangely misunderstood by Krause, who creates out of them an outer court, as if the reading were ἐν τῇ ἔξω αὐλῇ. The passage merely refers to the persons in the ὕπαιθρον of the peristyle, who are said ' to play without,' in contradistinction to those in the apodyterion.

Vitruvius' account of the other parts of the gymnasium is much more difficult to comprehend. ' Extra autem disponantur porticus tres, una ex peristylio exeuntibus, duæ dextra atque sinistra stadiatæ; ex quibus una, quæ spectaverit ad septentrionem, perficiatur duplex, amplissima latitudine : altera simplex, ita facta, uti in partibus, quæ fuerint circa parietes et quæ erunt ad columnas, margines habeant, uti semitas, non minus pedum denum mediumque excavatum, uti gradus bini sint in descensu a marginibus sesquipedem ad planitiem, quæ planities sit ne minus pedes XII.' The reading of the manuscripts, though evidently incorrect, has here been given, since the violent alteration of Perrault, ' alteræ simplices, ita factæ, &c.' seems to give the passage quite a false meaning. The two parallel arcades alone were *stadiatæ*, as the third, which was that first entered on coming out of the gymnasium, was not designed for exercises. *Stadiatæ* is explained by Stratico and Krause to mean ' of the length of a stadion,' but the more probable interpretation is that given by Marini, Schneider, &c. ' provided with a stadium.' The space in the middle certainly resembles a stadium, and at all events corresponds to the name δρόμος. For these reasons the only alteration we would propose would be to read *factæ* instead of *facta*, in the above passage. When Vitruvius adds, ' Hæc autem porticus ξυστὸς apud Græcos vocitatur,' the *hæc* shows that the porticus simplex is that intended.

But the greatest difficulty with regard to the arrangement,

lies in the equivocal expression, ' extra autem disponantur. porticus tres.' If these really lay behind the first-mentioned parts of the gymnasium, it seems strange that Virtruvius did not, as usual, employ the word *introrsus* or *post*, instead of *extra*, which Palladio has actually supposed to mean that the arcades now in question surrounded the *palæstra* on the outside. This writer makes the *porticus duplex* run parallel to, and touch, the inner peristyle, where the ephebeion is; and the *xystus* in the same manner he supposes to lie on the opposite side; the gymnasium is thus extended on the two flanks, and not backwards, as in the accompanying plan. Such a construction presents great difficulties, and can hardly be reconciled with the words, 'post xystum autem stadium.' Nor is Newton's arrangement free from difficulties, for according to it the space within the arcades could have had no greater area, and certainly no greater breadth, than the Hypæthron of the peristyle, and this would hardly leave room for the 'silvas aut platanonas ambulationes et stationes,' which we are told that it comprised. All this part of Vitruvius description abounds with difficulties, which are perhaps incapable of solution.

Another question not easily answered is, by whom, and for what exercises, the gymnasia and palæstræ were used. It is manifest, from the law of Solon, and from Antipho, that boys must be supposed to have frequented the gymnasium; and this entirely overthrows Krause's supposition, that in the gymnasia the ephebi were chiefly exercised, in the xysti the athletæ, and the boys in the palæstræ. Besides, Aristophanes, *Aves*, 141, mentions a παῖς ὡραῖος ἀπὸ γυμνασίου, and Plato, *Leg.* vi. p. 764, wishes for γυμνάσια καὶ διδασκαλεῖα for maidens as well as for boys, and hence the supposition that it was not till a later period that the gymnasia were used as the exercise-ground for boys, falls to the ground. Theophrastus, *Char.* 21, τῶν δὲ γυμνασίων ἐν τούτοις διατρίβειν, οὗ ἂν ἔφηβοι γυμνάζωνται, seems to imply that there were both γυμνάσια ἐφήβων and γυμνάσια παίδων; but those here referred to could only have been small institutions, such as were above denominated palæstræ. For Athens had only three gymnasia at the time in question, the Lyceion, the Cynosarges, and the Academia; and that these were not thus appropriated is beyond a doubt. Another supposition would be that these gymnasia served for persons of all ages, and that there were divisions for the different degrees of age; and at a later period this was certainly the case, as we learn from Dio Chrysost. *Orat.* xxviii. p. 533 : ἀποδυσαμένου δ' οὐκ ἔστιν ὅστις ἄλλον ἐθεᾶτο, πολλῶν μὲν παίδων, πολλῶν δὲ ἀνδρῶν γυμναζομένων. But this can hardly apply to Athens at any early period, for the law of Solon quoted by Æschines expressly forbids seniors entering the boys' places of exercise : Οἱ δὲ τῶν παίδων διδάσκαλοι ἀνοιγέτωσαν μὲν τὰ διδασκαλεῖα μὴ πρότερον ἡλίου ἀνιόντος, κλειέτωσαν δὲ πρὸ ἡλίου δύνοντος. καὶ μὴ ἐξέστω τοῖς ὑπὲρ τὴν τῶν παίδων ἡλικίαιν οὖσιν εἰσιέναι τῶν παίδων ἔνδον ὄντων, ἐὰν μὴ υἱὸς διδασκάλου ἢ ἀδελφὸς, ἢ θυγατρὸς ἀνήρ. ἐὰν δέ τις παρὰ ταῦτ' εἰσίῃ, θανάτῳ ζημιούσθω. καὶ οἱ γυμνασίαρχαι τοῖς Ἑρμαίοις μὴ ἐάτωσαν συγκαθιέναι μηδένα τῶν ἐν ἡλικίᾳ τρόπῳ μηδενί· ἐὰν δὲ ἐπιτρέπῃ καὶ μὴ ἐξείργῃ τοῦ γυμνασίου, ἔνοχος ἔστω ὁ γυμνασιάρχης τῷ τῆς ἐλευθέρων φθορᾶς νόμῳ. It is doubtful whether the διδασκαλεῖα here mentioned are merely the schools of the grammarians, or, which is improbable, those also of the *Pædotribæ.* Plato, except in *Leg.* vii. p. 794, always opposes διδασκαλεῖα to γυμνάσια. Pollux also takes διδασκαλεῖον as synonymous with γραμματεῖον and παιδαγωγεῖον, and indeed the word always occurs in this sense. So that Æschines either quotes the law incorrectly, or extends to the Pædotribæ an expression which only properly applies to schoolmasters. With regard to the latter part of this law we must suppose the words τοῦ γυμνασίου to refer to one of the larger gymnasia, and that its intention was to prohibit the admission of adults during the feast of the *Hermæa.* At the period of this festival the ordinary discipline of the pædotribæ and pædagogues would be relaxed, and the law in question might therefore be found necessary. Plato, *Lys.* p. 206, where the boys celebrate the Hermæa in a palæstra, might be advanced against the supposition that the law refers to one of the gymnasia, but to this we may reply, that in Plato's time Solon's law was no longer in force.

The results of the foregoing inquiry may be summed up as follows. Instead of confining the gymnasia to the ephebi, and the xysti to the athletæ, it appears more probable that they were opened to persons of all ages; and an additional argument in favour of this would be the size of the smaller palæstræ, which were not large enough to admit of several of the exercises, such as shooting with the bow, and hurling the javelin or discus. Thus Antipho, speaking of a boy who has killed another, says, μελετῶν μετὰ τῶν ἡλίκων ἀκοντίζειν ἐπὶ τῷ γυμνασίῳ. The gymnasia also have been frequently regarded merely as places of instruction for beginners, whereas they were frequented by adults, and even old people often repaired thither for the sake of wholesome exercise. See Plato, *de Republ.* v. p. 452 : ὥσπερ τοὺς γέροντας ἐν τοῖς γυμνασίοις, ὅταν ῥυσσοὶ καὶ μὴ ἡδεῖς τὴν ὄψιν, ὅμως φιλογυμναστῶσι. Also Xenoph. *Symp.* 2, 18 : ἢ ἐπ' ἐκείνῳ γελᾶτε, ὅτι οὐ δεήσαι συγγυμναστὴν ζητεῖν, οὐδ' ἐν ὄχλῳ, πρεσβυτὴν ὄντα, ἀποδύεσθαι. Wealthy persons may have had rooms in their own houses appropriated to this purpose. Xenoph. *de Republ. Athen.* 2, 10 : Καὶ γυμνάσια καὶ λουτρὰ καὶ ἀποδυτήρια τοῖς μὲν πλουσίοις ἐστὶν ἴδια ἐνίοις. Also Theophr. *Char.* 22 : αὐλίδιον παλαιστρικὴν κόνιν ἔχον καὶ σφαιριστήριον. Still it is very improbable that this was frequently the case so early as the time of Xenophon, although after that of Alexander the practice became common.

In the second place, we arrive at the conclusion that the palæstræ were not mere training schools for boys; but that on the contrary they were used to some extent by the athletæ also. Krause unnecessarily restricts the latter to the xysti alone. That they practised in the xystus, Vitruvius certainly says; but he does not use the word *athletæ* in any strict sense : and besides, the use of the xystus does not preclude that of the palæstra also. But the positive testimony of Plutarch is far more important. He tells us, *de San. Tuend.* 18 : (κελεύσομεν) ἐν τῷ ξυστῷ καὶ ταῖς παλαίστραις διαλέγεσθαι τοῖς ἀθληταῖς. Again, *Symp.* ii. 4, he says : τὸν οὖν τόπον ἐν ᾧ γυμνάζονται πάντες οἱ ἀθληταὶ παλαίστραν καλοῦμεν : and then expressly states that the palæstra was properly the school for wrestling and the pancration : οὔτε γὰρ δρόμον, οὔτε πυγμὴν ἐν παλαίστραις διαπονοῦσιν, ἀλλὰ πάλης καὶ παγκρατίου τὸ περὶ τὰς κυλίσεις. For running and boxing the xystus was assigned, because the palæstra was unadapted for those exercises; while for the πάλη and παγκράτιον the xysti had no suitable space, since, according to Vitruvius, they were only twelve feet broad, and were still further confined by the raised pathways on each side.

The exercises of the ephebi may be supposed to have taken

x 2

place mainly in the gymnasia, and it is in reference to them that the gymnasiarchs are specially mentioned; but they must not be entirely excluded from the palæstræ. And, indeed, though γυμνάσιον and παλαίστρα may originally have been different in meaning, yet γυμνάσιον is used to denote the exercise-place generally, and the two words are sometimes interchanged.

Krause's work contains a very complete and satisfactory account of the various kinds of exercises, and to it the reader is referred. He says nothing, however, as to the hours at which the boys were taught gymnastics, or how this was combined with the rest of the instruction they received; and in the absence of positive information on this head, we must be content with conjecture. The chief point to be determined is, whether these two branches of education were synchronous or not. As has been mentioned in the Excursus on *Education*, Aristotle and Plato require that boys should be under the παιδοτρίβης till their tenth year, and after that attend the school of a grammarian for three years. Still, we can hardly suppose that during these three years they gave up gymnastic instruction entirely; and this would certainly not appear to have been the case from Plautus, *Bacch.* iii. 3, 23, though we are ignorant how much of Roman custom is mixed up with his account:

> Ante solem exorientem nisi in palæstram veneras,
> Gymnasii præfecto haud mediocres pœnas solveres. . . .
> Inde de hippodromo et palæstra ubi revenisses domum,
> Cincticulo præcinctus apud magistrum in sella adsideres :
> Cum librum legeres, si unam peccavisses syllabam,
> Fieret corium tam maculosum, quam est nutricis pallium.

The most natural supposition would be that the boys varied their occupations, and that those who had spent all the morning in the school of the grammarian went to the gymnasium in the afternoon, and *vice versâ*.

Adults indulged in the lighter exercises, and in the bath, as a preparation for dinner. So Xenophon, *Symp.* 1, 7, speaking of Callias' guests, says : Ἔπειτα δὲ αὐτῷ οἱ μὲν γυμνασάμενοι καὶ χρισάμενοι, οἱ δὲ καὶ λουσάμενοι παρῆλθον. Also Lucian, *Lexiph.* 5, after describing at length a visit to the gymnasium, and the accompanying bath, adds : κἀπειδὴ καιρὸς ἦν ἐπ᾽ ἀγκῶνος ἐδειπνοῦμεν. The ξυστοὶ or δρόμοι, also ξυστοὶ δρόμοι or κατάστεγοι δρόμοι, were used for regular constitutionals, which seem to have

been but seldom taken outside the town.   See Plato. *Phædr.*
p. 227 : τῷ δὲ σῷ καὶ ἐμῷ ἑταίρῳ πειθόμενος Ἀκουμενῷ κατὰ τὰς
ὁδοὺς ποιοῦμαι τοὺς περιπάτους. φησὶ γὰρ ἀκοπωτέρους τῶν ἐν τοῖς
δρόμοις εἶναι.   Also Xenoph. *Œcon.* 11, 15 ; Plato, *Euthyd.* p. 273.
Cf. Poll. ix. 43.

But the gymnasia, especially at Athens, were also the favourite
places in which sophists and rhetoricians instructed their assembled pupils, or engaged in intellectual conversation with those
who might chance to gather round.   Socrates was often to be
found sitting on the benches of the exedræ, and conversing with
his pupils or the sophists, while a crowd of listeners stood near.
See *Euthyd.* p. 271.   This was not the case with the large gymnasia only : each of the palæstræ seems to have been selected by
some sophist or other for the delivery of his lectures.   Thus in
Plato, *Lysias,* p. 204. Miccos the sophist takes immediate possession of the newly-built palæstra.   This proves that Solon's law
forbidding the entrance of adults was now obsolete.   Cf. Antipho,
de Cæde Invol. p. 672 ; Æschin. *in Timarch.* p. 145.   In Sparta
mere lookers-on were not admitted ; Plato, *Theæt.* p. 169 : Λακεδαιμόνιοι μὲν γὰρ ἀπιέναι ἢ ἀποδύεσθαι κελεύουσι.   At Athens,
however, and probably elsewhere, the gymnasia were crowded by
spectators, and served as regular places of conversation and social
amusement.

EXCURSUS I. TO SCENE VI.

THE MEALS.

'ΟΡΩ πάντα τοῖς ἀνθρώποις ἐκ τριττῆς χρείας καὶ ἐπιθυμίας ἠρτημένα δι' ὧν ἀρετή τε αὐτοῖς ἀγομένοις ὀρθῶς, καὶ τοὐναντίον ἀποβαίνει κακῶς ἀχθεῖσι. ταῦτα δ' ἐστὶν ἐδωδὴ μὲν καὶ πόσις . . . καὶ ἔρως . . . are the words in which Plato (*Leg.* vi. p. 782) maintains that the appetites are the main-springs of human action, and that from them moral worth and its opposite proceed. Be this as it may, at all events the gratification of these appetites has ever been a main concern of life, and the peculiarities hence arising must ever, therefore, hold a prominent place in any description of national or of local manners. It would be foreign to this purpose to give a detailed account of the various dishes, though such might be readily constructed from Aristophanes and Plutarch, or from the tedious alphabetical catalogue of Athenæus, the most comprehensive, and at the same time the most insipid, of all compilers. It will be more useful for us to glance at the kinds of food most usual, and at the changes introduced at different periods, taking occasion by the way to demonstrate the progress of luxury ; and then to investigate more at length the usages customary at social and convivial repasts.

In early times, the more cultivated Greeks do not seem to have attached much importance to the mere enjoyments of eating. It is true that the simplicity for which Athenæus praises the Homeric age, when bread and roasted flesh formed the sole materials of a royal meal, had long since yielded to a greater diversity of dishes ; but the dainties afterwards in vogue were at all events unknown in the days of Herodotus. Cf. i. 133. Antiphanes also, ap. Athen. iv. p. 130, terms the Greeks generally, μικροτράπεζοι, φυλλοτρῶγες. The abstemiousness of the Spartans is proverbial. They were accustomed from their youth to despise all the refinements of the culinary art, and to disregard everything beyond mere nourishment. See the characteristic anecdote in Plutarch, *de Esu Carn.* i. 5 : Καίτοι χαρίεν γε τὸ τοῦ Λάκωνος, ὃς ἰχθύδιον ἐν πανδοκείῳ πριάμενος τῷ πανδοκεῖ σκευάσαι παρέ-

ὄωκεν. αἰτοῦντος δὲ ἐκείνου τυρὸν καὶ ὄξος καὶ ἔλαιον, 'Αλλ' εἰ
-αῦτα εἶχον, εἶπεν, οὐκ ἂν ἰχθὺν ἐπριάμην. Cf. Id. de San.
Tuend. 12 : οἱ Λάκωνες ὄξος καὶ ἅλας δόντες τῷ μαγείρῳ τὰ
λοιπὰ κελεύουσιν ἐν τῷ ἱερείῳ ζηνεῖν. These simple tastes may
be regarded as an original national peculiarity, and not as consequent on the stringent regulations of Lycurgus; for before the
time of this legislator they were ἁβροδίαιτοι, as they are styled
by Plutarch, Apophth. Lac. p. 900.

The coarser natures of the Bœotians, on the other hand, led
them to indulge in gross and plentiful repasts; and the luxury of
the Corinthians was conspicuous, though Sicilian gormandising
exceeded everything. The meals of the Athenians, on the contrary, are ridiculed by the comedians for their simplicity. Athen.
iv. p. 131 : Λυγκεὺς δ' ἐν Κενταύρῳ διαπαίζων τὰ 'Αττικὰ δεῖπνά
φησι·

> Μάγειρ', ὁ θύων ἐστὶν ὁ δειπνίζων τ' ἐμὲ
> 'Ρόδιος, ἐγ ὸ δ' ὁ κεκλημένος Περίνθιος.
> οὐδέτερος ἡμῶν ἥδεται τοῖς 'Αττικοῖς
> δείπνοις. ἀηδία γάρ ἐστιν 'Αττικὴ,
> ὥσπερ ξενική. παρέθηκε πίνακα γὰρ μέγαν
> ἔχοντα μικροὺς πέντε πενακίσκους ἐν οἷ . .
> ὄψιν μὲν οὖν ἔχει τὰ τοιαῦτα ποικίλην
> ἀλλ' οὐδέν ἐστι τοῦτο πρὸς τὴν γαστέρα.

Unquestionably the symposium which succeeded the meal was
considered by the Athenians as the main thing, and as affording
opportunity for a higher species of enjoyment. So in the Symposia of Xenophon and Plato the pleasure is wholly intellectual,
not sensual, as is remarked by Plutarch, Symp. vi. p. 817. Plato's
entertainments were noted for their frugality, and we are told that
a chief dish with him was figs, hence he was called φιλόσυκος.
Plutarch, Symp. iv. 4, 2 ; cf. de San. Tuend. 9.

From the earliest times it was usual to take three meals a day,
and though the hours of these repasts remained essentially un-
altered, still the same names were not always used to denote
them. With regard to the Homeric usage, we have the statements of Eustathius, ad Odyss. ii. 20, though we need not pin
our faith to his somewhat amusing etymologies : 'Ιστέον δ' ὅτι
τρισὶ τροφαῖς ἐχρῶντο οἱ παλαιοί · ὧν τὸ πρῶτον ἐκαλεῖτο ἄρι-
στ▪ν, γινόμενον πάνυ πρωΐ, ἅμ' ἠοῖ φαινομέ ηφι, ἄρεος ἱσταμέ-
▪.υ, ὡς καὶ ἡ τοῦ ὀνόματος ἐτυμολογία δηλοῖ. εἶτα τὸ δεῖπιον,

μεθ' ὃ ἔδει πονεῖν, ὃ καὶ ἄριστόν φασί τινες. τρίτον δὲ δόρπος
ἐναντίον ἀρίστῳ, ἡνίκα δόρυ παύεται. ὅπερ ἡμεῖς παρὰ τὸ δεῖν
▸ὅτε ὕπνου δεῖπνον καλοῦμεν. And Palamedes, in a fragment of
Æschylus, ap. Athen. i. p. 11, is made to say : σῖτον δ' εἰδέιαι
διώρισα, ἄριστα, δεῖπνα, δόρπα θ' αἱρεῖσθαι τρία. But these expressions are not used in their strict sense by Homer. Thus
ἄριστον occurs once only in the *Iliad* (xxiv. 124), and once in
the *Odyssey* (xvi. 2) ; while δεῖπνον, which means a meal generally,
without reference to the time, is elsewhere used instead : but for
the meal taken in the middle of the day there is no special name.
Cf. Eustath. ad *Il.* xi. 86 ; ad *Odyss.* xvi. 2.

The usage afterwards was changed, for in the Attic dialect, at
least, δεῖπνον came to be used, invariably, of the evening meal
(δόρπον), while the mid-day meal was called ἄριστον, and the first
breakfast received the name ἀκράτισμα. Instead of this word,
Plutarch also uses πρόπομα (*Symp.* i. 6, 3), which has elsewhere
quite another meaning. Plutarch also says, *Symp.* viii. 6, 4 : καὶ
τὸ μὲν ἄριστον ἐδόκει τῷ ἀκρατίσματι ταὐτὸν εἶναι. This may
mean that the same meal which was formerly called ἄριστον afterwards received the name ἀκράτισμα : or, when no great accuracy
of expression was required, the early breakfast might also be called
ἄριστον. So Plutarch, *de Alex. Fort.* 6 : ἠρίστα μὲν ὀρθροῦ κα-
θεζόμενος, ἐδείπνει δὲ πρὸς ἑσπέραν βαθεῖαν. But in this case
of course no other breakfast followed. Cf. *Alex.* 23.

The ἀκράτισμα, or proper breakfast, was taken quite early,
directly after rising. So Aristoph. *Aves*, 1285, says, ἔωθεν ἐξ εὐνῆς. It consisted of bread, dipped in neat wine, ἄκρατος, and
hence the name. Plutarch, *Symp.* viii. 6, 4 : Φασὶ γὰρ ἐκείνους
(τοὺς ἀρχαίους) ἐργατικοὺς ἅμα καὶ σώφρονας ὄντας ἔωθεν ἐσθίειν
ἄρτον ἐν ἀκράτῳ καὶ μηδὲν ἄλλο. διὸ τοῦτο μὲν ἀκράτισμα καλεῖν, διὰ τὸν ἄκρατον. Cf. Schol. ad Theocr. i. 51. Both these
passages refer to a very early period ; but Athenæus, i. p. 11,
mentions the custom as still existing in his own time. He also
quotes a fragment of Aristomenes :

Ἀκρατιοῦμαι μικρὸν, εἶθ' ἥξω πάλιν,
ἄρτου δὶς ἢ τρὶς ἀποδακών.

It is not so easy to assign a fixed hour for the ἄριστον. In
Xenophon's *Anabasis* this meal is repeatedly mentioned ; but of
course on a march, and in the field, it would often be impossible

to adhere to any given hour. Suidas places it περὶ ὥραν τρίτην. This would be mid-way between sun-rise and noon, and at the equinoxes would be about nine o'clock. But we have various reasons for distrusting this account. For the time of πλήθουσα ἀγορὰ chiefly embraces the fourth, fifth, and sixth hours, and this was the usual period for going to market—often to buy the materials for breakfast—and therefore the ἄριστον must be fixed nearer noon. This also agrees best with Aristoph. *Vesp.* 605–612, where the Heliast is spoken of as sitting down to the ἄριστον when the Court rises, which would hardly be the case so soon as the third hour. See Xenoph. *Œcon.* xi. 14, seq. down to εἶτα δὲ ἀριστῶ. Cf. Plutarch, *Arat.* 6, 7. According to this, the ἄριστον would appear to have been the mid-day meal, answering to the Roman *prandium*; and this indeed Plutarch expressly states; *Symp.* viii. 6, 5: τὸ ἄριστον ἐκλήθη πράνδιον ἀπὸ τῆς ὥρας. ἔνδιον γὰρ τὸ δειλινόν. Cf. Ruhnk. *ad Tim.* p. 63. This meal consisted, in part at least, of hot dishes, and therefore often required the services of the cook. Antiphanes, ap. Athen. i. p. 11: ἄριστον ἐν ὅσῳ ὁ μάγειρος ποιεῖ.

The chief meal, as among the Romans, was the third, the δεῖπνον, though perhaps it was served somewhat later than the Roman *cœna*. See Aristoph. *Eccles.* 652:

σοὶ δὲ μελήσει,
ὅταν ᾖ δεκάπουν τὸ στοιχεῖον λιπαρὸν χωρεῖν ἐπὶ δεῖπνον.

Unfortunately our knowledge of the γνώμων is not sufficient to enable us accurately to ascertain the hour here intended. See Note 3 to Scene XII. That the meal in question was usually late, is plain from Lysias, *de Cæd. Erat.* p. 26: Σώστρατος ἦν μοι ἐπιτήδειος καὶ φίλος. τούτῳ ἡλίου δεδυκότος ἰόντι ἐξ ἀγροῦ ἀπήντησα . . . καὶ ἐλθόντες οἴκαδε ὡς ἐμὲ ἀναβάντες εἰς τὸ ὑπερῷον ἐδειπνοῦμεν. So too, in the passage just quoted from Plutarch, we read that Alexander dined πρὸς ἑσπέραν βαθεῖαν.

The Greeks did not call it a regular meal, if a person ate alone, without any company. See Plutarch, *Symp.* vii. p. 869: ἐπεὶ μόνος ἐδείπνησε, βεβρωκέναι, μὴ δεδειπνηκέναι σήμερον. Cf. Alexis, apud Athen. ii. p. 47:

Ἐπὰν ἰδιώτην ἄνδρα μονοσιτοῦντ᾽ ἴδῃς,
ἢ μὴ ποθοῦντ᾽ ᾠδὰς ποιητὴν καὶ μέλη,
τὸν μὲν ἰδιώτην τοῦ βίου τὸν ἥμισυν

ἀπολωλεκέναι νόμιζε, τὸν δὲ τῆς τέχνης
τὴν ἡμίσειαν. ζῶσι δ' ἀμφότεροι μόλις.

Before proceeding to describe the details of one of these entertainments, it will be well to enumerate the various kinds of convivial meals, and the occasions which gave rise to them.   In
ancient times public or domestic sacrifices afforded the most frequent opportunities for banquets, and in after times this continued to be the case. See Antiph. *de Venef.* p. 612 ; Isæus, *de
Astyphil. Hered.* p. 243. The public feasts were mostly δαῖτες,
in the strict sense of the word, when each guest got his apportioned
share of meat, and also bread, and even wine. Plutarch, *Symp.*
ii. 10, 1 : τὰ πλεῖστα τῶν δείπνων δαῖτες ἦσαν, ἐν ταῖς θυσίαις
ἑκάστῳ μερίδος ἀποκληρουμένης . . . ὅπερ νῦν γίνεται, κρέας προ-
θέμενον καὶ ἄρτον, ὥσπερ ἐκ φάτνης ἰδίας ἕκαστον εὐωχεῖσθαι.
See Böckh, *Public Econ. of Athens,* p 211. Perhaps this custom
was not universal ; indeed Plutarch mentions it as newly instituted
in his native city, and he adds that it had displeased many.   On
the other hand, the μερίδες are mentioned as something usual.
Id. *Prov. Alex.* 35 ; Athen. viii. p. 365.

Birthdays also gave occasion for these banquets, and not only
the birthdays of members of the family itself (Lucian, *Somn. s.
Gall.* 9), but those also of esteemed persons, or of the renowned
dead : Plutarch, *Symp.* viii. 1 : Τῇ ἕκτῃ τοῦ Θαργελιῶνος ἱστα-
μένου τὴν Σωκράτους ἀγαγόντες γενέθλιον, τῇ ἑβδόμῃ τὴν Πλάτωνος ἤγομεν.   Other occasions which may be mentioned were
funerals ; the departure or arrival of a friend ; the gaining of a
victory (νικητήρια, Xenoph. *Symp.*; Plutarch, *Phoc.* 20), and
similar events.

It was very common for several to club together, and have a
feast at their joint expense. This could be done in two ways.
Each either contributed his share, συμβολή, in money, or brought
his own provisions with him.   The former method was very
usual among young people, and was called ἀπὸ συμβολῶν δειπνεῖν. See Lucian, *Lexiph.* 6 ; Terent. *Eun.* iii. 4 :

> Heri aliquot adolescentuli coiimus in Piræo,
> In hunc diem ut de symbolis essemus.

The feast came off at the house of an hetæra, or of one of the con-
tributors, or at a freedman's. See Terence, *Ib.* iii. 5, 60 ; Aristoph. *Acharn.* 1210 ; Athen. viii. p. 365 ; Lucian, *Dial. Mer.* vii.

The Homeric ἔρανος (*Odyss*. i. 225) is of similar significance ;
and at the time of Hesiod, at all events, such meals were usual.
Opp. 722 :

> Μηδὲ πολυξείνου δαιτὸς δυσπέμφελος εἶναι
> ἐκ κοινοῦ. πλείστη δὲ χάρις, δαπάνη τ᾽ ὀλιγίστη.

See also Eustath. *ad Il.* xvi. 784 ; *ad Odyss.* i. 225 ; Athen. viii.
pp. 362, 365. In these passages, however, the second kind of
entertainment may perhaps be meant, where each brought his
share of the provisions with him ; a custom which is alluded to
by Xenophon, *Mem.* iii. 14, 1 : Ὁπότε δὲ τῶν ξυνιόντων ἐπὶ τὸ
δεῖπνον οἱ μὲν μικρὸν ὄψον, οἱ δὲ πολὺ φέροιεν, ἐκέλευεν ὁ Σωκράτης τὸν παῖδα τὸ μικρὸν ἢ εἰς τὸ κοινὸν τιθέναι, ἢ διανέμειν ἑκάστῳ τὸ μέρος, κ.τ.λ. This was also called a δεῖπνον ἀπὸ
σπυρίδος, from the food being brought in baskets. Athen. viii.
p. 365 : οἴδασι δὲ οἱ ἀρχαῖοι καὶ τὰ νῦν καλούμενα ἀπὸ σπυρίδος δεῖπνα. Cf. Aristoph. *Acharn.* 1138 :

> τὸ δεῖπνον, ὦ παῖ, δῆσον ἐκ τῆς κίστιδος.

Pic-nic parties were often made up to dine in the country, especially on the sea-shore. Plutarch, *Symp.* iv. 4 : Τί δ᾽ οἱ πολλοὶ
βούλονται, πρὸς θεῶν, ὅταν ἡδέως γενέσθαι παρακαλοῦνι ες ἀλλήλους,
λέγωσι, Σήμερον ἀκτάσωμεν, οὐχὶ τὸ παρ᾽ ἄκτῃ δεῖπνον ἥδιστον
ἀποφαίνουσιν, ὥσπερ ἐστίν ; οὐ διὰ τὰ κύματα καὶ τὰς ψηφῖ-
δας᾽ ... ἀλλ᾽ ὡς ἰχθύος ἀφθόνου καὶ νεαροῦ τὴν παράλιον τράπεζαν
εὐποροῦσαν.

We now come to entertainments given at one person's private
expense. The invitations were often given on the same day, and
by the host in person, who sought out, in the market-place or the
gymnasium, those whom he desired to invite. A lively picture
of this free and easy custom may be found at the commencement
of Plato's *Symposion*, p. 175 : Ὦ Ἀριστόδημε, εἰς καλὸν ἥκεις,
ὅπως συνδειπνήσῃς᾽ εἰ δ᾽ ἄλλου τινὸς ἕνεκα ἦλθες, εἰσαῦθις ἀνα-
βαλοῦ. ὡς καὶ χθὲς ζητῶν σε, ἵνα καλέσαιμι, οὐχ οἷός τ᾽ ἦν ἰδεῖν.
At a later period greater formality was observed ; for instance,
Plutarch, *Sept. Sap. Conv.* 1, says that Periander sent a carriage
for each of his guests, and goes on to relate that the Sybarites invited women to banquets a year beforehand, that they might have
their toilets in perfect readiness. Cf. Athen. xii. p. 521.

It was not thought a breach of good manners to bring to a
friend's house an uninvited guest, ἄκλητος, αὐτόματος. Thus in

Plato's *Symposion*, p. 174, Socrates brings Aristodemos with him ;
presently Alcibiades drops in, and afterwards κωμασταὶ πολλοί.
Thus Crates, who was welcome everywhere, was called θυρεπανοίκ-
της ; Diog. Laert. vi. 86 ; and Lucian says of Demonax : ἄκλητος
εἰς ἣν τύχοι παριὼν οἰκίαν ἐδείπνει. *Demon.* 63. But these were
men of distinction, whom every one was proud of having for
guests. Still it was very usual for persons to come αὐτεπάγγελ-
τοι. Lucian, *Lexiph.* 9 ; *Conv. s. Lapith.* 12. How politely the
host behaved on such occasions we see from the reception Agathon gives Aristodemos. Plutarch has devoted a whole chapter to the discussion of the propriety of a guest's bringing an
uninvited person with him ; *Symp.* vii. 6 : Τὸ δὲ τῶν ἐπικλήτων
ἔθος οὓς νῦν σκιὰς καλοῦσιν, οὐ κεκλημένους αὐτοὺς, ἀλλ' ὑπὸ τῶν
κεκλημένων ἐπὶ τὸ δεῖπνον ἀγομένους ἐξητεῖτο, πόθεν ἔσχε τὴν
ἀρχήν. He makes the custom originate with Socrates, the instance in Plato's *Symposion* being probably the earliest with
which he was acquainted. It may be easily believed that parasites, such as Philippos in Xenophon's *Symposion*, and, in after-
times, the notorious sophists, should have often abused this privilege. The Cyrenæans especially seem to have been in bad
odour in this matter. See Alexis, ap. Athen. xii. p. 510 :

> κἀκεῖ γὰρ ἄν τις ἐπὶ τὸ δεῖπνον ἕνα καλῇ,
> πάρεισιν ὀκτωκαίδεκ' ἄλλοι, καὶ δέκα
> ἅρματα, συνωρίδες τε πεντεκαίδεκα.

On such occasions it was expected that the guests should have
paid some attention to their toilets, and should also have made
previous use of the bath, and of unguents. Socrates, when he
went to Agathon's, was λελουμένος τε καὶ τὰς βλαύτας ὑποδεδε-
μένος· ἃ ἐκεῖνος ὀλιγάκις ἐποίει. Plato, *Symp.* p. 174. Those also
who went with him to Callias' were οἱ μὲν γυμνασάμενοι καὶ
χρισάμενοι, οἱ δὲ καὶ λουσάμενοι, though the invitation had been
only just received. In this case some of the guests went on
horseback, since the host resided in the Piræus.

The time of arriving was an understood thing ; though occasionally it was more accurately fixed. The guests were sometimes
late, and this, though it did not cause much confusion, was yet
looked on as a mark of carelessness and overweening. So in
Plutarch. *Symp.* viii. 6, Polycharmos says of himself, οὐδέποτε
κληθεὶς ἐπὶ δεῖπνον ὕστατος ἀφικόμην. At a later period more

attention was paid to this point, as we clearly see from Lucian,
de Merc. Cond. 14: σὺ δ' ἐσθῆτα καθαρὰν προχειρισάμενος καὶ
σεαυτὸν ὡς κοσμιώτατα σχηματίσας, λουσάμενος ἥκεις, δεδιὼς μὴ
πρὸ τῶν ἄλλων ἀφίκοιο. ἀπειρόκαλον γὰρ, ὥσπερ καὶ τὸ ὕστατον ἥκειν φορτικόν. Cf. Schol. ad Theocr. vii. 24. It was not
usual to wait for the defaulters, but the meal was commenced
without them; and this we read was the case at Agathon's, who
was the pink of politeness. See Plato, Symp. p. 175.

In the historic period the practice was to recline at meals,
though in the heroic ages a sitting posture was customary ; but
it is not known at what time the change took place. From
Aristoph. Equit. 1163, it might perhaps be conjectured that the
alteration was contemporaneous with the disuse of the Ionic
chiton ; and in a fragment of Phocylides we have :

> Χρὴ δ' ἐν συμποσίῳ κυλίκων περινισσομενάων
> ἡδέα κωτίλλοντα καθήμενον οἰνοποτάζειν.

But at Sparta the change seems to have been effected before the
Persian wars. Whether it was before Alcman's time, as Müller
affirms, is at least doubtful. The assertion is certainly untenable,
if its only foundation is the fragment of Alcman which has been
preserved by Athenæus, iii. p. 111 :

> κλῖναι μὲν ἑπτὰ καὶ τόσαι τράπεσδαι.

This isolated expression of an erotic poet cannot be taken as a
proof of the ordinary Spartan custom. In Crete, only, the old
custom remained unchanged. See Müller's Dorians. Though
for eating we may think it incommodious, yet for drinking a
recumbent posture is at all events well suited. See Plutarch,
Symp. vii. 10 : ὥσπερ ἡ κλίνη τοῖς πίνουσι τῆς καθέδρας ἀμείνων,
ὅτι τὸ σῶμα κατέχει καὶ ἀπολύει κινήσεως ἁπάσης. Cf. Athen. x.
p. 428. Females and boys always sat, and the same is the case
with the rustic folks described by Dio Chrysostom, Orat. vii.
p. 243. It is so also in the antiques, and when recumbent females
occur they are always hetæræ. See the following woodcuts; also
Winkelm. Monum. ined. 200 ; and Alciphr. Epist. i. 39. An
anomaly is presented by an Etruscan painting, in Gerhard, Pit-
ture Tarquiniensi, where on each κλίνη a man and a modestly-
dressed female recline together.

The couches, and their arrangement, were much the same as
at Rome. See Gallus, p. 471. There was a difference, however,

in the manner in which the guests were distributed on the κλῖναι.
Among the Greeks only two persons reclined on each κλίνη,
instead of three; as appears from Plato, *Symp.* p. 175, where
Agathon says: Σὺ δ', Ἀριστόδημ:, παρ' Ἐρυξίμαχον κατακλίνου;
and then adds: δεῦοο, Σώκρατει, παρ' ἐμὲ κατάκεισο. And afterwards, when Alcibiades comes in, and finds all the seats occupied,
Agathon places him between himself and Socrates, and says:
ὑπολύετε, παῖδες, Ἀλκιβιάδην, ἵνα ἐκ τρίτων κατακέηται, this
being an exception to the general rule. So Herodotus, ix. 16,
speaking of the feast given by Attaginos to fifty Persians and the
same number of Greeks, says: καί σφεων οὐ χωρὶς ἑκατέρους κλῖναι,
ἀλλὰ Πέρσην τε καὶ Θηβαῖον ἐν κλίνῃ ἑκάστῃ. ὡς δὲ ἀπὸ δείπνου ἦσαν, διαπινόντων τὸν Πέρσην τὸν ὁμόκλινον Ἑλλάδα γλῶσ-
σαν ἱέντα εἴρεσθαι, κ. τ. λ. In works of art the same rule is
mostly observed, though three, or even more, occasionally recline
on the same couch. See Millin, *Peint. d. Vas. Gr.* i. pl. 38, 58,
76. See also the woodcuts in this and the following Excursus.

Agathon, it seems, appointed the place of each guest; and
this was mostly, if not always, the case. Plutarch, who devotes
a whole chapter to the subject, decides that it is best for the
host to assign the χώραι. *Symp.* i. 2. More congenial with
Roman than Grecian habits is what we read in Athenæus, i.
p. 47: μετὰ ταῦτα ἀναστάντες κατεκλίνθημεν, ὡς ἕκαστος ἤθελεν,
οὐ περιμείναντες ὀνομακλήτορα, τὸν τῶν δείπνων ταξίαρχον. As
was also the case among the Romans, certain places were more
honourable than others, and absurd contentions sometimes occurred among the guests. See Lucian, *Conviv. s. Lapith.* 9,
Deor. dial. 13; Plutarch, *Sept. Sap. Conv.* 3. The place of honour
seems to have been that next the master of the house. Theophr.
Char. 21: Ὁ δὲ μικροφιλότιμος τοιοῦτός τις, οἷος σπουδάσαι ἐπὶ
δεῖπνον κληθεὶς παρ' αὐτὸν τὸν καλέσαντα κατακείμενος δειπνῆσαι. Hence Socrates lies next Agathon, who himself lies first
on the κλίνη, or *superior*, as the Romans said.

Before reclining, the guests first sat down upon the couches,
in order that the attendants might take off their sandals and
wash their feet (ὑπολύειν and ἀπονίζειν). Plato, *Symp.* pp. 175,
213. In some reliefs they are represented as standing during the
performance of the ablution. See *Marbles of the Brit. Mus.* ii. 4.
This is also seen in the accompanying Plate.

A frequently occurring representation of Dionysos entering the house of Icarius ; from a terracotta. (*Terracottas in the British Mus.* pl. 25.) The act of ablution is being performed by a Satyr ; we may also notice the sitting posture of Erigone, with her feet resting on a footstool ; also the περίστρωμα of the couch, which reaches to the ground, and has a broad border either woven or embroidered on it ; and lastly the αὐλαία with which the wall is hung.

Even in Phocion's time, people were so extravagant as to use wine and perfumed essences, instead of water. Plutarch, *Phoc.* 20 : Ὡς δ' ἐλθὼν ἐπὶ τὸ δεῖπνον ἄλλην τε σοβαρὰν ἑώρα παρασκευὴν, καὶ ποδονιπτῆρας οἴνου δι' ἀρωμάτων προσφερομένους τοῖς εἰσιοῦσι, κ.τ.λ.

We see from numberless antiques that the posture used, the σχῆμα τῆς κατακλίσεως (Plutarch, *Symp.* v. 6), was with the left arm resting on the cushion behind, προσκεφάλαιον, the right hand being thus left free. This is called by Lucian ἐπ' ἀγκῶνος δειπνεῖν. *Lexiph.* 6. A passage in Aristoph. *Vesp.* 1210, amusingly illustrates this stage of the repast :

ΦΙΛ. πῶς οὖν κατακλίνω, φράζ ἀνύσας. ΒΔΕΛ. εὐσχημόνως.

ΦΙΛ. ὡδὶ κελεύεις κατακλιθῆναι; ΒΔΕΛ. μηδαμῶς.

ΦΙΛ. πῶς δαί; ΒΔΕΛ. τὰ γόνατ' ἔκτεινε, καὶ γυμναστικῶς
    ὑγρὸν χύτλασον σεαυτὸν ἐν τοῖς στρώμασιν.
    ἔπειτ' ἐπαίνεσόν τι τῶν χαλκωμάτων·
    ὀροφὴν θέασαι· κρεκάδι' αὐλῆς θαύμασον·
    ὕδωρ κατὰ χειρός· τὰς τραπέζας εἰσφέρειν·
    δειπνοῦμεν· ἀπονενίμμεθ'· ἤδη σπένδομεν.

Before the dishes were brought in, slaves handed round water
(the Homeric χέρνιψ) for washing the hands, κατὰ χειρὸς ἐδόθη,
Alexis, apud Athen. ii. p. 60. Hence Philoxenos the parasite, in
a dispute as to which was the best water, wittily decided that it
was τὸ κατὰ χειρός. Athen. iv. p. 156.

Nothing in the shape of knives and forks being in use, it was
of course indispensable for the hands to be again washed at the
conclusion of the meal. See *Gallus*, p. 477. In eating solid food
the fingers only were used. See the passage of Plutarch quoted
in the Excursus on *Education*, p. 236. So too mention is made
of persons whose hands were particularly callous, or who wore
gloves to enable them to take the food quite hot. Thus Chrysip-
pus, ap. Athen. i. p. 5, relates that the notorious gourmand Philoxenos was accustomed, when at the baths, to dip his fingers in
hot water, and to gargle his mouth with it, as a preparation for
the perils of the banquet. See Cratinus, ap. Id. vi. p. 241 :

    Κόρυδον τὸν χαλκότυπον πεφύλαξο,
    ἢν μὴ σοὶ νομιεῖς αὐτὸν μηδὲν καταλείψειν.
    μηδ' ὕψον κοινῇ μετὰ τούτου πώποτε δαίσῃ,
    τοῦ Κορύδου, προλέγω σοι· ἔχει γὰρ χεῖρα κραται'ν,
    χαλκῆν, ἀκάματον, πολὺ κρείττω τοῦ πυρὸς αὐτοῦ.

Also a fragment of Aristophanes, ap. Id. iv. p. 161 :

    ἐπεὶ παράθες αὐτοῖσιν ἰχθῦς ἢ κρέας,
    κἂν μὴ κατεσθίωσι καὶ τοὺς δακτύλους,
    ἐθέλω κρέμασθαι δεκάκις.

Forks were certainly not used, and no mention occurs of knives,
except in a fragment of Pherecrates, ap. Poll. x. 89 :

    Μάχαιραν ἆρ' ἐνέθηκας ; οὔ. τί μ' εἴργασαι ;
    ἀμάχαιρος ἐπὶ βόεια νοστήσω κρέα,
    ἀνὴρ γέρων, ἀνόδοντος.

The only implement commonly employed was the spoon, μυστίλη,
μύστρον, or μύστρος, Pollux, *ib.*; where γλῶσσα, the Roman *ligula*,
as well as κοχλιώρυχον, mean the same thing. See the remarks on

the *cochlear* in *Gallus,* p. 478. These μυστίλαι, or κοῖλα μύστρα, were of metal: golden ones are mentioned by Athenæus, iii. p. 126. Often, however, a hollow piece of bread served as a substitute. See Aristoph. *Equites,* 1167, where the sausage-seller presents the Demos with such an one. Also Suidas: μυστίλην. ψωμόν. κοῖλον ἄρτον, ὃν ἐποίουν, ἵνα ζωμὸν δι' αὐτοῦ ῥοφῶσι. Cf. Eustath. *ad Odyss.* iii. 457.

Neither table-cloths nor table-napkins were used. The χειρόμακτρον was merely a towel, which was handed round when they washed their hands. Aristoph. apud Athen. ix. p. 410:

> φέρι, παῖ, ταχέως κατὰ χειρὸς ὕδωρ,
> παράπεμπε τὸ χειρόμακτρον.

To cleanse the hands during the meal, the crumb of bread was used, which was kneaded to a dough (ἀπομάττεσθαι, ἀπομαγδαλία). Poll. vi. 93 : τὸ δὲ ἐκμαγεῖον καὶ χειρόμακτρον ἂν προσείποις. οἱ δὲ πάλαι ταῖς καλουμέναις ἀπομαγδαλίαις ἐχρῶντο, αἳ ἦσαν τὸ ἐν τῷ ἄρτῳ μαλακὸν καὶ σταιτῶδες, εἰς ὃ ἀποψησάμενοι τοῖς κυσὶν αὐτὸ παρέβαλλον. Or, according to the lexicographer Pausanias, a kind of dough was specially prepared for this purpose; Eustath. *ad Odyss.* xix. 92 : Παυσανίας δέ φησιν, ὅτι ἀπομαγδαλιὰ σταῖς, ὃ ἔφερον ἐπὶ τὸ δεῖπνον, εἰς ὃ τὰς χεῖρας ἀποματτόμενοι, εἶτα κυσὶν ἔβαλλον. Athenæus, iv. p. 148, following Harmodios, would seem to confine this usage to Phigalia; but this is a mistake, for ἀπομαγδαλίαι are mentioned by Aristophanes, *Equit.* 414, and 819; which latter passage proves that they were not restricted to the cook, as the Scholiast affirms. Lucian, *de Merc. Cond.* 15, speaks of a later, and indeed a Roman custom. With him χειρόμακτρον τιθέμενον (*mantele sternere*) is to be understood of a table-cloth.

We are told so little about the attendance, at least by the authors of the better period, that it is even doubtful whether the guests brought with them their own slaves, or not. In Plato's *Symposion,* p. 212, Alcibiades is certainly accompanied by ἀκόλουθοι: but whether they stopped to wait on him is not said, though Agathon's slaves would seem to have discharged all the offices required. Later writers unequivocally mention slaves who came with, and stood behind, their masters. See Lucian, *Hermot.* 11: παραλαβὼν τὰ κρέα, ὁπόσα τῷ παιδὶ κατόπιν ἑστῶτι παρεδεδώκει. And at the banquet of Aristænetos, described by

Y

Lucian, *Conviv. seu Lapith.* 15, 11, and 36, each guest was attended by his own servant, as well as by one of the host's domestics.
Cf. Athen. iv. p. 128.

From an expression of Agathon's, we see that at that period
it was the custom to entrust to a slave the superintendence of the
whole arrangements, and of the rest of the slaves. He says:
ἀλλ' ἡμᾶς, ὦ παῖδες, τοὺς ἄλλους ἑστιᾶτε. πάντως παρατίθετε
ὅ,τι ἂν βούλησθε, ἐπειδάν τις ὑμῖν μὴ ἐφεστήκῃ, ὃ ἐγὼ οὐδεπώποτε
ἐποίησα. νῦν οὖν νομίζοντες, καὶ ἐμὲ ὑφ' ὑμῶν κεκλῆσθαι ἐπὶ δεῖπνον
καὶ τούσδε τοὺς ἄλλους, θεραπεύετε, ἵνα ὑμᾶς ἐπαινῶμεν. Plato,
Symp. p. 175. This ἐφεστηκὼς is the τραπεζοποιὸς of Athenæus,
iv. p. 170, and nearly corresponded to the Roman *structor.* See
Poll. vi. 13, and iii. 41 : ὁ δὲ πάντων τῶν περὶ τὴν ἑστίασιν ἐπιμελούμενος, τραπεζοποιός. Athenæus ii. p. 49, also alludes to a
custom of presenting each guest, before the meal commenced, with
a bill of fare, γραμματίδιον. This, however, could scarcely have
been a universal practice, though it may have been adopted for
convenience at extensive entertainments.

Before proceeding to discuss the materials of one of these large
banquets, we may devote a few lines to those articles of food
which in earlier times formed the ordinary diet of all classes, and
which, at a later period, still constituted the staple of consumption among the lower orders. The words of Demaratus (Herodot. vii. 102), τῇ Ἑλλάδι πενίη μὲν ἀεί κοτε σύντροφός ἐστι,
certainly apply to their meals, in ancient times. The Greeks
then contented themselves with what barely sufficed for suste-
nance, though the colonies of Ionia and Magna Græcia had long
adopted a more luxurious style of living. A staple article of diet
with the Greeks was the μάζα, something similar to the *puls* of
the ancient Romans. It was prepared in various ways, of which
several are mentioned by Pollux, vi. 76. Cf. Aristoph. *Equit.* 1104,
1165; *Acharn.* 834; and *Vesp.* 610, where we have φυστὴ μάζα,
which the Scholiast says was ἐξ ἀλφίτων καὶ οἴνου, and therefore
was also called οἰνοῦττα. See Poll. vi. 23, 76. A similar dish is
mentioned by Thucyd. iii. 49: ἤθιον ἅμα ἐλαύνοντες οἴνῳ καὶ ἐλαίῳ
ἄλφιτα πεφυρμένα. 'What gluttons the Persians were to come
after our porridge, when they had such plenty !' was the exclamation of Pausanias on seeing the loaded tables of the Persians after
the battle of Platæa: Plutarch, *Apophth. Lac.* i. p. 919. This

μάζα continued to be the food of the lower classes till a later period; Lucian, *Tim.* 56; *Navig.* 46. Wheaten-flour, ἄλευρα, was used in making it, as well as the ἄλφιτα, which was of barley. Plato, *de Republ.* ii. p. 372: θρέψονται δὲ ἐκ μὲν τῶν κριθῶι ἄλφιτα σκευαζόμενοι, ἐκ δὲ τῶν πυρῶν ἄλευρα; τὰ μὲν πέψαντες, τὰ δὲ μάξαντες; μάζας γενναίας καὶ ἄρτους ἐπὶ κάλαμόν τινα παραβαλλόμενοι, ἢ φύλλα καθαρὰ κατακλινέντες ... εὐωχήσον-ται αὐτοί τε καὶ τὰ παιδία ;

After the μάζα comes bread, which was sometimes homebaked, and made of wheat or barley-meal, but was more frequently purchased in the market of the ἀρτοπῶλαι or ἀρ οπώλιδες. See *Vespæ*. According to Athenæus, iii. p. 109, where the various kinds are discussed at great length, the bread of Athens was reputed to be the best.

Other simple articles of diet were green vegetables, such as μαλάχη, mallow (πρώτη τροφὴ, Plutarch, *Sept. Sap. Conv.* 14), θρίδαξ, salad or lettuce, ῥάφανος, cabbage ; also κύαμοι, beans, φακαῖ, linseed, θέρμοι, lupines. Besides these, herbs of sundry sorts, onions and leeks, κρόμυον, βολβὸς, σκόροδον, were in great repute. Aristoph. *Acharn.* 760; Xenoph. *Symp.* iv. 7 ; Lucian, *Tim.* 56 ; *Lexiph.* 10.

With regard to butcher's meat, lamb, pork, and goats' flesh seem to have been preferred. Sausages, too, ἀλλᾶντες, and χορδαὶ, were very common. See Aristoph. *Acharn.* 1119. That black-puddings were also in request, appears from Aristoph. *Equit.* 208 :

> ὁ δράκων γάρ ἐστι μικρὸν, ὁ δ' ἀλλᾶς αὖ μακρόν.
> εἶθ' αἱματοπώτης ἐστὶν ὅ τ' ἀλλᾶς χὠ δράκων.

Cf. Sophilos, ap. Athen. iii. p. 125 :

> χορδήν τιν' αἱματῖτην αὐτῷ σκευάσαι
> ἐκέλευσε ταυτιὴν ἐμέ.

But fish, especially in towns near the sea, was preferred to everything else. To this dish the word ὄψον was applied *par excellence*. Athen. vii. p. 276: Εἰκότως πάντων τῶν προσοψη-μάτων ὄψων καλουμένων ἐξενίκησεν ὁ ἰχθὺς διὰ τὴν ἐξαίρετον ἐδωδὴν μόνος οὕτως καλεῖσθαι, διὰ τοὺς ἐπιμανῶς ἐσχηκότας πρὸς ταύτην τὴν ἐδωδήν. Cf. Plutarch, *Symp.* iv. 4, 2. It is a remarkable fact, to which Plato calls attention, that Homer, though he talks of catching fish, never mentions them in any way as an article of food. Plato, *de Republ.* iii. p. 404 ; so also Plutarch *de Iside et Osir.* 8. This was cert inly not owing to any religious prejudice, as was the case among the Egyptian priests and the Pythagoreans : perhaps rather the occupation of the fisherman was not agreeable to the ta-te of those times. So Plato, *Leg.* vii. p. 823, calls it, as well as fowling, an ἀργὸς θήρα, and ἔρως οὐ σφόδρα ἐλευθέριος, and gives his approval only to the chase. At an after period, fish not only formed a main article of subsistence, but also a chief object of the gourmand's attention. So Demosthenes, *de Fals. Leg.* p. 412, wishing to stigmatise Philocrates as a glutton and a spendthrift, says, πόρνας ἠγόραζε, καὶ ἰχθῦς περιιών : these being certainly the two chief objects of Athenian extravagance. An alphabetical list of the favourite sorts of fish occupies the greater part of the seventh book of Athenæus, pp. 281-330. We shall here only allude to the ἀφύαι, because they were not only much eaten by the better classes, but were also a dainty with the lower orders at Athens. Chrysippos, apud Athen. vii. p. 285 : Τὴν ἀφύην τὴν μὲν ἐν Ἀθήναις διὰ τὴν δαψίλειαν ὑπερορῶσι καὶ πτωχικὸν εἶναί φασιν ὄψον. Whether they were pilchards, anchovies, or herrings, matters little. There were several kinds, of which the most prized was the ἀφρῖτις. Schol. ad Aristoph. *Equit.* 643 : σφόδρα δὲ καὶ μέχρι νῦν παρὰ τοῖς Ἀθηναίοις σπουδάζεται. Besides fresh fish, the Hellespont and the Euxine supplied Greece with ταρίχη, pieces of large fish cured, which formed a cheap and favourite food. See Athen. iii. p. 116.

The daily provisions were generally prepared by the female slaves, under the superintendence of their mistress. See Excursus on *The Women.* Athenæus, xiv. p. 658, remarks that no comic writer, except Poseidippos, mentions a cook among the house-slaves : οὐδὲ γὰρ ἂν εὕροι τις ὑμῶν δοῦλον μάγειρόν τινα ἐν κωμῳδίᾳ, πλὴν παρὰ Ποσειδίππῳ μόνῳ. δοῦλοι δ᾽ ὀψοποιοὶ παρῆλθον ὑπὸ πρώτων Μακεδόνων, κ.τ.λ. On occasions requiring unusual culinary skill, there were plenty of cooks to be hired, as we see abundantly from the comic writers. So also Aristippos answered, when he was reproached, ὅτι δίκην ἔχων ἐμισθώσατο ῥήτορα · ‘ Καὶ γὰρ, ὅταν δεῖπνον ἔχω, μάγειρον μισθοῦμαι.’ Diog. Laert. ii. 72. These professional cooks often came from towns celebrated for their refinements in this art, the μηχανήματα and σοφίσματα of cookery, as Xenophon expresses it, *Hier.* i. 22. In comedy two different masks were used, one for the foreign,

the other for the native cook. Athen. xiv. p. 659 : ἐκάλουν δ᾽ οἱ
παλαιοὶ τὸν μὲν πολιτικὸν μάγειρον Μαίσωνα, τὸν δ᾽ ἐκτόπιον
Τέττιγα. Cf. Poll. iv. 148. And Antiphanes, ap. Athen. i. p. 27,
praises ἐξ Ἠλίδος μάγειρος. But the most celebrated of all seem
to have been those of Sicily. Plato, de Republ. iii. p. 404 : Σικελικὴν ποικιλίαν ὄψων. There were also books treating of the art of
cookery. Plato, Gorg. p. 518 : Μίθαικος ὁ τὴν ὀψοποιίαν ξυγγε-
γραφὼς τὴν Σικελικήν. Philoxenes of Cythera composed a poem,
entitled Δεῖπνον, which contained directions for cooking a large
banquet; this is alluded to by the comedian Plato, ap. Athen. i.
p. 5, in the words, Φιλοξένου καινή τις ὀψαρτυσία. Callimachos
also, as we are told by Athenæus, xiv. p. 643, mentions πλακουν-
τοποιϊκὰ συγγράμματα by four different authors. But the most
renowned work of the kind was the Gastrology of Archestratos,
which Chrysippos called the metropolis of the epicurean philosophy. Athen. iii. p. 104 : εἰκότως ἂν ἐπαινέσειε τὸν καλὸν Χρύ-
σιππον, κατιδόντα ἀκριβῶς τὴν Ἐπικούρου φύσιν, καὶ εἰπόντα,
μητρόπολιν εἶναι τῆς φιλοσοφίας αὐτοῦ τὴν Ἀρχεστράτου γα-
στρολογίαν, ἣν πάντες οἱ τῶν φιλοσόφων γαστρίμαργοι θεογονίαν
τινὰ αὐτῶν εἶναι λέγουσι τὴν καλὴν ταύτην ἐποποιίαν.

A tediously minute account of the πανοῦργα ὀψάρια καὶ
ὑποτρίμματα is given by Athenæus; and there are also numerous notices in Aristophanes; e.g. Acharn. 873, 969, 1042, 1090;
Vesp. 493, 508, etc.

Here, however, we have only space for a few general remarks on a banquet on a large scale. In the first place, the
question arises, whether the Greeks commenced with a pro-
mulsis or gustus like the Romans. At the time here principally
referred to, namely, before the Roman conquest, this was probably not the case; at all events, these preliminaries did not
take the shape of a regular course. In the time of later writers,
such as Plutarch (Symp. viii. 9, 3), and Athenæus (ii. pp. 58–64),
it had become usual, and is denoted by the word πρόπομα.
Athenæus also quotes Phylarchos : Φύλαρχος . . . φησὶν οὕτως, εἰ
μνήμης εὐτυχῶ · πρόπομά τι πρὸ τοῦ δείπνου περιεφέρετο καθὼς
εἰώθει τὸ πρῶτον. But this πρόπομα has nothing in common with
the Roman gustus; it was only a draught preceding the meal.
Still it is not to be denied that certain things were taken as a
whet to the appetite. See Aristoph. Acharn. 1112 :

ἀλλ' ἢ πρὸ δείπνου τὴν μίμαρκυν κατέδομαι.

At a later period the ψυχραὶ τράπεζαι, as Plutarch calls them, served this purpose; they consisted of oysters and other shell-fish, and raw vegetables, as salad and so forth. At an earlier period these were brought on at the conclusion of the meal. Cf. Athen. ii. p. 101.

It is uncertain whether, as among the Romans, the viands were brought in upon a tray, and set on a table standing in the centre of the κλῖναι, or whether, as in Homer, every guest, or at least every κλίνη, had a separate table. The latter is more probable, from the universal occurrence of the phrases, εἰσφέρειν and ἀφαιρεῖν τὰς τραπέζας: and that this refers not to the dishes, but to the tables themselves, is evident from a fragment of the Δεῖπνον of Philoxenos, apud Athen. iv. p. 146:

> Εἰς δ' ἔφερον διπλόοι παῖδες λιπαρῶπα τράπεζαν
> ἄμμι, ἑτέραν δ' ἕτεροι,
> ἄλλοι δ' ἑτέραν,
> μέχρι οὗ πλήρωσαν οἶκον.

Cf. Antiphanes, ap. Id. ii. p. 60. The custom in Arcadia appears to have been different, μίαν πᾶσι τράπεζαν εἰς τὸ μέσον παρατιθέασι: Theopompos, ap. Id. iv. p. 149. Besides, in all monuments representing *symposia*, before each κλίνη stand one, and sometimes several tables, τρίποδες or τράπεζαι, as is seen in the accompanying cut, and in those in the following Excursus. Pollux takes τράπεζαι to mean the trays, *repositoria*. He says, vi. 83: Ἦσαν δέ τινες πρῶται τράπεζαι, καὶ δεύτεραι, καὶ τρίται. καὶ τρίποδες μὲν, ἐφ' ὧν ἔκειντο . . . αἱ δὲ ἐπιτιθέμεναι καὶ αἱρόμεναι τράπεζαι, ἃς νῦν μαγίδας καλοῦσιν. Id. x. 81: καὶ μὴν καὶ τὰ ἐπιτιθέμενα τοῖς τρίποσι τράπεζαι καλοῦνται, καὶ μαγίδες. According to this, viands were served up on each of these small tables, and this agrees with the antiques. But we see from Plato, *de Republ.* i. p. 354, that the separate dishes were also handed round: ὥσπερ οἱ λίχνοι τοῦ ἀεὶ παραφερομένου ἀπογεύονται, ἁρπάζοντες πρὶν τοῦ προτέρου μετρίως ἀπολαῦσαι. Protagorides, ap. Athen. iv. p. 150, mentions as a peculiarity of Egyptian meals, that no τράπεζαι were employed: Τρίτη δ' ἐστὶν ἰδέα δείπνων Αἰγυπτιακὴ, τραπεζῶν μὲν οὐ παρατιθεμένων, πινάκων δὲ περιφερομένων. This is what Martial, vii. 48, calls *cœna ambulans*.

Ordinary joints, poultry, and fish, among which the Copaic

A vase-painting of a Symposion, from Millin, *Peint. d. Vas.* II. pl. 58. Three young and two older men are on a κλίνη, resting the left arm on the striped προσκεφάλαια (ὑπαγκώνια). Before the κλίνη stand two tables. Three of the men hold aloft the κύλιξ, with the forefinger through the handle. The fourth holds a phiala, and the fifth a rhyton also. In the middle Comos beats the tympanum.

eels are particularly celebrated (Aristoph. *Acharn.* 879; *Pax*, 1005), formed of course the staple dishes, but hares (Aristoph. *passim*), κίχλαι, fieldfares, and many other things, were favourite delicacies.

When all had eaten enough, the tables were removed, which was called αἴρειν, ἀπαίρειν, ἐκφέρειν, βαστάζειν τὰς τραπέζας. The floor, on which bones, fruit-shells, &c. had been thrown, was then swept, and water was handed round for the guests to wash their hands, ἀπονίψασθαι, whereupon the meal, δεῖπνον, properly so called, was closed with a libation. Chaplets and ointments were then usually, though not invariably, handed round. So a frag·ment of Menander (Mein. p. 94):

> Εἶτ᾽ εὐθὺς οὕτω τὰς τραπέζας αἴρετε
> μύρα, στεφάνους ἑτοίμασον, σπονδὰς ποίει.

See also Plato, Com. ap. Athen. xv. p. 665, and Philyllios, ap Id. ix. p. 408. A distinction between the expressions κατὰ χει-ρὸς and ἀπονίψασθαι is drawn by the grammarian Aristophanes, apud Athen. ix. p. 408: παρὰ γὰρ τοῖς παλαιοῖς τὸ μὲν πρὸ ἀρίστου καὶ δείπνου λέγεσθαι κατὰ χειρὸς, τὸ δὲ μετὰ τοῦτ᾽ ἀπονίψασθαι. Cf. Pollux, vi. 92: καὶ νίψασθαι μὲν τὸ πρὸ τῆς τροφῆς· ἀπονίψασθαι δὲ τὸ μετὰ τὴν τροφήν. This usage of the words appears, however, from other passages, not to have been observed. See Philoxenos, ap. Athen. iv. 147; and Plato, *Symp.* p 175. Along with the water, σμῆγμα or σμῆμα, which supplied the place of soap, was usually handed round, and, as with us, it was often scented. Hence ενώδης γῆ, and σμήματα ἰρινόμικτα, which occur in Philoxenos and Antiphanes, ap. Athen. ix. p. 409.

The meal was concluded by the σπονδαὶ, or libation 'to the good genius.' Xenoph. *Symp.* 2, 1; Plato, *Symp.* p. 176; Diod. Sic. iv. 3: φασὶν ἐπὶ τῶν δείπνων, ὅταν ἄκρατος οἶνος διδῶται πᾶσιν, ἐπιλέγειν 'ἀγαθοῦ δαίμονος·' ὅταν δὲ μετὰ τὸ δεῖπνον διδῶται κεκραμένος ὕδατι ' Διὸς Σωτῆρος' ἐπιφωνεῖν. Philochoros, ap. Athen. ii. p. 38: Καὶ θεσμὸν ἔθετο ('Αμφικτύων) προσφέρεσθαι μετὰ τὰ σῖτα ἄκρατον μόνον ὅσον γεύσασθαι, δεῖγμα τῆς δυνάμεως τοῦ ἀγαθοῦ θεοῦ. τὸ δὲ λοιπὸν ἤδη κεκραμένον ὁπόσον ἕκαστος βούλεται· προσεπιλέγειν δὲ τού-ῳ τὸ τοῦ Διὸς Σω-τῆρος ὄνομα. Instead of the formula, ἀγαθοῦ δαίμονος, it was also customary to say 'ὑγιείας,' and the goblet out of which this libation was made, was called μετάνιπτρον, or μετανιπτρίς, be-

cause it was used μετὰ τὸ ἀπονίψασθαι. See the passages cited
by Pollux, vi. 31, and by Athenæus, xi. p. 488; xv. p. 693.
Plutarch is the only author who says this ceremony took place to
the sound of the flute. Plut. *Sept. Sap. Con.* 5; *Symp.* vii. 8,
4. Cf. Plato, *Symp.* p. 176.

This libation being concluded, the πότος, συμπόσιον, or κῶμος
then commenced. Plato, *Symp.* p. 176 : σπονδὰς σφᾶς ποιήσασθαι καὶ ᾄσαντας τὸν θεὸν . . . τρέπεσθαι πρὸς τὸν πότον. The
dessert, δεύτεραι τράπεζαι, was now served up. In earlier times
this consisted merely of olives, figs, nuts, &c., which were invariably accompanied by salt, either pure or mixed with spice, to
bring out the flavour of the wine, as well as to induce thirst.
Plutarch, *Symp.* iv. 4, 3 : οὐ μόνον τοίνυν πρὸς τροφὴν ἀλλὰ
καὶ πρὸς ποτὸν ὄψον εἰσὶν οἱ ἅλες. Cf. P.aut. *Curc.* iv. 4, 5 ;
Pers. iii. 3, 23 : *nunquam delinget salem.* The expression, *lin-
gere salem* (ἅλα λείχειν, Diog. Laer. vi. 57), shows how it was
taken. So also the *concha salis puri*, Hor. *Sat.* i. 3, 14 ; and *Od.*
i. 16, 14. But the Greek authors are more explicit respecting
this custom : thus Athen. ix. p. 366 : καὶ ἅλας δὲ ἡδυσμένους ὁρῶ
ἐν ἄλλαις παροψίσιν. This answers to the *(sal) odoribus additis*,
Plin. *Nat. Hist.* xxxi. 7, 41 : and the ἅλας θυμίτας, Aristoph.
Acharn. 1099. So also the proverb, οἱ περὶ ἅλα καὶ κύμινον, said
of those who stuck to the salt and cummin, and neglected the
sweetmeats. Plutarch, *Symp.* iv. 1, 3. A kind of cake strewed
with salt, ἐπίπαστα, was also eaten with the wine. Cf. Aristoph.
Equit. 103, 1089 : ἐπίπαστα λείχειν. See also the Scholiast on
both places. The passage which seems to allude most explicitly
to eating salt with wine is one in Herodotus, i. 133, where the
Persian luxury is compared with Greek frugality : σίτοισι δὲ ὀλί-
γοισι χρέωνται (οἱ Πέρσαι), ἐπιφορήμασι δὲ πολλοῖσι, καὶ οὐκ ἁλέσι,
καὶ διὰ τοῦτό φασι Πέρσαι, τοὺς Ἕλληνας σιτεομένους πεινῶντας
παύεσθαι, ὅτι σφι ἀπὸ δείπνου παραφορέεται οὐδὲν λόγου ἄξιον.
εἰ δέ τι παραφέροιτο, ἐσθίοντας ἂν οὐ παύεσθαι. Here the proper
reading is undoubtedly, καὶ οὐκ ἅλεσι, if not ἁλάσι. The Persians
may well have thought the ἅλες of a Grecian dessert, οὐδὲν λόγου
ἄξιον. Lastly, we may refer to the proverb, ἁλίαν τρυπᾶν, Philost. *Epist. Apoll. Tyan.* 7, with which compare Pers. *S t.* v.
138 : *regustatum digito terebrare salinum.*

In the times of the middle and later comedy, when all sorts

of sweetmeats had been introduced, the mention of ἅλες seldom
occurs; yet in the account which Anaxandrides gives of the
wedding feast of Iphicrates, ἅλες are introduced along with σκό-
οοδον, κρόμνον and σίλφιον. At this later period the δεύτεραι
τράπεζαι had a variety of names, as ἐπιδόρπια, ἐπιδειπνα, ἐπιφο-
ρήματα, ἐπαίκλια (Eustath. ad Il. xviii. 215), τὸ ἐντελὲς δεῖπνον
(Lucian, Conv. s. Lapith. 38), ῥωγαλεύματα, &c. But the names
which most frequently occur are δεύτεραι τράπεζαι and τραγήματα. See the fragment of Aristotle's treatise περὶ μέθης, apud
Athen. xiv. p. 641 : Τὸ μὲν οὖν ὅλον διαφέρειν τράγημα βρώματος
νομιστέον ὅσον ἔδεσμα τρωγαλίου. τοῦτο γὰρ πάτριον τοὔνομα τοῖς
Ελλησιν, ἐπεὶ ἐν τραγήμασι τὰ βρώματα παρατίθενται. διόπερ
οὐ κακῶς ἔοικεν εἰπεῖν ὁ πρῶτος δευτέραν προσαγορεύσας τράπεζαν. ὄντως γὰρ ἐπιδορπισμός τις ὁ τραγηματισμός ἐστι, καὶ
δεῖπνον ἕτερον παρατίθεται τραγήματα. Here we should probably read, ἐπεὶ ἐν τραγήμασι καὶ βρώματα παρατίθενται. In
Aristotle's time various ἐδέσματα—properly so called—as hares,
ducks, and game of different sorts, were brought in along with
the dessert. See Athen. iii. p. 101, and xiv. p. 642.

The chief object of the dessert, besides the pleasure to the
palate which its dainties afforded, was to keep up the desire of
drinking. See Aristot. Probl. xxii. 6: Διὰ τί τὰ τραγήματα
ἐδεστέον ; ἢ ἕνεκα τοῦ πιεῖν ἱκανόν; οὐ γὰρ μόνον ποτέον τῆς
δίψης χάριν τῆς ἐκ τοῖς σιτίοις, ἀλλὰ καὶ μετὰ τὸ σιτίον. Cheese
was usually introduced, and the most celebrated was that of
Sicily. See the fragments of Antiphanes and Hermippos, apud
Athen. i. p. 27, and of Philemon, ap. Id. xiv. p. 658. Aristophanes, too, frequently alludes to it. That which came from
Tromileia in Achaia was also in high repute, as we see from the
last-named passage in Athenæus. Dried figs, ἰσχάδες, were also
eaten, and although those of Attica were very fine-flavoured,
gourmands preferred those from Rhodes. Hermippos, ap. Athen.
i. p. 27. Olives also were introduced, especially those that had
ripened on the tree and become quite shrivelled (ῥυσοὶ καὶ δρυπε-
τεῖς): dates from Syria and Egypt, for the fruit of the Grecian
palm was not eatable (Plutarch, Symp. viii. 4, 1); nuts, κάρυα,
a term which comprehended all ἀκρόδρυα, and therefore almonds
and chestnuts (ὀπτὰ κάρυα, Aristot. Probl. xxii. 7); also fresh

fruit of course. On this subject consult the second and third
books of Athenæus, *passim*.

Cakes also, for which, as aforesaid, Athens was renowned,
were a principal feature of the dessert. See Thucyd. i. 126 : ἐπιχώρια θύματα. Athenæus, in his third and fourteenth books,
mentions several sorts, differing in materials and shape, many of
which may appertain to the Roman era. The most usual form
was round, and hence the seed of the mallow was called πλακοῦς.
Athen. ii. p. 58 : Φανίας δὲ ἐν τοῖς φυτικοῖς φησι, τῆς ἡμέρου
μαλάχης ὁ σπερματικὸς τύπος καλεῖται πλακοῦς, ἐμφερὴς ὢν αὐτῷ.
Cf. Aristoph. *Acharn.* 1125 : πλακοῦντος τυρόγωτος κύκλος.

THE SYMPOSIA.

THE Roman *comissatio* was quite independent of the *cœna*, as has been shown in *Gallus*. p. 125, note, and in like manner the συμπόσιον or πότος of the Greeks must not be confounded with the δεῖπνον. It is true that δεῖπνον was usually followed by the πότος, as is the case in many instances already cited; yet the scenes are changed, and fresh personages frequently enter on the stage. During the meal no wine was brought on table, and we must consider as an exception to the rule the account in Athenæus, iii. p. 125 : ὅτι δ᾽ ἔπινον καὶ γλυκὺν οἶνον μεταξὺ ἐσθίοντες, Ἀλεξίς φησιν ἐν Δρωπίδῃ.

> Εἰσῆλθεν ἡ 'ταίρα φέρουσα τὸν γλυκὺν
> ἐν ἀργυρῷ ποτηρίῳ πετάχνῳ τινὶ, κ.τ.λ.

At all events, unmixed wine was not drunk till after the libation. Cf. Plutarch, *Symp.* viii. 9, 3.

These symposia were enlivened by varied conversation, music, dancing, and other arts, together with games and divertissements of all sorts. It is this mirthful and joyous tone that gives the chief zest to the graceful narrative of Xenophon, the vivid freshness and truthfulness of which at once convince us that it is taken from the life. And not less interesting is the story of Plato, so redolent of soul and imagination, and whose matter and form almost tempt us to forget that a discussion so artfully planned could never have been improvised. It was an unhappy thought of Plutarch's—if indeed the work be his—to range beside these masterpieces the tedious disputation of his seven sages, whose wire-drawn subtleties are only exceeded by the tasteless absurdities of the Deipnosophists in Athenæus. Of quite a different order is Lucian's Lapithan feast, which though, according to his wont, somewhat caricatured, yet teems with pleasant satire and humorous strokes of character. The *dramatis personæ* in Xenophon and Plato are, it is true, of so highly intellectual a cast, that we cannot take their conversation to represent the average tone of an ordinary convivial meeting; yet, with some modifications, these compositions will serve as valuable sketches to aid us in the composition of a more unpretending picture.

The Greeks, besides wine, οἶνος ἀμπέλινος, knew of no other drink except water. It is true that Diodorus Siculus, iv. 2, relates that Dionysos invented a drink from barley: εὑρεῖν δ' αὐτὸν καὶ τὸ ἐκ τῆς κριθῆς κατασκευαζόμενον πόμα τὸ προσαγορευόμενον μὲν ὑπ' ἐνίων ζύθος, οὐ πολὺ δὲ λειπόμενον τῆς περὶ τὸν οἶνον εὐωδίας. The names βρῦτος and πίνος are applied to this by Eustathius, ad Il. xi. 637; xxii. 283; and this mead-like drink was probably common in Egypt (see Herodot. ii. 77), as was the palm-wine in the palm-regions of Asia (Herodot. i. 193, 194); but there is nothing to lead us to suppose that such liquors were ever introduced into Greece; and indeed the abundance of the more generous beverage rendered any substitute unnecessary. Wine therefore was the ordinary drink of all, even of slaves and journeymen, though what they got was mostly sorry stuff. See Demosth. adv. Lacr. p. 933: τό, τε οἰνάριον τὸ Κῷον, ὀγδοήκοντα στάμνοι ἐξεστηκότος οἴνου, καὶ τὸ τάριχος ἀνθρώπῳ τινὶ γεωργῷ παρεκομίζετο ἐν τῷ πλοίῳ ... τοῖς ἐργάταις τοῖς περὶ τὴν γεωργίαν χρῆσθαι. Plutarch, Comp. Arist. c. Cat. 4: πιεῖν, ὃν ἐργάται πίνουσι καὶ θεράποντες, οἶνον. The extraordinary cheapness of the wine makes these passages intelligible, and accounts too for its somewhat excessive use. For its price, see Böckh's Public Econ. of Athens, p. 98. In the very earliest ages wine was regarded as the chief source of joy, and agreeably to this idea, Musæus and Eumolpus made the reward of the virtuous in Hades to consist in perpetual intoxication. Plato, de Republ. ii. p. 363: εἰς ᾅδου γὰρ ἀγαγόντες τῷ λόγῳ καὶ κατακλίναντες, καὶ συμπόσιον τῶν ὁσίων κατασκευάσαντες ἐστεφανωμένους ποιοῦσι τὸν ἅπαντα χρόνον ἤδη διάγειν μεθύοντας, ἡγησάμενοι κάλλιστον ἀρετῆς μισθὸν μέθην αἰώνιον. Sobriety was in no case one of the prime virtues of the Athenian; even Plato is of opinion that a man ought to become intoxicated at the Dionysia; Leg. vi. p. 775: πίνειν δὲ εἰς μέθην οὔτε ἄλλοθί που πρέπει, πλὴν ἐν ταῖς τοῦ τὸν οἶνον δόντος θεοῦ ἑορταῖς. Symposia, at all times, were apt to end in intoxication, and were therefore forbidden in Sparta and Crete. Mim. p 320. Still Plutarch tells an anecdote of Agesilaos as symposiarch: Apophth. Lac. i. p. 830. Cf. Id. Cleom. 13; Athen. x. p. 432.

With regard to the Grecian wines, and the various qualities

and excellences of the different growths, very little is known ; and
the Greeks were by no means such connoisseurs in this respect as
the Romans   Wine was bought from samples, as we see from
Lucian, *Hermot.* 58 ; Eurip. *Cycl.* 149 ; but provided it suited
their taste, people were not very particular as to what hill or
district it came from.   In early times the general name οἶνος was
ordinarily used.   Demosthenes, *adv. Lacr.* p. 935, enumerates a
few of the chief districts where it was grown : πᾶν γὰρ δήπου
τοὐναντίον εἰς τὸν Πόντον οἶνος εἰσάγεται ἐκ τῶν τόπων τῶν περὶ
ἡμᾶς, ἐκ Πεπαρήθου καὶ Κῶ, καὶ Θάσιος καὶ Μενδαῖος.   If we add
to the wines here mentioned those of Chios, Lesbos, Naxos, and
the Πράμνιος, the names of the more celebrated sorts are exhausted.   A few others are mentioned by Strabo, xiv. 1, 15, 47 ;
and Athen. i. p. 28, seq.   Chian wine, probably, was the most
costly, as appears from the defence of Demetrius before the
Areopagus ; Athen. iv. p. 167 : Ἀλλὰ καὶ νῦν, εἶπεν, ἐλευθερίως
ζῶ. καὶ γὰρ ἑταίραν ἔχω τὴν καλλίστην καὶ ἀδικῶ οὐδένα, καὶ
πίνω Χῖον οἶνον.   The Pramnian, on the other hand, which was
famous in Homer's time, was not liked at Athens, because it was
harsh, αὐστηρός.   Athen. i. p. 30 : οἴῳ Ἀριστοφάνης οὐχ ἥδεσθαι
Ἀθηναίους φησὶ λέγων, τὸν Ἀθηναίων δῆμον οὔτε ποιηταῖς ἥδεσθαι
σκληροῖς καὶ ἀστεμφέσιν οὔτε Πραμνίοις σκληροῖς οἴνοις συνάγουσι
τὰς ὀφρῦς τε καὶ τὴν κοιλίαν, ἀλλ' ἀνθοσμίᾳ καὶ πέπονι νεκταρο-
σταγεῖ.   Aristophanes frequently refers to the Thasian wine.
No mention is made, in early times, of Italian wines ; though it
is probable that in the palmy days of the Italian and Sicilian
cities the growth was cultivated, and the produce shipped to
Greece, as was the case with the Sicilian cheese and other articles
of consumption.   Theopompos, however, ap. Athen. i. p. 26, appears well acquainted with them, and mentions their individual
peculiarities ; and in Lucian, *Navig.* 13, the person who dreams
that he is rich, determines for the future to have nothing but
οἶνον ἐξ Ἰταλίας on his table.   Nevertheless, Pollux, vi. 16, says :
οὔπω γὰρ οἱ παλαιοὶ τὸν Ἰταλιώτην ἀκριβῶς ᾔδεσαν.   The colours
of the wines were red, μέλας, white, and yellow. Athen. i. p. 32 :
τῶν οἴνων ὁ μὲν λευκὸς, ὁ δὲ κιρρὸς, ὁ δὲ μέλας.   See *Gallus*,
p. 491.   The red is said to have been grown first in Chios ;
Athen. i. p. 26 : Θεόπομπος δέ φησι, παρὰ Χίοις πρώτοις γενέσθαι
τὸν μέλανα οἶνον . . . ὁ δὴ λευκὸς οἶνος ἀσθενὴς καὶ λεπτός. ὁ δὲ
κιρρὸς πέττει ῥᾷον, ξηραντικὸς ὤν.

Different sorts were occasionally mixed together. See Theophrastus, apud Athen. i. p. 32; Plutarch, *Symp.* iv. 1, 2. The addition of sea-water to wine is first mentioned by Dioscor. v. 27; Plutarch, *Quæst. Nat.* 10; Athen. i. p. 26. Plutarch also relates that the casks were smeared with pitch, and that the Eubeans mixed resin with the wine. *Symp.* v. 3, 1. Spiced wine was common in the time of the new comedy. Pollux, vi. 1: τὸ δὲ -ρίμμα πόμα ἦν μετὰ ἀρωμάτων παρὰ τοῖς νέοις κωμικοῖς. Also Athen. i. p. 31: ἐχρῶντο δ' οἱ ἀρχαῖοι καὶ πώματί τινι ἐξ ἀρω- μάτων κατασκευαζομένῳ, ὃ ἐκάλουν τρίμμα. Honey was also added; Theophrast. ap. Athen. i. p. 32: τὸν ἐν τῷ πρυτανείῳ διδόμενον θαυμαστὸν εἶναι τὴν ἡδονήν. ἠρτυμένος γάρ ἐστιν. ἐμ- βάλλουσι γὰρ εἰς τὰ κεράμια σταῖς μέλιτι φυράσαντες, ὥστε τὴν ὀσμὴν ἀπ' αὐτοῦ, τὴν δὲ γλυκύτητα ἀπὸ τοῦ σταιτὸς λαμβάνειι τὸν οἶνον. The mixture of *unguenta* with wine, which was practised by the Romans (see *Gallus*, p. 493), is here and there mentioned among the Greeks. Æl. *Var. Hist.* xii. 31: Τί δὲ, οὐκ ἐκεῖνα τοῖς Ἕλλησι τρυφῆς ἀπόδειξις; μύρῳ γὰρ οἶνον μιγ- νύντες οὕτως ἔπινον καὶ ὑπερηναγκάζοντο τὴν τοιαύτην κρᾶσιν, καὶ ἐκαλεῖτο ὁ οἶνος μυῤῥινίτης. In support of this he quotes Philippides, a poet of the new comedy. Cf. Plutarch, *Sept. Sap. Conv.* 3. Lastly, the Greeks prepared by boiling an ἕψημα οἶνου. answering to the Roman *sapa* and *defrutum.* Athen. i. p. 31: ἐχρῶντο γὰρ ἐφθοῖς οἴνοις. See *Gallus*, p. 486.

Age was considered a recommendation; see Pind. *Ol.* 9, 52: αἰνεῖ δὲ παλαιὸν μέν οἶνον. See Eubul. ap. Athen i. p. 26; and Alexis, ap. Id. ii. p. 36:

> οἶνον δὲ τὸν παλαιότατον σπουδάζομεν.

Cf. Plutarch, *Non Posse Suav.* 4. But it is doubtful whether they kept wine so long as the Romans did. From Athen. xiii. p. 584, we see that sixteen years was considered a very great age for wine: ἐπιδόντος δέ τινος οἶνον ἐν ψυκτηριδίῳ μικρὸν καὶ εἰπόντος ὅτι ἑκκαιδεκαέτης, Μικρός γε, ἔφη, ὡς τοσούτων ἐτῶν. Cf. Lucian, *Lexiph.* 6.

The wine was mixed either with hot or cold water before being drunk. Cf. *Gallus*, pp. 491, 494. The *calda* was not peculiar to the Romans, and θερμὸν ὕδωρ is often mentioned, and in the pure Greek period See Xenoph. *Memor.* iii. 13, 3: Plato, *de*

Republ. iv. p. 437; Athen. viii. p. 352. and iii. p. 123, where a number of instances are collected. There seems to have been a vessel expressly designed for keeping water hot; this perhaps is the ἰπνολέβης of Lucian, *Lexiph.* 8. When the wine was mixed with cold water, this was obtained as fresh as possible, and, even at an early period, snow was employed to keep it cool; πόσις διὰ χιόνος. See Alexis, ap. Athen. iii. p. 124:

> καὶ χιόνα μὲν πίνειν παρασκευάζομεν.

Dexicrates, ap. Id.: Εἰ δὲ μεθύω, καὶ χιόνα πίνω, κ.τ.λ. This was attempted even in summer. Xenoph. *Memor.* ii. 1, 30: οἴνους δὲ πολυτελεῖς παρασκευάζῃ καὶ τοῦ θέρους χιόνα περιθέ-ουσα ζητεῖς. Athenæus mentions ice-houses; but the common way was merely to cover the snow or ice with chaff. Plutarch, *Symp* vi. 6, 1: Καὶ γὰρ ἀχύροις σπαργανοῦντες αὐτὴν καὶ περιστέλ-λοντες ἱματίοις ἀγνάπτοις ἐπὶ πολὺν χρόνον διατηροῦσι. Snow seems to have been a regular article of traffic at Athens, as it is now at Naples. Euthycles, ap. Athen. *supra*: πρῶτος μὲν εἶδεν εἰ χιών ἐστ' ὠνία. It was often mixed with the wine itself, as we see from the sarcasm of Gnathæna, related by Machon, ap. Athen. xiii. p. 579:

> Παρὰ Γναθαίνῃ Δίφιλος πίνων ποτὲ,
> ψυχρόν γ'. ἔφη τἀγγεῖον, ὦ Γνάθαιν' ἔχεις.
> Τῶν σῶν γὰρ, εἶπεν, ἐπιμελῶς, ὦ Δίφιλε,
> εἰς αὐτό γ' ἀεὶ δραμάτων ἐμβάλλομεν.

Straining, so usual among the Romans, is seldom mentioned. Epilycus, however, ap. Athen. i. p. 28, mentions Χῖος καὶ Θάσιος ἠθημένος. Cf. Poll. vi. 18: σακκίας δὲ ὁ διυλισμένος, καὶ σακτὸς παρ' Εὐπόλιδι. Id. x. 75; and Dioscor. v. This was most likely done through wool. There are doubtful allusions to this practice in Plato, *Symp.* p. 175, and Aristoph. *Vespæ*, 701.

Wine was always drunk diluted, and to drink it ἄκρατος was looked on as a barbarism. Plato, *Leg.* i. p. 637. According to Ælian, *Var. Hist.* ii. 37, Zaleucos imposed a law upon the Locrians, according to which any person doing so, even if sick, unless by the prescription of the physician, was punishable with death. The custom of diluting wine can be traced up to the earliest period, and its origin is referred to Amphictyon. Athen. ii. p. 38: Φιλόχορος δέ φησιν Ἀμφικτύονα τὸν Ἀθηναίων βασιλέα, μαθόντα παρὰ Διονύσου τὴν τοῦ οἴνου κρᾶσιν, πρῶτον κεράσαι. Eustath.

ad Odyss. xvii. 205. The usage continued long in force, and any
departure from it was not only considered a sign of great intemp-
erance, but as highly injurious, both mentally and corporeally.
From Herodotus, vi. 84, we learn that the Spartans fancied
Cleomenes had gone mad by drinking neat wine, a habit he had
learned from the Scythians: ἐκ τούτου δὲ μανῆναί μιν νομίζουσι
Σπαρτιῆται. So Mnesitheos, apud Athen. ii. p. 36 :

> ἐὰν δ' ἴσον ἴσῳ προσφέρῃ, μανίαν ποιεῖ·
> ἐὰν δ' ἄκρατον, παράλυσιν τῶν σωμάτων.

Cf. Plato, *Leg.* vi. p. 773 ; Plutarch, *An seni resp. ger.* 13 : μαινό-
μενον θεὸν ἑτέρῳ θεῷ νήφονι- σωφρονίζεσθαι κολαζόμενον. Cf. Id.
de Aud. Poët. 1 : ἀφαιρεῖ ἡ κρᾶσις τοῦ οἴνου τὸ βλάπτον. And
from the prevalence of this custom, οἶνος always means diluted
wine, κεκραμένος being understood, unless ἄκρατος is expressly
mentioned.   Plutarch, *Conjug. Prœc.* 20 : τὸ κρᾶμα, καίτοι ὕδατος
μετέχον πλείονος, οἶνον καλοῦμεν.

The proportions of the mixture varied with the habits of the
drinkers.   Plutarch, *de Pyth. Or.* 23 : ὁ μὲν γὰρ οἶνος, ὡς ἔλεγε
Χαιρήμων, τοῖς τρόποις κεράννυται τῶν πινόντων. Id. *Symp.* v.
4, 2 : πρεσβυτέρους ὄντας εἰδὼς, οὐχ ὑδαρεῖ χαίροντας, ἀλλ' ἀκρα-
τοτέρῳ, καθάπερ οἱ ἄλλοι γέροντες, ἐπιτεῖναι κελεύει τὴν κρᾶσιν.
Cf. Aristot. *Probl.* iii. 3. In Sparta ἀκρατέστερον πίνειν was called
ἐπισκυθίζειν. Herod. vi. 84; Chamæl. ap. Athen. x. p. 427.
With regard to the usual proportions, see *Gallus*, p. 129, note.
There was always more water than wine; and the mixture ἴσον
ἴσῳ, half and half, was repudiated as highly intoxicating. From
Athenæus, Plutarch, and Eustathius, we gather that the usual
proportions were six parts of water to two, three, or four of wine.
The first of these, which is recommended by Hesiod, was considered ὑδαρὴς by most people, and was called βατράχοις οἰνοχοεῖν.
See Pherecrates, apud Athen. x. p. 430.   But some wines would
bear this quantity of water; see Poll. vi. 18 : ἐπήνουν δὲ οἶνον τὸν
τρία φέροντα, τουτέστι τὸ τριπλοῦν του ὕδατος. Such wine is called
πολυφόρος by Aristophanes, *Plut.* 853.   The opposite to this is
αὐτόκρας.   Poll. vi. 24.

The mixing took place, according to ancient custom, in a large
bowl, hence called κρατήρ ; and from this it was distributed into
the cups of the drinkers.   Procl. ad Hesiod. Ἔργ. 744 : ὁ μὲν
γὰρ κρατὴρ προὔκειτο κοινὸς ἐν ταῖς τραπέζαις · ἐκ δὲ τῆς οἰνοχόης

One of the richest of the compositions depicting Greek Symposia: from a vase in *Mus. Borb.* v. 51. See Gerhard and Panofka, *Neapel's ant. Bildwerke*, p. 340. On a κλίνη hung with gorgeous drapery,—before which stand three small tables, τρίποδες, and the Crater in the centre,—four youths are lying (the fifth on the right seems standing behind), and between them sit three *hetaerae*, one of whom is a *psaltria*. The man to the left holds a drinking cup and rhyton. On the tables are all sorts of τραγήματα. Whether the object on the right-hand table is intended for a lamp is hard to discover from the engraving in the *Mus. Borb.*

ἀρυόμενοι ἔπινον οἱ συνδειπνοῦντες. The οἰνοχόη answered the same purpose as our ladle ; see Poll. vi. 19 ; x. 75. The passage in Hesiod, μηδέποτ' οἰνοχόην τιθέμεν κρητῆρος ὕπερθεν πινόντων, probably refers to some superstitious belief that it was unlucky to lay the ladle across the κρατὴρ, an act which might imply a cessation of the carouse. The οἰνοχόη was quite different in form from the κύαθος, being shaped more like a tankard, as we see from many antiques. Panofka, *Recherches*, Pl. v. 101. These craters are found in representations of Bacchic scenes, as well as of mere symposia. See Stuart, *Antiq. of Ath.* vol. i. ch. iv. pl. 11. See also the accompanying plate.

The custom of mixing all the wine at once lasted till a late period, as appears from Theophrastus, *Char.* 13, where one feature of the character of a περίεργος is said to be πλείω δὲ ἐπαναγκάσαι τὸν παῖδα κεράσαι, ἢ ὅσα δύνανται οἱ παρόντες ἐκπιεῖν. But occasionally the water and the wine were mixed in the separate goblets. Xenophanes, ap. Athen. xi. p. 782 :

> Οὐδέ κεν ἐν κύλικι πρότερον κεράσαιέ τις οἶνον
> ἐγχέας, ἀλλ' ὕδωρ, καὶ καθύπερθε μέθυ.

Theophr. *Ib.*: Ἐπεὶ καὶ τὰ περὶ τὴν κρᾶσιν ἐναντίως εἶχε τὸ παλαιὸν τῷ νῦν παρ' Ἕλλησιν ὑπάρχοντι. οὐ γὰρ τὸ ὕδωρ ἐπὶ τὸν οἶνον ἐπέχεον, ἀλλ' ἐπὶ τὸ ὕδωρ τὸν οἶνον. The mixture in the crater was from time to time renewed according to the requirements of the guests. Eubulos, ap. Athen. ii. p. 36 :

> Τρεῖς γὰρ μόνους κρατῆρας ἐγκεραννύω
> τοῖς εὖ φρονοῦσι· τὸν μὲν ὑγιείας ἕνα,
> ὃν πρῶτον ἐκπίνουσι· τὸν δὲ δεύτερον
> ἔρωτος ἡδονῆς τε· τὸν τρίτον δ' ὕπνου,
> ὃν ἐκπιόντες οἱ σοφοὶ κεκλημένοι
> οἴκαδε βα^ρίζουσ'. ὁ δὲ τέταρτος οὐκ ἔτι
> ἡμέτερός ἐστ', ἀλλ' ὕβρεως· ὁ δὲ πεμπτὸς βοῆς·
> ἕκτος δὲ κώμων· ἕβδομος δ' ὑπωπίων.
> ὁ δ' ὄγδοος κλητῆρος· ὁ δ' ἔνατος χολῆς·
> δέκατος δὲ μανίας, ὥστε καὶ βάλλειν ποιεῖ.

To conduct the symposion, παιδαγωγεῖν συμπόσιον, (Plato, *Leg.* i. p. 641,) an ἄρχων τῆς πόσεως, συμποσίαρχος, or βασιλεὺς, was selected, and to his behests the company had to submit. He was generally chosen by the throw of the *astragali*; see *Gallus*, p. 499 ; Plato, however, makes Alcibiades elect himself to this office. *Symp.* p. 213 : ἄρχοντα οὖν ὑμῖν αἱροῦμαι τῆς πόσεως, ἕως ἂν ὑμεῖς ἱκαιῶς πίητε, ἐμαυτόν.

The symposiarch determined the proportions of the mixture, and the number of the κύαθοι; he could also impose fines, and so forth. On this subject Lucian, *Saturn.* 4, is tolerably explicit:

ἔτι καὶ βασιλέα μόνον ἐφ' ἁπάντων γενέσθαι τῷ ἀστραγάλῳ κρατήσαντα, ὡς μήτε ἐπιταχθείης γελοῖα ἐπιτάγματα καὶ αὐτὸς ἐπιτάττειν ἔχοις, τῷ μὲν αἰσχρόν τι περὶ αὐτοῦ ἀναβοῆσαι, τῷ δὲ γυμνὸν ὀρχήσασθαι καὶ ἀράμενον τὴν αὐλητρίδα τρὶς τὴν οἰκίαν περιελθεῖν. The practical jokes do not appear to have been remarkably novel or ingenious; for a specimen, see Plutarch, *Symp.* i. 4, 3: προστάττοντες ᾄδειν ψελλοῖς, ἢ κτενίζεσθαι φαλακροῖς, ἢ ἀσκωλιάζειν χωλοῖς. Ὥσπερ Ἀγαπήτορι τῷ Ἀκαδημαϊκῷ λεπτὸν ἔχοντι καὶ κατεφθινηκὸς τὸ σκέλος ἐπηρεάζοντες οἱ ξυμπόται πάντας ἐκέλευσαν ἐπὶ τοῦ δεξιοῦ ποδὸς ἑστῶτας ἐκπιεῖν τὸ ποτήριον ἢ ζημίαν καταβαλεῖν. τοῦ δὲ προστάσσειν περιελθόντος εἰς αὐτὸν ἐκέλευσε πάντας, οὕτως πιεῖν ὡς ἂν αὐτὸν ἴδωσι· καὶ κεραμίου κενοῦ κομισθέντος εἰς τοῦτο τὸν ἀσθενῆ πόδα καθεὶς ἐξέπιε τὸ ποτήριον, οἱ δ' ἄλλοι πάντες, ὡς ἐφαίνετο πειρωμένοις ἀδύνατον ἀπέτισαν τὴν ζημίαν. The system of proposing questions in turn occurs in Plato, *Symp.* p. 214.

As the way in which the symposion went off depended in a great measure on the symposiarch, Plato requires that he should be a wise and sober person. *Leg.* i. p. 640 : νήφοντά τε καὶ σοφὸν ἄρχοντα μεθυόντων δεῖ καθιστάναι. Cf. Aristot. *de Repub.* ii. 12. The domestics occupied with the cyathos and crater were under his control, even in a stranger's house; these were called οἰνοχόοι, and οἰνηροὶ θεράποντες, and were usually young slaves; and if no symposiarch had been selected, the guests themselves called for what they wanted. See Xenoph. *Symp.* 2, 26.

The dexterity of the οἰνοχόοι was chiefly shown in handing the cylix and other vessels. Pollux, vi. 95 : Οἱ δὲ οἰνοχόοι τὰ ἐκπώματα ἐκπλυνόντων τε καὶ διανιπτόντων καὶ κλυζόντων καὶ καθαιρόντων. καὶ τὰς φιάλας ἐπὶ τῶν δακτύλων ἄκρων ἐχέτωσαν, προσφέροντες τοῖς συμπόταις εὐλαβῶς. Also Theagenes, ap. Heliod. *Æthiop.* vii. 27 : καὶ ἄκροις τοῖς δακτύλοις ἐποχῶν τὴν φιάλην. Cf. Xenoph. *Cyrop.* i. 3, 8. It is a mistake to suppose that they had also γυναῖκας οἰνοχόους : into this error Eustathius, *ad Odyss.* i. 146, was led by Athenæus, x. p. 425. The single instance there alleged, from the court of Ptolemy Philadelphus, proves nothing. Hetæræ, however, may occasionally have discharged the office.

Before proceeding to the carouse, the company usually agreed upon the τρόπος τῆς πόσεως. Plato, *Symp*. p. 176 : τίνα τρόπον ἥδιστα πιώμεθα ; from which passage it appears that πίνειν ὅσον ἂν ἕκαστος βούληται, ἐπάναγκες δὲ μηδὲν εἶναι, was not usually allowable, but that every one was subject to the symposiarch, who could force him to drink ; πίνειν πρὸς βίαν, ἀναγκάζεσθαι. Drinking a prescribed quantity was a usual punishment : see also the next Excursus. It was customary, at least at Athens, to drink out of small goblets, or, at all events, to begin with them, afterwards resorting to larger. Diog. Laert. i. 103 : Ἕλληνες ἀρχόμενοι μὲν ἐν μικροῖς πίνουσι, πλησθέντες δὲ ἐν μεγάλοις. Some of these were of a tolerable size, holding twenty κύαθοι, or nearly two sevenths of a χοῦς, i. e. about a quart. See Alexis, ap. Athen. x. p. 431 :

> Οὐ συμποσίαρχος ἦν γὰρ, ἀλλὰ δήμιος,
> ὁ Χαιρέας κυάθους προπίνων εἴκοσιν.

But this is nothing to what is told of Alcibiades and Socrates. Plato, *Symp*. p. 213 : ἀλλὰ φερέτω Ἀγάθων εἴ τί ἐστιν ἔκπωμα μέγα · μᾶλλον δὲ οὐδὲν δεῖ. ἀλλὰ φέρε, παῖ, φάναι, τὸν ψυκτῆρα ἐκεῖνον, ἰδόντα αὐτὸν πλέον ἢ ὀκτὼ κοτύλας χωροῦντα. τοῦτον ἐμπλησάμενον πρῶτον μὲν αὐτὸν ἐκπιεῖν, κ.τ.λ. Eight *cotylæ* equalled two thirds of a χοῦς, more than half a gallon. According to Ephippos, apud Athen. x. p. 434, Alexander drained off a goblet holding two χοῦς, or a gallon and a half. Such vessels might well be termed λουτρὰ or φρέατα ; not to mention that they had to be emptied without taking breath, ἀπνευστὶ or ἀμυστὶ πίνειν. Plutarch, *Symp*. iii. 3 ; Alexis, ap. Athen. x. p. 431 ; Lucian *Lexiph*. 8. But of course the custom varied in different places. See Athen. xi. p. 463 : ὅτι τρόποι εἰσὶ πόσεων κατὰ πόλεις ἴδιοι, ὡς Κριτίας παρίστησιν ἐν τῇ Λακεδαιμονίων πολιτείᾳ διὰ τούτων, ὁ μὲν Χῖος καὶ Θάσιος ἐν μεγάλων κυλίκων ἐπιδέξια, ὁ δ' Ἀττικὸς ἐκ μικρῶν ἐπιδέξια, ὁ δὲ Θετταλικὸς ἐκπώματα προπίνει ὅτῳ ἂν βούλωνται μεγάλα. This ἐπιδέξια, or properly ἐπὶ δεξιὰ was observed not only in drinking, but in everything that the guests did in order. Thus Plato *de Repub*. iv. p. 420 : ἐπὶ δεξιὰ διαπίνειν. Id. *Symp*. p. 214 : ἐπὶ δεξιὰ λόγον εἰπεῖν. *Ib*. p. 223 : ἐπαινεῖν and πίνειν ἐπὶ δεξιά. The προπίνειν φιλοτησίας was exactly like drinking toasts or healths. Athen. xi. p. 498 : πληροῦντες γὰρ προέπινον ἀλλήλοις μετὰ προσαγορεύσεως. So in Heliodor. *Æthiop.* iii. 11 : προέπινεν ὁ Θεαγένης, καὶ ἄκων, ἑκάστῳ φιλοτησίαν. See Lucian, *Gall.* 12.

The conversation was of an unrestrained and varied kind; and it was the inborn vivacity and ready wit of the Athenian that lent these symposia their principal charm. Intellectual colloquies, such as those described by Xenophon and Plato, were naturally of rare occurrence, and were even thought out of place; so Plutarch says, *Symp.* i. 1, 1 : μὴ δεῖν, ὥσπερ οἰκοδέσποιναν, ἐν οἴνῳ φθέγγεσθαι φιλοσοφίαν. When games and other pastimes were introduced, every one present took part in them, and the company never relapsed into such a passive state as at Rome, where ἀκροάματα and θεάματα, lectures, concerts, contests of gladiators, and mimes, were put in requisition to fill up the pauses in the repast : and so utter was the want of genuine taste, that even the dialogues of Plato were dramatised for this purpose. See Plutarch, *Symp.* vii. 8, 1. At Philip's court, according to Demosthenes, still more insipid amusements were devised; *Olynth.* ii. p. 23 : λοιποὺς δὴ περὶ αὐτὸν εἶναι λῃστάς (αὐλητὰς Herm.) καὶ κόλακας, καὶ τοιούτους ἀνθρώπους, οἵους μεθυσθέντας ὀρχεῖσθαι τοιαῦτα, οἷα ἐγὼ νῦν ὀκνῶ πρὸς ὑμᾶς ὀνομάσαι. δῆλον δ᾽ ὅτι ταῦτ᾽ ἐστὶν ἀληθῆ· καὶ γὰρ οὓς ἐνθένδε πάντες ἀπήλαυνον, ὡς πολὺ τῶν θαυματοποιῶν ἀσελγεστέρους ὄντας, Καλλίαν ἐκεῖνον τὸν δημόσιον καὶ τοιούτους ἀνθρώπους, μίμους γελοίων καὶ ποιητὰς αἰσχρῶν ἀσμάτων, ὧν εἰς τοὺς συνόντας ποιοῦσιν ἕνεκα τοῦ γελασθῆναι. At the courts of the successors of Alexander things reached a still lower ebb. Thus we are told that naked Thessalian women danced before Antigonos. Athen. xiii. p. 607. But pure Greek manners began, from this period, rapidly to decline.

Music and the dance were certainly favourite amusements at the symposia. Female flute-players were indispensable for the sacrifice; they usually remained in attendance, and there are but few antiques representing symposia where either they or citharistriæ are not present. Plato would willingly have dispensed with them; as we see from *Symp.* p. 176 : τὴν μὲν ἄρτι εἰσελθοῦσαν αὐλητρίδα χαίρειν ἐᾶν αὐλοῦσαν ἑαυτῇ, ἢ ἐάν γε βούληται, ταῖς γυναιξὶ ταῖς ἔνδον. He uses stronger language still in *Protag.* p. 347 : ὅπου δὲ καλοὶ κἀγαθοὶ ξυμπόται καὶ πεπαιδευμένοι εἰσὶν, οὐκ ἂν ἴδοις οὔτ᾽ αὐλητρίδας, οὔτε ὀρχηστρίδας, οὔτε

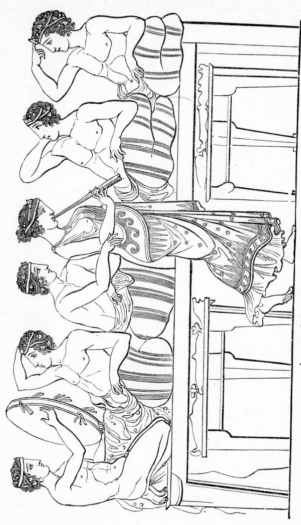

A vase-painting from Tischbein, *Engrav.* II. 55.

Symposion of four young men, listening to the music of the flute-player, who is accompanied by a tympanist.

ψαλτρίας, ἀλλὰ αὐτοὺς αὐτοῖς ἱκανοὺς ὄντας ξυνεῖναι. Plutarch, *Symp.* vii. 7, 8, differs on this point from Plato, and indeed the latter seems rather too severe in his strictures on music and dancing.

In many cases still graver objections might be urged against the presence of these flute-players, and most likely they were often but little removed from hetæræ. In Plautus they are always such, and the same is unequivocally apparent in many vase-paintings. See a curious story related by the Stoic Persæus, apud Athen. xiii. p. 607. On the subject of the other amusements, the games, and so forth, consult the notes to Scene VI., as well as the following Excursus.

THE GAMES.

OF the various games enumerated by Pollux, ix 7, under the title, Περὶ τῶν ἐν συμποσίοις παιδιῶν, many were peculiar to the symposion, while others were merely the amusements of children; the discussion of the latter would be foreign to our present purpose, though it is curious to notice that several of them are practised with little change even at the present day.

The songs called σκόλια, inasmuch as they were often improvised on the occasion, here claim mention. See Ilgen, Σκόλια, h. e. Carm. Conviv. Græc.

From a very early period, guessing riddles, αἰνίγματα or γρῖφοι, was another favourite intellectual amusement. The distinction drawn between these two words by Pollux, vi. 107, seems hardly to be borne out by the usage of the best period; he says: τῶν μὲν συμποτικῶν αἴνιγμα καὶ γρῖφος. τὸ μὲν παιδιὰν εἶχεν, ὁ δὲ γρῖφος καὶ σπουδήν. See Plato, de Republ. v. p. 479; cf. Athen. x. p. 452, where a mere jest is called γρῖφος; also in Diogenes Laertius, i. 91, the word αἴνιγμα is applied to the old riddle of Cleobulos on the year:

> Εἷς ὁ πατήρ, παῖδες δὲ δυώδεκα· τῶν δέ χ᾽ ἑκάστῳ
> παῖδες ἔασι τριήκοντ᾽ ἄνδιχα εἶδος ἔχουσαι.
> ᾗ μὲν λευκαὶ ἔασιν ἰδεῖν, ᾗ δ᾽ αὖτε μέλαιναι.
> ἀθάνατοι δέ τ᾽ ἐοῦσαι ἀποφθίνουσιν ἅπασαι.

The same word is also used of the earnest riddle of the Sphinx: Œd. Tyr. 393. Γρῖφος, on the other hand, is used of the silliest witticisms; as in Aristoph. Vespæ, 20. Athenæus also, who has preserved a great number of these riddles, uses both words without distinction, and even turns the Pythagorean sayings αἰνίγματα. Clearchos, apud Athenæus, x. p. 448, says: γρῖφος πρόβλημα ἐπιπαιστικόν, προστακτικὸν τοῦ διὰ ζητήσεως εὑρεῖν τῇ διανοίᾳ, τὸ προβληθέν, τιμῆς ἢ ἐπιζημίου χάριν εἰρημένον. The fine here alluded to for not guessing right was to drink a certain quantity of wine; οἱ δὲ μὴ εἴποντες οἷς προσετάττετο ἔπινον τὸ ποτήριον. Occasionally the wine was mixed with salt water; Id. p. 458: λεκτέον ἤδη καὶ τίνα κόλασιν ὑπέμενον οἱ μὴ λύσαντες τὸν προτεθέντα γρῖφον. ἔπινον οὗτοι ἅλμην παραμισγομένην τῷ αὑτῶν ποτῷ καὶ ἔδει προσενέγκασθαι τὸ ποτήριον ἀπνευστί. See Pollux, vi. 107: καὶ ὁ μὲν λύσας γέρας εἶχε κρεῶν τινα περιφορὰν, ὁ δὲ ἀδυνατήσας, ἅλμης ποτήριον ἐκπιεῖν. The reward for solving the riddle usually consisted of chaplets and tæniæ, cakes and sweetmeats; sometimes it was a kiss; Clearchos, ap. Athen. x. p. 458: καὶ ἐπὶ τούτοις ἆθλα μὲν τοῖς νικῶσι φιλήματα. In other contests also, such fines and rewards were common, and the company in some cases adjudicated them by ballot. See Xenoph. *Symp.* 5, 8: Ἀλλὰ διαφερόντων, ἔφη, τὰς ψήφους, ἵνα ὡς τάχιστα εἰδῶ, ὅ,τι με χρὴ παθεῖν ἢ ἀποτῖσαι. And again, τῷ νικήσαντι μὴ ταινίας ἀλλὰ φιλήματα ἀναδήματα παρὰ τῶν κριτῶν γενέσθαι.

One of the most favourite of these diversions was the Cottabos, a game said to be of Sicilian origin, and in which success depended mainly on manual dexterity. On this subject, a few words may here suffice, since it has been discussed at length by Jacobs. In spite of the circumstantial accounts given by Athenæus, xv. p. 666, Pollux, vi. 109, and the Scholiasts to Aristophanes, *Pax*, and to Lucian, *Lexiphanes*, 3, there still appears to be a hopeless obscurity attaching to some of the peculiarities of this game.

There were two sorts of cottabos, subject to manifold variations; Groddeck makes out nine. The one was called κότταβος κατακτός, Aristoph. *Pax*, 1243, and this is the most difficult of explanation. The Scholiast to Lucian, *Lexiph.* 3, whose account is not plagiarised from Athenæus, and is more intelligible than the others, informs us that a shaft or staff, χάραξ, was erected, and to the extremity of this was attached the beam of a pair of scales, ζυγός, while from either end of this depended the scale-plates, πλάστιγγες: and beneath these scale-plates little figures were placed, ἀνδριανταρίων ταῖς πλάστιγξιν ὑποκειμένων. One of the players now took a mouthful of wine or water and spirted it in a continuous stream upon one of the plates. If he succeeded in hitting this so as to fill it, it descended and struck the head of the little brass figure beneath; but rose again from the weight of the opposite scale, which, descending in its turn, hit the second figure, so that they both sounded in succession. Other accounts differ widely from this, though the discordance is probably owing to variations in the method in which the game was played.

Firstly, it is generally stated that the wine was not taken
into the mouth, but jerked out of a cup, the hand being bent
(συνεστραμμένῃ τῇ χειρὶ) and the arm curved (ἀπ' ἀγκύλης). This
may have been an alteration introduced at a later date. Cf. Poll.
vi. 111. Other authorities state that there was only one scale, and
one figure, called Manes. But, according to Athenæus, xv. p. 667,
this was not all, for beneath this Manes stood a basin into which
the liquid must fall : τὸ δὲ καλούμενον κατακτὸν κοττάβιον
τοιοῦτόν ἐστι· λυχνίον ἐστὶν ὑψηλὸν ἔχον τὸν Μάνην καλούμενον,
ἐφ' ὃν τὴν καταβαλλομένην ἔδει πεσεῖν πλάστιγγα, ἐντεῦθεν δ'
ἔπιπτεν εἰς λεκάνην ὑποκειμένην πληγεῖσαν τῷ κοττάβῳ. This
agrees with the Scholion to Aristoph. Pax, 343, where it is
further stated that the Manes stood under water in this basin,
and that the scale-plate had to sink so sharply as to hit his head
below the water : ῥάβδος ἦν μακρὰ πεπηγμένη ἐν τῇ γῇ καὶ ἑτέρα
ἐπάνω αὐτῆς κινουμένη, ὡς ἐπὶ ζυγίου. εἶχε δὲ πλάστιγγας δύο
ἐξηρτημένας καὶ κρατῆρας δύο ὑποκάτω τῶν πλαστίγγων, καὶ ὑπὸ
τὸ ὕδωρ ἀνδριὰς ἦν χαλκοῦς κεχρυσωμένος. τοῦτο δὲ ἦν ἐν τοῖς
συμποσίοις. καὶ πᾶς τῶν παιζόντων ἀνίστατο ἔχων φιάλην γέ-
μουσαν ἀκράτου καὶ μηκόθεν ἱστάμενος ἔπεμπεν ὅλον τὸν οἶνον
ὑπὸ μίαν σταγόνα εἰς τὴν πλάστιγγα, ἵνα γεμισθεῖσα βαρυνθῇ
καὶ κατελθῇ καὶ κατελθοῦσα κρούσῃ εἰς τὴν κεφαλὴν τοῦ ὑπὸ τὸ
ὕδωρ κεκρυμμένου καὶ ποιήσῃ ἦχον. καὶ εἰ μὲν χυθῇ τοῦ οἴνου,
ἐνίκα καὶ ᾔδει, ὅτι φιλεῖται ὑπὸ τῆς ἐρωμένης, εἰ δὲ μὴ, ἡττᾶτο.
ἐλέγετο δὲ ὁ ἀνδριὰς ὁ ὑπὸ τὸ ὕδωρ κεκρυμμένος Μάνης. Pollux
says that the scale-plate, κοτταβεῖον, as he calls it, hung from
the ceiling, and he compares it to the plate of a candelabrum,
λυχνίου ἐπίθεμα.

The second species, δι' ὀξυβάφων, is less difficult to comprehend.
On the surface of a vessel containing water a number of small
empty bowls and such like things were set floating ; into these
the wine was spirted in order to sink them. Athen. xv. p. 667 :
Ἕτερον δ' ἐστὶν εἶδος παιδιᾶς τῆς ἐν λεκάνῃ. αὕτη δ' ὕδατος πλη-
ροῦται, ἐπινεῖ τε ἐπ' αὐτῆς ὀξύβαφα κενά, ἐφ' ἃ βάλλοντες τὰς
λάταγας ἐκ καρχησίων ἐπειρῶντο καταδύειν. The other accounts
are to the same effect, with the exception of that given by Pollux,
who says : τὸ δέ τι ἦν κοίλη τις καὶ περιφερὴς λεκανὶς, ἣν καὶ
χάλκειον καὶ σκάφην ἐκάλουν. ἐῴκει δὲ πόλῳ τῷ τὰς ὥρας δεικ-
νύντι ... τὸ δὲ χάλκειον ἐπεπλήρωτο μὲν ὕδατος, ἐπεπόλαζε δ' αὐτῷ

σφαῖρα, καὶ πλάστιγξ καὶ Μάνης, καὶ τρεῖς μυρίναι, καὶ τρία ὀξύβαφα. ὁ δὲ ὑγρᾷ τῇ χειρὶ τὸν κότταβον ἀφεὶς καὶ τούτων τινὸς
τυχὼν εὐδοκιμεῖ. Cf Schol. to Aristoph. *Pax*, 1210. The liquid
so spirted was called λάταξ or λατάγη, whence λαταγεῖν. The
game itself, the entire apparatus, and also the wine that was spirted,
were all called κότταβος. Without further entering into the subject, or attempting to reconcile the apparently contradictory accounts, it may suffice to refer to the passages quoted by Athenæus,
which agree in the main with the description that has been given.

The game served also as a kind of love-oracle. Prizes were
sometimes given, and at all events the player won the ὀξύβαφα
which he had succeeded in sinking. Millingen, *Peint. d. vases gr.*
p. 11, supposes, with very little ground, that he has found the cottabos represented on a vase. Also in Winkelmann's *Monum. Ined.*
200, a tall λυχνίον is seen standing without a lamp; but what it
represents is doubtful. There is, however, one relief, *Marbles of
the Brit. Mus.* ii. 4, which not improbably refers to the game.
At the lower end of a couch stands a shaft bearing a large basin.
Out of this (Combe, however, says *behind it,* which makes all
the difference,) rises a second pillar, surmounted by a Hermes-
shaped figure, on the head of which rests something like a discus.
This agrees very well with the account of Athenæus, already
quoted: λυχνίον ἐστὶν ὑψηλὸν ἔχον τὸν Μάνην καλούμενον, ἐφ'
ὃν τὴν κατταβαλλομένην ἔδει πεσεῖν πλάστιγγα, ἐντεῦθεν δ' ἔπιπτεν εἰς λεκάνην ὑποκειμένην πληγεῖσαν τῷ κοττάβῳ.

The χαλκισμὸς was also a game requiring manual dexterity.
The account given of it by Pollux, ix. 118, is as follows : Ὁ μὲν
χαλκισμὸς, ὀρθὸν νόμισμα ἔδει συντόνως περιστρέψαντας ἐπι-
στρεφόμενον ἐπιστῆσαι τῷ δακτύλῳ · ᾧ τρόπῳ μάλιστα τῆς παιδιᾶς ὑπερήδεσθαί φασι Φρύνην τὴν ἑταίραν. This is wrongly
explained by Prof. K. W. Müller. The manner in which the game
was really played is described in Scene v. p. 75. The account
given by Eustathius, *ad Il.* xiv. 291, is perhaps clearer than that
in Pollux. He says : ἀλλ' ἦν ὁ χαλκισμὸς ὀρθοῦ νομίσματος
θετέον χαλκοῦ στροφὴ καὶ σύντονος περιδίνησις, μεθ' ἦν ἔδει τὸν
παίζοντα ἐπέχειν ὀρθῷ τῷ δακτύλῳ τὸ νόμισμα εἰς ὅσον τάχος
πρινὴ καταπεσεῖν.

The ἱμαντελιγμὸς may also be reckoned in this class of games,
though success in it depended mainly upon chance. A strap was

doubled, and rolled up in the shape of a disk; the player then took a nail or some pointed instrument and stuck it between the folds, and if, on unrolling the strap, the nail was inside the doubling, he had won. Poll. ix. 118 : Ὁ δὲ ἱμαντελιγμὸς διπλοῦ ἱμάντος λαβυρινθώδης τίς ἐστι περιστροφὴ, καθ' ἧς ἔδει καθέντα παττάλιον τῆς διπλόης τυχεῖν· εἰ γὰρ μὴ λυθέντος ἐμπεριείληπτο τῷ ἱμάντι τὸ παττάλιον, ἥττητο ὁ καθείς. Cf. Eustath. ad Il. xiv. 214.

The πεττεία, on the other hand, was a game wherein all depended on skill and calculation, and bore some resemblance to our chess. There were several varieties of this game, and those who have written on the subject have fallen into some confusion from neglecting the distinctions. The game with πεσσοί is very ancient, and Penelope's suitors played at it in the house of Odysseus (Odyss. i. 107) ; but it would be absurd to describe the Homeric πεττεία, when the mere name is all that Homer mentions. Nor can we attach any value to the explanation given by Apion, ap. Athen. i. p. 16, since we cannot ascertain how much is due to a later period. Afterwards there were at least two quite different kinds. For an account of the first variety see Pollux, ix. 97 ; ἐπειδὴ δὲ ψῆφοι μέν εἰσιν οἱ πεσσοὶ, πέντε δὲ ἑκάτερος εἶχε τῶν παιζόντων ἐπὶ πέντε γραμμῶν, εἰκότως εἴρηται Σοφοκλεῖ,

καὶ πεσσὰ πεντέγραμμα καὶ κύβων βολαί.

τῶν δὲ πέντε τῶν ἑκατέρωθεν γραμμῶν μέση τις ἦν ἱερὰ καλουμένη γραμμή. The same, in substance, are the descriptions given by Eustath. ad Od. i. 107 ; Schol. ad Plato, Leg. vii. p. 820 ; Hesychius ; and Schol. ad Theocr. Id. vi. 18. From these writers we learn that each player had five pieces, and five lines to move on, and that the piece standing on the centre line was not moved except in case of extreme necessity : hence the proverb : κινεῖν τὸν ἀφ' ἱερᾶς. But why this move was only made then, or what was the nature of the game, is unknown ; and our informants appear to have had no very clear notions of it themselves. In the language of a later period, the game or the table on which it was played was called ζατρίκιον.

There is rather less obscurity about the second kind of πεττεία, by which the first appears to have been gradually supplanted. This is also called πόλις, or, more correctly, πόλεις. Poll. ix. 98 : Ἡ δὲ διὰ πολλῶν ψήφων παιδιὰ πλινθίον ἐστι, χώρας ἐν γραμμαῖς ἔχον διακειμένας· καὶ τὸ μὲν πλινθίον καλεῖται πόλις, τῶν δὲ ψήφων ἑκάστη κύων. διῃρημένων δὲ εἰς δύο τῶν ψήφων ὁμοχρόων κατὰ τὰς χρόας ἡ τέχνη τῆς παιδιᾶς ἐστι περιληψει τῶν δύο ψήφων ὁμοχρόων τὴν ἑτερόχρουν ἀναιρεῖν. It thus appears to have been somewhat similar to our chess or draughts. The separate squares, which Pollux calls χῶραι, were also denominated πόλεις. See Zenob. *Prov. Cent.* v. 67; Plutarch, *Prov. Alex.* v p. 1254; Plato, *de Republ.* iv. p. 423.

The move forward was called θέσθαι τὴν ψῆφον; moving backward, or recalling a move, ἀναθέσθαι. Harpocr. s. v. ἀναθέσθαι. Plato, *Hipparch.* p. 229; *Leg.* x. p. 903. To give the adversary an advantage was called κρεῖσσον διδόναι. Eurip. *Suppl.* 409:

> ἓν μὲν τόδ' ἡμῖν, ὥσπερ ἐν πεσσοῖς, δίδως
> κρεῖσσον.

This passage seems to hint that the better player gave his adversary something at the commencement of the game.

The chief object of the player consisted in so shutting up his opponent's pieces that he was unable to move. Plato, *de Republ.* vi. p. 487: ὥσπερ ὑπὸ τῶν πεττεύειν δεινῶν οἱ μὴ, τελευτῶντες ἀποκλείονται καὶ οὐκ ἔχουσιν ὅ,τι φέρωσιν. Polyb. i. 84: πολλοὺς ἀποτεμνόμενος καὶ συγκλείων, ὥσπερ ἀγαθὸς πεττευτής. Cf. Plato, *Eryx*, p. 395. According to Pollux, when a piece got between two hostile ones, it was beaten or taken away. The game was by no means an easy one, and good players were rare. Cf. Plato, *Polit.* p. 292; Id. *de Republ.* ii. p. 374: πεττευτικὸς δὲ ἢ κυβευτικὸς ἱκανὸς οὐδ' ἂν εἷς γένοιτο, μὴ αὐτὸ τοῦτο ἐκ παιδὸς ἐπιτηδεύων, ἀλλὰ παρέργῳ χρώμενος;

The διαγραμμισμὸς was a game analogous to, if not identical with, that just described. See Poll. ix. 99; Eustath. *ad Il.* vi. p. 633: παιδιά τις ὁ διαγραμμισμός. ἐγίνετο δὲ, φασὶν, αὕτη κυβείας οὖσα εἶδος διὰ τῶν ἐν πλινθίοις ψήφων ἑξήκοντα, λευκῶν τε ἅμα καὶ μελαινῶν. Whether the game alluded to in an obscure epigram of Agathias, *Anthol.* ix. 482, was a species of πεττεία, can hardly, perhaps, be determined. That the *ludus latrunculorum* and *duodecim scriptorum* of the Romans originated from the Greek πεττεία, admits of no doubt, though the differences are considerable. See *Gallus*, p. 502.

The invention of the πεσσοὶ was traditionally ascribed to

A A

Palamedes. Alcidamas, *Palam*. pp. 74, 76. Cf. Eurip. *Iphig. in Aul.* 194. Plato, on the other hand, names the Egyptian Theuth as the inventor of the πεττεία and κυβεία : *Phædr*. p. 274. These games were universal favourites throughout Greece. See Poll. vii. 203; ix. 48.

Of the games of chance the ἀστραγαλισμὸς claims the first mention. The regular game has been fully described in *Gallus*, pp. 499–502. But the astragals or knuckle-bones were used in other games, for instance, in the ἀρτιασμὸς, which was principally a children's game. See *Gallus*, p. 504. There are many antiques representing children playing at this game. See *Marbles of the Brit. Mus.* ii. 31. So the children of Medea, in a wall-painting in *Mus. Borb.* v. 33. The game was also called ζυγὰ ἢ ἄζυγα, and in vulgar parlance, μονὰ καὶ ζυγὰ, or μονζύγα, 'odd and even.' See Schol. ad Aristoph. *Plut.* 816. The same game is described in the Paris Gloss to v. 1057 : πόσους ὀδόντας εἶπεν ἀντὶ τοῦ πόσα ἔχεις κάρυα. παιδιὰ γάρ ἐστι τοιαύτη· δραξάμενός τις καρύων καὶ ἐκτείνας τὴν χεῖρα ἐρωτᾷ, πόσα ; καὶ ἂν ἐπιτύχῃ, λαμβάνει ὅσα ἔχει ἐν τῇ χειρί· ἐὰν δὲ ἁμάρτῃ κατὰ τὴν ἀπόκρισιν, ἀποτίνει ὅσα ἂν ὁ ἐρωτήσας εὑρεθείη ἔχων. There was another game of skill, not chance, which was played with these astragals, or knuckle-bones, and which is still a favourite amusement of schoolboys in our own day. Five astragals or pebbles were laid on the palm of the hand ; the player then threw them up, and tried to catch them on the back of the hand : this was called πενταλιθίζειν. Poll. ix. 126 : Τὰ δὲ πεντάλιθα. ἤτοι λιθίδια, ἢ ψῆφοι, ἢ ἀστράγαλοι πέντε ἀνερρίπτουντο, ὥστε ἐπιστρέψαντα τὴν χεῖρα δέξασθαι τὰ ἀναρριφθέντα κατὰ τὸ ὀπισθέναρ, ἢ εἰ μὴ πάντα ἐπίσταται, ἢ τῶν ἐπιστάντων ἐπικειμένων ἀναιρεῖσθαι τὰ λοιπὰ τοῖς δακτύλοις. He adds that it was more of a women's game, γυναικῶν δὲ μᾶλλόν ἐστιν ἡ παιδιά, and this, as well as his whole account, is corroborated by a monochromatic painting of Niobe's visit to Latona, where the girls are represented playing at this game. *Antich. d'Ercol.* i. pl. 1.

Lastly comes the regular game of dice, κυβεία. See *Gallus*, p. 499. This was mostly played for money, a circumstance which was frequently urged as an objection against the game, since many were ruined by it. See Lysias, *in Alcib.* p. 541: κατακυβεύσας τὰ ὄντα. Cf. Æschin. *in Timarch.* p. 115.

The places where this game was carried on were called κυβεῖα, and also σκιράφεια, because the original locality was near, or in, the temple of Athena Sciras. See Eustath. *ad Oydss.* i. 107 : καὶ ὅτι ἐσπουδάζετο ἡ κυβεία οὐ μόνον παρὰ Σικελοῖς, ἀλλὰ καὶ Ἀθηναίοις· οἳ καὶ ἐν ἱεροῖς ἀθροιζόμενοι ἐκύβευον, καὶ μάλιστα ἐν τῷ τῆς Σκιράδος Ἀθηνᾶς τῷ ἐπὶ Σκίρῳ. ἀφ᾽ οὗ καὶ τὰ ἄλλα κυβευτήρια σκιράφεια ὠνομάζετο. Cf. the *Etym. M.*, Suidas, Harpocration, and Steph. *de Urb.*, s. v. Σκίρος. All places of the kind were afterwards called σκιράφεια. Isocr. *Areop.* 18, p. 202 ; Lucian, *Lexiph.* 10. We need not suppose that the τηλία, mentioned by Æschines, *in Timarch.* p. 79, refers to the ἀβάκιον or dice-board, for the reference is rather to cock-fighting. Still Pollux, vii. 203, and x. 150, enumerates this among the ὀργάνα κυβευτικά. Cf. Eustath. *ad Odyss.* i. 107.

There was another game in which πεσσοὶ and κύβοι were both used at once. Plato, *de Republ.* x. p. 604 : ὥσπερ ἐν πτώσει κύβων, πρὸς τὰ πεπτωκότα (δεῖ) τίθεσθαι τὰ αὑτοῦ πράγματα, ὅπῃ ὁ λόγος ἐρεῖ βέλτιστ᾽ ἂν ἔχειν. In reference to this, Plutarch, *de Tranquill. Anim.* 5, says : Κυβείᾳ γὰρ ὁ Πλάτων τὸν βίον ἀπείκασεν, ἐν ᾧ καὶ βαλεῖν δεῖ τὰ πρόσφορα, καὶ βαλόντα χρῆσθαι καλῶς τοῖς πεσοῦσι. See *Anthol. Pal.* ix. 767. A similar game is referred to by Ovid, *Art. Am.* ii. 203. A host of other games, many of them requiring neither πεσσοὶ nor κύβοι, are classed by Pollux and others under the common name κυβεία.

THE SLAVES.

ONE of the most striking anomalies in the character of the
Greeks is, that though they acknowledged above all other
nations the value of personal freedom, and kept a jealous guard
against everything that threatened it from within, and were ready
to resist to the death any encroachment made upon it from without
—still they did not recognise the equal claims of all to this blessing, but withheld it from millions of their fellow-men, whom they
made mere passive instruments of their will, and reduced to a
condition little superior to that of domestic animals. This strange
contradiction may be partly due to their assumption that the barbarians were creatures of a naturally inferior order to themselves;
though there was nothing in the habits of those nations which could
excuse such arrogance. But the root of slavery lies everywhere,
and must be rather sought in the general disinclination to menial
labour, and that abhorrence of servitude, based on false notions of
liberty, which first made the possession of slaves desirable. In
process of time this grew into an imperious necessity, which
refused to take into consideration the justice or injustice of the
case; and as there now existed a class of men which had, by
birth and education, become divested of all the habits and feelings
that were regarded as the essential characteristics of an ἐλεύθερος,
the notion of their belonging to a different race of mankind seemed
justified and strengthened.

And this explains the fact, that even Plato, benevolent and
humane as he was, never dreamt of excluding the slave-element
from his ideal of a state which was to include nothing inconsistent
with nature or with reason; and hence, too, he thought it necessary
to give different laws for the free-man and the slave; so that,
where verbal censure was sufficient for the former, the latter was
to receive corporal chastisement; and where the free were fined
for an offence, the slaves were executed. No doubt such a distinction seemed desirable, to mark the difference between a slave
and his master, and great severity might be also necessary to keep

down a class of men who had few feelings in common with those above them, and who in numbers were far their superiors. Aristotle, profound, but dispassionate, could not blink the question, ' What makes the slave a slave ? ' though he does not trouble himself to enquire whether, in its origin, slavery presented anything irrational, and contrary to the universal rights of men ; but proceeds to show, from a comparison between the present characters of the two, that the relative position occupied by the slave is that which is his due. Of course he falls into numerous contradictions, as, for instance, when he starts the question, πότερόν ἐστιν ἀρετή τις δούλου παρὰ τὰς ὀργανικὰς καὶ διακονικὰς ἄλλη τιμιωτέρα τούτων, οἶον σωφροσύνη καὶ ἀνδρία καὶ δικαιοσύνη . . . εἴτε γὰρ ἔστι, τί διοίσουσι τῶν ἐλευθέρων; εἴτε μή ἐστιν, ὄντων ἀνθρώπων καὶ λόγου κοινωνούντων, ἄτοπον. De Republ. i. 13, p. 1259. His solution, which is quite in keeping with the notions of his age, is worth nothing, as the premises are false. Assuming that slaves belong to an ἕτερον γένος, he supposes the existence of a special ἀρετὴ δούλων, while he entirely ignores the πρῶτον ψεῦδος of the case.

The question as to the abstract injustice of slavery, he disposes of by an artificial argument, wherein he shows that it is ever the natural destination of the κρεῖσσον to rule over the χεῖρον, as the soul over the body, the husband over the wife, and he thus arrives at the conclusion, that there are also φύσει δοῦλοι. He adds : ἐστι γὰρ φύσει δοῦλος ὁ δυνάμενος ἄλλου εἶναι (διὸ καὶ ἄλλου ἐστίν). Aristotle, moreover, pronounces a slave to be merely a piece of property ; de Republ. i. 4 : καὶ ὁ δοῦλος κτῆμά τι ἔμψυχον, and makes him in fact little more than a machine possessed of life ; Eth. Nicom. viii. 13, p. 1161 : ὁ γὰρ δοῦλος ἔμψυχον ὄργανον, τὸ δ' ὄργανον ἄψυχος δοῦλος. The verses of Philemon (Fragm. p. 410, Mein.) contain a sounder judgment than all the reasoning of the philosopher :

κἂν δοῦλός ἐστι (ἢ τις) σάρκα τὴν αὐτὴν ἔχει·
φύσει γὰρ οὐδεὶς δοῦλος ἐγενήθη ποτέ·
ἡ δ' αὖ Τύχη τὸ σῶμα κατεδουλώσατο.

And : gain, p. 364 :

Κἂν δοῦλος ᾖ τις, οὐδὲν ἧττον, δέσποτα
ἄνθρωπος οὗτός ἐστιν, ἂν ἄνθρωπος ᾖ.

The Greek slaves were in a far more tolerable condition than those at Rome, as we shall presently see. Sparta forms the only exception, with respect to the inhuman barbarities practised against the Helots. See Plutarch, *Lyc.* 28 ; Xenoph. *de Rep. Athen.* 1, 11. The abuse made by the Spartans of their power is entirely in unison with the character of that people, as is shown by Limburg Brower, *Hist. de la Civil. Mor. et Rélig. d. Grecs*, iii. p. 261. But it is not our purpose to consider the state of a nation living, like the Helots, in serfdom to another race ; and hence the Thessalian Penestæ, the Heracleote Mariandynæ, and the Cretan Clarotæ or Aphamiotæ, will be also excluded from our notice. Cf. Plato, *Leg.* vi. p. 776 ; Poll. iii. 83.

With regard to the origin of slavery, the Hellenes are said to have possessed no slaves in the earliest times. Thus Herodotus, vi. 137, speaking of the Athenians, says, οὐ γὰρ εἶναι τοῦτον τὸν χρόνον σφίσι κω οὐδὲ τοῖς ἄλλοις Ἕλλησι οἰκέτας. See also a fragment of Pherecrates, apud Athen. vi. p. 263. In the Homeric period, however, we find slave universal ; but at that time the slaves were mostly captives, δοριάλωτοι, who served their captor ; though this was not universally the case, for captives are made articles of sal in Homer. See *Odyss.* xv. 483. In the march of civilization, when predatory excursions had grown less frequent, there was no method by which slaves could be obtained except by purchase. But δοριάλωτοι and ἀργυρώνητοι or χρυσώνητοι were always distinguished. Isocr. *Platæens.* 9, p. 406. By degrees, however, the Hellenes grew ashamed of enslaving their own countrymen, and it became customary to set captives free for a certain ransom, which, if they were too poor to pay it, was often discharged by wealthy burghers, as a sort of *Leiturgia.* At the same time the traffic in barbarians and others increased proportionably. Timæus, apud Athen. vi. p. 264: Οὐκ ἦν πάτριον τοῖς Ἕλλησιν ὑπὸ ἀργυρωνήτων τὸ παλαιὸν διακονεῖσθαι. Theopompus, apud Id. p. 265: Χῖοι πρῶτοι τῶν Ἑλλήνων μετὰ Θετταλοὺς καὶ Λακεδαιμονίους ἐχρήσαντο δούλοις, τὴν μέντοι κτῆσιν αὐτῶν οὐ τὸν αὐτὸν τρόπον ἐκείνοις . . . Χῖοι δὲ βαρβάρους κέκτηνται τοὺς οἰκέτας καὶ τιμὴν αὐτῶν καταβάλλοντες. The principle, that none but barbarians should be held as slaves, is nowhere more strongly enunciated than in Plato, *de Republ.* v. p. 469: Μηδὲ Ἕλληνα ἄρα δοῦλον ἐκτῆσθαι μήτε αὐτοὺς, τοῖς τε ἄλλοις Ἕλλησιν οὕτω συμβουλεύειν: Cf. Id. *Leg.* vi. p. 777.

At Athens, as elsewhere, there was a regular slave-market,

where the slaves stood ready for selection. Harpocr. Κύκλοι, Δείναρχος ἐν τῷ κατὰ Καλλαίσχρου. κύκλοι ἐκαλοῦντο οἱ τόποι, ἐν οἷς ἐπωλοῦντό τινες. ὠνομάσθησαν δὲ ἀπὸ τοῦ κύκλῳ περιε- στάναι τοὺς πωλουμένους. The place is also called by Pollux, iii. 78, πρατὴρ λίθος, which is analogous to the Latin phrases, *lapis, de lapide emtus,* unless this refers to sale by auction. The slaves thus exposed were naked, or had to strip at the desire of the purchaser. Lucian, *Eunuch.* 12 : οἱ μὲν ἠξίουν ἀποδύσαντας αὐτὸν ὥσπερ τοὺς ἀργυρωνήτους ἐπισκοπεῖν. The law also made the seller responsible for any concealed defect. Plato, *Leg.* xi. p. 916 ; Dio Chrysost. *Orat.* x. p. 300. The market seems to have been held on fixed days. as for instance on the ἔνη καὶ νέα or νουμηνία. See Aristoph. *Equit.* 43 :

> οὗτος τῇ προτέρᾳ ιουμηνίᾳ
> ἐπρίατο δοῦλον, βυρσοδέψην Παφλαγόνα.

On this the Scholiast remarks : ἐν δὲ ταῖς νουμενίαις οἱ δοῦλοι ἐπω- λοῦντο καὶ οἱ στρατηγοὶ ἐχειροτονοῦντο. So Alciphr. *Epist.* iii. 38 : Φρύγα οἰκέτην ἔχω πονηρὸν, ὃς ἀπέβη τοιοῦτος ἐπὶ τῶν ἀγρῶν. ὡς γὰρ τῇ ἔνῃ καὶ νέα κατ' ἐκλογὴν τοῦτον ἐπριάμην, Νουμήνιον μὲν εὐθὺς ἐθέμην καλεῖσθαι. The prices of course varied according to age and qualities. Ample details will be found in Böckh, *Public Econ. of Athens,* p. 67. The most usual prices were from one to ten minæ ; though old and useless creatures went for even less, while on the other hand trustworthy men who could act as fore- men or overseers occasionally fetched far higher sums. Xenoph. *Memor.* ii. 5, 2 : Τῶν γὰρ οἰκετῶν ὁ μὲν που δύο μνῶν ἄξιός ἐστιν, ὁ δ' οὐδ' ἡμιμναίου, ὁ δὲ πέντε μνῶν, ὁ δὲ καὶ δέκα. Νικίας δ' ὁ Νικηράτου λέγεται ἐπιστάτην εἰς τἀργύρια πρίασθαι τα- λάντου. Plato, *Amat.* p. 135 : καὶ γὰρ τέκτονα μὲν ἂν πρίαιο πέντε ἢ ἓξ μνῶν ἄκρον · ἀρχιτέκτονα δὲ οὐδ' ἂν μυρίων δραχμῶν. The story runs that when somebody asked Aristippos what he would charge for instructing his son, he demanded one thousand drachmæ ; on which the father answered, that he could purchase a slave for that sum. Plutarch, *de Educ.* 7. Of course slaves who were artisans by trade varied much in value, according to their skill, and the difficulty of the craft they followed. Demosth. *in Aphob.* i. p. 816 : μαχαιροποιοὺς (κατέλιπεν ὁ πατὴρ) τριά- κοντα καὶ δύο ἢ τρεῖς, τοὺς μὲν ἀνὰ πέντε μνᾶς ἢ καὶ ἓξ, τοὺς δ' οὐκ ἐλάττονος ἢ τριῶν μνῶν ἀξίους ... κλινοποιοὺς δ' εἴκοσι τὸν

ἀριθμὸν τετταράκοντα μνῶν ὑποκειμένους. Two minæ would thus
be the average, and this was also the price paid in another instance: Demosth. *adv. Spud.* p. 1030. Slaves employed in
ordinary field or house-work were naturally worth much less.
It does not appear that the Greeks ever paid such enormous sums
as were sometimes given in Rome. See *Gallus*, p. 201.

Next to the purchased slaves, called by Plato, *Polit.* p. 289,
ἀναμφισβητήτως δοῦλοι, came those born in the house, οἰκότριβες.
Suidas: οἰκότριψ, δοῦλος οἰκογενής. Ammonius: Οἰκότριψ καὶ
οἰκέτης διαφέρει. οἰκότριψ μὲν γὰρ ὁ ἐν τῇ οἰκίᾳ διατρεφόμενος,
ὃν ἡμεῖς θρεπτὸν καλοῦμεν· οἰκέτης δὲ ὁ δοῦλος ὁ ὠνητός. παρὰ
δὲ Σόλωνι ἐν τοῖς ἄξοσιν οἰκεὺς κέκληται ὁ οἰκότριψ. They were
either the offspring of the master and a female slave, or of two
slaves, and in this case were called ἀμφίδουλοι. Eustath. *ad
Odyss.* ii. 290. If the parents were οἰκότριβες, their offspring
were called οἰκοτρίβαιοι. Poll. iii. 76. The relative number of
such slaves, and the frequency of slave-marriages, has not been
ascertained. Men frequently lived with a female slave as παλ-
λακή (see Excursus on *The Women*), and the children resulting
from this intercourse were only free by exception. See Demosth.
in Aristocr. p. 637. With regard to the intercourse of the slaves,
a mere intimation occurs in Xenophon, *Œcon.* 9, 5: μήτε τεκνοποιῶνται οἱ οἰκέται ἄνευ τῆς ἡμετέρας γνώμης. Also Plato, *Leg.*
xi. p. 930, says: δούλη μὲν ἐὰν συμμίξῃ δούλῳ ἢ ἐλευθέρῳ, ἢ ἀπε-
λευθέρῳ, πάντως τοῦ δεσπότου ἔστω τῆς δούλης τὸ γεινώμενον.
ἐὰν δέ τις ἐλευθέρα δούλῳ συγγίγνηται τοῦ δεσπότου ἔστω τὸ
γιγνόμενον τοῦ δούλου. ἐὰν δ' ἐξ αὑτοῦ δούλης ἢ ἐκ δούλου ἑαυτῆς
καὶ περιφανὲς τοῦτ' ᾖ, τὸ μὲν τῆς γυναικὸς αἱ γυναῖκες εἰς ἄλλην
χώραν ἐκπεμπόντων σὺν τῷ πατρί· τὸ δὲ τοῦ ἀνδρὸς οἱ νομοφύλακες
σὺν τῇ γεννησάσῃ.

An insolvent debtor was liable to become the slave of his
creditor, before the time of Solon, who forbade this δανείζειν
ἐπὶ σώματι, though the practice seems to have continued
in other states. See Isocr. *Plataeens.* 19, p. 414: μικρῶν ἕνεκα
συμβολαίων δουλεύειν. It was also the case in Athens when a
captive in war did not repay the ransom which another had
advanced for him. Demosth. *adv. Nicostr.* p. 1250: ὅτι καὶ οἱ
νόμοι κελεύουσι, τοῦ λυσαμένου ἐκ τῶν πολεμίων εἶναι τὸν λυ-
θέντα, ἐὰν μὴ ἀποδιδῷ τὰ λύτρα·

The number of slaves was very considerable, not only in Athens, but throughout Greece. According to Ctesicles, apud Athen. vi. p. 272, at a census of the population of Attica taken under Demetrius Phalereus, the number of free burghers was found to be twenty-one thousand, of resident aliens ten thousand, and of slaves four hundred thousand. Hence the statement of Thucydides (vii. 27) becomes intelligible, that in the Decelian war, ἀνδραπόδων πλέον ἢ δύο μυριάδες ηὐτομολήκεσαν. According to Timæus, Corinth possessed 460,000 slaves, and Ægina, as we learn from Aristotle, 470,000. But the number at Chios appears to have been the greatest. See Thucyd. viii. 40. For an estimate of the proportions of the free and slave populations, see Böckh, *Public Econ. of Athens*, pp. 30–39, and Wachsmuth, *Hellen. Alterthumsk.* ii. 1, p. 44. Slavery was not introduced into Phocis and Locris till a late period, according to Timæus, apud Athen. vi. p. 264, though little reliance can be placed on this author.

Although the number of private slaves possessed by individual burghers was sometimes very considerable, yet the Greeks seem to have fallen far behind the Romans in this respect. See *Gallus*, p. 203. The father of Demosthenes possessed fifty slaves, as that orator informs us; *in Aphob.* i. p. 823. In other instances the number was far greater. Thus Nicias let out a thousand to the Thracian mines, and Hipponicos six hundred. Plutarch, *Nic.* 4 ; Xenoph. *de Vect.* 4, 14 ; Böckh, *Public Econ. of Athens*, p. 37. Aristotle's friend Mnason also had a thousand. Timæus, apud Athen. vi. p. 264. In early times few were retained in the house, most of them being employed in various handicrafts. At a later period, however, domestic slaves became much more numerous. See Aristot. *de Republ.* ii. 3 : ὥσπερ ἐν ταῖς οἰκετικαῖς διακονίαις οἱ πολλοὶ θεράποντες ἐνίοτε χεῖρον ὑπηρετοῦσι τῶν ἐλαττόνων. Cf. Dio Chrysost. *Orat.* xiii. p. 434. There is no systematic account of the number of domestics in a large establishment, though a few hints may be gathered from the following passages. Thus according to Plutarch, *Apophth. Reg.* i. p. 696, Xenophanes complained to Hiero, μόλις οἰκέτας δύο τρέφειν, which was certainly a mark of great poverty. Again, the family of Æschines, consisting of himself, his wife, mother, and three children, was waited on by seven attendants, and this is brought

forward as a sign of very straitened circumstances. Æschin.
Epist. 12, p. 698. So an escort of four slaves by which the
hetæra Gnathæniou was attended to the Piræus, is mentioned
as insignificant; Machon, ap. Athen. xiii. p. 582:

> Πανηγύρεως οὔσης ποθ' ἡ Γναθαίνιον
> εἰς Πειραιᾶ κατέβαινε πρὸς ξένον τινὰ
> ἔμπορον ἐραστὴν εὐτελῶς ἐπ' ἀστράβης,
> τὰ πάντ' ἔχουσ' ὀνάρια μεθ' ἑαυτῆς τρία.
> καὶ τρεῖς θεραπαίνας καὶ νέαν τιτθὴν μίαν.

To go out without a single attendant was a sign of great indigence. See Aristoph. *Eccl.* 593; also Lysias, *in Diogit.* p. 903,
where a complaint is made of the children being dismissed, *οὐ
μετὰ ἀκολούθου*. And when Phocion's wife allowed herself to
be attended by only one female slave, it was considered so unusual, that it even came to be mentioned in the theatre. Plutarch, *Phoc.* 19. Men also had often three or more slaves to
attend them when from home. Demosth. *in Mid.* p. 565: *καὶ
τρεῖς ἀκολούθους ἢ τέτταρας αὐτὸς ἔχων διὰ τῆς ἀγορᾶς σοβεῖ*
Xenoph. *Memor.* i. 7, 2: *ὅτι ἐκεῖνοι σκεύη τε καλὰ κέκτηνται καὶ
ἀκολούθους πολλοὺς περιάγονται*. In later times the escort was
probably much more numerous. Lucian, *Imag.* 2, speaking of
the appearance of a lady of distinction, says: *θεραπεία δὲ πολλή,
καὶ ἄλλη περὶ αὐτὴν παρασκευὴ λαμπρά, καὶ εὐνούχων τι πλῆθος,
καὶ ἅβραι πάνυ πολλαί*. But it is not always clear whether this
author is portraying Greek or Roman manners; in this case,
however, the lady was of Smyrna. From these instances we
may fairly conclude that even at an early period the number of
domestic slaves was very considerable.

But of the fifty to one thousand slaves that are mentioned as
the property of one master, the majority were employed as artisans, either for their master, or on their own account, paying
him a daily sum. The great difference between the Roman and
Grecian systems consists in the fact that the Greeks looked on
their slaves as a capital yielding interest, while at Rome they
only attended to the wants of their master, or ministered to his
luxury and pride. See Athen. vi. p. 272: Ἀλλὰ Ῥωμαίων
ἕκαστος . . . πλείστους ὅσους κεκτημένος οἰκέτας. καὶ γὰρ μυρίους καὶ
δισμυρίους καὶ ἔτι πλείους δὲ πάμπολλοι κέκτηνται, οὐκ ἐπὶ προσόδοις
δέ, ὥσπερ ὁ τῶν Ἑλλήνων ζάπλουτος Νικίας, ἀλλ' οἱ πλείους τῶν
Ῥωμαίων συμπροϊόντας ἔχουσι τοὺς πλείστους. It is true that the

Roman slave also worked in the *familia urbana* as a mechanic
or artist, but only to supply the immediate wants of his master;
while the Greek was an operative supported by the proceeds of
his labour. Aristot. *de Republ.* iii. 4, p. 1277: δούλου δ᾽ εἴδη
πλείω λέγομεν· αἱ γὰρ ἐργασίαι πλείους, ὧν ἓν μέρος κατέχουσιν
οἱ χερνῆτες. οὗτοι δ᾽ εἰσὶν, ὥσπερ σημαίνει καὶ τοὔνομ᾽ αὐτοὺς,
οἱ ζῶντες ἀπὸ τῶν χειρῶν, ἐν οἷς ὁ βάναυσος τεχνίτης ἐστίν
Æschines mentions the daily sum which each had to pay. *In
Timarch.* p. 118: χωρὶς δὲ οἰκέτας δημιουργοὺς τῆς σκυτοτομικῆς
τέχνης ἐννέα ἢ δέκα, ὧν ἕκαστος τούτῳ δύ᾽ ὀβολοὺς ἀπέφερε τῆς
ἡμέρας, ὁ δ᾽ ἡγεμὼν τοῦ ἐργαστηρίου τριώβολον. A similar
arrangement was made with regard to those working in the
mines. Xenoph. *de Vect.* 4, 14: ὅτι Νικίας ποτὲ ὁ Νικηράτου
ἐκτήσατο ἐν τοῖς ἀργυρίοις χιλίους ἀνθρώπους, οὓς ἐκεῖνος Σωσίᾳ
τῷ Θρᾳκὶ ἐξεμίσθωσεν, ἐφ᾽ ᾧ ὀβολὸν μὲν ἀτελῆ ἑκάστου τῆς
ἡμέρας ἀποδιδόναι. See also the ἀνδράποδα μισθοφοροῦντα mentioned by Isæus, *de Ciron. Hered.* p. 219. Cf. Plato, *Leg.* v.
p. 742. When a slave undertook on his own account the labour
of a harvest or vintage, his case was the same. See Demosth.
adv. Nicostr. p. 1253. It would even appear that slaves were
occasionally allowed to hire farms on their own account. See
Plato, *Leg.* vii. p. 806.

The second method was to make the slaves work as artisans
in their master's shop or factory, his profit being derived from
the sale of their wares. Thus the father of Demosthenes possessed two workshops; Demosth. *in Aphob.* p. 816: μαχαιροποιοὺς μὲν τριάκοντα καὶ δύο ἢ τρεῖς, ἀφ᾽ ὧν τριάκοντα μνᾶς
ἀτελεῖς ἐλάμβανε τοῦ ἐνιαυτοῦ τὴν πρόσοδον. κλινοποιοὺς δ᾽ εἴκοσι
τὸν ἀριθμὸν τετταράκοντα μνῶν ὑποκειμένους, οἳ δώδεκα μνᾶς
ἀτελεῖς αὐτῷ προσέφερον. Cf. Id. *in Olympiod.* p. 1170;
Xenoph. *Memor.* ii. 7, 6; iii. 11, 4. This was most likely the
method pursued when the manufacture undertaken required a
large fixed capital.

If the master cultivated his lands himself, as Ischomachos
did (Xenoph. *Œcon.* 12, 2), he employed numerous slaves under
an overseer, ἐπίτροπος, who was himself also a slave, and on
whom the entire management frequently devolved, the possessor
devoting himself to public duties, or other employments. Aristot.
de Republ. i. 7: ἃ γὰρ τὸν δοῦλον ἐπίστασθαι δεῖ ποιεῖν, . . . αὐτὸ:

δὲ πολιτεύονται ἢ φιλοσοφοῦσιν. The house-steward was called
ταμίας; indeed this word is often used as synonymous with
οἰκονόμος and ἐπίτροπος. This ταμίας or ταμία superintended
all the domestic arrangements, and kept the household stores
under lock and seal, giving out what was required. See Xenoph.
Œcon. 9, 11; Aristoph. Vespæ, 612. He received, for this purpose, a signet-ring from his master. Aristoph. Equites, 947:

> καὶ νῦν ἀπόδος τὸν δακτύλιον, ὡς οὐκ ἔτι
> ἐμοὶ ταμιεύσεις.

The ταμίας must not be confounded with the ἐπίτροπος and
οἰκονόμος mentioned by Lucian, de Merc. Cond. 12. The reference is in this case to Roman customs; and the οἰκονόμος, who
is also paymaster of the household, answers to the Roman dis-
pensator. See Gallus, p. 204. Of the other domestic slaves
each had his peculiar duties. Among them may be mentioned
the οἰνοχόος, the ἀγοραστής (see Excursus on The Markets and
Commerce, p. 287), the ὑδροφόρος (Lucian, Vit. Auct. 7), and
the λασανοφόρος (Plutarch, Apophth Reg. i. p. 723).

A word or two now on the female domestics. Their number
was naturally less than that of the men. Some of them were
employed in manufacturing articles for sale. Thus in Æschines,
in Timarch. p. 118, we have mentioned: γυνὴ ἀμόργινα ἐπιστα-
μένη ἐργάζεσθαι καὶ ἔργα λεπτὰ εἰς τὴν ἀγορὰν ἐκφέρουσα. The
number thus engaged could not, however, have been large, and
most of the feminine labours, as weaving, embroidering and the
like, were also performed by men. In wealthy families a considerable number of women were probably employed in personal
services, and we should recollect that multitudes of articles which
we are accustomed to purchase ready-made, were in those times
prepared at home. In addition to the male slaves, we only find
δύο θεραπαίνας καὶ παιδίσκην mentioned as belonging to the slender
establishment referred to by Isæus, de Ciron. Her. p. 219; but
in more opulent houses several females were employed at the
mill, and in the kitchen, as well as in keeping things clean and
tidy. Then there were the spinners, nurses, chambermaids, and
lady's-maids, κομμώτριαι. Of these last, one often held a more
confidential position near her mistress, and was called ἅβρα.
See Suidas; also Eustath. ad Odyss. xix. 28: ἔστι δὲ ἅβρα κατὰ
Παυσανίαν ἡ σύντροφος καὶ παρὰ χεῖρα θεράπαινα. Cf. Alciphr.

Epist. i. 34. Female slaves born in the house were called σηκίδες.
Poll. iii. 76. A general term for female slaves is δουλάρια. See
Lucian, *Lexiph.* 25.

There were no learned slaves, as at Rome, nor any slaves who
merely ministered to pleasure, as dancers, actors, or musicians.
This, however, was the case at a later period, when the influence
of Roman manners began to be felt. See Lucian, *Amor.* 10:
Χαρικλεῖ γε μὴν πολὺς ὀρχεστρίδων καὶ μουσουργῶν εἴπετο. Yet
the rich kept blacks and eunuchs; the former from mere vanity
and love of show. Theophr. *Char.* 21: (μικροφιλοτίμου) ἐπι-
μεληθῆναι ὅπως αὐτῷ ὁ ἀκόλουθος Αἰθίοψ ἔσται. But the eunuchs
were prized for their reputed fidelity. See Herodotus, viii. 105.
Cf Heliodor. *Æthiop.* viii. 17. Hence they were employed as
treasurers; Plutarch, *Demetr.* 25: ἐπιεικῶς γὰρ εἰώθεσαν εὐνού-
χους ἔχειν γαζοφύλακας. In Lucian, *Imag.* 2, we have a πλῆθος
εὐνούχων, and the porter in the house of Callias is an eunuch.
Plato, *Protag.* p. 314. There is no ground for the supposition
that they were kept to guard the women.

The artisan slaves were naturally more independent than
those employed in domestic services. The latter were provided
by their master with clothes, food, and even wine. See Aristoph.
Vespæ, 442. This was not the case with the artisans, except
when they were working on their lord's account: when they only
paid him a fixed sum per diem, they found themselves in everything. The master, nevertheless, had to make good all damage
that his slaves might do to others, as was enjoined by a law of
Solon. Lysias, *in Theomn.* p. 362: εἰκῆος καὶ δούλης τὴν βλά-
βην ὀφείλειν. Cf. Demosth. *in Nicostr.* p. 1253: Meier and
Schömann, *Att. Proc.* pp. 477, 573. Upon the whole the position of the Greek slave, in reference to his master, was far pre-
ferable to that of the Roman, and this is principally to be
attributed to the character of the Athenian, which led him to
establish a confidential relation between himself and his domestic.
Hence the mute obedience of the Roman, and the familiar gar-
rulity of the Greek slave. See the amusing anecdote related by
Plutarch, *de Garrul.* 18. P. Piso had ordered his slaves never
to speak about anything unless when asked. On one occasion
he had invited Clodius to a banquet. The guests arrived, all but
Clodius. Piso repeatedly sent the slave who had carried the

invitation to look if he were coming. At last he asked him
whether he was sure he had invited Clodius. 'Quite sure,'
replied the slave. 'Why doesn't he come then?' inquired Piso.
'Because he declined the invitation,' answered the slave. 'And
why didn't you tell me that before?' 'Because you never asked
me,' was the slave's reply. Plutarch adds: Οὕτως μὲν 'Ρωμαϊκὸς
οἰκέτης· ὁ δὲ Ἀττικὸς ἐρεῖ τῷ δεσπότῃ σκάπτων, ἐφ' οἷς γεγό-
νασιν αἱ διαλύσεις, οὕτως μέγα πρὸς πάντα ὁ ἐθισμός ἐστι. Cf.
Aristot. de Republ. v. 11, p. 1313; Xenoph de Republ. Ath. 1,
12. Euripides, Phœn. 390, asserts that the greatest hardship of
a slave's fate was being denied the παρρησία:

> IO.   τί φυγάσιν τὸ δυσχερές ;
> ΠΟ. ἓν μὲν μέγιστον, οὐκ ἔχει παρρησίαν.
> IO. δούλου τόδ' εἶπας, μὴ λέγειν, ἅ τις φρονεῖ.

This is however of but limited application, and as far as Athens
is concerned, is contradicted by Demosthenes, Phil. iii. p. 111 :
ὑμεῖς τὴν παρρησίαν ἐπὶ μὲν τῶν ἄλλων οὕτω κοινὴν οἴεσθε δεῖν
εἶναι πᾶσι τοῖς ἐν τῇ πόλει, ὥστε καὶ τοῖς ξένοις καὶ τοῖς δούλοις
αὐτῆς μεταδεδώκατε. καὶ πολλοὺς ἄν τις οἰκέτας ἴδοι παρ' ὑμῖν
μετὰ πλείονος ἐξουσίας, ὅτι βούλονται, λέγοντας ἢ πολίτας ἐν
ἐνίαις τῶν ἄλλων πόλεων. Of course the position of a slave
depended a good deal on the character of his master, and on the
extent to which the slave was an accessory to dubious transactions. See Lucian, Asin. 5 : Δοῦλοι γὰρ τὰ δεσποτῶν ἐπί-
στανται καὶ καλὰ καὶ αἰσχρά. Plato requires a master always to
preserve a grave deportment in the intercourse with his slaves.
Leg. vi. p. 777.

But if these people were allowed more liberty at Athens, this
did not proceed from the recognition of their natural rights; and
even the laws for their protection are due to other motives than
the love of justice Xenophon, de Republ. Athen. i. 10, says that
it was forbidden to strike a slave at Athens, for fear of hitting
a free-man by mistake, as these, in dress and appearance, were
not superior to the slaves and the metœci; but this regulation
applied only to strange slaves, and not to one's own. It appears
to have been allowable to institute a γραφὴ ὕβρεως for injury
done to a slave. See Æschin. in Timarch. p. 41 : Ἄν τις Ἀθηναίων ἐλεύθερον παῖδα ὑβρίσῃ, γραφέσθω ὁ κύριος τοῦ παιδὸς πρὸς
τοὺς θεσμοθέτας, κ.τ.λ. ἔνοχοι δὲ ἔστωσαν ταῖσδε ταῖς αἰτίαις καὶ

οἱ εἰς τὰ οἰκετικὰ σώματα ἐξαμαρτάνοντες. Also Demosth. *in Mid.*
p. 529 : Ἐάν τις ὑβρίσῃ εἴς τινα, ἢ παῖδα, ἢ γυναῖκα, ἢ ἄνδρα, τῶν
ἐλευθέρων ἢ τῶν δούλων, ἢ παράνομόν τι ποιήσῃ εἰς τούτων τινά,
γραφέσθω πρὸς τοὺς θεσμοθέτας ὁ βουλόμενος Ἀθηναίων, οἷς ἔξεστιν
κ. τ. λ. The idea entertained by Meier and Schömann, *Att. Proc.*
p. 321, that a δίκη αἰκίας could be instituted, but not a γραφὴ
ὕβρεως, and that both the orators referred to one and the same
law, seems erroneous. In Demosthenes, *in Nicostr.* p. 1251, a
free-born lad, παιδάριον ἀστὸν, is sent into a garden to demolish
a rose-bed, and this seems to militate against the assumption that
a γραφὴ ὕβρεως might be brought for an assault upon a slave;
for the complainant adds: ἵν' εἴπερ καταλαβὼν αὐτὸν ἐγω πρὸς
ὀργὴν δήσαιμι ἢ πατάξαιμι, ὡς δοῦλον ὄντα γραφήν με γράψαιτο
ὕβρεως. But if we investigate the matter more narrowly, it will
appear that the inference is inadmissible; because it is not a
question of ὕβρις at all, since the criteria are wanting, viz. the
ἄρχεσθαι χειρῶν ἀδίκων, and the προπηλακισμός, See Aristot.
Rhet. ii. 24, p. 1402. There is no doubt that if a slave had been
dispatched to devastate the garden, and the owner had chastised
him, an action of ὕβρις could not possibly have been supported :
there would have been a better pretext for one on account of
maltreating the free-born lad, though this would have had small
shadow of justice.

Neither does it seem probable that Xenophon, or whoever was
the author of the treatise *de Republica Athenensium*, alleged the
above-mentioned reason for the law against striking slaves, merely
out of hostility to the Athenian democracy. See Æschin. *in
Timarch.* p. 42 : οὐ γὰρ ὑπὲρ τῶν οἰκετῶν ἐσπούδακεν ὁ νομοθέτης,
ἀλλὰ βουλόμενος ἡμᾶς ἐθίσαι πολὺ ἀπέχειν τῆς τῶν ἐλευθέρων
ὕβρεως, προσέγραφε, μηδ' εἰς τοὺς δούλους ὑβρίζειν. Cf. Plato,
Leg. vi. p. 777. With regard to the difference between the
punishments imposed on the slave and the free-man, the leading
distinction appears to be that in every instance a corporal penalty
is inflicted on the former, while in the case of the latter this is
only the last resource. Demosth. *in Timocr.* p. 752 : καὶ μὴν εἰ
θέλοιτε σκέψασθαι παρ' ὑμῖν αὐτοῖς, ὦ ἄνδρες δικασταὶ, τί δοῦλον ἢ
ἐλεύθερον εἶναι διαφέρει, τοῦτο μέγιστον ἂν εὕροιτε, ὅτι τοῖς μὲν
δούλοις τὸ σῶμα τῶν ἀδικημάτων ἀπάντων ὑπεύθυνόν ἐστι, τοῖς
δ' ἐλευθέροις ὕστατον τοῦτο προσήκει κολάζειν. Hence the differ-

ence in the kinds of evidence required in a court of justice in
behalf of the one or the other. Antipho, *de Choreut.* p. 778:
καὶ ἐξείη μὲν τοὺς ἐλευθέρους ὅρκοις καὶ πίστεσιν ἀναγκάζειν, ἃ
τοῖς ἐλευθέροις μέγιστα καὶ περὶ πλείστου ἐστίν. ἐξείη δὲ τοὺς
δούλους ἐτέραις ἀνάγκαις, ὑφ᾽ ὧν, καὶ ἦν μέλλωσιν ἀποθανεῖσθαι
κατειπόντες, ὅμως ἀναγκάζονται τἀληθῆ λέγειν. One of the most
degrading features of the slave's position was that when maltreated
he was not allowed to defend himself. Plato, *Gorg.* p. 483: οὐδὲ
γὰρ ἀνδρὸς τοῦτό γ᾽ ἐστὶ τὸ πάθημα, τὸ ἀδικεῖσθαι, ἀλλὰ ἀνδρα-
πόδου τινὸς, ᾧ κρεῖττον τεθνάναι ἐστὶν ἢ ζῆν, ὅστις ἀδικούμενος καὶ
προπηλακιζόμενος μὴ οἷός τέ ἐστιν αὐτὸς αὑτῷ βοηθεῖν, μηδὲ ἄλλῳ,
οὗ ἂν κήδηται. If the injury were done by a stranger, the master
might take the matter up, and lodge a complaint, since the slave
himself could not sue, or be sued; but the only defence he had
against his owner's cruelty was by taking refuge in the Theseion,
or at some other altar, whereupon the master might be forced to
sell him. See Petit, *Leg. Att.* p. 258; Meier and Schömann,
Att. Proc. pp. 403, 557. Public slaves, who had no master to
bring an action of αἰκία, appear to have sought protection in a
similar manner. See Æschin. *in Timarch.* p. 83: τῇ δὲ ὑστεραίᾳ
ὑπεραγανακτήσας τῷ πράγματι ὁ Πιττάλακος ἔρχεται γυμνὸς εἰς
τὴν ἀγορὰν καὶ καθίζει ἐπὶ τὸν βωμὸν τὸν τῆς μητρὸς τῶν θεῶν.

The custom of scattering sweet-meats, καταχύσματα, about
the house on the entrance of a newly-purchased slave, seems, at
first sight, to contrast strangely with this ill-treatment of his
person. Demosth *in Steph.* i. p. 1123: καὶ ἦ τὰ καταχύσματα
αὐτοῦ κατέχεε τόθ᾽, ἡνίκα ἐωνήθη, ταύτῃ συνοικεῖν. Aristoph.
Plut. 768:

> φέρε νῦν ἰοῦσ᾽ εἴσω κομίσω καταχύσματα
> ὥσπερ νεωνήτοισιν ὀφθαλμοῖς ἐγώ.

But this was done, not on the slave's account, but for the sake of
a good omen, as the Scholiast tells us. Cf. Poll. iii. 77; also
Harpocration and Suidas, s. v. καταχύσματα. There was also a
custom of beating and driving a slave out of doors, on a certain
day in the year, as a personification of want and worthlessness.
Plutarch, *Symp.* vi. p. 851: καλεῖται δὲ Βουλίμου ἐξέλασις· καὶ τῶν
οἰκετῶν ἕνα τύπτοντες ἀγνίαις ῥάβδοις διὰ θυρῶν ἐξελαύνουσιν
ἐπιλέγοντες, Ἔξω βούλιμον, ἔσω δὲ πλοῦτον καὶ ὑγίειαν.

The method of using slaves as witnesses is quite in accordance

with the rest of the treatment they experienced. Their simple
testimony passed for nothing, unless extorted by the rack, except
perhaps when they came forward as μηνυταὶ, in cases of heavy
crimes, such as murder ; see Plato, *Leg.* xi. p. 937 ; Antipho, *de
Cæde Vol.* p. 633. Thus Demosthenes *in Onet.* i. p. 874, says :
δούλων δὲ βασανισθέντων οὐδένες πώποτ' ἐξηλέγχθησαν, ὡς οὐκ
ἀληθῆ τὰ ἐκ τῆς βασάνου εἶπον. Also Isæus, *de Ciron. Her.*
p. 202 : καὶ ὁπόταν δοῦλοι καὶ ἐλεύθεροι παραγένωνται καὶ δέῃ
εὑρηθῆναί τι τῶν ζητουμένων, οὐ χρῆσθε ταῖς τῶν ἐλευθέρων μαρ-
τυρίαις, ἀλλὰ τοὺς δούλους βασανίζοντες οὕτω ζητεῖτε εὑρεῖν τὴν
ἀλήθειαν τῶν γεγενημένων. This was called ἐκ τοῦ σώματος, or
ἐν τῷ δέρματι τὸν ἔλεγχον διδόναι. Demosth. *adv. Timoth.*
p. 1200. The possibility of obtaining evidence of this kind tended
to depreciate the judicial value of the voluntary testimony of freemen. Thus Lycurgus, *in Leocr.* p. 160, says : βασανίζειν καὶ
τοῖς ἔργοις μᾶλλον ἢ τοῖς λόγοις πιστεύειν. The orators of course
decry or extol such evidence, just as it suits their purpose. Thus
Antipho, *de Choreut.* p. 778, declares it worthy of confidence,
and again *de Cæde Herod.* p. 720, rejects it as unsafe.

The punishments inflicted on slaves were almost invariably
corporal. No mention occurs of any that were merely ignomi-
nious, as the Roman *furca.* See *Gallus,* p. 223. Beating with
rods, thongs, or whips, was very common. As negroes have been
flogged till a pipe could be leisurely smoked out, so, if not in
Greece, at least in Etruria, a somewhat similar barbarity seems
to have been practised. Plutarch, *de Cohib. Ira,* 11 : Ἀριστοτέ-
λης ἱστορεῖ κατ' αὐτὸν ἐν Τυρρηνίᾳ μαστιγοῦσθαι τοὺς οἰκέτας
πρὸς αὐλόν.

Fetters, πέδαι, were often fastened on the feet, not only by
way of punishment, but also to prevent the escape of the slaves,
especially of those who worked in the fields or mines. Athen. vi.
p. 272 : καὶ αἱ πολλαὶ δὲ αὗται Ἀττικαὶ μυριάδες τῶν οἰκετῶν
δεδεμέναι εἰργάζοντο τὰ μέταλλα. The ποδοκάκη or ποδοκάκκη
was a cumbrous fetter employed as a punishment for offenders.
See Lysias, *in Theomn.* p. 356 ; Demosth. *in Timocr.* p. 733.
Cf. Suidas, s. v. Identical with, or similar to this, was the χοῖνιξ.
Aristophanes puns on its double sense of a measure and a fetter.
Vesp. 440 :

            οὓς ἐγὼ 'δίδαξα κλάειν τέτταρ' ἐς τὴν χοίνικα.

Something of the same kind was the σφαλός. Poll. viii. 72. The
ξύλον was an elaborate apparatus, in which the culprit was fixed,
with his neck, hands, and feet, in five different holes. Aristoph.
Equites, 1049 :

δῆσαι σ' ἐκέλευε πεντεσυρίγγῳ ξύλῳ.

See Scholiast on the passage. Suidas is wrong in taking this to
be synonymous with the ποδοκάκη. The κλοιὸς, again, was something of the same kind, but only fastened the neck and the hands.
Xenoph. *Hist. Gr.* iii. 3, 11 : ἐκ τούτου μέντοι ἤδη δεδεμένος καὶ
τὼ χεῖρε καὶ τὸν τράχηλον ἐν κλοιῷ, μαστιγούμενος καὶ κεντού-
μενος αὐτός τε καὶ οἱ μετ' αὐτοῦ κατὰ τὴν πόλιν περιήγοντο.
See also Lucian, *Toxar.* 29 : καὶ πονήρως εἶχεν, οἷον εἰκὸς χαμαὶ
καθεύδοντα καὶ τῆς νυκτὸς οὐδὲ προτείνειν τὰ σκέλη δυνάμενον ἐν
τῷ ξύλῳ κατακεκλεισμένα· τῆς μὲν γὰρ ἡμέρας ὁ κλοιὸς ἤρκει καὶ
ἡ ἑτέρα χεὶρ πεπεδημένη, εἰς δὲ τὴν νύκτα ἔδει ὅλον καταδεδέ-
σθαι. From this passage it appears that this instrument did not
necessarily fasten the hands, and would then be merely a collar
for the neck, the same as is elsewhere called περιδέραιον. Lucian,
Lexiph. 10. According to the Scholiast on Aristoph. *Plut.* 476,
κύφων is identical with κλοιός. These punishments were also
judicially imposed on freemen in the case of certain crimes ; but
they were the usual correctives applied to slaves. The τύμπανα,
however, (Aristoph. *Plut.* 476 ; Lysias, *in Agor.* p. 480,) the
στρέβλαι, and the τροχὸς, (Antiph. *de Venef.* p. 615,) are the
instruments of the δήμιος or δημόκοινος only.

Branding was a very common punishment, especially for running away, theft, and similar offences. Thus Aristoph. *Aves*, 759 :
δραπέτης ἐστιγμένος. A mark of some kind was branded on the
forehead, and many strove to conceal it under the hair. Diphilos,
apud Athen. vi. p. 225 :

κόμην τρέφων μὲν πρῶτον ἱερὰν τοῦ θεοῦ,
ὡς φησίν. οὐ διὰ τοῦτό γ', ἀλλ' ἐστιγμένος
πρὸ τοῦ μετώπου παραπέτασμ' αὐτὴν ἔχει.

Captives taken in war were sometimes thus dealt with in cases of
peculiar animosity. See Plutarch, *Pericl.* 26 : Οἱ δὲ Σάμιοι τοὺς
αἰχμαλώτους τῶν Ἀθηναίων ἀνθυβρίζοντες ἔστιζον εἰς τὸ μέτωπον γλαῦκας· καὶ γὰρ ἐκείνους οἱ Ἀθηναῖοι σάμαιναν.

The penalty of death could only be inflicted with the sanction
of the law, and not merely at the will of the master, as among the
Romans. Antipho, *de Cæde Herod.* p. 727 : καίτοι οὐδὲ οἱ τοὺς

δεσπότας ἀποκτείναντες, ἐὰν ἐπ' αὐτοφώρῳ ληφθῶσιν, οὐδ' οὗτοι
θνήσκουσιν ὑπ' αὐτῶν τῶν προσηκόντων, ἀλλὰ παραδιδόασιν αὐτοὺς
τῇ ἀρχῇ κατὰ νόμους ὑμετέρους πατρίους. See also Eurip. Hecub.
289 :

> νόμος δ' ἐν ὑμῖν τοῖς τ' ἐλευθέροις ἴσος
> καὶ τοῖσι δούλοις αἵματος κεῖται πέρι.

It is difficult to determine to what extent the character of the
slaves themselves might render necessary such harsh treatment ;
for it is from the accounts given by their masters that we gather
all our information on the subject. It would be absurd to deny
that among the multitudes of slaves in Greece there were not a
great number of intelligent and worthy, nay, even noble-minded
persons. Thus Plato, Leg. vi. p. 776, says : πολλοὶ γὰρ ἀδελφῶν
ἤδη δοῦλοι καὶ υἱέων τισὶ κρείττους πρὸς ἀρετὴν πᾶσαν γενόμενοι
σεσώκασι δεσπότας καὶ κτήματα τάς τε οἰκήσεις αὐτῶν ὅλας.
Aristotle, too, despite his theory, is obliged to confess that nature
sometimes errs, and accords to slaves the qualities of freemen :
De Republ. i. 5. That the affecting instance of Tyndarus in The
Captives of Plautus was founded on fact, we cannot doubt. On
the other hand, it is no doubt true that there were many who,
by the degradation of their nature, their want of fidelity to their
masters, and their vices of all kinds, might seem to deserve their
lot. See Plato, Phæd. p. 69.

But the real blame lay often with the master, and the badness
of the slave was an index of the character of his owner, and of his
domestic arrangements. Plato, Leg. vi. p. 777 : Ταῦτα δὴ διαλα-
βόντες ἕκαστοι τοῖς διανοήμασιν, οἱ μὲν πιστεύουσί τε οὐδὲν γένει
οἰκετῶν, κατὰ δὲ θηρίων φύσιν κέντροις καὶ μάστιξιν οὐ τρὶς μόνον
ἀλλὰ πολλάκις ἀπεργάζονται δούλας τὰς ψυχὰς τῶν οἰκετῶν· οἱ
δ' αὖ τἀναντία δρῶσι τούτων πάντα. Cf. Xenophon, Œcon. 3, 4.
The ordinary sentiments of the slave are nowhere better portrayed
than in the dialogue between Æacos and Xanthias, in Aristoph.
Ranæ, 745 :

> Α.　　　μάλα γ' ἐποπτεύειν δοκῶ,
> ὅταν καταράσωμαι λάθρα τῷ δεσπότῃ.
> Ξ. τί δὲ τονθορύζων, ἡνίκ' ἂν πληγὰς λαβὼν
> πολλὰς ἀπίῃς θύραζε ;　Α. καὶ τόθ' ἥδομαι.
> Ξ. τί δὲ πολλὰ πράττων ;　Α. ὡς, μὰ Δί', οὐδὲν οἶδ' ἐγώ.
> Ξ. Ὁμόγνιε Ζεῦ· καὶ παρακούων δεσποτῶν
> ἅττ' ἂν λαλῶσι ;　Α. καὶ μάλα πλεῖν ἢ μαίνομαι.
> Ξ. τί δὲ τοῖς θύραζε ταῦτα καταλαλῶν ;　Α. ἐγώ ;
> μὰ Δί', ἀλλ' ὅταν δρῶ τοῦτο, κἀκμιαίνομαι.

Cf. Plutarch, *Non Posse Su·v.* 8. It was from this coarse and grovelling way of thinking usual among slaves, that every ignoble desire was called ἡδονὴ ἀνδραποδώδης. Plato, *Epist.* vii. p. 335; Aristot. *Eth. Nic.* iii. 10, 11; Plutarch, *Amat.* 4. They seem to have been considered incapable of noble feelings, and their chief praise was to commit no crime. Philostr. *Vit. Apoll. Tyan.* iii. 25 : ἔπαινον ποιοῦνται τῶν ἀνδραπόδων τὸ μὴ κλέπτειν αὐτά.

Runaway slaves were not uncommon, even when there was no war to encourage their desertion. See Plato, *Protag.* p. 310; Xenoph. *Memor.* ii. 10, 1. On this account, when out of doors, the slave preceded his master, instead of going behind. Theophr. *Char.* 18 : καὶ τὸν παῖδα δὲ ἀκολουθοῦντα κελεύειν αὐτοῦ ὄπισθεν μὴ βαδίζειν, ἀλλ᾽ ἔμπροσθεν, ἵνα φυλάττηται αὐτῷ, μὴ ἐν τῇ ὁδῷ ἀποδράσῃ. Slave-rebellions actually took place once and again, (Athen. vi. p. 272; Plato, *Leg.* vi. p. 777,) and that such outbreaks were constant causes of apprehension, we see from Plato, *de Republ.* ix. p. 578.

Slaves were sometimes manumitted by the state as a reward for certain services, such as informing against criminals, or good conduct in war; but the master was always indemnified. Plato, *Leg.* xi. p. 914. At other times they obtained their freedom by paying their owner the sum which he had given for them. See Petit, *Leg. Att.* p. 259; Meier and Schömann, *Att. Proc.* pp. 405, 559. Nevertheless these freed-men, ἀπελεύθεροι, always remained in a sort of dependence on the master, and the neglect of their duties gave rise to the δίκη ἀποστασίου. This explains the law proposed by the orator Lycurgus, Plutarch, *Dec. Orat. Vit.* iv. p. 377 : μηδενὶ ἐξεῖναι Ἀθηναίων, μηδὲ τῶν οἰκούντων Ἀθήνησιν, ἐλεύθερον σῶμα πρίασθαι ἐπὶ δουλείᾳ ἐκ τῶν ἁλισκομένων ἄνευ τῆς τοῦ προτέρου δεσπότου γνώμης. These ἀπελεύθεροι always remained δοῦλοι, if not οἰκέται also. See Athen. vi. p. 267 : Διαφέρειν δέ φησι Χρύσιππος δοῦλον οἰκέτου . . . διὰ τὸ τοὺς ἀπελευθέρους μὲν δούλους ἔτι εἶναι, οἰκέτας δὲ τοὺς μὴ τῆς κτήσεως ἀφειμένους. They certainly often continued wholly in the service of their former master, (Isæus, *de Philoctem. Her.* p. 134,) and were then perhaps in a better position than if they had tried to support themselves independently. So a fragment of Philemon (Mein. p. 418):

Ὡς κρεῖττόν ἐστι δεσπότου χρηστοῦ τυχεῖν,
ἢ ζῆν ταπεινῶς καὶ κακῶς ἐλεύθερον.

Still their feelings toward the προστάτης were very frequently not of the most friendly kind. Demosth. *in Timocr.* p. 739: πονηρῶν καὶ ἀχαρίστων οἰκετῶν τρόπους ἔχοντες, καὶ γὰρ ἐκείνων, ὦ ἄ. δ., ὅσοι ἂν ἐλεύθεροι γένωνται οὐ τῆς ἐλευθερίας χάριν ἔχουσι τοῖς δεσπόταις, ἀλλὰ μισοῦσι μάλιστα ἀνθρώπων ἁπάντων, ὅτι συνίσασιν αὐτοῖς δουλεύσασιν.

In conclusion, it may be remarked that, besides the slaves, there were many of the poorer classes, especially among the ξένοι or μέτοικοι, who performed the same services for hire, μισθωτοί. Plato, *de Republ.* ii. p. 371: οἱ δὴ πωλοῦντες τὴν τῆς ἰσχύος χρείαν, τὴν τιμὴν ταύτην μισθὸν καλοῦντες, κέκληνται, ὡς ἐγῷμαι, μισθωτοί. Id. *Polit.* p. 290: οὕς γε ὁρῶμεν μισθωτοὺς καὶ θῆτας πᾶσιν ἑτοίμους ὑπηρετοῦντας. Cf. Aristot. *de Republ.* i. 11. Such people were hired, not only as artisans and farm-servants, but also as domestics. Thus Plato, *Lys.* p. 208: ἔστι τις ἡνίοχος, παρὰ τοῦ πατρὸς μισθὸν φέρων. The women who engaged themselves as nurses have been mentioned already, and the out-door attendants were also hired sometimes. Theophr. *Char.* 22: μισθοῦσθαι εἰς τὰς ἐξόδους παιδίον ἀκολουθῆσον. Occasionally the services of a poor relation were made use of in this capacity. Isæus, *de Dicæog. Her.* p. 94. Lastly, there were messengers, like our ticket-porters, waiting about the market-place at Athens, who were ready to run errands or do jobs at a moment's notice. Poll. vii. 132: δύο γὰρ ὄντων τῶν κολωνῶν, ὁ μὲν ἵππειος ἐκαλεῖτε . . . ὁ δ᾽ ἦν ἐν ἀγορᾷ παρὰ τὸ Εὐρυσάκειον, οὗ συνῄεσαν οἱ μισθαρνοῦντες. Cf. Suidas and Harpocration, s. v. Κολωνίτης.

EXCURSUS TO SCENE VIII.

THE DOCTORS.

AN account of the medical practice of the Greeks, or an estimate of the scientific acquirements of their physicians, would require a knowledge of medicine itself, as well as a deep study of the medical literature of the ancients. But such an attempt would be foreign to the object of this work, which professes only to describe the details of daily life. Yet it will not be uninstructive to cast our eyes for awhile from cheerful scenes to the sick chamber and the bed of suffering, and to learn the means of succour resorted to on such trying occasions. We shall describe the doctor's person and ordinary appearance; we shall investigate his position in society, the repute in which his art was held, his behaviour towards the sick, the amount of his fee, and we shall see how he at one time paid visits, at another received his patients at home. These particulars will be collected not so much from the medical writings of antiquity, as from the incidental notices which are found elsewhere.

In the first place we may remark that the science of healing and its professors were regarded in a much higher point of view in Greece than at Rome. See *Gallus*, p. 207. The arts of healing and divination were, in the very earliest times, considered as most intimately connected with each other; and this notion prevailed in a later age. See Eustath. *ad Il.* i. 63: κοινή πώς ἐστι τέχνη ἰατρικὴ καὶ μαντική. Since, moreover, the science was regarded as of divine origin, and since the doctors continued, in a certain sense, to be accounted the successors of Asclepios, this belief naturally increased the respect for the profession. Inherited from the son of Apollo by the Asclepiadæ, by them transmitted to their successors, the art was ever accounted divine; and, greatly as the ἰατρικὴ τέχνη of later times differed from the simple treatment pursued of yore, the doctors always looked on Asclepios as their πρόγονος, and themselves as his ἔκγονοι. Plato, *Symp.* p. 186: πάντα τὰ τοιαῦτα τούτοις (τοῖς ἐναντίοις) ἐπιστηθεὶς ἔρωτα ἐμποιῆσαι καὶ ὁμόνοιαν ὁ ἡμέτερος πρόγονος Ἀσκληπιὸς, ὥς φασιν οἵδε οἱ ποιηταὶ καὶ ἐγὼ πείθομαι, συνέστησε τὴν ἡμετέραν τέχνην. Cf. Id. *de Republ.* iii. p. 406.

Many however looked on the art and its professors with great contempt. Thus of Pausanias, the Lacedæmonian, we read in Plutarch, *Apophth. Lac.* i. p. 921: κράτιστον δὲ ἔλεγε τοῦτον ἰατρὸν εἶναι τὸν μὴ κατασήποντα τοὺς ἀῤῥωστοῦντας, ἀλλὰ τάχιστα θάπτοντα. Again, Aristophanes, *Nubes*, 332, designates them as swindlers; and in *Plutus*, 407, we read:

> τίς δῆτ᾽ ἰατρός ἐστι νῦν ἐν τῇ πόλει :
> οὔτε γὰρ ὁ μισθὸς οὐδὲν ἔστ᾽, οὔθ᾽ ἡ τέχνη.

Athenæus, also, calls them charlatans and pedants ; ix. p. 377 : Μέγας δ᾽ ἐστὶ σοφιστὴς καὶ οὐδὲν ἥττων τῶν ἰατρῶν εἰς ἀλαζονείαν καὶ ὁ παρὰ Σωσιπάτρῳ μάγειρος. Cf. xv. p. 666. The caricature too in Plautus, *Menæch*. v. 3–5, is perhaps from a Grecian original. Yet it would be unfair to infer from these passages that the profession generally was looked down upon in Greece. Incompetent doctors there were, no doubt, as now; but there were others possessed of great experience and skill. See Antipho, *Tetral.* iii. p. 689 : νῦν δὲ πολλαῖς ἡμέραις ὕστερον πονηρῷ ἰατρῷ ἐπιτρεφθεὶς διὰ τὴν τοῦ ἰατροῦ μοχθηρίαν, καὶ οὐ διὰ τὰς πληγὰς ἀπέθανε. προλεγόντων γὰρ αὐτῷ τῶν ἄλλων ἰατρῶν, εἰ ταύτην τὴν θεραπείαν θεραπεύσοιτο, ὅτι ἰάσιμος ὢν διαφθαρήσοιτο, δι᾽ ὑμᾶς τοὺς συμβούλους διαφθαρεὶς ἐμοὶ ἀνόσιον ἔγκλημα προσέβαλεν.

At Rome it was usual to have a house-physician in the number of the slaves, those who healed for money being looked on with distrust. The elder Cato contented himself with a recipe-book, *commentarius*, which probably contained all sorts of prescriptions for particular cases. See *Gallus*, p. 208. In Greece, also, there were numerous works on medical subjects, as we see from Xenophon, *Memor.* iv. 2, 10 : πολλὰ γὰρ καὶ ἰατρῶν ἐστι συγγράμματα. Yet these general treatises were not held sufficient for the individual cases that might occur, and this ἰατρεύεσθαι κατὰ γράμματα was considered useless. A doctor was therefore consulted on every occasion. See Euripides, apud Stob. *Tit.* C. 3, p. 308 :

> Πρὸς τὴν νόσον τοι καὶ τὸν ἰατρὸν χρεὼν
> ἰδόντ᾽ ἀκεῖσθαι, μὴ 'πιτακτὰ φάρμακα
> διδόντ᾽, ἐὰν μὴ ταῦτα τῇ νόσῳ πρέπῃ.

Cf. Aristot. *de Republ.* iii. 16, p. 1287 : ὅτι τὸ κατὰ γράμματα

ἰατρεύεσθαι φαῦλον, ἀλλὰ καὶ αἱρετώτερον χρῆσθαι τοῖς ἔχουσι
τὰς τέχνας. He adds, however, that when the doctor was sus-
pected of having been tampered with, the γράμματα would be
then consulted. Cf. Plato, *Polit.* p. 298 : ὃν μὲν γὰρ ἐθελήσωσιν
ἡμῶν τούτων ἑκάτεροι σώζειν, ὁμοίως δὴ σώζουσιν · ὃν δ᾽ ἂν λω-
βᾶσθαι βουληθῶσι, λωβῶνται τέμνοντες καὶ καίοντες . . . καὶ δὴ καὶ
τελευτῶντες ἢ παρὰ ξυγγενῶν ἢ παρά τινων ἐχθρῶν τοῦ κάμνοντος,
χρήματα μισθὸν λαμβάνοντες ἀποκτιννύασιν. The doctor, if he
wished to play false, had the law in his favour, as it naturally
acquitted him of all responsibility in case anything happened
to his patient. See Antipho. *Tetral.* iii. p. 694 : εἰ δ᾽ ἔτι καὶ ὑπὸ
τοῦ ἰατροῦ ἀπέθανεν, ὡς οὐκ ἀπέθανεν, ὁ μὲν ἰατρὸς οὐ φονεὺς
αὐτοῦ ἐστιν, ὁ γὰρ νόμος ἀπολύει αὐτόν. Also Philemon, apud
Stob. *Tit.* CII. 6, p. 333 :

> μόνῳ δ᾽ ἰατρῷ τοῦτο καὶ συνηγόρῳ
> ἔξεστιν, ἀποκτείνειν μὲν, ἀποθνήσκειν δὲ μή.

Plin. *Nat. Hist.* xxix. 1, 6 : ‘Medico tantum hominem occidisse
impunitas summa est.’ Cf. Plato, *Leg.* ix. p. 865. Still, in certain cases, they seem to have been legally accountable for their
treatment. See Aristot. *de Republ.* iii. 10, p. 1281 : ὥσπερ οὖν
ἰατρὸν δεῖ διδόναι τὰς εὐθύνας ἐν ἰατροῖς, οὕτω καὶ τοὺς ἄλλους
ἐν τοῖς ὁμοίοις.

It also appears that a permission from the state to practise
was always required, and even though no public examination took
place, yet every one desirous of being allowed to practise, had to
show that he had been the pupil of a medical man. See Xenoph.
Memor. iv. 2, 5 : Ἁρμόσεις δ᾽ ἂν οὕτω προοιμιάζεσθαι καὶ τοῖς
βουλομένοις παρὰ τῆς πόλεως ἰατρικὸν ἔργον λαβεῖν. ἐπιτήδειον
γὰρ αὐτοῖς εἴη τοῦ λόγου ἄρχεσθαι ἐντεῦθεν · ‘ Παρ᾽ οὐδενὸς μὲν
πώποτε, ὦ ἄνδρες Ἀθηναῖοι, τὴν ἰατρικὴν τέχνην ἔμαθον, οὐδ᾽ ἐζή-
τησα διδάσκαλον ἐμαυτῷ γενέσθαι τῶν ἰατρῶν οὐδένα · διατετέλεκα
γὰρ φυλαττόμενος οὐ μόνον τὸ μαθεῖν τι παρὰ τῶν ἰατρῶν, ἀλλὰ
καὶ τὸ δόξαι μεμαθηκέναι τὴν τέχνην ταύτην. ὅμως δέ μοι τὸ
ἰατρικὸν ἔργον δότε· πειράσομαι γὰρ ἐν ὑμῖν ἀποκινδυνεύων μανθάνειν.’ That this ἰατρικὸν ἔργον refers in this instance to a public
salaried appointment does not seem probable, though the fact
cannot be disputed that there were medical men regularly retained in the pay of the state. Thus in Aristoph. *Acharn.* 1029,

Dicæopolis says to the countryman, who begs him for some
ointment for his eyes :

ἀλλ', ὦ πόνηρ', οὐ δημοσιεύων τυγχάνω.

At the same time he directs him πρὸς τοὺς Πιττάλου. The Scholiast says : δημοσίᾳ χειροτονούμενοι ἰατροὶ καὶ δημόσιοι προῖκα
ἐθεράπευον. Cf. Plato, *Gorg.* p. 455 : ὅταν περὶ ἰατρῶν αἱρέσεως
ᾖ τῇ πόλει ξύλλογος. But Plato also distinctly mentions the two
classes ; those in the pay of the state, and those not. *Polit.* p.
259 : εἴ τῷ τις τῶν δημοσιευόντων ἰατρῶν ἱκανὸς συμβουλεύειν,
ἰδιωτεύων αὐτός. So Strabo, iv. 1, 291, speaking of the introduction of Greek customs into Gaul, says : σοφιστὰς γοῦν ὑποδέ-
χονται τοὺς μὲν ἰδίᾳ, τοὺς δὲ αἱ πόλεις κοινῇ μισθούμεναι, καθάπερ
καὶ ἰατρούς. Democedes, also, had practised for a year in Ægina,
on his own account, before he was taken into the public pay.
Herodot. iii. 131. The salary was sometimes, as in this instance,
very considerable. Democedes at first received from the Ægi-
netans a talent per annum. Next year the Athenians sent for
him, and paid him one hundred minæ, and at last Polycrates of
Samos secured his services at a salary of two talents. See Bockh,
Public Econ. of Athens, p. 120.

In addition to this salary, the patient paid a fee, as we see
from Aristotle, *ib.* : ἄρνυνται τὸν μισθὸν τοὺς κάμνοντας ὑγιάσαν-
τες. We certainly cannot draw the inference from this passage
that the fee was conditional upon recovery. Besides the general
expression μισθὸς, there were other more honourable terms for
the fee, as, for instance, σῶστρα and ἰατρεῖα. Poll. iv. 186 :
ἰδίως δὲ ἰατρῷ μὲν σῶστρα, σωτήρια καὶ ἰατρεῖα. Sometimes the
doctor demanded his fee in advance, before he attempted the cure.
Thus Aspasia, wife of Cyrus the Younger, when a girl, had a
tumour on her face : Δείκνυσι γοῦν αὐτὴν ὁ πατὴρ ἰατρῷ. ὁ δὲ
ὑπέσχετο ἰάσασθαι εἰ λάβοι τρεῖς στατῆρας. ὁ δὲ ἔφατο μὴ ἔχειν.
ὁ δὲ ἰατρὸς μηδὲ αὐτὸς εὐπορεῖν φαρμάκου. Ælian, *Var. Hist.*
xii. 1. See also Achill. Tat. iv. 15. Occasionally, the reason
for this procedure was, because the doctor had to provide the
remedies at his own expense, as we see from the passage in Ælian;
and this is confirmed by Plato, *Polit.* p. 298.

The physicians were under the necessity of dispensing their own
drugs, as there were no apothecaries' shops where the prescriptions could be made up. The booths of the φαρμακοπῶλαι were

of an entirely different nature. These people were nothing better than quacks and mountebanks, who, among other things, vended specifics, compounded by themselves without the aid of a qualified doctor, and which were adapted merely for common disorders. They also cried their nostrums about the streets. Lucian, *pro Merc. Cond.* 7: τὸ δ᾽ ὅλον ἐκείνῳ τῷ φαρμακοπώλῃ ἔοικας, ὃς ἀποκηρύττων βηχὸς φάρμακον, καὶ αὐτίκα παύσειν τοὺς πάσχοντας ὑπισχνούμενος, αὐτὸς μεταξὺ σπώμενος ὑπὸ βηχὸς ἐφαίνετο. See Plutarch, *de Prof. in Virt.* 8. They probably carried serpents about with them, to aid their mysterious feats of jugglery; at least this would appear to be the meaning of the fragment of Aristophanes, preserved by Pollux, x. 180 :

> καὶ τοὺς μὲν ὄφεις, οὓς ἐπιπέμπεις
> ἐν κίστῃ που κατασήμηναι,
> καὶ παῦσαι φαρμακοπωλῶν.

Among other wares they dealt in burning-glasses, as we see from Aristoph. *Nub.* 766 :

> ΣΤ. ἤδη παρὰ τοῖσι φαρμακοπώλαις τὴν λίθον
> ταύτην ἑώρας, τὴν καλήν, τὴν διαφανῆ,
> ἀφ᾽ ἧς τὸ πῦρ ἅπτουσι ;   ΣΩ. τὴν ὕαλον λέγεις ;

Indeed the word φάρμακον has so many significations, that it is not clear whether the φαρμακοτρίβαι, mentioned by Demosthenes, *in Olympiod.* p. 1171, were employed in grinding drugs, colours, or something else.

The regular doctor always made up his own medicines, often mixing them with something sweet, to conceal the unpleasant taste. Plutarch, *de Educ. Puer.* 18: καθάπερ ἰατροὶ τὰ πικρὰ τῶν φαρμάκων τοῖς γλυκέσι χυμοῖς καταμιγνύντες τὴν τέρψιν ἐπὶ τὸ συμφέρον πάροδον εὗρον. Cf. Xenoph. *Memor.* iv. 2, 17.

Some patients called at his ἰατρεῖον, or ἐργαστήριον, as it was also called; others he visited at their own dwellings. See Plato, *Leg.* iv. p. 720: ἰατρεύουσι περιτρέχοντες καὶ ἐν τοῖς ἰατρείοις περιμένοντες. Such an ἰατρεῖον was at once a bathing establishment, apothecary's shop, and surgery hence boxes, πυξίδες or κυλικίδες, (Athen. xi. p. 480; Eustath. *ad Odyss.* v. 296,) cupping-glasses, syringes, bathing apparatus, and so forth, were to be seen scattered about. A very complete picture of such a shop occurs in a fragment of Antiphanes, apud Pollux, x. 46 :

κατεπκευασμένο:
λαμπρότατον ἰατρεῖον ἐν χαλκῖς πάνυ
λουτηρίοισιν, ἐξαλίπτροις, κυλικίσιν,
σικύαισιν, ὑποθέτοισι.

The doctors had also their assistants or pupils, who carried their instructions into effect. Plato, *Leg.* iv. p. 720. Thus we find Timarchos with Euthydicos, a doctor in the Piræus. See Æschin. *in Timarch.* p. 65 : οὗτος γὰρ πρῶτον πάντων μὲν, ἐπειδὴ ἀπηλλάγη ἐκ παίδων ἐκάθητο ἐν Πειραιεῖ ἐπὶ τοῦ Εὐθυδίκου ἰατρείου, προφάσει μὲν τῆς τέχνης μαθητής. To these ἰατρεῖα those persons resorted who wished to take some medicine on the spot, for a slight indisposition ; Plato, *Leg.* i. p. 646. But others also came, who were labouring under severer complaints, Lamachos, for instance : Aristoph. *Acharn.* 1022.

The assistants seem to have been partly slaves, and these had principally to attend to those of their own class. That a slave could set up as doctor on his own account does not appear to have been the case. A very interesting passage about these slave-doctors, from which it appears that they were not remarkably delicate or conscientious in their treatment of their patients, is to be found in Plato, *Leg.* iv. p. 720 : ᾿Αρ᾿ οὖν καὶ ξυννοεῖς, ὅτι δούλων καὶ ἐλευθέρων ὄντων τῶν καμνόντων ἐν ταῖς πόλεσι, τοὺς μὲν δούλους σχεδόν τι οἱ δοῦλοι τὰ πολλὰ ἰατρεύουσι περιτρέχοντες καὶ ἐν τοῖς ἰατρείοις περιμένοντες ; καὶ οὔτε τινὰ λόγον ἑκάστου περὶ νοσήματος ἑκάστου τῶν οἰκετῶν οὐδεὶς τῶν τοιούτων ἰατρῶν δίδωσιν, οὐδ᾿ ἀποδέχεται· προστάξας δ᾿ αὐτῷ τὰ δόξαντα ἐξ ἐμπειρίας, ὡς ἀκριβῶς εἰδὼς, καθάπερ τύραννος, αὐθαδῶς οἴχεται ἱποπηδήσας πρὸς ἄλλον κάμνοντα οἰκέτην. Freemen, on the contrary, especially the more wealthy, had none but freemen for their medical attendants, who proceeded to work in a very careful and conscientious manner. Plato, *ibid.* : ὁ δὲ ἐλεύθερος ὡς ἐπὶ τὸ πλεῖστον τὰ τῶν ἐλευθέρων νοσήματα θεραπεύει τε καὶ ἐπισκοπεῖ καὶ ταῦτα ἐξετάζων ἀπ᾿ ἀρχῆς καὶ κατὰ φύσιν τῷ κάμνοντι κοινούμενος αὐτῷ τε καὶ τοῖς φίλοις ἅμα μὲν αὐτὸς μανθάνει τι παρὰ τῶν νοσούντων, ἅμα δέ καθόσον οἷός τέ ἐστι, διδάσκει τὸν ἀσθενοῦντα αὐτόν.

It was a rule of Hippocrates that a physician should maintain a becoming exterior, avoiding everything likely to cause an unpleasant impression on the patient. The hair and beard were to be carefully trimmed, and his dress to be even elegant. See Galen,

in Hippocr. *Epid.* xvii. 2, p. 138 : καὶ πρὸς τούτοις γε αὐτὸς ὁ
ἰατρὸς, ὃν πρῶτόν τε καὶ μάλιστα τάς τε χεῖρας ἔχειν δεῖ κα-
θαρωτάτας καὶ τὸ πρόσωπον τὰς τρίχας ἐπί τε τοῦ γενείου καὶ
κεφαλῆς. ἐφεξῆς δὲ καὶ τὰ ἄλλα μόρια τοῦ σώματος, ὥσπερ γε
καὶ τὴν ἐσθῆτα λαμπράν. His deportment should be equally
devoid of servility and of self-importance, he should be calm and
collected, and very guarded in expressing opinions as to the state
of the patient. This wholesome advice was not always observed,
according to Galen ; he says, p. 144 : ἰατροὶ δέ τινές εἰσιν, οἳ
μέχρι τοσούτου μωραίνουσιν, ὡς καὶ τοῖς κοιμωμένοις ἐπεισιέναι
μετὰ ψόφου ποδῶν, φωνῆς μείζονος, ὑφ' ὧν ἐνίοτε διεγερθέντες οἱ
νοσοῦντες ἀγανακτοῦσι κ.τ.λ. He also tells a story of a physician
who, when a sick person enquired the chance of his recovery,
answered him with the line :

κάτθανε καὶ Πάτροκλος, ὅπερ σέο πολλὸν ἀμείνων

Galen adds : ἔνιοι δὲ τῶν νῦν ἰατρῶν, . . . τραχέως καὶ αὐτοὶ προσ-
φέρονται τοῖς νοσοῦσιν, ὡς μισηθῆναι, καθάπερ ἄλλοι τινὲς ἐξ
ὑπεναντίου δουλοπρεπῶς κολακεύοντες ἐξ αὐτοῦ τούτου κατεφρο-
νήθησαν. Lucian, *adv. Indoct.* 29, gives an account of the strata-
gems of incompetent practitioners who sought to blind people's
eyes to their incapacity by the elegance of their apparatus : ὅτι
καὶ οἱ ἀμαθέστατοι τῶν ἰατρῶν τὸ αὐτὸ σοὶ ποιοῦσιν, ἐλεφαντί-
νους νάρθηκας καὶ σικύας ἀργυρᾶς ποιούμενοι, καὶ σμίλας χρυσο-
κολλήτους· ὁπόταν δὲ χρήσασθαι τούτοις δέῃ, οἱ μὲν οὐδὲ ὅπως
χρὴ μεταχειρίσασθαι αὐτὰ ἴσασι. παρελθὼν δέ τις εἰς τὸ μέσον
τῶν μεμαθηκότων φλεβοτόμον εὖ μάλα ἠκονημένον ἔχων, ἰοῦ τἆλλα
μεστὸν ἀπήλλαξε τῆς ὀδύνης τὸν νοσοῦντα. Cf. Xenoph. *Œcon.*
15, 7.

The Greek physician was likewise a surgeon. In Plutarch.
de San. Tuend. 15, we have an account of a bold attempt at
opening the larynx of a man who had swallowed a fish-bone.
The operation, however, proved fatal. It has been usually asserted that the ancients considered it a πρᾶγμα ἀνοσιώτατον to
dissect a human body. But instances do occur, though we are
told of none made especially for scientific purposes. See Steph.
de Urb. s. v. Ἀνδανία, where it is related that the Lacedæmonians,
having made the hero Aristomenes prisoner, cut open his body to
see whether it contained anything extraordinary : ἀνατεμόντες
ἐσκόπουν, εἰ παρὰ τοὺς λοιπούς ἐστί τι. καὶ εὗρον σπλάγχνον

ἐξηλλαγμένον, καὶ τὴν καρδίαν ἐασεῖιαν. See also Pau an. iv. 9, 5; Eustath, *ad Il.* i. 189. It was not till long afterwards that the science of healing became divided into separate branches, such as the arts of oculists, dentists, &c. See Lucian, *Lexiph.* 4. The passage in Dio Chrysostom, *Orat.* viii. p. 277, is hardly explicit enough to enable us to determine whether this was the case as early as the time of Diogenes the Cynic. He says: ἔλεγε θαυμάζειν, ὅτι εἰ μὲν ἔφη ὀδόντας ἰᾶσθαι, πάντες ἂν αὐτῷ προσῄεσαν οἱ δεόμενοι ὀδόντα ἐξελέσθαι. καὶ, νὴ Δία, εἰ ὑπέσχετο ὀφθαλμοὺς θαραπεύειν, πάντες ἄνθρωποι ὀφθαλμοὺς αὐτῷ ἐπεδείκνυον· ὁμοίως δὲ εἰ σπληνὸς ἢ ποδάγρας ἢ κορύζης εἰδέναι φάρμακον. Cf. *Gallus,* p. 208. The ἰατραλεῖπται seem to have been distinguished by their attempting to cure diseases by means of embrocations, combined with bodily exercise and strict régimen. See Plato, *de Republ.* iii. p. 406 : Ἡρόδικος γὰρ . . . μίξας γυμναστικὴν ἰατρικῇ, κ. τ. λ.

The Greek doctors were perpetually encountered by difficulties arising from the stupidity, distrustfulness, and blind superstition of the time. Thus when the plague was raging at Athens, during the Peloponnesian war, it was confidently believed that all the wells had been poisoned; see Thucyd. ii. 48 : ὥστε καὶ ἐλέχθη ὑπ' αὐτῶν, ὡς οἱ Πελοποννήσιοι φάρμακα ἐσβεβλήκοιεν ἐς τὰ φρέατα. Still more general was the superstition that certain persons, by incantations, tying of magic knots, and other secret arts, were able to afflict people with diseases, μαγευτικὴ or φαρμακεία, the different *nuances* being termed μαγγανεία, γοητεία, and so forth. It is worthy of note that even Plato, who often mentions this belief, could not wholly bring himself to attribute it to mere superstition. In one passage, *de Republ.* ii. p. 364, he does seem to pronounce it an imposture; but in the Laws, where he treats the subject more at large, he appears to be undecided on this point. He distinguishes between two kinds of φαρμακεία ; of which the first is σώματι σώματα κακουργοῦσα, i. e. by means of poison. Of the other he says: ἄλλη δὲ ἣ μαγγανείας τέ τισι καὶ ἐπῳδαῖς . . . ταῦτ' οὖν καὶ περὶ τὰ τοιαῦτα ξύμπαντα οὔτε ῥᾴδιον ὅπως ποτὲ πέφυκε γιγνώσκειν, οὔτ', εἴ τις γνοίη, πείθειν εὐπετὲς ἑτέρους. His law on the subject is as follows : ἐὰν δὲ καταδέσεσιν ἢ ἐπαγωγαῖς, ἤ τισιν ἐπῳδαῖς, ἢ τῶν τοιούτων φαρμακείων ὡντινωνοῦν δόξῃ ὅμοιος εἶναι βλάπτοντι. *Leg.* xi. p. 933.

Under these circumstances the use of counter-charms, ἀλεξιφάρμακα, was very natural. Plato, *Polit.* p. 280. Sympathetic
cures were frequently tried; see Theocr. ii. 91. An important
passage occurs in Demosthenes, *in Aristogit.* p. 793: ἀλλ᾿ ἐφ᾿ οἷς
ὑμεῖς τὴν μιαρὰν Θεοδωρίδα, τὴν Λημνίδα, τὴν φαρμακίδα καὶ αὐτὴν, καὶ τὸ γένος ἅπαν ἀπεκτείνατε, ταῦτα λαβὼν τὰ φάρμακα
καὶ τὰς ἐπῳδὰς παρὰ τῆς θεραπαίνης αὐτῆς . . . μαγγανεύει καὶ φε-
νακίζει καὶ τοὺς ἐπιλήπτους φησὶν ἰᾶσθαι. The usages customary
on such occasions are enumerated in an interesting fragment of
Menander (*Meineke*, p. 42):

Περιμαξάτωσάν σ᾿ αἱ γυναῖκες, ἐν κύκλῳ
καὶ περιθειωσάτωσαν, ἀπὸ κρουνῶν τριῶν
ὕδατι περίρραν᾿, ἐμβαλὼν ἅλας, φακούς.

These were called περικαθαρτήρια, and the accompanying songs
or charms, ἐπῳδαὶ, were considered essential to success. Thus
Socrates says ironically: καὶ ἐγὼ μὲν εἶπον, ὅτι αὐτὸ μὲν εἴη φύλλον τι, ἐπῳδὴ δέ τις ἐπὶ τῷ φαρμάκῳ εἴη, ἢν εἰ μέν τις ἐπᾴδοι
ἅμα καὶ χρῷτο αὐτῷ, παντάπασιν ὑγιᾶ ποιοῖ τὸ φάρμακον· ἄνευ
δὲ τῆς ἐπῳδῆς οὐδὲν ὄφελος εἴη τοῦ φύλλου. Plato, *Charm.*
p. 155. Those who practised these arts were called φαρμακοὶ,
φαρμακίδες, γόητες, &c. Cf. Eustath. *ad Il.* xi. 739; *ad Odyss.*
i. 260.

EXCURSUS TO SCENE IX.

THE BURIALS.

A VERY prominent feature in the Greek character was the pious conscientiousness with which they discharged those duties which were held to be due from the living to the dead. Among other nations of antiquity we find, it is true, a more pompous ceremonial, and usages more loudly expressive of grief, ending even in the bloody tragedy of self-sacrifice; we observe moreover a gloomy and superstitious veneration for the carefully-treasured relics of defunct kindred; but that modest piety which discharges the last labour of love to the departed, tending carefully the sepulchre, and testifying by often-recurring gifts an enduring recollection, is nowhere so distinctly traceable as among the Greeks. Originally, no doubt, a prudential consideration of the pernicious effects which the non-burial of the dead might have upon the living, may have given rise to the superstition that the unburied dead wandered restlessly about the earth. But as early as the time of Homer this discreet notion had been forgotten, and it was undoubtingly believed that an honourable interment was the happiest lot for the departed, and to provide it the most sacred duty of the survivor. Hence the wish expressed by Odysseus, when his bark is wrecked, that he had fallen before Troy, for then he says, τῷ κ' ἔλαχον κτερέων. In later times, also, splendid obsequies were held to be essential to human happiness: λέγω τοίνυν, ἀεὶ καὶ παντὶ, καὶ πανταχοῦ κάλλιστον εἶναι ἀνδρὶ πλουτοῦντι . . . ὑπὸ τῶν αὐτοῦ ἐκγόνων καλῶς καὶ μεγαλοπρεπῶς ταφῆναι. Plato, *Hipp. Maj.* p. 291.

Hence, except in cases of peculiar animosity, it was a rule among the Greeks not to deprive a fallen foe of the rites of sepulture. Thus in Euripides, *Suppl.* 524, Theseus is made to say:

> νεκροὺς δὲ τοὺς θανόντας, οὐ βλάπτων πόλιν,
> οὐδ' ἀνδροκμῆτας προσφέρων ἀγωνίας,
> θάψαι δικαιῶ, τὸν Πανελλήνων νόμον
> σώζων. τί τούτων εστὶν οὐ καλῶς ἔχον ;

In cases where passion and hatred caused a departure from this rule, the procedure met with strong disapprobation. See Isocrates,

Plataeens. p. 416 : ἔστι δ᾽ οὐκ ἴσον κακὸν ..υδ᾽ ὅμοιον τοὺς τεθνεῶ-
τας ταφῆς εἴργεσθαι καὶ τοὺς ζῶντας πατρίδος ἀπ̣οστερεῖσθαι καὶ
τῶν ἄλλων ἀγαθῶν ἁπάντων, ἀλλὰ τὸ μὲν δειιότερ͞ον τοῖς κωλύουσιν
ἢ τοῖς ἀτυχοῦσιν, κ.τ.λ. And a notion actually existed that
animals, and even insects, were capable of a like respect to the
dead of their kind. Cf. Plutarch, *de Sol. Anim.* 11.

How much more natural therefore was it that in civil life the
duty of sepulture was looked on as a very holy one; so that when
the law absolved children from all other duties to unworthy
parents, it still made it incumbent on them to provide for them a
suitable interment. So the law of Solon cited by Æschines, *in
Timarch.* p. 40 : μὴ ἐπάναγκες εἶναι τῷ παιδὶ ἡβήσαντι τρέφειν τὸν
πατέρα, μήτε οἴκησιν παρέχειν, ὃς ἂν ἐκμισθώσῃ ἑταιρεῖν· ἀποθανόντα δὲ θαπτέτω καὶ τἄλλα ποιείτω τὰ νομιζόμενα. Individual
instances of neglect, such as that mentioned by Demosthenes, *in
Erat.* p. 786, are referred to in terms which sufficiently show the
horror with which such unnatural conduct was generally regarded.
See also Lysias, *in Phil.* p. 883 ; Isæus, *de Philoctem. Hered.*
p. 143 ; *de Nicostr. Hered.* p. 78. But all these were examples
of abandoned people, and mostly outcasts in the public esteem.
Ordinary feeling imposed even on strangers coming across a
corpse, the duty of at least covering it with earth, should a formal
interment be found impracticable. Ælian, *Var. Hist.* v. 14.
Again, the very words used to designate funeral rites, such as τὰ
δίκαια, νόμιμα or νομιζόμενα, προσήκοντα, show that obsequies
were supposed to be claimed by the departed as their due.

The barbarous usages that accompanied the interments of
earlier ages were gradually changed during the march of civilization. Plato, *Min.* p. 315 : ὥσπερ καὶ ἡμᾶς αὐτοὺς οἶσθά που καὶ
αὐτὸς ἀκούων, οἵοις νόμοις ἐχρώμεθα προτοῦ περὶ τοὺς ἀποθανόντας
ἱερεῖά τε προσφάττοντες πρὸ τῆς ἐκφορᾶς τοῦ νεκροῦ καὶ ἐγχυτριστρίας
μεταπεμπόμενοι. οἱ δ᾽ αὖ ἐκείνων πρότεροι αὐτοῦ καὶ ἔθαπτον ἐν
τῇ οἰκίᾳ τοὺς ἀποθανόντας. ἡμεῖς δὲ τούτων οὐδὲν ποιοῦμεν. At
Athens this change was in a great measure wrought by the law of
Solon. See Demosth. *in Macart.* p. 1071 ; cf. Plutarch, *Sol.* 12 ;
Lyc. 27.

The best detailed account of the funeral ceremonies is that given
by Lucian, *de Luctu,* 10 ; and there is no reason to suppose that at
that period any material changes had taken place. The first thing

done on a person's death was to insert an obolos in his mouth as
a ναῦλον for the ferryman of Hades : ἐπειδάν τις ἀποθάνῃ τῶν
οἰκείων, πρῶτα μὲν φέροντες ὀβολὸν ἐς τὸ στόμα κατέθηκαν αὐτῷ,
μισθὸν τῷ πορθμεῖ ναυτιλίας γενησόμενον. Thus in Aristophanes,
Ran. 140, Dionysos is attended by Xanthias, and therefore has
to pay for two :

> ἐν πλοιαρίῳ τυννουτωὶ σ' ἀνὴρ γέρων
> ναύτης διάξει, δὔ ὀβωλὼ μισθὸν λαβών.

This ναῦλον was also called δανάκη. Hesychius : Δανάκη, νομισ-
μάτιόν τι βαρβαρικὸν (Περσικὸν) δυνάμενον πλέον ὀβολοῦ ὀλίγῳ
τινί. ἐλέγετο δὲ καὶ ὁ τοῖς νεκροῖς διδόμενος ὀβολός.

A curious confirmation of these passages was obtained on
opening a grave in Cephallenia, when the coin was discovered
still sticking between the teeth of the skeleton. Stackelberg,
die Gräber der Hellenen, p. 42. The dead were provided there-
with as soon as possible, it being thought that their transit would
be thus expedited. See Lucian, *Catapl.* 18 : ἀδικεῖς, ὦ Χάρων,
ἔωλον ἤδη νεκρὸν ἀπολιμπάνων. ἀμέλει γράψομαί σε παρανόμωι
ἐπὶ τοῦ Ῥαθαμάνθυος.

According to Lucian, *de Luctu*, 11, the corpse was next washed,
anointed with the most precious perfumes, crowned with flowers,
and dressed in a splendid garment : Μετὰ ταῦτα δὲ λούσαντες
αὐτοὺς, ὡς οὐχ ἱκανῆς τῆς κάτω λίμνης λουτρὸν εἶναι τοῖς ἐκεῖ, καὶ
μύρῳ τῷ καλλίστῳ χρίσαντες τὸ σῶμα πρὸς δυσωδίαν ἤδη βια-
ζόμενον, καὶ στεφανώσαντες τοῖς ὡραίοις ἄνθεσι, προτίθενται λαμ-
πρῶς ἀμφιέσαντες, ἵνα μὴ ῥιγῷεν δηλονότι παρὰ τὴν ὁδὸν, μηδὲ
γυμνοὶ βλέποιντο τῷ Κερβέρῳ. These offices were not performed
by a hireling and stranger, as the Roman *pollinctor*, but by the
nearest female relatives. Isæus, *de Philoctem. Her.* p. 143 ; *de
Ciron. Her.* p. 209. Hence the demand of Antigone, Eurip.
Phœniss. 1667 :

> σὺ δ' ἀλλὰ νεκρῷ λουτρὰ περιβαλεῖν μ' ἔα.

The corpse was always dressed in white. It may be objected
that Plato appears to mention this as a distinctive mark in the
obsequies of an ἱερεὺς, *Leg.* xii. p. 947. There are, however, many
other passages which show that this was always the colour used
Archilochus, ap. Plutarch, *de Aud. Poët.* 6 :

> εἰ κείνου κεφαλὴν καὶ χαρίεντα μέλη
> Ἥφαιστος καθαροῖσιν ἐν εἵμασιν ἀμφεπονήθη.

C C

Cf. Pausan. iv. 13, 1; and Artemidor. *Oneirocr.* ii. 3 : Ἀνδρὶ δὲ νοσοῦντι λευκὰ ἔχειν ἱμάτια θάνατον προαγορεύει διὰ τὸ τοὺς ἀποθανόντας ἐν λευκοῖς ἐκφέρεσθαι· τὸ δὲ μέλαν ἱμάτιον σωτηρίαν προσημαίνει. οὐ γὰρ οἱ ἀποθανόντες, ἀλλ' οἱ πενθοῦντες τοὺς ἀποθνήσκοντας τοιούτοις χρῶνται ἱματίοις. In Lucian, *Philops.* 32, some youngsters endeavour to frighten Democritus by dressing themselves νεκρικῶς ἐσθῆτι μελαίρῃ, but this, despite the verdict of the Scholiast, ὅτι τοὺς νεκροὺς οἱ παλαιοὶ μελαίναις στολαῖς ἀμφιέννυσαν, is no argument against the statement above; because death, as well as night, and her children, dreams, was also imagined to be μελάμπεπλος. Eurip. *Alc.* 860 ; Aristoph. *Ran.* 1336.

The use of garlands appears to have been universal. See Aristoph. *Eccles.* 538 ; *Lysist.* 602. These were brought by relations and friends, especially on the demise of young persons. So in Alciphron, *Epist.* i. 36, an hetæra complains : ἐγὼ δὲ ἡ τάλαινα θρηνῳδὸν, οὐκ ἐραστὴν, ἔχω, στεφάνιά μοι καὶ ῥόδα, ὥσπερ ἀώρῳ τάφῳ πέμπει. They were composed of the flowers in season, στεφανώσαντες τοῖς ὡραίοις ἄνθεσι, as Lucian says. The leaves of the parsley, σέλινον, appear to have been more usual than anything else. See note 7, p. 135.

It is also asserted that a honey-cake, μελιτοῦττα, was given to the corpse. In Aristoph. *Lysist.* 601, we have:

μελιτοῦτταν ἐγὼ καὶ δὴ μάξω.
λαβὲ ταυτὶ καὶ στεφάνωσαι.

The Scholiast says : ἡ μελιτοῦττα ἐδίδοτο τοῖς νεκροῖς ὡς εἰς τὸν Κέρβερον, καὶ ὀβολὸς τῷ πορθμεῖ, στέφανος, ὡς τὸν βίον διηγωνισμένοις. That this explanation is right is however far from certain.

The corpse was thus laid out (προτίθεσθαι, πρόθεσις) on a bed (κλίνη) in the house. The Scholiast on Aristophanes, *Lysist.* 611, says : τοὺς νεκροὺς γὰρ οἱ ἀρχαῖοι προετίθεσαν πρὸ τῶν θυρῶν καὶ ἐκόπτοντο. But this was certainly not the case at Athens, and by a law of Solon it was expressly commanded, τὸν ἀποθανόντα προτίθεσθαι ἔνδον, ὅπως ἂν βούληται. Demosth. *in Macart.* p. 1071. This ceremony seems to have been not only a piece of pageantry, but also in some respects a measure of police. Poll. viii. 65 : καὶ αἱ προθέσεις δὲ διὰ τοῦτο ἐγίγνοντο, ὡς ὁρῷτο ὁ νεκρὸς, μή τι βιαίως πέπονθε. It served also to guard against

the burial of a person in a trance. Plato, *Leg.* xii. p. 959. For
an account of this πρόθεσις, see Aristophanes, *Eccles.* 1030 :

> ὑποστόρεσαί νυν πρῶτα τῆς ὀριγάνου,
> καὶ κλήμαθ' ὑπόθου ξυγκλάσασα τέτταρα,
> καὶ ταινίωσαι, καὶ παράθου τὰς ληκύθους,
> ὕδατός τε κατάθου τοὔστρακον πρὸ τῆς θύρας.

This custom of laying the bed with ὀρίγανος and broken vine-
branches does not appear to be elsewhere mentioned. Near the
bed were placed earthen vessels painted, which were called by the
general name λήκυθαι. Cf. *ibid.* v. 538 and 994. The κλίνη was
an ordinary bedstead, with a προσκεφάλαιον to support the head
and back. Lysias, *in Eratosth.* p. 395 : ἀλλὰ τῶν φίλων ὁ μὲν
ἱμάτιον, ὁ δὲ προσκεφάλαιον, ὁ δὲ ὅ,τι ἕκαστος ἔτυχεν, ἔδωκεν εἰς
τὴν ἐκείνου ταφήν. The face of the corpse was turned to the
door, ἀνὰ πρόθυρα τετραμμένος. Eustath. *ad Iliad.* xix. 212.

Before the house-door was placed a vessel of water, called
ἀρδάνιον, in order that visitors on leaving the house might purify
themselves ; and inasmuch as the house of mourning, with all
belonging to it, was considered polluted by the presence of the
corpse, this water had to be obtained from another house. Poll.
viii. 65 : καὶ οἱ ἐπὶ τὴν οἰκίαν τοῦ πενθοῦντος ἀφικνούμενοι ἐξιόν-
τες ἐκαθαίροντο ὕδατι περιρραινόμενοι. τὸ δὲ προὔκειτο ἐν ἀγγείῳ
κεραμέῳ ἐξ ἄλλης οἰκίας κεκομισμένον. τὸ δὲ ὄστρακον ἐκαλεῖτο
ἀρδάνιον. See also Hesychius and Suidas, s. v. ἀρδάνιαι.

The relatives and friends, as well as others not particularly
connected with the deceased, were present in the house, and
around the bed the females lamented and wept. The best notion
of such a scene may be derived from Plato's regulations as to the
burial of an ἱερεὺς, though we must bear in mind that the description is probably ideal to some extent. *Leg.* xii. p. 947 : τελευτή-
σασι δὲ προθέσεις τε καὶ ἐκφορὰς καὶ θήκας διαφόρους εἶναι τῶν
ἄλλων πολιτῶν. λευκὴν μὲν τὴν στολὴν ἔχειν πᾶσαν, θρήνων δὲ
καὶ ὀδυρμῶν χωρὶς γίγνεσθαι. κωρῶν δὲ χορὸν πεντεκαίδεκα καὶ
ἀρρένων ἕτερον περιϊσταμένους τῇ κλίνῃ ἑκατέρους οἷον ὕμνον πεποιημένον ἔπαινον εἰς τοὺς ἱερέας ἐν μέρει ἑκατέρους ᾄδειν, εὐδαι-
μονίζοντες ᾠδῇ διὰ πάσης τῆς ἡμέρας. In more ancient times the
scenes of woe were offensively exaggerated ; but Solon curtailed
the ceremony, and forbade the excessive lamentations of the
women. Plutarch, *Sol.* 12, and 21 : Ἀμυχὰς δὲ κοπτομένων καὶ

τὸ θρηνεῖν πεποιημένα, καὶ τὸ κωκύειν ἄλλον ἐν ταφαῖς ἑτέρωι⸗
ἀφεῖλεν. ἐναγίζειν δὲ βοῦν οὐκ εἴασεν, οὐδὲ συντιθέναι πλέον ἱμα⸗
τίων τριῶν. It is doubtful, however, to what extent this law was
complied with. The chorus of virgins at the gate of Agamemnon indulges in all the more extravagant manifestations of grief,
such as beating the breast, lacerating the cheeks, rending their
garments. Æschyl. *Choëph.* 20–28; cf. Eurip. *Hecub.* 642.
The poet, it is true, may have only been faithfully portraying
the customs of early times, or indulging in an allowable poetical
exaggeration; but there are other reasons for supposing that these
rude manifestations of woe prevailed till a later period. Thus
Plutarch praises his wife for omitting them on the death of her
child. *Consol. ad Uxor.* 3: Καὶ τοῦτο λέγουσιν οἱ παραγενόμενοι
καὶ θαυμάζουσιν, ὡς οὐδὲ ἱμάτιον ἀνείληφας πένθιμον, οὐδὲ σαυτῇ
τινα προσήγαγες ἢ θεραπαινίσιν ἀμορφίαν καὶ αἰκίαν. Cf. Lucian,
de Luctu, 12 : Οἰμωγαὶ δὲ ἐπὶ τούτοις καὶ κωκυτὸς γυναικῶν, καὶ
παρὰ πάντων δάκρυα, καὶ στέρνα τυπτόμενα, καὶ σπαραττομένη
κόμη, καὶ φοινισσόμεναι παρειαί. καί που καὶ ἐσθὴς καταρρήγνυται
καὶ κόνις ἐπὶ τῇ κεφαλῇ πάσσεται, καὶ οἱ ζῶντες οἰκτρότεροι τοῦ
νεκροῦ. οἱ μὲν γὰρ χαμαὶ καλινδοῦνται πολλάκις, καὶ τὰς κεφαλὰς
ἀράττουσι πρὸς τὸ ἔδαφος. The ancient works of art also bear
out this representation; see *Mus. Capit.* iv. 40. A law of Charondas went beyond that of Solon; it forbade all manner of lamen-
tation and weeping for the dead. Stob. *Tit.* xliv. 40: Χρὴ δὲ καὶ
τῶν τελευτώντων ἕκαστον τιμᾶν, μὴ δακρύοις, μηδὲ οἴκτοις, ἀλλὰ
μνήμῃ ἀγαθῇ καὶ τῇ τῶν κατ' ἔτος ὡραίων ἐπιφορᾷ. Solon also
enacted that, except the nearest female relatives, no women under
sixty years of age should enter the house before the interment.
Demosth. *in Macart.* p. 1071 : γυναῖκα δὲ μὴ ἐξεῖναι εἰσιέναι
εἰς τὰ τοῦ ἀποθανόντος, μηδ' ἀκολουθεῖν ἀποθανόντι, ὅταν εἰς τὰ
σήματα ἄγηται, ἐντὸς ἑξήκοντ' ἐτῶν γεγονυῖαν, πλὴν ὅσαι ἐντὸς
ἀνεψιαδῶν εἰσί.

The laying out of the corpse took place on the second day after
death. An early burial was thought to be pleasing to the defunct.
Eustath. *ad Iliad.* viii. 410: νεκροῦ μείλιγμα μὲν ἡ ὠκεῖα ταφή.
And in Homer the shade of Patroclos demands of his friend—

θάπτε με ὅττι τάχιστα, πύλας Ἀΐδαο περήσω.

Il. xxiii. 71. Cf. Xenoph. *Memor.* i. 2, 53. Also Isæus, *de*
Philoctem. Her. p. 143, mentions it as a matter of grave reproach

that the corpse had been allowed to lie two days without any
preparations having been made for the πρόθεσις. This indeed is
not mentioned in the law of Solon, which however is very imper-
fectly quoted by Demosthenes; though the deficiency is amply
supplied by Antipho, *de Chor.* p. 782.

On the following day the ἐκφορά legally took place. According to Plato, *Leg.* xii. p. 960, the early morning was the time,
πρὸ ἡμέρας ἔξω τῆς πόλεως εἶναι, and this is corroborated by
Demosthenes, *ibid.*: ἐκφέρειν δὲ τὸν ἀποθανόντα τῇ ὑστεραίᾳ, ᾗ
ἂν προθῶνται, πρὶν ἥλιον ἐξέχειν. In other places, and perhaps
in later times, the burial took place as early as the second day.
See Callimachus *Epigr.* 15; Diog. Laert. i. 122. On the other
hand, Timoleon's burial is put off several days, to allow of the
arrival of distant friends. Plutarch, *Timol.* 39.

The corpse was carried to the place of interment upon the
κλίνη. Who the bearers were is doubtful: it is not likely that
there were special νεκροθάπται for the purpose, though a passage
in Pollux, vii. 195, would seem to imply that this was the case;
εἶεν δ᾽ ἄν τινες καὶ νεκροφόροι καὶ ταφεῖι. No early writer
mentions them, and it would seem more probable that relatives
performed the office. In particular cases, when an extraordinary
distinction was designed for the dead, youths (ephebi) were
specially selected for the purpose. Plato, *Leg.* xii. p. 947: ἔωθεν
δ᾽ εἰς τὴν θήκην φέρειν αὐτὴν μὲν τὴν κλίνην ἔκατον τῶν νέων
τῶν ἐν τοῖς γυμνασίοις, οὓς ἂν οἱ προσήκοντες τοῦ τελευτήσαντος
ἐπόψονται. Also Plutarch, *Timol.* 39: καὶ τὸ λέχος οἱ ψήφῳ τῶν
νεανίσκων προκριθέντες ἔφερον. The corpse of Demonax was borne
by sophists. Lucian, *Demon.* 67; cf. Plutarch, *Philop.* 21.

Hired θρηνῳδοὶ preceded or followed the corpse, like the *præ-
ficæ*, the *cornicines* and *tubicines* of the Romans. Plato, *Leg.* vii.
p. 800: οἷον οἱ περὶ τοὺς τελευτήσαντας μισθούμενοι Καρικῇ τινι
μούσῃ προπέμπουσι τοὺς τελευτήσαντας. It is remarkable that
Plato uses the masculine gender, whereas women, Καρίναι, are
elsewhere mentioned. Hesychius: Καρίναι, θρηνῳδοὶ μουσικαὶ,
αἱ τοὺς νεκροὺς τῷ θρήνῳ παραπέμπουσαι πρὸς τὰς ταφὰς καὶ τὰ
κήδη. παρελαμβάνοντο δὲ αἱ ἀπὸ Καρίας γυναῖκες. Comparing
this passage with Pollux, iv. 75, it appears that they were flute-
players. Lucian also, *de Luctu,* 20, mentions a hired θρηνῳδὸς,

though probably he is referring to the πρόθεσις rather than to
the ἐκφορά. See Schol. ad Aristoph. *Vesp.* 289.

The rest of the procession consisted of the relations, and others
who chose to join it; the men before, and the women behind,
according to Solon's law, apud Demosth. *in Macart.* p. 1071:
βαδίζειν δὲ τοὺς ἄνδρας πρόσθεν, ὅταν ἐκφέρωνται, τὰς δὲ γυναῖκας
ὄπισθεν. Plato arranges his funeral procession much in the same
way: πρώτους δὲ προϊέναι τοὺς ἠϊθέους, τὴν πολεμικὴν σκευὴν
ἐνδεδυκότας ἑκάστους . . . καὶ τοὺς ἄλλους ὡσαύτως. παῖδας δὲ περὶ
αὐτὴν τὴν κλίνην ἔμπροσθεν τὸ πάτριον μέλος ἐφυμνεῖν. καὶ κόρας
ἑπομένας ἐξόπισθεν ὅσαι τ' ἂν γυναῖκες τῆς παιδοποιήσεως ἀπηλ-
λαγμέναι τυγχάνωσι. Women who were not at least first cousin's
children to the deceased were not allowed to follow, except in the
case of those above sixty years of age. Demosth. *ibid.*: μηδ'
ἀκολουθεῖν ἀποθανόντι, ὅταν εἰς τὰ σήματα ἄγηται, ἐντὸς ἑξήκοντ
ἐτῶν γεγονυῖαν, πλὴν ὅσαι ἐντὸς ἀνεψιαδῶν εἰσίν. The case of a
daughter following her step-mother is mentioned by Lysias, *de
Cæd. Erat.* p. 11. The rule seems also to be violated in Terence,
Andr. i. 1, 90.

There has been a great deal of discussion as to whether the
corpse was buried or burnt. Lucian, *de Luctu*, 21, says, ὁ μὲν
Ἕλλην ἔκαυσεν, ὁ δὲ Πέρσης ἔθαψεν, and this sweeping conclusion
is adopted by Böttiger without reserve or limitation. Wachsmuth, on the contrary, says, 'In the historical period interment
was universal.' *Hellen. Alterthumsk.* ii. 2, p. 79. But neither
are right; for, in the first place, there is abundant evidence that
burning the corpse was not restricted to the heroic age, but was
practised in every period. See Plato, *Phæd.* p. 115: ἵνα Κρίτων
ῥᾷον φέρῃ, καὶ μὴ, ὁρῶν μου τὸ σῶμα ἢ καόμενον ἢ κατορυττόμενον,
ἀγανακτῇ ὑπὲρ ἐμοῦ, ὡς δεινὰ ἄττα πάσχοντος. See also Plutarch,
de Aud. pöet. 6. So Isæus, *de Nicostr. Her.* p. 78: οὔτ' ἔκαυσεν,
οὔτε ὠστολόγησεν. And the legend of Solon's ashes being strewed
about Salamis, although pronounced by Plutarch ἀπίθανος παν-
τάπασι καὶ μυθώδης, shows that his cremation was pre-supposed.
But to come to historical facts, we read that Timoleon was
actually burnt. Plutarch, *Timol.* 39: τῆς κλίνης ἐπὶ τὴν πυρὰν
τεθείσης. Cf. Id. *Philop.* 21: τὸ δὲ σῶμα καύσαντες αὐτοῦ, καὶ
τὰ λείψανα συνθέντες εἰς ὑδρίαν. Also in Lycon's will, apud

Diog. Laert. v. 70, it is ordered : περὶ δὲ τῆς ἐκφορᾶς καὶ καύσεως ἐπιμελεθήτωσαν Βούλων καὶ Καλλῖνος μετὰ τῶν συνήθων. Cf. Plutarch, *Dec. Or. Vit.* p. 405; Lucian, *Nigr.* 30. How then, in the face of these examples, can it be affirmed that interment was exclusively practised at any period ?

On the other hand, there is the clearest evidence to show that the dead were also inhumed in the proper sense of the word. The word θάπτειν, it is true, proves nothing, as it is applied to all modes of sepulture, and is even used with regard to ashes after burning. Dionys. Hal. *Ant. Rom.* v. 48 : ἐμέλλησαν αὐτὸν . . . καίειν τε καὶ θάπτειν. The proper expression for inhumation is κατορύττειν, as in Plato, *Phœd.* p. 115, *supra*, where it is opposed to καίειν. It is doubtful whether σοροὶ, πύελοι, ληνοὶ, and δροῖται, mean actual coffins for unburnt corpses, or receptacles for ashes. Cf. Homer, *Ilias*, xxiii. 91; xxiv. 795. But all doubts respecting a later period are removed by a fragment of Phere-crates, apud Pollux, x. 150, where κατορύττειν is used in connexion with ληνοὶ; see also Aristoph. *Lysistr.* 600 ; *Vesp.* 1365; Eurip. *Suppl.* 531. That inhumation was customary in very early times is shown by the tales of opened graves. See the legend about the bones of Theseus, which were brought from Scyros to Athens, in consequence of a Delphic oracle. Plutarch, *Thes.* 36 : εὑρέθη δὲ θήκη τε μεγάλου σώματος, αἰχμή τε παρακειμένη χαλκῆ καὶ ξίφος. But the custom is proved to a certainty by the contest between Athens and Megara for the possession of Salamis, where the claims of each party were based on the different modes of burial. Plutarch, *Sol.* 10 : Θάπτουσι δὲ Μεγαρεῖς πρὸς ἕω τοὺς νεκροὺς στρέφοντες· Ἀθηναῖοι δὲ πρὸς ἑσπέραν. Ἱρέας δ' ὁ Μεγαρεὺς ἐνιστάμενος λέγει, καὶ Μεγαρέας πρὸς ἑσπέραν τετραμμένα τὰ σώματα τῶν νεκρῶν τιθέναι. Cf. Ælian, *Var. Hist.* v. 14 ; vii. 19 ; Diog Laert. i. 48. Also Pausanias, ii. 7, 3, speaking of the Sicyonians, says, τὸ μὲν σῶμα γῇ κρύπτουσι. At Sparta also, the custom of inhumation was the prevailing one. Plutarch, *Lyc.* 27 ; Thucyd. i. 134.

These passages prove beyond dispute that burying and burning were practised coevally. In Lucian's time also, burying must have been customary, notwithstanding what he says (ὁ μὲν Ἕλλην ἔκαυσε, κ. τ. λ.), for otherwise there would be no point in his proverbs, τὸν ἕτερον πόδα ἐν τῇ σορῷ ἔχων, (*Hermot.* 78,) and υἱόμενος ἐπιβήσειν αὐτὸν τοῦ σοροῦ. (*Mort. dial.* vi. 4.) Cf. Appuleius, *Metam.* iv. p. 277; and x. p. 699, where a Greek original is probably alluded to.

But setting aside all this weight of documentary evidence, the co-existence of both methods is proved incontestably by the excavations of ancient Grecian graves. In Magna Græcia several unburnt skeletons have been discovered surrounded by earthen vases. Böttiger, it is true, is loth to admit that these were Grecian corpses, but this objection has been set at rest by the discovery, in Greece itself, of undisturbed skeletons, in addition to the remains of corpses that have been burnt. See Stackelberg's invaluable work, *Die Gräber der Hellenen.* One custom might, no doubt, have been more common than the other at any particular period; but neither was totally superseded till the extension of Christianity by degrees put an end to burning.

In some cases the coffins were of wood. Thus in Thucydides, i. 34, λάρνακες κυπαρίσσιναι are mentioned. More usually, however, they were the work of the potter. For their forms, see Stackelberg, Pl. 7 and 8. According to him, the oldest form was a three-sided prism, constructed of tiles, which were sometimes ornamented with arabesques: as in Pl. 5 and 6. The coffin of a child given in Pl. 8 is very interesting; it is in one piece, and is a regular πύελος or μάκτρα, oval and trough-shaped, and varnished black, with a red stripe running round. Those discovered at Capua and Nola are rather vaults of masonry than coffins. They were constructed of stones or tiles, with slabs placed on the low vertical walls so as to form a kind of gable roof. But there were also coffins of stone in Greece; and if we may trust the genuineness of the letter produced by Pollux. x. 150, the remarkable properties of the *lapis sarcophagus* from Assos were known in Plato's time. Cf. Plin. *Nat. Hist.* ii. 96; xxxvi. 17.

There are no certain accounts as to whether the body was burnt at the place of sepulture, or at a spot appropriated to the purpose, καῦστρον. If Terence, *Andr.* i. 1, 100, is to be received as an authority, the former was the case: ' sequimur ; ad sepulchrum venimus; in ignem imposita est.' Timoleon's corpse, however, does not appear to have been burnt at the place of sepulture. The remains were collected and placed in a cinerary made of clay or bronze. See Isæus, *de Nicostr. her.* p. 78; Sophocl. *Electr.* 54, 747.

The tombs, θῆκαι, τάφοι, μνήματα, μνημεῖα, and σήματα, were not all placed in one common spot appropriated to the purpose. In ancient times, according to Plato, a person's own house was used as his place of sepulture, in order that the remains of the defunct might be as near as possible to his friends. Plato, *Min.* p. 315. But it was afterwards forbidden to bury within the city, chiefly, no doubt, from an idea of the contamination arising from the contact or neighbourhood of corpses. This was the case in Athens at least, and Sicyon, though the feeling was far from being universal throughout Greece. Lycurgus, in order to accustom the Spartans to survey death without fear or aversion, allowed or rather commanded burials within the city. Plutarch, *Lycurg.* 27; *Apophth. Lac.* i. p. 954. This, however, is only in keeping with the other peculiarities of Spartan customs and legislation. Cf. Thucyd. i. 134. At Tarentum all the graves, in obedience to an oracle, were in a particular quarter of the city. Polyb. viii. 30 : Τὸ γὰρ πρὸς ἕω μέρος τῆς τῶν Ταραν- τίνων πόλεως μνημάτων ἐστὶ πλῆρες διὰ τὸ τοὺς τελευτήσαντας ἔτι καὶ νῦν θάπτεσθαι παρ' αὐτοῖς πάντας ἐντὸς τῶν τειχῶν κατά τι λόγιον ἀρχαῖον. This was likewise the case at Megara ; Pausan. i. 43, 2 : εἰσὶ δὲ τάφοι Μεγαρέων ἐν τῇ πόλει. Timoleon's ashes were buried in the market-place of Syracuse, and a gymnasium, called after his name, was built over the spot; Plutarch, *Timol.* 39. Many other instances might be adduced. On the other hand, Plutarch, *Arat.* 53, speaking of Sicyon, says : νόμου ὄντος ἀρ- χαίου, μηδένα θάπτεσθαι τειχῶν ἐντὸς, ἰσχυρᾶς τε τῷ νόμῳ δεισιδαι- μονίας προσούσης. The very necessity of a special law, however, shows that burial within the walls must have been usual else- where. But at Athens even the cenotaphs of the fallen warriors were outside the walls, on the road to the Academy ; (Thucyd. ii. 34; Pausan. i. 29, 4 ;) and at Delos, from the time of Peisis- tratos, no graves were allowed in sight of the temple, and, after the sixth year of the Peloponnesian war, nowhere at all on the island. Thucyd. iii. 104 : τότε δὲ πᾶσα ἐκαθάρθη τοιῷδε τρόπῳ θῆκαι ὅσαι ἦσαν τῶν τεθνεώτων ἐν Δήλῳ, πάσας ἀνεῖλον, καὶ τὸ λοιπὸν προεῖπον, μήτε ἐναποθνήσκειν ἐν τῇ νήσῳ, μήτε ἐντίκτειν, ἀλλ' ἐς τὴν Ῥήνειαν διακομίζεσθαι.

Those Athenians who possossed a piece of land, frequently left directions to have themselves buried in it, and hence the graves were often in the fields; see Demosth. *in Euerg.* p. 1159. A more usual choice, however, was by some frequented roadside Thus the family sepulchre of Isocrates was near the Cynosarges, and that of Thucydides by the Melitic gate. Plutarch *Dec. Or. Vit.* p. 363. So too on a child's tombstone we read,

ἣν γονέες πενθοῦντες ἐπὶ τρίοδου κατέθαψαν.

See *Corp. Inscr.* p. 545, no. 1003. But for those who neither possessed such ground, nor the means of purchasing it, there was a public place of burial. At Athens this was the space between the Itonic gate and the road to the Piræus, and the gate leading thither was hence called the Grave-gate,—Ἠρίαι πύλαι. Theophr. *Char.* 14 : πόσους οἴει κατὰ τὰς Ἠρίας πύλας ἐξενηνέχθαι νεκρούς; *Etym. M.* : Ἠρίαι πύλαι Ἀθήνησι διὰ τὸ τοὺς νεκροὺς ἐκφέρεσθαι ἐκεῖ ἐπὶ τὰ ἠρία, ὅ ἐστι τοὺς τάφους. Cf. Pollux, ix. 15; Harpocr. s. v. Ἠρία.

These tombs remained the inviolable property of the family, and no stranger was ever allowed to be buried therein; so that even before a court of justice this was brought forward as evidence of consanguinity. Demosth. *in Eubul.* p. 1307 : ἔθαψε τούτους εἰς τὰ πατρῷα μνήματα, ὧν ὅσοιπέρ εἰσι τοῦ γένους κοινωνοῦσι. καὶ τούτων οὐδεὶς οὐκ ἀπεῖπε πώποτε, οὐκ ἐκώλυσεν, οὐ δίκην ἔλαχε. καίτοι τίς ἄν ἐστιν, ὅστις εἰς τὰ πατρῷα μνήματα τοὺς μηδὲν ἐν γένει προσήκοντας τιθέναι ἐάσαι. Id. *in Macart.* p. 1077 : ἀλλὰ καὶ μνήματος ὄντος κοινοῦ ἅπασι τοῖς ἀπὸ τοῦ Βουσέλου γενομένοις, κ. τ. λ. Burying in another's grave was forbidden by a law of Solon. Cic. *de Leg.* ii. 26 : 'de sepulcris autem nihil est apud Solonem amplius quam, ne quis ea deleat, neve alienum inferat.'

The construction of these tombs has been completely ascertained by excavations. Setting aside the mere heaps of earth or stones, χώματα, κολῶναι, τύμβοι, they may be classified in four principal divisions: shafts, στῆλαι—regular columns, κίονες—small temple-shaped edifices, ναΐδια, or ἡρῷα—and horizontal gravestones, τράπεζαι. Cicero, *de Leg.* ii. 25, extols the ancient simplicity of Old-Athenian burials: but his account is not corroborated by any Greek author. Above the hillock a stone monument was usually erected, and this frequently at so great an expense, that, after Solon's time, it was found necessary to curb the practice

by law. Cicero, *de Leg.* ii. 26 : ' ne quis sepulcrum faceret ope-
rosius, quam quod decem homines effecerint triduo.' Cf. Plato,
Leg. xii. p. 959 : χῶμα δὲ μὴ χωννύναι ὑψηλότερον πέντε ἀνδρῶν
ἔργον, ἐν πένθ' ἡμέραις ἀποτελούμενον. λίθινα δὲ ἐπιστήματα μὴ
μείζω ποιεῖν ἢ ὅσα δέχεσθαι τὰ τοῦ τετελευτηκότος ἐγκώμια βίου,
μὴ πλείω τεττάρων ἡρωϊκῶν στίχων. This sumptuary enactment
does not seem, however, to have remained long in force, as great
sums continued to be spent on the erection of monuments. Thus
one—a modest erection—is mentioned as costing twenty-five
minæ ; Lysias, *in Diogit.* p. 905. So Phormio erects one to his
wife at an expense of more than two talents; Demosth. *in Steph.*
i. p. 1125. Of the monument to Isocrates, we are told by Plutarch, *Dec. Orat. Vit.* p. 364 : αὐτῷ δὲ Ἰσοκράτει ἐπὶ τοῦ μνήματος ἐπῆν κίων τριάκοντα πηχῶν, ἐφ' οὗ σειρὴν πηχῶν ἑπτὰ συμβο-
λικῶς. According to Cicero, *ibid.*, Demetrius Phalereus again
tried unsuccessfully to restrain this sumptuousness. ' Sepulchris
autem novis finivit modum; nam super terræ tumulum noluit
quid statui, nisi columellam tribus cubitis ne altiorem, aut men-
sam, aut labellum, et huic procurationi certum magistratum
præfecerat.'

The στῆλαι, in their strict signification—for the word often
denotes tombs generally—were slabs of stone standing upright,
rather than pillars. Upon these usually rested an ἐπίθημα,
sometimes gable-shaped, sometimes rounded like a coping-tile,
and mostly ornamented with arabesques. Often too they were
adorned with reliefs or paintings. Pausan ii. 7, 4. See Stackelberg, Pl. 1–6. The Sicyonian grave-stones were all of one
peculiar form. Pausan. ii. 7, 3 : λίθον δὲ ἐποικοδομήσαντες κρη-
πῖδα κίονας ἐφιστᾶσι καὶ ἐπ' αὐτοῖς ἐπίθημα ποιοῦσι κατὰ τοὺς
ἀετοὺς μάλιστα τοὺς ἐν τοῖς ναοῖς.

The regular columns, κίονες, very frequently occur on vases.
See Stackelberg, Pl. 44–46; Millin, *Peint. d. Vas.* i. 16 ; ii. 29,
51; Millingen, *Peint. d. Vas.* 39. The *mensa* mentioned by
Cicero was a cubical or other four-cornered stone, having a flat
surface above, while on the sides there were perhaps reliefs. See
Plutarch, *Dec. Orat. Vit.* p. 364: ἦν δὲ καὶ αὐτοῦ τράπεζα πλησίον ἔχουσα ποιητάς τε καὶ τοὺς διδασκάλους αὐτοῦ, ἐν οἷς καὶ
Γοργίαν εἰς σφαῖραν ἀστρολογικὴν βλέποντα, αὐτόν τε τὸν Ἰσο-
κράτην παρεστῶτα. The *labella* are probably identical with

the πύελοι or ληνοί, and so perhaps are many of the so-called sarcophagi.

The inscription contained, in addition to the name of the deceased, a few notices about his life in an epigrammatic form, admonitions addressed to the survivors, and frequently imprecations on any one who should touch or desecrate the tomb. For example, see Böckh, *Corp. Inscr.* p. 531, no. 916: Παραδίδωμι τοῖς καταχ-θονίο[ι]ς θεοῖς τοῦτο τὸ ἡρῷον φυλάσσειν, Πλούτωνι καὶ Δήμητρι καὶ Περσεφόρῃ καὶ Ἐρ[ι]νύσι καὶ πᾶσι τοῖς κατα[χ]θονίοις θεοῖς. εἴ τις ἀποκοσμήσει τοῦτο τὸ ἡρῷον ἢ ἀναστομ[ώ]σει ἤ τι καὶ ἕτερον μετακινήσει ἢ αὐτὸς ἢ δι᾽ ἄλλου, μὴ γῆ βατή, μὴ θάλασσα πλωτὴ [ἔσται], ἀλλὰ ἐκριζωθήσεται πανγενεί. πᾶσι τοῖς κακοῖς πεῖραν δώσει καὶ φρείκῃ καὶ π[υ]ρε[τῷ τριταίῳ] καὶ τεταρταίῳ καὶ ἐλέφαντι. καὶ ὅσα κακὰ καὶ [ὀλέθρια] γίνεται, ταῦτα γενέσθω τῷ τολμήσαντι ἐκ τούτου τοῦ ἡρῷου μετακινῆσαί τι. Also *ib.* p. 541, nos. 989, 990. 991; and *Gallus*, p. 522. Many directed that slaves should keep watch by the tomb. Lucian, *Nigr.* 30. In some places, however, the epitaphs were usually short and simple. Thus Pausanias, ii. 7, 3, speaking of Sicyon, says: ἐπίγραμμα δὲ ἄλλο μὲν γράφουσιν οὐδέν, τὸ δὲ ὄνομα ἐφ᾽ ἑαυτοῦ καὶ οὐ πατρόθεν ὑπειπόντες κελεύουσι τὸν νεκρὸν χαίρειν. Lycurgus would not even allow the name to be inscribed. Plutarch, *Lyc.* 27. One Diodoros wrote a special work περὶ μνημάτων. Plutarch, *Themist.* 32 ; *Dec. Orat. Vit.* p. 406. Age seems to have made no difference, for monuments with inscriptions were erected to children who died in early infancy. *Corp. Inscr.* p. 544, n. 997 ; p. 500, no. 632 ; p. 535, no. 942.

Various effects were put into the tomb along with the corpse, such as earthen vessels, and certainly the λήκυθοι which had served at the πρόθεσις, in like manner as, in case of burning, they were placed on the pyre. This was a very ancient custom, as is seen from what Agesilaos found on opening the reputed grave of Alcmene. Plutarch, *de Gen. Socr.* 5. Within were discovered : ψέλλιον χαλκοῦν οὐ μέγα καὶ δύο ἀμφορέες κεράμεωι γῆν ἔχοντες ἐντὸς ὑπὸ χρόνου λελιθωμένην ἤδη καὶ συμπεπηγυῖαν. To whomsoever this grave belonged, it was at all events one of very ancient date, as is shown by the brazen tablets inscribed with strange characters. The invaluable collections of painted vases which we possess were all discovered in tombs, and the style of the

painting shows that the practice endured over the best period of
Grecian art. The time of the decline of the custom can be known
only from conjecture It is certain, however, that it was so
utterly forgotten in Greece at Cæsar's time, that when, on the
rebuilding of Corinth, graves were discovered containing such
vessels, these were regarded by the Romans as curiosities, and
eagerly bought up. See Strabo, viii. 6, 23.

In the walled graves of Magna Græcia these vessels either
stand round the corpse, or hang on the walls; so also in the
earthen coffins. In the coffin of a child which has been already
mentioned, p. 392, there were fifteen vessels of various shapes,
among which were four large *lecythi*, as well as four sitting
figures of earthenware. Mirrors, trinkets, and so forth, were
also put into the tomb. See Stackelberg, Pl. 72.

The burial was followed by a funeral-feast, περίδειπνον. Lucian, de *Luctu*, 24: ἐπὶ πᾶσι δὲ τούτοις τὸ περίδειπνον, καὶ πάρ-
εισιν οἱ προσήκοντες καὶ τοὺς γονέας παραμυθοῦνται τοῦ τετελευτηκότος, καὶ πείθουσι γεύσασθαι ὡς οὐκ ἀηδῶς, μὰ Δί, οὐδ' αὐτοὺς
ἀναγκαζομένους, ἀλλ' ἤδη ὑπὸ λιμοῦ, τριῶν ἑξῆς ἡμερῶν ἀπηυδη-
κότας. See Cic. *Leg.* ii. 25. It was naturally held in the house of
the nearest relative. When Demosthenes was selected to deliver
the funeral oration for those who had fallen at Chæroneia, their
parents and brothers agreed to celebrate the περίδειπνον at his
house. he being regarded as the representative of all. Demosth.
de *Coron.* p. 321: ἀλλὰ δέον ποιεῖν αὐτοὺς τὸ περίδειπνον, ὡς παρ'
οἰκειοτάτῳ τῶν τετελευτηκότων, ὥσπερ τἄλλ' εἴωθε γίγνεσθαι, τοῦτ'
ἐποίησαν παρ' ἐμοί. Cf. Id. *in Macart.* p. 1071. On these occasions the deceased person was regarded as the host. Artemidor.
Oneirocr. v. 82 : Ἔθος μὲν γὰρ τοῖς συμβιώταις καὶ εἰς τὰ τῶν
ἀποθανόντων εἰσιέναι καὶ δειπνεῖν. ἡ δὲ ὑποδοχὴ λέγεται γενέσθαι
ὑπὸ τοῦ ἀποθανόντος κατὰ τιμὴν τὴν ἐκ τῶν συμβιωτῶν εἰς τὸν
ἀποθανόντα. Cf. Plutarch, *Frag.* v. p. 881.

On the succeeding days various sacrifices took place. Poll.
viii. 146: Προθέσεις, ἐκφοραὶ, τρίτα, ἔννατα, τριακάδες, ἐναγίσματα, χοαὶ, τὰ νενομισμένα. First come the τρίτα, which happened on the third day. Aristoph. *Lysistr.* 611:

μῶν ἐγκαλεῖς, ὅτι οὐχὶ προὐθέμεσθά σε;
ἀλλ' ἐς τρίτην γοῦν ἡμέραν σοι πρῷ πάνυ
ἥξει παρ' ἡμῶν τὰ τρίτ' ἐπεσκευασμένα.

Schol. : ἐπειδὴ τῇ τρίτῃ τὸ τῶν νεκρῶν ἄριστον ἐφέρετο. But
the most important sacrifice was the ἔνατα or ἔννατα, which took
place on the ninth day, and formed the conclusion of the regular
obsequies. Æschin, in Ctesiph. p. 617; Isæus, de Ciron. Her.
p. 224. In what the ἔνατα consisted does not clearly appear,
though from Plautus, Aul. ii. 4, 45, it would seem to have been
a formal feast prepared for the dead. Cf. Id. Pseud. iii. 2, 4.
But the mourning of the survivors was not yet complete. See
Æschin. in Ctesiph. p. 468; Plutarch, Demosth. 22. At Athens
it probably terminated on the thirtieth day, as may be inferred
from Lysias, de Cæde Erat. p. 15 : ἔδοξε δέ μοι, ὦ ἄνδρες, ἐψιμυθιῶσθαι, τοῦ ἀδελφοῦ τεθνεῶτος οὔπω τριάκονθ᾽ ἡμέρας. Cf. Poll.
i. 66 ; and Harpocr. s. v. τριακάς. At Sparta Lycurgus ordered
that the mourning should finish sooner ; Plutarch, Lycurg. 27 :
Χρόνον δὲ πένθους ὀλίγον προσώρισεν, ἡμέρας ἕνδεκα· τῇ δὲ δωδε-
κάτῃ θύσαντας ἔδει Δήμητρι λύειν τὸ πένθος. With regard to the
custom at Argos, see Plutarch, Quæst. Gr. 24.

The outward signs of mourning consisted in a studied avoidance of everything betokening joy and happiness; the usual dress
was laid aside, and even the hair was cut off. From the very
earliest times the customs of cutting off the hair and putting on
black garments appear to have prevailed. See Æschyl. Choëph
7 ; Eurip. Helen. 1087.

> ἐγὼ δ᾽ ἐς οἴκους βᾶσα βοστρύχους τεμῶ,
> πέπλων τε λευκῶν μέλανας ἀνταλλάξομαι.

Iphig. in Aul. 1416 :

> μήτ᾽ οὖν γε τὸν σὸν πλόκαμον ἐκτέμῃς τριχος,
> μήτ᾽ ἀμφὶ σῶμα μέλανας ἀμπίσχῃ πέπλους.

Cf. Isæus, de Nicostr. Her. p. 71. These customs endured till
a very late period. Plutarch, Consol. ad Ux. 4 : κουρὰς συγχω-
ρεῖν πενθίμους καὶ βαφὰς ἐσθῆτος μελαίνης. Athen. xv. p. 675.
Thus also on the death of any very popular personage, as a
general, it sometimes happened that all the army cut off their
hair and the manes of their horses; a custom also practised by
the barbarians. Plutarch, Pelop. 33 ; Herodot. ix. 24. So Alexander on the death of Hephæstion, had the folly to cause the
battlements of several towns to be razed. Plutarch, Alex. 72 :
εὐθὺς μὲν ἵππους τε κεῖραι πάντας ἐπὶ πένθει καὶ ἡμιόνους ἐκέλευσε καὶ τῶν πέριξ πόλεων ἀφεῖλε τὰς ἐπάλξεις. Cf. Id. Pelop.

34 ; and Ælian, *Var. Hist.* vii. 8. After all this, it is not easy
to understand the meaning of a passage in Plutarch, *Quæst. Rom.*
14, where he says : καὶ γὰρ παρ' ῞Ελλησιν, ὅταν δυστυχία τις
γένηται, κείρονται μὲν αἱ γυναῖκες, κομῶσι δὲ οἱ ἄνδρες, ὅτι τοῖς
μὲν τὸ κείρεσθαι, ταῖς δὲ τὸ κομᾶν σύνηθές ἐστιν. In this assertion he is supported by Artemidorus, *Oneirocr.* i. 19, though the
statement appears to be contradicted by Athenæus, xv. p. 675 ;
by Eustathius, *ad Iliad.* ii. 6 ; and even by Plutarch himself, *de
Superst.* 7. These passages appear to be irreconcilable, unless we
suppose the custom to have altered.

The mourning dress was, as we have seen, generally black ;
hence the boast of Pericles : οὐδεὶς δι' ἐμὲ τῶν ὄντων 'Αθηναίων
μέλαν ἱμάτιον περιεβάλετο. Plutarch, *Peric.* 38. Black garments were worn not only in cases of death, but also on other
occasions of mourning. Lysias, *in Agorat.* p. 469 : καὶ δὴ καὶ
Διονυσόδωρος μεταπέμπεται τὴν ἀδελφὴν τὴν ἐμὴν εἰς τὸ δεσμω-
τήριον, γυναῖκα ἑαυτοῦ οὖσαν. πυθομένη δ' ἐκείνη ἀφικνεῖται μέλαν
τε ἱμάτιον ἠμφιεσμένη, ὡς εἰκὸς ἦν ἐπὶ τῷ ἀνδρὶ αὐτῆς, τοιαύτῃ
συμφορᾷ κεχρημένῳ. Cf. Aristoph. *Acharn.* 1023. In different
states, however, the custom varied ; at Argos, for instance, the
colour of mourning was white. Plutarch, *Quæst. Rom.* 26 : ἐν
δὲ ῞Αργει λευκὰ φοροῦσιν ἐν τοῖς πένθεσι, ὡς Σωκράτης φησὶν,
ὑδατόκλυστα. It should also be observed that in every case a
black himation only is mentioned ; and it is the more probable
that the chiton was not changed, because dark-coloured under-
garments were frequently worn in common life.

The graves were piously and assiduously tended by the surviving relatives ; the light in which they were regarded is shown
by the mention of them in the climax of the impassioned harangue
before the battle of Salamis. Æschyl. *Pers.* 408 :

ὦ παῖδες 'Ελλήνων, ἴτε

ἐλευθεροῦτε πατρίδ', ἐλευθεροῦτε δὲ

παῖδας, γυναῖκας, θεῶν τε πατρῴων ἕδη,

θήκας τε προγόνων· νῦν ὑπὲρ πάντων ἀγων

See also Lycurg. *in Leocr.* p. 141 : τί γὰρ χρὴ παθεῖν τὸν ἐκλι-
πόντα μὲν τὴν πατρίδα, μὴ βοηθήσαντα δὲ τοῖς πατρῴοις ἱεροῖς,
ἐγκαταλιπόντα δὲ τὰς τῶν προγόνων θήκας ; It was also usual,
at the Docimasia of the Athenian Archons, to enquire whether
the candidate had neglected the graves of his forefathers. Xenoph.

Memor. ii. 2, 13 : Καὶ, νὴ Δία, ἐάν τις τῶν γονέων τελευτησάν-
των τοὺς τάφους μὴ κοσμῇ, καὶ τοῦτο ἐξετάζει ἡ πόλις ἐν ταῖς
τῶν ἀρχόντων δοκιμασίαις. Cf. Dinarch. *in Aristog.* p. 86 ; Isocr.
Platæens. p. 418. On stated days the tombs were crowned and
adorned with *tæniæ*, and various offerings were made. One of
the ceremonies in honour of the dead was the γενέσια, mentioned
as a Grecian custom by Herodotus, iv. 26, and which has been
variously explained. The most reasonable solution of the difficulty is that which the etymology would indicate, namely, that
it was the festival on the birth-day of the defunct ; and this is
confirmed by the will of Epicurus ; Diog. Laert. x. 18 : σκοπού-
μενοι εἴς τε τὰ ἐναγίσματα τῷ τε πατρὶ καὶ τῇ μητρὶ, καὶ τοῖς
ἀδελφοῖς, καὶ ἡμῖν εἰς τὴν εἰθισμένην ἄγεσθαι γενέθλιον ἡμέραν ἑκάστου ἔτους τῇ προτέρᾳ δεκάτῃ τοῦ Γαμηλιῶνος. See also Suidas ;
Ammonius ; and Lobeck on Phryn. p. 104. Besides this there
was another festival held on the anniversary of the day when
the person died. At Athens also there was a public festival in
honour of the dead, called νεκύσια. Hesychius : Γενέσια, ἑορτὴ
πένθιμος Ἀθηναίοις· οἱ δὲ τὰ νεκύσια. καὶ ἐν τῇ ἡμέρᾳ τῇ γῇ θύουσι.
These were what are called ἀποφράδες ἡμέραι, by Plato, *Leg.* vii.
p. 800. Tim. *Lex.* p. 41 : Ἀποφράδες ἡμέραι, ἐν αἷς τοῖς κατοιχο-
μένοις χοὰς ἐπιφέρουσιν.

The process of sacrificing at the grave was called ἐναγίζειν,
and the sacrifice itself ἐνάγισμα, usually χοαί ; and, when combined with bloody offerings, αἱμακουρίαι. Æschylus, *Pers.* 615–
624, enumerates the ingredients of which the χοαὶ consisted—
namely, milk, honey, water, wine, olives, and flowers. But this
was not all, for regular banquets were set out, and burnt in
honour of the dead. Lucian, *Char. s. Contempl.* 22 : Τί οὖν ἐκεῖνοι στεφανοῦσι τοὺς λίθους καὶ χρίουσι μύρῳ ; οἱ δὲ καὶ πυρὰν
νήσαντες πρὸ τῶν χωμάτων, καὶ βόθρον τινὰ ὀρύξαντες καίουσί
τε ταυτὶ τὰ πολυτελῆ δεῖπνα καὶ εἰς τὰ ὀρύγματα οἶνον καὶ με-
λίκρατον, ὡς γοῦν εἰκάσαι, ἐγχέουσιν. Cf. Id. *de Merc. Cond.* 28 ;
Artemidor. *Oneirocr.* iv. 81. Solon forbade any but relatives to
take part in these rites ; he also forbade the sacrifice of heifers.
Plutarch, *Sol.* 21 ; Böckh, ad Pind. *Olymp.* i. p. 112.

It was considered a pious duty to visit the grave, not only on
these fixed days, but at other times, from a belief that the presence
of those who had been friends of the deceased in this life, was as

agreeable, as the approach of his enemies was hateful. Isæus, *de Astyph. Her.* p. 232: καὶ τὸν ἐμὸν πατέρα ἀσθενοῦντα ἐπὶ τὸ μνῆμα ἤγαγον, εὖ εἰδότες, ὅτι ἀσπάζοιτο αὐτὸν Ἀστύφιλος. Again, p. 242, a dying person wills that certain parties should not approach his tomb. Cf. Sophocl. *Ajax*, 1372 :

> σὲ δ', ὦ γεραιοῦ σπέρμα Λαέρτου πατρὸς,
> τάφου μὲν ὀκνῶ τοῦδ' ἐπιψαύειν ἐᾶν,
> μὴ τῷ θανόντι τοῦτο δυσχερὲς ποιῶ.

It now only remains to allude to the particular cases in which, from religious or political causes, the burial was omitted altogether, or was performed in an extraordinary manner; or when, it being impossible to recover the body, vicarious ceremonies only were performed. Firstly, the bodies of those struck by lightning were either left uninterred, or at least were not placed in a tomb with others, since they were looked on as struck by the deity, and therefore ἱεροὺς νεκρούς. See Eurip. *Suppl.* 935 :

> Θ. τὸν μὲν Διὸς πληγέντα Καπανέα πυρὶ —
> A. ἢ χωρὶς, ἱερὸν ὡς νεκρὸν, θάψαι θέλεις ;
> Θ. ναί. τοὺς δέ γ' ἄλλους πάντας ἐν μᾷ πυρᾷ.

Also Artemid. *Oneirocr.* ii. 9 : οὐδεὶς γὰρ κεραυνωθεὶς ἄτιμός ἐστιν ὅθεν γε καὶ ὡς θεὸς τιμᾶται . . . οὐ γὰρ οἱ κεραυνωθέντες μετατίθενται, ἀλλ' ὅπου ἂν ὑπὸ τοῦ πυρὸς καταληφθῶσιν, ἐνταῦθα θάπτονται. Cf. Philost. *Imag.* ii. 31; and Plutarch, *Sympos.* iv. 2, 3. Malefactors also, who had been condemned to death, were left unburied, though this appears to have been intended as an aggravation of their punishment. At Athens there was a place where such corpses were thrown, and the same was the case at Sparta. Plutarch, *Themist.* 22 ; Thucyd. i. 134. Traitors to their country were also denied burial ; as for instance was the case with Polynices, Ajax, and also, according to the legend, with Palamedes. See Philostr. *Heroic.* 7 ; Dio Chrysost. *Orat.* xxxi. p. 580 ; Thucyd. *ibid.* The right hands of those who had committed suicide were hacked off, but burial was not refused them. Æschin. *in Ctesiph.* p. 636 : καὶ ἐάν τις αὐτὸν διαχρήσηται, τὴν χεῖρα τὴν τοῦτο πράξασαν χωρὶς τοῦ σώματος θάπτομεν. Plato thinks that such should be buried privately, and without any monument. *Leg.* ix. p. 873 : θάπτειν ἀκλεεῖς αὐτοὺς, μήτε στήλαις, μήτε ὀνόμασι δηλοῦντας τοὺς τάφους. Perhaps such burials took place at night, which was certainly the case in special instances ; so

Cassandra prophesies concerning Agamemnon ; Eurip. *Troades*, 448 :

> ἣ κακὸς κακῶς ταφήσει νυκτὸς, οὐκ ἐν ἡμέρᾳ.

Those who had died a violent death were interred with particular formalities. To symbolise the pursuit of the murderer, which was incumbent on the relations, a lance was carried in front of the procession, and stuck upright by the grave, and this was watched for three days. Cf. Demosth. *in Euerg.* p. 1160 : πρῶτον μὲν ἐπενεγκεῖν δόρυ ἐπὶ τῇ ἐκφορᾷ καὶ προαγορεύειν ἐπὶ τῷ μνήματι, εἴ τις προσήκων ἐστὶ τῆς ἀνθρώπου· ἔπειτα τὸ μνῆμα φυλάττειν ἐπὶ τρεῖς ἡμέρας. Cf. Harpocr. s. v. ἐπενεγκεῖν δόρυ. Eurip. *Troad.* 1137. When the body could not be obtained, as in the case of those who had been lost at sea, a fictitious burial took place. Charit. iv. 1 : καὶ γὰρ εἰ μὴ τὸ σῶμα εὕρηται τοῦ δυστυχοῦς, ἀλλὰ νόμος οὗτος ἀρχαῖος Ἑλλήνων, ὥστε καὶ τοὺς ἀφανεῖς τάφοις κοσμεῖν. Eurip. *Helen.* 1241 :

> Ἕλλησίν ἐστι νόμος, ὃς ἂν πόντῳ θάνῃ . . .
> κενοῖσι θάπτειν ἐν πέπλων ὑφάσμασιν.

In Chariton the εἴδωλον of Chæreas is carried on the κλίνη. But he is not a writer to be trusted implicitly on such matters ; and perhaps the Roman custom, at the funerals of the emperors, of placing the wax effigy of the deceased on the lectus, may have given rise to such a fiction. Also in the public funerals of those warriors who had fallen in battle a similar representative ceremony took place. Thucyd. ii. 34 : μία δὲ κλίνη κενὴ φέρεται ἐστρωμένη τῶν ἀφανῶν, οἳ ἂν μὴ εὑρεθῶσιν ἐς ἀναίρεσιν. Cf. Plutarch, *Quæst. Rom.* 5.

The chief works on the burial-usages of the ancients are Meursius, *de Funere*; Guther, *de Jure Manium*; Laurentius, *de Fun. Ant.*; Quensted, *de Sepult. Vet.* But all these writers refer more to the Roman usages than the Greek, and blend both together after a strange fashion. Stackelberg's work, *Die Gräber der Hellenen*, Berl. 1837, is of more value than all of them.

EXCURSUS TO SCENE X.

THEATRE-GOING.

OMITTING all enquiry as to the structure of the theatre, the method of scenic representation, and the numberless appliances of the stage, we shall confine ourselves to the spectators, and collect a few particulars as to who they were, what was their appearance, how they manifested their approval or disapproval of the performance, and how Greek character and manners were displayed in the theatre.

Who then were the spectators? The answer to this question is by no means easy, but nevertheless of much importance to any one who would arrive at a just comprehension of the habits of the Greek people, since its solution involves our estimate of the social position of the women, the efficiency of the educational system, and moreover our verdict as to the Athenian drama, and the appropriateness of the characters introduced upon the stage.

Böttiger was the first to assert that the females of Athens were not present at the dramatic representations; and he further affirmed that no young Athenian was allowed to visit the theatre before his eighteenth year, at which period he was admitted among the ephebi. These positions were attacked by Schlegel and Böckh, and Böttiger has even contradicted himself by inadvertently speaking of women and children being present at the theatre. *Kl. Schr.* ii. p. 279. Heindorf, Welcker, Voss, and Jacobs, also agree that women were among the audience. Of late the question has again been mooted by Meier, who thinks that maidens and respectable women did not often go to the theatre at Athens. And finally Passow comes to the conclusion that the Athenian females were present at tragedies, but not at comedies.

All the passages bearing on the subject have been again and again brought forward in the course of the controversy, but it is worthy of remark, that among them all, there is not one positively deciding the matter either way. Those who argue against the presence of the women rely mainly on the assumed seclusion of the sex, and also on the absence of clear positive assertions to the contrary; while their opponents rest chiefly on sundry passages which appear, in their natural sense, to refer to the presence of women among the auditors. But before entering on this discussion, we would first enquire whether there was anything in the nature of the tragic drama which might render it undesirable for women to be present. In tragedy itself, that most solemn species of poetry, which, full of earnestness and propriety, essayed to convey to mankind warning and instruction couched in the noblest language; that held up to him the nothingness of man, and the might of the deity; the perniciousness of passion, the high value of just and dispassionate action, and the slow, yet sure, punishment of transgression; in short, the sublimest picture of human doing and suffering; — in such representations nothing can be discovered rendering it unfit for women to be spectators. It would indeed be strange if the Greeks, with whom poetry was such a generally acknowledged means of forming the mind, had denied this advantage to the women, unless other reasons existed for this step. It will therefore be necessary to fall back on Böttiger's assertion, that it would have been considered the height of impropriety for a modest woman to appear openly among men.

We will now investigate certain passages bearing on the subject; and here it will not be desirable merely to confine ourselves to Athens, nor to the Aristophanic period alone. First then for the later writers on the subject, who are by far the most explicit. Thus in Lucian's dialogue, *de Saltatione*, § 5, the sophist Craton, who objects to mimic dances, is made to say, Ἔτι γὰρ τοῦτό μοι τὸ λοιπὸν ἦν, ἐν βαθεῖ τούτῳ πώγωνι καὶ πολιᾷ τῇ κόμῃ καθῆσθαι μέσον ἐν τοῖς γυναίοις καὶ τοῖς μεμηνόσιν ἐκείνοις θεαταῖς, κ. τ. λ. And Plutarch, *Consol. ad Uxor.* 5, praising the εὐτέλεια of his wife, says: οὔτε τῶν πολιτῶν (οὐδείς ἐστιν), ᾧ μὴ θέαμα παρέχεις ἐν ἱεροῖς καὶ θυσίαις, καὶ θεάτροις τὴν σεαυτῆς ἀφέλειαν. But these passages prove little, since they allude to a period when Greek manners had been considerably modified by Roman influence. Again, Phintys, apud Stob. *Tit.* lxxiv. 61, speaking of the occasions on which it was allowable for a woman to make her appearance in public, says: ἔπειτα μήτε ὀρφνᾶς ἀνισταμένας, μήτε ἑσπέρας, ἀλλὰ πλαθούσας ἀγορᾶς καταφανέα γινομέναν τὰν ἔξοδον ποιεῖσθαι θεωρίας ἕνεκά τινος ἢ ἀγορασμῶ οἰκήω. Here however it does not necessarily follow that this word θεωρία relates to the theatre at all. Cf. Poll. ii. 56. Moreover, the passage which Pollux, x. 67, cites from Aristophanes is inconclusive, as we are ignorant of the context. The same objection applies also to a fragment of Alexis, ap. Poll. ix. 44. Aristoph. *Thesmoph.* 832–841, and *Eccles.* 23, are not applicable to the question. The Scholiast's explanation of the latter passage was probably manufactured by himself for the occasion. But a third passage of Aristophanes, *Ranæ*, 1049, seems conclusive as to the fact that noble ladies were present at the representation of tragedies, such as the *Phædra* of Euripides, and were deeply shocked at the insults to their sex.

Much weight, moreover, should be attached to Plato, *Leg.* ii. p. 658. To illustrate the influence of age and education on the judgment, he supposes a contest between jugglers, comedians, tragedians, and rhapsodists, and then says : εἰ μὲν τοίνυν τὰ πάνυ σμικρὰ κρίνοι παιδία, κρινοῦσι τὸν τὰ θαύματα ἀποδεικνύντα . . . ἐὰν δέ γ᾽ οἱ μείζους παῖδες, τὸν τὰς κωμῳδίας· τραγῳδίαν δὲ αἵ τε πεπαιδευμέναι τῶν γυναικῶν καὶ τὰ νέα μειράκια καὶ σχεδὸν ἴσως τὸ πλῆθος πάντων, κ.τ.λ. If women had been systematically excluded from the theatre, it would be difficult to account for their preference for tragedy. Equally conclusive is *Leg.* vii. p. 817, where, when the tragedians and actors apply for admission into the new state, the citizens reply : μὴ δὴ δόξητε ἡμᾶς ῥᾳδίως γε οὕτως ὑμᾶς ποτε παρ᾽ ἡμῖν ἐάσειν σκηνάς τε πήξαντας κατ᾽ ἀγορὰν καὶ καλλιφώνους ὑποκριτὰς εἰσαγομένους μεῖζον φθεγγομένους ἡμῶν ἐπιτρέψειν ὑμῖν δημηγορεῖν πρὸς παῖδάς τε καὶ γυναῖκας καὶ τὸν πάντα ὄχλον κ.τ.λ. The most decisive passage in Plato, however, is in *Gorg.* p. 502 : ΣΩ. Οὐκοῦν ἡ ῥητορικὴ δημηγορία ἂν εἴη, ἢ οὐ ῥητορεύειν δοκοῦσί σοι οἱ ποιηταὶ ἐν τοῖς θεάτροις ; ΚΑΛ. Ἔμοιγε. ΣΩ. Νῦν ἄρα ἡμεῖς εὑρήκαμεν ῥητορικήν τινα πρὸς δῆμον, τοιοῦτον, οἷον παίδων τε ὁμοῦ καὶ γυναικῶν καὶ ἀνδρῶν, καὶ δούλων καὶ ἐλευθέρων, ἣν οὐ πάνυ ἀγάμεθα. Here we find it stated in plain words that the δῆμος in the theatre consisted of men, women, and children, of slaves and free. That hetæræ visited the theatre there can be no doubt at all. See Athen. iv. p. 157, where the nickname Θεατροτορύνη is applied to Melissa, from her appearance in the theatre being the signal for disturbance. Still none of the above passages mention as a fact the presence of women on any

particular occasion. But fortunately such evidence is supplied
by an anecdote of Alcibiades contained in a fragment of the
peripatetic Satyros, ap. Athen. xii. p. 534 : ὅτε δὲ χορηγοίη πομ-
πεύων ἐν πορφυρίδι, εἰσιὼν εἰς τὸ θέατρον ἐθαυμάζετο οὐ μόνον
ὑπὸ τῶν ἀνδρῶν, ἀλλὰ καὶ ὑπὸ τῶν γυναικῶν. The place alluded
to is Athens, and the period that of the Peloponnesian war.

The well-known legend of the fright of the women on the
appearance of the chorus in the *Eumenides*, may be a later
invention or exaggeration, as is the opinion of Hermann and
Böttiger. It does not come to us on sufficiently good or early
authority to do us any service in the present argument.

But on a Greek vase found at Aulis there is a remarkable
painting of a Grecian theatre (Millin, *Peint. d. Vas.* ii. pl. 55, 56),
which, from the view of the temple of the Acropolis above, is evidently that of Dionysos at Athens. It is in three compartments,
one of which represents a portion of the stage, and the other two
the seats for the spectators; one division of the seats is empty,
and in the other and larger one, we see two women in the long
chiton and himation ; one sitting, the other standing. Behind
them is a third female figure, in a chiton only, and beside her a
youth in a chlamys. That these figures are made to stand for
the entire audience will surprise no one who is acquainted with
the conventions usual in the vase-paintings. This vase then
seems almost conclusive on the question.

The women do not appear, however, to have been present at
the comedy, at least in early times. The passages cited below to
prove the admission of the boys, afford specific proof that the
women were excluded, and indeed the grossness of the dialogue
can only be excused on the supposition that none of the female
sex were among the auditors.

Boys were allowed to be present at both comic and tragic representations. This may be gathered, more especially as regards
tragedy, from the passages of Plato already cited. *Leg.* ii.
p. 658; *Ib.* vii. p. 817; *Gorg.* p. 502. To these may be added
Pausan. i. 2, 3 : λέγεται μὲν δὴ καὶ ἄλλα οὐκ ἀληθῆ παρὰ τοῖς
πολλοῖς, οἷα ἱστορίας ἀνηκόοις οὖσι καὶ ὁπόσα ἤκουον εὐθὺς ἐκ
παίδων ἔν τε χοροῖς καὶ τραγῳδίαις πιστὰ ἡγουμένοις. And in
Theophr. *Char.* 9. a sign of ἀναισχυντία is said to be : καὶ ξένοις
δὲ αὐτοῦ θέαν ἀγορασας μὴ δοὺς τὸ μέρος θεωρεῖν· ἄγειν δὲ καὶ

τοὺς υἱεῖς εἰς τὴν ὑστεραίαν καὶ τὸν παιδαγωγόν. It need not excite surprise that the women are not here mentioned, since they sat apart in a separate portion of the theatre. Another passage is Isæus, *de Ciron. Her.* p. 206 : ἀλλὰ καὶ εἰς Διονύσια εἰς ἀγρὸν ἦγεν ἀεὶ ἡμᾶς, καὶ μετ' ἐκείνου (τοῦ πάππου) τε ἐθεωροῦμεν καθήμενοι παρ' αὐτόν, κ. τ. λ. With respect to the comedies, clear proof may be derived from the comedians themselves. See Aristoph. *Nub.* 537 :

> ὡς δὲ σώφρων ἐστὶ φύσει, σκέψασθ'· ἥτις πρῶτα μὲν
> οὐδὲν ἦλθε ῥαψαμένη σκύτινον καθειμένον
> ἐρυθρὸν ἐξ ἄκρου, παχὺ, τοῖς παιδίοις ἵν' ᾖ γέλως.

See also *Pax*, 50 :

> ἐγὼ δὲ τὸν λόγον γε τοῖσι παιδίοις,
> καὶ τοῖσιν ἀνδρίοισι, καὶ τοῖς ἀδράσι,
> καὶ τοῖς ὑπερτάτοισιν ἀνδράσιν φράσω.

Cf. *Ib.* 766. So too a fragment of Eupolis apud Aristot. *Ethic. Nic.* iv. 2 : γελῶσιν, ὡς ὁρᾷς, τὰ παιδία. Also for a later period, see Lucian, *de Gymn.* 22 : καὶ μέντοι καὶ ἐς τὸ θέατρον συνάγοντες αὐτοὺς δημοσίᾳ παιδεύομεν ὑπὸ κωμῳδίαις καὶ τραγῳδίαις, ἀρετάς τε ἀνδρῶν παλαιῶν καὶ κακίας θεωμένους, ὡς τῶν μὲν ἀποτρέποιντο, ἐπ' ἐκεῖνα δὲ σπεύδοιεν.

It is true that this seems in opposition to the otherwise strict discipline in which youths were kept ; and it is not very comprehensible how an Autolycos or a Charmides could have been spectators of an Aristophanic comedy. The universal license of the Dionysia may perhaps have countenanced a departure of this kind from ordinary rules. Probably also the custom was not universal, and some fathers may have been too careful of their sons to allow them to be present on such occasions.

The spectators then were men, boys, and, as far as tragedy is concerned, women. To these, on Plato's authority, we must add slaves. *Gorg.* p. 502. The above cited passage of Theophrastus shows that the pedagogues, who were slaves, were present ; and it was no doubt usual for an attendant, ἀκόλουθος, to accompany his master to the theatre. Moreover, Theophrastus (*Char.* 2) introduces the κόλαξ as taking the cushion from the slave, and placing it himself for the object of his attentions : καὶ τοῦ παιδὸς ἐν τῷ θεάτρῳ ἀφελόμενος τὰ προσκεφάλεια αὐτὸς ὑποστρῶσαι. Cf. Æschin. *in Ctesiph.* p. 467. But it is doubtful whether these slaves remained in the theatre, and whether others

might go thither by themselves. At all events, it was not allowed
in Rome at the time when the prologue to the *Pœnulus* of Plautus
was written (v. 23):

> Servi ne obsideant, liberis ut sit locus.

Nor were the pedisequi allowed to remain (v. 40):

> Dum ludi fiunt, in popinam pedisequi
> Irruptionem facite.

But at Athens, where the relation between slave and freeman
was on a different footing, the former may very possibly have
been admitted, from the period when money was paid for entrance.

This entrance-money, θεωρικὸν, was, from the time of Pericles,
paid out of the treasury to the poorer classes, and by degrees to
all the burghers. It amounted to two oboles, which went to the
contractor of the building, ἀρχιτέκτων, or to the person who
rented the theatre, θεατρώνης, who was also called θεατροπώλης,
from his selling the seats. But it seems from Plato, *Apol.* p. 26,
that a higher charge was made for the better places (Alciphr.
iii. 20: τὸ καλὸν τοῦ θεάτρου), and scme were as high as a
drachma apiece. It will be unnecessary to pursue this subject
further, since it has been very fully discussed in Böckh's *Public
Econ. of Athens*, pp. 219–226.

That certain parts of the house were assigned to certain
classes, as at Rome, may possibly be inferred from Aristoph.
Equit. 704 :

> ἰδοῦ προεδρίαν· οἷον ὕψομαί σ' ἐγὼ
> ἐκ τῆς προεδρίας ἔσχατον θεώμενον.

This inference is confirmed by a passage of Alexis, ap. Poll. ix.
44, to which reference has already been made :

> ἐνταῦθα περὶ τὴν ἐσχάτην δεῖ κερκίδα
> ὑμᾶς καθιζούσας θεωρεῖν, ὡς ξένας.

See also a very remarkable passage in Demosthenes, *in Mid*
p. 572, where the πάρεδρος of an archon forcibly ousts a person
who is not sitting in his proper place : ἕτερος ἀδικεῖν ποτ' ἔδοξεν
ὑμῖν περὶ τὰ Διονύσια, καὶ κατεχειροτονήσατ' αὐτοῦ παυεδρεύοντος
ἄρχοντι τῷ υἱεῖ, ὅτι θέαν τινὸς καταλαβόντος ἥψατο, ἐξείργων
ἐκ τοῦ θεάτρου : and Demosthenes himself thinks that his conduct should have been : τοῖς ὑπηρέταις ἐξείργειν εἰπεῖν, οὐκ αὐτὸς
τύπτειν. Ulpian, however, explains it, that he had got into
another person's seat.

We may assert with confidence that the women sat separate

from the men, and this opinion is supported by the inscriptions
of the theatre at Syracuse; for an excellent account of which the
reader is referred to a paper by Göttling, in the *Rhein. Mus.*
1834, p. 103 sqq. This theatre consisted of three stories, separated
by passages, διαζώματα, eight feet wide. The whole of the seats
throughout all three stories were divided into nine κατατομὰς or
κερκίδας, (*cuneos*,) and the inscriptions on most of them are
still legible. On the first κιρκὶς to the east nothing can be
deciphered; on the second is inscribed ΒΑΣΙΛΙΣΣΑΣ ΝΗΡΗΙ-
ΔΟΣ; on the third, ΒΑΣΙΛΙΣΣΑΣ ΦΙΛΙΣΤΙΔΟΣ; on the
fourth, ΒΑΣ . . . ΝΟΣ. Proceeding further to the west the inscriptions are more defaced, and on the fifth and seventh Göttling could only make out a few disconnected letters. Landolina,
however, who saw the inscriptions toward the end of the last
century, was able to read on the fifth, or centre one, ΔΙΟΣ ΟΛΥ
. . . ΙΟΥ; and on the seventh, Η . ΑΚΛΕΟΣΕ . ΦΡΟΝΙΟΥ;
though on the eighth and ninth compartments he could decipher
nothing intelligible. From this it would seem that on the centre
and four western compartments there were male names, and
female ones on the four to the east (those namely to the right of
the spectator). This can scarcely be supposed a fortuitous
arrangement; on the contrary, it is probable that the seats of the
women were denoted by female, and those of the men by male,
names. These inscriptions were the appellations of the whole
κατατομὴ, and do not denote the seats of individuals, as Göttling
has satisfactorily shown. Cf. Panofka, *Lettera sopra una In-
scriz. del Teatro Syracus.*

The ὑπηρέται mentioned by Demosthenes in the passage just
quoted, (*in Mid.* p. 572,) are the ῥαβδοφόροι or ῥαβδοῦχοι employed to preserve order, and answer to the *præcones* of the Roman
theatre, who also oust (*suscitant*) those who are not in their
proper places. See Schol. ad Aristoph. *Pax*, 718.

The representations began early in the morning, and places
were taken ἕωθεν. Philochoros, apud Athen. xi. p. 464, says:
Ἀθηναῖοι τοῖς Διονυσιακοῖς ἀγῶσι τὸ μὲν πρῶτον ἠριστηκότες καὶ
πεπωκότες ἐβάδιζον ἐπὶ τὴν θέαν καὶ ἐστεφανωμένοι ἐθεώρουν,
παρὰ δὲ τὸν ἀγῶνα πόντα ᾠνοχοεῖτο καὶ τραγήματα παρεφέρετο,
καὶ τοῖς χοροῖς εἰσιοῦσιν ἐνέχεον πίνειν καὶ διηγωνισμένοις, ὅτ'
ἐξεπορεύοντο ἐνέχεον πάλιν· μαρτυρεῖν δὲ τούτοις καὶ Φερεκράτη

τὸν κωμικὸν, ὅτι μέχρι τῆς καθ' ἑαυτὸν ἡλικίας οὐκ ἀσίτους εἶναι
τοὺς θεωροῦντας.   This statement that they breakfasted first can
only be true of the earliest period, for that it was not so in the
time of Aristophanes is clear from *Aves*, 784 :

οὐδέν ἐστ' ἄμεινον, οὐδ' ἥδιον. ἢ φῦσαι πτερά.
αὐτίχ' ὑμῶν τῶν θεατῶν εἴ τις ἦν ὑπόπτερος,
εἶτα πεινῶν τοῖς χοροῖσι τῶν τραγῳδῶν ἤχθετο,
ἐκπετόμενος ἂν οὗτος ἠρίστησεν ἐλθὼν οἴκαδε,
κᾷτ' ἂν ἐμπλησθεὶς ἐφ' ἡμᾶς αὖθις αὖ κατέπτετο.

According to all accounts, however, the performances commenced
at a very early hour.   See Æschin. *in Ctesiph.* p. 467 : καὶ ἅμα
τῇ ἡμέρᾳ ἡγεῖτο τοῖς πρέσβεσιν εἰς τὸ θέατρον.   So Demosth. *in
Mid.* p. 538: ἐγὼ δ' ὑπ' ἐχθροῦ νήφοντος ἔωθεν . . . ὑβριζόμην. This
practice continued till a late period.   Plutarch, *Non Posse Suav.*
13 : Τί λέγεις, ὦ 'Επίκουρε ; κιθαρῳδῶν καὶ αὐλητῶν ἔωθεν ἀκροασό-
μενος εἰς τὸ θέατρον βαδίζεις, κ.τ.λ.   Eating and drinking were
permitted in the theatre ; but many only sat out part of the performance, while others did not come till late, when the money-
taker was gone, and they could get in for nothing.   The βδελυρὸς
did this ; Theophr. *Char.* 30 : καὶ ἐπὶ θέαν τηνικάδε πορεύεσθαι
ἄγων τοὺς υἱεῖς, ἡνίκα προῖκα ἀφιᾶσιν οἱ θεατρῶναι.   Others, however, were present the whole time.   Dio Chrysost. *Or.* xxvii. p.
528 : καὶ τούτων (τῶν θεατῶν) ὅσοι σφόδρα ἐσπουδακότες εἰς τὸ
πρᾶγμα, διατελοῦσιν οὐθὲν ἄλλο πράττοντες ἐξ ἑωθινοῦ.

The audience did not scruple to evince their disapprobation
either of actors or of individual spectators, by loud whistling
and clucking.   Demosth. *in Mid.* p. 586 : ὑμῶν οἱ θεώμενοι τοῖς
Διονυσίοις εἰσιόντα εἰς τὸ θέατρον τοῦτον (Μειδίαν) ἐσυρίττετε καὶ
ἐκλώζετε. ὥστε ἃ μίσους ἐστὶ σημεῖα ταῦτ' ἐποιεῖτε.   Cf. Æschin.
in Ctesiph. p. 467.   On the other hand, those who were distinguished and beloved were received with marks of universal
respect.   Thus at the Olympic games, when Themistocles entered,
the whole assembly rose with one accord ; see Pausan. viii. 50, 3
Similar demonstrations occurred in other instances. Lucian, *Demon.* 63.   The method of applauding poets and players was by
clapping the hands and by loud acclamations : this was called θορυ-
βεῖν, or ἐπισημαίνειν. Athen. viii. p. 350.   See Aristoph. *Equit.*
546, where the poet himself incites the spectators to applaud :

αἴρεσθ' αὐτῷ πολὺ τὸ ῥόθιον. παραπέμψατ' ἐφ' ἕνδεκα κώπαις
θόρυβον χρηστὸν ληναΐτην.

Lucian, *de Salt.* 83, relates that an actor played the mad Ajax
so naturally that τό γε θέατρον ἅπαν συνεμεμήνει τῷ Αἴαντι, καὶ
ἐπήδων καὶ ἐβόων, καὶ τὰς ἐσθῆτας ἀπερρίπτουν. This, however,
seems rather to pertain to the Roman custom, *togam jactare.*
It has been supposed that certain passages were encored, the
audience raising a loud cry of αὖθις (*da capo*). This may perhaps be inferred from the analogous case in Xenoph. *Symp.*
9, 4 : Οἱ δὲ συμπόται ὁρῶντες ἅμα μὲν ἐκρότουν, ἅμα δὲ ἐβόων
'αὖθις.' The ordinary mode of expressing disapprobation was
by hissing ; thus Demosthenes says to Æschines, who had been a
bad tragic actor, ἐξέπιπτες, ἐγὼ δ' ἐσύριττον. *De Coron.* p. 315
The audience, however, were not always content with this, but
sometimes proceeded to beat an actor who displeased them, so
that the tragic Agon became an ἀγὼν περὶ ψυχῆς. See Demosth.
de Coron. p. 314 : μισθώσας σαυτὸν τοῖς βαρυστόνοις ἐπικαλου-
μένοις ἐκείνοις ὑποκριταῖς, Σιμύλῳ καὶ Σωκράτει, ἐτριταγωνίστεις,
σῦκα καὶ βότρυς καὶ ἐλάας συλλέγων ὥσπερ ὀπωρώνης ἐκεῖνος ἐκ τῶν
ἀλλοτρίων χωρίων, πλείω λαμβάνων ἀπὸ τούτων, ἢ τῶν ἀγώνων οὓς
ὑμεῖς περὶ τῆς ψυχῆς ἠγωνίζεσθε. ἦν γὰρ ἄσπονδος καὶ ἀκήρυκτος
ὑμῖν ὁ πρὸς τοὺς θεατὰς πόλεμος· ὑφ' ὧν πολλὰ τραύματ' εἰληφὼς
εἰκότως τοὺς ἀπείρους τῶν τοιούτων κινδύνων ὡς δειλοὺς σκώπτεις.
That these τραύματα are to be taken literally appears from a
second passage, *de Falsa Leg.* p. 449 : ἐμοὶ δὲ δοκεῖτε ἀτοπώτατον
ἁπάντων ἂν ποιῆσαι, εἰ ὅτε μὲν τὰ Θυέστου καὶ τῶν ἐπὶ Τροίᾳ κακὰ
ἠγωνίζετο, ἐξεβάλλετε αὐτὸν καὶ ἐξεσυρίττετε ἐκ τῶν θεάτρων καὶ
μόνον οὐ κατελεύετε οὕτως, ὥστε τελευτῶντα τοῦ τριταγωνιστεῖν
ἀποστῆναι. See the anecdote of the parodist Hegemon, Athen.
ix. p. 406 : εἰσῆλθε δέ ποτε καὶ εἰς τὸ θέατρον διδάσκων κωμῳ-
δίαν, λίθων ἔχων πλῆρες τὸ ἱμάτιον· οὓς βάλλων εἰς τὴν ὀρχήστραν
διαπορεῖν ἐποίησε τοὺς θεατάς. καὶ ὀλίγον διαλιπὼν εἶπε, Λίθοι
μὲν οἵδε. βαλλέτω δ' εἴ τις θέλει. For the poet himself sometimes received a reception of this kind, or was forcibly expelled
from the theatre, as was the case with Diphilus. Athen. xiii.
p. 583.

But it would be wrong to argue from these instances that the
profession of a player was despised ; on the contrary, talented
actors were honoured and regarded. See Plutarch, *Apophth.*
Lac. i. p. 848. At a later time troops of despised and ill-paid
actors went about Greece, and they seem even to have consisted

of slaves. See Lucian, *Icaromen.* 29 : (σοφισταὶ) ἐοικότες μάλιστα τοῖς τραγικοῖς ἐκείνοις ὑποκριταῖς, ὧν ἦν ἀφέλης τὰ προσωπεῖα καὶ τὴν χρυσόπαστον ἐκείνην στολὴν, τὸ καταλειπόμενόν ἐστι γελοῖον, ἀνθρώπιον ἑπτὰ δραχμῶν ἐς τὸν ἀγῶνα μεμισθωμένον. Lucian does not speak in much higher terms even of actors who were in considerable repute. *Merc. Cond.* 5 : ἐνίοτε δὲ μαστιγούμενοί τινες αὐτῶν ὡς ἂν τῷ θεάτρῳ δόκῃ. Cf. *Necyom.* 16 ; *Nigrin.* 8 ; Dio Chrysost. *Orat.* x. p. 302 ; Plutarch, *de Sera Num. Vind.* 9. At this period, however, the stage was at a very low ebb.

If what has been said shows that the behaviour of the spectators was somewhat coarse, (see Theoph. *Char.* 11,) yet there is at the same time abundant proof of the attention with which they followed the piece, and of their fine taste and correct discrimination, which allowed no ἀσχημονεῖν on the part of the actor or poet to pass without expressions of disapprobation. Cf. Plutarch, *de Aud. Poet.* 12.

Of course the tragic representations were listened to with more gravity and tranquillity than the comedies. The deep impression made by the former on the feelings of the Athenian, who was easily moved to sympathy and pity, is well shown by what Lycon says of Callippides in Xenoph. *Symp.* 3, 11 : ὃς ὑπερσεμνύνεται, ὅτι δύναται πολλοὺς κλαίοντας καθίζειν. Cf. Isocr. *Paneg.* p. 98 ; Plutarch, *de Esu Carn.* ii. 5 ; Dio Chrysost. *Orat.* xxiii. p. 427 ; Lucian, *de Gymn.* 3. The wonderful effect produced on the monster Alexander of Pheræ by the representation of the *Troades* (or the *Hecuba*?) of Euripides, is recorded by Plutarch, *de Alex. Fort.* 1 : Ἀλέξανδρος δὲ ὁ Φεραίων τύραννος . . . θεώμενος τραγῳδὸν ἐμπαθέστερον ὑφ' ἡδονῆς διετέθη πρὸς τὸν οἶκτον· ἀναπηδήσας οὖν ἐκ τοῦ θεάτρου θᾶττον ἢ βάδην ἀπῄει, δεινὸν εἶναι λέγων, εἰ τοσούτους ἀποσφάττων πολίτας ὀφθήσεται τοῖς Ἑκάβης καὶ Πολυξένης πάθεσιν ἐπιδακρύων. Cf. *Pelop.* 29 ; Ælian, *Var. Hist.* xiv. 40.

In the comedies, on the other hand, the spectators were often requested to laugh and applaud, and many poets strove further to effect this by throwing nuts and figs among them (Aristoph. *Plut.* 797, *Vesp.* 58) ; so that it may be supposed there was no lack of noise and uproar.

EXCURSUS TO SCENE XI.

THE DRESS.

IN the discussion of this voluminous subject, the difficulties arise from the superfluity, instead of the paucity of those materials—both literary and artistic—which classical antiquity has transmitted to us. Indeed, to explain the names and peculiarities of all the various articles of Greek attire with which we are acquainted, would be utterly beyond the scope and limits of the present treatise.

The older writers on the subject, Ferrarius and Rubenius, as well as Montfaucon, are out of date, owing to the immense amount of material which has been discovered since their time, and Winkelmann is far from having exhausted even the special department he has chosen. One of the chief labourers in this field is Böttiger, whose numerous isolated memoirs are very valuable, though they are deficient in unity of purpose, and moreover give no notion of every-day Greek costume. Müller's *Handbuch der Archäol.* contains many very valuable hints, and his *History of the Dorians*, ii. pp. 271-278, conveys a very satisfactory idea of the dress of that people.

In the following pages an attempt will be made to describe, in the first place, the general national dress, and afterwards to review the casual peculiarities brought about by time, fashion, or foppery.

Upon the whole, the same remark applies to the Greek dress as to the Roman, that its separate portions continued, from the earliest to the latest period, essentially unchanged. It was characterised by great simplicity, which is partly attributable to the mildness of the climate, partly to the inborn taste for simple nobleness of form. There was no pinching up the proportions of the body, no multiplicity of garments drawn one over another, and no useless display of heterogeneous ornaments.

The articles of Greek costume may be divided into two chief classes, ἐνδύματα; and ἐπιβλήματα or περιβλήματα, generally ἀναβολή.

The sole ἔνδυμα was the chiton, and this, at an early period,

was different among the different races, till at last the more useful
Doric species got into vogue, and perhaps became general.   This
last, as worn by the men, was a short woollen shirt, without
sleeves; while the Ionic race, and more especially the Athenians,
wore a longer linen chiton.   It is hard to say whether this was
in use in Athens before the historic period, or whether it was first
introduced there from the Ionic colonies.   The account given by
Thucydides (i. 6) must be familiar to every one. Speaking of the
Athenians, he says: οὐ πολὺς χρόνος, ἐπειδὴ χιτῶνάς τε λινοῦς
ἐπαύσαντο φοροῦντες καὶ χρυσῶν τεττίγων ἐνέρσει κρωβύλον ἀναδούμενοι τῶν ἐν τῇ κεφαλῇ τριχῶν. ἀφ' οὗ καὶ Ἰώνων τοὺς πρεσβυτέρους κατὰ τὸ ξυγγενὲς ἐπιπολὺ αὕτη ἡ σκευὴ κατέσχε.
Müller, however, in his *Dorians,* ii. p. 278, rejects this testimony,
and assigns the invention of this chiton to the more effeminate
inhabitants of Ionia.   Nevertheless the Greek historian's account
is strongly supported by the fact that the epithet ἑλκεχίτωνες is
applied by Homer (*Il.* xiii. 685) to the Ionians, among whom the
Athenians are comprehended.   Pausanias (i. 19, 1) mentions a
rather improbable legend, that Theseus came to Athens in a dress
of this sort, and was laughed at by the Athenians: οἷα δὲ χιτῶνα
ἔχοντος αὐτοῦ ποδήρη καὶ πεπλεγμένης δὲ εὐπρεπῶς οἱ τῆς κόμης,
ὡς ἐγίνετο κατὰ τὸν τοῦ Δελφινίου ναὸν, οἱ τὴν στέγην οἰκοδο-
μοῦντες ἤροντο σὺν χλευασίᾳ, ὅτι δὴ παρθένος ἐν ὥρᾳ γάμου πλα-
νᾶται μόνη.   This story is, moreover, at variance with the statements of Herodotus, v. 88, who assigns a much later epoch for
the adoption of the Ionic chiton by the Athenian women.

The time when this antique dress fell into disuse admits of
more accurate determination. Thucydides says, οὐ παλὺς χρόνος,
and it is pretty certain that it still was in fashion at the time of
the Persian war.   See Heraclid. Pont. ap. Athen. xii. p. 512 : καὶ
ἡ Ἀθηναίων πόλις, ἕως ἐτρύφα, μεγίστη τε ἦν καὶ μεγαλοψυχο-
τάτους ἔ-ρεφεν ἄνδρας. ἁλουργῆ μὲν γὰρ ἠμπίσχοντο ἱμάτια,
ποικίλους δ' ὑπέδυνον χιτῶνας, κορύμβους δ' ἀναδούμενοι τῶν τριχῶν χρυσοῦς τέττιγας περὶ τὸ μέτωπον καὶ τὰς κόμας ἐφόρουν·
ὀκλαδίας τε αὐτοῖς δίφρους ἔφερον οἱ παῖδες, ἵνα μὴ καθίζοιεν ὡς
ἔτυχεν. καὶ οὗτοι ἦσαν οἱ τοιοῦτοι, οἱ τὴν ἐν Μαραθῶνι νικήσαν-
τες μάχην καὶ μόνοι τὴν τῆς Ἀσίας ἁπάσης δύναμιν χειρωσάμενοι.
We have also the authority of Aristophanes, who often combines
the description of these antiquely dressed forefathers with the

mention of the exploits at Marathon. See *Equit.* 1330; *Nub.* 984.
It is also clear from Aristophanes that at the time of the Peloponnesian war this dress had gone out entirely, and the epoch of the
adoption of the shorter chiton may be fixed at that period when
Pericles was at the head of affairs. Eustath. *ad Il.* xiii. 689 :
μέχρι γὰρ, φασὶ, τῆς Περικλέους στρατηγίας ποδήρεις εἶχον χιτῶνας, φοροῦντες καὶ τέττιγας.

The chiton, which from this time formed the universal attire
of the men, had two varieties of form. Poll. vii. 47 : χιτὼν δέ, ὁ
μὲν ἀμφιμάσχαλος ἐλευθέρων σχῆμα. ὁ δὲ ἑτερομάσχαλος οἰκετῶν.
It is by no means necessary to suppose that even the ἀμφιμάσχαλος invariably possessed sleeves; there were often merely arm-
holes, though the shoulders were always covered. See Hesychius;
Suidas; and Schol. ad. Aristoph. *Equit.* 882. The ἑτερομάσχαλος
had an arm-hole only for the left arm, leaving the right, with a
part of the breast, quite bare, and hence it was also called ἐξωμίς.
See Hesychius; Phot. *Lex.* p. 25 ; Schol. to Aristoph. *Vesp.* 444 ;
and Heliod. *Æthiop.* iii. 1 : τὸ μὲν ζῶσμα ἑκάστῳ χιτῶνα λευκὸν
εἰς ἀγκύλην ἀνέστελλε. χεὶρ δὲ ἡ δεξιὰ σὺν ὤμῳ καὶ μαζῷ παρα-
γυμνουμένη πέλεκυν δίστομον ἐπεκράδαινεν. See also Pausan. v.
16, 2 : χιτὼν ὀλίγον ὑπὲρ γόνατος καθήκει, τὸν ὦμον ἄχρι τοῦ
στήθους φαίνουσι τὸν δεξιόν. But the ἐξωμὶς was not only a chiton,
but could also serve as an ἱμάτιον or περίβλημα. Hesychius, at
least, asserts this to have been the case : ᾿Εξωμίς· χιτὼν ὁμοῦ καὶ
ἱμάτιον. τὴν γὰρ ἑκατέρου χρείαν παρεῖχεν· καὶ χιτῶνα μὲν διὰ
τὸ ζώννυσθαι, ἱμάτιον δὲ, ὅτι τὸ ἕτερον μέρος ἐβάλλετο. παρ᾿ ὃ
καὶ οἱ κωμικοὶ ὁτὲ μὲν ᾿Ενδῦθι, ὁτὲ δὲ Περιβαλοῦ. The same
meaning appears to attach to a passage of Ælius Dionysius, ap.
Eustath. *ad Il.* xviii. 595 : χιτῶνος εἶδος καὶ ἡ ἐξωμίς· ἐξωμὶς
γὰρ, φησὶ, χιτὼν ἅμα καὶ ἱμάτιον τὸ αὐτό. Pollux, however,
states that there were two different garments, both of which bore
the same name, exomis. He says : ἡ δ᾿ ἐξωμὶς καὶ περίβλημα
ἦν, καὶ χιτὼν ἑτερομάσχαλος. This view is supported by the
artistic remains, one of the most important of which is a relief
figured in the *Mus. Pio-Clem.* iv. pl. 11, representing an Hephæstos clad in the exomis, which is no chiton, but an indubitable himation. Cf. Stuart and Revett, *Antiq. of Athens*, ii. 4,
p. 36, and iii. 1, pl. 8. On the other hand, instances of the
genuine χιτὼν ἑτερομάσχαλος occur in two polychromatic vase-

paintings, given by Stackelberg. *Die Gräber der Hellenen*, pl. 47, 48, of one of which the accompanying woodcut is a copy.

Charon, in the Exomis and sailor's cap : from a polychromatic Lecythos in Stackelberg's *Gräber der Hellenen*, Pl. 47.

The exomis was not only the dress of the slaves, but of the working classes generally, and hence it is worn by Hephæstos in the relief above mentioned. By Hesychius the ἑτερομάσχαλος is called ἐργατικὸς, and a Scholion to Aristoph. *Equit.* 882, says : ἦν δὲ καὶ ἑτερομάσχαλος ὁ τῶν ἐργατῶν, οὗ τὴν μίαν μασχάλην ἐρ̇ρ̇απτον. In the *Lysistrata* the Chorus of old men is clad in the exomis; v. 662, τὴν ἐξωμίδ᾽ ἐκδυώμεθα. See also Poll. iv. 118, 119; Plaut. *Mil.* iv. 4, 43.

There is some difficulty in determining whether the chiton was worn next to the skin, ἀμέσως πρὸς τῇ σαρκὶ, or whether there was an under garment or shirt beneath it. Eustathius, who is always thinking of the customs of later times, when a *tunica interior* had long been worn, frequently speaks ambiguously on the subject. See *ad Il.* xviii. 416; xvi. 224 ; xviii. 25 : Χιτῶνα δὲ νῦν τὸ ἐπιπολάζον ἱμάτιον ἔφη καὶ οὐκ ἐξ ἀνάγκης τὸ ἀμέσως ἐπικεχυμένον τῷ σώματι, εἰ μὴ ἴσως μονοείμων ἔτυχεν εἶναι ὁ Ἀχιλλεύς. It is true that an article of dress is often mentioned, which apparently differed from the regular chiton. It is called χιτω-ίσκος when worn by the men, and χιτώνιον in the case of women; and though Plutarch once uses the former name for both sexes, yet the latter word is exclusively restricted to the female garment. Lucian, *Lexiph.* 25 : ὅτε χιτώνιον μὲν καὶ τὸν ἀνδρεῖον ᾦου λέγεσθαι, δουλάρια δὲ καὶ τοὺς ἄῤῥενας· ἅ τις οὐκ οἶδεν, ὅτι χιτώνιον μὲν γυναικὸς ἐσθὴς, δουλάρια δὲ τὰ θήλεα κα-λοῦσι. Eustath. *ad Il.* xviii. 595 : ὁ δὲ ἀνδρεῖος χιτωνίσκος, ὅ τινες ἐπενδύτην, τὸ δὲ βραχὺ χιτωνισκάριον· χιτώνιον δὲ καὶ χιτω-νάριον λεπτὸν ἔνδυμα γυναικεῖον πολυτελές. See also Plutarch, *de Gen. Socr.* 14 : σοὶ δὲ, ὦ πάτερ, Μιλησίαν χλαμύδα, τῇ δὲ μητρὶ παραλουργὸν ὠνησόμεθα χιτώνιον. Cf. Aristoph. *Lysistr.* 150. The word χιτωνίσκος is, however, used for an article of female dress by Plutarch, *Mul. Virt.* 26, where he says, speaking of Xenocrita : παρεκαλύψατο τῷ χιτωνίσκῳ τὸ πρόσωπον, but the reason is because the Cuman women had to wear male attire. Cf. *Alcib.* 39.

As an article of female costume, χιτώνιον seems to mean an under shift, as will presently be shown. But when Böttiger as-sumes that the χιτωνίσκος filled an analogous position in male attire, and proceeds to explain μονοχίτων of one who only wore the chitoniscos, without an upper chiton, and ἀχίτων, on the other hand, of one who wore no under shirt, he is quite wrong. For the chitoniscos is only a short chiton, not a shirt worn under the chiton, but, as Eustathius says, ἐπιπολάζων. It is the chiton of the men, and, as may be proved by many passages, it is the outer (or rather only) visible one. Thus Antiphanes, apud Athen. xii. p. 545, describing an Academic, says,

λευκὴ χλανὶς, φαιὸς χιτωνίσκος καλός.

See Demosth. *in Mid.* p. 583 : ὥστε με, ὦ ἄ. Ἀ., φοβηθέντα τὸν ὑμέτερον θόρυβον, θοἰμάτιον προέσθαι καὶ μικροῦ γυμνὸν ἐν τῷ χιτωνίσκῳ γενέσθαι. Cf. Æschin. *in Timarch.* p. 142 : Lysias *in Theomn.* p. 350. An opposite conclusion would seem to be de-rivable from Aristoph. *Ran.* 1067 : χιτῶνά γ᾽ ἔχων οὔλων ἐρίων ὑπένερθε. The ὑπένερθε will be found, however, if the context be considered, to refer to the ῥάκια or *tribonion* before mentioned. See also *Aves*, 944. The clearest proof however is from Plato, *Hipp. Min.* p. 368, where the articles of Hippias' wardrobe are

E E

one by one enumerated by Socrates. We have signet, sandals, girdle, καὶ τὸ ἱμάτιον καὶ τὸν χιτωνίσκον. A third garment, if worn, would have been infallibly mentioned.

Thus, then, the ἱμάτιον, χλαῖνα, or χλανὶς, and the χιτὼν or χιτωνίσκος, appear universally as the two sole articles of male dress, and there is no such thing as an inner shirt. And μονοχί-των denotes one who wore no περιβόλαιον over the chiton, i. q. οἰοχίτων : see *Odyss.* xiv. 488. Cf. Pythænetos, ap. Athen. xiii. p. 589. On the other hand, ἀχίτων denotes one who wore the himation only, without the chiton, which was often done by per- sons of a simple and austere manner of life. See Xenoph. *Memor.* i. 6, 2, where Antiphon says to Socrates : καὶ ἱμάτιον ἠμφίεσαι οὐ μόνον φαῦλον, ἀλλὰ τὸ αὐτὸ θέρους τε καὶ χειμῶνος, ἀνυπό- δητός τε καὶ ἀχίτων διατελεῖς. Ælian, *Var. Hist.* vii. 13, speaking of Agesilaos, says : γέρων ἤδη ὢν ἀνυπόδητος πολλάκις καὶ ἀχίτων προῄει, τὸν τρίβωνα περιβαλλόμενος αὐτὸς, καὶ ταῦτα ἑωθινὸς ἐν ὥρᾳ χειμερίῳ. Cf. Plutarch, *Apophth. Lac.* i. p. 838. And Dio- dorus Siculus, xi. 26, says of Gelon : ἀχίτων ἐν ἱματίῳ προσελ- θῶν, κ.τ.λ. It would indeed have been an unexampled instance of τρυφὴ for a Spartan, who from his twelfth year had been clad only in a tribon, to put on a double chiton. See Plutarch, *Lyc.* 16 : Γενόμενοι δὲ δωδεκαετεῖς ἄνευ χιτῶνος ἤδη διετέλουν, ἐν ἱματίῳ εἰς τὸν ἐνιαυτὸν λαμβάνοντες. Cf. Diog. Laert. vi. 13 ; and vii. 169.

The ἐπίβλημα or περίβλημα of the Greeks, the ἱμάτιον Ἑλληνικὸν, as Lucian (*de Merc. Cond.* 25) calls it, in contra- distinction to the Roman toga, was a large square cloth. This is expressly stated in the story of those Greeks who, under the Roman rule, had adopted the toga, and which they again ex- changed for the national dress, in order to escape the oppressions of Mithridates. Posidonius, ap. Athen. v. p. 213 : τῶν δ᾽ ἄλλων Ῥωμαίων οἱ μὲν θεῶν ἀγάλμασι προσπεπτώκασιν, οἱ δὲ λοιποὶ με- ταμφιεσάμενοι τετράγωνα ἱμάτια τὰς ἐξ ἀρχῆς πατρίδας πάλιν ὀνομάζουσι. See *Gallus,* p. 410. The method of adjustment was exactly the same as in the older and simpler way of wearing the toga, described in *Gallus,* pp. 412, 413. It was first thrown over the left shoulder, and then round the back to the right side, and then above the right arm or below it, and again brought over the left shoulder or arm. This was called ἐπὶ δεξιὰ ἀναβάλλεσ-

θαι or ἀμπισχνεῖσθαι; and according to a man's skill or awkward-
ness in doing it, was he pronounced genteel, or clownish and
un-Greek. The token of the ἀνελεύθερος and ἀπαίδευτος is expressly stated by Plato, *Theœt.* p. 175, to be ἀναβάλλεσθαι μὴ
ἐπίστασθαι ἐπιδέξια ἐλευθέρως. Cf. Athen. i. p. 21: Ἔμελε δὲ
αὐτοῖς καὶ τοῦ κοσμίως ἀναλαμβάνειν τὴν ἐσθῆτα καὶ τοὺς μὴ
τοῦτο ποιοῦντας ἔσκωπτον. See also Aristoph. *Aves.* 1565, where
Poseidon says to the barbarian:

> οὗτος, τί δρᾷς; ἐπ' ἀριστέρ' οὕτως ἀμπέχει;
> οὐ μεταβαλεῖς θοἰμάτιον ὡς ἐπὶ δεξιά;

At an earlier period it was the fashion, as with the Romans (*cohi-
bere brachium*), to keep the right hand in the garment, ἐντὸς τὴν
χεῖρα ἔχειν), a rule which does not apply to orators alone. Æschin.
in Timarch. p. 52; Demosth. *de Falsa Leg.* p. 420; Müller,
Handb. d. Archäol. pp. 85, 468. Many adhered to this ancient
custom; Phocion, for instance, as we are told by Duris, apud
Plutarch, *Phoc.* 4.

The himation reached properly to the knee at least, and a
shorter ἀναβολὴ was considered unbecoming. Theophr. *Char.* 4:
(ἀγροίκου) ἀναβεβλημένος ἄνω τοῦ γόνατος καθιζάνειν, ὥστε τὰ
γυμνὰ αὐτοῦ φαίνεσθαι. Philetærus, ap. Athen. i. p. 21: Ἀμφὶ
στέρνοις φᾶρος οὐ καθήσεις, μηδ' ἀγροίκως ἄνω γόνατος ἀμφέξει;
Usually it reached even lower. Quint. *Instit.* xi. 3, 143: 'Togas
veteres ad calceos usque demittebant, ut Græci pallium.' Cf.
Böttiger, *Vasengemälde*, p. 56. Still, when Athens was at her
zenith, so long a garment would have been thought a mark of
luxury and pride. Plato, *Alcib.* i. p. 122; Demosth. *de Falsa
Leg.* p. 422: καὶ διὰ τῆς ἀγορᾶς πορεύεται, θοἰμάτιον καθεὶς ἄχρι
τῶν σφυρῶν. Even in Lucian's time it was thought a sign of
τρυφή. See *Amor.* 3: φαιδρὰ μὲν ἐσθὴς μέχρι ποδῶν τὴν τρυφὴν
θειμένη.

The Spartans wore a short mantle of coarse texture, called
τρίβων or τριβώνιον. Those who aped Spartan customs, the
Λακωνίζοντες, and the philosophers of the cynic and stoic schools,
naturally adopted it also. See Thucyd. i. 6; Plato, *Protag.*
p. 342; Aristot. *Ethic. Nic.* iv. 13: Müller, *Dorians*, ii. p. 279.
Of course a good deal would depend on a man's means and condition, and the lower classes would frequently content themselves
with such a garment. See Isæus, *de Dicæog. Her.* p. 94; Aristoph.
Vesp. 116, 1131; *Eccl.* 850.

The boys at Athens used, in early times, to wear the simple chiton, but towards the period of the Peloponnesian war it became usual for them to wear an upper garment also. See Aristoph. *Nubes*, 964, 987. The boys of Sparta, as above-mentioned, were allowed the chiton only till their twelfth year; afterwards the tribon was their sole article of dress, in winter as well as summer. Xenoph. *de Republ. Laced.* 2, 4: Καὶ ἀντί γε τοῦ ἱματίοις διαθρύπτεσθαι, ἐνόμισεν ἑνὶ ἱματίῳ δι' ἔτους προσεθίζεσθαι, νομίζων οὕτω καὶ πρὸς ψύχη καὶ πρὸς θάλπη ἄμεινον ἂν παρασκευάσασθαι. Plutarch, *Dec. Or. Vit.* iv. p. 379: ἱμάτιον ἓν καθ' αὑτὸ ἐφόρει τοῦ χειμῶνος καὶ τοῦ θέρους.

After the Athenian lad had attained to the age of an ephebus, his proper dress was the chlamys, a garment entirely different from

the himation. It originally came from Thessaly or Macedon,
whence it seems to have been spread over all Greece. Poll. vii. 46 :
τὰς δὲ Θετταλικὰς χλαμύδας Θετταλικὰ πτερὰ ὠνόμαζον, καὶ ἐν-
τεθετταλίσμεθα ἔλεγον τὸ χλαμυδοφοροῦμεν. The clearest description of its form is in Plutarch, *Alex.* 26, where its shape is compared to that of the city of Alexandria : κυκλοτερῆ κόλπον ἦγον,
οὗ τὴν ἐντὸς περιφέρειαν εὐθεῖαι βάσεις, ὥσπερ ἀπὸ κρασπέδων
εἰς σχῆμα χλαμύδος, ὑπελάμβανον ἐξ ἴσου συνάγουσαι τὸ μέγεθος.
It is also represented very frequently in vase-paintings, and other
artistic remains. See the accompanying wood-cut, which represents Œdipus before the Sphinx, and is taken from Tischbein,
Engrav. ii. 24. The chlamys which he wears appears to be of
an oblong quadrangular shape. It has a purple border, and tassels
at the four corners. It was fastened by a button on the right
shoulder, and sometimes also across the breast, and the tassels
which hang down are the πτερὰ or πτέρυγες. Hesychius :
Θετταλικὰ πτερά· τοῦτο εἴρηται διὰ τὸ πτέρυγας ἔχειν τὰς Θετταλικὰς χλαμύδας. Πτέρυγες δὲ καλοῦνται αἱ ἑκατέρωθεν γωνίαι,
διὰ τὸ ἐοικέναι πτέρυξιν. The time when this garment got into
vogue throughout Greece is unknown. The first mention of it is
said to occur in Sappho. Poll. x. 124 : οἱ μέντοι Ἀττικοὶ τὸ
λεπτὸν χλανίδα, τὸ δὲ ἱππικὸν χλαμύδα, ὡς Θετταλῶν. πρώτην
δέ φασι χλαμύδα ὀνομάσαι Σαπφὼ ἐπὶ τοῦ Ἔρωτος εἰποῦσαν,
Ἐλθόντ᾽ ἐξ ὀρανῶ πορφυρέαν ἔχοντα προϊέμενον χλαμύν. Pollux
rightly calls it τὸ ἱππικὸν, for it is the proper riding coat, and
was worn on journeys. Müller, *Dorians,* ii. p. 278. Other names,
such as χλαῖνα, χλανὶς, &c. refer not so much to the form as to
the material which was adopted.

The dress of the women was in its main features the same as
that of the men, though distinguished by various additions. Care,
however, must be taken to distinguish between the two chitons,
the Doric and the Ionic. The Doric was a very simple woollen
shift, perhaps consisting only of two short pieces of cloth, sewed
together up to the breast (at least on one side), while the parts
covering the breast and back were fastened over the shoulders,
and thus formed arm-holes. The σχιστὸς of the virgins, alluded
to in the Excursus on *The Gymnasia,* p. 298, is only one species.
For this garment see the accompanying figure of Nike, which is
copied from Stackelberg, *Gräb. der Hell.* pl. 60. The σχιστὸς

which she wears can only be called a mixture of Doric and Ionic.
It should however be remarked that artists represented the longer
chiton with the diploidion, open in the same manner as in the
figure, so that the proper Doric σχιστὸς is only to be seen on the
Amazons, *Marbles in the Brit. Mus.* iv. 16; and in the *Mus.
Borb.* iv. 21

The Ionic chiton, on the other hand, was an ample shift, falling
in many folds down to the feet, and with broad sleeves, which
were variable in length.   It was of linen or of similar material.
Cf. Herodot. v. 87: ἐφόρεον γὰρ δὴ πρὸ τοῦ αἱ τῶν Ἀθηναίωι
γυναῖκες ἐσθῆτα Δωρίδα τῇ Κορινθίᾳ παραπλησιωτάτην· μετέβαλ-
λον ὦν ἐς τὸν λίνεον κιθῶνα, ἵνα δὴ περόνῃσι μὴ χρέωνται.   ἔστι

A Bronze from Herculaneum, *Mus. Borb.* ii. 6.

Here the adjustment of the chiton is complete. On the shoulders are the clasps which fasten together the πτέρυγες. The chiton is girded under the bosom, and the upper part, which is thus made to hang over (κόλπος), forms a parallel line with the diploïdion.

A Bronze from Herculaneum. *Mus. Borb.* ii. 4.

The girl is just in the act of fastening the chiton over the right shoulder, and we see how the lappet, διπλοΐδιον, is caused by this means. On the side where the seam is, joining the πτέρυγες, are two purple stripes.

εἰ ἀληθεῖ λόγῳ χρεωμένοισι οὐκ Ἰὰς αὕτη ἡ ἐσθὴς τὸ παλαιὸν ἀλλὰ Κάειρα· ἐπεὶ ἥ γε Ἑλληνικὴ ἐσθὴς πᾶσα ἡ ἀρχαίη τῶν γυναικῶν ἡ αὐτὴ ἦν, τὴν νῦν Δωρίδα καλέομεν.

The διπλοῖς, διπλοΐδιον, or ἡμιδιπλοΐδιον, is intimately connected with the chiton, or rather is a part of it. Böttiger supposes this diploidion, or the ἐπωμὶς, to have been a separate article of dress, a kind of double mantle, which at last came to be drawn on like a tunic. In the case of the sleeved chiton, which was not fastened with a clasp over the shoulder, this may have been the case, but originally, and in most instances, it was nothing more than the turn-over or lappet of the chiton itself. This is very clearly seen in many vase-paintings; but no antiques show the arrangement of this garment more unmistakably than the two bronzes from Herculaneum which are here engraved. The parts covering the breast and back are much too long, and hence this flap or turn-over, which in some cases falls as low as the hips, or lower; and inasmuch as the chiton was double so far as this reached, it was called διπλοΐδιον. When the lappet was formed on the breast only, or on the back, instead of on both, it may have borne the name ἡμιδιπλοΐδιον; or perhaps this name was used when the flap did not double the chiton more than half way down There is no passage which determines which of these two meanings properly attaches to the word. This diploidion was also called ἐπωμὶς, because it was fastened over the shoulders by agraffes. Müller, it is true, supposes that ἐπωμὶς merely means the end which was fastened across the shoulder. *Handb. d. Archäol.* p. 472. In support of this position he adduces Eurip. *Hec* 553:

> λαβοῦσα πέπλους ἐξ ἄκρας ἐπωμίδος
> ἔρρηξε λαγόνος ἐς μέσον παρ' ὀμφαλόν.

He also cites a fragment of Chæremon, apud Athen. xiii. p. 608:

> ἔκειτο δ' ἡ μὲν λευκὸν εἰς σεληνόφως
> φαίνουσα μαστὸν λελυμένης ἐπωμίδος.

In these passages, however, the word ἐπωμὶς may just as well be understood of the garment itself, and it is evidently taken in this sense by Pollux, vii. 49: Καὶ ἴδια δὲ γυναικῶν ἐπωμὶς, διπλοΐδιον, ἡμιδιπλοΐδιον, κ.τ.λ. So too a fragment of Apollodorus, ap. Suidas, s. v. ἐγκομβώσασθαι:

> τὴν ἐπωμίδα
> πτύξασα διπλῆν ἄνωθεν ἐνεκομβωσάμην

Müller also takes ἔγκυκλον as synonymous with diploidion; but
this is very doubtful. The Scholiast to Aristoph. *Thesmoph.* 261,
very properly observes: δῆλον δὲ, ὅτι τὸ ἔγκυκλον ἱμάτιον, ὁ δὲ
κροκωτὸς ἔνδυμα: and again, *Lysistr.* 114, we have τοὔγκυκλον
τουτὶ καταθεῖσαν. Pollux, however, understands the word to
mean a coloured border. See vii. 53.

The sleeves of the proper Ionic chiton seem quite closed, and

A female from Millin, *Peint. d Vas.* II. 70. She is dressed in a long chiton,
without sleeves, and fastened over the shoulders (ἐπωμίς). The diploidion is
bordered with a coloured edge; below it is the lappet (κόλπος) caused by the
girdle; on the right side near the seam are two parallel stripes (ῥάβδοι or
παρυφαί). The small shawl-shaped himation (ἀμπεχόνιον) has also a purple
border (παρυφὲς or παραλουργές, Poll.) at each end. She wears shoes, covering
the whole foot, and in her left hand is a parasol (σκιάδειον), of the usual form.

hang down in folds like broad pouches; but they were often slit
open from the shoulder on the upper side, and fastened with
clasps, so that the arm might be seen. This sort Böttiger very
improperly terms χιτὼν σχιστός.

The Ionic chiton was generally much longer than the body,
and was so drawn up by the girdle as just to reach to the feet.
The fold or lappet (κόλπος) which was by this means caused
under the breast or lower (according to the position of the
girdle), forms a parallel line with the border of the diploidion.
See Figure on p. 423. When the chiton was not girded, but
hung loose from the top, it was called ὀρθοστάδιος, or συμμε-
τρία χιτών. Poll. vii. 48 : χιτὼν ὀρθοστάδιος ὁ οὐ ζωννύμενος.
Phot. Lex p. 346 : Ὀρθοστάδιοι οἱ στατοὶ χιτῶνες· οἱ γὰρ συ-
ρόμενοι συρτοί. The chiton was called συρτὸς before it was girt
up; it was never worn with a train. Sometimes it had below a
flounce with folds, and was then called στολιδωτός. Poll. vii. 54 :
εἴη δ᾽ ἄν τις καὶ στολιδωτὸς χιτών. στολίδες δέ εἰσιν αἱ ἐξεπί-
τηδες ὑπὸ δεσμοῦ γιγνόμεναι κατὰ τέλη τοῖς χιτῶσιν ἐπιπτυχαί.
μάλιστα ἐπὶ λινῶν χιτωνίσκων. Cf. Xenoph. Cyrop. vi. 4, 2.

The girdle used by women is called ζώνιον or στρόφιον.
Ptolem. Ascal. de differ. voc. 87 : ζώνην λέγουσι τὴν τοῦ ἀνδρός·
ζώνιον δὲ τὸ γυναικός. Mœr. Att. p. 124 ; Poll. vii. 67 ; Aristoph. Thesm. 139 ; Lysistr. 72. This must be distinguished
from the band placed around the breast (usually) under the
chiton. It was called by several names, of which the most usual
are ταινία, μίτρα, ἀπόδεσμος, and στηθόδεσμος. Poll. vii. 65 :
τὸ δὲ τῶν μαστῶν τῶν γυναικείων ζῶσμα ταινίαν ὠνόμαζον καὶ
ταινίδιον. Cf. Anthol. Pal. v. 199 ; Anacr. 20, 13. The ἀπόδεσμος
corresponds to the fascia pectoralis (see Gallus, p. 432), but is
also generally a bosom-band. Lucian, Dial. Mer. xii. : ἡ δὲ φιλή-
σασα μεταξὺ τῶν μαστῶν ὑπὸ τῷ ἀποδέσμῳ παρεβύσατο. The
manner of wearing it is seen in a bronze, figured in the Antich.
d'Erc. vi. 17, 3. The body-band, περίζωμα, was different, being
used as a περὶ τῇ κοιλίᾳ ζῶσμα. Poll. vii. 65. The Greek women
had an infinity of means for improving the figure, though few,
perhaps, beside hetæræ made use of them. Alexis, ap. Athen.
xiii. p. 568, gives a long catalogue :

οὐκ ἔχει τις ἰσχία·
ὑπενέδυσ᾽ ἐρραμμέν᾽ αὐτήν, ὥστε τὴν εὐπυγίαν
ἀναβοᾶν τοὺς εἰσιδόντας. κοιλίαν ἀδρὰν ἔχει·

σ<i>τηθί</i> ἔστ' αὐταῖσι τούτων, ὦ ' ἔχουσ' οἱ κωμικοί.
ὀρθὰ προσθεῖσαι τοιαῦτα γοῦν αὐτῶν τῆς κοιλίας,
ὡσπερεὶ κόντοισι τούτοις εἰς τὸ πρόσθ' ἀπήγαγον.

The ἐπίβλημα, or upper garment of the women, in all essential
points resembled the himation of the males; hence the same might
serve for both man and wife. Ælian, *Var. Hist.* vii. 9 : ἡ Φωκίωνος γυνὴ τὸ Φωκίωνος ἱμάτιον ἐφόρει καὶ οὐδὲν ἐδεῖτο οὐ κρο-
κωτοῦ, οὐ Ταραντίνου, οὐκ ἀναβολῆς, οὐκ ἐγκυκλίου, οὐ κεκρυφάλου,
οὐ καλύπτρας, οὐ βαπτῶν χιτωνίσκων. The same author relates
that Xantippe refused to go out in her husband's himation, which
is likely enough. The usual name for this female himation is
ἀμπεχόνη or ἀμπεχόνιον, and the use of the diminutive shows
that smaller shawl-like garments were also worn. See the figure
with the σκιάδειον, p. 426. The word πέπλος, with the exception of the Panathenaic, denotes any article of apparel ordinarily
used. See Poll. vii. 49. If there was originally a particular garment called by this name, it must have become obsolete.

Before proceeding to describe these garments further, let us
return a moment to the question whether the χιτὼν and ἀμπεχόνη sufficed for a woman's attire, or whether an under shift
was also worn. Even at Athens this was probably not universally the case, still, most likely, it was pretty general. It is true
that there is no monument which distinctly represents one chiton
over the other; though the χιτώνια mentioned above can certainly
be nothing else than such under-shifts. But it is clear from
Aristophanes that these could never have been worn alone, not
even in the house, for it would have been next to nudity. *Lysistr.* 150 :

εἰ γὰρ καθοίμεθ' ἔνδον ἐντετριμμέναι
κἂν τοῖς χιτωνίοισι τοῖς ἀμοργίνοις
γυμναὶ παρίοιμεν.

In the *Adoniazusæ* of Theocritus, Praxagora, while washing herself, is clad in her chitonion ; she then puts on the περονατρίς
or upper ἔνδυμα, and the ὀμπέχονον. Still plainer, however, is
what Athenæus says of the celebrated Phryne, xiii. p. 590 : διόπερ
οὐδὲ ῥᾳδίως ἦν αὐτὴν ἰδεῖν γυμνήν. ἐχέσαρκον γὰρ χιτώνιον ἠμπεί-
χετο καὶ τοῖς δημοσίοις οὐκ ἐχρῆτο βαλανείοις. So too the artifice
of Hyperides, at the conclusion of his oration in her defence :
περιρρήξας τοὺς χιτωνίσκους γυμνά τε τὰ στέρνα ποιήσας, κ. τ. λ.

In the following engraving, taken from Tischbein, *Engrav-ings*, i. pl. 59, one of the women, who are here performing their ablutions, has on such a short thin shift, ἐξωμίς, which has all the peculiarities of a χιτώνιον, for it reaches scarcely half down the thigh, and is quite διαφανές, (Aristoph. *Lysistr.* 48,) and ἐχέσαρκον, like that of Phryne.

We will next speak of the materials of the several articles of Greek dress. After the linen chiton of the men had fallen into disuse, sheep's wool was the only material employed, the fabric being of coarser or finer texture, according to circumstances. The most celebrated wool came from Miletus. Aristoph. *Lysistr.* 729 ; Strabo, xii. 7, 16 : φέρει δ' ὁ περὶ τὴν Λαοδίκειαν τόπος προβάτων ἀρετὰς, οὐκ εἰς μαλακότητας μόνον τῶν ἐρίων, ᾗ καὶ τῶν Μιλησίων διαφέρει, ἀλλὰ καὶ εἰς τὴν κοραξὴν χρόαν. See *Gallus*, p. 442. For winter wear the chiton was made of much stouter cloth, and shagged on one or both sides. Thus in Aristophanes, *Ran.* 1067, we have : χιτὼν οαλων ἐρίων : and Pollux, vii. 57, mentions the χιτὼν δασὺς, μαλλωτὸς or ἀμφίμαλλος. The χλαῖνα, which was probably like the ordinary himation in form, only of

thicker stuff, was worn in winter. See Aristoph. *Aves,* 714,
where the appearance of the swallow is said to indicate

ὅτε χρὴ χλαῖναν πωλεῖν ἤδη καὶ ληδάριόν τι πρίασθαι.

Also Hesych.: χλαῖνα ἱμάτιον χειμερινόν. Cf. Suidas; Aristoph.
Vesp. 738, 1132; *Ranæ,* 1459. In summer, on the other hand,
was worn a garment of lighter material, θερίστρια, which Winkelmann mistakes for a veil. See Hesychius; and Poll. vii. 48.
In Theocr. xv. 69, Praxinoe wears a θερίστριον at the season of
the festival of Adonis. The λήδιον, or ληδάριον, was also a light
summer-garment, and so, probably, was the χλανίς also.

The female attire was made from other materials besides wool
and linen. The byssus claims the first mention, though the subject is obscure, since the ancients appear to have called various
stuffs by this name. The byssus of our naturalists is quite distinct, being a tuft of silky threads secreted by a family of mol-
lusks, of which the *Pinna marina* is the type. This also was
known to the ancients. See Tertull. *de Pallio,* 3; Man. Philes.
de Anim. Propr. 88. But the byssus used for garments was a
vegetable product, consisting of the fibres of certain plants. In
this all writers, ancient and modern, agree; but what the plants
were is not so easy to say. Herodotus, ii. 86, speaks of it in
reference to the Egyptian mummies: κατειλίσσουσι πᾶν τὸ σῶμα
σινδόνος βυσσίνης τελαμῶσι κατατετμημένοισι. It has been generally supposed that mummies, at least those of the first and
second classes, were enveloped in swathes of cotton; and if this
was the case, Herodotus must have taken βύσσος for cotton.
[Recent microscopical investigations, however, tend to show that
the fibres of the mummy-cloth are of flax, not cotton.] Again,
Herodotus, vii. 181, mentions βύσσος as a bandage for wounds,
a purpose to which cotton is not at all adapted. Cf. Id. ii.
37; Plin. *Nat. Hist.* xix. 1, 2. Philostratus, moreover, *Vit.
Apollon.* ii. 20, says: καὶ βύσσῳ δὲ τοὺς φανερωτέρους αὐτῶν
(Ἰνδῶν) φασιν ἐστάλθαι, τὴν δὲ βύσσον φύεσθαι δένδρου φασίν.
It is not unlikely that the thicker cotton fabrics may have been
confounded with linen. Anything resembling linen was probably often called so, and this may explain the uncertainty of
the expression. See Plutarch, *de Pythiæ Orac.* 4; and Poll.
vii. 76: καὶ μὴν καὶ τὰ βύσσινα καὶ ἡ βύσσος λίνου τι εἶδος παρ'
Ἰνδοῖς. ἤδη δὲ καὶ παρ' Αἰγυπτίοις ἀπὸ ξύλου τι ἔριον γίγνεται

ἐξ οὗ τὴν ἐσθῆτα λίνου ἄν τις μᾶλλον φαίη προσεοικέναι, πλὴν
τοῦ πάχους. On the whole, the best authorities have inclined
to the opinion that by βύσσος cotton is meant. See Forster, *de
Bysso Antiquorum*, p. 47 ; Bottiger, *Aldobrand. Hochz.* p. 127 ;
Sprengel, *Hist. rei Herb.* i. p. 15. There can however be no
doubt that several fabrics, essentially different from each other,
all bore this name. The usual byssus was white, like cotton ;
but there was also one kind of a yellow colour. Philostr. *Vit.
Apollon.* ii. 20: καὶ ἠσθῆναι τῇ βύσσῳ φησὶν ὁ Ἀπολλώνιος,
ἐπειδὴ ἔοικε φαιῷ τρίβωνι. Empedocles, apud Plutarch, *de Def.
Orac.* 4: βύσσῳ δὲ γλαυκῆς κρόκου καταμίσγεται. Pausan. vii.
21, 7 ; and v. 5, 2 ; ἡ δὲ βύσσος ἡ ἐν τῇ Ἠλείᾳ λεπτότητος μὲν
εἴνεκα οὐκ ἀποδεῖ τῆς Ἑβραίων, ἔστι δὲ οὐχ ὁμοίως ξανθή. Cf.
Plin. xix. 1, 4. But the enormous price of this yellow byssus,
which grew around Elis, makes it probable that it was used
for cauls and other ornaments, but hardly for whole dresses.
According to Voss, ad Virg. *Georg.* ii. 120, the true byssus is
the yellow cotton (*Gossypium religiosum?*); but the question is,
what he means by the true byssus, for Herodotus certainly is
not thinking of the yellow kind, and that grown at Elis was
evidently not the common article. It seems then that we must
assume that, originally, there was a great resemblance among
a variety of stuffs, owing to a similarity in the style of manufacture; and the confusion and perhaps intentional imitation
which took place will account for the contradictory nature of
the descriptions which have come down to us. See Wedel,
de Purp. et Bysso ; Bertolini, *de Bysso Ant.* ; Heeren, *Ideen*, i.
1, p. 106.

The period at which cotton garments were introduced into
Greece is uncertain. The fragment of Empedocles, quoted by
Plutarch, is too brief to afford us any information as to the use of
byssus for clothing; a βύσσινον φάρος, however, is mentioned,
with reference to the same period, in a fragment of the *Laocoon*
of Sophocles, apud Dionys. Halic. *Ant. Rom.* i. 48. Plutarch,
also, *de Virt. et Vit.* 2, affirms that at the Homeric period, wool
and linen, only, were known. There is a remarkable passage in
Diogenes Laertius, (vi. 90,) referring to the surveillance exercised
by the *Astynomi* over luxuriousness in dress ; where the obscure
expression σινδὼν may originally denote linen, but in any case of
foreign manufacture. He says: ὑπὸ τῶν Ἀθήνησιτ ἀστυνόμων

ἐπιτιμηθείς, ὅτι σινδόνα ἠμφίεστο, ἔφη, Καὶ Θεόφραστον ὑμῖν δείξω
σινδόνα περιβεβλημένον. ἀπιστούντων δὲ ἀπήγαγεν ἐπὶ κουρεῖον
καὶ ἔδειξε κειρόμενον. See Poll. vii. 72 ; Phot. *Lex.* p. 512 :
Σινδονίτης χιτών· λινοῦς. But since Herodotus mentions the
σινδὼν βυσσίνη, it would appear that fabrics of cotton were also
called by this name. Hence, if in the above story from Diogenes
Laertius robes of cotton are meant, it will follow that this was, at
that period, a very unusual dress for men ; but how early women
made use of this material does not appear. Cf. Art. *Byssus* in
the *Real-Encyklop. d. Class. Alterth.*

Another somewhat similar material was a very fine sort of flax,
which derived its name from the island Amorgos, where the best
was grown. Aristoph. *Lysistr.* 150, mentions χιτώνια ἀμόργινα,
and these are doubtless synonymous with the διαφανῆ χιτώνια
of v. 48. See Æschin. *in Timarch.* p. 118 : γυναῖκα ἀμόργινα
ἐπισταμένην ἐργάζεσθαι καὶ ἔργα λεπτὰ εἰς τὴν ἀγορὰν ἐκφέρου-
σαν. The garments thus made were particularly delicate and
transparent, and seem to have resembled those of byssus. Harpocr. Ἀμοργός· ἔστι παραπλήσιόν τι βύσσῳ. Pollux. vii. 74,
says : Τὰ δὲ ἀμόργινα γίγνεσθαι μὲν τὰ ἄριστα ἐν τῇ Ἀμοργῷ.
λίνου δ' οὖν καὶ ταύτας εἶναι λέγουσιν. ὁ δὲ ἀμόργινος χιτὼν
καὶ ἀμοργὶς ἐκαλεῖτο. This last assertion is, however, erroneous,
as appears from Aristophanes, *Lysistr.* 735, 737, and the Scholion thereon : τῆς λινοκαλάμης. ἔστι δὲ ἡ ἀμοργὶς ὅμοιον ἀλεπί-
στῳ λίνῳ. The material was exported raw, and manufactured
abroad.

The history of the silk manufacture is enveloped in still greater
obscurity, and the writers on the subject deal in the most extravagant assertions. With regard to early times this need excite no
surprise, considering the distance of the country that produced the
material, and the fables which the silk-dealers purposely spread
abroad. See Voss, ad Virg. *Georg.* ii. 121. But it is strange
that the Macedonian conquest did not introduce more accurate
information. Aristotle, it is true, appears to be acquainted with
the species (*Bombyx mori*, Linn.) by which the silk is produced ;
but from his account of its metamorphoses, and his description of
the larva, it would appear that he knew nothing about the insect
from personal observation. He says, *Hist. Anim.* v. 17 : ἐκ δέ
τινος σκώληκος μεγάλου, ὃς ἔχει οἷον κέρατα καὶ διαφέρει τῶν
ἄλλων, γίγνεται τὸ πρῶτον μὲν μεταβαλόντος τοῦ σκώληκος κάμπη,

ἔπειτα βομβύλιος, ἐκ δὲ τούτου νεκύδαλος· ἐν ἓξ δὲ μησὶ μετα-
βάλλει ταύτας τὰς μορφὰς πάσας. Ἐκ τούτου τοῦ ζώου καὶ τὰ
βομβύκια ἀναλύουσι τῶν γυναικῶν τινες ἀναπηνιζόμεναι κἄπειτα
ὑφαίνουσι. Πρώτη δὲ λέγεται ὑφῆναι ἐν Κῷ Παμφίλου Πλάτεω
θυγάτηρ. Pliny, *Nat. Hist.* vi. 17, 20, and xi. 22, 23, has merely
reproduced Aristotle's account, with the addition of a few blunders
from other sources; while Strabo, xv. 1, 21, follows Nearchus, and
gravely states that silk came ἔκ τινων φλοιῶν ξαινομένης βύσσου.
The traditions followed by Pausanias, vi. 26, 4, and Eustathius,
ad Dionys. Perieg. 753, are still more absurd. The latter takes
σηρικὰ to be a different thing from silk, and Pollux, vii. 76,
fancies it was made from something resembling spiders' webs.

Silk came both in a raw and manufactured state to the West;
and in the latter case, perhaps, was called σηρικά. By far the
larger quantity, however, was imported in a raw condition, and
was then denominated μέταξα. Procop. *Bell. Pers.* i. 20; *Bell.
Goth.* iv. 17. Cf. Hesychius, s. v. Σῆρες. The cocoons, on arrival, were first unwound (according to Aristotle on the isle of
Cos), and the βομβύκινα were then woven from the thread. The
obscurity of Aristotle's words, ἀναλύουσιν ἀναπηνιζόμεναι κἄπειτα
ὑφαίνουσι, and still more of Pliny's, vi. 17, 20, 'unde geminus
feminis labor, redordiendi fila rursumque texendi,' has given rise
to the erroneous notion that the webs, already finished, were again
unravelled. Forster, *de Bysso Ant.* 16, shares in this error. The
word ἀναλύειν refers only to the cocoons, as is correctly remarked
by Salmasius and Schneider.

In all probability silken garments were not used in Greece till
a late period, but the Asiatics wore them from the earliest times;
for the ἐσθῆτες Μηδικαὶ, which Herodotus (iii. 84, vii. 116) mentions as gifts of honour, were certainly of silk, as Procopius expressly states: *Bell. Pers.* i. 20: (μέταξα) ἐξ ἧς εἰώθεσαν τὴν ἐσθῆτα ἐργάζεσθαι, ἣν πάλαι μὲν Ἕλληνες Μηδικὴν ἐκάλουν, τὰ δὲ νῦν
σηρικὴν ὀνομάζουσιν. In Aristotle's time the manufacture was
still very limited in Greece; for his words are, ἔνιαι τῶν γυναικῶν. This, to be sure, does not prove that silk dresses were not
imported; but the silence of the writers of the time, and the
enormous price which the article maintained at a later period,
shows that its use must have been extremely limited. In after
times silk chitons even are mentioned. Alciphr. *Epist.* i. 39:

βόμβυξ δ' ἦν τὸ χιτώνιον. Cf. *Gallus*, p. 442 ; and Art. *Bombyx*, in the *Real-Encycl. d. Class Alterth.*

It cannot therefore be doubted that the notorious Coän robes were a gauze-like silk fabric ; but the εἵματα διαφανῆ, often alluded to at an earlier period, must have been of another material, βύσσια or ἀμόργινα. See Aristoph. *Lysistr.* 48 : διαφανῆ χιτώνια. Philemon, Fragm. (p. 387, Mein.) : ἱμάτια διαφαίνοντα. These were often employed by artists, as through them the contour of the form was pretty visible. See the woodcut, p. 460. Also, *August.* iii. 105 ; *Marm. Oxon.* 5 ; *Mus. Borb.* iii. 36. Lucian, *Amor.* 41, aptly terms such a dress an εἰς πρόφασιν ἐσθής. Cf. Hippolochus, apud Athen. iv. p. 129 : εἰσβάλλουσιν αὐλητρίδες καὶ μουσουργοὶ καὶ σαμβυκίστριαί τινες 'Ρόδιαι, ἐμοὶ μὲν γυμναὶ δοκῶ, πλὴν ἔλεγόν τινες αὐτὰς ἔχειν χιτῶνας.

The manufacture of asbestos fabrics at Carystos in Euboea may be mentioned as a curiosity. Strabo, x. 1, 6 ; Steph. Byz. s. v. Κάρυστος. Clothes of such a material were never actually worn.

Furs were not required, on account of the mildness of the climate, and indeed are scarcely mentioned. Athenæus, v. p. 220, tells a story of a sophist who used to wear a sheep-skin. Cf. Böttig. *Vasengem.* iii. p. 186 ; and the derivation of the name Λοκροὶ 'Οζολαὶ, given by Pausanias, x. 38, 1 ; see also Philostr. *Vit. Apollon.* i. 2.

Chitons of leather are mentioned by Pollux, vii. 70 : καὶ σκύτινοι δὲ ἦσαν ἐσθῆτες καὶ χιτὼν ἐκ δέρματος. In the time of Pausanias the poorer classes in Euboea and Phocis wore chitons of hogs' hides. Pausan. viii. 1, 2 : χιτῶνας τους ἐκ τῶν δερμάτων τῶν ὑῶν, οἷς καὶ νῦν περί τε Εὔβοιαν ἔτι χρῶνται καὶ ἐν τῇ Φωκίδι, ὁπόσοι βίου σπανίζουσιν.

The next enquiry is as to the colour of the dresses. In the first place we must protest against the very prevalent notion that in the rank of the free burghers, and indeed among all respectable females, with few exceptions, nothing but white was worn. This assertion has been repeatedly made by Böttiger ; he affirms that ' so long as the ancient Hellenic world, and, later, Rome, kept free from admixture with the barbarians,—which of course was not the case under the later Roman emperors,—white was the prevailing colour worn by the respectable females and among

the higher classes, and at Athens purple and other colours were
even considered the marks of immodest women.' *Kl. Schr.*
iii. p. 44. In one of his latest essays, however, he states his
views in a materially modified form. He there says, 'Though
the Greek women unquestionably wore coloured garments, and,
as is clear from the pictures of Polygnotus, often wore dresses of
yellow, and of variable colours, yet these are very different from
stripes and flaring patterns.' *Kl. Schr.* i. p. 293. This more
recent opinion is certainly that which will best bear examination.
On this subject we read in Pollux, vii. 55 : αἱ δὲ ἀπὸ χρωμάτων
ἐσθῆτες καλούμεναι, ἁλουργὶς, πορφυρὶς, φοινικὶς καὶ φοινικοῦς χιτὼν, βατραχίς. αὗται μὲν ἀνδρῶν. Γυναικῶν δὲ, κροκωτὸς, κρο-
κώτιον, παραλουργὶς, ὀμφάκινον. τούτῳ δὲ τῷ χρώματι καὶ ᾽Αλέξ-
ανδρον ἥδεσθαι λέγουσι, τὸ δὲ ὑδροβαφὲς εἴη ἂν ἱμάτιον, ὃ νῦν
ψυχροβαφὲς καλοῦσιν. ἔστι δὲ καὶ κίλλιον ἐσθῆτος χρῶμα, τὸ
νῦν ὀνάγρινον καλούμενον. καὶ κίλλον γὰρ τὸν ὄνον οἱ Δωριεῖς,
καὶ κιλλακτῆρα τὸν ὀνηλάτην. φαιὸν δὲ καὶ μέλαν ἀλλήλοις ἐστὶν
ἐγγύς. καὶ τὸ κοκκοβαφὲς δὲ καλεῖται ἀπὸ τοῦ χρώματος. Here
there is an express distinction drawn between those colours which
were worn by the men, and those which were confined to the
women. In another place the same writer mentions the colours
appropriated to particular characters on the stage ; and we should
bear in mind that comedy, especially the new, was an imitation
of the manners of ordinary life. Poll. iv. 118 : κωμικὴ δὲ ἐσθὴς
ἐξωμίς. ἔστι δὲ χιτὼν λευκὸς ἄσημος ... γερόντων δὲ φόρημα ἱμάτιον,
καμπύλη · φοινικὶς ἢ μελαμπόρφυρον ἱμάτιον, φόρημα νεωτέρων.
πήρα, βακτηρία, διφθέρα, ἐπὶ τῶν ἀγροίκων. καὶ πορφυρᾷ δὲ
ἐσθῆτι ἐχρῶντο οἱ νεανίσκοι. οἱ δὲ παράσιτοι μελαίνῃ ἢ φαιᾷ ...
῾Η δὲ γυναικῶν ἐσθὴς κωμικῶν, ἡ μὲν τῶν γραῶν μηλίνη, ἢ ἀερίνη,
πλὴν ἱερειῶν · ταύταις δὲ λευκή · ... ἡ δὲ τῶν νέων λευκὴ ἢ βυσσίνη.
ἐπικλήρων δὲ λευκὴ, κροσσωτή. πορνοβοσκοὶ δὲ χιτῶνι βαπτῷ καὶ
ἀνθεινῷ περιβολαίῳ ἐνδέδυνται, κ.τ.λ. From this passage it must
not be inferred that because a young man, in contrast to a γέρων,
wears a dark-coloured garment, μελαμπόρφυρον, and a lad a bright
purple one, πορφυρᾷ ἐσθὴς, that therefore they were always so
clad ; on the contrary, we only conclude that a coloured robe was
not unusual in common life among the higher orders, or they
would never have thus appeared in one on the stage.

Besides, it would be wonderful if that passion for magnificence

in dress which was so prevalent in Ionia, had not exercised some
influence on the costume of the mother-country. The Ionians
selected remarkably brilliant colours for their attire, though this
certainly was not the case at Athens, at least till a very late
period. See a fragment of Democritus of Ephesus, ap. Athen.
xii. p. 525 : Τὰ δὲ τῶν Ἰώνων ἰοβαφῆ καὶ πορφυρᾶ καὶ κρόκινα
ῥόμβοις ὑφαντά. καὶ σαράπεις μήλινοι καὶ πορφυροῖ καὶ λευκοὶ,
οἱ δὲ ἀλουργεῖς. καὶ καλασίρεις Κορινθιουργεῖς. εἰσὶ δὲ αἱ μὲν
πορφυραῖ τούτων, αἱ δὲ ἰοβαφεῖς, αἱ δὲ ὑακίνθιναι· λάβοι δ' ἄν τις
καὶ φλογίνας καὶ θαλασσοειδεῖς. There is distinct proof, moreover,
that in the mother-country the use of coloured garments partially
prevailed, even among the men. Thus there must be some meaning in the line in Aristoph. *Plut.* 533 :

οὔθ' ἱματίων βαπτῶν δαπάναις κοσμῆσαι ποικιλομόρφων.

See also Xenoph. *Œcon.* 10, 3 : ἐπιδεικνύς γε ἀργύριον κίβδηλον
καὶ ὅρμους ὑποξύλους, καὶ πορφυρίδας ἐξιτήλους φαίην ἀληθινὰς
εἶναι. Plutarch, *de Tranq. An.* 10 : ἡ πορφύρα τριῶν μνῶν. The
reply of Socrates shows that a garment is here meant. Occasionally we even meet with notices of the dress of individuals.
Thus Chamæleon, ap. Athen. ix. p. 374, says of the comedian
Anaxandrides : ἐφόρει ἀλουργίδα καὶ κράσπεδα χρυσᾶ. See Ælian,
Var. Hist. xii. 32 : Ἐμπεδοκλῆς δὲ ὁ Ἀκραγαντῖνος ἀλουργεῖ
ἐχρήσατο, καὶ ὑποδήμασι χαλκοῖς. Ἱππίαν δὲ καὶ Γοργίαν ἐν
πορφυραῖς ἐσθῆσι προϊέναι διαρρεῖ λόγος. Cf. *Ib.* xii. 11 ; Athen
xii. p. 543. In these passages, it is true, such coloured clothes
are mentioned as something remarkable; and no doubt it was
not everybody that wore them, but they certainly were used on
festive occasions, and doubtless frequently by ἁβροδίαιτοι. See
Lucian, *Bis Accus.* 17 : ἀφήρει τε τοὺς στεφάνους . . . καὶ ἐπὶ τῇ
πορφυρίδι ἠσχύνετο. The whole passage may be referred to as
giving a striking picture of an Athenian dandy.

Dark-coloured chitons appear to have been not at all unusual
See especially a fragment of Antiphanes, apud Athen. xii. p. 544,
where the costume of the academicians is described :

λευκὴ χλανὶς, φαιὸς χιτωνίσκος καλὸς,
πιλίδιον ἁπαλὸν, εὔρυθμος βακτηρία,
βαιὰ τράπεζα. τί μακρὰ δεῖ λέγειν ; ὅλως
αὐτὴν ὁρᾶν γὰρ τὴν Ἀκαδημείαν δοκῶ.

Here the φαιὸς χιτωνίσκος is certainly not black, but either

brown, as manufactured from the undyed wool of the brown
sheep, or else grey. See Phot. *Lex.* p. 637 : χρῶμα σύνθετον ἐκ
μέλανος καὶ λευκοῦ · ἤγουν μύϊνον. Cf. Suidas, s. v. φαιός.

Coloured dresses were prevalent to a far greater extent among
the female sex. In theory, no doubt, white was considered the
most becoming for a discreet and modest woman. See Phintys,
apud Stob. *Tit.* lxxiv. 61 : περὶ δὲ τῶ κόσμω τῶ περὶ τὸ σῶμα
δοκεῖ μοι οὕτως. Δεῖ λευχείμονα ἤμεν καὶ ἀπλοϊκὰν, καὶ ἀπερίσ·
σευτον. Ἐσεῖται δὲ τοῦτο, αἴκα μὴ διαφανέεσσι, μηδὲ διαποικίλοις,
μηδὲ ἀπὸ βέμβικος ὑφασμένοις χρᾶται τοῖς περὶ τὸ σῶμα, ἀλλὰ
μετρίοις καὶ λευκοχρωμάτοις. Evidently enough this advice is
directed against the prevailing practice. What is related of
Polygnotus by Pliny, *Nat. Hist.* xxxv 9, 35, ' primus mulieres
lucida veste pinxit,' may indicate a change in attire which took
place after the Persian war, or rather perhaps an improvement in
the art of painting and the preparation of pigments; and it is
certain that the painter would never have ventured on this step,
if, as Böttiger supposes, coloured clothes had been at Athens the
legal distinction of hetæræ ; nor does it follow, because he was
the first to paint women in brilliant colours, that his predecessors
had attired their females in white only. The polychromatic vase-
paintings and terracottas published by Stackelberg, in his *Gräber
der Hellenen,* which represent figures from the life, are the more
valuable, inasmuch as they corroborate, in the most striking
manner, many of the statements made by Pollux. Though in
most instances the colours have been much faded by age, yet
the ground tone still remains ; and the fact that white as well as
coloured chitons and himatia occur, demonstrates that the scenes
are from every-day life. Thus in Plate 44, 2, are represented two
female figures, one of whom wears a dark upper garment (ἀμπεχόνη) with a white border, over a pale yellow sleeved-chiton.
The latter, which looks like nankeen, is probably of byssus.
Cf. Philostr. *Vit. Apollon.* ii. 20 : καὶ ἠσθῆναι τῇ βύσσῳ φησὶν ὁ
Ἀπολλώνιος, ἐπειδὴ ἔοικε φαιῷ τρίβωνι. This colour frequently
occurs in women's dress. The himation, with its white border,
is what is called περίλευκον by Pollux, vii. 51 : τὰ δὲ περίλευκα
τοὐναντίον εἴη ἂν ὕφασμα ἐκ πορφύρας ἢ ἄλλου χρώματος, ἐν τῷ
περιδρόμῳ λευκὸν ἐνυφασμένον. The second figure is in a gold-
brown diploïs, also with a white edging. In Pl. 45, 1, are seen

two females, one of whom wears a white chiton with sleeves, under a red himation ; while the second is wrapped in a red mantle. Pl. 46, 2, is especially interesting. One of the women who stand at the tomb is clad in an ample blue cloak, which entirely conceals the under garment; the other wears a short and close-fitting purple chiton, without sleeves, the seam of which is adorned with a tolerably broad border of yellow. This border consists of upright indentations, which are seen elsewhere on monochromatic vase-paintings ; see Tischbein, *Engrav.* i. 15 ; Millin. *Peint.* i. 52, 61. But under this dress the woman seems to have also a chitonion of the usual yellow colour, the sleeves of which are visible. On these poly-chromatic *lecythæ* there are also representations of men in coloured garments ; for instance in Pl. 45, 2, is seen a young man in a red cherry-coloured chlamys; and the shades in Charon's bark wear red himatia. See Pl. 48. Charon's exomis, however, is grey or brown, which was the usual colour for sailors. Plaut. *Mil.* iv. 4, 43 :

Palliolum habeas ferrugineum ; nam is colos thalassicu'st.

Indeed the garb of the working classes was always dark-coloured. Artemidor. *Oneirocr.* ii. 3, p. 132 : οὐ γὰρ πρὸς ἔργῳ ὄντες οἱ ἄνθρωποι, καὶ μάλιστα οἱ τὰς βαναύσους τέχνας ἐργαζόμενοι λευ-κοῖς ἱματίοις χρῶνται. The terracottas given in Stackelberg's work go also to show that white was by no means the only colour worn either by men or women, and that perhaps it was only the very staring and brilliant tints, ἀνθεινὰ χρώματα, which were avoided by sober-minded and respectable women; this view, moreover, is excellently borne out by Artemidor. *Oneirocr.* ii. 3, p. 135 : Γυναικὶ δὲ ποικίλη καὶ ἀνθηρὰ ἐσθὴς συμφέρει, μάλιστα δὲ ἑταίρᾳ καὶ πλουσίᾳ· ἡ μὲν γὰρ διὰ τὴν ἐργασίαν, ἡ δὲ διὰ τὴν τρυφὴν ἀνθηραῖς ἐσθῆσι χρῶνται.

It would seem from Pollux, iv. 120, that damsels belonging to the upper classes wore only the white or yellowish chiton, for he says : ἡ δὲ τῶν νέων (ἐσθὴς) λευκὴ ἢ βυσσίνη. He does not here refer to the ἀμπεχόνη, a garment which belongs indeed more to the matrons than the maidens, who, being rarely abroad, did not require it. It is strange that he alludes to no particular costume for the hetæræ. He mentions, as suitable to women, first, the κροκωτὸς (χιτὼν), probably a chiton with a saffron-coloured diploïdion. See Aristoph. *Eccl.* 331 :

τῆς γυναικὸς ἐξελήλυθα
τὸ κροκωτίδιον ἀμπισχόμενος, οὑνδί τοι

Cf. Id. *Thesmoph.* 253 : τὸν κροκωτὸν πρῶτον ἐνδύου λαβών.
Pollux gives an erroneous explanation of this word : he says, ὁ δὲ
κροκωτὸς ἱμάτιον, having manifestly in view Aristoph. *Ranæ*, 46 ;
but in that passage there is not the slightest allusion to an
himation. The κροκωτὸς was also occasionally worn by men,
though of course not as a diploïs. Cf. Suidas, s. v. κροκωτὸς, and
Diog. Laert. vii. 169. It certainly was never of silk, as is affirmed
by the Scholiasts to Aristoph. *Ranæ*, 46.

The other colours mentioned by Pollux are ὀμφάκινον, perhaps
olive-green ; μήλινον, apple-green or yellow ; ἀέρινος, not only
azure, but a variety of tints, even to a bright grey. There is
much more obscurity about the ὑδροβαφὲς, which Pollux, doubtingly, compares with ψυχροβαφές. If with this we compare the
ὑδάτινα βράκη in Theocr. xxviii. 11, and the ὑδατόκλυστα of Plutarch, *Quæst. Rom.* 26, it would almost seem that we are to suppose
watered cloth (moiré) to be meant, and the same sort of thing is
probably intended by the *undulata vestis* of Pliny, *Nat. Hist.* viii.
48, 74, and the *cumatile* (κυματῶδες) of Plautus, *Epid.* ii. 2, 49.

The ornaments of the chiton may be divided into horizontal
borders, vertical stripes, figures irregularly embroidered, and
lastly, regular patterns running over the whole garment. The first
kind of ornament ran along the bottom edge, or round the hole
for the neck, and consisted either of simple coloured stripes or of
ornamental patterns. They were called πέζαι. Poll. vii. 62 : αἱ
δὲ παρὰ τὰς ὤας παρυφαὶ καλοῦνται πέζαι καὶ πεζίδες, καὶ περί-
πεζα τὰ οὕτω παρυφασμένα. These stripes also were apparently
many-coloured. The diploïdion of the figure of Νίκη, on p. 422,
has a narrow blue stripe close to the lower edge, and above that
a broader one of red ; probably too it was shaded off. See a fragment of Menander, apud Athen. ii. p. 163 :

> τῆς σκιᾶς τὴν πορφύραν
> πρῶτον ἐνυφαίνουσ᾽ · εἶτα μετὰ τὴν πορφύραν
> τοῦτ᾽ ἔστιν, οὐδὲ λευκὸν, οὐ ἐ πορφύρα,
> ἀλλ᾽ ὥσπερ αὐγὴ τῆς κρόκης κεκραμένη.

These borders were usually woven in, but sometimes were sewn
on, and, when faded, replaced by new ones. Poll. vii. 64 : περι-
ὖσαι δὲ ἔλεγον τῶν παλαιῶν ἱματίων τὰς ὤας ἀφελόντα καινὰς
παραθεῖναι. Phot. *Lex.* p. 405 : τὸ ἀπολῆγον τοῦ χιτῶνος, ὃ
ἡμεῖς ὦαν (sic) λέγομεν · πρότερον γὰρ ὑπὲρ τοῦ μὴ τρίβεσθαι
δέρμα προβάτων προσέρραπτον. (?)

The vertical stripes frequently appear on the two sides of the
chiton, where the πτέρυγες are sewn together, and are therefore
always double.   They are also often seen in front, also doubled,
and are either on the chiton, and reach down to the feet, or are
only on the diploïdion.   See the woodcuts on pp. 423, 424, 426 ;
also Tischbein, *Engrav.* i. 4.   The general name for these stripes
was ῥάβδοι or πάρυφοι.   Poll. vii. 53 : αἱ μέντοι ἐν τοῖς χιτῶσι
πορφυραῖ ῥάβδοι πάρυφοι καλοῦνται.   Cf. Id. vii. 65 ; and Hesychius, s. v. Ὀχθοιβοι, which he supposes to mean these stripes,
although this seems a mistake.   In Millin. *Peint. des Vases Gr.* i.
Pl. 38, may be seen a chiton with long sleeves reaching to the
hand, and which has a singular ornament.   An arabesque runs
from the breast to the lower seam, and a similar one passes down
the whole length of the sleeve.   Such sleeve-ornaments also occur
on men's chitons, being perhaps borrowed from the tragic costume.
See Tischbein, *Engrav.* i. 3.

On the himatia also of both men and women are to be seen
similar borders, which sometimes run right round, and sometimes
appear to be only on the two seamed sides of the oblong cloth.   To
the former kind Pollux refers the words περίνησα and ἔγκυκλον.
The second is said by Hesychius to be comprehended under the
dubious term παράπηχυ.   Cf. Phot. *Lex.* p. 388.   Pollux seems
to assign a different signification to this word.   He says, vii. 53 :
τὸ δὲ παράπηχυ ἱμάτιον ἦν τι λευκὸν πῆχυν πορφυροῦν ἔχον
παρυφασμένον.   τὸ δὲ παρυφὲς καὶ παραλουργὲς τὸ ἑκατέρωθεν
ἔχον παρυφασμένην πορφύραν.   Ἴωνες δὲ αὐτὸ καλοῦσι πηχυαλές.

Fringes also, κροσσοί, θύσανοι, were appended to the garments,
and tassels at the corners, as in the Roman toga ; these were not
for ornament merely, but for the purpose of keeping down the
dress by their weight.   Poll. vii. 64 ; iv. 120.

The third class of ornaments consisted of flowers, stars, and so
forth, embroidered or woven in, and scattered all over the chiton,
which was then called χιτὼν κατάστικτος.   Poll. vii. 55 : ὁ δὲ
κατάστικτος χιτών ἐστιν ὁ ἔχων ζῶα ἢ ἄνθη ἐνυφασμένα.   καὶ
ζωωτὸς δὲ χιτὼν ἐκαλεῖτο καὶ ζωδιωτός.   Plato, *de Republ.* viii.
p. 557 : ἱμάτιον ποικίλον, πᾶσιν ἄνθεσι πεποικιλμένον.   These are
very commonly represented on vases.

Fourthly come the dresses of regular patterns.   In a very
ancient and remarkable vase-painting in Millin. ii. Pl. 61, are

seen two Attic maidens, who are being offered to the Minotaur.
They are enveloped in garments of a chessboard-looking pattern;
which the artist could never have borrowed entirely from his own
invention. A somewhat similar device occurs elsewhere for tur-
bans. See Plaut. *Epid.* ii. 2, 40, where the *vestis impluviata* is
probably something of the sort.

There are but few names of dresses which yet remain to be
mentioned; some of these are of a general import, others are peculiar to the lower classes and the slaves. The word ξυστίς is very
insufficiently explained by Böttiger to mean an embroidered purple
coat. The grammarians give a variety of explanations, such as
ποδῆρες ἔνδυμα and τραγικὸν ἔνδυμα, again, χλανὶς κωμική, ἱμάτιον
πορφυροῦν, ἱππικὸν ἔνδυμα, or λεπτὸν ὕφασμα, κ. τ. λ. See Harpocr.; Hesych.; Phot.; Schol. ad Aristoph. *Nub.* 70; Schol. ad
Theocr. ii. 74. That it was not exclusively an ἔνδυμα, nor belonged merely to the tragic or comic stage, but might also denote
a female robe of state, is evident from Theocr. ii. 74:

> ἐγὼ δέ οἱ ἂ μεγάλοιτος
> ὡμάρτευν, βσσοιο καλὸν σύροισα χιτῶνα
> κἀμφιστειλαμένη τὰν ξυστίδα τὰν Κλεαρίστας.

The name ξυστίς does not refer to the shape at all, but merely to
the material and ornaments. Thus it is correctly observed by
Pollux, vii. 49 : ξυστίς, ἔνδυμά τε ὁμοῦ καὶ περίβλημα, καὶ χιτών.
The best proof of this is that rich coverlets, στρώματα, are also
thus designated. See Poll. vi. 10; x. 42.

The name ἐφεστρίς also refers more to a cloth or coverlet than
to a garment of any particular shape. Hence Pollux, x. 42,
reckons it among the στρώματα, as well as the χλαῖνα, though
this, too, served also as a robe. Nevertheless, it is clear that it
resembled the chlamys, being, like that garment, fastened by a
clasp. The word is used for an himation in Xenophon, *Symp.*
4, 38; but in Lucian, *Dial. Meretr.* ix., it denotes a garment
resembling a chlamys : ἑώρακα δὲ κἀγὼ αὐτὸν ἐφεστρίδα περι-
πόρφυρον ἐμπεπορπημένον. See also Id. *Contempl.* 14; Artemidor.
Oneirocr. ii. 3 : χλαμὺς, ἣν ἔνιοι μανδύην, οἱ δὲ ἐφεστρίδα, οἱ δὲ
βίρρον καλοῦσι. In Heliod. *Æthiop.* iii. 6, it is used for the
ἀμπεχόνη of the women. In Agathias, apud Suidas, it is used
both for this, and also for a soldier's chlamys.

The διφθέρα was a coat of skins used by herdsmen and countryfolks. Aristoph. *Nubes*, 71 :

> "Οταν μὲν οὖν τὰς αἶγας ἐκ τοῦ Φελλέω,
> ὥσπερ ὁ πατήρ σου, διφθέραν ἐνημμένος.

Schol. : ποιμενικὸν δὲ περιβόλαιον ἡ διφθέρα. Ἀττικοὶ δὲ λέγουσιν, ἣν νῦν ἰσάλην καλοῦμεν. ἔστι δὲ ἐκ δέρματος. It could be drawn over the head. Poll. vii. 70: (Περὶ σκυτίνων ἐσθήτων) διφθέρα δὲ στεγανὸς χιτὼν ἐπίκρανον ἔχων. See Aristoph. *Vesp.* 444; Plato, *Crit.* p. 53; Lucian, *Tim.* 12. A herdsman wearing the διφθέρα is represented in the *Mus. Pio-Clem.* iii. 34. Probably the σισύρα was something similar, but serving more as an himation than a chiton. It was also a κώδιον, see Aristoph. *Eccles.* 418, and it appears to have been mostly used as a coverlet, as was shown in Note 8 to Scene VIII. It also served the purpose of a cloak; and sometimes was not a skin, but was made of coarse thick cloth. Lucian, *Rhet. Præc.* 16 : ἡ πορφύρα μόνον ἔστω καλὴ καὶ εὐανθὴς, κἂν σισύρα τῶν παχειῶν τὸ ἱμάτιον ᾖ. Cf. Longus, *Past.* ii. p. 35.

The κατωνάκη was a dress for slaves, probably used only in the country : it was a chiton of coarse cloth, with the lower hem trimmed with sheep-skin. See Aristoph. *Lysistr.* 1151 ; Athen. vi. p. 271; Poll. vii. 68 ; Müller, *Dorians*, ii. p. 38. The lower orders, and especially seafaring folks, wore a kind of matting, φορμός. Pausan. x. 29, 2 : ὁ δὲ Ἑλπήνωρ ἀμπέχεται φορμὸν ἀντὶ ἐσθῆτος, σύνηθες τοῖς ναύταις φόρημα. There are a number of other names which refer either to trivial variations of attire, or to articles introduced from abroad, but they need not be discussed here, being irrelevant to the general Greek customs.

We will now say a word or two on the head-coverings worn by the men; the women used nothing of the kind, and their nets, cauls, and head-dresses will be treated of in the Excursus on *The Hair and Beard*. The men did not wear any covering on the head, either at the gymnasia or when going about the city. So Anacharsis, in Lucian, *de Gymn.* 16, speaking of the fierceness of the sun, says : τὸν γὰρ πῖλόν μοι ἀφελεῖν οἴκοθεν ἔδοξεν, ὡς μὴ μόνος ἐν ὑμῖν ξενίζοιμι τῷ σχήματι But something of the kind was required in certain trades, and was also worn on journeys. They may be divided into two sorts, hats with brims, and caps with none, though both kinds were known by the common term κυνῆ and πῖλος. The πέτασος is the best known form of the first kind ; it was of Thessalian or Macedonian origin, like the chlamys, and quite appertained to it, and hence was commonly worn by the ephebi and those who appeared in the chlamys. Poll. x. 164 : Τὸ δὲ τῶν ἐφήβων φόρημα πέτασος καὶ χλαμύς. Hesych. Πέτασος, τὸ τῶν ἐφήβων φόρημα. The best illustrations of its use are the reliefs of the Parthenon, and many other monuments. The variations, which are very numerous, always occur in the brim. The ephebi from the Parthenon wear a petasos, the brim of which is bent downwards, and has four arch-shaped cuts, by which means four corners are formed, one of which projects right over the forehead. Another variety is seen on the Bellerophon in Tischbein, *Engrav.* i. 3, where the brim is entire, and bent upwards. The petasos of Hermes has often a very small brim. See Winkelm. iv. Pl. 7. a. But the invariable characteristic of all is the round arched crown. See the figure of Œdipus, p. 420. In Sophocl. *Œd. Col.* 315, Ismene wears such a hat, ἡλιοστερὴς κυνῆ Θεσσαλίς : and the only explanation of a female wearing such an article may be found in the equally unusual apparition of a virgin on such a journey. Cf. Böttiger, *Furienmaske*, p. 123.

The καυσία, also Macedonian in its origin, much resembled the petasos, only that it had a higher crown, flat at the top, and a horizontal brim, quite round, and often very broad. Tischbein, *Engrav.* i. 10. Probably the Arcadian κυνῆ resembled it. Böttiger erroneously supposes that this κυνῆ had a kind of shade, παραπέτασμα, on the brim, which was bent downwards. The mistake appears to have arisen from a misconception of Aristoph. *Aves*, 1202. Iris no doubt had a rainbow round her head, when she appeared on the stage, and this ring may have resembled the shade of an Arcadian sombrero. Concerning the καυσία, see Müller, *Ueber die Makedoner*, p. 48.

The cap-shaped coverings for the head vary but little ; they were generally semi-oval in shape. They were worn by the boatmen, and consequently Charon is thus represented. See the woodcut on p. 416; also Stackelberg, *Die Gräber der Hell.* Pl. 47 and 48. The same is also the case with Odysseus and Cadmos ; Millingen, *Uned. Mon.* i. 27. The artisans also wore them, and therefore Hephæstos usually has one; Hirt, *Bilderb.* Pl. vi. 1, 2 ;

Terracottas in the Brit. Mus. 10. The workmen of the Argo wear
a similar cap with a somewhat broad rim running round it.

The colour of these hats and caps was various. That of
Charon in the preceding woodcut should be red; while Plautus,
Mil. iv. 4, 42, mentions a *causia ferruginea* among the *ornatus
nauclericus*. On another lecythos in Stackelberg (Pl. 45, 2), a
young man in a chlamys wears a white petasos with red rim.
In Macedonia a purple καυσία was a mark of honour, bestowed
by kings. Plutarch, *Eumen.* 8: Ἐξῆν γὰρ Εὐμένει καὶ καυσίας
ἁλουργεῖς καὶ χλαμύδας διανέμειν, ἥτις ἦν δωρεὰ βασιλικωτάτη
παρὰ Μακεδόσι. Cf. Id. *Demetr.* 41. Occasionally, and especially
in early times, the material may have been leather; afterwards it
was generally felt, and hence all head-coverings go by the name of
πῖλοι. On this subject see Mongèz, *sur les Vêtemens des Anciens.
Mém. de l'Institut. Royal*, iv.; Clarac, *Musée de Sculpt.* ii. p. 49;
and *Gallus.* p. 408

EXCURSUS II. TO SCENE XI.

THE SHOES.

IN-DOORS the Greeks always went about unshod, and even when abroad the use of a foot-covering was by no means universal. Already in the heroic ages we find persons putting on the πέδιλα just before going out, not on a journey, but for a common walk. See *Iliad*, ii. 44; *Odyss.* ii. 4; xvii. 2. At a later period the custom continued the same. Shoes were only worn to protect the feet from injury in the street: at home they were never used, and at a stranger's were put off before reclining to the meal. See Excursus on *The Meals*, p. 318. Effeminate persons, in winter-time, may possibly have covered their feet with something at home; but this was not the rule; and many even went barefoot out of doors both in summer and winter. Plato, *de Republ.* ii. p. 372; Lucian, *Navig.* 1. At Sparta, in the case of younger persons, this was actually compulsory by law. Xenoph. *de Republ. Laced.* 2, 3: Ἀντί γε μὴν τοῦ ἁπαλύνειν τοὺς πόδας ὑποδήμασιν ἔταξεν, ἀνυποδησίᾳ κρατύνειν, νομίζων, εἰ τοῦτο ἀσκήσειαν, πολὺ μὲν ῥᾷον ἂν ὀρθιάδε βαίνειν, ἀσφαλέστερον δὲ πρανῆ καταβαίνειν. Plato, *Leg.* i. p. 633. And even aged people did the same. Ælian, *Var. Hist.* vii. 13: Ἀγησίλαος ὁ Λακεδαιμόνιος γέρων ἤδη ὢν ἀνυπόδητος πολλάκις καὶ ἀχίτων προῄει . . . καὶ ταῦτα ἑωθινὸς ἐν ὥρᾳ χειμερίῳ. At Athens, too, it was usual for those of simple habits never to wear anything on the feet, except on special occasions, when propriety demanded it. Plato, *Symp.* p. 220; cf. Xenoph. *Mem.* i. 6, 2. Of this Socrates was by no means a solitary instance, and it was also done by persons of consequence and wealth, such as Lycurgus the orator; Plutarch *Dec. Or. Vit.* iv. p. 379: ὑπεδέδετο ταῖς ἀναγκαίαις ἡμέραις. So also Phocion; Plutarch, *Phoc.* 4. It was a special mark of the stricter philosophic sects, and, as such, affected by the later beard-philosophers. Lucian, *Icaromen.* 31.

With these exceptions, it was usual to wear sandals or some such thing out of doors; and masters also gave them to their slaves, at least in winter-time. See Aristoph. *Vespæ*, 448.

In spite of numberless varieties of form, the foot-coverings of the Greeks may be divided into two chief classes, sandals and shoes. But there are so many transition forms, that a complete set of gradations may be adduced, from the simple sandal up to the quasi-boot or endromis. Sandals bound under the foot are the genuine ὑποδήματα; and the often-repeated assertion of Salmasius (ad Tertull. *de Pallio*, p. 387), that ὑπόδημα denotes the regular shoe, and σανδάλιον the sandal, is entirely erroneous. The passage on this subject in Pollux, vii. 84, stood in the old editions: λέγοις δ' ἂν καὶ ὑποδήματα κοῖλα, βαθέα, εἰς μέσην τὴν κνήμην ἀνήκοντα. τὰ δὲ οὐκ οἶδα εἰ μόνον ἀποχρῶι ἐστιν εἰπεῖν ὑποδήματα. It has, however, been thus corrected by Kühn from the MSS.: τὰ δὲ οὐ (μὴ) κοῖλα αὐτὸ μόνον ἀποχρῶν ἐστιν εἰπεῖν ὑποδήματα.

The σανδάλιον or σάνδαλον is the first transition form to the shoes which covered the upper part of the foot. For it had a thong across the toes, which grew into a small upper leather, and was called ζυγὸς or ζυγόν. Aristoph. *Lysistr.* 416:

> Ὦ σκυτοτόμε τῆς μου γυναικὸς τοῦ ποδὸς
> τὸ δακτυλίδιον πιέζει τὸ ζυγὸν,
> ἄθ' ἁπαλὸν ὄν· τοῦτ' οὖν σὺ τῆς μεσημβρίας
> ἐλθὼν χάλασον, ὅπως ἂν εὐρυτέρως ἔχῃ.

Scholiast: μέρος τοῦ σανδαλίου· ... ζυγὸς γὰρ καλεῖται ὁ περικεί-μενος τοῖς γυναικείοις σανδαλίοις ἱμᾶς κατὰ τοὺς δακτύλους πρὸς τὸ συνέχειν ἐξαγόμενον τὸν πόδα. So also Hesychius, and Pollux, vii. 81. Without this ζυγὸν the sandal was no σανδάλιον; and hence Böttiger has wrongly interpreted a passage in Strabo, vi. 1, 8: τινὰς δὲ καὶ σανδάλια ὑποδουμένας ἄζυγα, τὸ μὲν ὑψηλὸν, τὸ δὲ ταπεινόν. The word ἄζυγα he explains, 'not having thongs over the feet;' whereas it evidently means, odd, not pairs, one of the sandals being high, another low. It is evident that this ζυγὸν was not a mere thong over the toes, because we read of sandals embroidered and ornamented even with gold. See Cephisodorus, apud Poll. vii. 87:

> σανδάλιά τε τῶν λεπτοσχιδῶν,
> ἐφ' οἷς τὰ χρυσᾶ ταῦτ' ἔπεστιν ἄνθεμα.

Also Clem. Alex. *Pæd.* ii. 11: Αἰσχρὰ γοῦν ἀληθῶς τὰ σανδάλια ἐκεῖνα, ἐφ' οἷς ἐστι τὰ χρυσᾶ ἀναθέματα (l. ἄνθεμα). In this respect the sandal was like a slipper; but it was fastened with thongs beside. Thus Pollux, vii. 92, says of the Tyrrhenian sandals: οἱ δὲ ἱμάντες ἐπίχρυσοι. σανδάλιον γὰρ ἦν. Generally, however, σανδάλια are appropriated to the women. See Hesychius: Σανδάλια, σάνδαλα, γυναικεῖα ὑποδήματα, ἃ καὶ βλαύτια. Hence it is clear that σανδάλια could not have been mere *sandals*, for these were worn by men also.

Mere sandals, made of cow's hide, are mentioned by Homer, *Odyss.* xiv. 24 ; and Hesiod, *Op.* 542 ; in later times such may have been worn by women in the house, or by the lower classes; but a stronger double-soled kind was worn on going out. See Winkelm. v. p. 41. Not only leather was employed, but cork was sometimes used to form the intermediate thickness of the sole. Concerning the manifold ways of fastening them, see *Gallus*, p. 425. The most usual plan was for a thong to go between the great and second toe, being fastened by a heart or leaf-shaped *fibula* to two side straps, or to another, which ran along the instep, and was then fastened to the back strap. Instead of thongs the poorer classes used σπάρτια, i.e. cords of twisted σπάρτος. See Athen. v. p. 220 : τὰ ὑποδήματα σπαρτίοις ἐνημμένον σαπροῖς. The thongs, however, were often so multiplied as to cover not only the foot, but the lower part of the leg up to the calf. See Millingen, *Peint. d. Vas.* Pl. 51 ; *Mus. Borb.* vii. 19. These, which were probably called ῥαΐδια, in some sort resembled shoes or boots with holes pierced in them, and therefore form a transition to the regular shoes, κοῖλα ὑποδήματα. These were made on a last, καλόπους, which was different, so as to suit each foot. They were worn both by men and women, and were like our high shoes, reaching to the ankle, and having a slit over the instep. See Millingen, *Peint. d. Vas.* Pl. 39 ; *Pitt. d'Ercol.* i. 13–28 ; *Mus. Borb.* vii. 20, 23–40.

The very numerous varieties of form mentioned by Pollux are difficult to specify and distinguish, owing to the brevity with which they are noticed. In this place we can only mention a few of the kinds which were most generally worn. The κρηπὶς is one of those names whose explanation is the most dubious. From the other signification of the word it might be supposed to mean a mere sole ; and this derives additional probability from the name being also applied to a kind of cake, which in form probably resembled this ὑπόδημα. Athen. xiv. p. 645 : Ἐμπέπτας . . . πύρινος ἄρτος κοῖλος καὶ σύμμετρος, ὅμοιος ταῖς λεγομέ-

ναις κρηπῖσιν, εἰς ἃς ἐντίθεται τὰ διὰ τοῦ τυροῦ σκευαζόμενα
πλακούντια. See also Poll. vi. 77. Cf. Suidas and Hesychius.
Athenæus also distinguishes between the κρηπὶς and the ὑπόδημα.
He says, xiv. p. 621 : καὶ τὸ μὲν παλαιὸν ὑποδήμασιν ἐχρῆτο,
ὥς φησιν ὁ Ἀριστοκλῆς, νῦν δὲ κρηπῖσι. Cf. Poll. vii. 91 : ἦν
δέ τι ὑπόδημα καὶ ὀπισθοκρηπίς. From these passages the κρηπὶς would appear to have been a high sandal, differing from the
simpler ὑπόδημα in having several thicknesses ; and in Pollux
it seems to be a sandal with a higher heel than usual. With
these accounts it is difficult to reconcile what is said of the κόλαξ
by Theophrastus, *Char.* 2 : καὶ συνωνούμενος δὲ κρηπῖδας τὸν πόδα
φῆσαι εἶναι εὐρυθμότερον τοῦ ὑποδήματος. Most likely it was
a sort of half-shoe, which only covered the fore-part of the foot,
and was fastened behind with thongs. See also Heliod. *Æthiop.*
iii. 3 : κρηπὶς μὲν αὐτοῖς ἱμάντι φοινικῷ διάπλοκος ὑπὲρ ἀστρά-
γαλον ἐσφίγγετο. Poll. vii. 85 : κρηπῖδες, τὸ μὲν φόρημα στρα-
τιωτικόν. Cf. Plutarch, *Alex.* 40. We cannot, however, confine
its use to soldiers. The Romans formed out of κρηπὶς the word

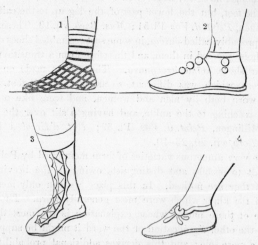

Fig. 1. Foot-covering belonging to a young man, from Tischbein, I. 14. Perhaps the name ῥαΐδια might be applied to it.

Fig. 2. Man's shoe, of a form which very frequently occurs. Millin. II 8.

Fig. 3. Half-boot of a male figure from Millin. II. 69 ; it seems slit down and
laced in front, though the lacing serves only for ornament.

Fig. 4. Woman's shoe, from Millingen, *Peint. d. Vas. Gr.* 39.

crĕpĭdă, which is certainly not equivalent to *solea*, as is assumed
by Heindorf, ad Hor. *Sat.* i. 3, 127. See Cic. *pro Rab.* 10; Liv.
xxix. 19.

Something more definite is known about the ἐμβάδες. They
were real shoes, and must therefore be reckoned among the κοῖλα
ὑποδήματα in a more extended sense. They were worn exclusively by men, as is seen from Aristophanes, *Eccles.* 47, 314 ;
Equit. 872. Also Suidas : ἐμβάς· τὰ ὑποδήματα τὰ ἀνδρεῖα. In
the time of Aristophanes they seem to have been the most usual
kind of common men's shoes, though they were not worn by the
higher classes. See Isæus, *de Dicæog. Her.* p. 94 : καὶ πρὸς τοῖς
ἄλλοις κακοῖς ὀνειδίζει καὶ ἐγκαλεῖ αὐτῷ, ὅτι ἐμβάδας καὶ τριβώνια
φορεῖ, ἀλλ' οὐκ ἀδικῶν, ὅτι ἀφελόμενος αὐτὸν τὰ ὄντα πένητα
πεποίηκεν. This of course refers principally to Athens ; for the
ἐμβὰς was not everywhere the same. Thus Herodotus, i. 195,
tells us that the Babylonians wore ὑποδήματα ἐπιχώρια, παραπλήσια τῇσι Βοιωτίῃσι ἐμβάσι. Pollux derives them from Thrace;
he says, vii. 85 : ἐμβάδες· εὐτελὲς μὲν τὸ ὑπόδημα, Θράκιον δὲ τὸ
εὕρημα· τὴν δὲ ἰδέαν κοθόρνοις ταπεινοῖς ἔοικεν.

The Λακωνικαὶ were also men's shoes, and probably bore some
resemblance to the ἐμβάδες. As the name imports, they originated at Lacedæmon, but were also very much worn in Athens.
Sometimes they are distinguished from the ἐμβάδες, at others they
are confounded with them. See Aristoph. *Vespæ*, 1157 ; *Eccles.*
314, 345, 507. Perhaps there were two sorts of Laconian shoes,
a εὐτελέστερον and a πολυτελέστερον ὑπόδημα; and in this case
the latter may be the Ἀμυκλαΐδες, which Pollux calls an ἐλευ-
θεριώτερον ὑπόδημα. See also Hesychius : Ἀμυκλαΐδες· εἶδος
ὑποδήματος πολυτελοῦς Λακωνικοῦ. Pollux proceeds to say that
the Laconian shoes were red: αἱ δὲ Λακωνικαὶ τὸ μὲν χρῶμα
ἐρυθραί. Hence they cannot be the so-called ἀπλᾶι, which the
Λακωνίζοντες wore along with the tribon. Demosth. *in Conon.*
p. 1267. Of these ἀπλᾶι Harpocration says: Καλλίστρατός φησι,
τὰ μονόπελμα τῶν ὑποδημάτων οὕτω καλεῖσθαι, i.e. they had only
one thickness of sole, and perhaps were not a regular shoe at all.

The βλαῦται or βλαυτία were shoes of a more elegant sort,
and were worn by men when they went out to dinner. Thus
shod, Socrates goes to Agathon's ; Plato. *Symp.* 174 : ἔφη γάρ οι
Σωκράτη ἐντυχεῖν λελουμένον τε καὶ τὰς βλαύτας ὑποδεδεμένον,

G G

ἃ ἐκεῖνος ὀλιγάκις ἐποίει   Cf. Aristoph. *Equites*, 889. Pollux,
vii. 87, calls them σανδαλίου τι εἶδος, and they were in fact a sort
of half-shoe, fastened round the ankles by thongs. This explains
Athen. xii. p. 543: χρυσοῖς ἀνασπαστοῖς ἐπέσφιγγε τῶν βλαυτῶν
τὰς ἀναγωγέας.

The foregoing names are those most frequently met with. We
may, however, mention the ἐνδρομίδες and καρβάτιναι, both worn
by men. The first were high shoes, or rather boots, which Pollux,
perhaps led astray by the etymology, mentions as being suited
for athletæ (iii. 155) ; though elsewhere (vii. 93) he assigns them
to Artemis : ἴδιον τῆς Ἀρτέμιδος τὸ ὑπόδημα. This is corroborated by a Scholion to Callim. *Hymn. in Del.* 238 : Ἐνδρομίδας,
κυρίως τῶν κυνηγῶν ὑποδήματα. Perhaps in essential points they
were the same as the κόθορνος. See Salmasius, ad Tertull. *de
Pallio*, p. 310. Singularly enough, the word has quite another
meaning in Latin ; signifying a warm garment. See Mart. iv. 19,
4 ; Juven. iii. 103. The καρβάτιναι, on the contrary, were probably the commonest foot-covering of the lower orders, and made
of undressed leather. Poll. vii. 88 : Καρβατίνη μὲν ἀγροικῶν ὑπόδημα. See Phot. *Lex.* p. 131 ; Hesychius ; Xenoph. *Anab.* iv. 5,
14. Many other names are mentioned, and probably this article
of costume was more subject to the caprices of fashion than any
other. Hence there were many kinds which were named after
the persons who had introduced them. Poll. vii. 89 : ἀπὸ δὲ
τῶν χρησαμένων, Ἰφικρατίδες, Δεινιάδες, Ἀλκιβιάδια, Σμινδυρίδια,
Μυνάκια ἀπὸ Μυνάκου. Shoes were imported in great quantities:
those from Sicyon, Σικυώνια, are often mentioned.

So likewise there were many kinds of women's shoes ; but
little more is known of them than the names which are recounted
by Pollux, vii. 92–94. Besides the σανδάλιον, Aristophanes
makes special mention of the Περσικὰ, which, according to the
best accounts, was a sort of common shoe, which covered the
whole foot. Hesychius : Περσικά· . . . εὐτελῆ ὑποδήματα. Steph.
Byz. : Πέρσαι. Καὶ Περσικαὶ εἶδος εὐτελοῦς ὑποδήματος. ἔοικε
δὲ γυναικεῖον εἶναι. Pollux is evidently mistaken in his account
of them. He says : ἴδια δὲ γυναικῶν ὑποδήματα Περσικά· λευκὸν
ὑπόδημα, μᾶλλον ἑταιρικόν. Probably they were not ma e right
and left, but suited either foot, like the κόθορνοι. With regard
to the κόθορνοι (not those of tragedy or the chase), see Schol. ad

Aristoph. *Eccl.* 346 : κόθορνος εἶδος ὑποδήματος, ἁρμόζον ἀμφοτέροις ποσί. Poll. vii. 90 : ὁ δὲ κόθορνος ἑκάτερος ἀμφοῖν τοῖν ποδοῖν. Suidas : ὑπόδημα ἀμφοτεροδέξιον. Photius, *Lex.* p. 176, says it was κοινὸν ἀνδρῶν καὶ γυναικῶν : but this is probably a confusion with the *cothurnus* of the chase. The βαυκίδες were a more elegant sort. See Pollux, vii. 94 : αἱ δὲ βαυκίδες πολυτελὲς ἦν ὑπόδημα, κροκοειδὲς, γυναικεῖον. The περιβαρὶς was a kind used for slaves. Poll. vii. 92. The Bœotian women wore a low purple shoe. Dicæarch. *Fragm.* p. 491 : ὑπόδημα λιτὸν, οὐ βαθὺ, φοινικοῦν δὲ τῇ χροίᾳ καὶ ταπεινόν· ὑσκλωτὸν δὲ, ὥστε γυμνοὺς σχεδὸν ἐκφαίνεσθαι τοὺς πόδας.

All these foot-coverings were generally of leather ; and hence the designation σκυτοτόμος includes the shoemaker. But other materials were occasionally used. Cf. Plato, *Symp.* p. 220 : ὑποδεδεμένων καὶ ἐνειλιγμένων τοὺς πόδας εἰς πίλους καὶ ἀρνακίδας. So Antiphanes, apud Athen. xii. p. 545 :

> λευκὴ χλανὶς. φαιὸς χινωνίσκος καλὸς,
> πιλίδιον ἁπαλὸν, εὔρυθμος βακτηρία.

The word πιλίδιον in this place certainly refers to a shoe, not a hat. So Poll. vii. 171 : οὐ μόνον δὲ ὁ ἐπὶ τῶν κεφαλῶν ἐπιτιθέμενος πῖλος οὕτως ἐκαλεῖτο, ἀλλὰ καὶ ὁ περὶ τοῖς ποσὶν, ὡς δηλοῖ Κρατῖνος ἐν Μαλθάκοις λέγων 'λευκοὺς ὑπὸ ποσσὶν ἔχων πίλους.' In Stackelb. *Gräber der Hell.* Pl. 45, is a young man who apparently wears boots of white felt. Such also were the shoes of Demetrius Polioicetes. Duris, apud Athen. xii. p. 535 : τὴν μὲν γὰρ ὑπόδεσιν, ἣν εἶχε, κατεσκεύαζεν ἐκ πολλοῦ δαπανήματος. ἦν γὰρ κατὰ μὲι τὸ σχῆμα τῆς ἐργασίας σχεδὸν ἐμβάτης, πίλημα λαμβάνων τῆ: πολυτελεστάτης πορφύρας· τούτῳ δὲ χρυσοῦ πολλὴν ἐνύφαινον ποικιλίαν ὀπίσω καὶ ἔμπροσθεν ἐνιέντες οἱ τεχνῖται. Felt socks were also worn inside the shoes or sandals. Hesiod, *Op.* 541 :

> ἀμφὶ δὲ ποσσὶ πέδιλα βοὸς ἶφι κταμένοιο
> ἄρμενα δήσασθαι πίλοις ἔντοσθε πυκάσσας.

These in some measure supplied the place of our stockings, as we see from Lucian, *Rhet. Prœc.* 15 : καὶ ἡ κρηπὶς Ἀττικὴ καὶ γυναικεία, τὸ πολυσχιδές· ἡ ἐμβὰς Σικυωνία, πίλοις τοῖς λευκοῖς ἐπιπρέπουσα. Also Poll. vii. 91 : ἃ δὲ πόδεια Κριτίας καλεῖ, εἴτε πίλους αὐτὰ οἰητέον εἴτε περιειλήματα ποδῶν, ταῦτα πέλυντρα καλεῖ ἐν Φοινίσσαις Αἰσχύλος,

> πέλυντρ' ἔχουσιν εὐθέτοις ἐν ἀρβύλαις

τὰ δὲ πέλυντρα εἶδος ὑποδήματος, ὥσπερ αὖ τὰ πόδεια ταὐτὸν
ἦν ταῖς ἀναξυρίσιν, ἃς σκελέας ἔνιοι ὀνομάζουσι. Hesych. σκε-
λεαί, τὰ τῶν σκελῶν σκεπάσματα. These are the *udones* of the
later Roman time.

Cork was often used for the stronger sole, κάττυμα ; it formed
the middle layer ; and women were very partial tu such shoes, as
they added to their apparent height, and yet were not heavy.
Xenoph. *Œcon.* 10, 2 : ὑποδήματα ἔχουσαν ὑψηλὰ, ὅπως μείζων
δοκοίη εἶναι ἢ ἐπεφύκει. So Alexis, apud Athen. xiii. p. 568,
speaking of the arts of the hetæræ, says :

> τυγχάνει μικρά τις οὖσα· φελλὸς ἐν ταῖς βαυκίσι ν
> ἐγκεκάττυται. μακρά τις· διάβαθρον λεπτὸν φορεῖ.

See Böttiger, *Ueber die Stelzenschuhe der Alten Griechinnen.*
Men's shoes were studded with nails, ἧλοι, to render them more
durable, but of course this was not considered *à la mode*; and
Theophrastus, *Char.* 4, mentions it as a mark of ἀγροικία. Still
it was not unusual on a journey, and even gold and silver nails
were sometimes used.

Being neatly shod was essential to propriety of attire. Hence
the frequent notices of the subject in Plato, as in *Protag.* p. 322,
Phæd. p. 64, *Hipp. Maj.* 294 ; cf. Lucian, *Imag.* 10 ; Theophr.
Char. 4. From these passages we see that a good fit was considered desirable, and the contrary a mark of ἀγροικία.

The most usual colour was either black, or the natural one of
the leather ; and the shoes were cleaned with a sponge. Aristoph,
Vesp. 600 :

> τὸν σπόγγον ἔχων ἐκ τῆς λεκάνης τάμβάδι' ἡμῶν περικωνεῖ.

Athen. viii. p. 351 : ἀπαντήσας δέ τινι τῶν γνωρίμων, ὡς εἶδεν
ἐσπογγισμένα τὰ ὑποδήματα καλῶς, συνηχθέσθη, ὡς πράττοντι
κακῶς, νομίζων, οὐκ ἂν οὕτως ἐσπογγίσθαι καλῶς, εἰ μὴ αὐτὸς
ἐσπόγγισεν. But it is evident from the foregoing passages that
both sexes also wore white and party-coloured shoes. For further
information on the subject, consult Ferrari and Rubens, *de Re
Vest.* ; Sperling, *de Crepidis (Gronov. Thes. ant. Gr.* ix.) ; and
Voss, *Mythol. Briefe*, i. pp. 132, 138.

HAIR AND BEARD.

THE Greeks bestowed great pains on that natural ornament of the head, the hair, οἰκεῖοι πῖλοι, as Plato calls it; and he is very adverse to having it covered up in any manner τῇ τῶν ἀλλοτρίων σκεπασμάτων περικαλυφῇ. *Leg.* xii. p. 942. Winkelmann (iii. p. 49) remarks that the natives of the south are endowed with a greater profusion of hair than the inhabitants of northern lands; and by the Greeks its growth was carefully cherished, as it was thought to contribute greatly to render the figure noble and attractive.

Moreover, a certain political significancy was attached to the hair; families, grades of rank, and of age, being thereby distinguished. Even Homer mentions the καρηκομόωντες Ἀχαιοὶ and the ὄπιθεν κομόωντες Ἄβαντες; and in after times the Athenians, who followed the Ionic fashion, were distinguished from the Spartans, who adhered to the old Doric. The latter allowed the hair, as being the cheapest of ornaments, τῶν κόσμων ἀδαπανώτατος, to grow long. Plutarch, *Apophth. Reg.* i. p. 754. Id. *Lyc.* 22: κομῶντες εὐθὺς ἐκ τῆς τῶν ἐφήβων ἡλικίας, μάλιστα περὶ τοὺς κινδύνους ἐθεράπευον τὴν κόμην, λιπαράν, τε φαίνεσθαι καὶ διακεκριμένην. Id. *Lysand.* 1: Λυσάνδρου δέ ἐστιν εἰκονικὸς (ἀνδριάς), εὖ μάλα κομῶντος ἔθει τῷ παλαιῷ καὶ πώγωνα καθειμένου γενναῖον. Οὐ γὰρ, ὡς ἔνιοί φασιν, Ἀργείων μετὰ τὴν μεγάλην ἧτταν ἐπὶ πένθει καρέντων οἱ Σπαρτιᾶται πρὸς τὸ ἀντίπαλον αὐτοῖς τὰς κόμας, ἀγαλλόμενοι τοῖς πεπραγμένοις, ἀνῆκαν. οὐδὲ Βακχιαδῶν τῶν ἐκ Κορίνθου φυγόντων εἰς Λακεδαίμονα ταπεινῶν καὶ ἀμόρφων διὰ τὸ κείρασθαι τὰς κεφαλὰς φανέντων, εἰς ζῆλον αὐτοὶ τοῦ κομᾶν ἦλθον· ἀλλὰ καὶ τοῦτο Λυκούργειόν ἐστι. Καί φασιν εἰπεῖν αὐτὸν, ὡς ἡ κόμη τοὺς μὲν καλοὺς εὐπρεπεστέρους ὁρᾶσθαι ποιεῖ, τοὺς δὲ αἰσχροὺς φοβερωτέρους. See also Heliod. *Æthiop.* ii. 20; Xenoph. *de Republ. Lac.* 11, 3. This practice was certainly not an institution of Lycurgus, but an old Doric fashion. Plutarch's assertion, that the Spartans adorned their hair before battle, or on the eve of any imminent danger, is derived from Herodotus, vii.

208, 209, where it is related that the spy of Xerxes found the
Spartans τὰς κόμας κτενιζομένους before the battle of Thermo-
pylæ. Cf. Müller, *Dorians*, ii. pp. 264, 282. Other passages,
however, seem to contradict these accounts. See Plutarch, *Alcib.*
23 : τοὺς πολλοὺς κατεδημαγώγει καὶ κατεγοήτευε τῇ διαίτῃ λα-
κωνίζων · ὥσθ᾽ ὁρῶντας ἐν χρῷ κουριῶντα καὶ ψυχρολουτοῦντα,
κ. τ. λ. Also Lucian, *Fugit.* 27 : γυναῖκα ἐν χρῷ κεκαρμένην εἰς
τὸ Λακωνικὸν, ἀρρενωπὴν καὶ κομιδῇ ἀνδρικήν. The only way of
reconciling the discrepancy is to suppose that Plutarch confounded
the habit of his own time with the earlier one ; for the Spartans had
long given up this antique fashion, certainly before the time of the
Achæan league. Pausan. vii. 14, 2 ; Philostr. *Vit. Apollon.* iii. 15.

It is stated that in Sparta it was on arriving at the age of an
ephebos that the hair was first allowed to grow, boys wearing it
cut short. Plutarch, *Lyc.* 16. Elsewhere, however, as at Athens,
the custom was exactly the reverse. There, as is well known,
cutting off the hair on the entering upon the age of an ephebos
was a solemn act, accompanied by religious ceremonies. A sacrifice,
called Οἰνιστήρια, was first made to Hercules. Hesychius says :
Ἀθήνησιν οἱ μέλλοντες ἐφηβεύειν πρὶν ἀποκείρασθαι τὸν μαλλὸν
εἰσέφερον Ἡρακλεῖ μέτρον οἴνου καὶ σπείσαντες τοῖς συνελθοῦσιν
ἐπεδίδουν πίνειν. ἡ δὲ σπονδὴ ἐκαλεῖτο Οἰνιστήρια. Cf. Phot. *Lex.*
p. 321 ; Eustath. *ad Il.* xii. 311. The hair was then usually conse-
crated to some deity, most usually perhaps to a neighbouring river-
god. Æschyl. *Choëph.* 6 : πλόκαμον Ἰνάχῳ θρεπτήριον. Pausan.
i. 37, 2 : ἀνάθημα κειρομένου τὴν κόμην τοῦ παιδός οἱ τῷ Κη-
φισσῷ. There was also an ancient custom of repairing for this
purpose to Delphi, and this Theseus is reported to have done.
Plutarch, *Thes.* 5 : Ἔθους δὲ ὄντος ἔτι τότε, τοὺς μεταβαίνοντας
ἐκ παίδων ἐλθόντας εἰς Δελφοὺς ἀπάρχεσθαι τῷ θεῷ τῆς κόμης
ἦλθε μὲν εἰς Δελφοὺς ὁ Θησεύς. And this custom had not fallen
into disuse, even in the age of Theophrastus, for among the marks
of μικροφιλοτιμία, he gives: τὸν υἱὸν ἀποκεῖραι ἀπαγαγὼν εἰς Δελ-
φούς. *Char.* 21.

The ephebi always appear with short hair; and so also do
the athletæ. Lucian, *Dial. Mer.* v. p. 290 : ἐν χρῷ ὤφθη αὐτή,
καθάπερ οἱ σφόδρα ἀνδρώδεις τῶν ἀθλητῶν ἀποκεκαρμένη. The
expression, κουρὰ ἐν χρῷ, means the hair cropped short and
smooth. Cf. Eustath. *ad Odyss.* ii. 376.

In manhood, on the contrary, the hair was worn longer, and the correct quantity, and the fashion of the cut, served quite as much to indicate the polished gentleman, as did the adjustment of the himation, or the fit and fashion of the shoes. See Lucian, *Lexiph.* 10. In Theophrastus, *Char.* 21, πλειστάκις ἀποκείρασθαι is mentioned as a sign of ridiculous vanity.

Hair-cutting was performed in the barbers' shops, κουρεῖα, which were also, however, frequented as mere lounging-places; ι.ence Theophrastus called them wineless symposia. Plutarch, *Symp.* v. 5 : Διὸ καὶ Θεόφραστος ἄοινα συμπόσια παίζων ἐκάλει ιὰ κουρεῖα διὰ τὴν λαλιὰν τῶν προσκαθιζόντων. A place of this kind, with the instruments and mirrors, is depicted by Lucian, *adv. Ind.* 29: τοὺς κουρέας τούτους ἐπίσκεψαι, καὶ ὄψει τοὺς μὲν ιεχνίτας αὐτῶν ξυρὸν καὶ μαχαιρίδας, καὶ κάτοπτρον σύμμετρον ἔχοντας, κ. τ. λ. Cf. Plutarch, *de Aud.* 8 ; Alciphr. *Epist.* iii. 66. The instruments used by the κουρεὺς are enumerated by Pollux, x. 140.

Besides cutting the hair, and trimming the beard, the κουρεὺς cleansed the nails, removed excrescences of the skin (τύλοι, warts?`, and other corporeal disfigurements. In small matters of this kind the εὐσχημονεῖν was carefully observed ; for instance, it was considered very unseemly to appear with nails unpared. Theophr. *Char.* 19 : Ὁ δὲ δυσχερὴς τοιοῦτός τις, οἷος λέπραν ἔχων καὶ τοὺς ὄνυχας μεγάλους περιπατεῖν. At Athens it does not seem to have been thought so much *infra dig.* for a person to pare his own nails as it was at Rome. (Cf. Hor. *Epist.* i. 7, 51 : 'Cultello proprios purgantem leniter ungues.') Thus in Xenophon, *Memor.* i. 2, 54, we have αὐτοί τε γὰρ αὐτῶν ὄνυχάς τε καὶ τρίχας καὶ τύλους ἀφαιροῦσι : but the mention of the hair in this passage shows that it can hardly apply to persons of the upper class ; and moreover it took place in the κουρεῖον, where there were ὀνυχιστήρια λεπτὰ for the purpose. See Posidippos, apud Poll. x. 140. People were also in the habit of using the τριχολάβιον to pluck out the hairs on the body, παρατίλλεσθαι and παραλεαίνεσθαι. This custom is said to have been first originated by the Tarentines. Athen. xii. p. 522 : Ταραντίνους δέ φησι Κλέαρχος ἐν τετάρτῳ βίων ... εἰς τοσοῦτον τρυφῆς προελθεῖν, ὥστε τὸν ὅλον χρῶτα παραλεαίνεσθαι καὶ τῆς ψιλώσεως ταύτης τοῖς λοιποῖς κατάρξαι. Cf. Poll. vii. 165.

After the extinction of the old Attic κρώβυλος, little is known
with certainty concerning the particular modes of wearing the
hair which were usual among the men. It is true that several
εἴδη κουρᾶς are mentioned by Pollux, ii. 29, as well as by other
writers; but how many of them were in ordinary use, and in what
their several peculiarities consisted, is left chiefly to conjecture;
nor do the portraits in Visconti's *Iconographie Grecque* afford
much certain information on the subject.

Black was probably the prevailing colour of the hair, though
blond is frequently mentioned. Thus even in Homer, ξανθαὶ
τρίχες are said to be ὑακινθίνῳ ἄνθει ὅμοιαι. *Odyss*. vi. 231.
Both colours could be produced artificially. Poll. ii. 35 : ἔλεγον
δὲ καὶ ξανθίζεσθαι τὴν κόμην καὶ μελαίνεσθαι. καὶ μέλασμα τὸ τῆς
κόμης βάμμα. This was practised not only by women, but also
by men, especially when the hair began to turn grey. Ælian,
Var. Hist. vii. 20 : Ἀνὴρ εἰς Λακεδαίμονα ἀφίκετο Κεῖος γέρων
ἤδη ὤν, τὰ μὲν ἄλλα ἀλαζών, ᾔδεῖτο δὲ ἐπὶ τῷ γήρᾳ καὶ διὰ ταῦτα
τὴν τρίχα πολιὰν οὖσαν ἐπειρᾶτο βαφῇ ἀφανίζειν. According to
Plutarch, *Apophth. Reg.* i. p. 709, this was done by Philip of
Macedon; and also by Demetrius Phalereus; see Duris, ap.
Athen. xii. p. 542 : τὴν τρίχα τὴν ἐπὶ τῆς κεφαλῆς ξανθιζόμενος.
The blond or yellow hair was much admired; and there was a
preparation which, being smeared on the hair, produced this tint
by exposure to the sun. Women, probably, often had recourse
to it. Menand. Fragm. (Mein. p. 235) :

τὴν γυναῖκα γὰρ
τὴν σώφρον' οὐ δεῖ τὰς τρίχας ξανθὰς ποιεῖν.

There is no necessity to suppose a reference to late Roman
usage in Plutarch, *Amat.* 25 : φάρμακον, ᾧ τὴν κόμην αἱ γυναῖκες
ἐναλειφόμεναι ποιοῦσι χρυσοειδῆ πυῤῥάν. The most detailed account is in Lucian, *Amor.* 40 : Τὸ δὲ πλεῖστον ἀναλίσκει ἡ πλοκὴ
τῶν τριχῶν. αἱ μὲν γὰρ φαρμάκοις ἐρυθαίνειν δυναμένοις πρὸς
ἡλίου μεσημβρίαν τοὺς πλοκάμους, ἴσα ταῖς τῶν ἐρίων χροιαῖς,
ξανθῷ μεταβάπτουσιν ἄνθει, τὴν ἰδίαν κατακρίνουσαι φύσιν· ὁπό-
σαις δὲ ἀρκεῖν ἡ μέλαινα χαίτη νομίζεται, τὸν γεγαμηκότων πλοῦτον ἀναλίσκουσιν, ὅλην Ἀραβίαν σχεδὸν ἐκ τῶν τριχῶν ἀπο-
πνέουσαι. Ointment was often applied; and those who contemned
the perfumes mentioned by Lucian, still used pure oil to assist
the growth of the hair, and render it soft. Plutarch, *Præc.
Conjug.* 29 ; Plato, *Protag.* p. 334.

No less attention was lavished on the beard, which was not looked on as a troublesome incumbrance, but as a dignified ornament of maturity and old age. Lucian, *Cyn.* 14; Epictet. *Dissert.* i. 16, 13. Hence the whiskers, πώγων, the moustachios, μύσταξ, πάππος, ὑπήνη, and the beard, γένειον, were allowed to grow (πωγωνοτροφεῖν). The words πώγων, ὑπήνη, and γένειον are often used for the hair on the face generally; but originally their meanings were restricted as above stated. Poll. ii. 80; Eubulos, ap. Id. x. 120.

None of these parts were shorn; but of course there were variations in the wear, according to race, abode, condition, and individual character. Compare, for instance, the busts of Solon and Lycurgus, Visconti, *Iconogr. Grecque,* Pl. 8 and 9; or those of Plato, Antisthenes, and Chrysippos: *Ib.* Pl. 18, 22, 23.

In general a strong full beard, πώγων βαθὺς or δασὺς, was held to be a sign of manliness and power. Cf. Aristoph. *Thesmoph.* 31. Still it was never allowed to go untrimmed, the κουρεὺς attending to it, as well as to the hair of the head, though this may have been neglected by the sophists and others. Thus Plato is ridiculed for the opposite extreme by Ephippos, ap. Athen. xi. p. 509 :

> εὖ μὲν μαχαίρᾳ ξύστ᾿ ἔχων τριχώματα,
> εὖ δ᾿ ὑποκαθιεὶς ἄτομα πώγωνος βάθη.

Cf. Aristoph. *Lysistr.* 1072. Alexander brought shaving into fashion, but there can be no doubt that it was partially adopted at a much earlier period, though the practice was certainly regarded as contemptible. See Aristoph. *Thesmoph.* 218. So too the courtiers of Philip are attacked by Theopompos, apud Athen. vi. p. 260 : τί γὰρ τῶν αἰσχρῶν ἢ δεινῶν αὐτοῖς οὐ προσῆν, ἢ τί τῶν καλῶν καὶ σπουδαίων οὐκ ἀπῆν ; οὐχ οἱ μὲν ξυρούμενοι καὶ λεαινόμενοι διετέλουν ἄνδρες ὄντες, οἱ δ᾿ ἀλλήλοις ἐτόλμων ἐπανίστασθαι πώγωνας ἔχουσι. Cf. Chrysippos and Alexis, apud Athen. xiii. p. 565. Yet Chrysippos expressly states that this new custom of shaving, probably derived from the East or Egypt, was introduced by Alexander. Τὸ ξύρεσθαι τὸν πώγωνα κατ᾿ Ἀλέξανδρον προῆκται, τῶν πρώτων οὐ χρωμένων αὐτῷ. Plutarch. *Thes.* 5, asserts that Alexander caused his soldiers' beards to be shaved, from motives of strategical caution : ὡς λαβὴν ταύτην ἐν ταῖς μάχαις οὖσαν προχειροτάτην. Cf. Id. *Apophth. Reg.* i. p. 714 ;

Eustathius, *ad Odyss*. xxi. 305. The innovation was stoutly resisted in many states, and was forbidden by special laws which do not seem to have had much effect; Chrysippos adduces a couple of instances: ἐν 'Ρόδῳ δὲ νόμου ὄντος, μὴ ξύρεσθαι, οὐδὲ ὁ ἐπιληψόμενος οὐδείς ἐστι, διὰ τὸ πάντας ξύρεσθαι. ἐν Βυζαντίῳ δὲ ζημίας ἐπικειμένης τῷ ἔχοντι κουρεῖ ξυρόν, οὐδὲν ἧττον πάντες χρῶνται αὐτῷ. Hence the practice seems to have been very universally and speedily adopted. Alexander's successors adhered to the new custom in their own persons, and most of the kings of the Macedonian dynasties are thus represented. There are a few exceptions, such as Philip V. and Perseus, (Visconti, *Iconogr*. Pl. 40,) as well as Ptolemæus Philadelphus on the celebrated Cameo-Gonzaga (*Mus. Odesc*. i. Pl. 15: Meyer, *Abbild. z. Kunstgesch*. Pl. 14). The same is also the case with the busts of poets, as Menander and Posidippus; of physicians, as Asclepiades; and even of philosophers, as Aristotle, which are all without beards. Visconti, Pl. 6, 32. Yet the sophists, for the most part, kept to the ancient fashion; and till a late period the πώγων βαθὺς continued to be the badge of the stoic Aretalogi: and so much did they affect it, that it gave rise to more than one proverb directed against them, as ἐκ πώγωνος σοφὸς, πωγωνοτροφία φιλόσοφον οὐ ποιεῖ, etc. See Plutarch, *de Iside et Osir*. 3 ; Lucian, *Demon*. 13 ; Gell. ix. 2.

A pleasant picture of the process of shaving is drawn by Alciphron, *Epist*. iii. 66 : ὡς γὰρ ἀφικόμην ξυριεῖσθαι τὴν γενειάδα βουλόμενος, ἀσμένως τε ἐδέξατο καὶ ἐφ ὑψηλοῦ θρόνου καθίσας, σινδόνα καινὴν περιθεὶς πρᾴως εὖ μάλα κατέφερέ μοι τῶν γνάθων τὸ ξυρὸν, ἀποψιλῶν τὸ πύκνωμα τῶν τριχῶν. Comp. Plaut. *Capt*. ii. 2, 16 ; Böttiger, *Sabina*, ii. p. 57 ; and Becker's *Gallus*, p. 428. Concerning the enigmatical Spartan decree, μὴ τρέφειν or κείρεσθαι τὸν μύστακα, see Valcken. ad Theocr. p. 288. But there is still much difficulty about it. Cf. Plutarch, *Agesil*. 30 ; Antiphanes, apud Athen. iv. p. 143.

The women doubtless wore their hair in manifold ways; the antiques, however, do not enable us to establish the prevalence of any definite fashions, or even to interpret the names that here and there occur. The extraordinary artificial coiffure of the virgins of the Pandroseum (the so-called Caryatides) has no more reference to the every-day costume than has their dress itself.

This observation will also apply to many varieties depicted on
the terracottas found in Attic tombs, and in this case, moreover,
we are ignorant of the period to which they belong. See Stackelberg, *Gräber der Hell*. Pl. 75–78. In by far the majority of
cases the long and luxuriant hair is neither braided nor curled,
but, if no other head-dress is worn, it is gathered together
and tied behind or over the crown in a knot. The forehead, at
the same time, is pretty well covered, as it was considered a
beauty to have a βραχὺ τῷ μετώπῳ μεταίχμιον. Cf Hor. *Od*.
i. 33, 5 : *tenuis frons*. There are nevertheless instances of a
more elaborate coiffure, for instance, in the busts of Aspasia, and
of Berenice, the wife of Ptolemæus Soter. See Visconti, *Iconogr*.
Pl. 15 and 52. In both the head is encircled with a wreath of
curiously twisted ringlets, which hang low down. Cf. Lucian,
Amor. 40 : σιδηρᾶ τε ὄργανα, πυρὸς ἀμβλεία φλογὶ χλιανθέντα
βίᾳ τὴν ἑλίκων οὐλότητα διαπλέκει. καὶ περίεργοι μὲν αἱ μέχρι
τῶν ὀφρύων ἐφειλκυσμέναι κόμαι βραχὺ τῷ μετώπῳ μεταίχμιον
ἀφιᾶσι· σοβαρῶς δὲ ἄχρι τῶν μεταφρένων οἱ ὄπισθεν ἐπισαλεύονται
πλόκαμοι. On the comic stage, long locks hanging down on
both sides belonged to the custom of hetæræ. Poll. iv. 153 :
Τὸ δὲ τέλειον ἑταιρικὸν τῆς ψευδοκόρης ἐστὶν ἐρυθρότερον καὶ
βοστρύχους ἔχει περὶ τὰ ὦτα. Cf. Lucian, *Bis Accus*. 31 : τὰς
τρίχας εὐθετίζουσαν εἰς τὸ ἑταιρικὸν καὶ φυκίον ἐντριβομένην, καὶ
τὼ ὀφθαλμὼ ὑπογραφομένην.

In vase-paintings we usually see the hair held together by
variously formed bandeaus, by a cap-like kerchief, a net, or something of the kind. And first of these stands the σφενδόνη, which,
as the name indicates, was a sling-shaped band, i.e. broad over
the forehead, and narrow at the sides. It was sometimes, perhaps, of metal, or merely of gilded leather : for of the somewhat
similar στλεγγὶς, we read in Pollux, vii. 179 : ἔστι δὲ καὶ ἕτερόν
τι στλεγγὶς, δέρμα κεχρυσωμένον, ὃ περὶ τὴν κεφαλὴν φοροῦσι.
Cf. Id. v. 96 ; Böttiger, *Vasengem*. iii. p. 225 ; and Gerhard,
Prodromus, p. 20, sqq. This band was also worn on the back
of the head, as an ὀπισθοσφενδόνη, and the two were often worn
at the same time. Böttiger, *Kl. Schr*. iii. p. 108. The forms of
these bandeaus are very numerous, and they were mostly ornamented in some way with gold, for Pollux, after enumerating their
names, adds : χρυσᾶ καὶ ἐπίχρυσα πάντα.

The cap-like head-coverings, the use of which is of great antiquity, may be divided into nets, hair-bags, and kerchiefs. They are all comprehended under the name κεκρύφαλος, though properly a distinction should be drawn between κεκρύφαλος, σάκκος, and μίτρα. The κεκρύφαλος proper was a net, which was worn both night and day, like the reticulum of the Roman ladies. See *Gallus*, p. 440; and the Article *Calantica*, in the *Real-Encyklop. d. Klass. Alterth.* It was merely netted or woven of threads; hence the makers were called κεκρυφαλοπλόκοι. Poll. vii. 179. The σακχυφάνται mentioned by Demosthenes, *in Olympiod.* p. 1170, are, it is true, said by Pollux, x. 192, to be the same as τοὺς πλέκοντας ταῖς γυναιξὶ τοὺς κεκρυφάλους, but the word has nevertheless a wider signification. Such hair-nets are not visible on vase-paintings, but they may be seen on the carefully executed frescoes of Herculaneum and Pompeii. See *Mus. Borb.* iv. 49; vi. 18; viii. 4; and fig. 1, *infra.* They seem to consist of gold threads, which agrees with Juven. ii. 96:

Reticulumque comis auratum ingentibus implet.

Cf. Petron. 97. They were also made of silk (Salmas. *Exerc. ad Solin.* p. 392), and of the costly gold-yellow byssus of Eleia, (Pausan. vii. 21, 7), as well as of commoner stuff. See Hesychius: τρίχαπτον· τὸ βομβύκινον ὕφασμα ὑπὲρ τῶν τριχῶν, τῆς κεφαλῆς ἁπτόμενον. Cf. Photius and Suidas. A different explanation of the word is, however, given by Pollux, x. 32: καὶ τρίχαπτον δέ φασι, πλέγμα ἐκ τριχῶν.

The σάκκοι or snoods, on the contrary, were often of thicker stuff, and sometimes covered the whole head, so that the hair

2   1   3   4

Different kinds of κεκρύφαλος   Fig. 1 is a regular κεκρύφαλος or hairnet, from a Pompeian fresco, Aphrodite and Eros; *Mus. Borb.* VIII. 5. The gauze drapery also deserves attention. Figs. 2 and 3 are from a vase-painting in Millin., *Peint. d. Vas.* II. 43. Fig. 4, a σάκκος, from Tischbein, *Engrav.* I. 14.

hung down on the neck like a pouch; occasionally the front part
was left bare; and sometimes it was open behind, so as to allow
a tuft of hair to hang out. See figs. 3 and 4; also Stackelberg,
Gräber der Hell. Pl. 68, 75, 76. From the peak of the snood
tassels sometimes depended. A head-dress of this kind is evidently
intended by the κεφαλὴ περίθετος, in Aristoph. *Thesmoph.* 257 :

> ΕΤΡ. κεκρυφάλου δεῖ καὶ μίτρας. ΑΓ. ἡδὶ μὲν οὖν
> κεφαλὴ περίθετος, ἥν ἐγὼ νύκτωρ φορῶ.

They were of divers materials—silk, byssus, and wool. See Poll
vii. 66. They usually were coloured, and often worked in patterns, like the kerchiefs. See Millingen, *Coghill*, Pl. 22 ; Millin.
Peint. des Vases Gr. i. Pl. 36, 37, 41, 58, 59 ; ii. 43 ; Stackelberg, Pl. 33, 34. Bladders were also used for the purpose; and
the πομφόλυγας of Aristophanes are explained in the same manner
by Mœr. Attic. p. 222 : Πομφόλυγας, τὰ δερμάτια, ἃ ἐπὶ τῶν
κεφαλῶν αἱ γυναῖκες ἔχουσιν. Ἀριστοφάνης Θεσμοφοριαζούσαις.
Cf. Mart. viii. 33, 19 :

> Fortior intortos servat vesica capillos.

A coloured kerchief was also wrapped round the hair, sometimes covering the entire head, at others only a part of it. This
was doubtless the μίτρα, which originally signified only a band,
and this must be its meaning in the above-quoted passage of
Aristophanes, where the κεκρύφαλος is also mentioned. The band
was by degrees worn broader and broader, till it at last merged
into the kerchief, and from this originated the snood itself.

For further details, see Böttiger, *Aldobr. Hochz.* pp. 79, 150 ;
Kl. Sch. ii. p. 245 ; *Sabina*, i. p. 143; also Junii *de Coma lib.*;
Hotoman, *de Barba*, in Pitisci *Lex.*; Ferrarii *Electa*, ii. 12 ;
Camill. Silvestr. ad Juven. iv. 103.

EXCURSUS TO SCENE XII.

THE WOMEN.

A VARIETY of views have been entertained on the social position of the Greek women, and their estimation in the eyes of the men. The majority of scholars have described them as despicable in the opinion of the other sex, their life as a species of slavery, and the gynæconitis as a place of durance little differing from the Oriental harem; while a few writers have stoutly contended for the historic emancipation of the fair sex among the Greeks. To the former class belong de Pauw, *Recherches sur les Grecs*; Meiners, *Gesch. des Weibl. Geschl.*; as well as Böttiger and Thöluck. This last writer was replied to by Jacobs, in his *Beitr. z. Gesch. d. Weibl. Geschl.* As usual, the truth lies between the contending parties. The assertions of the former are manifestly exaggerated; while Jacobs, without undertaking the necessary research, has assigned to the Grecian women in general a position analogous to that which they occupied in the heroic age. The former view, though in a modified and less objectionable form, has been again espoused by Limburg-Brower, in his *Hist. de la Civilis. Morale et Relig. des Grecs.*

It cannot be denied that the women of Homer occupy a more honourable position in the household than those of the so-called historic period. The reason of the change cannot be ascertained, as we have no certain accounts of the intervening centuries, during which had been effected an entire revolution in the modes of life among the Greeks. For instance, the vice of παιδεραστία is utterly unknown to Homer; and again, while he describes the husband as almost buying the bride from her parents, the father now gave a dowry with his daughter. We need, then, no longer wonder that the women, at the later period, were less respected and more restrained, and that the marriage relationship was less tender and endearing.

It is no part of the purpose of this work to dwell upon the Homeric period. That subject is complete in itself, and the sources of information are by no means difficult of access. We

may refer especiaɪɪ,
alter, and Helbig, Die ~
alters.

We shall here strictly confine ourselves to the historic ᴜpoch.
At this time, and in the very focus of civilisation, the women
were regarded as a lower order of beings, neglected by nature iɪɪ
comparison with man, both in point of intellect and heart; incapable of taking part in public life, naturally prone to evil, and
fitted only for propagating the species and gratifying the sensual
appetites of the men. Of course the invectives of the notorious
misogynist Euripides, or the complaints of pestered husbands in
the comedians, must not be adduced as proof; though, on the
other hand, they cannot be entirely ignored. Passages such as
that in the *Hippolytus* of Euripides, v. 615–621, are nothing
but rhetorical exaggerations. See Athen. xiii. p. 557 : Εἰπόντος
Σοφοκλεῖ τινος, ὅτι μισογύνης ἐστὶν Εὐριπίδης, "Εν γε ταῖς τραγῳδίαις, ἔφη ὁ Σοφοκλῆς· ἐπεὶ ἔν γε τῇ κλίνῃ φολογύνης. So also
the παίδων ἐραστὴς in Lucian, *Amor.* 38, praises this outburst
of the poet; but this is only in keeping with his assigned character. Cf. Hipponax, ap. Stob. *Tit.* lxviii. 8 :

> Δύ' ἡμέραι γυναικός εἰσιν ἥδισται·
> ὅταν γάμῃ τις κἀκφέρῃ τεθνηκυῖαν.

Also Plaut. *Asin.* i. 1, 30 ; *Mil.* iii. 1, 91 ; Achill. Tat. i. 7.
But such expressions prove nothing as to the general opinion.
We may regard, however, as the deeply-rooted sentiment of
Greek antiquity, the confession of Iphigenia in the *Iphigenia in
Aulide* of Euripides, v. 1373 :

> εἷς γ' ἀνὴρ κρείσσων γυναικῶν μυρίων,

And the habit of regarding the wife as a necessary evil of the
household is shown by the words of Menander (p. 190, Mein.) :

> ἀνάγκη γὰρ γυναῖκ' εἶναι κακόν,
> ἀλλ' εὐτυχής ἐσθ' ὁ μετριώτατον λαβών.

A great number of such passages as the foregoing might be
easily collected from the dramatists and others. But far greater
weight should be attached to the voices of the most thoughtful,
liberal, and unprejudiced philosophers of antiquity, who have,
without any bitterness or comic exaggeration, deliberately pronounced that nature assigns to woman a place far beneath that
of man. It is true that Aristotle considers the putting women

see *de Republ*. i. 2,
.....early enunciates his opi-
.... says: τὸ ἄρρεν πρὸς τὸ θῆλυ
φύσει τὸ μὲν κρεῖττον, τὸ δὲ χεῖρον, τὸ μὲν ἄρχον, τὸ δ᾽ ἀρχό-
μενον. Cf. *Hist. Anim.* ix. 1. Plato, too, with all his mildness,
benevolence, and love of justice, says, *Leg.* vi. p. 781 : λαθραιότε-
ρον μᾶλλον καὶ ἐπικλοπώτερον ἔφυ τὸ θῆλυ: and he proceeds to
say that the women must be so much the more curbed, ὅσῳ ἡ
θήλεια φύσις ἐστὶ πρὸς ἀρετὴν χείρων τῆς τῶν ἀρρένων. See also
Aristot. *de Republ.* ii. 9, p. 1270 ; and Id. *Probl.* xxix. 11 : Διὰ
τί δεινότερον γυναῖκα ἀποκτεῖναι ἢ ἄνδρα ; καίτοι βέλτιον τὸ ἄρρεν
τοῦ θήλεος φύσει. Cf. Stob. *Tit.* lxxiii. 62. All this expresses
the prevalent notion ; and the only ἀρετὴ of which woman was
thought capable in that age differed but little from that of a
faithful slave. See Plato, *Meno*, p. 71.

In some cases, doubtless, a woman's virtues ensured her a
greater share of affection ; and, again, a great dower, or her own
natural character, might occasionally give her the upper hand
in the household ; but the general notion mentioned above always
prevailed. Except in her own immediate circle, a woman's existence was scarcely recognised; and though now and then an
extraordinary instance of female σωφροσύνη was publicly recognised, yet the homage was clearly intended for the husband. See
Plutarch, *Phoc.* 19.

Among the Dorians, and especially at Sparta, where the
women enjoyed a much greater degree of freedom than among
the Ionico-Attic race, and where the attempt of Lycurgus to
place the women under stricter regulations is said to have failed,
their position may have been somewhat different; but even there
the woman had only a physical worth. Aristot. *de Republ.* ii. 9 ;
Plutarch, *Lyc.* 14 ; Id. *Agis.* 7.

Intimately connected with this vilipending of the woman was
her utter want of independence, in consequence of which she
was, at least in Athens, considered a minor all her life long. But
little is said of this in connexion with judicial and public matters, yet quite enough to show how the case was regarded by the
law. See Thucyd. ii. 45 ; Plutarch, *de Mul. Virt.* 1. Thus it
was enacted, that everything that a man did by the counsel or
request of a woman should be null. Demosth. *in Olymp.* p.

1183 : καὶ ἄκυρά γε ταῦτα πάντα ἐνομοθέτησεν εἶναι Σόλων, ὅ,τι
ἄν τις γυναικὶ πειθόμενος πράττῃ, ἄλλως τε καὶ τοιαύτῃ (πόρνῃ).
They were not allowed to conclude any bargain, or transaction
of consequence, on their own account.   Isæus, *de Aristarchi
Hered.* p. 259 : ὁ γὰρ νόμος διαρρήδην κωλύει, παιδὶ μὴ ἐξεῖναι
συμβάλλειν μηδὲ γυναικὶ πέρα μεδίμνων κριθῶν.   Plato, it is true,
proposes that this concession should be made them, but this is
only a notion of his own. See *Leg.* xi. p. 937.

  Their education from early childhood corresponded to the
rest of their treatment.   As has been already stated, there were
no educational institutions for girls, nor any private teachers at
home.   Their whole instruction was left to the mother and the
nurses, through whose means they obtained, perhaps, a smat-
tering ἐν γράμμασι, and were taught to spin and weave, and
similar female avocations. This was certainly the case at Athens
How it was in other states does not appear, but it was probably
much the same elsewhere, except at Sparta. Hence there were no
scientific or even learned ladies, with the exception of the hetæræ.
See, however, Eurip. *Hippol.* 635. They were also almost entirely deprived of that most essential promoter of female culture,
the society of the other sex. They were excluded from intercourse
not only with strangers, but also with their nearest relations,
and they saw but little even of their fathers or husbands; for the
men lived more abroad than at home, and even when at home
they inhabited their own apartments. Κεχωρίσθαι ἄνδρας γυναικῶν
was an established maxim, as Herodotus says, v. 18 : and to this
Plato also adheres, when desirous of introducing Syssitia of the
women : see *Leg.* vii. p. 806. A more confidential intercourse
would seem to be indicated by passages such as Demosth. *in Neær.*
p. 1382 ; and Æschin. *in Timarch.* p. 178 ; but we cannot infer
that anything like instructive and improving conversation took
place.

  Thus the gynæconitis, though not exactly a prison, nor yet
an ever-locked harem, was still the confined abode allotted, for
life, to the female portion of the household; and Plato rightly
calls the women γένος εἰθισμένον δεδυκὸς καὶ σκοτεινὸν ζῆν. *Leg.*
vi. p. 781. This applies especially to the maidens, who lived in
the greatest seclusion till their marriage, and, so to speak, regularly under lock and key, κατάκλειστοι (Callim. *Fragm.* 118),

θαλαμευόμεναι, and φρουρούμεναι (Aristæn. ii. *Ep.* 5). See also Phocylides, 203 :

Παρθενικὴν δὲ φύλασσε πολυκλείστοις θαλάμοισι,
μηδέ μιν ἄχρι γάμων πρὸ δόμων ὀφθῆναι ἐάσῃς.

Cf. Eurip. *Iphig. in Aul.* 728 ; Sophocl. *Œdip. Colon.* 344. They never quitted the shades of the παρθενὼν, except on special occasions, such as to be spectators of a festal procession, or to swell its pomp ; and probably it was on such opportunities that a tender passion first arose ; as we see from the use made of such circumstances by the comedians. But no παρθένος ἐλευθέρα ever takes part in the action of a comedy. No such instance occurs in the pieces preserved to us by the Romans, except in the *Persa* of Plautus, where, however, the appearance of the parasite's daughter is owing to the father's pretended sale of her as a slave. In tragedy it was allowed, though Euripides says, *Orest.* 108 :

ἐς ὄχλον ἕρπειν, παρθένοισιν οὐ καλόν.

The material of tragedy was taken from the domain of the epic, and, as we learn from Homer, the virgins in his time enjoyed more liberty.

After marriage these restrictions were mitigated at Athens, though at Sparta, on the contrary, the married women lived in stricter seclusion than the others, who were purposely allowed to have intercourse with the men. See Müller, *Dorians*, ii. p. 273. In fact, it is impossible to deny that a gross mistake prevailed at Sparta respecting the destination and natural disposition of women, and an education such as was there practised necessarily induced bold and unfeminine manners, which to us seem highly repulsive. Plutarch, *Compar. Lyc. c. Num.* 3 ; Aristot. *de Rep.* ii. 9 ; and the Excursus on *The Gymnasia*, p. 297.

Returning to the Attic women, we find that after marriage they were still, in a great measure, confined to the gynæconitis, which no strange man was allowed to enter. It was also considered unbecoming for the young wife to leave the house without her husband's knowledge ; and, in fact, she seldom quitted it : she was thus restricted for the most part to the society of her female slaves ; and her husband, if he chose to exercise it, had the power of keeping her in confinement. The doubt which has been thrown upon these assertions renders it necessary to substantiate them by the production of the original authorities.

Now first with regard to the οἰκουρεῖν, or continuous staying at home, we find this universally mentioned as a woman's first duty. See Eurip. *Troad.* 649 :

> πρῶτον μὲν, ἔνθα κἂν προσῇ, κἂν μὴ προσῇ
> ψόγος γυναιξὶν, αὐτὸ τοῦτ᾽ ἐφέλκεται
> κακῶς ἀκούειν, ἥτις οὐκ ἔνδον μένει,
> τούτου πόθον παρεῖσ᾽, ἔμιμνον ἐν δόμοις.

Also Menand. Fragm. (p. 87, Mein.) :

> Τοὺς τῆς γαμετῆς ὅρους ὑπερβαίνεις, γύναι,
> τὴν αὐλίαν· πέρας γὰρ αὔλιος θύρα
> ἐλευθέρᾳ γυναικὶ νενόμιστ᾽ οἰκίας.

These passages certainly express the universal opinion hereon, though their critical value may be called in question, on the ground that Euripides was a μισογύνης, and that Menander refers to a special case. No such objection, however, can be urged against the extract from the treatise περὶ γυναικὸς σωφροσύνης of Phintys the Pythagorean, which has been preserved by Stobæus, *Tit.* lxxiv. 61 : "Ἴδια μὲν ἀνδρὸς τὸ στραταγὲν, τὸ πολιτεύεσθαι καὶ δαμαγορέν. ἴδια δὲ γυναικὸς τὸ οἰκουρὲν καὶ ἔνδον μένεν, καὶ ἐκδέχεσθαι καὶ θεραπεύεν τὸν ἄνδρα. Further on she specifies the cases in which a wife might be permitted to go abroad. So also Aristophanes speaks of the wrath of the husbands when their wives leave the house unknown to them ; nor is there the slightest ground for supposing him to exaggerate; *Thesmoph.* 793 :

> κἂν ἐξέλθῃ τὸ γύναιόν ποι, κᾆθ᾽ εὕρητ᾽ αὐτὸ θύραισιν,
> μανίας μαίνεσθ᾽.

See also *Pax*, 980. And hence when the news of the defeat of Chæroneia reached Athens, and we might have expected that the eager anxiety of the moment would have caused the women to leave the house, we find them only at the doors. Lycurg. *in Leocr.* p. 165 : ὁρᾶν δ᾽ ἦν ἐπὶ μὲν τῶν θυρῶν γυναῖκας ἐλευθέρας περιφόβους, καταπεπτηχυίας καὶ πυνθανομένας, εἰ ζῶσι, τὰς μὲν ὑπὲρ ἀνδρὸς, τὰς δ᾽ ὑπὲρ πατρὸς, τὰς δ᾽ ὑπὲρ ἀδελφῶν, κ.τ.λ., and even this the orator calls ἀναξίως αὐτῶν καὶ τῆς πόλεως ὁρωμένας. Much the same took place at Thebes, after the overthrow of the foreign domination. Plutarch, *de Gen. Socr.* 33 : Αἱ δὲ γυναῖκες, ὡς ἑκάστη περὶ τοῦ προσήκοντος ἤκουσεν, οὐκ ἐμμένουσαι τῶν Βοιωτῶν ἤθεσιν ἐξέτρεχον πρὸς ἀλλήλας καὶ διεπυνθάνοντο παρὰ τῶν ἀπαντώντων . . . Οὐδεὶς δὲ ἐκώλυε. Cf. Xenoph. *Œcon.* vii 30.

Older females were not so straitly guarded as those of younger years, as may be gathered from the words of Hyperides, apud Stob. *Tit.* lxxiv. 33 : Δεῖ τὴν ἐκ τῆς οἰκίας ἐκπορευομένην ἐν τοι-αύτῃ καταστάσει εἶναι τῆς ἡλικίας, ὥστε τοὺς ἀπαντῶντας πυνθά-νεσθαι, μὴ τίνος ἐστὶ γυνὴ, ἀλλὰ τίνος μήτηρ. Cf. Eurip. *Androm.* 858, *Heraclid.* 474 ; and Plato, *de Republ.* ix. p. 579, where it is said of tyrants : καταδεδυκὼς ἐν τῇ οἰκίᾳ τὰ πολλὰ ὡς γυνὴ ζῇ. And lastly, the tortoise, on which the Aphrodite Urania of Phidias was supported, was considered as a symbol of this secluded existence of the women. Plutarch, *de Iside et Osir.* 76 : Τῷ δὲ τῆς ’Αθηνᾶς (εἰκάσματι) τὸν δράκοντα Φειδίας παρέθηκε, τῷ δὲ τῆς ’Αφροδίτης ἐν ῞Ηλιδι χελώνην, ὡς τὰς μὲν παρθένους φυλακῆς δεομένας, ταῖς δὲ γαμεταῖς οἰκουρίαν καὶ σιωπὴν πρέπουσιν. Cf. Id. *Conjug. Prœc.* 32 ; Pausan. vi. 25, 2.

As regards going abroad, we may take in their full extent the words of Aristophanes, *Lysistr.* 16 : χαλεπή τοι γυναικῶι ἔξοδος. Apart from the consideration of toilet and household occupations, the women were detained at home by special restric-tions. Thus Athenæus, xii. p. 521, informs us, on the authority of Phylarchos, that a law was in force at Syracuse, which forbade free-women to go out at all after sunset; or even in the daytime, ἄνευ τῶν γυναικονόμων, ἀκολουθούσης αὐτῇ μιᾶς θεραπαινίδος. To a similar effect was a law of Solon's ; Plutarch, *Sol.* 21 : ’Επέστησε δὲ καὶ ταῖς ἐξόδοις τῶν γυναικῶν καὶ τοῖς πένθεσι καὶ ταῖς ἑορταῖς νόμον ἀπείργοντα τὸ ἄτακτον καὶ ἀκόλαστον· ... μήτε νύκτωρ πορεύεσθαι πλὴν ἁμάξῃ κομιζομένην, λύχνου προφαίνοντος. The γυναικονόμοι are not mentioned in the latter law, but there were such officers at Athens, though whether at so early a period is doubtful. See Poll. viii. 112 ; Hesych. s. v. Πλάτανος. Be-sides their other duties they had to watch over the ἐξόδους of the women, as is clear from Aristot. *de Republ.* iv. 15, p. 1300 : παιδονόμος δὲ καὶ γυναικονόμος, καὶ εἴ τις ἄλλος ἄρχων κύριός ἐστι τοιαύτης ἐπιμελείας, ἀριστοκρατικὸν, δημοκρατικὸν δ' οὔ. πῶς γὰρ οἷόν τε κωλύειν ἐξιέναι τὰς τῶν ἀπόρων. Also *ib.* vi. 8, p. 1323 : τούτων δ' ἔνιαι φανερῶς εἰσιν οὐ δημοτικαὶ τῶν ἀρχῶν, οἷον γυναι-κονομία καὶ παιδονομία· τοῖς γὰρ ἀπόροις ἀνάγκη, χρῆσθαι καὶ γυναιξὶ καὶ παισὶν ὥσπερ ἀκολούθοις διὰ τὴν ἀδουλίαν. Somewhat similar is Plato's appointment of women, as ἐπίσκοποι of morals. *Leg.* vi. p. 784.

It is scarcely possible that, in accordance with the Syracusan law, women were never allowed to go out except by the permission of the gynæconomi, and doubtless this would not apply to excursions away from home. In the above-mentioned treatise of Phintys, περὶ γυναικὸς σωφροσύνης, the third place is taken by the ἐκ τῶν ἐξόδων τῶν ἐκ τᾶς ἰδίας οἰκίας. She thinks the occasions on which the women should be allowed to go out are, religious ceremonies, to be spectators of a festival, and to purchase household necessaries. She says: Τὰς δὲ ἐξόδως ἐκ τᾶς οἰκίας ποιεῖσθαι τὰς γυναῖκας τὰς δαμοτελέας θυηπολούσας τῷ ἀρχαγέτᾳ θεῷ τᾶς πόλιος ὑπὲρ αὐτᾶς καὶ τῶ ἀνδρὸς καὶ τῶ παντὸς οἴκω· ἔπειτα μήτε ὀρφνᾶς ἀνισταμένας, μήτε ἑσπέρας, ἀλλὰ πλαθούσας ἀγορᾶς καταφανέα γινομέναν τὰν ἔξοδον ποιεῖσθαι, θεωρίας ἕνεκά τινος, ἢ ἀγορασμῷ οἰκήω μετὰ θεραπαίνας μιᾶς, ἢ καττὸ πλεῖστον δύο εὐκόσμως χειραγωγουμέναν. We are hardly justified in assuming that so much liberty was usually allowed, and our surprise is by no means lessened when we find that she goes on to recommend a walk for the improvement of the complexion, instead of the use of rouge. Whether this ever actually took place, or whether it is merely a theoretical suggestion of her own, we cannot determine; no mention ever occurs of such a thing, and at all events no such promenading was in vogue in Attica; and the γυναικεία ἀγορὰ at Athens would hardly be visited by respectable females, as has been shown in the Excursus on *The Markets and Commerce*, p. 287. At those festivals, however, from which men were excluded, the women had an opportunity of seeing something of each other; and they enjoyed themselves all the more on account of their ordinary seclusion. Cf. Isæus, *de Pyrrhi Her.* p. 66; Aristoph. *Thesmoph.* 795.

No respectable lady thought of going out without a female slave, as we see from the Syracusan law above quoted; and the husband always assigned one to his wife; and how indispensable such an attendant was thought, we see from the example of the ἀνελεύθερος, who hired a slave for the purpose, when wanted. Theophr. *Char.* 22: τῇ γυναικὶ μὴ πρίασθαι θεράπαιναν, ἀλλὰ μισθοῦσθαι εἰς τὰς ἐξόδους παιδίον ἀκολουθῆσον. At a later period the number of these attendants was greatly increased. Lucian, *Imag.* 2: θεραπεία δὲ πολλὴ καὶ ἄλλη περὶ αὐτὴν παρασκευὴ λαμπρά, καὶ εὐνούχων τι πλῆθος, καὶ ἅβραι πάνυ πολλαὶ, κ. τ. λ. Cf. Excursus on *The Slaves*, p. 362.

Under such circumstances there could not have been much
interchange of visits, except among relatives, though they were
not entirely omitted.   See Naumachios, apud Stob. *Tit.* lxxiv. 7 :

> μήτε γραῦν ποτε σοῖσι κακὴν δέξαιο μελάθροις·
> πολλῶν γρῆες ἔπερσαν ἐΰκτιτα δώματα φώτων.
> μηδὲ μὲν ἀκριτόμυθον ἑταιρίσσαιο γυναῖκα·
> κεδνὰ κακοὶ φθείρουσι γυναικῶν ἤθεα μῦθοι.

Here ἐλεύθεραι γυναῖκες cannot be meant ; but they are in another
passage ; Euripides, *Androm.* 926.   There is no doubt that elderly
and experienced women used to visit and offer their assistance at
childbeds and in cases of illness.   Quite different, however, from
the regular Grecian custom was that prevalent at Alexandria.
See Theocrit. xv.

We see, then, that there were very severe restrictions on the
freedom of the Greek women, with the exception of those of the
lowest class.   Yet many writers have gone further, and have
asserted that husbands often kept their wives under lock and
key, and even placed their seals on the door of the gynæconitis,
for the sake of additional security.   Perhaps a jealous and suspicious man might now and then have ensured his wife's fidelity
by fastening the μέσαυλος ; but the passages quoted in proof of
this seem of no great weight.   Thus we have the tirade in Eurip.
Androm. 932 :

> πρὸς τάδ᾽ εὖ φυλάσσετε
> κλήθροισι καὶ μοχλοῖσι δωμάτων πύλας.

This, however, does not refer to the door of the women's apartments, but to the house-door, and the end proposed was to get
rid of the visits of other women.   See also Aristoph. *Thesmoph.*
414 :

> εἶτα διὰ τοῦτον ταῖς γυναικωνίτισιν
> σφραγῖδας ἐμβάλλουσιν ἤδη καὶ μόχλους,
> τηροῦντες ἡμᾶς. καὶ προσέτι Μολοττικοὺς
> τρέφουσι, μυρμολυκεῖα τοῖς μοιχοῖς, κύνας.

We must not suppose this to be by any means intended as a
representation of actual life ; it is merely meant as a persiflage
on passages of Euripides, such as that in the fragment of the
Danaë, v. 58 :

> πατὴρ δέ μιν κλήσας
> ἐν παρθενῶσι σφραγῖσι δέμας φυλάσσει.

More weight may be attached to a seriously-meant passage of
Menander, apud Stob. *Tit.* lxxiv. 27 :

ὅστις δὲ μοχλοῖς καὶ διὰ σφραγισμάτων
σώζει δάμαρτα, δρᾶν τι δὴ δοκῶν σοφὸν,
μάταιός ἐστι καὶ φρονῶν οὐδὲν φρονεῖ.

But if we consider that these Euripido-Aristophanic inventions became almost proverbial, we shall hardly be disposed to argue as to facts from Menander's hypothetical expressions. Tholuck, moreover, is quite wrong in asserting that the gynæconitis was guarded by eunuchs, a notion which he may perhaps have culled from Barthelemy or Potter.

Such a method of treatment naturally had the effect of rendering the girls excessively bashful, and even prudish ; but the proverbial modesty of the Attic virgins, which arose from this, stood in agreeable contrast to the wantonness of other Greek damsels, and the pert forwardness of those at Sparta. See the remarkable account of the Lydian girls given by Herodotus, i. 93 : Τοῦ γὰρ δὴ Λυδῶν δήμου αἱ θυγατέρες πορνεύονται πᾶσαι, συλλέγουσαι σφίσι φερνὰς, ἐς ὃ ἂν συνοικήσωσι τοῦτο ποιέουσαι. ἐκδιδόασι δὲ αὐταὶ ἑωυτάς. Strabo, xi. 13, 16, relates the same thing of the Armenian damsels, and those of Tuscany did likewise. See Plaut. Cist. ii. 3, 20 :

non enim hic, ubi ex Tusco modo
Tute tibi indigne dotem quæras corpore.

It is especially noticeable that the Lydians and Tuscans, whose other customs were so similar as to lead to the inference of a common origin, should also resemble each other in this strange usage. Such enormities were quite unknown to the Greeks, and branding was the punishment inflicted in the few cases of the sort. But at Athens, and indeed in most other cities, the Spartan γύμνωσις and ἄνεσις must have been thought very repulsive. See the Excursus on The Gymnasia, p. 298, and the passage there quoted from Euripides, Andromache, 586. There was as great a diversity between the manners of the Spartan and Athenian virgin as between the χιτὼν σχιστὸς of the former, and the modest dress of the latter, which so carefully concealed the person. Even the married woman shrunk back and blushed if she chanced to be seen at the window by a man. Aristoph. Thesmoph. 797. And thus the whole behaviour of the women, and not at Athens only, was most modest and retiring. Indeed it sometimes lapsed into a simplicity very amusing. See Plutarch, de Cap. ex Inim. Util. 7 : Ὁ Ἱέρων ὑπό τινος τῶν ἐχθρῶν εἰς τὴν

δυσωδίαν ἐλοιδορήθη τοῦ στόματος· ἐλθὼν οὖν οἴκαδε πρὸς τὴν
γυναῖκα, Τί λέγεις, εἶπεν, οὐδὲ σύ μοι τοῦτο ἔφρασας ; ἡ δὲ οὖσα
σώφρων καὶ ἄκακος, Ὤιμην, εἶπεν, ὅτι τοιοῦτο πάντες ὄζουσιν οἱ
ἄνδρες. Cf. Id. *Apophth. Reg.* p. 695 ; *Conjug. Præc.* 29.

On the one hand, the men were very careful as to their
behaviour in the presence of women, though they were quite
strangers to those minute attentions which constitute the gallantry
of the moderns. On the other hand, the conjugal rights and
relations were carefully respected, and the men were ceremoniously
observant of that etiquette which debarred them from the society
of the other sex. Thus it was considered a grievous infraction of
the rights of a married couple, as well as a gross piece of vulga-
rity, for a man to enter an abode of women in the absence of the
master. We have a remarkable instance of the conscientious observance of this rule, in a case where a friend or relation who is
called in to give assistance, does not venture to cross the threshold.
See Demosth. *in Euerg.* p. 1157 : προσελθὼν δὲ ὁ Ἀγνόφιλος προσ-
κληθεὶς ὑπὸ τοῦ θεράποντος τοῦ Ἀρθεμίωνος, ὅς ἐστί μοι γείτων,
εἰς μὲν τὴν οἰκίαν οὐκ εἰσῆλθεν· οὐ γὰρ ἡγεῖτο δίκαιον εἶναι μὴ
παρόντος γε τοῦ κυρίου. Again, in the same speech, the plaintiff
excuses his having entered the house of his opponent, on the plea
of this person being unmarried. *Ibid.* p. 1150 : καὶ ἐπεπύσμην·
αὐτὸν ὅτι οὐκ εἴη γεγαμηκώς. And in a case similar to the former one, Lysias accuses Simon of a gross ὕβρις for forcing his way
into the gynæconitis. Lysias, *adv. Simon.* p. 139 : ἐλθὼν ἐπὶ τὴν
οἰκίαν τὴν ἐμὴν νύκτωρ μεθύων, ἐκκόψας τὰς θύρας εἰσῆλθεν εἰς
τὴν γυναικωνῖτιν, ἔνδον οἰσῶν τῆς τε ἀδελφῆς τῆς ἐμῆς καὶ τῶν
ἀδελφιδῶν, αἳ οὕτω κοσμίως βεβιώκασιν, ὥστε καὶ ὑπὸ τῶν οἰκείων
ὁρώμεναι αἰσχύνεσθαι.

Offensive language before females was held very culpable.
See Demosth. *in Mid.* p. 540 : τῆς ἀδελφῆς ἔτ᾽ ἔνδον οὔσης τότε
καὶ παιδὸς οὔσης κόρης ἐναντίον ἐφθέγγοντο αἰσχρὰ καὶ τοιαῦτα,
οἷα ἂν ἄνθρωποι τοιοῦτοι φθέγξαιντο. Hiero punished Epichar-
mos for a similar offence. Plutarch, *Apophth. Reg.* p. 696 : Ἐπί-
χαρμον δὲ τὸν κωμῳδοποιόν, ὅτι τῆς γυναικὸς αὐτοῦ παρούσης
εἶπέ τι τῶν ἀπρεπῶν, ἐζημίωσε. Cf. Terent. *Heaut.* v. 4, 19 :
' pudet dicere hac præsente verbum turpe ' (i.e. the word *scortum*).
A beautiful observance, had it sprung from true moral grounds, and
not rather from motives of respect to the κύριος, whoever he might

be. Besides which, even the strong current of popular opinion
was not able to prevent frequent breaches of this custom.

Marriage, in reference to the procreation of children, was considered by the Greeks as a necessity enforced by their duties to
the gods, to the state, and to their ancestors; and they also took
into account the advantages which the wedded state possessed
with regard to household arrangements. Aristot. *Ethic. Nic.* viii.
14, p. 1162 : οἱ δ᾽ ἄνθρωποι οὐ μόνον τῆς τεκνοποιίας χάριν συν-
οικοῦσιν, ἀλλὰ καὶ τῶν εἰς τὸν βίον. Until a very late period,
at least, no higher considerations attached to matrimony, nor
was strong attachment a frequent cause of marriage. Yet it
would be too much to assert with Müller, *Dorians*, ii. p. 292,
that there is no instance of an Athenian falling in love with
a free-born woman, and marrying her from violent passion.
Now, firstly, this is actually related of Callias, who, in order to
obtain the sister of Cimon, paid the debt of her father. Plutarch,
Cim. 4 : ἐπεὶ δὲ Καλλίας, τῶν εὐπόρων τις ᾿Αθήνῃσιν, ἐρασθεὶς
προσῆλθε, τὴν ὑπὲρ τοῦ πατρὸς καταδίκην ἐκτίνειν ἕτοιμος ὢν
πρὸς τὸ δημόσιον. Cf. Demosth. *adv. Bœot.* ii. p. 1016. Secondly,
how often do the comedians describe a youth desperately en-
amoured of a girl; and they surely would not have done so had
not such a thing sometimes occurred. We may cite the instances
of Charinus and Pamphilus in the *Andria* of Terence, of Antipho
in the *Phormio*, and many others. And if we remember the
Antigone and Hæmon of Sophocles, can we assert that the ἔρως
ἀνίκατος μάχαν was at work for hetæræ only? Still it must be
admitted that sensuality was the soil from which such passion
sprung, and none other than a sensual love was acknowledged
between man and wife. This is very distinctly stated by Pausanias, in Plato, *Symp.* p. 181 ; cf. Plutarch, *Amat.* 4.

But in the greater number of cases there was no such previous inclination, as is shown by the way in which marriages
were usually arranged. The ordinary motives are laid down by
Demosthenes, *in Neær.* p. 1386 : τὰς μὲν γὰρ ἑταίρας ἡδονῆς
ἕνεκ᾽ ἔχομεν· τὰς δὲ παλλακὰς τῆς καθ᾽ ἡμέραν θεραπείας τοῦ σώματος. τὰς δὲ γυναῖκας τοῦ παιδοποιεῖσθαι γνησίως καὶ τῶν ἔνδον
φύλακα πιστὴν ἔχειν. This agrees with Antipho, *de Venef.* p. 613,
where the παλλακὴ follows Philoneos to the sacrifice, and waits
upon him and his guests at table. In this case she was the

absolute property of her master, as we see from *Ib.* p. 611 : *κα.*
ῆν αὐτῷ παλλακὴ ἣν ὁ Φιλόνεως ἐπὶ πορνεῖον ἔμελλε καταστῆσαι.
Sometimes, however, the παλλακὴ occupied a higher position.
This is seen from the law quoted by Demosthenes, *in Aristocr.*
p. 637 : *ῆ ἐπὶ δάμαρτι, ἢ ἐπὶ μητρὶ, ἢ ἐπ' ἀδελφῇ, ἢ ἐπὶ θυγατρὶ,*
ἢ ἐπὶ παλλακῇ ἣν ἂν ἐπ' ἐλευθέροις παισὶν ἔχῃ. Here we should
notice the distinction between ἐλεύθεροι and γνήσιοι. Cf. Lysias,
de Cœde Eratosth. p. 34. In the heroic age it was quite usual to
keep a παλλακὴ as well as the lawful wife ; but there is no passage
directly informing us whether this was subsequently allowable,
though it most likely was not, since we know that if a husband
brought an hetæra into the house, it was a legal ground for separation. Andocid. *in Alcib.* p. 117. See also Eurip. *Androm.* 891.
It is stated by Diog. Laert. ii. 26, and by Athenæus. xiii. p. 556,
that in the time of Socrates a Psephisma made it lawful, *γαμεῖν*
μὲν ἀστὴν μίαν, παιδοποιεῖσθαι δὲ καὶ ἐξ ἑτέρας. This assertion
must be received with suspicion, in spite of the authorities adduced. The thing itself might no doubt sometimes occur. Cf.
Hermann, *Griech. Staatsalt.* p. 254.

In regular marriage, on the other hand, in which the wife as
γαμετὴ is opposed to the παλλακὴ, the chief object was, as Demosthenes expresses it, *παιδοποιεῖσθαι γνησίως,* though this intention was not made so prominent at Athens as at Sparta, where,
as Plutarch tells us, the women were married for nothing else *ἢ*
ἐπὶ τὸ τῆς τεκνώσεως ἔργον, and the husband often resigned his
rights to some more potent individual, though the marriage continued undissolved. Plutarch, *comp. Lyc. c. Num.* 3 : *Ὁ δὲ Λά-*
κων οἴκοι τῆς γυναικὸς οὔσης παρ' αὐτῷ, καὶ τοῦ γάμου μένοντος
ἐπὶ τῶν ἐξ ἀρχῆς δικαίων, μετεδίδου τῷ πείσαντι τῆς κοινωνίας
εἰς τέκνωσιν. πολλοὶ δὲ, ὥσπερ εἴρηται, καὶ παρακαλοῦντες εἰσῆ-
γον ἐξ ὧν ἂν ἐδόκουν μάλιστα παῖδας εὐειδεῖς καὶ ἀγαθοὺς γενέ-
σθαι. Cf. Xenoph. *de Rep. Lac.* 1, 8 ; and Goguet, *Orig. des Lois,*
v. p. 427.

At Athens, too, and probably in the other Grecian states as
well, the generation of children was considered the chief end of
marriage. Xenoph. *Memor.* ii. 2, 4 : *Καὶ μή που τῶν γε ἀφρο-*
δισίων ἕνεκα παιδοποιεῖσθαι τοὺς ἀνθρώπους ὑπολάμβανε, κ.τ.λ.
Cf. Demosth. *pro Phorm.* p. 953. Here, however, the sacredness
of the married state was not sacrificed to this eager desire of

posterity, nor were state-interests in this case the only
motives

There were three considerations by which the duty of marriage
was enforced. First, respect to the gods; for it was considered to
be incumbent on every one to leave behind him those who should
continue to discharge his religious obligations. Plato, *Leg.* vi.
p. 773 : ἀεὶ τῷ θεῷ ὑπηρέτας ἀνθ' αὑτοῦ παραδιδόναι. Secondly,
obligation to the state : since by generating descendants, its continuance was provided for. Entirely consonant with the Spartan
institutions was such a subordination of individual inclination to
the demands of the public weal. See Plutarch, *Lyc.* 15 : οὐ μὴν
ἀλλὰ καὶ ἀτιμίαν τινὰ προσέθηκε τοῖς ἀγάμοις. εἴργοντο γὰρ ἐν
ταῖς γυμνοπαιδιαῖς τῆς θέας· τοῦ δὲ χειμῶνος οἱ μὲν ἄρχοντες
αὐτοὺς ἐκέλευον ἐν κύκλῳ περιϊέναι τὴν ἀγορὰν, οἱ δὲ περιϊόντες
ᾖδον εἰς αὑτοὺς ᾠδήν τινα πεποιημένην ὡς δίκαια πάσχοιεν, ὅτι
τοῖς νόμοις ἀπειθοῦσι· τιμῆς δὲ καὶ θεραπείας, ἣν νέοι πρεσβυτέροις παρεῖχον, ἐστέροντο. See Aristo, apud. Stob. *Tit.* lxvii. 16;
Poll. viii. 40 ; Clearch. apud Athen. xiii. p. 555. These passages
relate to Sparta, but at Athens, and probably in all or most of
the other states, there were no such express penalties on celibacy.
Something of the kind, it is true, is hinted at by Plutarch, *de
Amore Prol.* 2 : Πρῶτον οὐκ ἀναμένει (τὰ ζῶα) νόμους ἀγάμου καὶ
ὀψιγάμου, καθάπερ οἱ Λυκούργου πολῖται καὶ Σόλωνος. Pollux,
also, not referring to Sparta, speaks of a γραφὴ ἀγάμου, though
such a process does not appear to have been ever instituted.
Laws of this kind, enforced by ἀτιμία, as well as fines, are no
doubt recommended by Plato, *Leg.* iv. p. 721, and vi. p. 774.
But here, as in many other instances, he leans more to the
Spartan than to the Attic principles of legislation. Thus he says
p. 773 : τὸν γὰρ τῇ πόλει δεῖ συμφέροντα μνηστεύειν γάμον ἕκαστον,
οὐ τὸν ἥδιστον αὐτῷ. Of the same tendency was the regulation to
the effect that the orators and generals should be married, as a
pledge of their fidelity to the state; see Dinarch. *in Demosth.*
p. 51. Nevertheless the number of bachelors seems to have been
very considerable ; and we see from the lengthy apologies for celibacy (*e.g.* Antipho, ap. Stob. *Tit.* lxviii. 37 ; Plaut. *Mil.* iii. 1),
how many, to avoid the trouble of maintaining a wife and children,
or from suspicion of the sex, remained single. Other causes also
are assigned by Fr. Schlegel, *Griechen und Römer*, p. 261.

A third consideration which induced persons to marry was
a regard for their own race and lineage; and this was not only
from the wish of seeing themselves perpetuated in the same, but
was chiefly in reference to the continuance of the duties to the
departed, inasmuch as the belief in the beneficial perception of
the offerings and tokens of love devoted to the manes made
obligatory the propagation of the family. See Isocrates, *Plat.* 24.
Hence those who were childless sought, by means of adoption, to
prevent the cessation of these usages. Isæus, *de Apollod. Her.*
p. 179 : πάντες γὰρ οἱ τελευτήσειν μέλλοντες πρόνοιαν ποιοῦνται
σφῶν αὐτῶν, ὅπως μὴ ἐξερημώσωσι τοὺς σφετέρους αὐτῶν οἴκους,
ἀλλ' ἔσται τις καὶ ὁ ἐναγιῶν καὶ πάντα τὰ νομιζόμενα αὐτοῖς
ποιήσων. διὸ κἂν ἄπαιδες τελευτήσωσιν, ἀλλ' οὖν ποιησάμενοι
καταλείπουσι.

In addition to these motives, considerations of an economical
nature entered into the case ; and many married chiefly in order
to obtain a trusty and skilful housekeeper. It is very rarely
that we meet with even a hint of any higher considerations. See,
however, the fragment of Musonius, apud Stob. *Tit.* lxvii. 20.

The choice of the bride seldom depended on previous, or at
least on intimate, acquaintance. More attention was generally
paid to the position of a damsel's family and the amount of her
dowry than to her personal qualities. This subject is enlarged
on by Plato, *Polit.* p. 310, and he utterly repudiates the principle
of looking out for a wife of equal condition and property : τὰ
πλούτου καὶ δυνάμεων διώγματα. That great regard was paid to
the proverb, τὴν κατὰ σαυτὸν ἔλα (Plutarch, *Educ. Puer.* 19),
is seen not only from many passages in Plato, but from frequent
expressions of the comedians, when rich men sue for the sisters or
daughters of their poorer neighbours. Thus, in the *Aulularia* of
Plautus, ii. 2, 58, where the wealthy Megadorus sues for the hand
of the daughter of the poor Euclio : 'Hoc magnum est periculum,
ab asinis ad boves transcendere, etc.' Cf. Xenophon, *Hier.* i. 27 ;
Plutarch, *Amat.* 2. If the rich objected to a dowerless bride, the
poor, on their side, had equal scruples about a rich alliance ; and
on this hinges the whole plot of the *Trinummus* of Plautus, in
which Lesbonicus strongly urges the impropriety of his undowered
sister being wedded by the rich Lysiteles. See Act iii. 2, 62.

Hence it was usual for a father to choose for his son a wife and one perhaps whom the bridegroom had never seen. Terent. *Andr.* i. 5, 14. Marriage was often adopted by the father as an expedient for putting an end to the debaucheries of his son, who received the lady as a sort of penalty inflicted on him. Terent. *Heaut.* v. 5; Plaut. *Trin.* v. 2, 59: 'si pro peccatis centum ducat uxores, parum est.' Achill. Tat. i. 8: Γάμον, εἶπεν, ἤδη σοι δίδωσιν ὁ πατήρ; τί γὰρ ἠδίκησας, ἵνα καὶ πεδηθῇς;

Such arrangements were unfavourable to the existence of real affection, and we cannot be surprised at the frequent prevalence of coldness, indifference, or discontent. Plato thinks these consequences might be prevented, by giving the young people more frequent opportunities of seeing one another. See *Leg.* vi. p. 177. No such previous intercourse was possible at Athens, and therefore couples might often find themselves mutually disappointed. Love after marriage was of unfrequent occurrence, though an instance is to be found in the *Hecyra* of Terence. It was probably still more unusual for the lady's inclinations to be consulted. The hard fate of maidens who were thus consigned for life to an unknown master, is forcibly described in a fragment of the *Tereus* of Sophocles, apud Stob. *Tit.* lxviii. 19. At first, as we might expect, there was an entire absence of confidence between the newly-married pair, and it was a long while before the shyness in the woman gave place to a more familiar tone. See the characteristic description Ischomachos gives of the behaviour of his wife soon after marriage. Xenoph. *Œcon.* 7, 10: ἐπεὶ ἤδη μοι χειροήθης ἦν καὶ ἐτιθασσεύετο, ὥστε διαλέγεσθαι, ἠρόμην αὐτὴν κ. τ. λ.

An essential consideration with the Attic burgher, ἄστος or Ἀθηναῖος, was that his bride should be also of that rank. For the children of such marriages only were γνήσιοι, and marriage between an ἀστὸς and a ξένη was forbidden. The two laws on this subject are produced by Demosthenes, *in Neær.* pp. 1350, 1363. For further details see Wachsmuth, *Hellen. Alterthumsk.* i. 2, p. 205. These laws, however, appear to have been frequently infringed. See Demosth. *ibid.* p. 1385.

Relationship was, with trifling limitations, no hindrance to marriage, which could take place within all degrees of ἀγχιστεία or συγγένεια, though naturally not in the γένος itself. See Isæus, *de Cir. Her.* p. 217: Κίρωνος θυγάτηρ ἢ ἀδελφὸς ἐγγυτέρω τοῦ γένους ἐστί; δῆλον γὰρ ὅτι θυγάτηρ. ἡ μὲν γὰρ ἐξ ἐκείνου νέγο

νεν, ὁ δὲ μετ' ἐκείνου. θυγατρὸς δὲ παῖδες ἢ ἀδελφός; παῖδες δή-
πουθεν· γένος γὰρ, ἀλλ' οὐχὶ συγγένεια τοῦτ' ἔστιν. The marriage
of brothers and sisters was only allowed in the case of their not
being ὁμομήτριοι. Demosth. *adv. Eubul.* p. 1304; Plutarch,
Themist. 32; Pausan. i. 7, 1; Achill. Tat. i. 3. But there is
strong reason to conclude that, except in the very earliest period,
such alliances were universally condemned. It seems also that
we should take in their full meaning such passages as Lysias,
in Alcib. p. 550, and Eurip. *Androm.* 175. Plato, too, carefully enumerates all the grades of relationship within which the
daughters might marry, in case the father died intestate, and he
makes no mention of any but collateral branches. *Leg.* xi. p. 925.
Cf. *ib.* viii. p. 838. The force of public opinion was not, however, sufficient to prevent the occasional occurrence of flagrant
cases. Andocid. *de Myst.* p. 61: γαμεῖ μὲν Ἰσχομάχου θυγατέρα·
ταύτῃ δὲ συνοικήσας οὐδ' ἐνιαυτὸν τὴν μητέρα αὐτῆς ἔλαβε. καὶ
συνῴκει ὁ πάντων σχετλιώτατος ἀνθρώπων τῇ μητρὶ καὶ τῇ θυ-
γατρί . . . καὶ εἶχεν ἐν τῇ οἰκίᾳ ἀμφοτέρας. See also Athen. xii.
p. 534.

It is well known that widows frequently married again; this
was often in compliance with the testamentary dispositions of
their husbands, as little regard being paid to their own wishes as
in the case of girls. See Isæus, *de Philoctem. Her.* p. 149; *de
Cir. Her.* p. 215; Demosth. *in Aphob.* i. p. 814. This custom
was of very ancient date, and it is asserted by Pausanias, ii. 21,
8, that Gorgophone, the daughter of Perseus, was the first widow
who married again! The words of Euripides (*Troad.* 669) are
at the most his own individual view, though they in some measure
agree with the law of Charondas, quoted by Stobæus, *Tit.* xliv.
40: Ὁ μητρυιὰν ἐπιγαμῶν μὴ εὐδοξείτω, ἀλλ' ὀνειδιζέσθω αἴτιος
ὢν οἰκείας διαστάσεως.

With regard to age, there does not seem to have been any fixed
time for marriage, except perhaps at Sparta. Plato is somewhat
inconsistent on this point. In the *de Republ.* p. 460, he suggests
τὰ εἴκοσιν ἔτη γυναικὶ, ἀνδρὶ δὲ τὰ τριάκοντα. Compare *Leg.*
vi. p. 785: γάμου δὲ ὅρον εἶναι, κόρῃ μὲν ἀπὸ ἑκκαίδεκα ἐτῶν εἰς
εἴκοσι τὸν μακρότατον χρόνον ἀφωρισμένον· κόρῳ δὲ ἀπὸ τριάκοντα μέχρι τῶν πέντε καὶ τριάκοντα. Aristotle, *de Republ.* vii.
16, p. 1335, thinks eighteen a good age for girls to marry, and

for men thirty-seven or less. It may be assumed that virgins did not often marry before their fifteenth year, nor men before their twentieth. See Xenoph. *Œcon.* 7, 5. Some exceptions are, however, mentioned. See Demosth. *adv. Bœot. προικ.* p. 1009; Pausan. iv. 19, 4; though both these passages show that it was unusual. Cf. Meier and Schömann, *Att. Proc.* p. 407.

Care was generally taken that the bride should be considerably the younger. See Eurip. apud Stob. *Tit.* lxxi. 3 :

> κακὸν γυναῖκα πρὸς νέαν ζεῦξαι νέον.
> μακρὸν γὰρ ἰσχὺς μᾶλλον ἀῤῥένων μένει,
> θήλεια δ' ἥβη θᾶσσον ἐκλείπει δέμας.

Sappho, Fragm. 20 : ἀλλ' ἐὼν φίλος ἀμῖν λέχος ἄρνυσο νεώτε-ρον. οὐ γὰρ τλάσομ' ἐγὼ ξυνοικεῖν οὖσα γερατέρα. Hence those girls who did not find a husband early were mostly fated not to marry at all. See Aristoph. *Lysist.* 597. Still it must not be concealed that there were other means, besides a father's aid, by which a husband might be procured. There appear to have been certain obliging dames who drove a trade in match-making, and were hence called προμνήστριαι or προμνηστρίδες. Xenoph. *Mem.* ii. 6, 36 : ἔφη γὰρ ('Ασπασία) τὰς ἀγαθὰς προμνηστρίδας μετὰ μὲν ἀληθείας τἀγαθὰ διαγγελλούσας δεινὰς εἶναι συνάγειν ἀνθρώ-πους εἰς κηδείαν, ψευδομένας δ' οὐκ ὠφελεῖν ἐπαινούσας. τοὺς γὰρ ἐξαπατηθέντας ἅμα μισεῖν ἀλλήλους τε καὶ τὴν προμνησαμένην. Poll. iii. 31 : καὶ προμνήστριαι μὲν αἱ συνάγουσαι τὸν γάμον. Cf. Lucian, *Deor. Dial.* xx. 16; Dio Chrysost. *Orat.* vii. p. 249. Some-times confidential female slaves discharged such duties, as in the *Pharmaceutria* of Theocritus. Cf. Charit. i. 2. But as pander-ing in its worst sense might easily lurk behind, the whole trade was in no very good repute. See Plato, *Theæt.* p. 150; Xenoph. *Symp.* 4, 61.

The usages and formalities of marriage were numerous. The solemn affiancing, ἐγγύησις, which was legally necessary, in order to render the marriage complete and binding, will not be dis-cussed here. The law itself is to be found in Demosthenes, *in Steph.* ii. p. 1134 ; see also Platner, *Beitr. z. Kenntn. d. Att. Rechts*, p. 109; Meier and Schömann, *Att. Proc.* p. 409; Hermann, *Staatsalterth.* p. 254; Wachsmuth, *Hell. Alterth.* ii. 1, p. 206. This public ratification must be carefully distinguished from the previous betrothal or consent of the bride. See Pindar, *Ol.* vii. 1 :

Φιάλαν ὡς εἴ τις ἀφνείας ἀπὸ χειρὸς ἑλὼν
ἔνδον ἀμπέλου καχλάζοισαν δρόσῳ
δωρήσεται
νεανίᾳ γαμβρῷ προπίνων οἴκοθεν οἴκαδε, πάγχρυσον κορυφὰν κτεάνων
συμποσίου τε χάριν κᾶδός τε τιμάσαις ἑὸν, ἐν δὲ φίλων
παριόντων θῆκέ μιν ζαλωτὸν ὁμόφρονος εὐνᾶς.

From this passage Böckh assumes that it was a prevalent Greek
custom to solemnise the affiancing at the banquet, by pledging
the future son-in-law; but this can hardly be borne out. The
instances adduced from Athenæus, xiii. p. 575, are neither of
them Greek; and moreover, in each case, the girl, and not the
father, drinks to the bridegroom, thus declaring her choice. All
this is entirely opposed to Greek customs.

At the same time that the affiancing took place, the dowry,
προὶξ or φερνὴ, was also settled upon the bride. This, however, was
scarcely so much of a legal requirement as the ἐγγύη, but rather was
an ancient usage, strictly complied with for the most part. See
Meier and Schömann, *Att. Proc.* p. 415. It might be a matter of
law, in so far as the κύριος of the bride was in some cases bound
to an ἔκδοσις with a dower; but its neglect was certainly not
attended with the same civil disadvantages as were entailed by
an omission of the ἐγγύησις. See Demosth. *adv. Bæot.* p. 1016,
where the legitimacy of the plaintiff, whose mother was ἄπροικος,
is nowise called in question, though the unseemliness of the marriage is made the subject of remark. Cf. Platner, *Beitr.* p. 110.
And for the very reason that it was considered more proper, and
because the woman took a higher position in her new household
when possessed of a dowry, rich burghers would often join in
portioning the sisters or daughters of those in humble circumstances. See Lysias, *de bon. Aristoph.* p. 659: ἔτι τοίνυν καὶ ἰδίᾳ
τισὶ τῶν πολιτῶν ἀποροῦσι συνεξέδωκε θυγατέρας καὶ ἀδελφάς.

There is no evidence enabling us to determine when this custom of giving dowers first began; though it was certainly long
before the time of Solon. In the heroic age, as above remarked,
the contrary was the case: the man won his bride by gifts, ἔδνα;
a custom so general that it cannot be disproved by *Odyss.* i. 227,
and ii. 196. Aristotle also mentions the early custom of buying
the bride, as he expresses it; *de Republ.* ii. 8, p. 1268: τοὺς γὰρ
ἀρχαίους νόμους λίαν ἁπλοῦς εἶναι καὶ βαρβαρικούς. ἐσιδηροφο-
οοῦντό τε γὰρ οἱ Ἕλληνες, καὶ τὰς γυναῖκας ἐωνοῦντο παρ᾽ ἀλλήλων.

We are also told that Solon introduced a law to restrict the amount of the φερνὴ which the bride brought her husband. Plutarch, *Sol.* 20 : τῶν δ' ἄλλων γάμων ἀφεῖλε τὰς φερνὰς, ἱμάτια τρία, καὶ σκεύη μικροῦ νομίσματος ἄξια κελεύσας, ἕτερον δὲ μηδὲν ἐπιφέρεσθαι τὴν γαμουμένην. οὐ γὰρ ἐβούλετο μισθοφόρον, οὐδ' ὤνιον εἶναι τὸν γάμον, ἀλλ' ἐπὶ τεκνώσει καὶ χάριτι καὶ φιλότητι γίνεσθαι τοῦ ἀνδρὸς καὶ γυναικὸς συνοικισμόν. Some doubt, however, is thrown upon this statement by the fact that no such restriction is mentioned by any of the Attic orators. The most probable conjecture seems to be that adopted by Bunsen, *de Jure Hered. Athen.* p. 43, and other writers, who suppose that by the φερνὴ mentioned by Plutarch is not meant the regular προίξ, but certain additional wedding-presents. This supposition is not free from difficulties, for the dowry did not solely consist of money, but included clothes and ornaments, ἱμάτια καὶ χρυσία, as well as slaves. See Eurip. *Iphig. in Aul.* 46 ; Diog. Laert. v. 13. In support of his position, Bunsen quotes a passage in which these gifts are distinguished from the προίξ. Demosth. *in Spud.* p. 1036 : ἅπερ ἔπεμψέ μοι χωρὶς τῆς προικός. But in Isæus, *de Cir. Her.* p. 199, things of this sort are not reckoned as separate presents, but are included in the dowry : ἐκείνων δὲ ἔτι ζώντων, ἐπεὶ συνοικεῖν εἶχεν ἡλικίαν, ἐκδίδωσιν αὐτὴν Ναυσιμένει, Χολαργεῖ, σὺν ἱματίοις καὶ χρυσίοις πέντε καὶ εἴκοσι μνᾶς ἐπιδούς. Most probably Solon's law was only directed against these presents, and its application was erroneously extended by Plutarch to the whole προίξ.

The intention assigned by Plutarch to this law, is the maintenance of the husband's independence, which might have been endangered by the reception of too large a dowry with his wife. This object receives Plato's sanction, and he recommends that no dowry should be allowed to exceed fifty drachmæ in value, ἐσθῆτος χάριν. See *Leg.* vi. p. 774. In fact, the Greek ladies must have presumed a good deal upon the strength of their fortunes ; for not only are the comedians full of complaints on this head, but other authors repeat the warning. See Plutarch, *de Educ. Puer.* 19 ; *Amator.* 7. On the other hand, fathers thought it a burden to portion their daughters, and hence female infants were more frequently exposed. In support of this, a host of passages might be adduced. See, for instance, Menander (p. 14, Mein.) :

χαλεπόν γε θυγάτηρ κτῆμα καὶ δυσδιάθετον.

See also Id. p. 24 :

> εὐδαιμονία τοῦτ' ἔστιν υἱὸς νοῦν ἔχων·
> ἀλλὰ θυγάτηρ κτῆμ' ἐστὶν ἐργῶδες πατρί.

By far the greater number of marriages seem to have taken place in winter. This is mentioned as the most suitable and usual time by Aristotle, *de Republ.* vii. 16. It is known also that the month Gamelion received its name from this circumstance. Certain days also were considered more proper than others. The fourth day of the month is named by Hesiod, *Opp.* 800, though it may be doubtful whether he means the fourth from the beginning. His words are :

> πεφύλαξο δὲ θύμῳ
> τετράδ' ἀλεύασθαι φθίνοντός θ' ἱσταμένου τε
> ἄλγεα θυμοβορεῖν· μάλα τοι τετελεσμένον ἦμαρ.
> ἐν δὲ τετάρτῃ μηνὸς ἄγεσθαι ἐς οἶκεν ἄκοιτιν.

Since the Greeks reckoned their months from the new moon, or the first appearance of the crescent, this is in tolerable accordance with Procl. ad Hesiod. *Opp.* 782 : διὸ καὶ Ἀθηναῖοι τὰς πρὸς σύνοδον ἡμέρας ἐξελέγοντο πρὸς γάμους καὶ τὰ Θεογάμια ἐτέλουν, τότε φυσικῶς εἶναι πρῶτον οἰόμενοι γάμον τῆς σελήνης οὔσης πρὸς ἡλίου σύνοδον. A contrary custom seems to be inferred by Pindar, *Isthm.* vii. 44 : ἐν διχομηνίδεσσιν δὲ ἑσπέραις ἐρατὸν λύοι κεν χαλινὸν ὑφ' ἥρωϊ παρθενίας. See also Eurip. *Iphig. in Aulid.* 717 : ὅταν σελήνης εὐτυχὴς ἔλθῃ κύκλος.

Cf. Dio Chrysost. *Or.* vii. p. 245 : καὶ ποιήσομέν γε τοὺς γάμους ἡμέραν ἀγαθὴν ἐπιλεξάμενοι. κἀγὼ, Πῶς, ἔφην, κρίνετε τὴν ἀγαθὴν ἡμέραν ; καὶ ὅς, Ὅταν μὴ μικρὸν ᾖ τὸ σελήνιον.

The wedding-day was preceded by several solemnities. The most important of these was the sacrifice to the tutelar gods of marriage, θεοὶ γαμήλιοι. This was called τὰ προτέλεια γάμων, or προγάμεια. Cf. Poll. iii. 38 ; Ruhnken, *ad Tim.* p. 188. There does not appear to be any authority for the statement frequently advanced, that this took place on the day preceding the wedding. The wedding-day itself seems to be intended in Achilles Tatius, ii. 12 : ἔθυεν οὖν τότε ὁ πατὴρ προτέλεια τῶν γάμων . . . καὶ δὴ ἐπέσχον ἐκείνην τὴν ἡμέραν τοὺς γάμους. It is worthy of remark, that the father is the person who makes the offering both here and in Eurip. *Iphig. in Aulid.* 718.

Diodorus Siculus, v. 73, names only Zeus and Hera as the deities thus sacrificed to. See, however, Phot. p. 464 : Προτελείαν

‍

ἡμέραν ὀνομάζουσιν, ἐν ᾗ εἰς τὴν ἀκρόπολιν τὴν γαμουμένην παρθένον ἄγουσιν οἱ γονεῖς ὡς τὴν θεὸν καὶ θυσίαν ἐπιτελοῦσιν. Here
ἡ θεὸς probably means Artemis, who, as well as Athene, had a
temple on the Acropolis. See Pollux, iii. 38 : διὰ τοῦτο καὶ "Ηρα
τελεία ἡ ζυγία. ταύτῃ γὰο τοῖς προτελείοις προὐτέλουν τὰς κόρας καὶ Ἀρτέμιδι καὶ Μοίραις. And this does not apply to Athens
alone, but also to Bœotia and Locris, as we are told by Plutarch,
Aristid. 20.   Cf. Eurip. Hippol. 1414 ; Lucian, de Syr. Dea, 60.

The ἀρκτεύεσθαι seems to have been an expiatory sacrifice
offered to Artemis Munychia or Brauronia, but at an earlier age,
perhaps in the tenth year. See Schol. ad Aristoph. Lysistr. 645 ;
also Harpocration and Suidas. We learn, too, that the προτέλεια
were also offered to various local deities, θεοῖς ἐγχωρίοις. Plutarch, Amat. Narr. 1 : ἕως ἡ κόρη κατὰ τὰ πάτρια ἐπὶ τὴν Κισ-
σόεσσαν καλουμένην κρήνην κατῄει ταῖς Νύμφαις τὰ προτέλεια
θύσουσα. But the offering to Aphrodite did not belong to the
προτέλεια, but took place either on the wedding-day (Plutarch,
Amator. 26), or was an after-offering made by the νεωστὶ γεγα-
μημέναι, as in Æschin. Epist. 10, p. 681.

A second ceremony, which appears to have been universally
observed, was the bath, which both bride and bridegroom took on
the wedding-day, in the water of a certain fountain or river. At
Athens it was the fountain Callirrhoë, called also, after the alterations of Peisistratos, Ἐννεάκρουνος, from which was fetched the
water for this λουτρὸν νυμφικόν. Aristoph. Lysistr. 378. See
Thucyd. ii. 15 : καὶ τῇ κρήνῃ τῇ νῦν μὲν τῶν τυράννων οὕτω
σκευασάντων Ἐννεακρούνῳ καλουμένῃ, τὸ δὲ πάλαι φανερῶν τῶν
πηγῶν οὐσῶν Καλλιῤῥόῃ ὠνομασμένῃ, ἐκείνῃ τε ἐγγὺς οὔσῃ τὰ
πλείστου ἄξια ἐχρῶντο. καὶ νῦν ἔτι ἀπὸ τοῦ ἀρχαίου πρό τε
γαμικῶν καὶ ἐς ἄλλα τῶν ἱερῶν νομίζεται τῷ ὕδατι χρῆσθαι. Cf.
Poll. iii. 43. Harpocration says that the water was brought by
a boy, the nearest relation of the bridegroom, and that he was
called λουτροφόρος. The passage is as follows : "Εθος ἦν τοῖς
γαμοῦσι λουτρὰ μεταπέμπεσθαι κατὰ τὴν τοῦ γάμου ἡμέραν. ἔπεμ-
πον δ' ἐπὶ ταῦτα τὸν ἐγγυτάτω γένους παῖδα ἄῤῥενα, καὶ οὗτοι
ἐλουτροφόρουν. ἔθος δὲ ἦν καὶ τοῖς ἀγάμοις ἀποθανοῦσι λουτροφο-
ρεῖν καὶ ἐπὶ τὸ μνῆμα ἐφίστασθαι (λουτροφόρον ἐπὶ τὸ μν.?).
τοῦτο δὲ ἦν παῖς ὑδρίαν ἔχων. λέγει περὶ τούτων Δείναρχος ἔν
τε τῷ κατὰ Θεοδότου καὶ ἐν τῇ κατὰ Καλλισθένους εἰσαγγελίᾳ.

Suidas and Photius say exactly the same. This express account
would not excite much attention, were it not contradicted by
several other passages. Thus Pollux, iii. 43, makes no mention
of a boy, but says: καὶ λουτρά τις κομίζουσα, λουτροφόρος. To
reconcile these conflicting accounts, we might assume that a girl
fetched water for the bride, and a boy for the bridegroom ; and
the first of these suppositions is supported by existing antiques,
but for the latter there is no corroborating evidence of any kind.
It is condemned, moreover, by the well-known passage in Demosthenes, in Leochar. p. 1086, from which we learn that it was
the custom to place some figure referring to water-carrying on
the tomb of one who had died single, as a symbol of celibacy.
We there read : οὐ πολλῷ δὲ χρόνῳ ὕστερον ... ἠῤῥώστησεν ὁ Ἀρ-
χιάδης καὶ τελευτᾷ τὸν βίον ἀπόντος τοῦ Μειδυλίδου ἄγαμος ὤν.
-τί τούτου σημεῖον; λουτροφόρος ἐφέστηκεν ἐπὶ τῷ τοῦ Ἀρχιάδου
τάφῳ. That a girl is here intended is seen from p. 1089, where
Demosthenes expressly says : καὶ ἡ λουτροφόρος ἐφέστηκεν ἐπὶ
τῷ τοῦ Ἀρχιάδου μνήματι. We are elsewhere informed that the
symbol was merely a vessel for carrying water, in fact a black
pitcher, hence also called λίβνς. Eustath. ad Iliad. xxiii. 141 :
καὶ τοῖς πρὸ γάμου τελευτῶσιν ἡ λουτροφόρος, φασίν, ἐπετίθετο
κάλπις εἰς ἔνδειξιν τοῦ ὅτι ἄλουτος τὰ νυμφικὰ καὶ ἄγονος ἄπεισι.
Such vessels are to be found on sepulchral pillars. See Stackelberg, pl. 1. Nevertheless, this sense of the word is distinctly
contradicted by Pollux, viii. 66 : τῶν δὲ ἀγάμων λουτροφόρος τῷ
μνήματι ἐφίστατο κόρη, ἀγγεῖον ἔχουσα ὑδροφόρον, ἢ ὑδρίαν, ἢ
πρόχουν, ἢ κρωσσὸν, ἢ κάλπιν. This testimony is confirmed by
the paintings on some Volscian vases, representing girls carrying
water, and the inscription over one of them, ΚΑΛΙΡΕ ΚΡΕΝΕ
(Καλλιῤῥῆ κρήνη), leaves no doubt as to the signification. See
Brönsted, Description of thirty-two ancient Greek vases, Pl. 27.

The expression used by Pollux, iii. 43, ἀλλαχόθι δὲ, ὅθεν ἂν
καὶ τύχοι, does not mean that in other places it was immaterial
what water was used, but that in each place water was fetched
from that spring which happened to be most in repute. At
Thebes, for instance, the bridal bath would be supplied from the
Ismenos. Running water was universally used for the purpose.
Eurip. Phœnis. 347, and Schol.; Böttig. Vasengem. i. p. 143.

In the tenth letter of Æschines, a somewhat similar custom is mentioned as prevalent in Troas. It was there usual for virgins to bathe in the Scamander before their marriage, and thus symbolically dedicate their virginity to the god, see p. 680 : νενόμισται δὲ ἐν τῇ Τρωάδι γῇ, τὰς γαμουμένας παρθένους ἐπὶ τὸν Σκάμανδρον ἔρχεσθαι καὶ λουσαμένας ἀπ' αὐτοῦ τὸ ἔπος τοῦτο, ὥσπερ ἱερόν τι ἐπιλέγειν· Λαβέ μου, Σκάμανδρε, τὴν παρθενίαν.

In Sparta the marriage was solemnised in a manner very different from that usual in Attica, and probably in the other states. As is well known, the bridegroom, of course with the parents' consent, carried off the bride by force. Plutarch, *Lyc.* 15 ; Müller, *Dorians,* ii. p. 293. A scene of the kind is very frequently represented on vases, but it is extremely doubtful whether these paintings refer to the usage in question. Many of them are intended for the rape of Thetis, and similar subjects. See also Achill. Tat. ii. 13 : Νόμου γὰρ ὄντος Βυζαντίοις, εἴ τις ἁρπάσας παρθένον φθάσας ποιήσει γυναῖκα, γάμον ἔχειν τὴν βίαν, προσεῖχε τούτῳ τῷ νόμῳ.

The bride was usually fetched away towards evening by the bridegroom, in a carriage, ἐφ' ἁμάξης. This was drawn by mules or oxen, and probably by horses also, and the bride sat between the bridegroom and παράνυμφος, who was a near relation or intimate friend, and was also called πάροχος. The most detailed account is that given by Harpocration : ζεῦγος ἡμιονικὸν ἢ βοεικὸν ζεύξαντες τὴν λεγομένην κλινίδα, ἥ ἐστιν ὁμοία διεέρῳ, τὴν τῆς νύμφης μέθοδον ποιοῦνται. Παραλαβόντες δὲ αὐτὴν ἐκ τῆς πατρῴας ἑστίας ἐπὶ τὴν ἄμαξαν ἄγουσιν ἐς τὰ τοῦ γαμοῦντος ἑσπέρας ἱκανῆς. Κάθηνται δὲ τρεῖς ἐπὶ τῆς ἁμάξης· μέση μὲν ἡ νύμφη, ἑκατέρωθεν δὲ ὅ τε νυμφίος, καὶ ὁ πάροχος. οὗτος δέ ἐστι φίλος ἢ συγγενὴς ὅτι μάλιστα τιμώμενος καὶ ἀγαπώμενος. Ἐπειδὴ δὲ ἡ ἄμαξα ὄχημα ἐλέγετο, ὁ ἐκ τρίτου ὁ παροχούμενος πάροχος ἐκλήθη. Καὶ ἀπὸ ταύτης τῆς συνηθείας, κᾶν πεζοὶ μετίωσί τινες κόρην, ὁ τρίτος συμπαρὼν πάροχος λέγεται. See also Poll. iii. 40, and x. 33 ; Schol. ad Aristoph. *Aves,* 1735. We find a team of oxen mentioned by Pausanias, ix. 3, 1 ; but horses are expressly named by Euripides, *Helen.* 723 :

> καὶ λαμπάδων μεμνήμεθ', ἃς τετραόροις
> ἵπποις τροχάζων παρέφερον · σὺ δ' ἐν δίφροις
> σὺν τῷδε νύμφη δῶι' ἔλειπες ὄλβιον.

In many places a symbolical custom prevailed of burning the

axle of the carriage on their arrival. Plutarch, *Quœst. Rom.* 29 :
Καὶ γὰρ παρ' ἡμῖν ἐν Βοιωτίᾳ καίουσι πρὸ τῆς θύρας τὸν ἄξονα
τῆς ἁμάξης, ἐμφαίνοντες δεῖν τὴν νύμφην ἐμμένειν ὡς ἀνῃρημένου
τοῦ ἀπάξοντος. The bridegroom is carried by bearers in Aristoph. *Pax*, 1341 ; but this was doubtless a deviation from the
rule for stage-convenience. The bridegroom escorted home in
this manner his first wife only. If he married again, the lady
was brought to him by a relative or friend, who was then called
νυμφαγωγός. See Poll. iii. 40 ; Hesychius says : Νυμφαγωγός·
ὁ μετερχόμενος ἑτέρῳ νύμφην καὶ ἄγων ἐκ τοῦ πατρὸς οἰκίας· ᾧ
πρότερον γεγαμηκότι οὐκ ἔξεστι μετελθεῖν· διὸ ἀποστέλλουσι τῶν
φίλων τινάς. κ. τ. λ.

The train, which was probably numerous, was preceded by
torches, δᾷδες νυμφικαί ; but by whom they were borne is not
certain. That the mother lighted the nuptial torch is seen from
Euripides, *Iphig. in Aul.* 722 ; and *Phœniss.* 344 :

> ἐγὼ δ' οὔτε σοι πυρὸς ἀνῆψα φῶς νόμιμον ἐν γάμοις,
> ὡς πρέπει ματέρι μακαρίᾳ.

On this passage the Scholiast says : ἔθος ἦν τὴν νύμφην ὑπὸ τῆς
μητρὸς τοῦ γαμοῦντος μετὰ λαμπάδων εἰσάγεσθαι. This assertion,
that the bride was escorted with torches by the mother of the
bridegroom, is nowhere corroborated ; and in any case it could
only be an escorting into the thalamos. In the *Helena*, 723, a
servant lights the procession, torches being of course borne by
several others of the escort. Cf. Aristoph. *Pax*, 1318. If we
may assume that the whole solemnity was intended as an imitation of the ἱερὸς γάμος, it will then seem probable that a special
δᾳδοῦχος, symbolical as it were of Hymen himself, preceded the
procession. This is the case on the celebrated cameo, Lipp. i.
843. Cf. Böttiger, *Kunstmyth.* ii. p. 444 ; *Aldobr. Hochz.* p. 142.

The bride and bridegroom were of course in festal attire; and
if the custom of the Homeric age still continued, the persons
composing the escort were also provided with holiday dresses.
See *Odyss.* vi. 27 :

> σοὶ δὲ γάμος σχεδόν ἐστιν, ἵνα χρὴ καλὰ μὲν αὐτὴν
> ἕννυσθαι, τὰ δὲ τοῖσι παρασχεῖν, οἵ κέ σ' ἄγωνται.

Suidas, s. v. βαπτὰ, following the error of the Schol. ad Aristoph. *Plut.* 530, says that the dress of the bridal pair was coloured. This may, perhaps, be assumed of the bride. See Achill.

Tat. ii. 11 : Ἐώνητο δὲ τῇ κόρῃ τὰ πρὸς τὸν γάμον· περιέραιεν μὲν λίθων ποικίλων· ἐσθῆα δὲ τὸ πᾶν μὲν πορφυρᾶν· ἔνθα δὲ ταῖς ἄλλαις ἐσθήσιν ἡ χώρα τῆς πορφύρας ἐκεῖ χρυσὸς ἦν. But this was certainly not the usual Greek custom, and with regard to the bridegroom the question is still more doubtful. The male part of the escort, at all events, went in white. Plutarch, Amat. 26 : καὶ νῦν ἑκὼν στέφανον καὶ λευκὸν ἱμάτιον λαβὼν. οἷός ἐστιν ἡγεῖσθαι δι' ἀγορᾶς πρὸς τὸν θεόν. The ἱμάτιον νυμφικὸν (ibid. 10) is only mentioned in contradistinction to the chlamys, with which Bacchon had come out of the gymnasium; but there is no reference to any particular colour. See also Pollux, iv. 119 : οἱ δὲ παράσιτοι μελαίνῃ ἢ φαιᾷ (χρῶνται) πλὴν ἐν Σικυωνίῳ λευκῇ, ὅτε μέλλει γαμεῖν ὁ παράσιτος. At any rate the dress must have differed in some way from the daily one, for Chariton, i. 6, says of the corpse of Callirrhoë : κατέκειτο μὲν Καλλιρρόη νυμφικὴν ἐσθῆτα περιειμένη.

Chaplets were certainly worn both by bride and bridegroom. Böttiger, Kunstmyth. p. 253 ; Schol. ad Aristoph. Pax, 869. The same was also the case with the attendants, according to Plutarch, supra. Also the doors of both the houses were ornamented with festive garlands. Plutarch, Amat. 10 : ἀνέστεφον ἐλαίᾳ καὶ δάφνῃ τὰς θύρας, κ.τ.λ. Perfumed ointment, μύρον, was a part of the bride's κόσμος. Xenoph. Symp. ii. 3 ; Aristoph. Plut. 529. Her head also was covered by a long veil, which will be spoken of presently.

In this manner the procession moved along to the song of Hymenæos with the accompaniment of flutes, towards the house of the bridegroom, whilst those who met it would pour forth congratulations and good wishes. See Aristoph. Pax, 1318 ; Chariton, i. 1 ; v. 5 ; Heliodor. Æthiop. x. 41. On arriving at the house they were saluted with a shower of sweetmeats, καταχύσματα, as was the custom also at Rome. Schol. ad Aristoph. Plut. 768 : καὶ ἐπὶ τοῦ νυμφίου περὶ τὴν ἑστίαν τὰ τραγήματα ἐκατέχεον εἰς σημεῖον εὐπορίας, ὡς καὶ Θεόπομπός φησιν ἐν Ἡδυκάρει ' φέρε σὺ τὰ καταχύσματα ταχέως κατάχει τοῦ νυμφίου καὶ τῆς κόρης.' Cf. Theopompus, ap. Harpocr. and Phot. p. 145.

Then followed the wedding-feast, γάμος, θοίνη γαμική. It was usually, though not always, held at the house of the bridegroom or of his parents. The most decisive passage, although of

a late period, is in Lucian, *Conviv. s. Lapithæ*, 5. Little weight
can be attached to the *Aulularia* of Plautus, as we do not know
how much is to be attributed to the influence of Roman habits
This banquet was not a mere matter of form, but was in
tended as an attestation of the ceremony : it being desirable, in
those times, to have as many witnesses as possible of the marriage, and such were the guests. Demosth. *in Onet.* i. p. 869 .
ἀλλὰ τῶν τοιούτων ἕνεκα καὶ γάμους ποιοῦμεν καὶ τοὺς ἀναγκαιο-
τάτους παρακαλοῦμεν, ὅτι οὐ πάρεργον, ἀλλ᾽ ἀδελφῶν καὶ θυγατέ-
ρων βίους ἐγχειρίζομεν, ὑπὲρ ὧν τὰς ἀσφαλείας μάλιστα σκοποῦμεν.
Athen. v. p. 185: ὡς νενόμισται ἄγειν συμπόσια περὶ τοὺς γάμους
τῶν τε γαμηλίων θεῶν ἕνεκα, καὶ τῆς οἱονεὶ μαρτυρίας. And, in
fact, the judicial proof that the wife was actually γαμετὴ, was
derived from the ἑπτιᾶσαι γάμους. Isæus, *de Cir. Hered.* pp. 201,
207, 208. Plutarch, *Symposiac.* iv. 3, adduces additional reasons
for the banquet, though this simple one is quite sufficient.

At this feast, contrary to the custom in other cases, the
women also were allowed to be present. Plato, *Leg.* vi. pp. 775,
784. But in Lucian, *Conviv.* 8, they occupy a particular table,
and the bride remains veiled : Δέον δὲ ἤδη κατακλίνεσθαι, ἁπάντων
σχεδὸν παρόντων, ἐν δεξιᾷ μὲν εἰσιόντων αἱ γυναῖκες ὅλον τὸν κλιν-
τῆρα ἐκείνων ἐπέλαβον οὐκ ὀλίγαι οὖσαι, καὶ ἐν αὐταῖς ἡ νύμφη,
πάνυ ἀκριβῶς ἐγκεκαλυμμένη, ὑπὸ τῶν γυναικῶν περιεχομένη. Also
in a fragment of Euangelos, apud Athen. xiv. p. 644, mention is
made of τέτταρες τράπεζαι γυναικῶν, ἐξ ἀνδρῶν. See also Eurip.
Iphig. in Aul. 712. In other cases, as at the Thesmophoria, the
women no doubt had a banquet to themselves. Isæus, *de Pyrrh.
Her.* p. 66.

The cakes, πέμματα, seem to have been an important part of
this feast, especially the symbolical sesame-cakes. See Schol. ad
Aristoph. *Pax,* 869 : ἐδόκουν γὰρ ἐν τοῖς γάμοις σήσαμον διδόναι,
ὅς ἐστι πλακοῦς γαμικὸς ἀπὸ σησάμου πεποιημένος διὰ τὸ πούλ-
γονον, ὡς φησι Μένανδρος. Among the persons busied at the
marriage, there was a woman who was called δημιουργὸς, whose
especial duty it was to attend to these cakes. Athen. iv. p. 172 ;
Poll. iii. 41.

The bride was led veiled to the bridal chamber, θάλαμος or
πασιὰς, which the bridegroom closed. This was called κατα-
κλάζειν τὴν νύμφην. See Theocr. xviii. 5, and the proverb, *ib.*

XV. 77 : ἐνδοῖ πᾶσαι, ὁ τὰν νυὸν εἶπ' ἀποκλάξας.   At Athens it
was enjoined by a law of Solon, that the bride should eat beforehand a quince, μῆλον κυδώνιον.   Plutarch, Sol. 20; Quæst
Rom. 65 ; Conjug. Præc. 1.   Before the door of the thalamos the
epithalamium was sung by a chorus of maidens.   Theocr. Id. xviii.:

> πρόσθε νεογράπτῳ θαλάμῳ χορὸν ἐστάσαντο
> δάδεκα ταὶ πρᾶται πόλιος, μέγα χρῆμα Λακαινᾶν—
> Ἄειδον δ' ἄρα πᾶσαι, ἐς ἓν μέλος ἐγκροτέοισαι
> πυσσὶ περιπλέκτοις· περὶ δ' ἴαχε δῶμ' ὑμεναίῳ.

On this the Scholiast observes : τῶν δ' ἐπιθαλαμίων τινὰ μὲν
ᾄδεται ἑσπέρας, ἃ λέγεται κατακοιμητικά. ἄτινα ἕως μέσης ινκτὸς
ᾄδουσι. τινὰ δ' ὄρθρια, ἃ καὶ προσαγορεύεται διεγερτικά.   τὸν
ἐπιθαλάμιον ᾄδουσιν αἱ παρθένοι πρὸ τοῦ θαλάμου, ἵνα τῆς παρ-
θένου βιαζομένης ὑπὸ τοῦ ἀνδρὸς ἡ φωνὴ μὴ ἐξακούηται, λανθάνῃ
δὲ κρυπτομένη διὰ τῆς τῶν παρθένων φωνῆς.   According to Pollux
the door was guarded by a friend of the bridegroom's, εἴργων
τὰς γυναῖκας βοηθεῖν τῇ νύμφῃ βοώσῃ.   But it is questionable
how many of these customs, heaped together at random by the
grammarians, will apply to Athens.

After the νὺξ μυστικὴ (Charit. iv. 4), the lady received presents from her husband, and both of them from their relations
and friends.   Since the bride now for the first time showed herself without a veil, these gifts were called ἀνακαλυπτήρια, ὀπτήρια,
and so forth; but on what day they were given is not very
clear.   Hesychius mentions the third day : Ἀνακαλυπτήριον, ὅτε
τὴν νύμφην πρῶτον ἐξάγουσι τῇ τρίτῃ ἡμέρᾳ.   He also says :
Ἐπαύλια· ἡ δευτέρα τῶν γάμων ἡμέρα οὕτως καλεῖται, ἐν ᾗ κομί-
ζουσι δῶρα οἱ οἰκεῖοι τῷ γεγαμηκότι καὶ τῇ νύμφῃ.   These latter
presents were also called ἀνακαλυπτήρια, for Harpocration says:
Ἀνακαλυπτήρια, δῶρα διδόμενα ταῖς νύμφαις . . . ὅταν τὸ πρῶτον
ἀνακαλύπτωνται . . . καλεῖται δὲ αὐτὰ καὶ ἐπαύλαια.   These passages
then are openly at variance, and we have the additional evidence
of Pollux, iii. 39, that ἐπαυλία (ἡμέρα) means the day after the
marriage.   The same author also mentions another usage, which
may throw some light on the subject.   He says : καὶ ἀπαύλια δέ,
ἐν ᾗ ὁ νυμφίος εἰς τοῦ πενθεροῦ ἀπὸ τῆς νύμφης ἀπαυλίζεται.   οἱ
δὲ τὰ διδόμενα δῶρα τῇ νύμφῃ καλοῦσιν ἀπαύλια.   ἡ δὲ ἀπαυλισ-
τηρία χλανὶς ἀπὸ τῆς νύμφης τῷ νυμφίῳ ἐν τοῖς ἀπαυλίοις πέμ-
πεται.   We may perhaps reconcile these accounts by supposing
that the day after the marriage was the ἐπαυλία ἡμερα, and that

then on the second day the ἀπαύλια were presented, the ἀνακαλυπτήρια not being given till the third day, when the bride
first appeared unveiled. And then the only error would be in
the account of Harpocration. Cf. Pausanias, apud Eustath. *ad
Iliad.* xxiv. 29. The gifts presented by relations and friends
were also calle1 προσφοραί. See Theophrastus, *Char.* 30 ; where
one of the characteristics of a mean person is to leave town for
awhile on the marriage of a friend, or of a friend's daughter : ἵνα
μὴ προσπέμψῃ προσφοράν. Certain antiques referring to these
wedding scenes are given by Müller, *Handb. d. Archäol.* p. 693.

From this time forward the gynæconitis was the woman's
regular abode, except that she shared with her husband the
thalamos, which might occasionally be quite detached from the
women's apartments. See Excursus on *The Grecian House,*
p. 266. The description of the household arrangements given in
Lysias, *de Cæde Eratosth.* p. 13, affords us some insight into this
department of domestic life. Euphiletos, who has been accused
of the murder, explains that he inhabits a house of two stories,
of which the upper was occupied by himself, and the lower by
his wife and children. The wife, however, sleeps above stairs,
separate from her child, and this made her presence in the
gynæconitis often necessary.

The husband and wife naturally took their meals together,
provided that no other men were dining with the master of the
house ; for no woman, who did not wish to be accounted a
μοιχὰς or ἑταίρα, could think, even in her own house, of participating in the symposia of the men, or even of being present
when her husband accidentally brought a friend home to dinner.
See Lysias, *ib.* p. 27. There are two passages which clearly show
the strictness with whi h this rule was adhered to. Isæus, *de
Pyrrhi Hered.* p. 22 : καίτοι οὐ δήπου γε ἐπὶ γαμετὰς γυναῖκας
οὐδεὶς ἂν κωμάζειν τολμήσειεν· οὐδὲ αἱ γαμεταὶ γυναῖκες ἔρχονται
μετὰ τῶν ἀνδρῶν ἐπὶ τὰ δεῖπνα, οὐδὲ συνδειπνεῖν ἀξιοῦσι μετὰ τῶν
ἀλλοτρίων, καὶ ταῦτι μετὰ τῶν ἐπιτυχόντων. Demosth. *in Neær.*
p. 1352 : καὶ συνέπινε καὶ συνεδείπνει ἐναντίον πολλῶν Νέαιρα αὕτη,
ὡς ἂν ἑταίρα οὖσα.

The province of the wife was the management of the entire
household, and the nurture of the children ; of the boys until
they were placed under a master, of the girls till marriage.

Plato, who, on this subject, rather approaches the Spartan principles, assigns as the sole occupation of the women, θεραπεία,
ταμιεία, παιδοτροφία. *Leg.* vii. p. 805 ; cf. Aristoph. *Lysistr.*
17. In consequence of the great inexperience of young wives,
who had been brought up in almost monastic seclusion, matters
were often managed very awkwardly at first. See the account
given of his wife by Ischomachos ; Xenoph. *Œcon.* 7, 4 : καὶ τί
ἂν ἐπισταμένην αὐτὴν παρέλαβον, ἣ ἔτη μὲν οὔπω πεντεκαίδεκα
γεγονυῖα ἦλθε πρὸς ἐμέ, τὸν δ' ἔμπροσθεν χρόνον ἔζη ὑπὸ πολλῆς
ἐπιμελείας, ὅπως ὡς ἐλάχιστα μὲν ὄψοιτο, ἐλάχιστα δ' ἀκούσοιτο,
ἐλάχιστα δ' ἔροιτο ; Cf. *ibid.* § 14.

It may perhaps not be amiss if we attempt to describe the
wife's occupations somewhat more in detail. The methods of
nursery management have already been treated of in the Excursus on *Education.* Next to the care of her children, her
attention was principally directed to that which went by the
comprehensive term ταμιεία. To this belonged, firstly, the
superintendence of all the moveable effects appertaining to the
house, the furniture and utensils, the clothes, stores, and slaves.
Occasionally she was not trusted to this extent. See Aristoph.
Thesmoph. 418. Also from Lysias, *de Cæde Eratosth.* p. 10, we
find that Euphiletos did not entrust the whole of his domestic
concerns to his wife till she had borne him a son, which he considered sufficient security for her behaviour. Aristophanes calls
wives the ἐπίτροποι and ταμίαι of the household. *Eccles.* 212 ;
Lysistr. 495. Among the higher classes, and in large establishments, the lady had a ταμία to assist her. Xenoph. *Œcon.* 9, 11.

Another chief duty of the wife consisted in the superintendence of the slaves and the assignment of their several domestic duties. Xenoph. *Œcon.* 7, 33. Hence Plato requires that
she should rise the first thing in the morning, as a pattern to
others. *Leg.* vii. p. 808. Cf. Aristoph. *Lysistr.* 18. The
labours of the female slaves, such as spinning, weaving, and so
forth, required particular attention. Xenoph. *Œcon.* 7, 6. When
Theano was asked how she intended to become renowned, (πῶς
ἔνδοξος ἔσται :) she answered with the Homeric line :

ἱστὸν ἐποιχομένη καὶ ἐμὸν λέχος ἀντιόωσα.

Stob. *Tit.* lxxiv. 32. Cf. Plutarch, *Mul. Virt.* 19. The wife
superintended the kitchen. In a Grecian house there was seldom

any professional cook; one being hired when occasion required.
The women usually cared for all the requirements of the meal, and
the lady of the house was not idle. Plato, *de Republ.* v. p. 455 :
ἢ μακρολογῶμεν τήν τε ὑφαντικὴν λέγοντες καὶ τὴν τῶν ποπάνων
τε καὶ ἐψημάτων θεραπείαν; ἐν οἷς δή τι δοκεῖ τὸ γυναικεῖον γένος
εἶναι, οὗ καὶ καταγελαστότατόν ἐστι πάντων ἡττώμενον.   Hence,
when the crowd of useless consumers was expelled from Platæa,
we read that one hundred and ten γυναῖκες σιτοποιοί were
retained. Thucyd. ii. 78.

Besides this, another momentous occupation devolved exclusively on the women; the nursing of the sick, not only of their
husbands and children, but also of the slaves. Xenoph. *Œcon.*
7, 37 : ὅτε ὅς ἂν κάμνῃ τῶν οἰκετῶν, τούτων σοι ἐπιμελετέον πάντων, ὅπως θεραπεύηται.   Cf. Demosth. *in Neær.* p. 1364.

The foregoing description is intended to apply to the household of a wealthy burgher of the higher class. The women of
the lower classes, having no slaves, had of course to discharge
many duties which were otherwise deemed unworthy of free
persons. It was not considered unbecoming to fetch water from
the fountain in the morning; nay, in the earliest times, this was
an office assigned to the daughters of the most distinguished
persons. We may mention the instances of Amymone and
Evadne, and Athene even meets Odysseus,

παρθενικῇ εἰκυῖα νεήνιδι, κάλπιν ἐχούσῃ.

Odyss. vii. 20; cf. Böckh, ad Pind. *Ol.* vi. p. 157. At a later
period, it is true that in the houses of the wealthy this was done
by the female slaves; but those of limited means, and not the
poorest classes merely, repaired to the fountain in person. An
interesting picture of such a scene at early dawn may be found
in Aristophanes, *Lysistr.* 327 :

νῦν δὴ γὰρ ἐμπλησαμένη τὴν ὑδρίαν κνεφαία
μόγις ἀπὸ κρήνης ὑπ' ὄχλου καὶ θορύβου,
καὶ πατάγου χυτρείου,
δούλῃσιν ὠστιζομένη
στιγματίαις θ', κ.τ.λ.

Cf. Pausan. iv. 20, 3 ; x. 18, 2.

As regards the moral tone maintained between man and
wife, it may be stated that the husband carefully abstained, in
his wife's presence, from doing anything that might derogate
from his dignity and respect in her estimation. How far the

notion of ἀσχημονεῖν extended, and how careful the husband was to behave as an ἐλεύθερος on all occasions, is clear from Demosthenes, *in Androt.* p. 609. Although we gather from this that there was a certain distance maintained between married persons, and that cordial familiarity was sacrificed to σεμνότης, still there would be modifications corresponding to differences of character and education; and thus we find man and wife joking pretty freely in Lysias, *de Cæde Eratosth.* p. 14, where, when Euphiletos sends his wife down into the gynæconitis to quiet the child, she pretends to refuse, and says: ἵνα σύγε πειρᾷς ἐνταῦθα τὴν παιδίσκην· καὶ πρότερον δὲ μεθύων εἶλκες αὐτήν. Κἀγὼ μὲν ἐγέλων. ἐκείνη δὲ ἀναστᾶσα καὶ ἀπιοῦσα προστίθησι τὴν θύραν, προσποιουμένη παίζειν, καὶ τὴν κλεῖν ἐφέλκεται.

Still it is an unquestionable fact that in many cases the wife was in reality the ruling power in the house, whether from her mental superiority, domineering disposition, or amount of dower. Aristot. *Ethic. Nic.* viii. 12, p. 1161: ἐνιοτε δὲ ἄρχουσιν αἱ γυναῖκες ἐπίκληροι οὖσαι. In Sparta, where the men were accounted ὑπήκοοι τῶν γυναικῶν (Plutarch, *Agis.* 7), and where the women, who were called δέσποιναι, even by the men, (Id. *Lyc.* 14,) were accustomed to rule over the house (τῶν οἴκων ἄρχουσαι κατὰ κράτος), perhaps the domestic tyranny of the women was rarer than at Athens. Plutarch, speaking of Themistocl s, says, *Apophth. Reg.* 10, and *Themist.* 18: Τὸν δ᾽ υἱὸν ἐντρυφῶντα τῇ μητρὶ καὶ δι᾽ ἐκείνην αὐτῷ σκώπτων ἔλεγε πλεῖστον τῶν Ἑλλήνων δύνασθαι· τοῖς μὲν γὰρ Ἕλλησιν ἐπιτάττειν Ἀθηναίους, Ἀθηναίους δ᾽ αὐτὸν, αὐτῷ δὲ τὴν ἐκείνου μη-έρα, τῇ μητρὶ δ᾽ ἐκεῖνον. This must not perhaps be taken too strictly, yet not to speak of the πολυθρύλητος Ξανθίππη, instances are not wanting where wives are designated as Λάμια and Ἔμπουσα. See a fragment of Menander, p. 144, Mein. Some wives indeed maintained their rights with their slippers in a most objectionable manner. Brunck, *Anal.* ii. p. 409:

> Εἰ δ᾽, οὐ σανδαλίῳ, φῂς, τύπτομαι, οὐδ᾽ ἀκολάστου
> οὔσης μοι γαμετῆς, χρή με μύσαντα φέρειν.

See also Aristoph. *Lysistr.* 657:

> ἆρα γρυκτόν ἐστιν ὑμῖν; εἰ δὲ λμπήσεις τί με,
> τῷδέ γ᾽ ἀψήκτῳ πατάξω τῷ κοθόρνῳ τὴν γνάθον.

The men might, at all events, console themselves with the reflec-

tion that Hercules was served no better by Omphale. Lucian,
Deor. Dial. xiii. 2 : παιόμενος ὑπὸ τῆς Ὀμφάλης χρωσῷ σανδάλῳ.
Cf. Westerh. ad Terent. *Eun.* vii. 8, 4 ; Menander, fragm. p. 68,
Mein.

The law imposed the duty of continence in a very unequal
manner.   Whilst the husband required from his wife the strictest
fidelity, and severely visited any dereliction on her part, he
would frequently allow himself to have intercourse with hetæræ.
Such conduct, though it was not exactly approved of, yet did
not meet with any marked censure, much less was it considered
a violation of matrimonial rights.   The passage in Isocrates,
Nicocl. p. 42, must be regarded as a protest against the general
opinion, which was indirectly countenanced even by the law.
For any transgression of the wife was heavily visited, as being
a civil injury done to the husband ; but when he was the
offender, no process was instituted unless the circumstances had
been peculiarly aggravated, and atimia was most certainly not
inflicted in any case.   The following passage refers without doubt
to Greek life, and a multitude of instances might be adduced
to show the correctness of the picture it presents.   Plaut. *Merc.*
iv. 6, 2 :

> Nam si vir scortum duxit clam uxorem suam,
> Id si rescivit uxor, impune est viro.
> Uxor viro si clam domo egressa est foras,
> Viro fit causa, exigitur matrimonio.
> Utinam lex esset eadem, quæ uxori est, viro !

When Aristotle, *de Republ.* vii. 16, p. 1335, demands that husband as well as wife should be visited with atimia for incontinence,
this is only an idea of his own, and is not borne out by facts.

Infidelity in the wife was judged most sharply.   It might
be supposed that, living in such strict seclusion, the women were
generally precluded from transgressing ; but it is clear that they
very frequently found means of deceiving their husbands.   So in
Lysias, *de Cæd. Erat.* p. 19, the woman who reveals to Euphiletos the infidelity of his wife, says : ἔστι δ᾽ Ἐρατοσθένης Οἰῆθεν
ὁ ταῦτα πράττων, ὃς οὐ μόνον τὴν σὴν γυναῖκα διέφθαρκεν, ἀλλὰ
καὶ ἄλλας πολλάς.   Cf. Demosth. *in Steph.* i. p. 1125.   It was
the boast of Sparta that adultery was unknown there.   When
Geradatas was asked what punishment was inflicted on the
adulterer, he replied, πῶς ἂν ἐν Σπάρτῃ μοιχὸς γένοιτο ; Plutarch,

Lyc. 15 ; *Apophth. Lac.* i. p. 909. This piece of braggadocio is
thus justly criticised by Limburg-Brower, in his *Hist. de la
Civil. Mor. et Relig. d. Gr.* iv. p. 165 : ' C'est comme qui diroit
que dans une bande de brigands il n'y avoit pas un seul voleur.'
But this was only intended by Plutarch to refer to the very
ancient times, for he names Geradatas as τῶν σφόδρα παλαιῶν
τινα, and contrasts with that period the εὐχέρεια of the Spartan
women at a later date. Cf. *De Tranq. An.* 6.

It is evident from Lysias, *de Cæde Eratosth.* p. 23, that the
female slaves were open to corruption, and that they had generally a good deal to do with the peccadilloes of their mistress ;
and indeed the artifices the adulterer employed to get into a house
could not have succeeded without the connivance of some of its
inmates. See the fragment of Xenarchos, apud Athen. xiii. p. 569 :

> μὴ κλίμακ᾽ οἰτησάμενον εἰσβῆναι λάθρᾳ,
> μηδὲ δι᾽ ὀπῆς κάτωθεν ἐκδῦναι στέγης,
> μηδ᾽ ἐν ἀχύροισιν εἰσενεχθῆναι τέχνῃ.

Actual bribery is moreover mentioned by Dio Chrysost. *Or.* vii.
p. 272 : καὶ νὴ Δία ἀργυρίου στάζοντος κατ᾽ ὀλίγον οὐδ᾽ εἰς τοὺς
τῶν παρθένων κόλπους μόνους, ἀλλ᾽ εἴς τε μητέρων, καὶ τροφῶν, καὶ
παιδαγωγῶν, καὶ ἄλλων πολλῶν καὶ καλῶν δώρων· τῶν μὲν κρύφα
εἰσιόντων διὰ τῶν στεγῶν, ἔστι δ᾽ οὗ φανερῶς κατ᾽ αὐτάς που τὰς
κλισίας. There was a special law directed against προαγωγεία,
which appears to have been extensively carried on by persons
who made it a regular profession. See Anaxandrides, apud
Stob. *Tit.* lxvii. 1. The main passage about the προαγωγοὶ is
in Æschines, *in Timarch.* p. 177 : καὶ τοὺς προαγωγοὺς γράφεσθαι
κελεύει, κἂν ἁλῶσι, θανάτῳ ζημιοῦν, ὅτι τῶν ἐξαμαρτάνειν, ἐπιθυ-
μούντων, ὀκνούντων καὶ αἰσχυνομένων ἀλλήλοις ἐντυγχάνειν, αὐτοὶ
τὴν ἀναίδειαν παρασχόντες ἐπὶ μισθῷ τὸ πρᾶγμα εἰς διάπειραν καὶ
λόγον κατέστησαν. Cf. *Ib.* p. 40 ; Xenoph. *Symp.* 4, 61 ; Plato,
Theæt. p. 150. These people not only arranged assignations.
but also offered their own abodes as places of rendezvous.
Hence ἀγωγεῖα (προαγωγεῖα ?) are mentioned among places of
evil repute by Pollux, ix. 48. And probably the ματρυλεῖα were
not very different. Cf. Id. vii. 201. Such was the house of
Orsilochos. Aristoph. *Lysistr.* 725. These things were occasionally done without any attempt at concealment, as we see from
Demosth. *in Steph.* i. p. 1125 : τίνος γυναῖκα διέφθαρκα, ὥσπερ

σὺ πρὸς πολλαῖς ἄλλαις ταύτην, ᾗ τὸ μνῆμα ᾠκοδόμησεν ὁ θεοῖς
ἐχθρὸς οὗτος πλησίον τοῦ τῆς δεσποίνης ἀνηλωκὼς πλέον ἢ τάλαντα δύο; καὶ οὐκ ᾐσθάνετο, ὅτι οὐχὶ τοῦ τάφου μνημεῖον ἔσται
τὸ οἰκοδόμημα, τοιοῦτον ὄν, ἀλλὰ τῆς ἀδικίας, ᾗ καὶ τὸ ἄγρα
ἠδίκηκεν ἐκείνη διὰ τοῦτον. The husband was not always entirely
ignorant of what was going on; and sometimes a pretty woman
was even married by way of speculation.   See Demosth. *in
Neær.* pp. 1358, 1367; cf. Plutarch, *de Aud. Poet.* 8.

The law left the punishment of the adulterer to the injured
husband, who was allowed to kill the offender if caught in the
act. Lysias, *de Cæde Eratosth.* p. 31 : διαρρήδην εἴρηται τοῦτον μὴ
καταγιγνώσκειν φόνου, ὃς ἂν ἐπὶ δάμαρτι τῇ ἑαυτοῦ μοιχὸν λαβὼν
ταύτην τὴν τιμωρίαν ποιήσηται. Cf. Demosth. *in Aristocr.* p.
637 ; Plutarch, *Sol.* 23. This law has been only partially preserved, though we are probably acquainted with its most important provisions. Thus we have a few words of it in Lucian,
Eunuch. 10: καὶ μοιχὸς ἑάλω ποτέ, ὡς ὁ ἄξων φησὶν, ἄρθρα ἐν
ἄρθροις ἔχων. A more important fragment, which refers to the
punishment inflicted on the woman, may be found in Demosthenes,
in Neær. p. 1374: Ἐπειδὰν δὲ ἕλῃ τὸν μοιχὸν, μὴ ἐξέστω τῷ
ἑλόντι συνοικεῖν τῇ γυναικί. ἐὰν δὲ συνοικῇ, ἄτιμος ἔστω. μηδὲ τῇ
γυναικὶ ἐξέστω εἰσιέναι εἰς τὰ ἱερὰ τὰ δημοτελῆ, ἐφ' ᾗ ἂν μοιχὸς ἁλῷ.
ἐὰν δὲ εἰσίῃ, νηποινεὶ πασχέτω, ὅ,τι ἂν πάσχῃ, πλὴν θανάτου.
See also *Ib.* p. 1367 : ἐὰν δὲ δόξῃ μοιχὸς εἶναι, παραδοῦναι αὐτὸν
κελεύει τοὺς ἐγγυητὰς τῷ ἑλόντι. ἐπὶ δὲ τοῦ δικαστηρίου ἄνευ
ἐγχειριδίου χρῆσθαι ὅ,τι ἂν βουληθῇ, ὡς μοιχῷ ὄντι. See also a
fragment of Menander (p. 130, Mein) :

> Οὐκ ἔστι μοιχοῦ πρᾶγμα τιμιώτερον.
> θανάτου γάρ ἐστιν ὤνιον.

This personal revenge was legally sanctioned in many other states
besides Athens. See Xenoph. *Hier.* 3, 3 : μόνους γοῦν τοὺς μοιχοὺς
νομίζουσι πολλαὶ τῶν πόλεων νηποινὰ ἀποκτείνειν. Plato also
permits it to its fullest extent in his ideal state. *Leg.* ix. p. 874.
On the other hand, after time for calm reflection had intervened,
it was not allowable to kill the culprit; but corporal chastisement
and the notorious ῥαφανίδωσις were even then permitted. Aristoph. *Nub.* 1083 ; Schol. ad *Plut.* 168. Sometimes a considerable sum of money was paid to escape a worse fate. Lysias,
de Cæde Eratosth. p. 28; Demosth. *in Neær.* p. 1367.

The wife was made infamous, as we see from the fragment of
the law quoted above.   A more detailed account is given by
Æschines *in Timarch.* 176 : τὴν γὰρ γυναῖκα, ἐφ᾽ ᾗ ἂν ἁλῷ μοιχὸς,
οὐκ ἐᾷ κοσμεῖσθαι, οὐδὲ εἰς τὰ δημοτελῆ ἱερὰ εἰσιέναι, ἵνα μὴ τὰς
ἀναμαρτήτους τῶν γυναικῶν ἀναμιγνυμένη διαφθείρῃ· ἐὰν δ᾽ εἰσίῃ
ἢ κοσμῆται, τὸν ἐντυχόντα κελεύει καταρρήγνύναι τὰ ἱμάτια καὶ
τὸν κόσμον ἀφαιρεῖσθαι, καὶ τύπτειν, εἰργόμενον θανάτου καὶ τοῦ
ἀνάπηρον ποιῆσαι.   The adulteress was never punished with
death ; and Heliodorus makes a mistake when he supposes this
possible at Athens.   See *Æthiop.* i. 11.   The man who received
her to wife was also punished with atimia.

A peculiar penalty was inflicted on the adulteress at Cymæ,
according to Plutarch, *Quæst. Græc.* 2.   He tells us that the
woman, after having been set up on a stone in the forum, was
then mounted on an ass, and having been led round the town,
was brought back to the stone : καὶ τὸ λοιπὸν ἄτιμον διατελεῖν,
Ὀνοβάτιν προσαγορευομένην.   Cf. Ælian, *Var. Hist.* xii. 12 :
ὅτι ἐν Κρήτῃ ἐν Γορτύνῃ μοιχὸς ἁλοὺς ἤγετο ἐπὶ τὰς ἀρχὰς καὶ
ἐστεφανοῦτο ἐρίῳ ἐλεγχθείς.   See also *ib.* xiii. 24 : Ζάλευκος ὁ
Λοκρῶν νομοθέτης προσέταξε τὸν μοιχὸν ἁλόντα ἐκκόπτεσθαι τοὺς
ὀφθαλμούς.   Cf. the law of Charondas, apud Stob. *Tit.* xliv. 40.

In all these cases the law commanded the marriage to be
annulled.   Separations were also of frequent occurrence, though
unaccompanied by any formalities.   The husband rejects the wife,
ἐκπέμπει ; or the wife leaves the husband, ἀπολείπει.   The procedure in this latter case has been discussed in a most satisfactory
manner by Meier and Schömann, *Att. Proc.* p. 413.   It may be
questioned, however, whether the husband could send back his
wife to her former κύριος, against her will, at least without some
special reason.   The theoretical recommendations of Plato, *Leg.*
vi. p. 784, and xi. p. 930, will of course prove nothing as to the
actual state of the case.   See however a fragment of Amphis, ap.
Athen. xiii. p. 559 :

> Εἶτ᾽ οὐ γυναικός ἐστιν εὐνοϊκώτερον
> γαμετῆς ἑταίρα ; πολύ γε καὶ μάλ᾽ εἰκότως.
> ἡ μὲν νόμῳ γὰρ καταφρονοῦσ᾽ ἔνδον μένει,
> ἡ δ᾽ οἶδεν ὅτι ἢ τοῖς τρόποις ὠνητέος
> ἄνθρωπός ἐστιν, ἢ πρὸς ἄλλον ἀπιτέον.

Hence it would appear that there were some legal restrictions on the husband's arbitrary power in getting rid of his wife. It is clear that barrenness was a frequent cause of separation, for we are told by Dio Chrysostom, *Or.* xv. p. 447, that childless women often procured supposititious children: βουλομένη κατασχεῖν ἑκάστη τὸν ἄνδρα τὸν ἑαυτῆς. However, the ἔκπεμψις and ἀπόλειψις were always held more or less disgraceful for the woman, as we see from a fragment of Anaxandrides, apud Stob. *Tit.* lxxiii. 1. The simple ἀπόλειψις is occasionally viewed with more indifference, as in Terence, *Andr.* iii. 3, 35, where the lady, it seems, is to be taken on trial. So too the story told of the cynic Crates by Diogenes Laertius, vi. 93: καὶ θυγατέρ' ᾽ἔδωκε μαθηταῖς αὐτοῦ, ἐκείνοις ἐπὶ πείρᾳ δοὺς τριάκονθ' ἡμέρας.

INDEX.

—————————

PRINTED BY
SPOTTISWOODE AND CO., NEW-STREET SQUARE
LONDON

MESSRS. LONGMANS, GREEN, & CO.'S
CLASSIFIED CATALOGUE
OF
WORKS IN GENERAL LITERATURE.

History, Politics, Polity, Political Memoirs, &c.

Abbott.—A HISTORY OF GREECE. By EVELYN ABBOTT, M.A., LL.D.
Part I.—From the Earliest Times to the Ionian Revolt. Crown 8vo., 10s. 6d.
Part II.—500-445 B.C. Cr. 8vo., 10s. 6d.

Acland and Ransome.—A HAND-BOOK IN OUTLINE OF THE POLITICAL HISTORY OF ENGLAND TO 1896. Chronologically Arranged. By A. H. DYKE ACLAND, M.P., and CYRIL RANSOME, M.A. Crown 8vo., 6s.

ANNUAL REGISTER (THE). A Review of Public Events at Home and Abroad, for the year 1897. 8vo., 18s.
Volumes of the ANNUAL REGISTER for the years 1863-1896 can still be had. 18s. each.

Amos.—PRIMER OF THE ENGLISH CONSTITUTION AND GOVERNMENT. By SHELDON AMOS, M.A. Cr. 8vo., 6s.

Arnold.— INTRODUCTORY LECTURES ON MODERN HISTORY. By THOMAS ARNOLD, D.D., formerly Head Master of Rugby School. 8vo., 7s. 6d.

Baden-Powell.—THE INDIAN VILLAGE COMMUNITY. Examined with Reference to the Physical, Ethnographic, and Historical Conditions of the Provinces; chiefly on the Basis of the Revenue-Settlement Records and District Manuals. By B. H. BADEN-POWELL, M.A., C.I.E. With Map. 8vo., 16s.

Bagwell.—IRELAND UNDER THE TUDORS. By RICHARD BAGWELL, LL.D. (3 vols). Vols. I. and II. From the first Invasion of the Northmen to the year 1578. 8vo., 32s. Vol. III. 1578-1603. 8vo., 18s.

Ball.—HISTORICAL REVIEW OF THE LEGISLATIVE SYSTEMS OPERATIVE IN IRELAND, from the Invasion of Henry the Second to the Union (1172-1800). By the Rt. Hon. J. T. BALL. 8vo., 6s.

Besant.—THE HISTORY OF LONDON. By Sir WALTER BESANT. With 74 Illustrations. Crown 8vo., 1s. 9d. Or bound as a School Prize Book, 2s. 6d.

Brassey (LORD).—PAPERS AND ADDRESSES.
NAVAL AND MARITIME, 1872-1893. 2 vols. Crown 8vo., 10s.
MERCANTILE MARINE AND NAVIGATION, from 1871-1894. Cr. 8vo., 5s.
IMPERIAL FEDERATION AND COLONISATION FROM 1880-1894. Crown 8vo., 5s.
POLITICAL AND MISCELLANEOUS, 1861-1894. Crown 8vo., 5s.

Bright.—A HISTORY OF ENGLAND. By the Rev. J. FRANCK BRIGHT, D.D.
Period I. MEDIÆVAL MONARCHY: A.D. 449-1485. Crown 8vo., 4s. 6d.
Period II. PERSONAL MONARCHY: 1485-1688. Crown 8vo., 5s.
Period III. CONSTITUTIONAL MONARCHY: 1689-1837. Cr. 8vo., 7s. 6d.
Period IV. THE GROWTH OF DEMOCRACY: 1837-1880. Crown 8vo., 6s.

Buckle.—HISTORY OF CIVILISATION IN ENGLAND. By HENRY THOMAS BUCKLE. 3 vols. Crown 8vo., 24s.

Burke.—A HISTORY OF SPAIN, from the Earliest Times to the Death of Ferdinand the Catholic. By ULICK RALPH BURKE, M.A. 2 vols. 8vo., 32s.

Chesney.—INDIAN POLITY: a View of the System of Administration in India. By General Sir GEORGE CHESNEY, K.C.B. With Map showing all the Administrative Divisions of British India. 8vo., 21s.

Corbett.—DRAKE AND THE TUDOR NAVY, with a History of the Rise of England as a Maritime Power. By JULIAN S. CORBETT. With Portrait, Illustrations and Maps. 2 vols. 8vo., 36s.

Creighton.—A HISTORY OF THE PAPACY FROM THE GREAT SCHISM TO THE SACK OF ROME (1378-1527). By M. CREIGHTON, D.D., Lord Bishop of London. 6 vols. Cr. 8vo., 6s. each.

Cuningham.—A SCHEME FOR IMPERIAL FEDERATION : a Senate for the Empire. By GRANVILLE C. CUNINGHAM of Montreal, Canada. Cr. 8vo., 3s. 6d.

History, Politics, Polity, Political Memoirs, &c.—*continued.*

Curzon.—PERSIA AND THE PERSIAN QUESTION. By the Right HON. GEORGE N. CURZON, M.P. With 9 Maps, 96 Illustrations, Appendices, and an Index. 2 vols. 8vo., 42s.

De Tocqueville.— DEMOCRACY IN AMERICA. By ALEXIS DE TOCQUEVILLE. 2 vols. Crown 8vo., 16s.

Dickinson.—THE DEVELOPMENT OF PARLIAMENT DURING THE NINETEENTH CENTURY. By G. LOWES DICKINSON, M.A. 8vo., 7s. 6d.

Froude (JAMES A.).

THE HISTORY OF ENGLAND, from the Fall of Wolsey to the Defeat of the Spanish Armada. 12 vols. Crown 8vo., 3s. 6d. each.

THE DIVORCE OF CATHERINE OF ARAGON. Crown 8vo., 3s. 6d.

THE SPANISH STORY OF THE ARMADA, and other Essays. Cr. 8vo., 3s. 6d.

THE ENGLISH IN IRELAND IN THE EIGHTEENTH CENTURY. 3 vols. Crown 8vo., 10s. 6d.

ENGLISH SEAMEN IN THE SIXTEENTH CENTURY. Crown 8vo., 6s.

THE COUNCIL OF TRENT. Cr. 8vo., 3s. 6d.

SHORT STUDIES ON GREAT SUBJECTS. 4 vols. Cr. 8vo., 3s. 6d. each.

CÆSAR: a Sketch. Cr. 8vo., 3s. 6d.

Gardiner (SAMUEL RAWSON, D.C.L., LL.D.).

HISTORY OF ENGLAND, from the Accession of James I. to the Outbreak of the Civil War, 1603-1642. 10 vols. Crown 8vo., 6s. each.

A HISTORY OF THE GREAT CIVIL WAR, 1642-1649. 4 vols. Cr. 8vo., 6s. each.

A HISTORY OF THE COMMONWEALTH AND THE PROTECTORATE, 1649-1660. Vol. I., 1649-1651. With 14 Maps. 8vo., 21s. Vol. II., 1651-1654. With 7 Maps. 8vo., 21s.

WHAT GUNPOWDER PLOT WAS. With 8 Illustrations and Plates. Crown 8vo., 5s.

Gardiner (SAMUEL RAWSON, D.C.L., LL.D.)—*continued.*

CROMWELL'S PLACE IN HISTORY. Founded on Six Lectures delivered in the University of Oxford. Crown 8vo., 3s. 6d.

THE STUDENT'S HISTORY OF ENGLAND. With 378 Illustrations. Cr. 8vo., 12s.

Also in Three Volumes, price 4s. each.

Vol. I. B.C. 55-A.D. 1509. 173 Illustrations.

Vol. II. 1509-1689. 96 Illustrations.

Vol. III. 1689-1885. 109 Illustrations.

Greville.—A JOURNAL OF THE REIGNS OF KING GEORGE IV., KING WILLIAM IV., AND QUEEN VICTORIA. By CHARLES C. F. GREVILLE, formerly Clerk of the Council. 8 vols. Crown 8vo., 3s. 6d. each.

HARVARD HISTORICAL STUDIES:

THE SUPPRESSION OF THE AFRICAN SLAVE TRADE TO THE UNITED STATES OF AMERICA, 1638-1870. By W. E. B. DU BOIS, Ph.D. 8vo., 7s. 6d.

THE CONTEST OVER THE RATIFICATION OF THE FEDERAL CONSTITUTION IN MASSACHUSETTS. By S. B. HARDING, A.M. 8vo., 6s.

A CRITICAL STUDY OF NULLIFICATION IN SOUTH CAROLINA. By D. F. HOUSTON, A.M. 8vo., 6s.

NOMINATIONS FOR ELECTIVE OFFICE IN THE UNITED STATES. By FREDERICK W. DALLINGER, A.M. 8vo., 7s. 6d.

A BIBLIOGRAPHY OF BRITISH MUNICIPAL HISTORY, including Gilds and Parliamentary Representation. By CHARLES GROSS, Ph.D. 8vo, 12s.

THE LIBERTY AND FREE SOIL PARTIES IN THE NORTH-WEST. By THEODORE CLARKE SMITH, Ph.D. 8vo., 7s. 6d.

Historic Towns.—Edited by E. A. FREEMAN, D.C.L., and Rev. WILLIAM HUNT, M.A. With Maps and Plans. Crown 8vo., 3s. 6d. each.

Bristol. By Rev. W. Hunt.	London. By Rev. W. J. Loftie.
Carlisle. By Mandell Creighton, D.D.	Oxford. By Rev. C. W. Boase.
Cinque Ports. By Montagu Burrows.	Winchester. By G. W. Kitchin, D.D.
Colchester. By Rev. E. L. Cutts.	York. By Rev. James Raine.
	New York. By Theodore Roosevelt.
Exeter. By E. A. Freeman.	Boston (U.S.). By Henry Cabot Lodge.

History, Politics, Polity, Political Memoirs, &c.—*continued.*

Joyce (P. W., LL.D.).

A SHORT HISTORY OF IRELAND, from the Earliest Times to 1608. Crown 8vo., 10s. 6d.

A CHILD'S HISTORY OF IRELAND, from the Earliest Times to the Death of O'Connell. With Map and 160 Illustrations. Crown 8vo., 3s. 6d.

Kaye and Malleson.—HISTORY OF THE INDIAN MUTINY, 1857-1858. By Sir JOHN W. KAYE and Colonel G. B. MALLESON. With Analytical Index and Maps and Plans. 6 vols. Crown 8vo., 3s. 6d. each.

Lang (ANDREW).

PICKLE THE SPY, or, The Incognito of Prince Charles. With 6 Portraits. 8vo., 18s.

ST. ANDREWS. With 8 Plates and 24 Illustrations in the Text by T. HODGE. 8vo., 15s. net.

Lecky (WILLIAM EDWARD HART-POLE).

HISTORY OF ENGLAND IN THE EIGH-TEENTH CENTURY.
Library Edition. 8 vols. 8vo.
Vols. I. and II., 1700-1760, 36s. Vols. III. and IV., 1760-1784, 36s. Vols. V. and VI., 1784-1793, 36s. Vols. VII. and VIII., 1793-1800, 36s.
Cabinet Edition. ENGLAND. 7 vols. Cr. 8vo., 6s. each. IRELAND. 5 vols. Crown 8vo., 6s. each.

HISTORY OF EUROPEAN MORALS FROM AUGUSTUS TO CHARLEMAGNE. 2 vols. Crown 8vo., 16s.

HISTORY OF THE RISE AND INFLUENCE OF THE SPIRIT OF RATIONALISM IN EUROPE. 2 vols. Crown 8vo., 16s.

DEMOCRACY AND LIBERTY. 2 vols. 8vo., 36s.

Macaulay (LORD).

THE LIFE AND WORKS OF LORD MAC-AULAY. '*Edinburgh*' *Edition.* 10 vols. 8vo., 6s. each.
Vols. I.-IV. HISTORY OF ENGLAND.
Vols. V.-VII. ESSAYS; BIOGRAPHIES; INDIAN PENAL CODE ; CONTRIBU-TIONS TO KNIGHT'S ' QUARTERLY MAGAZINE '.
Vol. VIII. SPEECHES ; LAYS OF ANCIENT ROME ; MISCELLANEOUS POEMS.
Vols. IX. and X. THE LIFE AND LETTERS OF LORD MACAULAY. By the Right Hon. Sir G. O. TREVE-LYAN, Bart.
This Edition is a cheaper reprint of the Library Edition of LORD MACAULAY'S *Life and Works.*

COMPLETE WORKS.
'*Albany*' *Edition.* With 12 Portraits. 12 vols. Crown 8vo., 3s. 6d. each.
Cabinet Edition. 16 vols. Post 8vo., £4 16s.
' *Edinburgh*' *Edition.* 8 vols. 8vo., 6s. each.
Library Edition. 8 vols. 8vo., £5 5s.

HISTORY OF ENGLAND FROM THE AC-CESSION OF JAMES THE SECOND.
Popular Edition. 2 vols. Cr. 8vo., 5s.
Student's Edit. 2 vols. Cr. 8vo., 12s.
People's Edition. 4 vols. Cr. 8vo., 16s.
Cabinet Edition. 8 vols. Post 8vo., 48s.
'*Edinburgh*' *Edition.* 4 vols. 8vo., 6s. each.
' *Albany*' *Edition.* 6 vols. Crown 8vo., 3s. 6d. each.
Library Edition. 5 vols. 8vo., £4.

CRITICAL AND HISTORICAL ESSAYS, WITH LAYS OF ANCIENT ROME, in 1 volume.
Popular Edition. Crown 8vo., 2s. 6d.
Authorised Edition. Crown 8vo., 2s. 6d., or 3s. 6d., gilt edges.
' *Silver Library* ' *Edition.* Crown 8vo., 3s. 6d.

CRITICAL AND HISTORICAL ESSAYS.
Student's Edition. 1 vol. Cr. 8vo., 6s.
People's Edition. 2 vols. Cr. 8vo., 8s.
' *Trevelyan' Edit.* 2 vols. Cr. 8vo., 9s.
Cabinet Edition. 4 vols. Post 8vo., 24s.
' *Edinburgh*' *Edition.* 4 vols. 8vo., 6s. each.
Library Edition. 3 vols. 8vo., 36s.

History, Politics, Polity, Political Memoirs, &c.—*continued.*

Macaulay (LORD).—*continued.*

ESSAYS which may be had separately, price 6*d.* each sewed, 1*s.* each cloth.

Addison and Walpole.	Ranke and Gladstone.
Croker's Boswell's Johnson.	Milton and Machiavelli.
Hallam's Constitutional History.	Lord Byron.
Warren Hastings.	Lord Clive.
The Earl of Chatham(Two Essays).	Lord Byron,and The Comic Dramatists of the Restoration.
Frederick the Great.	

MISCELLANEOUS WRITINGS.

People's Edition. 1 vol. Cr. 8vo., 4*s.* 6*d.*
Library Edition. 2 vols. 8vo., 21*s.*
Popular Edition. Cr. 8vo., 2*s.* 6*d.*
Cabinet Edition. Including Indian Penal Code, Lays of Ancient Rome, and Miscellaneous Poems. 4 vols. Post 8vo., 24*s.*

SELECTIONS FROM THE WRITINGS OF LORD MACAULAY. Edited, with Occasional Notes, by the Right Hon. Sir G. O. Trevelyan, Bart. Cr. 8vo., 6*s.*

MacColl. — THE SULTAN AND THE POWERS. By the Rev. MALCOLM MACCOLL, M.A., Canon of Ripon. 8vo., 10*s.* 6*d.*

Mackinnon. — THE UNION OF ENGLAND AND SCOTLAND: a Study of International History. By JAMES MACKINNON, Ph.D., Examiner in History to the University of Edinburgh. 8vo., 16*s.*

May.—THE CONSTITUTIONAL HISTORY OF ENGLAND since the Accession of George III. 1760-1870. By Sir THOMAS ERSKINE MAY, K.C.B. (Lord Farnborough). 3 vols. Crown 8vo., 18*s.*

Merivale (THE LATE DEAN).

HISTORY OF THE ROMANS UNDER THE EMPIRE. 8 vols. Cr. 8vo., 3*s.* 6*d.* each.

THE FALL OF THE ROMAN REPUBLIC: a Short History of the Last Century of the Commonwealth. 12mo., 7*s.* 6*d.*

GENERAL HISTORY OF ROME, from the Foundation of the City to the Fall of Augustulus, B.C. 753-A.D. 476. With 5 Maps. Crown 8vo., 7*s.* 6*d.*

Montague.—THE ELEMENTS OF ENGLISH CONSTITUTIONAL HISTORY. By F. C. MONTAGUE, M.A. Cr. 8vo., 3*s.* 6*d.*

Richman.—APPENZELL: Pure Democracy and Pastoral Life in Inner-Rhoden. A Swiss Study. By IRVING B. RICHMAN, Consul-General of the United States to Switzerland. With Maps. Crown 8vo., 5*s.*

Seebohm (FREDERIC).

THE ENGLISH VILLAGE COMMUNITY Examined in its Relations to the Manorial and Tribal Systems, &c. With 13 Maps and Plates. 8vo., 16*s.*

THE TRIBAL SYSTEM IN WALES: being Part of an Inquiry into the Structure and Methods of Tribal Society. With 3 Maps. 8vo., 12*s.*

Sharpe.—LONDON AND THE KINGDOM: a History derived mainly from the Archives at Guildhall in the custody of the Corporation of the City of London. By REGINALD R. SHARPE, D.C.L., Records Clerk in the Office of the Town Clerk of the City of London. 3 vols. 8vo., 10*s.* 6*d.* each.

Smith.—CARTHAGE AND THE CARTHAGINIANS. By R. BOSWORTH SMITH, M.A., With Maps, Plans, &c. Cr. 8vo., 3*s.* 6*d.*

Stephens.—A HISTORY OF THE FRENCH REVOLUTION. By H. MORSE STEPHENS, 8vo. Vols. I. and II., 18*s.* each.

Stubbs.—HISTORY OF THE UNIVERSITY OF DUBLIN, from its Foundation to the End of the Eighteenth Century. By J. W. STUBBS. 8vo., 12*s.* 6*d.*

Sutherland.—THE HISTORY OF AUSTRALIA AND NEW ZEALAND, from 1606-1890. By ALEXANDER SUTHERLAND, M.A., and GEORGE SUTHERLAND, M.A. Crown 8vo., 2*s.* 6*d.*

Taylor.—A STUDENT'S MANUAL OF THE HISTORY OF INDIA. By Colonel MEADOWS TAYLOR, C.S.I., &c. Cr. 8vo., 7*s.* 6*d.*

Todd.—PARLIAMENTARY GOVERNMENT IN THE BRITISH COLONIES. By ALPHEUS TODD, LL.D. 8vo., 30*s.* net.

History, Politics, Polity, Political Memoirs, &c.—*continued*.

Wakeman and Hassall.—ESSAYS INTRODUCTORY TO THE STUDY OF ENGLISH CONSTITUTIONAL HISTORY. By Resident Members of the University of Oxford. Edited by HENRY OFFLEY WAKEMAN, M.A., and ARTHUR HASSALL, M.A. Crown 8vo., 6s.

Walpole.—HISTORY OF ENGLAND FROM THE CONCLUSION OF THE GREAT WAR IN 1815 TO 1858. By SPENCER WALPOLE. 6 vols. Crown 8vo., 6s. each.

Wood-Martin.—PAGAN IRELAND: an Archæological Sketch. A Handbook of Irish Pre-Christian Antiquities. By W. G. WOOD-MARTIN, M.R.I.A. With 512 Illustrations. Crown 8vo., 15s.

Wylie.—HISTORY OF ENGLAND UNDER HENRY IV. By JAMES HAMILTON WYLIE, M.A., one of H.M. Inspectors of Schools. 4 vols. Crown 8vo. Vol. I., 1399-1404, 10s. 6d. Vol. II. 15s. Vol. III. 15s. Vol. IV. 21s.

Biography, Personal Memoirs, &c.

Armstrong.—THE LIFE AND LETTERS OF EDMUND J. ARMSTRONG. Edited by G. F. SAVAGE ARMSTRONG. Fcp. 8vo., 7s. 6d.

Bacon.—THE LETTERS AND LIFE OF FRANCIS BACON, INCLUDING ALL HIS OCCASIONAL WORKS. Edited by JAMES SPEDDING. 7 vols. 8vo., £4 4s.

Bagehot. — BIOGRAPHICAL STUDIES. By WALTER BAGEHOT. Cr. 8vo., 3s. 6d.

Blackwell.—PIONEER WORK IN OPENING THE MEDICAL PROFESSION TO WOMEN: Autobiographical Sketches. By Dr. ELIZABETH BLACKWELL. Cr. 8vo., 6s.

Buss.—FRANCES MARY BUSS AND HER WORK FOR EDUCATION. By ANNIE E. RIDLEY. With 5 Portraits and 4 Illustrations. Crown 8vo., 7s. 6d.

Carlyle.—THOMAS CARLYLE: a History of his Life. By JAMES ANTHONY FROUDE. 1795-1835. 2 vols. Crown 8vo., 7s. 1834-1881. 2 vols. Crown 8vo., 7s.

Digby.—THE LIFE OF SIR KENELM DIGBY, *by one of his Descendants*, the Author of 'The Life of a Conspirator,' 'A Life of Archbishop Laud,' etc. With 7 Illustrations. 8vo., 16s.

Duncan.—ADMIRAL DUNCAN. By the EARL OF CAMPERDOWN. With 3 Portraits. 8vo., 16s.

Erasmus.—LIFE AND LETTERS OF ERASMUS. By JAMES ANTHONY FROUDE. Crown 8vo., 6s.

FALKLANDS. By the Author of 'The Life of Sir Kenelm Digby,' 'The Life of a Prig,' etc. With Portraits and other Illustrations. 8vo., 10s. 6d.

Faraday. — FARADAY AS A DISCOVERER. By JOHN TYNDALL. Cr. 8vo., 3s. 6d.

FOREIGN COURTS AND FOREIGN HOMES. By A. M. F. Crown 8vo., 7s. 6d.

Fox.—THE EARLY HISTORY OF CHARLES JAMES FOX. By the Right Hon. Sir G. O. TREVELYAN, Bart.
Library Edition. 8vo., 18s.
Cabinet Edition. Crown 8vo., 6s.

Halifax.—THE LIFE AND LETTERS OF SIR GEORGE SAVILE, BARONET, FIRST MARQUIS OF HALIFAX. With a New Edition of his Works, now for the first time collected and revised. By H. C. FOXCROFT. With 2 Portraits. 2 vols. 8vo., 36s.

Hamilton.—LIFE OF SIR WILLIAM HAMILTON. By R. P. GRAVES. 8vo. 3 vols. 15s. each. ADDENDUM. 8vo., 6d.

Havelock.—MEMOIRS OF SIR HENRY HAVELOCK, K.C.B. By JOHN CLARK MARSHMAN. Crown 8vo., 3s. 6d.

Haweis.—MY MUSICAL LIFE. By the Rev. H. R. HAWEIS. With Portrait of Richard Wagner and 3 Illustrations. Crown 8vo., 7s. 6d.

Holroyd.—THE GIRLHOOD OF MARIA JOSEPHA HOLROYD (Lady Stanley of Alderly). Recorded in Letters of a Hundred Years Ago, from 1776-1796. Edited by J. H. ADEANE. With 6 Portraits. 8vo., 18s.

Jackson.—STONEWALL JACKSON AND THE AMERICAN CIVIL WAR. By Lieut.-Col. G. F. R. HENDERSON, York and Lancaster Regiment. With 2 Portraits and 33 Maps and Plans. 2 vols. 8vo., 42s.

Biography, Personal Memoirs, &c.—*continued.*

Lejeune.—MEMOIRS OF BARON LE-JEUNE, Aide-de-Camp to Marshals Berthier, Davout, and Oudinot. Translated. 2 vols. 8vo., 24s.

Luther.—LIFE OF LUTHER. By JULIUS KÖSTLIN. With Illustrations from Authentic Sources. Translated from the German. Crown 8vo., 3s. 6d.

Macaulay.—THE LIFE AND LETTERS OF LORD MACAULAY. By the Right Hon. Sir G. O. TREVELYAN, Bart., M.P.
Popular Edit. 1 vol. Cr. 8vo., 2s. 6d.
Student's Edition. 1 vol. Cr. 8vo., 6s.
Cabinet Edition. 2 vols. Post 8vo., 12s.
Library Edition. 2 vols. 8vo., 36s.
'Edinburgh Edition.' 2 vols. 8vo., 6s. each.

Marbot.—THE MEMOIRS OF THE BARON DE MARBOT. Translated from the French. 2 vols. Crown 8vo., 7s.

Max Müller.—AULD LANG SYNE. By the Right Hon. Professor F. MAX MÜLLER. With Portrait. 8vo., 10s. 6d.

Meade. — GENERAL SIR RICHARD MEADE AND THE FEUDATORY STATES OF CENTRAL AND SOUTHERN INDIA : a Record of Forty-three Years' Service as Soldier, Political Officer and Administrator. By THOMAS HENRY THORNTON, C.S.I., D.C.L. With Portrait, Map and 16 Illustrations. 8vo., 10s. 6d. net.

Nansen.—FRIDTJOF NANSEN, 1861-1893. By W. C. BRÖGGER and NORDAHL ROLFSEN. Translated by WILLIAM ARCHER. With 8 Plates, 48 Illustrations in the Text, and 3 Maps. 8vo., 12s. 6d.

Newdegate.—THE CHEVERELS OF CHEVEREL MANOR. By Lady NEWDIGATE-NEWDEGATE, Author of ' Gossip from a Muniment Room'. With 6 Illustrations from Family Portraits. 8vo., 10s. 6d.

Place.—THE LIFE OF FRANCIS PLACE. By GRAHAM WALLAS. 8vo., 12s.

Rawlinson.—A MEMOIR OF MAJOR-GENERAL SIR HENRY CRESWICKE RAWLINSON, Bart., K.C.B. By GEO. RAWLINSON, M.A., F.R.G.S., Canon of Canterbury. With an Introduction by Field-Marshal LORD ROBERTS of Kandahar, V.C. With Map, 3 Portraits and an Illustration. 8vo., 16s.

Reeve.—MEMOIRS OF THE LIFE AND CORRESPONDENCE OF HENRY REEVE, C.B., D.C.L., late Editor of the ' Edinburgh Review' and Registrar of the Privy Council. By J. KNOX LAUGHTON, M.A. 2 vols. 8vo.

Romanes.—THE LIFE AND LETTERS OF GEORGE JOHN ROMANES, M.A., LL.D., F.R.S. Written and Edited by his Wife. With Portrait and 2 Illustrations. Cr. 8vo., 6s.

Seebohm.—THE OXFORD REFORMERS —JOHN COLET, ERASMUS AND THOMAS MORE : a History of their Fellow-Work. By FREDERIC SEEBOHM. 8vo., 14s.

Shakespeare.—OUTLINES OF THE LIFE OF SHAKESPEARE. By J. O. HALLIWELL-PHILLIPPS. With Illustrations and Facsimiles. 2 vols. Royal 8vo., £1 1s.

Shakespeare's TRUE LIFE. By JAS. WALTER. With 500 Illustrations by GERALD E. MOIRA. Imp. 8vo., 21s.

Verney.—MEMOIRS OF THE VERNEY FAMILY.
Vols. I. and II. DURING THE CIVIL WAR. By FRANCES PARTHENOPE VERNEY. With 38 Portraits, Woodcuts and Facsimile. Royal 8vo., 42s.
Vol. III. DURING THE COMMONWEALTH. 1650-1660 By MARGARET M. VERNEY. With 10 Portraits, &c. Royal 8vo., 21s.

Wellington.—LIFE OF THE DUKE OF WELLINGTON. By the Rev. G. R. GLEIG, M.A. Crown 8vo., 3s. 6d.

Wills.—W. G. WILLS, DRAMATIST AND PAINTER. By FREEMAN WILLS. With Photogravure Portrait. 8vo., 10s. 6d.

Travel and Adventure, the Colonies, &c.

Arnold.—SEAS AND LANDS. By Sir EDWIN ARNOLD. With 71 Illustrations. Cr. 8vo., 3s. 6d.

Baker (Sir S. W.).
EIGHT YEARS IN CEYLON. With 6 Illustrations. Crown 8vo., 3s. 6d.
THE RIFLE AND THE HOUND IN CEYLON. With 6 Illustrations. Cr. 8vo., 3s. 6d.

Ball.—THE ALPINE GUIDE. By the late JOHN BALL, F.R.S., &c., President of the Alpine Club. A New Edition, Reconstructed and Revised on behalf ot the Alpine Club, by W. A. B. COOLIDGE.
Vol. I. THE WESTERN ALPS . The Alpine Region, South ot the Rhone Valley, from the Col de Tenda to the Simplon Pass. With 9 New and Revised Maps. Crown 8vo., 12s. net.

Travel and Adventure, the Colonies, &c.—*continued.*

Bent.—THE RUINED CITIES OF MASH-
ONALAND : being a Record of Excava-
tion and Exploration in 1891. By J.
THEODORE BENT. With 117 Illustrations. Crown 8vo., 3*s*. 6*d.*

Brassey.—VOYAGES AND TRAVELS OF
LORD BRASSEY, K.C.B., D.C.L., 1862-
1894. Arranged and Edited by Captain
S. EARDLEY-WILMOT. 2 vols. Cr.
8vo., 10*s.*

Brassey (The late LADY).

A VOYAGE IN THE 'SUNBEAM'; OUR
HOME ON THE OCEAN FOR ELEVEN
MONTHS.

  Cabinet Edition. With Map and 66
  Illustrations. Crown 8vo., 7*s*. 6*d.*
  Silver Library Edition. With 66
  Illustrations. Crown 8vo., 3*s*. 6*d.*
  Popular Edition. With 60 Illustra-
  tions. 4to., 6*d.* sewed, 1*s.* cloth.
  School Edition. With 37 Illustrations.
  Fcp., 2*s.*cloth, or 3*s.*white parchment.

SUNSHINE AND STORM IN THE EAST.

  Cabinet Edition. With 2 Maps and
  114 Illustrations. Crown 8vo.,7*s.*6*d.*
  Popular Edition. With 103 Illustrations. 4to., 6*d.* sewed, 1*s.* cloth.

IN THE TRADES, THE TROPICS, AND
THE 'ROARING FORTIES'.
  Cabinet Edition. With Map and 220
  Illustrations. Crown 8vo., 7*s*. 6*d.*
  Popular Edition. With 183 Illustra-
  tions. 4to., 6*d.* sewed, 1*s.* cloth.

THREE VOYAGES IN THE 'SUNBEAM'.
Popular Edition. With 346 Illustrations. 4to., 2*s.* 6*d.*

Browning.—A GIRL'S WANDERINGS
IN HUNGARY. By H. ELLEN BROWN-
ING. With Map and 20 Illustrations.
Crown 8vo., 3*s*. 6*d.*

Churchill.—THE STORY OF THE MA-
LAKAND FIELD FORCE. By Lieut.
WINSTON L. SPENCER CHURCHILL.
With Maps and Plans. Cr. 8vo., 7*s*. 6*d.*

Crawford. — SOUTH AMERICAN
SKETCHES. By ROBERT CRAWFORD,
M.A. Crown 8vo., 6*s.*

Froude (JAMES A.).

OCEANA : or England and her Colonies.
With 9 Illustrations. Crown 8vo.,
3*s*. 6*d.*

THE ENGLISH IN THE WEST INDIES :
or the Bow of Ulysses. With 9 Illustrations. Cr. 8vo., 2*s.* bds., 2*s.* 6*d.* cl.

Howitt.—VISITS TO REMARKABLE
PLACES, Old Halls, Battle-Fields,
Scenes illustrative of Striking Passages
in English History and Poetry. By
WILLIAM HOWITT. With 80 Illustra-
tions. Crown 8vo., 3*s*. 6*d.*

Knight (E. F.).

THE CRUISE OF THE 'ALERTE': the
Narrative of a Search for Treasure on
the Desert Island of Trinidad. With
2 Maps and 23 Illustrations. Crown
8vo., 3*s*. 6*d.*

WHERE THREE EMPIRES MEET: a Nar-
rative of Recent Travel in Kashmir,
Western Tibet, Baltistan, Ladak,
Gilgit, and the adjoining Countries.
With a Map and 54 Illustrations.
Cr. 8vo., 3*s*. 6*d.*

THE 'FALCON' ON THE BALTIC: a
Voyage from London to Copenhagen
in a Three-Tonner. With 10 Full-
page Illustrations. Cr. 8vo., 3*s*. 6*d.*

Lees and Clutterbuck.—B. C. 1887:
A RAMBLE IN BRITISH COLUMBIA. By
J. A. LEES and W. J. CLUTTERBUCK.
With Map and 75 Illustrations. Cr. 8vo.,
3*s*. 6*d.*

Max Müller.—LETTERS FROM CON-
STANTINOPLE. By Mrs. MAX MÜLLER.
With 12 Views of Constantinople and
the neighbourhood. Crown 8vo., 6*s.*

Nansen (FRIDTJOF).

THE FIRST CROSSING OF GREENLAND.
With numerous Illustrations and a
Map. Crown 8vo., 3*s*. 6*d.*

ESKIMO LIFE. With 31 Illustrations.
8vo., 16*s.*

Oliver.—CRAGS AND CRATERS: Rambles in the Island of Réunion. By
WILLIAM DUDLEY OLIVER, M.A.
With 27 Illustrations and a Map. Cr.
8vo., 6*s.*

Travel and Adventure, the Colonies, &c.—*continued.*

Smith.—CLIMBING IN THE BRITISH ISLES. By W. P. HASKETT SMITH. With Illustrations by ELLIS CARR, and Numerous Plans.

Part I. ENGLAND. 16mo., 3*s*. 6*d*.

Part II. WALES AND IRELAND. 16mo., 3*s*. 6*d*.

Stephen. — THE PLAYGROUND OF EUROPE. By LESLIE STEPHEN. New Edition, with Additions and 4 Illustrations. Crown 8vo., 6*s*. net.

THREE IN NORWAY. By Two of Them. With a Map and 59 Illustrations. Cr. 8vo., 2*s*. boards, 2*s*. 6*d*. cloth.

Tyndall.—THE GLACIERS OF THE ALPS: being a Narrative of Excursions and Ascents. An Account of the Origin and Phenomena of Glaciers, and an Exposition of the Physical Principles to which they are related. By JOHN TYNDALL, F.R.S. With 61 Illustrations. Crown 8vo., 6*s*. 6*d*. net.

Vivian.—SERVIA: the Poor Man's Paradise. By HERBERT VIVIAN, M.A. 8vo., 15*s*.

Sport and Pastime.

THE BADMINTON LIBRARY.

Edited by HIS GRACE THE DUKE OF BEAUFORT, K.G., and

A. E. T. WATSON.

Complete in 28 Volumes. Crown 8vo., Price 10*s*. 6*d*. each Volume, Cloth.

* The Volumes are also issued half-bound in Leather, with gilt top. The price can be had from all Booksellers.

ARCHERY. By C. J. LONGMAN and Col. H. WALROND. With Contributions by Miss LEGH, Viscount DILLON, &c. With 2 Maps, 23 Plates, and 172 Illustrations in the Text. Crown 8vo., 10*s*. 6*d*.

ATHLETICS. By MONTAGUE SHEARMAN. With 6 Plates and 52 Illustrations in the Text. Crown 8vo., 10*s*. 6*d*.

BIG GAME SHOOTING. By CLIVE PHILLIPPS-WOLLEY.

Vol. I. AFRICA AND AMERICA. With Contributions by Sir SAMUEL W. BAKER, W. C. OSWELL, F. C. SELOUS, &c. With 20 Plates and 57 Illustrations in the Text. Crown 8vo., 10*s*. 6*d*.

Vol. II. EUROPE, ASIA, AND THE ARCTIC REGIONS. With Contributions by Lieut.-Colonel R. HEBER PERCY, Major ALGERNON C. HEBER PERCY, &c. With 17 Plates and 56 Illustrations in the Text. Crown 8vo., 10*s*. 6*d*.

BILLIARDS. By Major W. BROADFOOT, R.E. With Contributions by A. H. BOYD, SYDENHAM DIXON, W. J. FORD, &c. With 11 Plates, 19 Illustrations in the Text, and numerous Diagrams. Crown 8vo., 10*s*. 6*d*.

COURSING AND FALCONRY. By HARDING COX and the Hon. GERALD LASCELLES. With 20 Plates and 56 Illustrations in the Text. Crown 8vo., 10*s*. 6*d*.

CRICKET. By A. G. STEEL, and the Hon. R. H. LYTTELTON. With Contributions by ANDREW LANG, W. G. GRACE, F. GALE, &c. With 12 Plates and 53 Illustrations in the Text. Crown 8vo., 10*s*. 6*d*.

CYCLING. By the EARL OF ALBEMARLE, and G. LACY HILLIER. With 19 Plates and 44 Illustrations in the Text. Crown 8vo., 10*s*. 6*d*.

Sport and Pastime—*continued.*

THE BADMINTON LIBRARY—*continued.*

DANCING. By Mrs. LILLY GROVE, F.R.G.S. With Contributions by Miss MIDDLETON, The Honourable Mrs. ARMYTAGE, &c. With Musical Examples, and 38 Full-page Plates and 93 Illustrations in the Text. Crown 8vo., 10s. 6d.

DRIVING. By His Grace the DUKE OF BEAUFORT, K.G. With Contributions by other Authorities. With 12 Plates and 54 Illustrations in the Text. Crown 8vo., 10s. 6d.

FENCING, BOXING, AND WREST-LING. By WALTER H. POLLOCK, F. C. GROVE, C. PREVOST, E. B. MITCHELL, and WALTER ARMSTRONG. With 18 Plates and 24 Illustrations in the Text. Crown 8vo., 10s. 6d.

FISHING. By H. CHOLMONDELEY-PEN-NELL.

Vol. I. SALMON AND TROUT. With Contributions by H. R. FRANCIS, Major JOHN P. TRAHERNE, &c. With 9 Plates and numerous Illustrations of Tackle, &c. Crown 8vo., 10s. 6d.

Vol. II. PIKE AND OTHER COARSE FISH. With Contributions by the MARQUIS OF EXETER, WILLIAM SENIOR, G. CHRISTOPHER DAVIES, &c. With 7 Plates and numerous Illustrations of Tackle, &c. Crown 8vo., 10s. 6d.

GOLF. By HORACE G. HUTCHINSON. With Contributions by the Rt. Hon. A. J. BALFOUR, M.P., Sir WALTER SIMPSON, Bart., ANDREW LANG, &c. With 32 Plates and 57 Illustrations in the Text. Cr. 8vo., 10s. 6d.

HUNTING. By His Grace the DUKE OF BEAUFORT K.G., and MOWBRAY MORRIS. With Contributions by the EARL OF SUFFOLK AND BERKSHIRE, Rev. E. W. L. DAVIES, G. H. LONG-MAN, &c. With 5 Plates and 54 Illustrations in the Text. Crown 8vo., 10s. 6d.

MOUNTAINEERING. By C. T. DENT. With Contributions by Sir W. M. CON-WAY, D. W. FRESHFIELD, C. E. MA-THEWS, &c. With 13 Plates and 95 Illustrations in the Text. Crown 8vo., 10s. 6d.

POETRY OF SPORT (THE).—Selected by HEDLEY PEEK. With a Chapter on Classical Allusions to Sport by ANDREW LANG, and a Special Preface to the Badminton Library by A. E. T. WAT-SON. With 32 Plates and 74 Illustrations in the Text. Crown 8vo., 10s. 6d.

RACING AND STEEPLE-CHASING. By the EARL OF SUFFOLK AND BERK-SHIRE, W. G. CRAVEN, the HON. F. LAWLEY, ARTHUR COVENTRY, and ALFRED E. T. WATSON. With Frontispiece and 56 Illustrations in the Text. Crown 8vo., 10s. 6d.

RIDING AND POLO. By Captain ROBERT WEIR, the DUKE OF BEAU-FORT, the EARL OF SUFFOLK AND BERKSHIRE, the EARL OF ONSLOW, &c. With 18 Plates and 41 Illustrations in the Text. Crown 8vo., 10s. 6d.

ROWING. By R. P. P. ROWE and C. M. PITMAN. With Contributions by C. P. SEROCOLD, F. C. BEGG, and S. LE B. SMITH. PUNTING. By P. W. SQUIRE. With 20 Plates and 55 Illustrations in the Text; also 4 Maps of the Oxford and Cambridge Boat-race and Metropolitan Championship Course, Henley Course, Oxford Course, and Cambridge Course. Crown 8vo., 10s. 6d.

SEA FISHING. By JOHN BICKERDYKE, Sir H. W. GORE-BOOTH, ALFRED C. HARMSWORTH, and W. SENIOR. With 22 Full-page Plates and 175 Illustrations in the Text. Crown 8vo., 10s. 6d.

Sport and Pastime—*continued.*

THE BADMINTON LIBRARY—*continued.*

SHOOTING.

Vol. I. FIELD AND COVERT. By LORD WALSINGHAM and Sir RALPH PAYNE-GALLWEY, Bart. With Contributions by the Hon. GERALD LASCELLES and A. J. STUART-WORTLEY. With 11 Plates and 94 Illustrations in the Text. Crown 8vo., 10s. 6d.

Vol. II. MOOR AND MARSH. By LORD WALSINGHAM and Sir RALPH PAYNE-GALLWEY, Bart. With Contributions by LORD LOVAT and LORD CHARLES LENNOX KERR. With 8 Plates and 57 Illustrations in the Text. Crown 8vo., 10s. 6d.

SKATING, CURLING, TOBOGGAN-ING. By J. M. HEATHCOTE, C. G. TEBBUTT, T. MAXWELL WITHAM, Rev. JOHN KERR, ORMOND HAKE, HENRY A. BUCK, &c. With 12 Plates and 272 Illustrations in the Text. Cr. 8vo., 10s. 6d.

SWIMMING. By ARCHIBALD SINCLAIR and WILLIAM HENRY, Hon. Secs. of the Life-Saving Society. With 13 Plates and 106 Illustrations in the Text. Cr. 8vo., 10s. 6d.

TENNIS, LAWN TENNIS, RACQUETS, AND FIVES. By J. M. and C. G. HEATHCOTE, E. O. PLEYDELL-BOUVERIE, and A. C. AINGER. With Contributions by the Hon. A. LYTTELTON, W. C. MARSHALL, Miss L. DOD, &c. With 12 Plates and 67 Illustrations in the Text. Crown 8vo., 10s. 6d.

YACHTING.

Vol. I. CRUISING, CONSTRUCTION OF YACHTS, YACHT RACING RULES, FITTING-OUT, &c. By Sir EDWARD SULLIVAN, Bart., THE EARL OF PEMBROKE, LORD BRASSEY, K.C.B., C. E. SETH-SMITH, C.B., G. L. WATSON, R. T. PRITCHETT, E. F. KNIGHT, &c. With 21 Plates and 93 Illustrations in the Text, and from Photographs. Crown 8vo., 10s. 6d.

Vol. II. YACHT CLUBS, YACHTING IN AMERICA AND THE COLONIES, YACHT RACING, &c. By R. T. PRITCHETT, THE MARQUIS OF DUFFERIN AND AVA, K.P., THE EARL OF ONSLOW, JAMES McFERRAN, &c. With 35 Plates and 160 Illustrations in the Text. Crown 8vo., 10s. 6d.

FUR, FEATHER AND FIN SERIES.

Edited by A. E. T. WATSON.

Crown 8vo., price 5s. each Volume.

*** *The Volumes are also issued half-bound in Leather, with gilt top. The price can be had from all Booksellers.*

THE PARTRIDGE. *Natural History,* by the Rev. H. A. MACPHERSON; *Shooting,* by A. J. STUART-WORTLEY; *Cookery,* by GEORGE SAINTSBURY. With 11 Illustrations and various Diagrams in the Text. Crown 8vo., 5s.

THE GROUSE. *Natural History,* by the Rev. H. A. MACPHERSON; *Shooting,* by A. J. STUART-WORTLEY; *Cookery,* by GEORGE SAINTSBURY. With 13 Illustrations and various Diagrams in the Text. Crown 8vo., 5s.

THE PHEASANT. *Natural History,* by the Rev. H. A. MACPHERSON; *Shooting,* by A. J. STUART-WORTLEY; *Cookery,* by ALEXANDER INNES SHAND. With 10 Illustrations and various Diagrams. Crown 8vo., 5s.

THE HARE. *Natural History,* by the Rev. H. A. MACPHERSON; *Shooting,* by the Hon. GERALD LASCELLES; *Coursing,* by CHARLES RICHARDSON; *Hunting,* by J. S. GIBBONS and G. H. LONGMAN; *Cookery,* by Col. KENNEY HERBERT. With 9 Illustrations. Cr. 8vo., 5s.

Sport and Pastime—*continued*.

FUR, FEATHER AND FIN SERIES—*continued*.

RED DEER. *Natural History*, by the Rev. H. A. MACPHERSON; *Deer Stalking*, by CAMERON OF LOCHIEL. *Stag Hunting*, by Viscount EBRINGTON; *Cookery*, by ALEXANDER INNES SHAND. With 10 Illustrations. Crown 8vo., 5s.

THE RABBIT. By J. E. HARTING, &c. With Illustrations. [*In preparation*.

WILDFOWL. By the Hon. JOHN SCOTT MONTAGU. With Illustrations. [*In preparation*.

THE SALMON. By the Hon. A. E. GATHORNE-HARDY. With Chapters on the Law of Salmon-Fishing by CLAUD DOUGLAS PENNANT; Cookery, by ALEXANDER INNES SHAND. With 8 Illustrations. Crown 8vo., 5s.

THE TROUT. By the MARQUESS OF GRANBY. With Chapters on Breeding by Colonel F. H. CUSTANCE; Cookery, by ALEXANDER INNES SHAND. With 12 Illustrations. Crown 8vo., 5s.

André.—COLONEL BOGEY'S SKETCH-BOOK. Comprising an Eccentric Collection of Scribbles and Scratches found in disused Lockers and swept up in the Pavilion, together with sundry After-Dinner Sayings of the Colonel. By R. ANDRE, West Herts Golf Club. Oblong 4to., 2s. 6d.

BADMINTON MAGAZINE (THE) OF SPORTS AND PASTIMES. Edited by ALFRED E. T. WATSON ('Rapier'). With numerous Illustrations. Price 1s. Monthly. Vols. I.-VI., 6s. each.

DEAD SHOT (THE): or, Sportsman's Complete Guide. Being a Treatise on the Use of the Gun, with Rudimentary and Finishing Lessons on the Art of Shooting Game of all kinds. Also Game-driving, Wildfowl and Pigeon-shooting, Dog-breaking, etc. By MARKS-MAN. With numerous Illustrations. Crown 8vo., 10s. 6d.

Ellis.—CHESS SPARKS; or, Short and Bright Games of Chess. Collected and Arranged by J. H. ELLIS, M.A. 8vo., 4s. 6d.

Folkard. — THE WILD-FOWLER: A Treatise on Fowling, Ancient and Modern; descriptive also of Decoys and Flight-ponds, Wild-fowl Shooting, Gunning-punts, Shooting-yachts, &c. Also Fowling in the Fens and in Foreign Countries, Rock-fowling, &c., &c., by H. C. FOLKARD. With 13 Engravings on Steel, and several Woodcuts. 8vo., 12s. 6d.

Ford.—THE THEORY AND PRACTICE OF ARCHERY. BY HORACE FORD. New Edition, thoroughly Revised and Re-written by W. BUTT, M.A. With a Preface by C. J. LONGMAN, M.A. 8vo., 14s.

Francis.—A BOOK ON ANGLING: or, Treatise on the Art of Fishing in every Branch; including full Illustrated List of Salmon Flies. By FRANCIS FRANCIS. With Portrait and Coloured Plates. Crown 8vo., 15s.

Gibson.—TOBOGGANING ON CROOKED RUNS. By the Hon. HARRY GIBSON. With Contributions by F. DE B. STRICK-LAND and 'LADY-TOBOGGANER'. With 40 Illustrations. Crown 8vo., 6s.

Graham.—COUNTRY PASTIMES FOR BOYS. By P. ANDERSON GRAHAM. With 252 Illustrations from Drawings and Photographs. Crown 8vo., 3s. 6d.

Lang.—ANGLING SKETCHES. By A. LANG. With 20 Illustrations. Crown 8vo., 3s. 6d.

Lillie.—CROQUET: its History, Rules, and Secrets. By ARTHUR LILLIE, Champion Grand National Croquet Club, 1872; Winner of the 'All-Comers' Championship,' Maidstone, 1896. With 4 Full-page Illustrations by LUCIEN DAVIS, 15 Illustrations in the Text, and 27 Diagrams. Crown 8vo., 6s.

Longman.—CHESS OPENINGS. By FREDERICK W. LONGMAN. Fcp. 8vo., 2s. 6d.

Madden.—THE DIARY OF MASTER WILLIAM SILENCE: A Study of Shakespeare and of Elizabethan Sport. By the Right Hon. D. H. MADDEN, Vice-Chancellor of the University of Dublin. 8vo., 16s.

Sport and Pastime—*continued.*

Maskelyne.—SHARPS AND FLATS : a Complete Revelation of the Secrets of Cheating at Games of Chance and Skill. By JOHN NEVIL MASKELYNE, of the Egyption Hall. With 62 Illustrations. Crown 8vo., 6s.

Park.—THE GAME OF GOLF. By WILLIAM PARK, Junr., Champion Golfer, 1887-89. With 17 Plates and 26 Illustrations in the Text. Crown 8vo., 7s. 6d.

Payne-Gallwey (Sir RALPH, Bart.).

LETTERS TO YOUNG SHOOTERS (First Series). On the Choice and Use of a Gun. With 41 Illustrations. Cr. 8vo., 7s. 6d.

LETTERS TO YOUNG SHOOTERS (Second Series). On the Production, Preservation, and Killing of Game. With Directions in Shooting Wood-Pigeons and Breaking-in Retrievers. With Portrait and 103 Illustrations. Crown 8vo., 12s. 6d.

LETTERS TO YOUNG SHOOTERS (Third Series). Comprising a Short Natural History of the Wildfowl that are Rare or Common to the British Islands, with Complete Directions in Shooting Wildfowl on the Coast and Inland. With 200 Illustrations. Cr. 8vo., 18s.

Pole.—THE THEORY OF THE MODERN SCIENTIFIC GAME OF WHIST. By WILLIAM POLE. Fcp. 8vo., 2s. 6d.

Proctor.—HOW TO PLAY WHIST: WITH THE LAWS AND ETIQUETTE OF WHIST. By RICHARD A. PROCTOR. Crown 8vo., 3s. 6d.

Ribblesdale.—THE QUEEN'S HOUNDS AND STAG-HUNTING RECOLLECTIONS. By LORD RIBBLESDALE, Master of the Buckhounds, 1892-95. With Introductory Chapter on the Hereditary Mastership by E. BURROWS. With 24 Plates and 35 Illustrations in the Text, including reproductions from Oil Paintings in the possession of Her Majesty the Queen at Windsor Castle and Cumberland Lodge, Original Drawings by G. D. GILES, and from Prints and Photographs. 8vo., 25s.

Ronalds.—THE FLY-FISHER'S ENTOMOLOGY. By ALFRED RONALDS. With 20 Coloured Plates. 8vo., 14s.

Thompson and Cannan. HAND-IN-HAND FIGURE SKATING. By NORCLIFFE G. THOMPSON and F. LAURA CANNAN, Members of the Skating Club. With an Introduction by Captain J. H. THOMSON, R.A. With Illustrations. 16mo., 6s.

Wilcocks. THE SEA FISHERMAN : Comprising the Chief Methods of Hook and Line Fishing in the British and other Seas, and Remarks on Nets, Boats, and Boating. By J. C. WILCOCKS. Illustrated. Crown 8vo., 6s.

Veterinary Medicine, &c.

Steel (JOHN HENRY).
A TREATISE ON THE DISEASES OF THE DOG. With 88 Illustrations. 8vo., 10s. 6d.
A TREATISE ON THE DISEASES OF THE OX. With 119 Illustrations. 8vo., 15s.
A TREATISE ON THE DISEASES OF THE SHEEP. With 100 Illustrations. 8vo., 12s.
OUTLINES OF EQUINE ANATOMY : a Manual for the use of Veterinary Students in the Dissecting Room. Crown 8vo., 7s. 6d.

Fitzwygram.--HORSES AND STABLES. By Major-General Sir F. FITZWYGRAM, Bart. With 56 pages of Illustrations. 8vo., 2s. 6d. net.

Schreiner. — THE ANGORA GOAT (published under the auspices of the South African Angora Goat Breeders' Association), and a Paper on the Ostrich (reprinted from the *Zoologist* for March, 1897). By S. C. CRONWRIGHT SCHRIENER. With 26 Illustrations. 8vo., 10s. 6d.

'Stonehenge.'—THE DOG IN HEALTH AND DISEASE. By 'STONEHENGE'. With 78 Wood Engravings. 8vo., 7s. 6d.

Youatt (WILLIAM).
THE HORSE. Revised and enlarged. By W. WATSON, M.R.C.V.S. With 52 Wood Engravings. 8vo., 7s. 6d.
THE DOG. Revised and enlarged. With 33 Wood Engravings. 8vo., 6s.

Mental, Moral, and Political Philosophy.
LOGIC, RHETORIC, PSYCHOLOGY, &c.

Abbott.—THE ELEMENTS OF LOGIC. By T. K. ABBOTT, B.D. 12mo., 3s.

Aristotle.

THE ETHICS: Greek Text, Illustrated with Essay and Notes. By Sir ALEXANDER GRANT, Bart. 2 vols. 8vo., 32s.

AN INTRODUCTION TO ARISTOTLE'S ETHICS. Books I.-IV. (Book X. c. vi.-ix. in an Appendix.) With a continuous Analysis and Notes. By the Rev. EDWARD MOORE, D.D. Cr. 8vo., 10s. 6d.

Bacon (FRANCIS).

COMPLETE WORKS. Edited by R. L. ELLIS, JAMES SPEDDING, and D. D. HEATH. 7 vols. 8vo., £3 13s. 6d.

LETTERS AND LIFE, including all his occasional Works. Edited by JAMES SPEDDING. 7 vols. 8vo., £4 4s.

THE ESSAYS: with Annotations. By RICHARD WHATELY, D.D. 8vo., 10s. 6d.

THE ESSAYS: Edited, with Notes. By F. STORR and C. H. GIBSON. Cr. 8vo., 3s. 6d.

THE ESSAYS. With Introduction, Notes, and Index. By E. A. ABBOTT, D.D. 2 vols. Fcp. 8vo., 6s. The Text and Index only, without Introduction and Notes, in One Volume. Fcp. 8vo., 2s. 6d.

Bain (ALEXANDER).

MENTAL SCIENCE. Crown 8vo., 6s. 6d.

MORAL SCIENCE. Crown 8vo., 4s. 6d.

The two works as above can be had in one volume, price 10s. 6d.

SENSES AND THE INTELLECT. 8vo., 15s.

EMOTIONS AND THE WILL. 8vo., 15s.

LOGIC, DEDUCTIVE AND INDUCTIVE. Part I., 4s. Part II., 6s. 6d.

PRACTICAL ESSAYS. Crown 8vo., 2s.

Bray.—THE PHILOSOPHY OF NECESSITY; or Law in Mind as in Matter. By CHARLES BRAY. Crown 8vo., 5s.

Crozier (JOHN BEATTIE).

HISTORY OF INTELLECTUAL DEVELOPMENT: on the Lines of Modern Evolution.

Vol. I. Greek and Hindoo Thought; Græco-Roman Paganism; Judaism; and Christianity down to the Closing of the Schools of Athens by Justinian, 529 A.D. 8vo., 14s.

Crozier (JOHN BEATTIE)—*continued.*

CIVILISATION AND PROGRESS; being the Outlines of a New System of Political, Religious and Social Philosophy. 8vo., 14s.

Davidson.—THE LOGIC OF DEFINITION, Explained and Applied. By WILLIAM L. DAVIDSON, M.A. Crown 8vo., 6s.

Green (THOMAS HILL). The Works of. Edited by R. L. NETTLESHIP.

Vols. I. and II. Philosophical Works 8vo., 16s. each.

Vol. III. Miscellanies. With Index to the three Volumes, and Memoir. 8vo., 21s.

LECTURES ON THE PRINCIPLES OF POLITICAL OBLIGATION. 8vo., 5s.

Hodgson (SHADWORTH H.).

TIME AND SPACE: a Metaphysical Essay. 8vo., 16s.

THE THEORY OF PRACTICE: an Ethical Inquiry. 2 vols. 8vo., 24s.

THE PHILOSOPHY OF REFLECTION. 2 vols. 8vo., 21s.

THE METAPHYSIC OF EXPERIENCE. 4 vols. I. General Analysis of Experience. II. Positive Science. III. Analysis of Conscious Action. IV. The Real Universe. 4 vols. 8vo., 36s. net.

Hume.—THE PHILOSOPHICAL WORKS OF DAVID HUME. Edited by T. H. GREEN and T. H. GROSE. 4 vols. 8vo., 56s. Or separately, Essays. 2 vols. 28s. Treatise of Human Nature. 2 vols. 28s.

James.—THE WILL TO BELIEVE, and other Essays in Popular Philosophy. By WILLIAM JAMES, M.D., LL.D., &c. Crown 8vo., 7s. 6d.

Justinian.—THE INSTITUTES OF JUSTINIAN: Latin Text, chiefly that of Huschke, with English Introduction, Translation, Notes, and Summary. By THOMAS C. SANDARS, M.A. 8vo., 18s.

Kant (IMMANUEL).

CRITIQUE OF PRACTICAL REASON, AND OTHER WORKS ON THE THEORY OF ETHICS. Translated by T. K. ABBOTT, B.D. With Memoir. 8vo., 12s. 6d.

FUNDAMENTAL PRINCIPLES OF THE METAPHYSIC OF ETHICS. Translated by T. K. ABBOTT, B.D. Crown 8vo., 3s.

Mental, Moral and Political Philosophy—*continued.*

Kant (IMMANUEL)—*continued.*

INTRODUCTION TO LOGIC, AND HIS ESSAY ON THE MISTAKEN SUBTILTY OF THE FOUR FIGURES. Translated by T. K. ABBOTT. 8vo., 6s.

Killick.—HANDBOOK TO MILL'S SYSTEM OF LOGIC. By Rev. A. H. KILLICK, M.A. Crown 8vo., 3s. 6d.

Ladd (GEORGE TRUMBULL).

OUTLINES OF DESCRIPTIVE PSYCHOLOGY : a Text-Book of Mental Science for Colleges and Normal Schools. 8vo., 12s.

PHILOSOPHY OF KNOWLEDGE : an Inquiry into the Nature, Limits and Validity of Human Cognitive Faculty. 8vo., 18s.

PHILOSOPHY OF MIND : an Essay on the Metaphysics of Psychology. 8vo., 16s.

ELEMENTS OF PHYSIOLOGICAL PSYCHOLOGY. 8vo., 21s.

OUTLINES OF PHYSIOLOGICAL PSYCHOLOGY. A Text-Book of Mental Science for Academies and Colleges. 8vo., 12s.

PRIMER OF PSYCHOLOGY. Crown 8vo., 5s. 6d.

Lutoslawski.—THE ORIGIN AND GROWTH OF PLATO'S LOGIC. By W. LUTOSLAWSKI. 8vo., 21s.

Max Müller (F.).

THE SCIENCE OF THOUGHT. 8vo., 21s.

THREE INTRODUCTORY LECTURES ON THE SCIENCE OF THOUGHT. 8vo., 2s. 6d. net.

Mill.—ANALYSIS OF THE PHENOMENA OF THE HUMAN MIND. By JAMES MILL. 2 vols. 8vo., 28s.

Mill (JOHN STUART).

A SYSTEM OF LOGIC. Cr. 8vo., 3s. 6d.

ON LIBERTY. Cr. 8vo., 1s. 4d.

CONSIDERATIONS ON REPRESENTATIVE GOVERNMENT. Crown 8vo., 2s.

UTILITARIANISM. 8vo., 2s. 6d.

Mill (JOHN STUART)—*continued.*

EXAMINATION OF SIR WILLIAM HAMILTON'S PHILOSOPHY. 8vo., 16s.

NATURE, THE UTILITY OF RELIGION, AND THEISM. Three Essays. 8vo., 5s.

Romanes.—MIND AND MOTION AND MONISM. By GEORGE JOHN ROMANES, LL.D., F.R.S. Crown 8vo., 4s. 6d.

Stock (ST. GEORGE).

DEDUCTIVE LOGIC. Fcp. 8vo., 3s. 6d.

LECTURES IN THE LYCEUM ; or, Aristotle's Ethics for English Readers. Edited by ST. GEORGE STOCK. Crown 8vo., 7s. 6d.

Sully (JAMES).

THE HUMAN MIND : a Text-book of Psychology. 2 vols. 8vo., 21s.

OUTLINES OF PSYCHOLOGY. Crown 8vo., 9s.

THE TEACHER'S HANDBOOK OF PSYCHOLOGY. Crown 8vo., 6s. 6d.

STUDIES OF CHILDHOOD. 8vo. 10s. 6d.

CHILDREN'S WAYS : being Selections from the Author's 'Studies of Childhood,' with some additional Matter. With 25 Figures in the Text. Crown 8vo., 4s. 6d.

Sutherland. — THE ORIGIN AND GROWTH OF THE MORAL INSTINCT. By ALEXANDER SUTHERLAND, M.A. 2 vols. 8vo., 28s.

Swinburne.—PICTURE LOGIC : an Attempt to Popularise the Science of Reasoning. By ALFRED JAMES SWINBURNE, M.A. With 23 Woodcuts. Crown 8vo., 5s.

Weber.—HISTORY OF PHILOSOPHY. By ALFRED WEBER, Professor in the University of Strasburg, Translated by FRANK THILLY, Ph.D. 8vo., 16s.

Whately (ARCHBISHOP).

BACON'S ESSAYS. With Annotations. 8vo., 10s. 6d.

ELEMENTS OF LOGIC. Cr. 8vo., 4s. 6d.

ELEMENTS OF RHETORIC. Cr. 8vo., 4s. 6d.

LESSONS ON REASONING. Fcp. 8vo., 1s. 6d.

Mental, Moral and Political Philosophy—*continued.*

Zeller (Dr EDWARD, Professor in the University of Berlin).

THE STOICS, EPICUREANS, AND SCEPTICS. Translated by the Rev. O. J. REICHEL, M.A. Crown 8vo., 15s.

OUTLINES OF THE HISTORY OF GREEK PHILOSOPHY. Translated by SARAH F. ALLEYNE and EVELYN ABBOTT. Crown 8vo., 10s. 6d.

Zeller (Dr. EDWARD)—*continued.*

PLATO AND THE OLDER ACADEMY. Translated by SARAH F. ALLEYNE and ALFRED GOODWIN, B.A. Crown 8vo., 18s.

SOCRATES AND THE SOCRATIC SCHOOLS. Translated by the Rev. O. J. REICHEL, M.A Crown 8vo., 10s. 6d.

ARISTOTLE AND THE EARLIER PERIPATETICS. Translated by B. F. C. COSTELLOE, M.A., and J. H. MUIRHEAD, M.A. 2 vols. Cr. 8vo., 24s.

MANUALS OF CATHOLIC PHILOSOPHY.

(Stonyhurst Series.)

A MANUAL OF POLITICAL ECONOMY. By C. S. DEVAS, M.A. Cr. 8vo.. 6s. 6d.

FIRST PRINCIPLES OF KNOWLEDGE. By JOHN RICKABY, S.J. Crown 8vo., 5s.

GENERAL METAPHYSICS. By JOHN RICKABY, S.J. Crown 8vo., 5s.

LOGIC. By RICHARD F. CLARKE, S.J. Crown 8vo., 5s.

MORAL PHILOSOPHY (ETHICS AND NATURAL LAW). By JOSEPH RICKABY, S.J. Crown 8vo., 5s.

NATURAL THEOLOGY. By BERNARD BOEDDER, S.J. Crown 8vo., 6s. 6d.

PSYCHOLOGY. By MICHAEL MAHER, S.J. Crown 8vo., 6s. 6d.

History and Science of Language, &c.

Davidson.—LEADING AND IMPORTANT ENGLISH WORDS · Explained and Exemplified. By WILLIAM L. DAVIDSON, M.A. Fcp. 8vo., 3s. 6d.

Farrar.—LANGUAGE AND LANGUAGES. By F. W. FARRAR, D.D., F.R.S., Cr. 8vo., 6s.

Graham.—ENGLISH SYNONYMS, Classified and Explained : with Practical Exercises. By G. F. GRAHAM. Fcap 8vo., 6s.

Max Müller (F.).

THE SCIENCE OF LANGUAGE, Founded on Lectures delivered at the Royal Institution in 1861 and 1863. 2 vols. Crown 8vo., 10s.

BIOGRAPHIES OF WORDS, AND THE HOME OF THE ARYAS. Crown 8vo., 5s.

Max Müller (F.)—*continued.*

THREE LECTURES ON THE SCIENCE OF LANGUAGE, AND ITS PLACE IN GENERAL EDUCATION, delivered at Oxford, 1889. Crown 8vo., 3s. net.

Roget. — THESAURUS OF ENGLISH WORDS AND PHRASES. Classified and Arranged so as to Facilitate the Expression of Ideas and assist in Literary Composition. By PETER MARK ROGET, M.D., F.R.S. Recomposed throughout, enlarged and improved, partly from the Author's Notes, and with a full Index, by the Author's Son, JOHN LEWIS ROGET. Crown 8vo., 10s. 6d.

Whately.—ENGLISH SY
E. JANE WHATELY

Political Economy and Economics.

Ashley.—ENGLISH ECONOMIC HISTORY AND THEORY. By W. J. ASHLEY. Cr. 8vo., Part I., 5s.   Part II., 10s. 6d.

Bagehot.—ECONOMIC STUDIES. By WALTER BAGEHOT. Cr. 8vo., 3s. 6d.

Brassey.—PAPERS AND ADDRESSES ON WORK AND WAGES. By Lord BRASSEY. Crown 8vo., 5s.

Channing.—THE TRUTH ABOUT AGRICULTURAL DEPRESSION: An Economic Study of the Evidence of the Royal Commission. By FRANCIS ALLSTON CHANNING, M.P., one of the Commission. Crown 8vo., 6s.

Devas.—A MANUAL OF POLITICAL ECONOMY. By C. S. DEVAS, M.A. Crown 8vo., 6s. 6d.

Dowell.—A HISTORY OF TAXATION AND TAXES IN ENGLAND, from the Earliest Times to the Year 1885. By STEPHEN DOWELL (4 vols. 8vo.). Vols. I. and II. The History of Taxation, 21s. Vols. III. and IV. The History of Taxes, 21s.

Jordan.—THE STANDARD OF VALUE. By WILLIAM LEIGHTON JORDAN. Crown 8vo., 6s.

Macleod (HENRY DUNNING).
BIMETALISM. 8vo., 5s. net.
THE ELEMENTS OF BANKING. Crown 8vo., 3s. 6d.
THE THEORY AND PRACTICE OF BANKING. Vol. I. 8vo., 12s. Vol. II. 14s.

Macleod (HENRY DUNNING)—*cont.*
THE THEORY OF CREDIT. 8vo. Vol. I. 10s. net. Vol. II., Part I., 10s. net. Vol. II. Part II., 10s. net.
INDIAN CURRENCY. 8vo., 2s. 6d. net.

Mill.—POLITICAL ECONOMY. By JOHN STUART MILL.
Popular Edition. Crown 8vo., 3s 6d.
Library Edition. 2 vols. 8vo., 30s.

Mulhall.—INDUSTRIES AND WEALTH OF NATIONS. By MICHAEL G. MULHALL, F.S.S.   With 32 Full-page Diagrams. Crown 8vo., 8s. 6d.

Soderini.—SOCIALISM AND CATHOLICISM. From the Italian of Count EDWARD SODERINI. By RICHARD JENERY-SHEE. With a Preface by Cardinal VAUGHAN. Crown 8vo., 6s.

Symes.—POLITICAL ECONOMY: a Short Text-book of Political Economy. With a Supplementary Chapter on Socialism. By J. E. SYMES, M.A. Crown 8vo., 2s. 6d.

Toynbee.—LECTURES ON THE INDUSTRIAL REVOLUTION OF THE 18th CENTURY IN ENGLAND. By ARNOLD TOYNBEE. With a Memoir of the Author by BENJAMIN JOWETT, D.D. 8vo., 10s. 6d.

Webb (SIDNEY and BEATRICE).
THE HISTORY OF TRADE UNIONISM. With Map and full Bibliography of the Subject. 8vo., 18s.
INDUSTRIAL DEMOCRACY: a Study in Trade Unionism. 2 vols. 8vo., 25s. net.
PROBLEMS OF MODERN INDUSTRY. 8vo., 7s. 6d.

STUDIES IN ECONOMICS AND POLITICAL SCIENCE.

Issued under the auspices of the London School of Economics and Political Science.

THE HISTORY OF LOCAL RATES IN ENGLAND: Five Lectures. By EDWIN CANNAN, M.A. Crown 8vo., 2s. 6d.

GERMAN SOCIAL DEMOCRACY. By BERTRAND RUSSELL, B.A. With an Appendix on Social Democracy and the Woman Question in Germany by ALYS RUSSELL, B.A. Cr. 8vo., 3s. 6d.

SELECT DOCUMENTS ILLUSTRATING THE HISTORY OF TRADE UNIONISM.
1. The Tailoring Trade. Edited by W. F. GALTON. With a Preface by SIDNEY WEBB, LL.B. Crown

⬛ONS OF RATES AND ⬛ LAURENCE, B.A., ⬛llege, Cambridge. [*In the press.*

DEPLOIGE'S REFERENDUM EN SUISSE. Translated with Introduction and Notes, by C. P. TREVELYAN, M.A.
[*In preparation*

SELECT DOCUMENTS ILLUSTRATING THE STATE REGULATION OF WAGES. Edited, with Introduction and Notes, by W. A. S. HEWINS, M.A.
[*In preparation.*

HUNGARIAN GILD RECORDS. Edited by Dr. JULIUS MANDELLO, of Budapest.
[*In preparation.*

THE RELATIONS BETWEEN ENGLAND AND THE HANSEATIC LEAGUE. By Miss E. A. MACARTHUR. [*In preparation.*

THE ECONOMIC POLICY OF COLBERT. By A. J. SARGENT, B.A. [*In preparation.*

Evolution, Anthropology, &c.

Clodd (EDWARD).

THE STORY OF CREATION : a Plain Account of Evolution. With 77 Illustrations. Crown 8vo., 3s. 6d.

A PRIMER OF EVOLUTION : being a Popular Abridged Edition of 'The Story of Creation'. With Illustrations. Fcp. 8vo., 1s. 6d.

Lang.—CUSTOM AND MYTH : Studies of Early Usage and Belief. By ANDREW LANG. With 15 Illustrations. Crown 8vo., 3s. 6d.

Lubbock.—THE ORIGIN OF CIVILISATION and the Primitive Condition of Man. By Sir J. LUBBOCK, Bart., M.P. With 5 Plates and 20 Illustrations in the Text. 8vo., 18s.

Romanes (GEORGE JOHN).

DARWIN, AND AFTER DARWIN : an Exposition of the Darwinian Theory, and a Discussion on Post-Darwinian Questions.
Part I. THE DARWINIAN THEORY. With Portrait of Darwin and 125 Illustrations. Crown 8vo., 10s. 6d.
Part II. POST-DARWINIAN QUESTIONS : Heredity and Utility. With Portrait of the Author and 5 Illustrations. Cr. 8vo., 10s. 6d.
Part III. POST-DARWINIAN QUESTIONS : Isolation and Physiological Selection. Crown 8vo., 5s.

AN EXAMINATION OF WEISMANNISM. Crown 8vo., 6s.

ESSAYS. Edited by C. LLOYD MORGAN, Principal of University College, Bristol. Crown 8vo., 6s.

Classical Literature, Translations, &c.

Abbott.—HELLENICA. A Collection of Essays on Greek Poetry, Philosophy, History, and Religion. Edited by EVELYN ABBOTT, M.A., LL.D. Crown 8vo., 7s. 6d.

Æschylus.—EUMENIDES OF ÆSCHYLUS. With Metrical English Translation. By J. F. DAVIES. 8vo., 7s.

Aristophanes.—The ACHARNIANS OF ARISTOPHANES, translated into English Verse. By R. Y. TYRRELL. Cr. 8vo., 1s.

Aristotle.—YOUTH AND OLD AGE, LIFE AND DEATH, AND RESPIRATION. Translated, with Introduction and Notes, by W. OGLE, M.A., M.D., F.R.C.P. 8vo., 7s. 6d.

Becker (W. A.). Translated by the Rev. F. Metcalfe, B.D.

GALLUS : or, Roman Scenes in the Time of Augustus. With 26 Illustrations. Post 8vo., 3s. 6d.

CHARICLES : or, Illustrations of the Private Life of the Ancient Greeks. With 26 Illustrations. Post 8vo., 3s. 6d.

Butler. — THE AUTHORESS OF THE ODYSSEY, WHERE AND WHEN SHE WROTE, WHO SHE WAS, THE USE SHE MADE OF THE ILIAD, AND HOW THE POEM GREW UNDER HER HANDS. By SAMUEL BUTLER, Author of 'Erewhon,' &c. With 14 Illustrations and 4 Maps. 8vo., 10s. 6d.

Cicero.—CICERO'S CORRESPONDENCE. By R. Y. TYRRELL. Vols. I., II., III. 8vo., each 12s. Vol. IV., 15s. Vol. V., 14s.

Homer. — THE ILIAD OF HOMER. Freely rendered into English Prose for the use of those that cannot read the original. By SAMUEL BUTLER, Author of 'Erewhon,' 'Life and Habit,' etc. Crown 8vo., 7s. 6d.

Horace.—THE WORKS OF HORACE, rendered into English Prose. With Life, Introduction, and Notes. By WILLIAM COUTTS, M.A. Crown 8vo., 5s. net.

Lang.—HOMER AND THE EPIC. By ANDREW LANG. Crown 8vo., 9s. net.

Lucan.—THE PHARSALIA OF LUCAN. Translated into Blank Verse. By Sir EDWARD RIDLEY. 8vo., 14s.

Mackail.—SELECT EPIGRAMS FROM THE GREEK ANTHOLOGY. By J. W. MACKAIL. Edited with a Revised Text, Introduction, Translation, and Notes. 8vo., 16s.

Rich.—A DICTIONARY OF ROMAN AND GREEK ANTIQUITIES. By A. RICH, B.A. With 2000 Woodcuts. Crown 8vo., 7s. 6d.

Classical Literature, Translations, &c.—*continued.*

Sophocles.—Translated into English Verse. By ROBERT WHITELAW, M.A., Assistant Master in Rugby School. Cr. 8vo., 8*s.* 6*d.*

Tacitus.—THE HISTORY OF P. CORNELIUS TACITUS. Translated into English, with an Introduction and Notes, Critical and Explanatory, by ALBERT WILLIAM QUILL, M.A., T.C.D. 2 Vols. Vol. I., 8vo., 7*s.* 6*d.*, Vol. II., 8vo., 12*s.* 6*d.*

Tyrrell.—TRANSLATIONS INTO GREEK AND LATIN VERSE. Edited by R. Y. TYRRELL. 8vo., 6*s.*

Virgil.—THE ÆNEID OF VIRGIL. Translated into English Verse by JOHN CONINGTON. Crown 8vo., 6*s.*

THE POEMS OF VIRGIL. Translated into English Prose by JOHN CONINGTON. Crown 8vo., 6*s.*

THE ÆNEID OF VIRGIL, freely translated into English Blank Verse. By W. J. THORNHILL. Crown 8vo., 7*s.* 6*d.*

THE ÆNEID OF VIRGIL. Translated into English Verse by JAMES RHOADES.
Books I.-VI. Crown 8vo., 5*s.*
Books VII.-XII. Crown 8vo., 5*s.*

Poetry and the Drama.

Allingham (WILLIAM).

IRISH SONGS AND POEMS. With Frontispiece of the Waterfall of Asaroe. Fcp. 8vo., 6*s.*

LAURENCE BLOOMFIELD. With Portrait of the Author. Fcp. 8vo., 3*s.* 6*d.*

FLOWER PIECES; DAY AND NIGHT SONGS; BALLADS. With 2 Designs by D. G. ROSSETTI. Fcp. 8vo., 6*s.*; large paper edition, 12*s.*

LIFE AND PHANTASY: with Frontispiece by Sir J. E. MILLAIS, Bart., and Design by ARTHUR HUGHES. Fcp. 8vo., 6*s.*; large paper edition, 12*s.*

THOUGHT AND WORD, AND ASHBY MANOR: a Play. Fcp. 8vo., 6*s.*; large paper edition, 12*s.*

BLACKBERRIES. Imperial 16mo., 6*s.*

Sets of the above 6 vols. may be had in uniform half-parchment binding, price 30*s.*

Armstrong (G. F. SAVAGE).

POEMS: Lyrical and Dramatic. Fcp. 8vo., 6*s.*

KING SAUL. (The Tragedy of Israel, Part I.) Fcp. 8vo., 5*s.*

KING DAVID. (The Tragedy of Israel, Part II.) Fcp. 8vo., 6*s.*

Armstrong (G. F. SAVAGE)—*continued.*

KING SOLOMON. (The Tragedy of Israel, Part III.) Fcp. 8vo., 6*s.*

UGONE: a Tragedy. Fcp. 8vo., 6*s.*

A GARLAND FROM GREECE: Poems. Fcp. 8vo., 7*s.* 6*d.*

STORIES OF WICKLOW: Poems. Fcp. 8vo., 7*s.* 6*d.*

MEPHISTOPHELES IN BROADCLOTH: a Satire. Fcp. 8vo., 4*s.*

ONE IN THE INFINITE: a Poem. Cr. 8vo., 7*s.* 6*d.*

Armstrong.—THE POETICAL WORKS OF EDMUND J. ARMSTRONG. Fcp. 8vo., 5*s.*

Arnold.—THE LIGHT OF THE WORLD: or, the Great Consummation. By Sir EDWIN ARNOLD. With 14 Illustrations after HOLMAN HUNT. Crown 8vo., 6*s.*

Beesly (A. H.).
BALLADS, AND OTHER VERSE. Fcp. 8vo., 5*s.*

DANTON, AND OTHER VERSE. Fcp. 8vo., 4*s.* 6*d.*

Bell (Mrs. HUGH).
CHAMBER COMEDIES: a Collection of Plays and Monologues for the Drawing Room. Crown 8vo., 6*s.*

FAIRY TALE PLAYS, AND HOW TO ACT THEM. With 91 Diagrams and 52 Illustrations. Crown 8vo., 6*s.*

Poetry and the Drama—*continued.*

Cochrane (ALFRED).

THE KESTREL'S NEST, and other Verses. Fcp. 8vo., 3s. 6d.

LEVIORE PLECTRO: Occasional Verses. Fcp. 8vo., 3s. 6d.

Douglas. — POEMS OF A COUNTRY GENTLEMAN. By Sir GEORGE DOUGLAS, Bart. Crown 8vo., 3s. 6d.

Goethe.

FAUST, Part I., the German Text, with Introduction and Notes. By ALBERT M. SELSS, Ph.D., M.A. Cr. 8vo., 5s.

THE FIRST PART OF THE TRAGEDY OF GOETHE'S FAUST IN ENGLISH. By THOS. E. WEBB, LL.D. New and Cheaper Edition, with the Death of Faust, from the Second Part. Crown 8vo., 6s.

Gurney (Rev. ALFRED, M.A.).

DAY-DREAMS: Poems. Cr. 8vo, 3s. 6d.

LOVE'S FRUITION, and other Poems. Fcp. 8vo., 2s. 6d.

Hampton.—FOR REMEMBRANCE. A Record of Life's Beginnings. Three Poetical Quotations for Every Day in the Year for Birth, Baptism, Death. Illustrative of our Life, Temporal, Spiritual, Eternal. Interleaved for Names. Compiled by the Lady LAURA HAMPTON. Fcp. 8vo., 3s. 6d.

Ingelow (JEAN).

POETICAL WORKS. 2 vols. Fcp. 8vo., 12s. Complete in One Volume. Crown 8vo., 7s. 6d.

LYRICAL AND OTHER POEMS. Selected from the Writings of JEAN INGELOW. Fcp. 8vo., 2s. 6d.; cloth plain, 3s. cloth gilt.

Lang (ANDREW).

GRASS OF PARNASSUS. Fcp. 8vo., 2s. 6d. net.

THE BLUE POETRY BOOK. Edited by ANDREW LANG. With 100 Illustrations. Crown 8vo., 6s.

Layard.—SONGS IN MANY MOODS. By NINA F. LAYARD. And THE WANDERING ALBATROSS, &C. By ANNIE CORDER. In one volume. Crown 8vo., 5s.

Lecky.—POEMS. By W. E. H. LECKY. Fcp. 8vo., 5s.

Lytton (THE EARL OF) (OWEN MEREDITH).

THE WANDERER. Cr. 8vo., 10s. 6d.

LUCILE. Crown 8vo., 10s. 6d.

SELECTED POEMS. Cr. 8vo., 10s. 6d.

Macaulay.—LAYS OF ANCIENT ROME, WITH IVRY, AND THE ARMADA. By Lord MACAULAY.

Illustrated by G. SCHARF. Fcp. 4to., 10s. 6d.

————————— Bijou Edition. 18mo., 2s. 6d., gilt top.

————————— Popular Edition. Fcp. 4to., 6d. sewed, 1s. cloth.

Illustrated by J. R. WEGUELIN. Crown 8vo., 3s. 6d.

Annotated Edition. Fcp. 8vo., 1s. sewed, 1s. 6d. cloth.

MacDonald (GEORGE, LL.D.).

A BOOK OF STRIFE, IN THE FORM OF THE DIARY OF AN OLD SOUL: Poems. 18mo., 6s.

RAMPOLLI: GROWTHS FROM A LONG-PLANTED ROOT; being Translations, new and old (mainly in verse), chiefly from the German; along with 'A Year's Diary of an Old Soul'. Crown 8vo., 6s.

Moffat.—CRICKETY CRICKET: Rhymes and Parodies. By DOUGLAS MOFFAT. With Frontispiece by Sir FRANK LOCKWOOD, Q.C., M.P., and 53 Illustrations by the Author. Crown 8vo., 2s. 6d.

Morris (WILLIAM).

POETICAL WORKS—LIBRARY EDITION. Complete in Ten Volumes. Crown 8vo., price 6s. each :—

THE EARTHLY PARADISE. 4 vols. 6s. each.

THE LIFE AND DEATH OF JASON. 6s.

THE DEFENCE OF GUENEVERE, and other Poems. 6s.

THE STORY OF SIGURD THE VOLSUNG, and the Fall of the Niblungs. 6s.

LOVE IS ENOUGH; or, The Freeing of Pharamond : a Morality; and POEMS BY THE WAY. 6s.

Poetry and the Drama—*continued.*

Morris (WILLIAM)—*continued.*

THE ODYSSEY OF HOMER. Done into English Verse. 6s.

THE ÆNEIDS OF VIRGIL. Done into English Verse. 6s.

Certain of the Poetical Works may also be had in the following Editions :—

THE EARTHLY PARADISE.

Popular Edition. 5 vols. 12mo., 25s. ; or 5s. each, sold separately.

The same in Ten Parts, 25s. ; or 2s. 6d. each, sold separately.

Cheap Edition, in 1 vol. Cr. 8vo., 7s. 6d.

LOVE IS ENOUGH ; or, The Freeing of Pharamond : a Morality. Square crown 8vo., 7s. 6d.

POEMS BY THE WAY. Square crown 8vo., 6s.

*** For Mr. William Morris's Prose Works, see pp. 22 and 31.

Nesbit.—LAYS AND LEGENDS. By E. NESBIT (Mrs. HUBERT BLAND). First Series. Crown 8vo., 5s. Second Series, with Portrait. Crown 8vo., 5s.

Riley (JAMES WHITCOMB).

OLD FASHIONED ROSES : Poems. 12mo., 5s.

A CHILD-WORLD : POEMS. Fcp. 8vo. 5s.

RUBÁIYÁT OF DOC SIFERS. With 43 Illustrations by C. M RELYEA. Crown 8vo., 6s.

THE GOLDEN YEAR. From the Verse and Prose of JAMES WHITCOMB RILEY. Compiled by CLARA E. LAUGHLIN. Fcp. 8vo.

Romanes.—A SELECTION FROM THE POEMS OF GEORGE JOHN ROMANES, M.A., LL.D., F.R.S. With an Introduction by T. HERBERT WARREN, President of Magdalen College, Oxford, Crown 8vo., 4s. 6d.

Russell.—SONNETS ON THE SONNET : an Anthology compiled by the Rev. MATTHEW RUSSELL, S.J. Crown 8vo., 3s. 6d.

Shakespeare.—BOWDLER'S FAMILY SHAKESPEARE. With 36 Woodcuts. 1 vol. 8vo., 14s. Or in 6 vols. Fcp. 8vo., 21s.

THE SHAKESPEARE BIRTHDAY BOOK. By MARY F. DUNBAR. 32mo., 1s. 6d.

Tupper.—POEMS. By JOHN LUCAS TUPPER. Selected and Edited by WILLIAM MICHAEL ROSSETTI. Crown 8vo., 5s.

Wordsworth. — SELECTED POEMS. By ANDREW LANG. With Photogravure Frontispiece of Rydal Mount. With 16 Illustrations and numerous Initial Letters By ALFRED PARSONS, A.R.A. Crown 8vo., gilt edges, 3s. 6d.

Wordsworth and Coleridge.—A DESCRIPTION OF THE WORDSWORTH AND COLERIDGE MANUSCRIPTS IN THE POSSESSION OF Mr. T. NORTON LONGMAN. Edited, with Notes, by W. HALE WHITE. With 3 Facsimile Reproductions. 4to., 10s. 6d.

Fiction, Humour, &c.

Allingham.—CROOKED PATHS. By FRANCIS ALLINGHAM. Cr. 8vo., 6s.

Anstey.—VOCES POPULI. Reprinted from 'Punch'. By F. ANSTEY. First Series. With 20 Illustrations by J. BERNARD PARTRIDGE. Cr. 8vo., 3s. 6d.

Beaconsfield (THE EARL OF).

NOVELS AND TALES.

Complete in 11 vols. Cr. 8vo., 1s. 6d. each.

Vivian Grey.	Sybil.
The Young Duke, &c.	Henrietta Temple.
Alroy, Ixion, &c.	Venetia.
Contarini Fleming, &c.	Coningsby.
	Lothair.
Tancred.	Endymion.

NOVELS AND TALES. The Hughenden Edition. With 2 Portraits and 11 Vignettes. 11 vols. Cr. 8vo., 42s.

Deland (MARGARET).

PHILIP AND HIS WIFE. Cr. 8vo., 2s. 6d.

THE WISDOM OF FOOLS : Stories. Cr 8vo., 5s.

OLD CHESTER TALES. Crown 8vo

Diderot. — RAMEAU'S NEPHEW : a Translation from Diderot's Autographic Text. By SYLVIA MARGARET HILL. Crown 8vo., 3s. 6d.

Dougall. — BEGGARS ALL. By L DOUGALL. Crown 8vo., 3s. 6d.

Fiction, Humour, &c.—*continued.*

Doyle (A. CONAN).

MICAH CLARKE : a Tale of Monmouth's Rebellion. With 10 Illustrations. Cr. 8vo., 3s. 6d.

THE CAPTAIN OF THE POLESTAR, and other Tales. Cr. 8vo., 3s. 6d.

THE REFUGEES: a Tale of the Huguenots. With 25 Illustrations. Crown 8vo., 3s. 6d.

THE STARK-MUNRO LETTERS. Cr. 8vo., 3s. 6d.

Farrar (F. W., Dean of Canterbury).

DARKNESS AND DAWN : or, Scenes in the Days of Nero. An Historic Tale. Cr. 8vo., 7s. 6d.

GATHERING CLOUDS : a Tale of the Days of St. Chrysostom. Crown 8vo., 7s. 6d.

Fowler (EDITH H.).

THE YOUNG PRETENDERS. A Story of Child Life. With 12 Illustrations by PHILIP BURNE-JONES. Cr. 8vo.. 6s.

THE PROFESSOR'S CHILDREN. With 24 Illustrations by ETHEL KATE BURGESS. Crown 8vo., 6s.

Froude.—THE TWO CHIEFS OF DUNBOY: an Irish Romance of the Last Century. By JAMES A. FROUDE. Cr. 8vo., 3s. 6d.

Gilkes.—KALLISTRATUS : An Autobiography. A Story of the Hannibal and the Second Punic War. By A. H. GILKES, M.A., Master of Dulwich College. With 3 Illustrations by MAURICE GREIFFENHAGEN. Crown 8vo., 6s.

Graham.—THE RED SCAUR : a Story of the North Country. By P. ANDERSON GRAHAM. Crown 8vo., 6s.

Gurdon.—MEMORIES AND FANCIES : Suffolk Tales and other Stories ; Fairy Legends ; Poems ; Miscellaneous Articles. By the late LADY CAMILLA GURDON, Author of 'Suffolk Folk-Lore'. Crown 8vo., 5s.

Haggard (H. RIDER).

HEART OF THE WORLD. With 15 Illustrations, Crown 8vo., 3s. 6d.

JOAN HASTE. With 20 Illustrations. Cr. 8vo., 3s. 6d.

THE PEOPLE OF THE MIST. With 16 Illustrations. Crown 8vo., 3s. 6d.

MONTEZUMA'S DAUGHTER. With 24 Illustrations. Crown 8vo., 3s. 6d.

SHE. With 32 Illustrations. Cr. 8vo. 3s. 6d.

Haggard (H. RIDER)—*continued.*

ALLAN QUATERMAIN. With 31 Illustrations. Crown 8vo., 3s. 6d.

MAIWA'S REVENGE. Crown 8vo., 1s. 6d.

COLONEL QUARITCH, V.C. Cr. 8vo., 3s. 6d.

CLEOPATRA. With 29 Illustrations Crown 8vo., 3s. 6d.

BEATRICE. Cr. 8vo., 3s. 6d.

ERIC BRIGHTEYES. With 51 Illustrations. Cr. 8vo., 3s. 6d.

NADA THE LILY. With 23 Illustrations. Cr. 8vo., 3s. 6d.

ALLAN'S WIFE. With 34 Illustrations. Crown 8vo., 3s. 6d.

THE WITCH'S HEAD. With 16 Illustrations. Crown 8vo., 3s. 6d.

MR. MEESON'S WILL. With 16 Illustrations. Crown 8vo., 3s. 6d.

DAWN. With 16 Illustrations. Crown 8vo. 3s. 6d.

Haggard and Lang.—THE WORLD'S DESIRE. By H. RIDER HAGGARD and ANDREW LANG. With 27 Illustrations. Crown 8vo., 3s. 6d.

Harte.— IN THE CARQUINEZ WOODS, and other Stories. By BRET HARTE. Cr. 8vo., 3s. 6d.

Hope.—THE HEART OF PRINCESS OSRA. By ANTHONY HOPE. With 9 Illustrations by JOHN WILLIAMSON. Crown 8vo., 6s.

Hornung.—THE UNBIDDEN GUEST. By E. W. HORNUNG. Cr. 8vo., 3s. 6d.

Jerome.—SKETCHES IN LAVENDER : Blue and Green. By JEROME K. JEROME, Author of 'Three Men in a Boat,' &c. Crown 8vo., 6s.

Joyce. — OLD CELTIC ROMANCES : Twelve of the most beautiful of the Ancient Irish Romantic Tales. Translated from the Gaelic. Cr. 8vo., 3s. 6d.

Lang.—A MONK OF FIFE : a Story of the Days of Joan of Arc. By ANDREW LANG. With 13 Illustrations by SELWYN IMAGE. Crown 8vo., 3s. 6d.

Levett-Yeats (S.).

THE CHEVALIER D'AURIAC. Crown 8vo., 6s.

A GALAHAD OF THE CREEKS, and other Stories. Crown 8vo., 6s.

THE HEART OF DENISE, and other Stories. Crown 8vo., 6s

Fiction, Humour, &c.—*continued.*

Lyall (EDNA).

THE AUTOBIOGRAPHY OF A SLANDER. Fcp. 8vo., 1s. sewed.

Presentation Edition. With 20 Illustrations by LANCELOT SPEED. Cr. 8vo., 2s. 6d. net.

THE AUTOBIOGRAPHY OF A TRUTH. Fcp. 8vo., 1s. sewed ; 1s. 6d. cloth.

DOREEN : The Story of a Singer. Cr. 8vo., 6s.

WAYFARING MEN. Crown 8vo., 6s.

HOPE THE HERMIT : a Romance of Borrowdale. Crown 8vo., 6s.

Melville (G. J. WHYTE).

The Gladiators.	Holmby House.
The Interpreter.	Kate Coventry.
Good for Nothing.	Digby Grand.
The Queen's Maries.	General Bounce.

Cr. 8vo., 1s. 6d. each.

Merriman.—FLOTSAM : a Story of the Indian Mutiny. By HENRY SETON MERRIMAN. With Frontispiece and Vignette by H. G. MASSEY, A.R.E. Crown 8vo., 3s. 6d.

Morris (WILLIAM).

THE SUNDERING FLOOD. Crown 8vo., 7s. 6d.

THE WATER OF THE WONDROUS ISLES. Crown 8vo., 7s. 6d.

THE WELL AT THE WORLD'S END. 2 vols., 8vo., 28s.

THE STORY OF THE GLITTERING PLAIN, which has been also called The Land of the Living Men, or The Acre of the Undying. Square post 8vo., 5s. net.

THE ROOTS OF THE MOUNTAINS, Written in Prose and Verse. Square crown 8vo., 8s.

A TALE OF THE HOUSE OF THE WOLFINGS. Written in Prose and Verse. Square crown 8vo., 6s.

A DREAM OF JOHN BALL, AND A KING'S LESSON. 12mo., 1s. 6d.

NEWS FROM NOWHERE ; or, An Epoch of Rest. Post 8vo., 1s. 6d.

** For Mr. William Morris's Poetical Works, see p. 19.

Newman (CARDINAL).

LOSS AND GAIN : The Story of a Convert. Crown 8vo. Cabinet Edition, 6s. ; Popular Edition, 3s. 6d.

CALLISTA : A Tale of the Third Century. Crown 8vo. Cabinet Edition, 6s. ; Popular Edition, 3s. 6d.

Oliphant.—OLD MR. TREDGOLD. By Mrs. OLIPHANT. Crown 8vo., 2s. 6d.

Phillipps-Wolley.—SNAP : a Legend of the Lone Mountain. By C. PHILLIPPS-WOLLEY. With 13 Illustrations. Crown 8vo., 3s. 6d.

Quintana.—THE CID CAMPEADOR ; an Historical Romance. By D. ANTONIO DE TRUEBA Y LA QUINTANA. Translated from the Spanish by HENRY J. GILL, M.A., T.C.D. Crown 8vo., 6s.

Rhoscomyl (OWEN).

THE JEWEL OF YNYS GALON : being a hitherto unprinted Chapter in the History of the Sea Rovers. With 12 Illustrations by LANCELOT SPEED. Crown 8vo., 3s. 6d.

BATTLEMENT AND TOWER : a Romance. With Frontispiece by R. CATON WOODVILLE. Crown 8vo., 6s.

FOR THE WHITE ROSE OF ARNO : A Story of the Jacobite Rising of 1745. Crown 8vo., 6s.

Sewell (ELIZABETH M.).

A Glimpse of the World.	Amy Herbert.
Laneton Parsonage.	Cleve Hall.
Margaret Percival.	Gertrude.
Katharine Ashton.	Home Life.
The Earl's Daughter.	After Life.
The Experience of Life.	Ursula. Ivors.

Cr. 8vo., 1s. 6d. each, cloth plain. 2s. 6d. each, cloth extra, gilt edges.

Stevenson (ROBERT LOUIS).

THE STRANGE CASE OF DR. JEKYLL AND MR. HYDE. Fcp. 8vo., 1s. sewed, 1s. 6d. cloth.

THE STRANGE CASE OF DR. JEKYLL AND MR. HYDE ; with Other Fables. Crown 8vo., 3s. 6d.

MORE NEW ARABIAN NIGHTS—THE DYNAMITER. By ROBERT LOUIS STEVENSON and FANNY VAN DE GRIFT STEVENSON. Crown 8vo., 3s. 6d.

THE WRONG BOX. By ROBERT LOUIS STEVENSON and LLOYD OSBOURNE. Crown 8vo., 3s. 6d.

Suttner.—LAY DOWN YOUR ARMS (*Die Waffen Nieder*) : The Autobiography of Martha Tilling. By BERTHA VON SUTTNER. Translated by T. HOLMES. Crown 8vo., 1s. 6d.

Taylor. — EARLY ITALIAN LOVESTORIES. Edited and Retold by UNA TAYLOR. With 12 Illustrations by H. J. FORD.

Fiction, Humour, &c.—*continued.*

Trollope (ANTHONY).
THE WARDEN. Cr. 8vo., 1s. 6d.
BARCHESTER TOWERS. Cr. 8vo., 1s. 6d.

Walford (L. B.).
LEDDY MARGET. Crown 8vo., 6s.
IVA KILDARE: a Matrimonial Problem. Crown 8vo., 6s.
Mr. SMITH: a Part of his Life. Crown 8vo., 2s. 6d.
THE BABY'S GRANDMOTHER. Crown 8vo., 2s. 6d.
COUSINS. Crown 8vo., 2s. 6d.
TROUBLESOME DAUGHTERS. Crown 8vo., 2s. 6d.
PAULINE. Crown 8vo., 2s. 6d.
DICK NETHERBY. Crown 8vo., 2s. 6d.
THE HISTORY OF A WEEK. Crown 8vo. 2s. 6d.
A STIFF-NECKED GENERATION. Crown 8vo. 2s. 6d.
NAN, and other Stories. Cr. 8vo., 2s. 6d.
THE MISCHIEF OF MONICA. Crown 8vo., 2s. 6d.
THE ONE GOOD GUEST. Cr. 8vo. 2s. 6d.
'PLOUGHED,' and other Stories. Crown 8vo., 2s. 6d.
THE MATCHMAKER. Cr. 8vo., 2s. 6d.

Watson.—RACING AND CHASING: a Volume of Sporting Stories and Sketches. By ALFRED E. T. WATSON, Editor of the 'Badminton Magazine'. With 52 Illustrations. Crown 8vo., 7s. 6d.

Weyman (STANLEY).
THE HOUSE OF THE WOLF. Cr. 8vo., 3s. 6d.
A GENTLEMAN OF FRANCE. Cr. 8vo., 6s.
THE RED COCKADE. Cr. 8vo., 6s.
SHREWSBURY. With 24 Illustrations. Crown 8vo., 6s.

Whishaw (FRED.).
A BOYAR OF THE TERRIBLE: a Romance of the Court of Ivan the Cruel, First Tzar of Russia. With 12 Illustrations by H. G. MASSEY, A.R.E. Cr. 8vo., 6s.
A TSAR'S GRATITUDE. Cr. 8vo., 6s.

Woods.—WEEPING FERRY, and other Stories. By MARGARET L. WOODS, Author of 'A Village Tragedy'. Crown 8vo., 6s.

Popular Science (Natural History, &c.).

Butler.—OUR HOUSEHOLD INSECTS. An Account of the Insect-Pests found in Dwelling-Houses. By EDWARD A. BUTLER, B.A., B.Sc. (Lond.). With 113 Illustrations. Crown 8vo., 3s. 6d.

Furneaux (W.).
THE OUTDOOR WORLD; or, The Young Collector's Handbook. With 18 Plates, 16 of which are coloured, and 549 Illustrations in the Text. Crown 8vo., 7s. 6d.
BUTTERFLIES AND MOTHS (British). With 12 coloured Plates and 241 Illustrations in the Text. Crown 8vo., 7s. 6d.
LIFE IN PONDS AND STREAMS. With 8 coloured Plates and 331 Illustrations in the Text. Cr. 8vo., 7s. 6d.

Hartwig (Dr. GEORGE).
THE SEA AND ITS LIVING WONDERS. With 12 Plates and 303 Woodcuts. 8vo., 7s. net.
THE TROPICAL WORLD. With 8 Plates and 172 Woodcuts. 8vo., 7s. net.
THE POLAR WORLD. With 3 Maps, 8 Plates and 85 Woodcuts. 8vo., 7s. net.

Hartwig (Dr. GEORGE)—*continued.*
THE SUBTERRANEAN WORLD. With 3 Maps and 80 Woodcuts. 8vo., 7s. net.
THE AERIAL WORLD. With Map, 8 Plates and 60 Woodcuts. 8vo., 7s. net.
HEROES OF THE POLAR WORLD. 19 Illustrations. Crown 8vo., 2s.
WONDERS OF THE TROPICAL FORESTS. 40 Illustrations. Crown 8vo., 2s.
WORKERS UNDER THE GROUND. 29 Illustrations. Crown 8vo., 2s.
MARVELS OVER OUR HEADS. 29 Illustrations. Crown 8vo., 2s.
SEA MONSTERS AND SEA BIRDS. 75 Illustrations. Crown 8vo., 2s. 6d.
DENIZENS OF THE DEEP. 117 Illustrations. Crown 8vo., 2s. 6d.
VOLCANOES AND EARTHQUAKES. 30 Illustrations. Crown 8vo., 2s. 6d.
WILD ANIMALS OF THE TROPICS. 66 Illustrations. Crown 8vo., 3s. 6d.

Helmholtz.—POPULAR LECTURES ON SCIENTIFIC SUBJECTS. By HERMANN VON HELMHOLTZ. With 68 Woodcuts. 2 vols. Crown 8vo., 3s. 6d. each.

Popular Science (Natural History, &c.).

Hudson (W. H.).

BRITISH BIRDS. With a Chapter on Structure and Classification by FRANK E. BEDDARD, F.R.S. With 16 Plates (8 of which are Coloured), and over 100 Illustrations in the Text. Crown 8vo., 7s. 6d.

BIRDS IN LONDON. With 17 Plates and 15 Illustrations in the Text. 8vo., 12s.

Proctor (RICHARD A.).

LIGHT SCIENCE FOR LEISURE HOURS. Familiar Essays on Scientific Subjects. 3 vols. Crown 8vo., 5s. each vol. Cheap edition, Crown 8vo., 3s. 6d.

ROUGH WAYS MADE SMOOTH. Familiar Essays on Scientific Subjects. Crown 8vo., 3s. 6d.

PLEASANT WAYS IN SCIENCE. Crown 8vo., 3s. 6d.

NATURE STUDIES. By R. A. PROCTOR, GRANT ALLEN, A. WILSON, T. FOSTER and E. CLODD. Crown 8vo., 3s. 6d.

LEISURE READINGS. By R. A. PROCTOR, E. CLODD, A. WILSON, T. FOSTER, and A. C. RANYARD. Cr. 8vo., 3s. 6d.

** For Mr. Proctor's other books see Messrs. Longmans & Co.'s Catalogue of Scientific Works.

Stanley.—A FAMILIAR HISTORY OF BIRDS. By E. STANLEY, D.D., formerly Bishop of Norwich. With 160 Illustrations. Crown 8vo., 3s. 6d.

Wood (Rev. J. G.).

HOMES WITHOUT HANDS : a Description of the Habitation of Animals, classed according to the Principle of Construction. With 140 Illustrations. 8vo., 7s. net.

Wood (Rev. J. G.)—*continued.*

INSECTS AT HOME . a Popular Account of British Insects, their Structure, Habits and Transformations. With 700 Illustrations. 8vo., 7s. net.

INSECTS ABROAD : a Popular Account of Foreign Insects, their Structure, Habits and Transformations. With 600 Illustrations. 8vo., 7s. net.

BIBLE ANIMALS : a Description of every Living Creature mentioned in the Scriptures. With 112 Illustrations. 8vo., 7s. net.

PETLAND REVISITED. With 33 Illustrations. Cr. 8vo., 3s. 6d.

OUT OF DOORS ; a Selection of Original Articles on Practical Natural History. With 11 Illustrations. Cr. 8vo., 3s. 6d.

STRANGE DWELLINGS : a Description of the Habitations of Animals, abridged from 'Homes without Hands'. With 60 Illustrations. Cr. 8vo., 3s. 6d.

BIRD LIFE OF THE BIBLE. 32 Illustrations. Crown 8vo., 3s. 6d.

WONDERFUL NESTS. 30 Illustrations. Crown 8vo., 3s. 6d.

HOMES UNDER THE GROUND. 28 Illustrations. Crown 8vo., 3s. 6d.

WILD ANIMALS OF THE BIBLE. 29 Illustrations. Crown 8vo., 3s. 6d.

DOMESTIC ANIMALS OF THE BIBLE. 23 Illustrations. Crown 8vo., 3s. 6d.

THE BRANCH BUILDERS. 28 Illustrations. Crown 8vo., 2s. 6d.

SOCIAL HABITATIONS AND PARASITIC NESTS. 18 Illustrations. Crown 8vo., 2s.

Works of Reference.

Longmans' GAZETTEER OF THE WORLD. Edited by GEORGE G. CHISHOLM, M.A., B.Sc. Imp. 8vo., £2 2s. cloth, £2 12s. 6d. half-morocco.

Maunder (Samuel).

BIOGRAPHICAL TREASURY. With Supplement brought down to 1889. By Rev. JAMES WOOD. Fcp. 8vo., 6s.

Maunder (Samuel)—*continued.*

TREASURY OF GEOGRAPHY, Physical, Historical, Descriptive, and Political. With 7 Maps and 16 Plates. Fcp. 8vo., 6s.

THE TREASURY OF BIBLE KNOWLEDGE. By the Rev. J. AYRE, M.A. With 5 Maps, 15 Plates, and 300 Woodcuts. Fcp. 8vo., 6s.

Works of Reference—*continued*.

Maunder (Samuel)—*continued.*

TREASURY OF KNOWLEDGE AND LIBRARY OF REFERENCE. Fcp. 8vo., 6s.

HISTORICAL TREASURY : Fcp. 8vo., 6s.

SCIENTIFIC AND LITERARY TREASURY. Fcp. 8vo., 6s.

THE TREASURY OF BOTANY. Edited by J. LINDLEY, F.R.S., and T. MOORE, F.L.S. With 274 Woodcuts and 20 Steel Plates. 2 vols. Fcp. 8vo., 12s.

Roget.—THESAURUS OF ENGLISH WORDS AND PHRASES. Classified and Arranged so as to Facilitate the Expression of Ideas and assist in Literary Composition. By PETER MARK ROGET, M.D., F.R.S. Recomposed throughout, enlarged and improved, partly from the Author's Notes and with a full Index, by the Author's Son, JOHN LEWIS ROGET. Crown 8vo., 10s. 6d.

Willich.—POPULAR TABLES for giving information for ascertaining the value of Lifehold, Leasehold, and Church Property, the Public Funds, &c. By CHARLES M. WILLICH. Edited by H. BENCE JONES. Crown 8vo., 10s. 6d.

Children's Books.

Buckland.—TWO LITTLE RUNAWAYS. Adapted from the French of LOUIS DESNOYERS. By JAMES BUCKLAND. With 110 Illustrations by CECIL ALDIN.

Crake (Rev. A. D.).

EDWY THE FAIR ; or, the First Chronicle of Æscendune. Crown 8vo., 2s. 6d.

ALFGAR THE DANE: or, the Second Chronicle of Æscendune. Cr. 8vo., 2s. 6d.

THE RIVAL HEIRS : being the Third and Last Chronicle of Æscendune. Crown 8vo., 2s. 6d.

THE HOUSE OF WALDERNE. A Tale of the Cloister and the Forest in the Days of the Barons' Wars. Crown 8vo., 2s. 6d.

BRIAN FITZ-COUNT. A Story of Wallingford Castle and Dorchester Abbey. Crown 8vo., 2s. 6d.

Lang (ANDREW)—EDITED BY.

THE BLUE FAIRY BOOK. With 138 Illustrations. Crown 8vo., 6s.

THE RED FAIRY BOOK. With 100 Illustrations. Crown 8vo., 6s.

THE GREEN FAIRY BOOK. With 99 Illustrations. Crown 8vo., 6s.

THE YELLOW FAIRY BOOK. With 104 Illustrations. Crown 8vo., 6s.

THE PINK FAIRY BOOK. With 67 Illustrations. Crown 8vo., 6s.

THE BLUE POETRY BOOK. With 100 Illustrations. Crown 8vo., 6s.

THE BLUE POETRY BOOK. School Edition, without Illustrations. Fcp. 8vo., 2s. 6d.

Lang (ANDREW)—*continued.*

THE TRUE STORY BOOK. With 66 Illustrations. Crown 8vo., 6s.

THE RED TRUE STORY BOOK. With 100 Illustrations. Crown 8vo., 6s.

THE ANIMAL STORY BOOK. With 67 Illustrations. Crown 8vo., 6s.

THE ARABIAN NIGHTS ENTERTAINMENTS. With Illustrations. Crown 8vo., 6s.

Meade (L. T.).

DADDY'S BOY. With Illustrations. Crown 8vo., 3s. 6d.

DEB AND THE DUCHESS. With Illustrations. Crown 8vo., 3s. 6d.

THE BERESFORD PRIZE. With Illustrations. Crown 8vo., 3s. 6d.

THE HOUSE OF SURPRISES. With Illustrations. Crown 8vo., 3s. 6d.

Praeger. (S. ROSAMOND).

THE ADVENTURES OF THE THREE BOLD BABES : Hector, Honoria and Alisander. A Story in Pictures. With 24 Coloured Plates and 24 Outline Pictures. Oblong 4to., 3s. 6d.

THE FURTHER DOINGS OF THE THREE BOLD BABES. With 25 Coloured Plates and 24 Outline Pictures. Oblong 4to., 3s. 6d.

Stevenson.—A CHILD'S GARDEN OF VERSES. By ROBERT LOUIS STEVENSON. fcp. 8vo., 5s.

Sullivan.—HERE THEY ARE! More Stories. Written and Illustrated by JAMES F. SULLIVAN. Crown 8vo., 6s.

Children's Books—*continued.*

Upton (FLORENCE K., and BERTHA).

THE ADVENTURES OF TWO DUTCH DOLLS AND A 'GOLLIWOGG'. With 31 Coloured Plates and numerous Illustrations in the Text. Oblong 4to., 6s.

THE GOLLIWOGG'S BICYCLE CLUB. With 31 Coloured Plates and numerous Illustrations in the Text. Oblong 4to., 6s.

Upton (FLORENCE K., and BERTHA)—*continued.*

THE VEGE-MEN'S REVENGE. With 31 Coloured Plates and numerous Illustrations in the Text. Oblong 4to., 6s.

THE GOLLIWOGG AT THE SEA-SIDE. With Coloured Plates and Illustrations in the Text. Oblong 4to., 6s.

Wordsworth.—THE SNOW GARDEN, and other Fairy Tales for Children. By ELIZABETH WORDSWORTH. With 10 Illustrations by TREVOR HADDON. Crown 8vo., 3s. 6d.

Longmans' Series of Books for Girls.
Price 2s. 6d. each.

ATELIER (THE) DU LYS: or an Art Student in the Reign of Terror.

BY THE SAME AUTHOR.

Mademoiselle Mori: a Tale of Modern Rome.	The Younger Sister. That Child. Under a Cloud.
In the Olden Time: a Tale of the Peasant War in Germany.	Hester's Venture. The Fiddler of Lugau. A Child of the Revolution.

ATHERSTONE PRIORY. By L. N. COMYN.

THE STORY OF A SPRING MORNING, &c. By Mrs. MOLESWORTH. Illustrated.

THE PALACE IN THE GARDEN. By Mrs. MOLESWORTH. Illustrated.

NEIGHBOURS. By Mrs. MOLESWORTH.

THE THIRD MISS ST. QUENTIN. By Mrs. MOLESWORTH.

VERY YOUNG; and QUITE ANOTHER STORY. Two Stories. By JEAN INGELOW.

CAN THIS BE LOVE? By LOUISA PARR.

KEITH DERAMORE. By the Author of 'Miss Molly'.

SIDNEY. By MARGARET DELAND.

AN ARRANGED MARRIAGE. By DOROTHEA GERARD.

LAST WORDS TO GIRLS ON LIFE AT SCHOOL AND AFTER SCHOOL. By MARIA GREY.

STRAY THOUGHTS FOR GIRLS. By LUCY H. M. SOULSBY, Head Mistress of Oxford High School. 16mo., 1s. 6d. net.

The Silver Library.
CROWN 8vo. 3s. 6d. EACH VOLUME.

Arnold's (Sir Edwin) Seas and Lands. With 71 Illustrations. 3s. 6d.

Bagehot's (W.) Biographical Studies. 3s. 6d.

Bagehot's (W.) Economic Studies. 3s. 6d.

Bagehot's (W.) Literary Studies. With Portrait. 3 vols. 3s. 6d. each.

Baker's (Sir S. W.) Eight Years in Ceylon. With 6 Illustrations. 3s. 6d.

Baker's (Sir S. W.) Rifle and Hound in Ceylon. With 6 Illustrations. 3s. 6d.

Baring-Gould's (Rev. S.) Curious Myths of the Middle Ages. 3s. 6d.

Baring-Gould's (Rev. S.) Origin and Development of Religious Belief. 2 vols. 3s. 6d. each.

Becker's (W. A.) Gallus: or, Roman Scenes in the Time of Augustus. With 26 Illustrations. 3s. 6d.

Becker's (W. A.) Charicles: or, Illustrations of the Private Life of the Ancient Greeks. With 26 Illustrations. 3s. 6d.

Bent's (J. T.) The Ruined Cities of Mashonaland. With 117 Illustrations. 3s. 6d.

Brassey's (Lady) A Voyage in the 'Sunbeam'. With 66 Illustrations. 3s. 6d.

Clodd's (E.) Story of Creation: a Plain Account of Evolution. With 77 Illustrations. 3s. 6d.

The Silver Library—*continued.*

Conybeare (Rev. W. J.) and Howson's (Very Rev. J. S.) Life and Epistles of St. Paul. With 46 Illustrations. 3s. 6d.

Dougall's(L.)Beggars All; a Novel. 3s.6d.

Doyle's (A. Conan) Micah Clarke : a Tale of Monmouth's Rebellion. With 10 Illustrations. 3s. 6d.

Doyle's (A. Conan) The Captain of the Polestar, and other Tales. 3s. 6d.

Doyle's (A. Conan) The Refugees : A Tale of the Huguenots. With 25 Illustrations, 3s. 6d.

Doyle's (A. Conan) The Stark Munro Letters. 3s. 6d.

Froude's (J. A.) The History of England, from the Fall of Wolsey to the Defeat of the Spanish Armada. 12 vols. 3s. 6d. each.

Froude's (J. A.) The English in Ireland. 3 vols. 10s. 6d.

Froude's (J. A.) The Divorce of Catherine of Aragon. 3s. 6d.

Froude's (J. A.) The Spanish Story of the Armada, and other Essays. 3s. 6d.

Froude's (J. A.) Short Studies on Great Subjects. 4 vols. 3s. 6d. each.

Froude's (J. A.) The Council of Trent. 3s. 6d.

Froude's (J. A.) Thomas Carlyle : a History of his Life.
1795-1835. 2 vols. 7s.
1834-1881. 2 vols. 7s.

Froude's (J. A.) Cæsar : a Sketch. 3s. 6d.

Froude's (J. A.) Oceana ; or, England and her Colonies. With 9 Illustrations. 3s. 6d.

Froude's (J. A.) The Two Chiefs of Dunboy : an Irish Romance of the Last Century. 3s. 6d.

Gleig's (Rev. G. R.) Life of the Duke of Wellington. With Portrait. 3s. 6d.

Greville's (C. C. F.) Journal of the Reigns of King George IV., King William IV., and Queen Victoria. 8 vols, 3s. 6d. each.

Haggard's (H. R.) She : A History of Adventure. 32 Illustrations. 3s. 6d.

Haggard's (H. R.) Allan Quatermain. With 20 Illustrations. 3s. 6d.

Haggard's (H. R.) Colonel Quaritch, V.C. : a Tale of Country Life. 3s.6d.

Haggard's (H. R.) Cleopatra. With 29 Illustrations. 3s. 6d.

Haggard's (H. R.) Eric Brighteyes. With 51 Illustrations. 3s. 6d.

Haggard's (H. R.) Beatrice. 3s. 6d.

Haggard's (H. R.) Allan's Wife. With 34 Illustrations. 3s. 6d.

Haggard's (H. R.) Heart of the World. With 15 Illustrations. 3s. 6d.

Haggard's (H. R.) Montezuma's Daughter. With 25 Illustrations. 3s. 6d.

Haggard's (H. R.) The Witch's Head. With 16 Illustrations. 3s. 6d.

Haggard's (H. R.) Mr. Meeson's Will. With 16 Illustrations. 3s. 6d.

Haggard's (H. R.) Nada the Lily. With 23 Illustrations. 3s. 6d.

Haggard's (H. R.) Dawn. With 16 Illustrations. 3s. 6d.

Haggard's (H. R.) The People of the Mist. With 16 Illustrations. 3s. 6d.

Haggard's (H. R.) Joan Haste. With 20 Illustrations. 3s. 6d.

Haggard (H. R.) and Lang's (A.) The World's Desire. With 27 Illus. 3s. 6d.

Harte's (Bret) In the Carquinez Woods, and other Stories. 3s. 6d.

Helmholtz's (Hermann von) Popular Lectures on Scientific Subjects. With 68 Illustrations. 2 vols. 3s. 6d. each.

Hornung's (E. W.) The Unbidden Guest. 3s. 6d.

Howitt's (W.) Visits to Remarkable Places. With 80 Illustrations. 3s. 6d.

Jefferies'(R.)The Story of My Heart : My Autobiography. With Portrait. 3s. 6d.

Jefferies' (R.) Field and Hedgerow. With Portrait. 3s. 6d.

Jefferies' (R.) Red Deer. 17 Illus. 3s. 6d.

Jefferies' (R.) Wood Magic : a Fable. 3s. 6d.

Jefferies' (R.) The Toilers of the Field. With Portrait from the Bust in Salisbury Cathedral. 3s. 6d.

Kaye (Sir J.) and Malleson's (Colonel) History of the Indian Mutiny of 1857-8. 6 vols. 3s. 6d. each.

Knight's(E.F.)The Cruise of the 'Alerte' : the Narrative of a Search for Treasure on the Desert Island of Trinidad. With 2 Maps and 23 Illustrations. 3s. 6d.

Knight's (E. F.) Where Three Empires Meet : a Narrative of Recent Travel in Kashmir, Western Tibet, Baltistan, Gilgit. With a Map and 54 Illustrations. 3s. 6d

Knight's (E. F.) The 'Falcon' on the Baltic. With Map and 11 Illustrations. 3s. 6d.

Koestlin's (J.) Life of Luther. With 62 Illustrations, &c. 3s. 6d.

Lang's (A.) Angling Sketches. 20 Illustrations. 3s. 6d.

Lang's (A.) A Monk of Fife. With 13 Illustrations. 3s. 6d.

The Silver Library—*continued.*

Lang's (A.) Custom and Myth: Studies of Early Usage and Belief. 3s. 6d.

Lang's (Andrew) Cock Lane and Common-Sense. With a New Preface. 3s. 6d.

Lees (J. A.) and Clutterbuck's (W.J.)B.C. 1887, A Ramble in British Columbia. With Maps and 75 Illustrations. 3s. 6d.

Macaulay's (Lord) Essays and Lays of Ancient Rome. With Portrait and Illustration. 3s. 6d.

Macleod's (H. D.) Elements of Banking. 3s. 6d.

Marbot's (Baron de) Memoirs. Translated. 2 vols. 7s.

Marshman's (J. C.) Memoirs of Sir Henry Havelock. 3s. 6d.

Merivale's (Dean) History of the Romans under the Empire. 8 vols. 3s. 6d. ea.

Merriman's (H. S.) Flotsam : a Story of the Indian Mutiny. 3s. 6d.

Mill's (J. S.) Political Economy. 3s. 6d.

Mill's (J. S.) System of Logic. 3s. 6d.

Milner's (Geo.) Country Pleasures: the Chronicle of a Year chiefly in a garden. 3s. 6d.

Nansen's (F.) The First Crossing of Greenland. With Illustrations and a Map. 3s. 6d.

Phillipps-Wolley's (C.) Snap: a Legend of the Lone Mountain. With 13 Illustrations. 3s. 6d.

Proctor's (R. A.) The Moon. 3s. 6d.

Proctor's (R. A.) The Orbs Around Us. 3s. 6d.

Proctor's (R. A.) The Expanse of Heaven. 3s. 6d.

Proctor's (R. A.) Other Worlds than Ours. 3s. 6d.

Proctor's (R. A.) Our Place among Infinities: a Series of Essays contrasting our Little Abode in Space and Time with the Infinities around us. Crown 8vo., 3s. 6d.

Proctor's (R. A.) Other Suns than Ours. 3s. 6d.

Proctor's (R. A.) Rough Ways made Smooth. 3s. 6d.

Proctor's (R. A.) Pleasant Ways in Science. 3s. 6d.

Proctor's (R. A.) Myths and Marvels of Astronomy. 3s. 6d.

Proctor's (R. A.) Light Science for Leisure Hours. First Series. 3s. 6d.

Proctor's (R. A.) Nature Studies. 3s. 6d.

Proctor's (R. A.) Leisure Readings. By R. A. PROCTOR, EDWARD CLODD, ANDREW WILSON, THOMAS FOSTER, and A. C. RANYARD. With Illustrations. 3s. 6d.

Rossetti's (Maria F.) A Shadow of Dante. 3s. 6d.

Smith's (R. Bosworth) Carthage and the Carthaginians. With Maps, Plans, &c. 3s. 6d.

Stanley's (Bishop) Familiar History of Birds. With 160 Illustrations. 3s. 6d.

Stevenson's (R. L.) The Strange Case of Dr. Jekyll and Mr. Hyde; with other Fables. 3s. 6d.

Stevenson (R. L.) and Osbourne's (Ll.) The Wrong Box. 3s. 6d.

Stevenson (Robt. Louis) and Stevenson's (Fanny van de Grift) More New Arabian Nights. — The Dynamiter. 3s. 6d.

Weyman's (Stanley J.) The House of the Wolf: a Romance. 3s. 6d.

Wood's (Rev. J. G.) Petland Revisited. With 33 Illustrations. 3s. 6d.

Wood's (Rev. J. G.) Strange Dwellings. With 60 Illustrations. 3s. 6d.

Wood's (Rev. J. G.) Out of Doors. With 11 Illustrations. 3s. 6d.

Cookery, Domestic Management, &c.

Acton.—MODERN COOKERY. By ELIZA ACTON. With 150 Woodcuts. Fcp. 8vo., 4s. 6d.

Bull (THOMAS, M.D.).

HINTS TO MOTHERS ON THE MANAGEMENT OF THEIR HEALTH DURING THE PERIOD OF PREGNANCY. Fcp. 8vo., 1s. 6d.

THE MATERNAL MANAGEMENT OF CHILDREN IN HEALTH AND DISEASE. Fcp. 8vo., 1s. 6d.

De Salis (Mrs.).

CAKES AND CONFECTIONS À LA MODE. Fcp. 8vo., 1s. 6d.

DOGS: a Manual for Amateurs. Fcp. 8vo., 1s. 6d.

DRESSED GAME AND POULTRY À LA MODE. Fcp. 8vo., 1s. 6d.

DRESSED VEGETABLES À LA MODE. Fcp. 8vo., 1s. 6d.

Cookery, Domestic Management, &c.—*continued*.

De Salis (Mrs.)—*continued*.

DRINKS À LA MODE. Fcp. 8vo., 1s. 6d.

ENTRÉES À LA MODE. Fcp. 8vo., 1s. 6d.

FLORAL DECORATIONS. Fcp. 8vo., 1s. 6d.

GARDENING À LA MODE. Fcp. 8vo.
Part I. Vegetables. 1s. 6d.
Part II. Fruits. 1s. 6d.

NATIONAL VIANDS À LA MODE. Fcp. 8vo., 1s. 6d.

NEW-LAID EGGS. Fcp. 8vo., 1s. 6d.

OYSTERS À LA MODE. Fcp. 8vo., 1s. 6d.

PUDDINGS AND PASTRY À LA MODE. Fcp. 8vo., 1s. 6d.

SAVOURIES À LA MODE. Fcp. 8vo., 1s. 6d.

SOUPS AND DRESSED FISH À LA MODE. Fcp. 8vo., 1s. 6d.

SWEETS AND SUPPER DISHES À LA MODE. Fcp. 8vo., 1s. 6d.

De Salis (Mrs.)—*continued*.

TEMPTING DISHES FOR SMALL INCOMES. Fcp. 8vo., 1s. 6d.

WRINKLES AND NOTIONS FOR EVERY HOUSEHOLD. Cr. 8vo., 1s. 6d.

Lear.—MAIGRE COOKERY. By H. L. SIDNEY LEAR. 16mo., 2s.

Poole.—COOKERY FOR THE DIABETIC. By W. H. and Mrs. POOLE. With Preface by Dr. PAVY. Fcp. 8vo., 2s. 6d.

Walker (JANE H.).

A BOOK FOR EVERY WOMAN.
Part I. The Management of Children in Health and out of Health. Cr. 8vo., 2s. 6d.
Part II. Woman in Health and out of Health. Crown 8vo, 2s. 6d.

A HANDBOOK FOR MOTHERS: being Simple Hints to Women on the Management of their Health during Pregnancy and Confinement, together with Plain Directions as to the Care of Infants. Cr. 8vo., 2s. 6d.

Miscellaneous and Critical Works.

Allingham.—VARIETIES IN PROSE. By WILLIAM ALLINGHAM. 3 vols. Cr. 8vo, 18s. (Vols. 1 and 2, Rambles, by PATRICIUS WALKER. Vol. 3, Irish Sketches, etc.)

Armstrong.—ESSAYS AND SKETCHES. By EDMUND J. ARMSTRONG. Fcp. 8vo., 5s.

Bagehot.—LITERARY STUDIES. By WALTER BAGEHOT. With Portrait. 3 vols. Crown 8vo., 3s. 6d. each.

Baring-Gould.—CURIOUS MYTHS OF THE MIDDLE AGES. By Rev. S. BARING-GOULD. Crown 8vo., 3s. 6d.

Baynes.—SHAKESPEARE STUDIES, AND OTHER ESSAYS. By the late THOMAS SPENCER BAYNES, LL.B., LL.D. With a Biographical Preface by Prof. LEWIS CAMPBELL. Crown 8vo., 7s. 6d.

Boyd (A. K. H.) ('**A.K.H.B.**').

And see MISCELLANEOUS THEOLOGICAL WORKS, p. 32.

AUTUMN HOLIDAYS OF A COUNTRY PARSON. Crown 8vo., 3s. 6d.

COMMONPLACE PHILOSOPHER. Crown 8vo., 3s. 6d.

CRITICAL ESSAYS OF A COUNTRY PARSON. Crown 8vo., 3s. 6d.

EAST COAST DAYS AND MEMORIES. Crown 8vo., 3s. 6d.

LANDSCAPES, CHURCHES AND MORALITIES. Crown 8vo., 3s. 6d.

LEISURE HOURS IN TOWN. Crown 8vo., 3s. 6d.

LESSONS OF MIDDLE AGE. Cr. 8vo., 3s. 6d.

OUR LITTLE LIFE. Two Series. Cr. 8vo., 3s. 6d. each.

OUR HOMELY COMEDY: AND TRAGEDY. Crown 8vo., 3s. 6d.

RECREATIONS OF A COUNTRY PARSON. Three Series. Cr. 8vo., 3s. 6d. each.

Miscellaneous and Critical Works—*continued.*

Butler (SAMUEL).

EREWHON. Cr. 8vo., 5s.

THE FAIR HAVEN. A Work in Defence of the Miraculous Element in our Lord's Ministry. Cr. 8vo., 7s. 6d.

LIFE AND HABIT. An Essay after a Completer View of Evolution. Cr. 8vo., 7s. 6d.

EVOLUTION, OLD AND NEW. Cr. 8vo., 10s. 6d.

ALPS AND SANCTUARIES OF PIEDMONT AND CANTON TICINO. Illustrated. Pott 4to., 10s. 6d.

LUCK, OR CUNNING, AS THE MAIN MEANS OF ORGANIC MODIFICATION? Cr. 8vo., 7s. 6d.

EX VOTO. An Account of the Sacro Monte or New Jerusalem at Varallo-Sesia. Crown 8vo., 10s. 6d.

CHARITIES REGISTER, THE ANNUAL, AND DIGEST. Volume for 1898 : being a Classified Register of Charities in or available in the Metropolis. With an Introduction by C. S. LOCH, Secretary to the Council of the Charity Organisation Society, London. 8vo., 4s.

Clough.—A STUDY OF MARY WOLLSTONECRAFT, AND THE RIGHTS OF WOMEN. By EMMA RAUSCHENBUSCH-CLOUGH, Ph.D. 8vo., 7s. 6d.

Dreyfus.—LECTURES ON FRENCH LITERATURE. Delivered in Melbourne by IRMA DREYFUS. With Portrait of the Author. Large crown 8vo., 12s. 6d.

Evans.—THE ANCIENT STONE IMPLEMENTS, WEAPONS, AND ORNAMENTS OF GREAT BRITAIN. By Sir JOHN EVANS, K.C.B., D.C.L., LL.D., F.R.S., etc. With 537 Illustrations. Medium 8vo., 28s.

Gwilt.—AN ENCYCLOPÆDIA OF ARCHITECTURE. By JOSEPH GWILT, F.S.A. Illustrated with more than 1100 Engravings on Wood. Revised (1888), with Alterations and Considerable Additions by WYATT PAPWORTH. 8vo., £2 12s. 6d.

Hamlin.—A TEXT-BOOK OF THE HISTORY OF ARCHITECTURE. By A. D. F. HAMLIN, A.M. With 229 Illustrations. Crown 8vo., 7s. 6d.

Haweis.—MUSIC AND MORALS. By the Rev. H. R. HAWEIS. With Portrait of the Author, and numerous Illustrations, Facsimiles and Diagrams. Cr. 8vo., 7s. 6d.

Hime. — STRAY MILITARY PAPERS. By Lieut.-Colonel H. W. L. HIME (late Royal Artillery). 8vo., 7s. 6d.

CONTENTS. — Infantry Fire Formations—On Marking at Rifle Matches—The Progress of Field Artillery—The Reconnoitering Duties of Cavalry.

Indian Ideals (No. 1).

NÂRADA SÛTRA : an Inquiry into Love (Bhakti-Jijnâsâ). Translated from the Sanskrit, with an Independent Commentary, by E. T. STURDY. Crown 8vo., 2s. 6d. net.

Jefferies (RICHARD).

FIELD AND HEDGEROW. With Portrait. Crown 8vo., 3s. 6d.

THE STORY OF MY HEART : my Autobiography. With Portrait and New Preface by C. J. LONGMAN. Crown 8vo., 3s. 6d.

RED DEER. With 17 Illustrations by J. CHARLTON and H. TUNALY. Crown 8vo., 3s. 6d.

THE TOILERS OF THE FIELD. With Portrait from the Bust in Salisbury Cathedral. Crown 8vo., 3s. 6d.

WOOD MAGIC : a Fable. With Frontispiece and Vignette by E. V. B. Cr. 8vo., 3s. 6d.

Johnson.—THE PATENTEE'S MANUAL: a Treatise on the Law and Practice of Letters Patent. By J. & J. H. JOHNSON, Patent Agents, &c. 8vo., 10s. 6d.

Joyce.—THE ORIGIN AND HISTORY OF IRISH NAMES OF PLACES. By P. W. JOYCE, LL.D. Seventh Edition. 2 vols. Crown 8vo., 5s. each.

Lang (ANDREW).

MODERN MYTHOLOGY. 8vo., 9s.

LETTERS TO DEAD AUTHORS. Fcp. 8vo., 2s. 6d. net.

BOOKS AND BOOKMEN. With 2 Coloured Plates and 17 Illustrations. Fcp. 8vo., 2s. 6d. net.

OLD FRIENDS. Fcp. 8vo., 2s. 6d. net.

LETTERS ON LITERATURE. Fcp. 8vo., 2s. 6d. net.

COCK LANE AND COMMON-SENSE. Crown 8vo., 3s. 6d.

THE BOOK OF DREAMS AND GHOSTS. Crown 8vo., 6s.

ESSAYS IN LITTLE. With Portrait of the Author. Crown 8vo., 2s. 6d.

Macfarren.—LECTURES ON HARMONY. By Sir G. A. MACFARREN. 8vo., 12s.

Madden.—THE DIARY OF MASTER WILLIAM SILENCE : a Study of Shakespeare and Elizabethan Sport. By the Right Hon. D. H. MADDEN. 8vo., 16s.

Miscellaneous and Critical Works—*continued.*

Max Müller (F.).

INDIA: WHAT CAN IT TEACH US ? Cr. 8vo., 3s. 6d.

CHIPS FROM A GERMAN WORKSHOP.
Vol. I. Recent Essays and Addresses. Cr. 8vo., 5s.
Vol. II. Biographical Essays. Cr. 8vo., 5s.
Vol. III. Essays on Language and Literature. Cr. 8vo., 5s.
Vol. IV. Essays on Mythology and Folk Lore. Crown 8vo., 5s.

CONTRIBUTIONS TO THE SCIENCE OF MYTHOLOGY. 2 vols. 8vo., 32s.

Milner. — COUNTRY PLEASURES: the Chronicle of a Year chiefly in a Garden. By GEORGE MILNER. Cr. 8vo., 3s. 6d.

Morris (WILLIAM).

SIGNS OF CHANGE. Post 8vo., 4s. 6d.
HOPES AND FEARS FOR ART. Cr. 8vo., 4s. 6d.
AN ADDRESS DELIVERED AT THE DISTRIBUTION OF PRIZES TO STUDENTS OF THE BIRMINGHAM MUNICIPAL SCHOOL OF ART, 21ST FEBRUARY, 1894. 8vo., 2s. 6d. net.

Orchard. — THE ASTRONOMY OF 'MILTON'S PARADISE LOST'. By T. N. ORCHARD. 13 Illustrations. 8vo., 6s. net.

Poore (GEORGE VIVIAN, M.D., F.R.C.P.).

ESSAYS ON RURAL HYGIENE. With 13 Illustrations. Crown 8vo., 6s. 6d.
THE DWELLING HOUSE. With 36 Illustrations. Crown 8vo., 3s. 6d.

Proctor. — STRENGTH : How to get Strong and keep Strong, with Chapters on Rowing and Swimming, Fat, Age, and the Waist. By R. A. PROCTOR. With 9 Illustrations. Cr. 8vo, 2s.

PROGRESS IN WOMEN'S EDUCATION IN THE BRITISH EMPIRE. Being the Report of the Education Section, Victorian Era Exhibition, 1897. Edited by the COUNTESS OF WARWICK. With 10 Illustrations. Crown 8vo., 6s.

Richmond. — BOYHOOD : a Plea for Continuity in Education. By ENNIS RICHMOND. Crown 8vo., 2s. 6d.

Rossetti.—A SHADOW OF DANTE : being an Essay towards studying Himself, his World, and his Pilgrimage. By MARIA FRANCESCA ROSSETTI. Crown 8vo., 3s. 6d.

Solovyoff.—A MODERN PRIESTESS OF ISIS (MADAME BLAVATSKY). Abridged and Translated on Behalf of the Society for Psychical Research from the Russian of VSEVOLOD SERGYEEVICH SOLOVYOFF. By WALTER LEAF, Litt. D. Cr. 8vo., 6s.

Soulsby (LUCY H. M.).

STRAY THOUGHTS ON READING. Small 8vo., 2s. 6d. net.
STRAY THOUGHTS FOR GIRLS. 16mo., 1s. 6d. net.
STRAY THOUGHTS FOR MOTHERS AND TEACHERS. Fcp. 8vo., 2s. 6d. net.
STRAY THOUGHTS FOR INVALIDS. 16mo., 2s. net.

Stevens.—ON THE STOWAGE OF SHIPS AND THEIR CARGOES. With Information regarding Freights, Charter-Parties, &c. By ROBERT WHITE STEVENS. 8vo., 21s.

Turner and Sutherland. — THE DEVELOPMENT OF AUSTRALIAN LITERATURE. By HENRY GYLES TURNER and ALEXANDER SUTHERLAND. With 5 Portraits and an Illust. Cr. 8vo., 5s.

White.—AN EXAMINATION OF THE CHARGE OF APOSTASY AGAINST WORDSWORTH. By WILLIAM HALE WHITE. Crown 8vo., 3s. 6d.

Miscellaneous Theological Works.

₊ *For Church of England and Roman Catholic Works see* MESSRS. LONGMANS & CO.'s *Special Catalogues.*

Balfour.—THE FOUNDATIONS OF BELIEF: being Notes Introductory to the Study of Theology. By the Right Hon. ARTHUR J. BALFOUR, M.P. 8vo., 12s. 6d.

Bird (ROBERT).

A CHILD'S RELIGION. Crown 8vo., 2s.
JOSEPH THE DREAMER. Cr. 8vo., 5s.

Bird (ROBERT)—*continued.*

JESUS, THE CARPENTER OF NAZARETH. Twelfth Edition. Crown 8vo, 5s.
To be had also in Two Parts, price 2s. 6d. each.
Part I.—GALILEE AND THE LAKE OF GENNESARET.
Part II.—JERUSALEM AND THE PERÆA.

Miscellaneous Theological Works—*continued.*

Boyd (A. K. H.) (' A.K.H.B.').

OCCASIONAL AND IMMEMORIAL DAYS: Discourses. Crown 8vo., 7s. 6d.

COUNSEL AND COMFORT FROM A CITY PULPIT. Crown 8vo., 3s. 6d.

SUNDAY AFTERNOONS IN THE PARISH CHURCH OF A SCOTTISH UNIVERSITY CITY. Crown 8vo., 3s. 6d.

CHANGED ASPECTS OF UNCHANGED TRUTHS. Crown 8vo., 3s. 6d.

GRAVER THOUGHTS OF A COUNTRY PARSON. Three Series. Crown 8vo., 3s. 6d. each.

PRESENT DAY THOUGHTS. Crown 8vo., 3s. 6d.

SEASIDE MUSINGS. Cr. 8vo., 3s. 6d.

'TO MEET THE DAY' through the Christian Year ; being a Text of Scripture, with an Original Meditation and a Short Selection in Verse for Every Day. Crown 8vo., 4s. 6d.

Gibson.—THE ABBÉ DE LAMENNAIS AND THE LIBERAL CATHOLIC MOVEMENT IN FRANCE. By the HON. W. GIBSON. With Portrait. 8vo., 12s. 6d.

Kalisch (M. M., Ph.D.).

BIBLE STUDIES. Part I. Prophecies of Balaam. 8vo., 10s. 6d. Part II. The Book of Jonah. 8vo., 10s. 6d.

COMMENTARY ON THE OLD TESTAMENT: with a new Translation. Vol. I. Genesis. 8vo., 18s. Or adapted for the General Reader. 12s. Vol. II. Exodus. 15s. Or adapted for the General Reader. 12s. Vol. III. Leviticus, Part I. 15s. Or adapted for the General Reader. 8s. Vol. IV. Leviticus, Part II. 15s. Or adapted for the General Reader. 8s.

Lang.—THE MAKING OF RELIGION. By ANDREW LANG. 8vo., 12s.

Macdonald (GEORGE).

UNSPOKEN SERMONS. Three Series. Crown 8vo., 3s. 6d. each.

THE MIRACLES OF OUR LORD. Crown 8vo., 3s. 6d.

Martineau (JAMES).

HOURS OF THOUGHT ON SACRED THINGS: Sermons. 2 Vols. Crown 8vo. 3s. 6d. each.

Martineau (JAMES)—*continued.*

ENDEAVOURS AFTER THE CHRISTIAN LIFE. Discourses. Cr. 8vo., 7s. 6d.

THE SEAT OF AUTHORITY IN RELIGION. 8vo., 14s.

ESSAYS, REVIEWS, AND ADDRESSES. 4 Vols. Crown 8vo., 7s. 6d. each. I. Personal; Political. II. Ecclesiastical ; Historical. III. Theological; Philosophical. IV. Academical; Religious.

HOME PRAYERS, with Two Services for Public Worship. Crown 8vo. 3s. 6d.

Max Müller (F.).

THE ORIGIN AND GROWTH OF RELIGION, as illustrated by the Religions of India. The Hibbert Lectures, delivered at the Chapter House, Westminster Abbey, in 1878. Crown 8vo., 5s.

INTRODUCTION TO THE SCIENCE OF RELIGION : Four Lectures delivered at the Royal Institution. Cr. 8vo., 3s. 6d.

NATURAL RELIGION. The Gifford Lectures, delivered before the University of Glasgow in 1888. Cr. 8vo., 5s.

PHYSICAL RELIGION. The Gifford Lectures, delivered before the University of Glasgow in 1890. Cr. 8vo., 5s.

ANTHROPOLOGICAL RELIGION. The Gifford Lectures, delivered before the University of Glasgow in 1891. Cr. 8vo., 5s.

THEOSOPHY ; or, PSYCHOLOGICAL RELIGION. The Gifford Lectures, delivered before the University of Glasgow in 1892. Cr. 8vo., 5s.

THREE LECTURES ON THE VEDANTA PHILOSOPHY, delivered at the Royal Institution in March, 1894. 8vo., 5s.

Romanes.—THOUGHTS ON RELIGION. By GEORGE J. ROMANES, LL.D., F.R.S. Crown 8vo., 4s. 6d.

Vivekananda.—YOGA PHILOSOPHY : Lectures delivered in New York, Winter of 1895-6, by the SWAMI VIVEKANANDA, on Raja Yoga ; or, Conquering the Internal Nature; also Patanjali's Yoga Aphorisms, with Commentaries. Crown 8vo., 3s. 6d.

50,000—9/98.   ABERDEEN UNIVERSITY PRESS.